A SOUND MIND

A SOUND MIND

How I fell in love with classical music (and decided to rewrite its entire history)

PAUL MORLEY

BLOOMSBURY PUBLISHING

NEW YORK · LONDON · OXFORD · NEW DELHI · SYDNEY

BLOOMSBURY PUBLISHING
Bloomsbury Publishing Inc.
1385 Broadway, New York, NY 10018, USA

BLOOMSBURY, BLOOMSBURY PUBLISHING, and the Diana
logo are trademarks of Bloomsbury Publishing Plc

First published in 2020 in Great Britain
First published in the United States 2020

ISBN: HB: 978-1-63557-026-7; eBook: 978-1-63557-025-0

Library of Congress Cataloging-in-Publication Data is available.

2 4 6 8 10 9 7 5 3 1

Typeset by Newgen KnowledgeWorks Pvt. Ltd., Chennai, India
Printed and bound in the U.S.A. by Berryville Graphics Inc., Berryville, Virginia

To find out more about our authors and books visit
www.bloomsbury.com and sign up for our newsletters.

Bloomsbury books may be purchased for business or promotional use.
For information on bulk purchases please contact Macmillan Corporate and
Premium Sales Department at specialmarkets@macmillan.com.

I am no connoisseur in art ... nevertheless, works of art do exercise a powerful effect on me, especially those of literature and sculpture, less often of painting ... [I] spend a long time before them trying to apprehend them in my own way, i.e. to explain to myself what their effect is due to. Wherever I cannot do this, as for instance with music, I am almost incapable of obtaining any pleasure. Some rationalistic, or perhaps analytic, turn of mind in me rebels against being moved by a thing without knowing why I am thus affected and what it is that affects me.

Sigmund Freud, 'The Moses of Michelangelo'

Without music, life would be a mistake.

Friedrich Nietzsche, *Twilight of the Idols*

For every discovery we need new sounds.

Anaïs Nin, *In Favour of the Sensitive Man and Other Essays* e.s.p.

Contents

The Question – Into the Unknown

*Musical notes by **Wolfgang Amadeus Mozart** circa 1800: 'Whence and how these ideas come I know not, nor can I force them.'*

The plane took off. It was obviously about to happen, but the way the ground fell away from underneath me still seemed very sudden and somehow, discreetly, violent.

I hoped that everything was under control, that the experts in control of my immediate fate knew what they were doing and in general felt good about their life and completely confident about the maintenance of the machine they were piloting. The behaviour of the visible professional staff in the cabin was inevitably relatively serene verging on the indifferent, even when rules and regulations were routinely explained to ensure our safety, considering how we were now beginning to hurtle through the air and there would be much less between the passengers and certain death than there had been an hour ago.

The noisy roar and erratic rattle of the plane as it arrowed upwards, drawing attention to the precariousness of my position, needed dealing with. I was still holding my phone after switching it to airplane mode, and since I had turned fifty my phone had become more of a music player than anything else. In my lifetime I had gone from the near-spiritual or theatrical ritual of the record – patiently picking dust from my record player's needle, dropping the stylus softly at the wobbly edge of a deeply black shiny record to connect with the groove, turning the disc over, filing all my albums in an order between thoughtful and chaotic – to a point where music was held inside some sort of space inside my phone that could be quickly connected to my mind. The twentieth-century record-playing ritual, filled with beloved gestures and pauses, hisses and clicks, had been replaced by a slick functionality

closer to fastening your seat belt on a plane than preparing for lift-off
into all space. Once the music was playing, though, it was still music,
and if you had made the right choice, still magical.

Needing to focus my mind, to turn one set of thoughts into another,
to push myself more into myself, I tucked some headphones into my
ears and turned to the Tidal streaming app, which is more or less where
my music collection now lives. Once, when it was vinyl, my music
collection might have needed a large van to move. When it was on
compact disc, it would still have needed a little planning to move,
especially if I wanted to carry it all around with me. A music collection
was now invisible, the abstract replacing the object, and relied on such
vulnerable things as battery power and connectivity. A portability that
had begun in the 1970s with the futuristic Sony Walkman from future-
perfect Japan, where you carried music of your choice to be played as
and when as you moved around, had rapidly extended over the next
forty years, turning the Walkman into a quaint period piece. By 2020
you could just speak aloud, asking a gadget for a certain piece of music
and out of nowhere it would appear somewhere between magically and
mechanically. The next stage in portability would be where all music
laid dormant inside your head and you thought it into action. Or music
became so abstract it is beyond reach.

Before I boarded my plane, ready for moments when there was no
wi-fi, I had downloaded a few albums – if that is what they are still
called. To some extent, this small group of albums, randomly selected
for hopefully temporary offline emergencies from a more consciously
compiled list, was now my record collection, although I would regularly
make changes to it. A quick scroll through what once would have
been the automatic Dylan, Hendrix, Coltrane or Joy Division took
me to what, at that moment, seemed the perfect sound, the perfect
thinking, to fight off the churning, lightly menacing whine of the
plane, and more significantly to take my mind off the loss of ground as
the plane vibrated into the sky. There was a dull shudder as the plane
was enveloped by churning cloud representing a basic struggle with
mortality. The plane breaking into a devious shake can make a two-
hour flight to the pleasures of Barcelona, which at the time were mostly
taken for granted, momentarily seem like a death sentence.

I chose a performance of three cello sonatas written across time
by a trio of German composers: Beethoven, born in 1770, Brahms,

born in 1833, six years after Beethoven died, and Hindemith, born in 1895, two years before Brahms died, and living through the twentieth century until 1963, six years after I was born, the year the Beatles broke through. I am not sure it had ever been released as a record, and the two musicians playing the music, the cellist Alessio Pianelli and the pianist Mario Montore, did not seem particularly famous.

I'd fallen for the combination of composers, the raw, open balance between the glide of the cello and the flight of the piano, and how technical and emotional thinking about music and the mystique of enlightenment had been passed through history from one composer to another, this journey beginning with the contemplation and calculation of J. S. Bach, and backwards beyond into a mysterious musical equivalent of a before-the-Common Era epoch.

Beethoven's Cello Sonata No. 4 shows how he was pulling away in 1815 from his early adoration of Mozart and Haydn into what became labelled as the 'late period' of his creative life. Original influences were shaken off, leaving his own internal urges and instincts for change as his greatest influence, a musical progress from pure imaginative efficiency to other-worldliness, compressed into his five works for cello and piano. The drama of Brahms' Cello Sonata No. 1 generates an ethereal fusion of cello and piano that made me think of all the weird air – the nothing and something – around the plane I was in rather than the late nineteenth century.

Finally, in this trio, Hindemith, one of the accepted founders of musical modernism along with Schoenberg, Stravinsky and Bartók, who as part of his intellectual research into the sensation and structure of sound composed sonatas for all the major instruments. His *Three Easy Pieces* for cello and piano from 1938, titled as though they are teaching pieces, easily cope with being bracketed with Brahms and Beethoven.

The fiery, serene sonatas take me into the clouds, through some worrying turbulence, peaking out into level peace high in the sky, where you're rapidly moving forward but don't seem to be moving at all, when the nerves can level out as well – the plane flies on and my life continues, but for a short while, in those vulnerable moments as the flight began, if something had gone wrong, and the ground furiously grabbed us back, the last piece of music I would ever hear in my life might have been one of these intimately immense sonatas. Brahms and Hindemith imagining where J. S. Bach would have been after Beethoven, or Bartók. Beethoven inventing a new musical language, so it is said, but to my ears, under the circumstances, an uncanny demonstration of the relationship between time, space and mind, thinking and body, between sound and silence, between inside and outside, bliss and tension, temporary and permanent, motion and emotion and, ultimately, between life and death. Just what I needed as I accelerated towards 500 miles an hour.

All three, using just two instruments, pressing so much feeling, knowledge and purpose into musical structures veering between tradition and adventure, while they had the chance, searching for evidence, before the possibility of everything, like a piece of music, because all things must pass, ends.

After such journeys when fast jet travel combined with fast new ways of hearing music, when progress seemed to be running ahead of itself, I started to increasingly wonder what the last piece of music that I'd ever hear would actually be. The final piece of music, the last song, before I died, paying attention to the very end, which is what listening to music is about. Paying attention. Hopefully to a brand new world that you want to be part of, or perhaps deal with when it seems more a threat than a delight. Paying attention whether you seem to be paying attention or not. Paying attention whatever the time of day, or whatever the stage of your life.

All the music I had listened to, and thought about, written about, collected, analysed, discovered, loved, all that I had rejected and dismissed, once or twice danced to, played once or again and again, coming down, after all that, to this one, last piece – that would become in my life a complete full stop, or maybe a question mark, even an exclamation mark.

Or, and this of course all depended on what the song or piece was, which I began to think about more and more, the conclusion could be a little less definite. A comma, a semicolon, perhaps an asterisk, suggesting there might be more to come, a form of collaboration with eternity that this last music might help me understand. If the whole event of my death seemed particularly and unexpectedly 'ironic', in quotation marks, or if it felt perversely a little unfinished, oddly provisional, annoyingly premature, a dash—

What music would do the job, be the full stop, or the dash, connecting me with elsewhere, chosen with care, as part of a deliberate slowing-down ritual, a closing event, or an accident, because my death was? And if it was an accident, was the last music something I had chosen to play, before the accident, which I didn't see coming, or something that I heard randomly, half watching a television show, or hearing something boom from a passing car, or while I was shopping in my local Co-Op? Would this piece be horribly commercial, sadly a slice of muzak, a charity choir crushing the life out of a favourite song or, terribly, something, the ultimate horror, by Phil Collins, definitely an experience to put inside scare quotes?

And if I could be in control, somehow establishing some isolation, a sanctuary, accepting the end was near and must not be interfered with by what the music critic in me had come to call the enemy – those with the affrontery to have different taste from me – how could I make sure that this last piece was something I chose? Something that I had prepared, as an event, after much consideration, a distillation of all of my musical loves, the sort of music I would be happy to have as my musical epitaph, something that made a little sense of the fact I had spent all of my working life judging, interpreting, celebrating, mythologising, hyping and listing music? The end of the trail of a life of music… And in choosing this piece, making my mind up that a certain musical selection was the one carrying me forth into an unknown, what kind of thinking and feeling would go into this decision?

To arrive at an answer, I needed to write a book, to explore once and for all what my thinking about music is, and along the way to help work out what that last music choice was; this very book, in fact, which becomes the story of how I worked out what I would be listening to in those final moments, and how the idea of what that music would be went through changes.

These changes were not just because I was going through changes, the sort of changes that tend to come as you helplessly – hopefully, given the alternative – drift closer to death, picking up pace, slipping out of the way, when you are perhaps twenty, or ten years from the moment to end all moments. They came about because music itself, at least in how it made it into my life, and how it made it into the wider world, was also going through changes, in terms of how it was distributed and made available, and just how much of it there now was. So much music that there seemed to be less and less care about what was played, less commitment to the idea of quality, as a route to the sublime, as if it was all the same, because it was all in the same place. The route to the sublime had become routine. Abundance had led to a diminishing of specialness.

Between the ages of fifty and sixty, the candidates for what that last piece could be had considerably expanded, because I was increasingly listening to music that spanned centuries. I wasn't less committed or less caring faced with all this music; I was more so. I couldn't help it. The 'more music' didn't disconcert me, because, as a long-time professional writer about music, I could make some sense of it all, and work out where a lot of it had come from and how it was part of history, make decisions about what had become of it; what did challenge me perhaps was where it was all going and what it meant to the making of music. What was music becoming?

The 'more – and more – music', the onslaught, simply gave me more to think about, and this became the kind of thinking that I began putting into large playlists – 'sonic sculptures', I called them, consciously made as artworks, some of which contained so much assembled music that they could last for days, and which I imagined being released from inside their virtual storage centre and floating off into space, spectacular evidence of life on earth.

I imagined them as artworks in the way I had imagined music writing to be an art. When I started, there didn't seem any other way of approaching it. Once writing about music became more polite or prosaic, and part of a social-media invasion and interruption of traditional rational thinking, it could seem that generating these playlists was the new form of writing about music. How you put together the playlists – even if just for yourself – expressed and explained your feelings about music. More than that, they were a musical act: you told stories, expressed emotions and created worlds through these playlists.

Previously, before music streaming, where all music was gathered in the one place because now it could be – if possibly on borrowed time, but then we all are – my music listening tended to be concentrated on music made, recorded and performed, coincidentally, or quite naturally enough, between the year I was born, 1957, and the beginning of the twenty-first century, as long as my life so far, the borrowed time, had lasted.

Before streaming, this music was limited to records and compact discs that I owned as objects, certain radio stations I listened to that had the time and inclination to feature my kind of music, and increasingly what repeats of *Top of the Pops* BBC Four showed, once they had edited out the actually evil presence of certain disc jockeys. (Pop music turned out to be a great cover not only for the occasional genius but also for the occasional psychopath.) The music I heard was heavily biased to that second half of the twentieth century, post-Presley, post-multitrack recording, post-seven-inch singles and post-albums-as-art. For a while, this was where my final piece was going to come from: music more or less made and released during my lifetime.

A love of jazz and the mental motoring and sensual seriousness of improvised music pushed me back deeper into the almighty tangle of the twentieth century, and an anti-herd fascination with the dismantled and dismantling sounds, risks and challenges of avant-garde music pushed me even further back to the beginning of the twentieth century, and the early murmurs, and anxieties, of modernism. In turn, that took me back to what I decided were definite sources of jazz and the conceptual avant-garde, in particular the artfully temporal and sacred secular French music written by Erik Satie, Claude Debussy and Maurice Ravel at the end of the nineteenth century and beginning of the twentieth century.

I hesitantly dipped back further in time, to Beethoven, Brahms and Mozart. There were definitely a few candidates among this music, at the heart of many of my structured playlists, that were high up on the list of a last, personal musical ceremony. I found myself playing this French music, and what came immediately after from Germany and Russia, from Stravinsky, Webern, Hindemith and Shostakovich, as I sat on planes that were taking off, or landing. Just in case…

I was ready; speeding away from the planet, or descending towards it, when something might happen to bring about the end of my time, playing early twentieth-century music, made about a century ago, cautiously generating a private ceremony. For me, this is what music had come to. This is where it had taken me. I could not imagine a world where I didn't make the sort of decision that led to me hearing Part I of Stravinsky's *Divertimento* from *Le Baiser de la fée* as a plane streaks into the sky. The music matching the speed of the machine I'm on and then keeping up with the flow of the movement through the air, and then the skimming across clouds in splendid isolation and the aiming towards whatever next, making you feel that life has been worthwhile, because it is filled with such radiant, ridiculous things as this – the flying and the music, two different ways of travelling outside yourself.

And then, astonishingly, after all this thinking through sound, music that moves through you as you move through space, which makes you realise that the lack of words in classical music is not an obstacle to meaning but a release of possibilities, an opening up of sensation, not a limiting, you are around to touch the ground and renew acquaintance with the solid and the ongoing, hearing Martha Argerich and Alexandre Rabinovitch play Schumann's *Andante and Variations* for two pianos in B-flat major.

This might not be rock 'n' roll in the way we have been led to believe, full of obvious psyching up and freaking out, and associated rites of passage, and it comes from the long-lost nineteenth century, but it can make today's world seem something else, and something amazing, even freaky, as if it was composed to be heard as you hit the ground strapped into a metal tube at a few hundred miles an hour surrounded by complete strangers midway through their own dizzying destinies. It would sound amazing right up to your very last moments, as you hit another sort of ground, an unbelievable underground, at a speed that, until it happens, you cannot even imagine.

Before finding this music, up until my fifties, the favourite possibilities for the final piece of music were settled around my teenage years, and the years I spent in my late teens and early twenties writing for the *New Musical Express*, where precocious alternative thinking about pop culture had smuggled itself into the mainstream. The sentimental years; the lost golden years you find yourself culturally compelled to repeat as you get older, however much you resist nostalgia, because the music has most vividly impressed itself upon your senses, and character, and of course your hairstyle and favourite style of trousers. The consolation of looking back to the music you listened to in your early years never fades away, and perhaps can recreate even right at the end equivalent feelings of hope and anticipation, of excitingly setting out on an adventure, not disappearing into the unrealistic unknown. It seems safe, and soothing, to play music that you loved as a twenty-year-old, as if nothing has changed in your life, your surroundings are still the same, and there is still everything to look forward to – the music says so, setting you up for what is to come, not showing you where you have been.

Also, as a rock critic who, I like to think, made a reputation in the late 1970s and early 1980s writing about Manchester punk, post-punk and what I called New Pop – odd, stylish, commercial kinky pop coming from the likes of Sparks, Bowie and Roxy Music, which now stretches electrically between the Human League and Billie Eilish – I found, as I got officially old, I was professionally expected to write about the same thing in different guises. All the anniversaries, rewindings, reunions, box sets, exhibitions, compilations and goodbyes for the rest of my life. It didn't matter how inappropriate it was, or how much I might want to be writing about other things, newer music, other arts, I was, at least as a formal music writer, stuck in the past whether I liked it or not.

Forty years after I left the North, thirty-five years after I stopped writing for the *NME* – considering myself at twenty-six too old – I still often get thought of as a northern *NME* writer. I might not want to settle down writing a narrative of nostalgia, but it often turns out that is what is expected from me. That's my job, that's my lot. To every person their little cross. Nostalgia is tricky if what turned you on as a young person were violations of the norm. Pop, it turned out, was a great cover for those wishing to violate the norm, and so was writing about it, until it became just another profession, and mostly a new form of professional mourning.

In the 1980s, the rock writer, once part of a slightly manic but influential and initially experimental self-consciously literary, even philosophical cult, grew more ordinary and visible, and much less adventurous. The few became the many. What had been a rare thing became common, a conventional career like pop performing itself, a formalised, often quasi-academic method of organising, interpreting and rating a torrent of songs and performances. By the end of the twentieth century the internet landed, or just popped out of the air, and reality itself was disturbed, possibly permanently disrupted, while print journalism was made to look increasingly vulnerable on the inevitable path to empty offices, howling winds and tumbleweed. Commenting on your favourite music became less an esoteric profession and more an everyday hobby, a load of centreless, directionless chatter.

Post-internet, one of the first things that happened, because in the end writing about rock required secluded, geek-framed enthusiasm, no grown-up qualifications and only a minimal amount of truly useful knowledge, was that everyone had a chance to try their hand at writing about rock music from the privacy of their own keyboard. Everyone could become famous and some sort of instant social historian once social media dominated the internet, but before that, in the internet's early days, before everyone was able to write and photograph the story of their lives, everyone could become a rock writer. In the early 1970s, there were scores of rock writers charged with giving contextual and critical shape to a new world, and there were five great ones. In the late 1970s and early 1980s there were a few hundred rock writers, and there were five great ones. By the 1990s there were thousands of rock writers, and five great ones. Being objective about it.

The internet was the end for anyone fancying writing about music in the way it had been written about after the method had been invented in the 1960s and consolidated in the 1970s, as something more ambitious and provocative than a convenient, practical consumer guide. It helped ensure that popular culture, once at the messy, furtive edge of things, became the mainstream. Everyone had an opinion, and even though it could be claimed there is nothing wrong with that, the disappointing thing was, the majority of those opinions were all the same and not particularly exceptional. Bestsellers' charts had once been the place where the voice of the majority was seen and heard; critics were responsible for ensuring there was more to art and entertainment than the simply popular. Increasingly, populist opinions were broadcast as though they were interesting, revealing and insightful, as if they showed intrinsic, constructive critical merit, not merely a dreary display of likes and dislikes.

Once everyone had the opportunity to distribute their opinions and attitudes, and could endlessly record their taste and draw attention to their favourite music, movies or TV, through endless blogs, vlogs, podcasts and online music forums, they picked up the same conditions and neuroses that the great rock writers had, without the ideological energy and literary ambition – the addiction to telling people about your loves and hates, the excitement of telling people all about yourself when previously no one really wanted to know, the snobbish elevated high you can feel when you are first to spot a secret new trend, a hot new movement. The internet meant that there were now millions of rock writers covering, celebrating and hyping, and explaining popular culture in ways that were unimaginable when there were just a few. Millions of music critics, and five great ones, and one or two of those are the same as they were in the 1970s.

Nostalgic against my better instincts, I could never bring myself to accept that the most important thing in a music review after about 1995 was the number of stars you handed out or marks out of ten. The discriminating, provocative, disruptive moods of the critic were replaced by the bland four and five stars, or the merely angry and mostly staged one or two stars. I had always believed it was about finding the language and structure to explain how and what the music made you feel. Also, because of the new sharing world, whatever I could write about the things I liked to write about, there were hundreds of people lined up fully prepared to do the same or similar, quite reasonably considering they could do it better than me and quite happy to grade what they were writing about as if it was a product, a hotel room, a train journey or an exam.

For those born during and after the 1980s there was no other way; sightings of the other way must have seemed a little Edwardian, even though all generations were now more or less interested in the proliferating trends and currents of popular culture as it more or less redirected reality itself. Everyone could find what they wanted now, quickly and efficiently, guided by genial, anonymous calculations, by ever-increasing playlists, by a proliferation of genres that almost bureaucratically processed and filed music for driving, sleeping, motivating, studying, eating, chilling, isolation, concentrating, shopping, swapping, dancing, night-time, Thursday. It became a world that was looking for user-friendly tips and advice, not manifestos, essays and rants, a world of irregular uniformity and conglomerated mediocrity, where the idea of quality and meaning was quickly replaced by convenience.

You can find information and guidance within seconds without coming into contact with a 1970s-style mostly white, mostly male rock writer, their peculiar personal habits, the narcissistic certainty that they are right, their dubious, far-fetched claims, their insane, illogical prejudices, their arcane, mystifying theories, a deep fear of losing control of their precious canon, and their insatiable desire to use too many words. Note how the first two or three waves of rock writers between the early 1960s and the early 1980s acted as though they were changing the world and, to some extent, ruling it, even though they had little experience of life and other cultures outside of their bedroom, their favourite gig venues and their record collection. The breed of eager, inbred, self-obsessed, self-important, naive, unsophisticated, holier-than-thou, mock-disruptive white male entrepreneurs who founded Apple, Google, Amazon, Facebook, Twitter, Instagram, Spotify, etc. shared many of the same introverted, defensively arrogant and immature, insular qualities of the early rock writers, their nerdy self-involvement, missionary zeal and self-righteous rebel gestures. They also thought they were agents of free expression and protest who were going to change the world, even run it. The big difference between them and the rock writers was that, scarily, they actually did.

The covering of music is all for the consumer now, the well-regulated customers, less for the nature and momentum, the wonderful warp and weave, of the culture, which ultimately has greater worth for the consumer and introduces them to better things and a wider, more varied selection. There is all the choice in the world, but less actual selective choosing than there used to be. At least, that's what I tell myself, still with this need to write about music because, on and off, it's something I have done since I was, well, a child. I had also become fascinated with how to write about music, and there was still plenty for me to find out about the practice and function.

I wasn't going to stop just because so many others were now doing it and the wider point of it was far less specific, less unprecedented than it was when I started. I needed to find new routes, new material and see if there could still be a purpose in the way I understood it, something other than being part of the promotions industry or one faceless component in a collective flowing in one forced direction.

This book, then, is not just the story of a search to find out what might be the final piece of music I would ever listen to, or to analyse the effects of streaming on the form and content of music, but it is also a book about what it is, and how it is, to write about music, what the motivation is, and what the satisfactions are, after doing it for forty years. And how I found the material to continue writing about music in a different, non-rock field, where there are perhaps still only a few hundred practitioners – and only five great ones.

Writing about rock and pop is now far too crowded for me, and the way I write about rock, drawing attention to myself for a variety of reasons, on the hunt for deeper meanings and stranger patterns, tends to infuriate those now looking simply for plain, useful, matter-of-fact, best-of-year information, for playlists and more new music to hear, even if all it leads to is more new music to listen to, or, if you've had enough, less. For personal reasons, to keep my writing, and thinking, and music listening fresh, I needed some new things to write about, even as more writing about music also came with there being fewer places to experiment with writing about music. Especially experimenting with writing about music if you wanted to write about Stravinsky and Schumann rather than Post Malone and Dave, yet another winner of the Mercury Prize.

In the middle of all these changes to my personal, professional circumstances, new music — and therefore new things to write about — started to fall into my lap and into my ears, especially when I was holding my music-playing iPhone. I had access to a small proportion of all the music ever made, which even then was more music than you could ever really hear more than once in your life. Sometime around 2010, the floodgates really opened. There was still only a proportion of all the music ever made, but the amount of music instantly available in my life was hundreds, probably thousands, of times more than it had ever been. Apple was soon promising they were giving us 50 million songs. Like this was a good thing, like it made sense, like it was to be expected. Aren't we lucky? But if, as the composer Mauricio Kagel once observed, finding an unexpected new piece of music you love listening to is the equivalent of getting some luck in your lives, is it possible for there to be too much luck? Should this sort of luck be compiled, processed and endlessly exposed in this way?

What came with all the music, all these millions of songs, a streaming, straightened-out deluge of good luck, was a collapsing of chronology, a collapsing of musical history, and the fulfilment of a promise once made by the philosopher-composer-teacher John Cage, where Duchamp meets Buddha, that eventually all music would exist at once. Cage was the son of an inventor and a *Los Angeles Times* society writer who believed that the primary act of musical performance was not making music but listening.

In 1965, at fifty-three, Cage had imagined the internet — the clear-thinking social prophet already fantasising about the glorious inevitability of such an operation — as something like a universal language, a universal culture and a universal common market. He anticipated instant television, instant newspapers, instant magazines and an instant telephone service; everybody linked to everybody everywhere at every moment. It seemed like a good idea at the time, or a good idea from the point of view of an intellectually curious, artistically busy, benevolent visionary who always valued good ideas and confidently believed this new world would all be about good ideas and positive, inclusive thinking. He did acknowledge there was also a possibility we would all become digital tourists overlapping each other in a state of terminal duplication. He wasn't the sort of philosopher to anticipate the nastiness, the brainwashing and the crowds baying, and posing, for attention.

He was also influenced by something said by his friend, the Indian music teacher Gita Sarabhai, who he remarked came into his life 'like an angel from India', completely changing the reasons why he wrote music: 'The purpose of music is to quiet and sober the mind, making it susceptible to divine influences.' This makes more sense the older you get, and roughly speaking takes you away, a little bit, from Iggy and the Stooges, as divine as that can seem and closer to, say, utopian experimental composer Morton Feldman. This soft, quiet, acutely responsible music, closer to silence than sound, finding new connections between the mind and the body, can become a weapon in an actual attack on the commercialisation of everything, especially music; Cage could see before most others how in contemporary civilisation everything is standardised, and everything is repeated, if deviously disguised as something constantly different. For Cage forgetfulness became important, so that you would not always be trapped into only contemplating and consuming what you were told to think about and buy. You could break out of those patterns. You could find yourself, not the person that others, with ulterior motives, following your every move, were making you become.

To forget was to avoid being completely taken over by what others decided you should be preoccupied with. Art, Cage decided, could help us forget, at least occasionally, so that we could resist being pummelled by the same things again and again. It could remind us that there were other worlds, sensations and objects to think about, not only what was placed in front of us for our comfort, which ultimately made us all addicts, pushed into a coma of apparent awareness. 'If art today didn't help us forget,' he noted, 'we would be submerged, drowned under those avalanches of rigorously identical objects.' The forgetfulness was actually a remembering — of ideas and energies that were not being controlled on your behalf, by forces narrowing and emptying your actual options even as it seemed you had all the choice you needed.

Once music had become so instant, so handy, some proposed that listening to music ceased to be an event, a special drama, and became simply another task, almost a duty, something to take for granted, not least because despite the amount of music just a touch or two away, it somehow didn't take up any actual space in our lives. It all fitted into a small gadget that could then fit inside our pockets or be held permanently in our hands, becoming another digit. In there somewhere, if you wanted to find them, there were works of art — distinctive examples of divine and/or difficult music that could help you forget how music was being made so ordinary by being made so plentiful.

There had always been lots of music for those of my age, which you could hear on the radio, and on records in the 1960s and 1970s, and see on television, especially after the 1980s and the arrival of MTV, followed by hundreds of channels inheriting its agitated, zealous visual and haphazard philosophical logic, whether news or entertainment. But before technological advances and various forms of media expansion created a vast library, or heaven, or mess of almost all the music that had ever been recorded that could be accessed, certain music remained out of reach if it wasn't being played on the radio or hadn't recently been released on a record that you could buy in your local record shop. The availability of music was sectioned off, siphoned off, it was reduced by various practical issues to being only a certain amount, and only accessible to a certain extent.

At about the same time I started to seriously wonder about that last piece of music I would ever hear, my farewell song, at the same time as my existence as a rock critic was gravely threatened, all music, as far as the eye could see, the ear could hear, seemed to become available. You didn't need to listen to it on the radio or buy it on disc; with a couple of pieces of equipment and a few subscriptions to certain remote but very accommodating companies nifty with their marketing, their informed, if automated, curating and their methods of processing coolness, you were able to have all of the music you could ever want.

Before this, the idea of hearing, say, some Mozart, let alone all of Mozart, seemed a difficult task, fraught with problems to do with what to play, and how to get hold of it. Once the streaming of music emerged, automatically dragging everything with it into the same place, he was now right in front of me. He was all mine. By accident more than intent, an entire of history of music was released into the world, as though for the first time – the release date of millions of pieces of music was always now. The music of Mozart was out now, all of the time.

All of music, a multitude of versions of all of Mozart, was suddenly easy to find. In one weekend, peculiarly trained to feel the need, feeling like a mountaineer abruptly faced with previously inaccessible new peaks to conquer, I could hear more or less everything Mozart had ever written. I could now speed through Mozart – the years he was alive, the years his music has been performed and recorded, by an endless supply of those who appreciate the sublime madness in the method – in a matter of days. It seemed churlish, even idiotic to ignore this sudden discovery of treasure and see what I made of it as both a listener to music and a writer about music. And to confirm the theory that in this new streaming setting all music exists at the same time; old music, previously hard to hear and assimilate, becomes new music. Everything is always new.

Old music becomes something new to write about, because in its new setting it has been rejuvenated and it comes to new life. For me, now, not just because of my age, but because I continue on a quest to find new sounds and new minds, there is Mozart as though it has only just happened. It is from history, from before my time, and therefore the time of pop, but it is now more part of the present than it has ever been. Can he still make sense during our troubled times, when things are in flux in a whole new way; can he still be relevant to those working out the role of music in clearing the way forward, of diagnosing cultural climate, of inspiring new thinking? Is it more than a mere accident of timing and technology that, wow, like the wizard some have always claimed he is, he makes this kind of abstract but persistent comeback?

The only problem I felt now that I was able to approach and pay attention to Mozart, as much as an inverse snobbery that had long dismissed him as irrelevant and old-fashioned, was a lingering inferiority complex – did I need somehow to have certain qualifications in order to understand and enjoy the music? Could I ever write about Mozart in the way I had written about the music I became an expert in covering, and, more importantly, would I ever be allowed to write anything at all about Mozart, especially in a country that had almost officially banned such intellectual and critical mobility? Should I keep my Mozart listening to myself, or was there still a reason, as a professional music writer, to pass on my experience, my new adventure, to use writing about a subject as I always had – in the first place, for me to discover, appreciate and to get my bearings?

I love and crave music of all sorts enough to be seduced by streamed music and all its information and take out subscriptions to all the streaming services, even as I am aware of its new, disorientating, overwhelming, even synthetic oddness, which one day will seem very natural, or be replaced as something old-fashioned, by something else even newer, odder and apparently, at least from a late twentieth-century point of view, less human. I realise that somehow music has become data, rather than knowledge, experience, emotion – but what data! As long as you can keep your wits about you and begin sifting all this data with prior knowledge of at least some music history.

When people ask me what I am listening to, expecting to hear from an alleged rock expert some new band or compelling discovery, the elusive latest happening, like the old days when such things mattered, or were made to matter, I now reply – I'm listening to Tidal, to Spotify and Apple, to YouTube Music, as though that is the one act, taking all music by whoever and whatever into its corporate body, its deadpan creative presence.

This made me think: what is all this music actually for, now that we appear to own it all, even if just virtually, in our own personal cloud, which fast becomes our own personal Jesus? Simply pleasure, nostalgia, consolation, relaxation, collection, sharing, completing the turning of the millions of songs into playlists that show off your signalled taste, hipness and discrimination, the sentimentally paraded trajectory of your life. Is all this gathering of musical material the creation of a vast library that might eventually sink under its own weight, or, really, its weightlessness – or something more, something that might be threatened by the very thing that is actually making music so easily accessible?

It's all so easy to find, but it is harder to pay attention to, at least as a collective – individual attention perhaps, if you have the will and need, but collectively the latest new thing is now destined to remain inside its own world, however popular and rated never likely to make an impact beyond its place. Even the most popular of pop music seems essentially a niche activity, a segment of pop culture, a portion of distraction, rather than the top of the bill. The idea of a teenage audience, which originally was the momentum behind pop music, the way out of a dreary environment, a tense domestic situation, the weirdness of the mind, has evolved, and teenagers, which becomes an age span stretching between, say, ten and forty or fifty, maybe a few years beyond, have different ways of fighting free of immediate restrictions, of generating personal space and possible independence.

Do we lose that sense of the greater purpose of music – once it is set inside the flat, if relentless and very helpful, music services – as this other language, this alien presence taking on the unknown, defending us against all kinds of threats, danger and tension? Will this near-monstrous availability of music, the over-engineered tethering of everything into one place, lead to stronger, more innovative music, and more awareness of its deeper powers, or weaken and break it up into mere patterns of fun, a bland, near-perfunctory amenity increasingly adrift from any rooted, evolving artistic, cultural or social context, except when the idea of 'rebellion', or resistance – the transmission of cool – is merely part of an inherited game plan, an established formula?

As much as there is now all music ready for us to quickly find, there is also the fact that it can easily go missing – the power can be turned off, the machines lost or broken, the playlists become narrower and narrower, inevitably marginalising the loftier, higher thinking, the bolder music, instead favouring music that is more ingenious product design, more zesty, zoned soundtrack to celebrity, to TikTok doodling, than challenging, visionary, reality-changing, life-altering sonic poetry.

Does it now become cut off from creative regeneration and new developments – no more indisputable masterpieces, no more real shocks to the system, or ruptures to the history – and simply reside inside a permanently open, well-lit store, a zoo, a static museum, a series of relics, anniversaries and greatest hits targeting shrinking communities stuck inside ever-multiplying and narrower aesthetic alcoves? Rather than being released by the streaming services, does music lose its freedom, and its freedom to be obscure and outlying, and become caged? Some parts of the zoo are visited a lot more than others, which start to become a little unlooked-after, a little overgrown, even sad.

The great music, the great songs, the bright, persuasive togetherness achieved by musicians and composers finding new ways to turn old music into new music has always, like the best art, helped us adapt to new ideas, to fundamental change, encouraged us to keep our wits about us, prepare for love and death, supplying clues about how to defend ourselves from the damaging consequences of those environmental, emotional and existential changes that result from often unregulated technological and economic advancements.

Art is ultimately what helps us deal with the turbulent, sometimes toxic force of change; it explains it, predicts it, contains it, is a necessary antidote to the rampaging forces of those claiming power, dictating morals, reducing freedom, setting us apart and shredding truth and beauty. It is the most vital corrective alternative to the self-generating entrepreneurial energy that generally exploits technological change and natural disaster, mostly to make money and take control of our interests. It is a mysterious, at best uncontrollable form of opposition to those who use the developments in technology to herd us into obedient, pacified communities whose sole function is ultimately to consume and download and disappear into a kind of censored, gated territory of lifestyle ease, merciless entertainment and moral indifference, until there's nothing left of what once seemed inviolably human.

At this point, in the middle of the sort of changes that will either end us or profoundly transform us, even replace us, there is an extraordinary, fast-evolving need for music, as an unclassifiable symbol of otherness and artistic endeavour, as a method of communicating thought about the vastness of the cosmos, the glory of love, the wonder of existence, the nature of our minds, the dreams of humans, which music is a mirror of, a maker of, beyond words and logic, and temporary, distracting societal pressure and overstimulating fashionable trends. As someone trained in the elastic, eccentric arts of rock criticism, where Roland Barthes and Susan Sontag, even J. G. Ballard and Philip K. Dick were as much an influence as Nik Cohn, Joan Didion, Richard Meltzer, Patti Smith and Lester Bangs, I still have these kind of thoughts, and they still seem important — but with the knowledge that they now are drowning in a world of instant ratings, Amazon reviews (no offence), perky spirit raising and scrappy, aggrieved, populist shouting.

Something about the fact that obscure, difficult music is now within easy reach – with a few touches on your phone and the ability to fund the many subscriptions – is fantastic, but it also makes me sad. It's progress, and you can never deny that, unless you're not thinking very deeply, but it's also a regression, possibly even a betrayal of all that imagination and ambition that led to the music existing in the first place, something that makes you think about what happens if music goes missing. Put into one engineered space, as it is being, a pasted-together lump sum of all musical achievement, it can easily disappear. When the power is turned off, or the batteries run out, or the terms of agreement change, or it just becomes one big musical mountain where millions of thoughts become just the one. Something is stored there, but it might be forgotten what it is, or what the point of it is.

Because of YouTube Music, Apple, Tidal, Amazon and Spotify, I currently have the best, biggest collection of music I have ever had, enough to take me to the end of time, through dozens of lifetimes, but increasingly it only exists as a technological illusion, a playlist containing playlists containing virtual remnants of records stored in the suspiciously convenient make-believe clouds, a collective memory of something that is fast becoming vague and somehow even quiet, or the subject of mere gossip. It's tantalising – hearing musically everything if you fancy it, and have the time, but knowing at any minute it could all be knocked down and taken away, my whole collection collapsing into the abyss. Here, but not here. Like me, I guess. Maybe this was how it was always meant to be, where it was all leading.

Perhaps, via streaming, music has only just begun. The streaming system is a protective vessel carrying music into the future, beyond whatever terribly unprecedented and life-threatening problems suddenly appear, where it will reconfigure itself in ways that will make the current streaming technology seem primitive. As always, to keep us sane, smart and positive in the middle of trying, relentlessly chaotic times where considered thought is taking a battering, music is going somewhere else, becoming something else, using whatever technology is available to fill our minds with the efforts, ingenuity and dreams of other hopeful minds. Even inside the machine, as the world falters, up in that mysterious cloud, pressed into a new kind of service, music keeps going. It keeps going for as long as we need it, not even stopping when we stop.

I can't be sure when I started writing or when I started using Google, and I can't pin down exactly when it was that I first thought about a final piece of music, the emergence of this anticipation, or apprehension, of my coming musical end, but slowly the idea started to grow on me. I suppose, as certain personal fixtures and fittings, certain faculties, started to shut down, it was something, an energy, or a nagging doubt, or a strange form of planning ahead, that was expanding and becoming something new. A part of me that was evolving, as I became intensely aware of how my life was leading to a very interesting climax. Once, despite the regular panic attacks, I didn't really believe it was actually going to happen. Not to me. After all, I was so filled with music, which by its very nature is so filled with life, showing no signs, as it happens, of ever coming to an end.

A last piece of music was nothing that I would have thought about early on in my life, as part of how and why I was listening to music, as fan and critic, enthusiastic amateur becoming zealous professional, the sheer pleasure of it all becoming entangled with curiosity and analysis and the sense of making a map that I would never finish. Not least because I still kept setting myself challenges. Once one part of the map seemed complete, to my satisfaction, I set out to draw another part. There would always be new territories to explore.

These new thoughts formed sometime in that rapid acceleration between fifty and sixty, as it became increasingly clear that there was an insurmountable distance between my age now and when I was listening to music as a teenager and the pseudo-something twenty-something years that followed. My approach to what music is, and what it means to me, my own understanding of its history and its relationship to reality, and what was beyond reality, had entered a very different place. I couldn't possibly have the same relationship with the music I had first loved as a kid, becoming a teenager, becoming a professional music journalist paid to have a form of expertise about the newest, brightest pop music.

Perhaps, in the end, I needed something new to write about, and something new to look forward to, even if what I was looking forward to was in fact the end of everything, or at least the end of me, and my musical taste, my musical story. I was needing a new country, or planet, a whole other history, to visit.

I was still writing professionally about music – and of course this tended to be rock and pop, in the old sense of 'file under pop', so that it could mean everything from Faust to Donny Hathaway, Autechre to Fiona Apple, Zappa to Abra, and was beginning to mean more obituaries – but mostly this writing was less and less for publications and more for the artists themselves. A certain amount of freedom was still allowed when you wrote liner notes, books and biographies commissioned by the artists, who were still looking for the kind of writing about music that once performed a function that could even be called creative and collaborative in terms of contributing to the context their music existed within. The sort of writing about music that helped musicians understand their own music more than a stark star rating or a capsule review ever did.

Streaming had begun to conceive of ways to nostalgically recreate the context of rock and pop music from the vinyl and compact-disc era – the idea of the new release as an event, sleeves, charts, photography, criticism, music-paper interviews, which is how your life and image as a musician could be measured and responded to – but essentially was responsible for its destruction, because it treated music as product, as content, not necessarily inspiration.

A certain momentum kept things going, up to a point, as if things were the same as the old days, but instead created a limbo. Music had been put into a new realm that was both dynamic and static. It had been changed, but it was not at all clear into what.

A true new context for popular music was not yet created and maybe it couldn't be; the sites with robotic orderliness were an oddly retrospective muddle of the systems, schedules, styles, sequences and shapes of the lingering past, all piled into one place, and the new shapeless, timeless new world, which was its own context, separated from the outside world that once required and supplied the context – effectively, the meaning, which, whether you were bothered about that or not, created the overall cultural excitement that lifted rock, soul, pop above being simply about the music and, increasingly, the award ceremonies.

Streaming, I decided, once that other, outside-world stuff was eradicated, pulled everything down to being just about the music, and in making all music equal, whatever its style, or historical place, or genre, or commercialism, or obscurity, its position in the canon as classic, cult or hit, it all became the same. From the same place, from the same time.

Essentially, it was the beginning of a new musical era, and inheriting my own instincts about how to make sense of music as an art form and as a cultural energy, I felt that it gave me some new opportunities to write about music as a going concern, where the history wasn't crashing into over-abundance and a tangled mass of timelines but entering an extraordinary, unprecedented transformation. The writer, I hoped, perhaps vainly, might still have a role in working out what all this would be, and what it could mean. The capacity for interpretation, courtesy of the vibrant imagination, hadn't completely broken down, beaten back by all this automation and mediatisation, all this unstoppable assistance and relentless guidance. Here was a new kind of psychic space made up of music. The music was for sale, but in a completely new kind of way, and it was also on show in a completely new kind of way. It was part of a very different way of living that seemed to require a very different way of thinking.

Habits picked up in the 1970s and 1980s meant my writing as a critic for the *Sunday Telegraph* and as a columnist for the *Observer Music Monthly* in the first decade of the twenty-first century seemed a little preoccupied with where music, as an art form, entertainment and/or business, was heading now that there was so much of it, and the context had been so radically transformed. Not just remade and repositioned by the streaming, but also by how there was now a collision of generations piling up with an interest in music that was once very much the concern of the young, those exploring and creating their future, which helped generate a certain tension that gave the music a delectable forbidden quality, however made-up that really was.

When almost everyone else was just carrying on as though the structure of commercial and more serious music was the same as it had been when there were vinyl records and pop charts, it seemed either obsessively crusty or over-theoretical to be worrying about what was happening to music, and what would happen next. In the middle of all this music, more music and more ways to find music, it seemed a little fussy and over-anxious to be thinking too hard about the impact of streaming on music itself.

Few were interested in hearing that we had reached the end of something, even if this was perhaps a more realistic method of maintaining energy. For me, there were plenty of think pieces about the effect of streaming on the music business, but not so many on the impact on musicians and how they made music, on listeners, and any logical, continuing historic shape. A music business wasn't going to keep music going; the ambition and motivation of musicians and their ideas was what would keep music alive. In fact, streaming was the new shape of the music business, as if all along that had been the most important part of music. The business. And perhaps, of course, it always has been: how the music was made, played, distributed, heard, bought, sold, collected – all of this was about business.

I found myself writing an increasing number of pieces that were definitely laments for the end of something, wondering what beginning this led to; the end of the vinyl single, and then the end of the vinyl album, of its essential structural unity, despite sentimental cultural attempts to convince an indifferent set of new audiences that these formats weren't doomed to drift off back into history, as outdated as wax cylinders, 78s and cassettes. Sweet, collectible objects, but increasingly as antique, as vintage, as art deco, as steam-age railway posters and transistor radios.

The record album as art form, as much as a commercial item, had a limited lifespan, and after that it was generational memory, a lingering love, from those who could not imagine an album-less world. A certain generation, never imagining that the album was a temporary arrangement, had lived through the entire lifespan of the album. It was a form and format that began in the late 1940s, became a rock object in the 1960s and started to run out of energy thirty years later as the internet began to colonise, or more accurately replace, reality. In some sense, for all its brand newness and technological novelty as a musical setting, the streaming site is also a nostalgic environment, to soothe the very anxiety it can provoke, having so violently removed a familiar world. It has replaced this familiar world with a combination of the convenient and the familiar – the collected music, carefully organised into sections, genres, lists – and the completely different – music now belongs in another place, which is removed from the world even as it is so inexorably embedded inside it.

I was well past fifty; my automatic subscriptions to the very conducive streaming services meant I was now regularly heading off onto numerous adventures through other music and discovering composers and performers that were new to me and, as far as I was concerned, were new, whether that was Anton Webern, Franz Schubert or John Dowland. I was voyaging further and further into time, and slowly beginning to wonder if it would be even possible for me to write about these new discoveries from what once seemed distant other centuries, or about contemporary music that was treated by the mainstream as though it was centuries old, but was now just twenty-first-century touches away on a smartphone.

As I was tentatively thinking about writing about music made often centuries before I was born, music I seemed forbidden from commenting on because of my class, status, media accreditation and general, common and highly regulated position as a rock critic, I would still occasionally be commissioned to write about that week's pop event. Despite everything I had done to escape the straitjacket of being seen only as some sort of certified expert in pop music, including writing a book in 2004 about the history of pop music that featured the avant-garde composer Alvin Lucier as the star of the story alongside Kylie Minogue, it appeared it would last until the day I died, however old, passing away following a final blast of pop by T. Rex or Lizzo. It was as though pop music was only about making you feel young, however old you were; even if in the end it couldn't stop the actual end result, however much the great pop song simulates or articulates the illusion of eternal life. Music can be the perfect fantasy, but it also needs to be rooted in a certain reality – the reality, the very different new adventure, of the end.

One day, deep into the 2010s, as I was listening to something severely smart by Webern, imagining this playing at the very end of me, taking my soul with it, and at the back of my mind wondering whether I could even begin to write about how much I enjoyed and wanted to understand his music, I was asked by the *Observer* for a topical piece about the respective merits of Harry Styles of boy band One Direction and the jaunty folk-pop troubadour Jake Bugg, who some possibly reasonably considered in this upside-down world as being closer to Bob Dylan or at least Donovan than George Formby. Always finding it hard to turn down a chance to write anything – if only to find out what I did indeed think about the pair, who had suddenly swum into my stream of attention, and of course to get paid, as though writing, representing the remarkable power of the mind, still has a value, before I finally accept the inevitable and reduce myself to reviewing for Amazon (no offence) – I sadly turned off the music. It was too distracting, too absorbing and too damned real. I resigned myself to one more ridiculous ageing-rock-critic, age-inappropriate challenge. Webern would have to wait. I am sure he was used to it.

AN ARTICLE WRITTEN ABOUT HARRY STYLES AND JAKE BUGG BY SOMEONE WITH ANTON WEBERN ON HIS MIND

The conflict between what is perceived as radiant, stable truth and what is merely the fraudulent and dubious opposite is a central element in the game of pop culture and, eventually, modern politics. There has to be some sort of dynamic to maintain momentum and fabricate interest, or the whole charade collapses. Pepsi versus Coke, Nicki Minaj versus Lil'Kim, Blur versus Oasis, Lily versus Cheryl, Apple versus Microsoft, Marvel versus DC, vampires versus werewolves, Tupac versus Biggie, Vans versus Converse, Backstreet Boys versus N'Sync, Jay Z versus Kanye, Snapchat versus literature. This week, to really help us work out what's right and what's wrong in these shifting, shattering times, battle has commenced between Harry Styles and Jake Bugg; between, so it seems, the fake and the authentic, the bright and the dull.

This contest is about as real as the affair between Harry and Taylor Swift, but these days, these flares of publicity, these highly coordinated and tightly targeted fictional campaigns, are where pop's remaining energy mostly resides. In a stylised mock-up of reality. In that sense, poor Bugg follows Swift into the Styles zone, who remains in the news, and in prime place on the shelf. Your first thought is that Styles and Bugg share the same publicist, and it's all following a script written by a student of Martin Amis, Charlie Brooker and Jackie Collins. The whole thing is arranged to create the equivalent of what in the vinyl era was properly called a single. These days, you don't have to release a single to create publicity, and develop a career, you just have to find someone to argue with, and engage in a tabloid-amplified exchange of views about how ugly/stupid/pointless the other one is, producing vapid tension that mirrors the times and is largely empty of actual, imaginative content.

Both of these personalities, these minor actors in a contrived drama, do better having a nemesis, giving them a little necessary old-style edge otherwise missing, and although in this battle it is meant to be clear who is Batman and who is the Joker, who is Beckham and who is Barton, either could take on both roles. The encounter roughs up Styles's scrubbed blandness and encourages the careful nurturing of him as the sort of appealing bad boy that will end up soloing with Robbie-ish gusto and Bowie-lite-lite mannerisms, and gives a little rugged boost to Bugg's scruffy blandness and suggests he may yet shake off his innocence and gain a little emotional heft. Possible endings for this little scuffle include the pair of them making up and appearing as buddies in a Danny Dyer remake of *Slade in Flame*, performing next year's Children in Need song as though they are the modern version of Bowie and Jagger, or being medically spliced together to become one freakish mini-icon, Stuggy Byle.

Up to now, to be honest, I couldn't muster up the enthusiasm to break into their fringes and get the measure of their skinny legs in order to tell them apart, because there seemed nothing in it for me. If I had to choose one I would prefer to chuck a shoe at, whether for love or hate, I would have a little trouble. Neither make music I recognise as music, and even Bugg, the one supported by rock sentimentalists as a refreshing teenage gem with something on his non-*X Factor* mind, produced with conscientious MOR-indie care, writes songs that seem me to leave very quickly on a jet plane in the direction of John Denver.

One Direction are obviously closer to being an artificially sweetened soft drink, a flavour of Pringles, a living soft toy, a ticket to ride, floppy fodder for future reality shows than a musical act of any interest to anyone with an interest in music. Bugg is touted as the Real Thing, Bragg-endorsed, very right-on 6 Music, earnest teenage angst with a capital Working Class, as though he is genuinely in the tradition of Cash and Strummer, with a voice pieced out of Pitney, Guthrie and Albarn. It's hard to believe, though, if such judgements still have any worth, that for all his songwriting talent and decorous musical taste he's any less formulaic and ultimately futile than One Direction, except slanted towards the 'so soft it's not really rock' rock of Cast, Athlete and Snow Patrol.

Bugg's mildly mischievous description of One Direction as 'not really a band', up there with his shruggy comment that Mumford and Sons look like posh farmers with banjos, does not suggest he has much of the wit and insight some reviewers claim. Or, perhaps, that he hasn't got the heart for confrontation. He's been forced into a corner by a media that prefers playground fights to artistic dignity, and he doesn't want to get too involved in this sort of pointless sniping, which drags attention away from his sincere, well-intentioned singer-songwriting and his summoning up a commentary on modern life that may or may not set the world on fire. Once you are tangled up in the popular imagination in stunt warfare with a well-trained teen idol it is very hard, down the line, to act as if what you do is in any way serious.

In that sense, Bugg cannot win. It's Styles all the way, because such set-up bitching and overexcited headlines cannot hurt his work, which is not concerned with the kind of credibility those born before 1990 would recognise. He does nothing conventionally creative, except for his undeniable skill at playing the role of Harry Styles. He plays Styles, odious and irritating to some, adorable and heroic to those more likely to be looking in his eyes or at his groin, with reasonable flair and neat timing. As a performer in the guise of a performer following orders in order to make a name for himself, he has an elastic, narcissistic presence that we will probably look back on as being more of a comment on the queasy, sleazy times than model moody lad Jake's sweet, underwhelming and deeply conventional desire to channel Buddy Holly, Donovan and Noel Gallagher.

On some show-business scale that allows us to actually measure the truth, Styles is closer to Bowie than Bugg is to Dylan. His getting matey with rational thinker Alain de Botton and hedonistic mentor Russell Brand and ripping Socrates from Wikipedia and tweeting it out is more militant than Bugg's old-time rambling on about booze and fags. And if pop is all about the pose, the masquerade, with music the mere decorative soundtrack, then again Styles is way out in front; Bugg is stuck in a square rock 'n' roll past now, as quaint-seeming as Perry Como, Styles effortlessly streaming through the liquid entertainmentscape, as modern as a ruined reputation, a Piers Morgan insult or a food scandal.

Ultimately, Bugg's presence, promoted as authentic and council-estate solid, lacks the complexity required to embody the kind of artistic integrity that makes sense now, rather than in 1956, 1966 or 1996. He can only work for those who wish pop life was how it used to be, back when life was safely seven inches and chart-fixated. It's difficult to appreciate if you might pine for the sixties of the Stones or the nineties of Oasis, but as things are now, Styles is the truth, authentic, perversely sophisticated, a groomed, blank symbol of what's left of pop: the daily hype, monstrous turnover and aimless, targeted pressure. Bugg is the plastic, phoney contestant, a weedy echo of an echo of an echo of the idea that to write your own songs based on personal experience of a local world and a wider universe can lead to genius. Pop is now about nothing other than generating the sort of publicity that can keep the idea of pop going for those still keen on wringing money out of the traditional concept of the teenage fan's desire for the teen idol. Songs are souvenirs of the generated publicity.

We should be able to vote on the result of these skirmishes, with the loser consigned to permanent obscurity. Now that this particular Bugg v. Styles tiff is happening right in front of me, and I find myself starting to actually care, as if it's all for real, I realise that I would vote for Styles, because I will enjoy more over the next few years seeing him professionally negotiate his future fame and desperately chase real purpose, perhaps to the point of personal risk. Troubadour Jake will just churn out more and more pasty, at best quite decent songs that rhyme, written for and about a world that doesn't exist any more.

PART TWO

The Learning – What Brought Me Here

Erik Satie *1909: 'I took to my room and let small things evolve slowly.'*

1. A POSSIBLE NEW ME

I was being asked to write about teenybop stars and faux feuds while in my mid-fifties, a few years after I had been featured in a BBC television documentary attempting to study composition at the world-renowned Royal Academy of Music. I hoped by accepting the challenge it might somehow persuade the *Observer* that, do you know what? He is so good on Harry Styles we should ask him for his no doubt very topical, even fashionable views on the life and death of Anton Webern.

I think I was asked by the BBC to make the programme not so much to check my skill at actually learning some authentic technical information about how to write classical music, but to see someone apparently very much from the rock world being thrown very much out of his comfort zone. It was all part of something I was going to learn more about – the difficulty of moving from one world to another without it being seen as some sort of gimmick.

I was seriously thinking that perhaps at my age, with an enduring desire to still write about music, it could be a way forward: to write about classical music. I naively thought studying classical basics in however contrived or controlled a way might actually create some openings as a classical critic. Naivety does not disappear in your fifties, believe me. If anything, it coats your personality even more. The idea, especially in Britain, especially in the media, that anyone can make a move from one 'speciality' to another without it being part of some entertainment set-up is spectacularly naive.

I took on the challenge. After all, at the time I was a columnist for the *Observer Music Monthly*, a final publishing attempt to pretend that there was still a role for the sort of intense, emotional and comprehensive music papers there had been between the 1970s and 1990s. I didn't quite fit there, but as one of the original creatures from the 1970s I was allowed to roam through where music had ended up, a sort of editor-at-large with no fixed brief, diagnosing the state of music with the benefit, or burden, of hindsight. As a contributor to the *OMM* and by doing the programme, I would get a chance to write about classical music, even if it was only to report how I was daring to pretend I could cross over from one world to another. I would perhaps be given permission, if only temporarily.

It would, of course, be a piece written about how I was going to be a fish out of water, and the expectation was that what I would really learn would have little to do with discovering classical music and more to do with discovering a possible new me. There would be some sort of story. A journey!

The next month I would be back in what seemed to be my comfort zone, writing about the end of this, or the change in that, or desperately trying to warn readers that the future of rock music was going to be made up of endless anniversaries and retrospective exhibitions, or interviewing Harry Styles and reviewing Adele.

The television experience actually did give me the opportunity to write for the *Observer* and get to mention Webern, the sort of thing I felt, for the sake of dignity, I should be doing in my fifties. I had, at least for the moment, something new to write about, which was the most important thing to me. Something new I knew very little about. The finding-out would be what I could write about. First though, in public, I had to play the role of befuddled newcomer – which came quite easy even as I pretended to be a nerveless, adaptable student – and here is the piece written for the *Observer Music Monthly* that allowed me to mention Webern and other adventurers and imagine I was transforming into writing about different music.

2. HOW TO BE A MATURE STUDENT; AN ARTICLE WRITTEN FOR THE OBSERVER MUSIC MONTHLY

In 2010, I spent some time studying composition at the Royal Academy of Music. The plan was for me to spend a year there, possibly more, taking a specially designed course that was intended to rapidly supply enough theory and technique to enable me to read a score and compose a serious piece of concert music avoiding the use of sampling, electronics and recording studios. Essentially the qualification that allowed me to enter the building to join some of the most talented and ambitious young musicians in the world – jumping years of necessary preparation, practice and patience – was that I had been hired by a television production company that had been commissioned by the BBC. My year at the Academy was to be filmed, and my progress, or not, was to be ruthlessly monitored for two TV documentaries that would be shown on BBC Four.

Possibly because of the success of a recent programme about pop music and style, where I discussed shoes with Jarvis Cocker, Kraftwerk's ties with New Order and noizy trousers with Noddy Holder, the music and arts department at the BBC had rewarded me with this chance to return, for better or worse, to formal learning for the first time since I left school at sixteen in 1973. I don't count the embarrassing few months I spent at Stockport College on a business studies course, leaving when my attendance record dipped below 10 per cent. As I missed classes at the college, my future educational direction, and my sensibility as listener, writer and thinker, was then defined by my susceptible teenage listening during daytime hours in a darkened bedroom to the first post-prog releases on the Virgin label, apart from Mike Oldfield – Henry Cow, Gong, Kevin Coyne, Robert Wyatt, Hatfield and the North – going to sleep to the endless, drifting, electro-heavenly sound of Fripp and Eno's *No Pussyfooting*, and reading Ballard, Burroughs, Beckett, Walter Benjamin and Roland Barthes, just counting the Bs. If this activity had been marked, I would have received the Ordinary National Diploma I never received in business studies.

At some point during the filming, 'the journey', as these programmes have become in a world where reality TV and accompanying fallout has profoundly distorted reality, the intention was no doubt that I would break down in tears faced with some frustrating setback, such as a general inability to understand the precious secrets of harmony buried beneath hundreds of years of consolidated music theory. Arguments would need to ensue, prejudices would be broken down or consolidated, and the music I wrote would either be the equivalent of 'Pauline Quirke plays the violin' or 'Phil Daniels makes his own cheese'. The bitter truth was my inexplicable inability to recognise the difference between major or minor chords being played on the piano, confirming for every musician I have ever given a bad review to that, as an unfortunate edit had me say during the first programme, 'I know nothing about music.'

Perhaps I could write the kind of music that, responding as a discriminating critic, I would not actually dismiss as a frivolous, totally fraudulent attempt to create a serious piece of music, something that could be actually played on my dream radio show between Milton Babbitt and the Books. Or would I end up with the kind of music that professional classical critics would sweetly pity, music causing friends and colleagues to avert their eyes. And ears.

There would be drama to come, but the real excitement for me was the thought of all the unexplored new music waiting to be discovered – music that would be new to me even if it was written hundreds of years ago, already beginning to appreciate how in an era of Arvo Pärt, John Surman, Múm, and Stars of the Lid, medieval music can sound as modern as anything.

I think this was something else that made the idea of learning composition at the Royal Academy so seductive. There would be new histories to follow, new obscurities to delight in, music that for me and many others had got away, the unique, the bizarre, the freakish, a reminder of the thrill it was to venture into the dangerous unknown, now that CD repackaging, middle-aged music magazines and internet access meant that every dark, remote corner of rock and pop was being comprehensively over-lit, gossiped about and repeatedly analysed.

The curious listener I had always been would be shown into new areas of existence where there existed collections of strange specimens for me to hear for the first time. Probably not what the production company and BBC Four was hoping for, but I was imagining a glorious cabinet of curiosities that I could enthusiastically introduce on television. The documentary series was given the title *How to Be a Composer*, and I was uncomfortable with what that promised; as a writer, you are often asked at talks and panels at literary festivals how to be a writer, as though the secret was something to do with work hours, tools and process. The whole internet-shaped world seemed more interested in constant tips than actual ideas and the impossibility of truly understanding where they come from and how you manage and manipulate them.

How to Be a Composer as a title seemed to propose that the viewer would be politely served with the secret of how to write music, as if it was the same for everyone, a basic, practical and very fixed list of techniques and instructions to follow. Mysteries would be solved, whereas I was in the mood to find new mysteries and relish their inexplicable energies, not try to pin anything down.

I was interested in the rootless, tangled imagination of the composer, which could not be so easily copied or recreated, rather than chasing down and summarising some instant formula, as if it was that simple. As though composing music was like knitting, a compression of learned information into a craft, which would leave out the particular, personal nature of the imagination, which is what makes a piece of music individual and not simply a pattern or texture given a regulated shape. It would miss out a kind of madness, and the whimsical thoughts, and complicated loneliness, and fear and self-loathing that leads to the creative freedom necessary to produce original art, but I had not been asked to ask more questions. I was expected to come up with answers, and be an amiable, accessible and satisfying guide to how to be a composer. I was also thinking of it being more 'How to Write About Classical Music', but the BBC wasn't going to allow me to use their resources to get some fast-tracked deluxe private education.

I started out with the intention of using it as an opportunity to become familiar with classical music; how else could I learn to write a piece – and ultimately write about the music – without knowing as much as possible about the music, where it had come from, and how the rules and regulations were made? As a lover of unusual music inspired by the beguiling and fantastically practical way Alex Ross summarised twentieth-century classical music in his inspiring book *The Rest is Noise*, I was beginning to feel that I needed to move outside my usual, often fairly far-out listening places to uncover vast areas of unusual music that I had missed out on. What tends to be called classical music, in its purest state, seems to value a necessary isolation in the making and hearing of music that is threatened in rock and pop by the current fad for incessant sharing and commercialised cool. Being part of a crowd is fine, but not all the time, and not when it compels everyone to think the same.

I thought my year at the Academy might help me understand why writing about classical music has lately rarely achieved the intensity and insight that rock criticism has – experimental, thought-provoking, metaphorical, original writing as opposed to the kind of formal, technical, distancing and often blandly controlled writing that classical music inspires.

I had never written about classical music, apart from, occasionally, reviewing a composer whose work had sailed close to the remote coastline of experimental rock – someone like Steve Reich or Karlheinz Stockhausen, and the classified-as-rock musicians they had inspired, Brian Eno and Kraftwerk, This Heat and John Cale. Getting this close to classical music, I would notice a strange, intimidated change in my approach, as though I was not allowed and possibly not ever able to write about, say, J. S. Bach in the same way as I would about the Rachels, or Stravinsky the way I write about Hot Chip, or Bartók the same way I would about Jóhann Jóhannsson.

Was this because I couldn't help but think that classical music is somehow too important, too special, too serious to be written about as though it is just sound to enjoy and feelings to share? Am I intimidated because I think I need to know something secret about its construction and place in history that I do not know, or do I think that actually it cannot take being written about as impressionistically, as spontaneously, as emotionally as I would write about modern and postmodern pop, because it is old, and presented, packaged, organised, sponsored in such ways as to merely confirm its oldness, its irrelevance, and ultimately its protected opaqueness? As a serious music specialist Alex Ross knew what he was doing and saying without it seeming cold, impenetrable and flat, and he could swing effortlessly from Björk to Busoni and back, but I got the feeling he'd studied more than me. So, back to school.

I had often passed the grand, imposing and oddly hushed-seeming Royal Academy along the Marylebone Road in central London, just by Regent's Park, a couple of hundred yards along from the tourist-swamped Madame Tussauds, and it always seemed about as likely that I would ever enter the Academy as I would the waxworks. When I did enter the building, nervously scrubbed up for a surprising first day at school, camera trailing me, definitely concerned that I was entering a sterile place of worship, an institution that trained obedient musicians not to enter the dynamic future flow of music but sink back into its static past, I came across unexpected action and activity. There was more buzz than hush.

I was soon mixing with teachers and pupils constantly engaged with the problems serious music faces in a frivolous age: some have resigned themselves to operating in a shadowy place at the farthest edges of the fragmenting new world, others to investigating how interest can be sustained in a music that, at its most dramatic and revealing, is about creating something that doesn't sound like anything you've ever heard before – music that requires a disappearing attention to detail to decode, let alone learn to love.

I found that the elevating passion and enthusiasm that in my world is consistently applied to the Velvets, Iggy and the Stooges, the Beach Boys, Joy Division, Radiohead, Roxy Music, David Bowie, or Ornette, Miles and Coltrane, was being unsentimentally given to the grandeur and gentleness of Mahler, the immense intricacy of Janáček, the unexpected violence of Richard Strauss, the livid insights of Ferruccio Busoni, the magic force of Schoenberg, the folk modernism of Bartók, the simply delicious complex music of Alban Berg, the ravishing perversities of Pierre Boulez, the speculative loveliness of Aaron Copland.

From the outside the building can make you think everyone inside is keeping themselves to themselves. But what I found on the other side of the heavy entrance doors were young composers, some of them occasionally alongside me in class, politely accepting my peculiar ageing presence, determined to refresh the long, apparently decaying history of concert music by working out how to remain faithful to its principles while absorbing influences from unusual and unexpected new sources. Classical music only stays alive if there are signs it still lives, not as it once did, but as it should do.

My intention was to use the year not only to learn about the basics of music making and playing, but also to see if I could work out a clear version of a history of classical music, one that would help provide me with a map of how music commonly described in this way has passed through the centuries. Not a map that suggested there is some kind of logical destination, but one that suggested it was possible to find all the music, that it was available and accessible for those with a sudden urge to find it. I wanted to find ways to demystify a vast, complex world that seemed locked away behind a socio-politically constructed stuffy public image, as if it is a music that belongs only to a conscribed elite

obsessed with ossified geniuses and their timeless masterpieces. An elite
dedicated to establishing carefully preserved hierarchical distinctions.

Classical music gives the impression of being run by a set of secret
societies apparently talking among themselves, using language that keeps
those not in the know at a distance. It seems to need a secret handshake to
gain admittance. Both sides of the fence seem happy with this arrangement.
When there are moves made to try and commercially brand the idea of
classical music, to make it more friendly in a world tightly defined only
by what succeeds commercially, the music's power, depth and beauty, the
fact that it has always looked to the future and expressed thoughts about
an artist's thoughts, emotions and states of being with a directness and
immediacy no other art form achieves, seems betrayed. It was as though
classical music can only survive as a gimmick, an unthreatening, soothing
and universally appealing form of charming eccentricity.

Those that sponsor the idea of classical music seem happy to present
it as something stripped of its radicalism, as safely separated from the
vital issues and crises of the day, and those that are indifferent to the
perceived pomp and ceremony of classical music are happy for it to curl
up and shrivel under the weight of its history.

The task the television programme had allowed me to set myself
seemed to suggest that the corny old story is true – at a certain stage
in your life, as you settle down or leave behind childish dreams of rock
'n' roll's primacy, you move from beer to wine, and from Dylan to
Bach. I actually wasn't keen at all on leaving Dylan behind. I did want
to find out whether it is right that, just because Bach is dead and his
music ancient – and often made to sound ancient, as though to let
it be touched with modern sensibility would threaten its essence and
pollute its specialness – it occupies another kind of place in the cultural
landscape and is set apart, for reasons that ultimately suit those who love
the music and those who do not. And was a similar destiny ultimately
awaiting Bob Dylan?

I wanted to find out what was more responsible for how classical music
is now generally perceived. The manner in which the music written
before the twentieth century had been tamed and archived for polite,
ordered and exclusive consumption, the dark, troubling edges of its
beauty smoothed away, gentility replacing agitation, the philosophical
furies that motivated the music jettisoned. Meaning that fans of Aphex
Twin and Animal Collective who might take to the convulsive joys of

Silvestre Revueltas or the crazed bleakness of Jean Sibelius would never consider such music to have anything to do with them and their lives, as it appears to be completely sealed off from contemporary reality.

Then there's the issue of whether the chaos of contemporary composition in the twentieth century, as various composers battled with the imposing past, a fraught, turbulent and nihilistic present and their own demons to produce a succession of inaccessible, demanding sounds, profoundly alienated audiences increasingly used to the glamorous thrills and sensual consolations of pop, musical theatre and jazz. Or is the ultimate exile of all forms of serious music – music that is a challenge, and helps you prepare for challenges – one major result of a colossal collective collapse of concentration, or the introduction of a new technologically cultivated form of concentration that finds solace and stimulation in ways that will soon make everything twentieth century and before, not just classical music, completely out of date?

Chasing new sounds to keep my interest in new music alive, because of those first tantalising teenage feelings I got hearing the serene, giddy strangeness of Stockhausen, which strangely echoed the strangeness of Faust and NEU!, I've always been interested in classical music, or at least that part of the music I got to through Fripp and Eno's deglazed glam drone *No Pussyfooting*, the post-wartime expanding, space-filling and emptying, mind-stretching experimental music that seeped through into rock and pop, dub and techno, ambient and trip hop, and elsewhere the German electronic music of the late 1960s and early 1970s, and the Jamaican dub of Lee 'Scratch' Perry using machines to summon up devastated ancestral rhythms – this helped me to Steve Reich, Philip Glass, Terry Riley, La Monte Young, George Crumb, Morton Feldman, John Cage, and therefore Claude Debussy and Erik Satie, the classical music that seems to bridge the pre-industrial classical with the post-industrial, which prepared the way for the experiments and insights of the modernists.

Inspired by works of the endlessly mobile, conceptually minded non-musician Brian Eno, a constantly persuasive but subversive democratiser of the successive questing compositional spirit that drove music forward from Chopin and Mozart to Wagner, Satie and Debussy, and then through the devastation of the twentieth century to Varèse and Cage via Stravinsky and Webern, I have previously been involved in the making of music. I had been a contributor to cryptic electro-pioneers Art of Noise, and to the electro chamber ensemble Infantjoy – using both projects to examine the music of Debussy and Satie, believing from a non-musician point of view that all recorded modern music began with these two French visionaries, and using the music we made to create the equivalent of a surreal biographical essay and imagine how they might work given access to modern recording equipment. I imagined them spanning the age of the score as the sole method of 'storing' music and the age of electronics, when music was stored by literally recording it, and bringing the sound to life. At the beginning of Debussy's and Ravel's lives the only way of passing music forward was through the score, a fundamental abstraction; by the end of their life, music could be passed forward through recordings, through its actual sound. At first, these recordings were literal, simply a copy of the music. Within decades, the recordings would become a more sophisticated method of making music, constructing structures and atmospheres that Debussy and Ravel started to do using only notes written on a page and their imagination.

I willed Debussy and Ravel closer to the world of pop than others would place them, although I would still feel I couldn't write about them with the same confidence and indeed exuberance as I did pop. It was as though normal feelings expressed in a non-technical way were somehow forbidden.

I have been a presence in a studio, applying judgement and creative commentary on the electronic construction of a piece of music to the extent that I effectively contributed to its composition. I can, though, play no musical instrument, and when my year started at the Academy I had no real idea what a 'bar' actually was. I did not know how long it was, what was inside it, how it was used, the way it connected the bar before it to the bar after it. I did not know the difference between a crotchet and a quaver. I indulged in critically, even sensually drooling over complex time signatures when used by Van der Graaf Generator and Soft Machine, or Cecil Taylor and Paul Motian, savouring the dissolving, distorting effect but never really understanding the actual methodology involved. It sounded from the outside like some sort of poetry, not part of a strict formula discovered over time to remind composers how certain effects could be achieved and refined. Would becoming an insider ruin this poetry for me, turning it into factors of knowledge?

To be honest, in all the time I have written about music, whether that was Gang of Four, Steve Reich, Chemical Brothers or Miles Davis, I have never thought about notes, chords, modulations, pitch relationships, tempo, timbre or cadences. This hasn't stopped me, for better or worse, writing millions of words about music, and aggressively advocating what I believed was great music, and what I thought was awful.

Once I started to study music, getting used to the mathematical element, the series of formulae refined over time to enable certain inspirations and instincts to be repeated and adjusted, what would happen to me as a critic, as a devoted but untutored lover of music? I'd made up my own intuitive standards of what music works and doesn't work, why it will last and why it won't. Would they become dislodged if I slipped from being a non-musician, working in and around music and having a point of view that proved professionally acceptable, to actually becoming a more official musician? What would change in the ways I listened and made sense of music if I knew some of what were to me its secrets, its science, its fluid, tantalising inner dimensions? Would this new knowledge ruin music for me, enrich the listening experience, or ultimately make no difference at all? Would it make me a better critic or mean that, somehow, I sacrificed the ability to successfully generate and arrange my critical decisions, effectively ruining me as a critic and music writer? Would it be like a golfer halfway through a fairly successful career hoping to extend it by riskily changing their swing? If I was, in fact, doing the equivalent of performing some kind of surgery on my swing, would I forget everything and plummet down the world rankings?

Perhaps in the new world where everyone's opinion and roughly compiled knowledge can be evenly distributed throughout the internet as though it all has equal validity, where the authoritative role of the critic has been near-fatally wounded by the inexorable spread of user-generated content, by constant access to music that can bypass the recommendations and knowledge of the traditional skilled gatekeepers, it wasn't so much of a risk to tamper with my critical swing. And the idea that I might perhaps learn how to compose modern contemporary music, possibly with an audience that can be counted in the hundreds, will ultimately be more lucrative than any continuing existence as a professional rock writer. The journalist, especially the rock journalist, displaced by the millions who can now recreate for free the duties of the rock critic, is facing up to seeing his role slip towards something approaching the relevance of a blacksmith. Oddly enough, the role of contemporary music composer, writing the type of music that most people will never hear but adding to the continuity of thinking and exploring that stretches back centuries, may yet outlast the conventional role of the print journalist.

The head of composition at the Royal Academy is Philip Cashian, whose own tartly seasoned, radically stylish music sounds as influenced as much by Frank Zappa, Gentle Giant and King Crimson as Charles Ives, Pierre Boulez and Harrison Birtwistle. If his music was on, say, the Leaf label, or folded into electronica on Warp, or given space on the 4AD or Bedroom Community labels, it would not actually be defined as classical music, and would be easily filed alongside Murcof, Jóhan Jóhannsson and Autechre.

As classical music, Cashian's music inherits different levels of expectation, and a certain sense that because it does not produce sounds as soothing and familiar and in all ways as rich as the canonised classical greats – even if their music was considered during its day painfully discordant and often quite unnerving – it is disappointing, even insulting. The fact that such a committed modernist, even postmodernist, as Cashian is the head of composition at the Academy – allowing for the fact that other departments necessarily operate within a less conscientiously contemporary framework – made me realise that the Academy does not hold the view that serious music is best presented as a kind of soporific, or that classical music is simply about reverent historical reconstruction.

Phil suggested the brainy, exuberant conductor/composer/scholar Christopher Austin to be my composition teacher. A passionate advocate of unfavoured and unfashionable twentieth-century romantic music, he's simultaneously a master at treating the ferociously reviled techniques of serial music – compositional procedures that rejected traditional tonality, initially dictated by Schoenberg – not as something that aggressively drains sensuality and destroys pleasure, but as a way of increasing musical vocabulary and compositional freedom. Consequently he can move freely from Rachmaninov to Elisabeth Lutyens, or from William Walton to Witold Lutosławski without worrying about their place in any canon, about their reputation for either lush, buttery sentimentality or agile cerebral intensity. For Chris, being one thing – emotionally tender – does not cancel out also being another thing – fiercely analytical.

I started to understand how Olivier Messiaen crosses back and forwards between the sensationally romantic and the provocatively idiosyncratic. I began to see how in essence Bartók and Milhaud were saying similar things to Schumann and Tchaikovsky – and ultimately Dylan and Van Morrison, Can and Godspeed You! Black Emperor – but using different voices and sounds, and responding to different environments, epochs, events and personal circumstances.

The young flautist Hannah Riddell was my notation teacher, a lover of baroque music patiently and passionately unveiling the history, meaning and value of the score as the central element in how various forms of music have crossed time. I became fascinated with the idea of the score as a kind of quasi-literary object that contained the original mysterious thinking of a great mind, enabling the lost, true thoughts of Bach, Mozart, Beethoven and Mahler to be repeatedly turned into sound and given life – any performance is merely an estimate, an interpretation of the marks and indications on the page, a hopefully inspired guess at what they were thinking, and the genius of the modern interpreter is to imagine as accurately as possible what on earth it was they were hearing in their mind, and how it might be brought up to date without sacrificing its connection with history.

I started to read scores – the marks, lines, symbols, codes, abbreviations and instructions making an exhilarating new kind of sense – as a kind of map of the imagination, and a way of delivering music across the delicate surface of old-fashioned paper deep into the future, even when fragile technology breaks down. Misunderstandings about how to interpret the mysteries of a score, or ideas provoked by gaps and spaces in the clarity of a score, lead to ideas about new forms of music. The score is a secret, but filled with sometimes blatant, sometimes discreet, clues about how to uncover its hidden truth. The score is sacred, but it's also something to break apart.

Both my teachers had ideas about the history of music and its repertoire that constantly surprised me, encouraging me to move into classical music not as though you needed history lessons to do so, but simply because it consists of various moments when musicians in the time when they were alive generated sound to express feelings, both about their time and sound itself, in a new way. Both found ways to teach me that negotiated the reality that in one way I had a tremendous amount of listening knowledge and could spend all day tracing routes between Ravel and Lee Morgan, Messiaen and extreme electronic musician Fennesz, Schubert and conceptual electronic duo Matmos, and in another, I had the musical ability of a three-year-old. I was a mutant, knowing too much, knowing very little.

This was where I was worried that the awareness of how childish I was in many areas would eradicate the self-taught expert, destroy all my confidence, and mean I would end the time I spend at the Academy not as any kind of composer, and also without the ability to write not only about classical music but about any music at all. The illusion of my critical faculties based on those first few years making it up as I went along at the *NME* would be fatally punctured.

Hannah would listen patiently while I defensively spent an improper amount of time explaining my patchy theories about how *musique concrète* – *concrète* more as a French word for 'real' than anything necessarily brutalist, music built up using a set of recorded, manipulated 'concrete' sounds that are then arranged into a piece of music, or a sonic montage – and primitive electronic music in the 1950s altered the entire way music could be made, creating sound that could be nonlinear and multidimensional.

Composition jumped nimbly from Edgard Varèse's *Ionisation* and Stockhausen's *Gesang der Jünglinge* to Wendy Carlos to Kraftwerk to Eno to Björk, technosonically subdividing and reaching through the recording studio into all modern pop music. And what about the way Stockhausen reduced music to 'information', even as he composed in order to represent a universe in continual expansion, perhaps anticipating how in the twenty-first century everything in the world would be turned into continually expanding information? And did you know that in 1937 George Gershwin died and Phillip Glass was born? Varèse was born in 1883, the year Wagner died. Debussy died in 1918, the year Leonard Bernstein was born. Isn't that interesting? I would wonder aloud – perhaps putting off the moment when I had to beat time in 9/8 or work out how many flats made up the key of F – what the actual function was of all artistic products in contemporary society? What is it all for, I would declaim, all these technical demands and musical directions, all these decrees and mandates? Hannah would then ask me to play 'Happy Birthday' on the piano from the sheet music in front of me, and not flinch as I ended up turning it into something more than a little unhappy.

I'd ask Chris if he felt that classical music, its enthralled, retrospective elevation and adulation of Mozart, Beethoven and Wagner, and the way it contains rigid conventions, has had a petrifying effect on everything it touches. I would ramble at length on the way classical music, as a direct or indirect source, lush or aggressive, even as it fell away from the popular imagination in the twentieth century, was an absolutely essential part in the impact of cinema, giving elevating weight and focus to images that needed completing with this kind of emotional power.

I would suggest that perhaps post-war classical music's lack of interest in alternative ways of realising and recording music – failing to properly, profoundly, absorb the revelatory lessons of jazz, resisting the studio multitracking that rapidly turned pop into an art and looking down on pop's ingenious, open-minded sonic advancements, stubbornly refusing to import the more audacious achievements in rock – has ultimately fixed nineteenth-century methods as absolute, after all the detours, movements, counter-movements and brave new procedures of the twentieth century. Chris would respond by playing me something by Ralph Vaughan Williams or a Malcolm Arnold piece inspired by Charlie Parker, urging me to shake off prejudices about music that had accumulated because of the way it is turned into a cultural commodity, blocking the light from its actual unspoilt majesty.

Theory, and the ultimate confidence trick of making up plausible history in the image of your own unstable preferences and prejudices, needed to be replaced by the purity of technique and order. Technique and precision that does threaten to limit inspiration, to trap composers inside outdated methods, but that leaves enough openings through which intelligence may penetrate, opening up new ways of generating and organising sound.

During the winter months of 2010 I turned into a willing, wide-eyed, if still slightly intimidated pupil, knowing that the more I learned, the more I knew how much there was to learn. I sat in on a seminar given by the Master of the Queen's Music, Sir Peter Maxwell Davies, about the cello suites of Bach. Such seminars are open to the public, although only a very few souls took up this amazing offer. And watching Max – look how familiar I was getting? – analyse how Bach's mind and music worked, as a mixture of the divinely mathematical and the naturally mysterious, was irresistible. He examined the remnants of a long-lost modernity, from when Bach was the most advanced musician in the known world, making progress like no one else, and his talk had a dreamlike quality, where the music he was discussing didn't come from the past, or the future, or the now, it actually purely came from 'music', which is nowhere and everywhere.

For me, one of my programmes could easily have been taken up by getting to understand Max's uncanny thinking about Bach's uncanny thinking, and the way he explained the music as something that can still be heard, if you broaden your conception of music, as though it is still as vivaciously modern, as sensationally brand new, as it was when it was first composed. The revelation was hearing Maxwell Davies promote music above time and fashion, because at its most powerful it leaves such constructs behind; it becomes pure energy. Music, something that I never took for granted but just assumed was exactly what I thought it was, changed shape in front of and inside me.

I waited to see what difference it would make to me as a writer, as a listener, as I got used to the idea of bars, and how you fill bars with the notes and indeed lack of notes that you definitely desired, and let the bars dissolve, and how you structured a piece so that it didn't seem like an arbitrary collection of sounds but a considered piece that accurately reflected not understanding of technique but the mystery of thought and the strange fluctuations of feeling. A change did start to happen. I began hearing music in a new way. It was as though the music expanded into and beyond itself. Listening to my favourite music as pure abstract sensation formed in distant, unknown ways merged with listening to it and realising how it existed as the result of a calculated but uninhibited series of spontaneous, experienced and surprising decisions that both accepted the limitations of arbitrarily arranged musical rules and strived to stretch outside them and find new ground. And indeed new rules, themselves to be broken.

You could detect in the music I cautiously started to write the influences of my three primary teachers. The music they played me as part of my learning – the best training of all is to listen, and then to think, not necessarily the easiest things to film – mixed in with instincts and enthusiasms I already had. Cashian played me a John Cage piece that I did not know, *One*, the result of some utterly ingenious Cageian score-play, one note transformed through shifting performance perceptions into something unbelievably gorgeous and evocatively trancelike, reminding me how Cage was writing profoundly winsome piano pieces in the dark, threatening middle of the twentieth century, before he turned to the noise in silence, the romance of chance, and various ways of musically connecting the mind and soul.

Austin constantly pushed at my snobby, narrow-minded, art-rock-inspired prejudices, showing me how a dynamically ornate piece by Malcolm Williamson was achieved with such spectacular economy. Hannah played me the elegant modernist Anton Webern generously, euphorically rewriting Bach using a combination of pure science and burning inspiration. It was a kind of transformative remix, the score as a virtual mixing desk, and it clarified for me how Reich, Glass, Nyman, Riley, Feldman had fused their take on the competitive battles of pre- and post-Second World War composing with rational traditions absorbed from the centuries before Bach, Handel and Vivaldi, when music consisted of simple, unadorned vocal lines pragmatically connecting fixed earthly desires with a mystical shifting cosmos.

Hearing these new things, making new connections, and thinking about what I was hearing and whether I could dare to try something similar, meant that, even if only to myself, for myself, even just having to write it down for the sake of this feature, I was beginning to write about classical music. Rightly or wrongly, and it took a kind of courage, and it certainly helped me place things in history, I was describing Anton Webern as an 'elegant modernist' and therefore beginning to get my bearings. I was making connections – as Wittgenstein said, what we call 'explanation' is a form of connection – and these connections were clearing the way forward.

I was hearing Mozart's pure, subtle and desperately despairing Adagio in B minor, written not long after the death of his father Leopold and in tribute clearly echoing the kind of church music Leopold would ask Mozart to play, and thinking of it as being as modern as the next moment. And in the sense that it is about life and death, a portrait of a man who was so alive and then so not, it was as modern as the next moment that does not come – as modern as anything can be. I hadn't expected it when I began studying at the Royal Academy, but Mozart, previously way beyond me, was becoming clearer, through the enclosed, and open-ended, beauty of the music, which I could now hear separated from the busyness and business – the pure image – of his name. The music was in fact nameless, unfixed even after there had been centuries of attempts to pin it down, and once I realised that, I could pay attention to it, and realise that it was paying attention to me.

I could put Mozart in the same paragraph as Webern and begin breaking down the history into a succession of breakthroughs and premonitions: Webern (Second Viennese School) considered Mozart's *Jupiter* Symphony, No. 41, in C major, his last one, at thirty-two, written in 1788, the year of the American Constitution and the year before the start of the French Revolution, to be Mozart's (First Viennese School) most important contribution to the symphonic form – the fiendish, almost atonal passage in the finale a primordial foreshadowing of early twentieth-century serialism to come.

I was making up a map, even if just for myself. There was no linear path of continuing progress in musical history, just sudden shocks and flashes that capture the 'time of now'. Within that, there was a series of developments I was able to follow that enabled me to create landing stations from where I could find new forms of music.

Early chant music, moving through successive periods of experiment and trial and error, evolved into increasingly sophisticated multi-instrumental contrapuntal music consisting of almost hallucinatory intense musical harmony. Each stage of composition involved breaking an old context, breaking up sounds, shaking up rhythms, stimulating new contexts, Beethoven abstracting Mozart, Wagner abstracting Beethoven, Schoenberg abstracting Wagner even as he respected Brahms, Ravel abstractly slipping between Debussy and Stravinsky, Satie abstractly shadowing them all. Harmony was abolished, and non-harmony led back to harmony, but this new harmony was now not the same as the old harmony, because it had come out of a period of non-harmony.

I began to see a territory of classical music, the way one thing leads to another, the way music moves forwards by becoming liberated from the historic implications loaded into it, in much the same way I have come to view the ebb and flow of pop music. Doing this allowed me to smash through the barriers erected around the music and get to it simply as it is, once all associations of time, history, fashion, prejudice and interpretation are stripped away – seeing Dowland or Shostakovich not as something that should only be appreciated in a very particular and formalised context, requiring sophisticated technical understanding and the correct clothing, but as liberated sound existing in a pure metaphysical space reflecting timeless thinking and emotion. For all the obstacles, the complexity of the history, the amount of music to digest, the succession of forms, the degrees of intellectualising, the repeated myths and ritualising, the mainstream indifference, a certain sort of vibrant simplicity took over. I began to view and understand music written even by the revered and mummified old masters as simply sounds being moved around through space and time in order to communicate feelings that spoken language or other artistic endeavours cannot come close to conveying.

As a composer, I roughly learned how to put together in one coherent space a hundred bars of notes that repeated themselves and spun off into connected patterns. I looked into the anatomy of sound, discerning how each sound is composed of its own vivid rhythms and vibrating tones, has momentum, erupts, vanishes. I began to view the entire history of music as a sequence of accumulating bars of music. These individual bars were like a constellation of sounds that connected with each other and formed a framework around history, and a history of thought. I tried to compose my own music, beginning with monotonous drones that emerged out of my love for the patient force, the philosophical application of Eno, Feldman and La Monte Young, then finding ways to thicken texture, introduce pitch and play with harmony. I still operated as I would have before, in an electronic context, generating musical sounds through instructions and non-musical suggestions, playing other music for reference points, needing such a collaborative input from Chris Austin that in the pop world he would be acting as 'producer', but this was all joined by a brand new musical vocabulary.

I decided to test the theory of how Ravel and Debussy influenced the questing, sensuous piano playing of Bill Evans and therefore the late 1950s jazz of Miles Davis by appropriating some Bill Evans chords and placing them in an orchestral context, writing my first ensemble piece. Eventually, which neglects to mention considerable help from a committed Chris as he sorted out realistic settings for my stolen chords, I had written down ready for orchestral performance *As If Toward Paradise* – the paradise being for me the enlightenment this late in my life of a suddenly revealed new musical universe. It was written for CoMA – Contemporary Music for All – a series of amateur music ensembles around the country who commission new pieces from schools such as the Academy, and from contemporary composers such as Michael Nyman and Andrew Poppy.

The moment I first heard those adapted Bill Evans chords turned into moving yet somehow motionless strings with inevitably huge echoes of jazz arranger Gil Evans, the camera got its teary moment. All my own work – give or take the help of my teacher and of course the genius of Bill and Gil Evans – and made majestic, if only to me, by being passed through the score via the concentration and contemplation of the players, turning those marks on paper into a souvenir of a very specific time and place, and very particular emotions. The music didn't explain what they were, but it wouldn't have existed or sounded like it did without them.

I felt myself becoming addicted to the idea of imagining a piece of music, defining the limits of the piece, what instruments to use, what form, how long, how free, writing it down, and then – eventually – hearing it performed by an orchestra or ensemble and discovering just how close the interpretation was to what I imagined in my mind. Somehow, in that unfathomable space between the imagined piece and the interpreted result lay some of the secrets of the fluctuating mystery of music, and I felt myself move a little, a very little, closer than ever to understanding them.

As I write, I am completing a string quartet. Yes, really, I am. At some point during the time I spent at the Royal Academy, the thought seemed to be the most exotic thing imaginable. The string quartet is such a difficult discipline, and very exposed, lacking the protection of blasting, chirping, rattling masses of instruments compensating for lazy, banal writing. It was the best way of demonstrating the changes there have been in my growing musical ability.

The greatest musicians of all time have surely said and done everything possible using two violins, a viola and a cello. This became the challenge. Could I find any kind of newness, anything at all that sounded authentic, having just learned how to begin to explain my thoughts about music not just through words but through the assembly and spacing of notes and time. And then, because during my year at the Academy one of my favourite writers, essayists and thinkers, the brilliant, troubled David Foster Wallace, committed suicide, I wanted to name this piece, and other pieces, using a title Wallace used for a number of short stories – 'Yet Another Example of the Porousness of Certain Borders'.

I also used it for a number of pieces, to describe how for me the borders between music, and between eras and styles in classical music, were falling apart. Using the title as a remembrance of Wallace — and one thing I learned about classical music was the importance of remembrance, as a religious, human and artistic act, the progressive-minded tying together of people, time and ideas, especially when such things were increasingly threatened — meant it had to at the very least demonstrate I had some genuine idea of what brilliance actually is and try to attain it in whatever way I could.

The studying and the filming had not been easy. The one or two days a week I had some lessons were enough for the television but not for any true learning. I only really had the time to learn fragments of technical scaffolding and develop a crush on the idea of the notation while only learning vaguely how to listen to a piece of music while following the score.

I now miss just how multidimensional and liberating writing the score can actually be. While I was working on the string quartet, having a favourite key to write in, and a tempo I wanted it to be, my teacher Chris gave me some clues and then left me to it. At that point I really was alone, where I apparently wanted to be. Again, not a place that is easily filmed, so the programme does not really transmit the anguish and panic I felt writing something that may have no life at all beyond the television show but which I had made important to myself, as if somehow it would explain me more than anything, as if that is in any way important, and also the awfulness of Wallace's death, and of suicide — each reported suicide of a celebrity or artist instantly taking me back to my father's suicide in 1977, reanimating the feelings, and confusion, and the grief I suppose I always looked to music to help explain. In a book I wrote about his suicide, I wondered about the last time he did various things — shaving, eating, driving — but I never wondered what the last piece of music he ever listened to had been. I didn't know much about what kind of music he liked, if any at all, really.

This kind of composing takes time, the kind of time that seems to take no time but in fact lasts for hours, with nothing to show for it but a few marks on a page, representing the outlining, the trying-out of ideas, many if not all of which may end up going nowhere. Somewhere in there is how to be a composer. To make up a few minutes of music that in effect plays with time and bends it into a structure that intends to defeat time, takes so much real time to complete, it is as though you are actually being punished by Time itself for daring to take it on.

At times the piece did seem to verge on the 'Pauline Quirke learns to play the violin', and at times, after I'd I spent hours moving one note around, struggling with trying to ensure the cello sounds as beautiful as I knew it should, to generate balanced but careering sound that was appropriately harrowing and inspiring, I heard what I can only describe as… something. I got a tantalising glimpse that I was on the verge of getting close to getting close to getting on the outside of understanding of knowing one day how to capture parts of what I had been hearing in the spellbinding, magical, demanding string quartets written by Beethoven, Debussy, Ravel, Schoenberg, Zemlinsky, Bartók, Elliott Carter, and when I get there, closer and closer to that closeness, then I can think of myself as a musician and not a writer/broadcaster/theorist playing at the idea of being a musician. And I could carry on as a music critic with a rapidly shrinking audience and a dubious social role but a newly earned swinging confidence that I do actually know what I'm talking about.

PART THREE

The Beginning – To *The Planets* and Beyond

Gustav Holst *circa 1921: 'I've learned what classical means. It means something that sings and dances through sheer joy of existence.'*

1. ON BEING A FUNKY YOUNGSTER

There was no particularly profound professional breakthrough or significant change as musician or music writer after my time at the Royal Academy. I hadn't become a bona fide musician and I hadn't forgotten how to be a writer.

There was no shattering of confidence or spoiling of instinct now that I had learned something of the technical and mechanical process of composing music, and I didn't feel that there was now some sort of obstacle in my way when it came to writing about music. It wasn't like finding out so much about the science of riding a bicycle that you were too self-conscious to ride one.

I did think that I had made a small breakthrough in terms of the confidence and knowledge necessary to write about classical music, but no arts editor was suddenly going to decide to ask me to write about it when I was so obviously a writer of the 1980s, of pop, of where I was when I was in my twenties. I was listening to a much wider range of music and working on my own sense of how it all fitted together, but I was still stuck in the land of being asked to write about what I was, officially, an expert in. Harry Styles, it seemed.

Eventually, an alert producer at Radio 3 remembered the Royal Academy programme, where I mentioned that the only orthodox, mainstream classical album I had bought as a teenager – and for many years after – was *The Planets* by Holst.

In the early 2000s a trend had developed in the media and the record industry towards working out, for the sake of some sort of diversity and inclusivity, and a new kind of customer, how to reach a mythical young audience with classical music. My recent provisional qualifications meant I had become a small part of this minor movement, as though someone who very clearly came from the world of pop and rock might help classical music reach a younger audience – or in another sense an older audience, but an older audience that had grown up, like me, during the age of rock and pop. As though I was capable of adding something funky and fashionable to the image of classical music, which was both flattering and completely absurd.

The whole point of this seemed a matter of survival, both commercially and culturally – if there were no younger or once-younger pop people to replace those listeners and enthusiasts who, bluntly, were dying off, then the music itself would die away as well. How to reach younger people, and the new old who had grown up with rock and pop? Make it clear there were critics and writers interested in rock and pop who were also interested in classical music. Case solved.

I was in my early fifties, but then it appeared the average age of a Radio 3 listener was in their early sixties, so here was another advantage to becoming a writer about classical music. In rock I was part of the older generation. In classical I was, relatively speaking, a youngster. Possibly a funky youngster.

Back when I really was a youngster, my first contact with classical music did not go well.

2. A FIRST CLASSICAL EXPERIENCE READ OUT ON RADIO 3

To my teenage self, the more mainstream classical music, the well-known composers with their stern, traditional position in an unattractively stable and slow, censoring grown-up world, was part of a universe I had no connection with. I could recognise names like Mozart and Beethoven, but of all available music, it was located elsewhere, the other side of large, forbidding and guarded gates that apparently needed special paperwork and arcane inside information to enter.

Classical seemed connected to a dreary, generalised sense of uninspiring worthiness that was fixed inside an ideologically suspect status quo, lacking the exhilarating suggestion of new beginnings, a pulsating sense of an exciting, mind-expanding tomorrow. There was something monstrous about it – as if on the other side there were lumbering dinosaurs and toothless dragons, refusing to accept they were extinct — but it did also tantalisingly hint at something that might be magical, that might be of use in the formation of a progressive new world, if only it wasn't so starched and evasive, or at least heavily protected by a mysterious inner circle.

Eventually, after a few years of teenage indifference to playing something classical on my own tatty, cheap but invaluable record player in the early 1970s, *The Planets* by Gustav Holst, written during the first two years of the First World War, ended up being the first classical album I ever bought. Perhaps I finally made the move because of hearing the mighty 'Mars' movement fit perfectly, like a skewed, supersonic slab of glam, as the show-business introduction to a Mott the Hoople concert at the Manchester Palace theatre in 1973 — just like Elvis would use Richard Strauss's Nietzsche-inspired *Also Sprach Zarathustra* to set up a barrage of swaggering, glittering rock 'n' roll.[1]

Or maybe I wanted *The Planets* because there it was, amidst the gaudy pick-and-mix sweets and plastic cutlery of Woolworth's, looking like it belonged with books about robots and time travel by Philip K. Dick and Isaac Asimov, on the bargain-priced Classics for Pleasure label. In hindsight, this is a little like finding Mahler's Ninth in Poundland.

A cheap album was especially seductive to an underfunded provincial teenager, especially if it looked like it came from space. Because *The Planets* album, unlike most classical albums I came across, had space and planets on the cover, it looked like it was a part of science fiction, along with *2001: A Space Odyssey* and the novels of Alfred Bester and Joanna Russ. It looked as though I could put it into my record collection between Tangerine Dream and Faust.

There was one album by Faust, *The Faust Tapes*, with a seductively radiant black-and-white cover featuring a mysteriously swirling Bridget Riley pop-art pattern that Virgin had released in 1973 for the price of a single, 48p, and which was many more estranged early 1970s teenagers' tunnel into mood-altering electronica and the mind-altering noise of noise. As soon as the needle dropped on the record, the hiss it made

---

[1] A youthful mock-metal group called Queen with a very lithe, worked-up, microphone-thrusting lead singer were Mott's unknown support group, and Holst's battling 'Mars' setting up the arrival of Mott perhaps taught them a lot about the pumping attractions of melodrama. Holst times Rory Gallagher multiplied by Judy Garland equals Queen.

previewing all sorts of hisses to come threaded through the music, you felt simultaneously bigger and smaller. Your mind swirled along with the black-and-white cover.

The price was a marketing gimmick, Richard Branson's hippy-corporate Virgin cracking the problem of how to sell unsettling chaotic anti-pop by putting it out at a pop price, and it sold around 50,000 copies, probably over fifty times what it would have done if it had been full price. The music – or to some the 'music', or to most the 'messing around', threading throughout the record with no pause, no relief, a constant, unseparated, colliding series of fragments of something else, crushed rhythms, stressed sound and thought patterns – could be taken as being at some exact, unstable midpoint between avant-garde jazz and Frank Zappa.

Many buyers were repelled by the apparently clearly stoned off-the-wall chaos, and felt they had paid perhaps 47p too much, and wished they'd not been greedy and spent the money instead on Slade's 'Cum on Feel the Noize'. Others, like me, perhaps ready for the jagged juxtaposition of hallucination, drone and dream from exposure to the Velvet Underground and Can – which turned out to be where David Bowie was coming from and going to – considered it one of the great purchases, the 48p setting you up for a lifetime of adventure.

In the early seventies, my teenage interest in the more obvious pop music very quickly became an interest in other music, an irresistible compulsion to find newer, more intoxicating thrills. Within months I had gone from televised, glistening glam rock and the endlessly replenished Top 40 to the Velvet Underground, Captain Beefheart, Henry Cow and Robert Wyatt. Back then you could move very quickly, inside your mind, inside your local record shop, guided by energetic, informed music papers and the wildly reticent anti-energy of John Peel – and the zany marketing meetings of Virgin Records – to go further and further out, into enticing, inspiring weirdness, into jazz, to its free, avant-garde limits, to the primitively achieved sophistication of Jamaican dub radically and mysteriously rewiring African rhythmical history, to experimental German electronic music and psychedelic rock influenced – or, more accurately, infected – by the likes of Stockhausen, Cage, Varèse and La Monte Young, where music became spatial, even heretical, and beautifully, futuristically strange, but somehow still pop.

The Planets was a few pence more than *The Faust Tapes*, but still cheap, within what at that stage was pocket-money price, and when you could only afford an album a month, it was an added bonus, a treasured addition to a record collection that was very slowly growing; I can now add a hundred albums to my Tidal library in a few minutes, which is not necessarily a better or worse experience but very different from how it was for me in 1973, when owning new albums was often a case of bargain-hunting, second-hand shops, scrounging, and looking for part-time work. Shoplifting was not out of the question either; using the money given to me by my parents to buy an O-level revision textbook to actually buy the first New York Dolls album, therefore having to slip the history revision book into my jacket pocket and hold my breath as I walked through the door of WH Smith's, feeling all eyes were on me. This made me the sort of rebel qualified to buy the rebel rock of the New York Dolls.

Some of that bargain-hunting and forbidden activity worked out, and the future was glimpsed. Some of it didn't work out, and the past made an unwelcome move to draw you in. I gambled on *The Planets*, faced with all those twinkling stars on the cover — suggesting one of my favourite places of all, which I would make the title of a fanzine I wrote three years later. *Out There.*

Hearing *The Planets* on record, James Loughran conducting the Manchester Hallé Orchestra, based a few miles from my house, was a big disappointment. There was, it seemed, no 'out there'. It sounded like it came from a quaint, chilly village hall; perhaps it being so local didn't help give it a feeling of otherness. It might have been the feeble budget quality, or because of the huge, hammy-sounding orchestra squashed through my tinny little bedroom speakers, but next to Iggy and the Stooges, Faust or Ornette Coleman it sounded frail and pompous, puny and passé, unattractively dense to the point of sludgy, and to my mind, which was much narrower than I thought, deeply conservative. There is a possibility that it was some kind of equivalent to how, it seems, a young child's taste buds are naturally repulsed by Brussels sprouts; at the time my hearing equivalent of taste buds were in no state to receive and in any way enjoy the unusual flavours and textures of the music. The fractured and intense un-pop of Faust was more to my taste when it came to music that mostly lacked words.

I could hear only blandness on *The Planets*. Whatever timeless, carefully organised esoteric mythical elements Holst had scrupulously pressed into his music seemed buried under puffed-up fuss and curlicue. Unlike György Ligeti and even Richard Strauss, which had been sent by director Stanley Kubrick into a post-time, post-human *2001: A Space Odyssey* cosmos along with speaking computer Hal and the godlike star child, it seemed embedded in a decaying drawing room from all our yesterdays. It sounded like it had been made in insipid non-Bridget Riley black and white, which seems weird to think now, when it is so clearly saturated with colour, every colour but black and white, and if there is black and white, somehow that is in colour.

The cover promised Space Age, as though the music would pour out of the pulsating machines of the pioneering underground German music I loved at the time – condescendingly labelled Krautrock by British rock critics – because it seemed like a point of departure, a utopian attempt to repair a ruined recent past and make new myths for a lost country; Holst's music seemed trapped in the age of steam, fit only for gloomy, scary establishment rituals.

The disappointing experience even put me off Isao Tomita's later jaunty electro-pop transformation of *The Planets* Suite into a synthesiser fantasy journey through space, closer in spirit to Kraftwerk, if also Liberace, a kinky blurring of kitsch, fanfare and vaulting synths that does make you realise how *The Planets* has the Shakespearean quality of being open to endless interpretation, from the baroque to the spectacular, the down-to-earth to the gravity-defying, the angry to the twee.

The contemporary zest and ideological dimension to forward-looking rock music rendered the likes of a stubborn, faceless orchestra playing a piece of music written in the second decade of the massive, history-clogged twentieth century irrelevant, and on the verge of extinction. And much of Holst's technique – borrowed and reconfigured from the flair and invention of Debussy and Schoenberg and their imaginative rejecting of the overblown, over-decorated nineteenth-century symphonic stuffiness – had influenced the industrial composers of Hollywood soundtracks, which made Holst's music sound clichéd and predictable.

Because of what it influenced, it felt as though *The Planets* was the rip-off, because on a budget record it sounded thinner and tamer than the music that borrowed and stole from it, which was engineered to ceremonially fill cinemas and make you feel it as much as hear it. In the 1970s its suspenseful extravagance already sounded oddly common because of all the things that it had been inspired by, and inspired, and where it had spilled; even more so by 1977, when John Williams — Steven Spielberg's one, chosen composer — efficiently and unashamedly ladled its ornamenting techniques and protocol into the anthems and musical motifs of *Star Wars*, when its impact on science fiction and fantasy soundtracks really picked up speed, and you would have to separate it from all the plagiarising, parodies, copies and tributes to ever get inside its awesome, technically stunning architecture.

John Williams followed the Bernard Herrmann principle established when Herrmann was working with Alfred Hitchcock on films such as *Vertigo*, where to represent the vertigo he appropriated the off-centre tonality of Debussy and Ravel, adding a necessary, tense, eerily stationary remorselessness which, on the quiet, also reflected the steady tones of Morton Feldman and La Monte Young.

Even if few knew it at the time, Herrmann's music was prototype minimalism filtered through the vainglorious pounding might of Wagner, to some extent bringing minimalism full circle, back to the static, non-assertive music of Debussy, undermining the heroically inflamed seriousness of Wagner with some welcome nonchalance. Debussy's discreet atmospheric opulence made his the perfect music to appropriate for film composition. There were all those instruments, but also a more flexible, and once established, endlessly modern sense of dynamic, as though the music was bringing with it the invention and illumination of electricity, which wouldn't go out of date.

Herrmann said that Hitchcock only made 60 per cent of the film and his music then had to finish it. (In a wider sense, it might be that reality itself, the reality that film explores, only goes so far and does so much, and music, in all its variety, finishes it.) The music Herrmann wound into place, deliberately rewiring influences and reference points, was intended, as with John Williams, to stir the memories of those who knew where the music came from and what it resembled, and to stimulate the subconscious of those who didn't. The intention was for the music to be familiar enough to not knock the filmgoer outside the world of the film but unfamiliar enough that it contained the surprise and tension to make that world completely original. The music came from our world, but belonged in this other, made-up world.

Film composition was not completely a musical task, which is why Stravinsky pointed out that so-called 'better' or more 'authentically classical' composers were not necessarily the right people to write the music. The best film composers were the best, most discriminating compilers of influences, the best curators of experience, and the best at knowing where the great musical moments in history were and fusing them with their own particular organisational and orchestral skills. Their greatest skill was in pastiche, and the most skilled of those – like Herrmann – were those who had enough technical know-how and originality to give their pastiches their own reason to exist outside the film images they were so deeply connected to. Their music managed to leave behind its own world and enter this one, which is where it had started.

Williams's music adapted the abilities of Herrmann to make film soundtracks a manipulative, comfortable mix of the subversive and the soothing, the thrilling and the avant-garde, and a component part of the vibrant, escapist Hollywood film. Both used logical extensions of Debussy's rich orchestration and his fluid blurring of harmonies, rhythms and forms, which naturally, in a late nineteenth-century setting, conveniently became known as impressionism, and the traces that passed through Holst into Herrmann and, to a lesser extent, Williams fulfilled Debussy's idealistic hope that cinema would be the perfect creation of poetry, vision and dreams.

The parochial, Cheltenham-born, nineteenth-century caution of Holst meant initially he was not totally convinced by the elusive Debussy and his new ways of arranging notes, but he became very taken by the uniquely scored discreet revolution of his three ultra-vivid, dreamily abstracted orchestral *Nocturnes*, premiered in 1901. A deeply subtle sense of alluring stillness, a propulsive indirectness, had coolly cut down to size the forward-charging big-orchestra movements of Wagner and his myth-mad cult followers. Debussy was a new way to produce fantastic visions through music and paint beautiful images with sound.

The knowing John Williams channelled ominous Stravinsky into the famous shark warning embedded into the pop masterpiece *Jaws* just like Herrmann had dropped cutting-edge Stravinsky into the slashing shower music scene in *Psycho*. Williams knew his way around the New World music of Dvořák and Ives, and he channelled Holst and Carl Orff, and the composers that Holst and Orff had channelled, like Brahms, Wagner, Strauss and Debussy, into the commercial films of Steven Spielberg and George Lucas, so that the combination of Hollywood power and a paraphrased classical music quickly became part of the sound-drenching blockbuster formula. One sort of magic mated with another.

The Williams-style bombast and merciless, tension-building muzak, as it became, saturated blockbuster films such as *The Terminator*, *Gladiator* and *The Lord of the Rings* and seemed to ruin the idea that *The Planets* was a hyper-alert sequence of highly emotional, expressive tone poems rooted in an experimental, eclectic sensibility, with hints of the mystical and ethereal.

I knew none of this when I bought the album and first heard it, quickly dismissing it as film muzak. I had other musical things on my mind. Eventually I realised that Holst was one of the prime sources for commercial film-music writers, not as derivative and facile as those composers. Holst was in fact the First Emperor of the blockbuster universe, which gave it the ubiquity that meant it was the one Holst work that became part of the international repertoire and that it was also then looked down upon by critics and purists for its charmless universality.

The Planets had enough presence in popular culture – not least because it had become one of the most-loved orchestral pieces of the twentieth century, a classical pop hit – to bring it to attention as though it had a glamorous quality, even if the music didn't appear to. Holst's *The Planets*, always given those cosmic, starry album sleeves as if to disguise his crusty Victorian Christian name, Gustav, which came from his Latvian grandfather, moved across the border between what was fixed as high and low art with a fair amount of freedom, especially on *The Planets*' legendary opening movement, the definitively ominous, tension-building 'Mars, the Bringer of War'. It had been used during the spooky title sequence for the BBC's original 1953 broadcast of *The Quatermass Experiment*, its insistent rhythms inevitably representing monstrous threats approaching from outer space; and in 1976, in Nic Roeg's *The Man Who Fell to Earth*, a different kind of invasion film, the dehydrated alien visitor from a waterless planet, played by David Bowie, a big fan as a child of the scratchily scary black-and-white

Quatermass programmes, drinks his first miraculous earthbound water as the Bringer of War stirs up unease.

In 1973, beloved British prog-pop group Manfred Mann turned the 'Jupiter, the Bringer of Jollity' fourth movement, historically verging on an alternative, more optimistically minded national anthem, into 'Joybringer', a sweet-natured, sunlit pop hit. And there was a sliver of 'Jupiter' amidst all of the cavorting counterculture and Stravinsky quotes on the second Frank Zappa and the Mothers of Invention album, 1967's *Absolutely Free*, blown into the wildly groovy 'Invocation & Ritual Dance of the Young Pumpkin'.

The Mars movement's brutal articulation of conflict was creepily regenerated by cerebral prog-rock aristocracy King Crimson as 'The Devil's Triangle' on their second 1970 album *In the Wake of Poseidon*, a piece enacting – or defying – potential human destruction written during the First World War transferred to the dark, disorientating Vietnam age. The sophisticated harmonic techniques of Holst, as much as Bartók, Sibelius and Stravinsky, inspired by resistance to dehumanising industrialisation and a quest for spiritual transcendence, were a key influence on the highfalutin conceits of prog-rock acts, inspiring a little weighty, clever-seeming dissonance, a little complicated highbrow messing with rhythm and tempo.

Ultimately engraved with its own distinctive programmatic narrative shape – it was clearly about something, in many ways the whole story of life itself, on the tantalising threshold of the supernatural – *The Planets* would become, for better or worse, a big influence on the awkward, tritely baroque idea of the prog-rock concept album, with its own bloated, self-involved aesthetic that needed urgent, almost therapeutic puncturing by punk rock. Astrology is interpreted as being the movement and relative position of celestial bodies having an influence on the course of natural earthly occurrences and human affairs, and Holst's *The Planets* actually did have an impact on musical human affairs, if you can call Emerson, Lake & Palmer human.

In some ways the follow-up to *The Planets* was conceived by the Munich-born composer and educator Carl Orff, who in the mid-1930s set the thirteenth-century poem 'O Fortuna' to rousingly energising, almost monstrously dramatic music as part of his twenty-five-movement 'scenic cantata' *Carmina Burana*. Through its overuse in films, trailers, jingles, commercials, sports events, Michael Jackson tours, video games and light-entertainment television shows by those looking for a quick route to profundity or to setting the mood for something menacing, sensational or cataclysmic, it has become one of the most recognisable pieces of twentieth-century music, almost a joke rather than a dauntless, majestic choral translation of arcane medieval thinking.

The Nazi regime adored it, hearing in its epic rhythms the marching columns of the Third Reich, and it seemed involved in the all-guns-blazing, dolled-up nonsense passions of Queen's 'Bohemian Rhapsody'.

In the 1960s and 1970s it was rinsed of its direct associations with fascist Germany, but with its grandiosity further embellished after it surged into popular culture, whipping up the waves for a surfer in a pungent Old Spice aftershave TV advert. Jerry Goldsmith won an Oscar for his 1976 Oscar-winning soundtrack to the Hollywood horror film *The Omen*, which inherited much of the Latin-loaded Satanic-sounding pomposity of 'O Fortuna', to the extent that some thought Orff had been used, and its regular use in the situation comedy *Only Fools and Horses* to underline Rodney's suspicions that Del Boy's son Damian is the Antichrist added to the general belief that 'O Fortuna' featured in *The Omen* and stood for fear and terror.

A few years later, it was the only non-Wagner original piece used in John Boorman's solemn, stylised, sword-and-sorcery, mud-and-myth retelling of the King Arthur legend *Excalibur*, misleading many for a time that it was by Wagner. Humourless sentimentalist Simon Cowell soaked *The X Factor* – the talent show as grotesque fantasy – with what by then had become its kitsch histrionics, often used to emphasise silliness rather than the esoteric. In a 2009 Radio 2 'People's Chart' of the most popular classical music of the twentieth century, it came top, above Ralph Vaughan Williams's *Fantasia on a Theme by Thomas Tallis*.

The Planets – and 'O Fortuna' – put me off large amounts of apparently non-experimental, orchestral classical music for years, convincing me there was nothing of interest for me there, unless it had influenced the electronic music of the German experimental musicians inspired by conceptual art and the harder-edged, abstract fringes of prog. Oddly, as time goes by, and not just because I'm getting older, or naturally losing interest in fresh, unplanned fashion-based excitement, most of pop and rock now sounds dated and even quaint, and *The Planets* seems to grow in sonic stature, containing more feeling, more intelligence and, ultimately, more provocative power.

It doesn't need the special multitrack and overdubbing effects of a recording studio to make music seem modern and charged up; the special effects, the sense of surprise, a bold treatment of tonality and structure was written into the music, and what it needs to give it new life is the equivalent of a great production, the perceptive conductor and scintillating orchestra setting it against a backdrop of all time and space. It perhaps sounded out of place in the 1970s not because it was from the past but because it was moving through time, heading into an unknown future where it would make more sense as a work of art. A future where I could catch up with it.

You did need to work at the music as well – to explore and understand the musical and artistic times it had emerged out of and into, to appreciate how Holst himself was struggling with his composing, as works as exploratory as *The Planets* were being received badly or even failing to reach performance, and also to investigate where such compositional discoveries went next. From Holst you can move through Ralph Vaughan Williams, Benjamin Britten, Michael Tippett and Harrison Birtwistle into either practical, down-to-earth, scenic Englishness, into the fields and forests, the rivers and hills, lambs and spires, pleasant views, charming villages, winding lanes and cloudy days, or into an other-worldly, less specifically nationalistic Englishness, as though England was actually located on an unknown planet the other side of the sun.

The Planets was where Holst overcame his frustrations that he was being ignored as a composer, and the crushing, almost paralysing, sense that he was failing. His music didn't come out of nowhere, as the ignorant pop fan would have thought. It was the sophisticated culmination of his probing early twentieth-century compositions written in his early thirties, including two ambitious operas, the monumental *Sita*, where mad king Wagner still ruled, the more delicate chamber opera *Sāvitri*, and a lengthy, adventurous, often deeply beautiful choral work, *The Cloud Messenger*.

The choral piece reflected Holst's interest in the Indian occult as well as its literature and music, which he was using to shake off the inflexible influence of his great first love, Wagner – although before that there was a brief infatuation with the light operetta of Gilbert and Sullivan – and find new methods of expression. He taught himself Sanskrit to open his mind still further to new, liberating influences, to material that would help his sense of spiritual enquiry and also help loosen his music.

The work-in-progress hybrid that lay between resisting the stern orders of Wagner and introducing the unorthodox romantic mystique of *The Cloud Messenger*'s message is why it was originally viewed with considerable hostility. It wasn't clear if he had broken the chains of Wagner and found a way to enter fully the very different twentieth century or was still trapped inside the mazy Wagner woods, only glimpsing an actually more fantastic world outside. The lacklustre reaction propelled Holst into a depression that he fought his way out of to write *The Planets*; the sound of falling in love with being human on a lonely planet spinning with such vivid, vulnerable life amidst infinite space.

You can hear the turbulent music of *The Planets* — and therefore big-budget science-fiction-movie music — moving into place throughout the Indian-inspired grandeur of *The Cloud Messenger*, and a crucial personal way of escaping the damned tug of Wagner by exploiting the intricate, Indian approach of juxtaposing sounds in mosaic form rather than embracing symphonic development. I didn't learn about this for a good forty years after I first heard it, and also how much his friend and fellow student Ralph Vaughan Williams admired *The Cloud Messenger*, although he did have one or two very particular, even niggly criticisms. It was his envy of Holst's sophisticated control of orchestral texture that motivated Vaughan Williams to study under Ravel in Paris and give his pastoral Englishness some greater, more alien power.

The Planets reflected Holst's interest in magic — the magic of music, and literature, and art — and in the new technology, and also, at another extreme, the magic of astrology, which he studied at length. The suite's seven movements, representing the seven ages of man, the characters of the known planets in the solar system, with associated astrological significance, began more plainly as 'Seven Pieces for Large Orchestra', inspired by Schoenberg's ultra-modern music-shaking *Five Pieces for Orchestra*. Schoenberg's own intense craving to escape nineteenth-century gravity helped Holst to fly free as well.

Schoenberg's revolutionary 1909 experimentation with the scale, colour and harmonic symmetry of an orchestra now sounds much more accessibly romantic than radically disturbing, but it became perceived as being the work where dissonance was liberated, an equivalent to the cubism of Picasso and Braque. A new, noisy, electric-powered, increasingly popularised industrial world was materialising, which seemed beyond words, and as always it was music that was first to describe it, to begin to explain it.

At the time, quickly responding to a new musical language coalescing structurally and conceptually, as tonality dissolved into atonality, on the way to the mind-bending emancipation of dissonance, the creatively restless Holst, after an initial suspicion of the stranger elements and unmoored abstraction, received *Five Pieces for Orchestra* with its almost scientific, definitely unromantic title as a revelation.

It was very much another clue to how make his way out of the high camp of Wagner, and the inspiration to look elsewhere for influence encouraged Holst into a more British romantic and melodic tradition of folk song and madrigals that could complete the escape. To orbit the planets, to mix the fuel he needed, Holst explored ancient Englishness and folk jigs as much as astrology and Indian exoticism. To tour further out into space, Holst dropped down the beanstalk from Wagnerland.

Composed as five untitled abstract pieces, a spare, expressive antidote to bombastic, symphonic, nineteenth-century excess, Schoenberg's *Five Pieces* needed individual titles – a sense of a story, of comforting meaning – to make them less oppressively remote and more saleable. Eventually, reluctantly, Schoenberg added titles to each of the five pieces, which wounded their position as hymns to the unknown, to the otherworldly purity of the spirit, not its earthbound distillation.

The Planets did have their titles and their story – and approachable concept – and this did make the suite more accessible and helped distribute what as the undramatically titled 'Seven Pieces' might well have remained sealed off into other less appealing, more academic zones. It was the concept, though, that actually cancelled it out as an intrepid, abstract piece following Schoenberg, and made it seem a quaint, crowd-pleasing entertainment. The friendly concept rubbed out the transcendental, captivating power of the music and, for a while at least to me, made it seem closer to the organised film-music ingenuity of John Williams than the penetrating, uncompromising, spiritual investigations of Schoenberg.

Forty years later, I am now at one with *The Planets* as an intrepid evocation of an evolving universe, and visit it regularly, becoming more familiar with different versions, different conductors and orchestras giving it their attitude, their take – or perhaps, their mere going through the motions – as if it really is a *Macbeth*, *Hamlet* or *King Lear*, the story of rebirth, of clairvoyance, this setting of the imagination against a backdrop of space and infinity, open to a multitude of readings from the warm and fuzzy to the magisterial and intimidating, from the severe to the sensational, the British and sensible to the galactic and all-conquering. Holst himself conducted the London Symphony Orchestra for the first studio recordings of *The Planets* in 1922/3 and 1926, for HMV, speeding his way through the session with crackling nervous energy you can sense today, the music already radiant with the sort of visual power that cinema and television would colonise and reshuffle in decades to come. Along with Elgar, Holst was one of the first composers to make records of his music.

There are versions by all the leading conductors relishing its invasion of musical history, a superstar cosmic crew of maestros: Rattle, Previn, Stokowski, Sargent, Herrmann, Bernstein, Susskind, Karajan, and Boult's belting 1945 version from Abbey Road Studios, Boult being the conductor who, in the words of Holst after a partial private performance in 1918 'first caused the Planets to shine'... all of them orbiting an idea of what Holst's own *Planets* sounded like in his mind, exploiting the imagined personalities, flaws, brilliance of the seven planets to make an overall wise, awed, fearful, loving judgement on the humanity of the one planet that was not directly featured, Earth.

For all its venturing forth, *The Planets* looks earthward, and in the end it looks inward, into the endlessly inquisitive mind of someone who grew up in the world of Oscar Wilde, William Morris, H. G. Wells, George Bernard Shaw and Arthur Conan Doyle and who, in the last years of his life, in the late 1920s and early 1930s, was promoting his work through the brand new 'wireless' broadcasts on the BBC. Disciple Ralph Vaughan Williams wrote after Holst's death that 'his music reaches into the unknown but it never loses touch with humanity'.

After years of keeping it in exile, *The Planets* has helped me find a way to get through the forbidding gates that once separated me from the icy, intimidating classical land beyond. I have located the correct paperwork, or perhaps it is just my age, now that I have made the clichéd late-life move from pop to classical, where pop is about the setting-up of life, the facing forward, being psyched up and ready for action, and classical is about the settling down, the closing in on the idea of death, and what is beyond that. Classical music when you are young can seem all about death, being mostly written by the long-dead, and filled with quiet, comfortless dread, and not something you wish to engage with... but as you get older, and find your way around this elaborate other land, you appreciate it is more about the astonishing privilege of being alive, on the astonishing verge of not being. And after a few days a week at the Royal Academy for a few months, I now know enough to understand how Holst's channelling, through *The Planets'* grandiose, romantic and warrior forces, of Debussy, Berlioz and Dvořák's then fresh techniques of orchestral colouring and evocative phrasing, of the primal, rarefied yearnings of Scriabin and Stravinsky, of Schoenberg's formidable testing and transcending of tonality, of ghostly post-Mahler and Wagner modernism, produced the definitive template for blockbuster movie soundtracks, for better or worse.

All that exuberant, escapist Hollywood force, music as enchanting, distracting special effect, is rooted in the interests of Holst in the occult, in magic and the paranormal, but also in the potential of music to read and describe the mind, and what Vaughan Williams described after hearing *The Planets* as the perfect equilibrium of the mystic and melodic sides of the composer's nature. I now also appreciate how Holst, more experimental, eclectic and intellectually curious than it seemed after my upsetting Classics for Pleasure misstep, helped usher in unusual new sound worlds and illuminate new paths; although, oddly and probably snobbily, I went into Holst backwards, from Schoenberg and Birtwistle, rather than the other way around.

It is King Crimson that can now sound dainty and dated next to a great, driven orchestra piling into *The Planets*; heavy metal, however noxious, sounds docile next to Holst's use of an orchestra to stretch the imagination and gloriously generate accelerating suspense. Pop sounds like yesterday, not as dynamically immediate as it was from the fifties to the nineties, where it was in the right time and place, responding to and helping create the world around it. I was in the right time and place as well.

The Planets sounds more and more like now, and its context is all of space, other forms of time, dimension and existence, not just the twenties, thirties and forties. It sounds massive and vigorous, chaos in spectacular harmony, its rhythms intensifying expectation and always building towards the future, which it saw into, and beyond, believing in music as a kind of alchemy that helps us cope with the relentless crises of everyday life, diagnoses our fate, and protects us from the demons and perils always out there, always about to invade and divert our lives.

There is a tradition in rock of being asked what the first single or album you ever bought was, and you hope that your reply is not too embarrassing. I am now delighted to say that when asked what my first ever classical album was, I can honestly say *The Planets* by Holst. At first, it might seem as embarrassing as saying *Boléro* by Ravel, another composer whose other work got blotted out by his pop-culture hit, his one-hit wonder; it is in the end not as poor a choice as I thought, when I felt it should be something more obviously avant-garde, even though it meant by the time I was ready to buy a second classical album not made by a composer who had influenced Brian Eno or Miles Davis, the vinyl album had come to the end of its time.

Beyond The Planets, *because there is more to Holst than Mars*

A Holst playlist for further exploration of the curious, lonely, unbeaten, sometimes crestfallen English imagination, this side of outer space:

1. *A Song of the Night*, Op. 19, No. 1
2. *Invocation*, for cello and orchestra
3. *Seven Part-Songs*: 'Say who is this?'
4. Short Pianoforte Trio in E major: III. Andante con moto
5. *The Mystic Trumpeter*
6. *The Perfect Fool*: 'Dance of Spirits of Fire' (arr. G. Poffenbarger for wind ensemble)
7. *Japanese Suite*: I. 'Prelude: Song of the Fisherman'
8. *Hammersmith*, Op. 52
9. *Brook Green Suite*
10. Symphony in F major, *The Cotswolds*: II. Elegy – Molto adagio (In Memoriam William Morris)
11. First Suite in E-flat major: I. Chaconne
12. *Choral Hymns from the Rig Veda* (Group 3, 1909–10) – translated from the Sanskrit by Gustav Holst, 'Hymn to the Waters'
13. *A Dirge for Two Veterans*
14. Scherzo for orchestra
15. Double Violin Concerto, Op. 49: II. Lament – Andante
16. *Suite de Ballet*, Op. 10: III. 'Scene de nuit'
17. 'In the Bleak Midwinter'

3. FURTHER BEYOND: A BRIEF HISTORY OF THE 'CLASSICS FOR PLEASURE' LABEL THAT SOMEHOW LEADS TO 'FROM A FOR AMAZON TO Z FOR ZAPPA'

When I was growing up, deep in the last century, the sort of comfortably lo-falutin and soft, accessible music presently found at the top of the current classical charts tended to be readily available, mostly in Woolworth's and WH Smith's, on the friendly, budget-priced, slightly camp and tacky Music for Pleasure label. MfP was formed in 1965 as a marketing collaboration between record label EMI and the book publisher Paul Hamlyn for the swift, no-nonsense selling of shoddy versions of passing trends and to deal with the then troubling problem of unwanted old stock.

The label released ex-catalogue albums, nostalgic compilations, soundtracks and soundalike tribute records at more or less half full price, sometimes by acts such as the Supremes, the Hollies, Joe Cocker and Count Basie, as well as the more lightweight likes of Russ Conway, Des O'Connor and Vince Hill, and pop music done up in various unashamedly groovy styles, bossa nova, funky and Tijuana styles being particularly popular.

Some MfPs you bought just because they were within pocket-money range, despite their junky feel, one or two because they were actually worth owning. The very fetching MfP *Relics of Pink Floyd* featuring slanted, Syd Barrett-era acid-pop like 'See Emily Play' and slanted, out-there space jams like 'Careful with That Axe, Eugene' – where Mersey Beat-style pop got Stockhausened, and/or stoned – was a cut-price portal through which many early seventies teenagers passed into the heady, wider world of pre-*Dark Side of the Moon* Floyd, where the group became a brand. *Relics* remains the Pink Floyd album I am fondest of.

The lingering vinyl collector in me still recommends you grab any quirky and/or creaky MfP gems you spot in your local charity shop, especially if you come across Bruce Forsyth's *Mister Entertainment*, Django Reinhardt's *Djangology*, *Strings for Pleasure Play the Best of Bacharach* or the *Best of Henry Mancini*, *Stereo Galaxy: A New World of Quality Sound*, and Geoff Love's *Big Bond Movie Themes*. Nice.

Alan Moorhouse's MfP bossa nova versions of the Beatles, Bach and Bacharach, so that, bargain-bin blissfully, you get in one barmy place 'Something', 'Minuet in G' and 'I Say a Little Prayer', is a fiver on eBay, but without the sleeve, which was a significant part of the MfP point — the cover of this album was a trio of photos presumably representing the mood of the Beatles, Bach and Bacharach with characters smooching in a Babycham party world somewhere between *Tales of the Unexpected, Abigail's Party* and *Made in Chelsea*. Moorhouse's *Rock Gently with Beethoven, Bach and Brahms*, released on another budget reissue label, Contour, must be mentioned, first for the cover — the three great composers reduced to stern postage-stamp sized cameos while a go-go girl, presented somewhere between innocently and cynically, wildly shakes her hair, not perhaps listening to Brahms's 'Lullaby' but promising actual musical fun, an early attempt at claiming classical really is fun and cool and, God help us, sexy — and also that the composer, bandleader and loungecore master Moorhouse co-wrote Lulu's 1969 Eurovision Song Contest entry 'Boom Bang-a-Bang', extending his clear fascination with the letter B. *Rock Gently*, incidentally, is less rock and more jazz-loungified Beethoven, Bach and Brahms presented as if the B-maestros actually made music to listen to arranged in the glossy near-swinging style of James Last while buying gypsy creams and Hamlet cigars at the supermarket.

Today's sectioned-off classical chart represents the most forcibly accessible zone of classical music, but which needs a different genre to describe it, useful to those interested in music that can be described as lovely, nice, unassuming, reflective, and, mostly, easy-on-the-ear accessible. It's a middle-of-the-road chart, although for some reason, those who appreciate this sort of middle-of-the-road music apparently need to be flattered and elevated by the use of the word 'classical'. (Really, I am picking holes in a chart that should be titled 'Accessible Music', or 'Comely', or 'Fifty Shades', and suggesting, perhaps, for an imaginary, romantic chart better suited to a more rigorous and challenging version of classical, that we return to a description of what is now called classical music that was in use up to the mid-twentieth century: permanent music, 'music of permanent interest'.) Perhaps the classical charts should be called 'Music for Pleasure', which could be branded as the label once was, with the friendly Reader's Digest-type line 'your kind of music'.

There was an MfP album of Yehudi Menuhin playing Carl Nielsen's Violin Concerto before it was fully decided to separate the classical albums from the trashy, occasionally enticing repackaged, funked-up pop albums. The Classics for Pleasure branch of MFP was launched in 1970, before it was pimped up by EMI in the 1990s, still faithful to the economising introductory principle and original Hallmark-card-level artwork. The original series featured many fair-to-quite-desirable albums that might be too strong for what the classical charts now are. They tended to be pressed on dubious-quality vinyl that suggested they were disposable records, meant to last only a few listens or, indeed, never played at all, just bought to suggest a nice middlebrow hint of culture on your record shelf.

The CfP catalogue, budget priced, many plucked from the popular, toe-tapping, gin-and-tonic end of the repertoire, but with a bit of depth, featured Mahler's Symphony No. 4, Bartók's Concerto for Orchestra, Britten's Violin Concerto, Vaughan Williams's *London* Symphony, Elgar's Symphony No. 1, Schubert's Symphony No. 5, all played by the London Philharmonic; Stravinsky and Beethoven played by the late 1950s Berlin Philharmonic; and Brahms symphonies and Rachmaninov played by the Manchester Hallé – so here was a great place to start listening or collecting classical music, through a low-priced catalogue created by Classics for Pleasure during the 1970s, looked down upon at the time, but clearly the work of people with some sort of vision.

The modern classical chart, invented to create the sense that there are classical-music bestsellers, makes me think of the Classics for Pleasure label. One particular Amazon classical chart I look at, which could have been anywhere post-vinyl between 2010 and 2020, and which would never change much, suggests it is stuffed and will be for the foreseeable future with André Rieu, the music of whom, for fans of alternative timelines, gives an excellent insight into what pop music would now be like if the Nazis had won the Second World War. In this world, the Beatles never replaced Mantovani, Liberace was the Elvis and Roger Whittaker the Dylan.

André Rieu's ornate, perfunctory, waltzing performances seem to be the ultimate confirmation of Debussy's 1913 fears, mirroring many fears about Spotify: that recording music would domesticate it, and that recorded music would lead to far too much music, underlining Schoenberg's early concerns that a surfeit of music 'would wear it out'. There were those who discovered music before recordings, who considered the recording of it and fixing it in place meant that by the second half of the twentieth century, music had become too familiar, and less miraculous, than it had been. There are those of us who discovered music as it was being recorded and released on vinyl records, which seemed like a miracle, and we now view the shift to downloads, clouds, apps, ringtones, jingles and a constant barrage of half-hearted, half-finished music as our loss of the miraculous, our tormenting torrent of familiarity. Presumably those living through what's happening now, considering the non-stop taking-it-for-granted sonic presence and constantly available musical history as their form of miracle, will see some kind of new era ruin everything for them.

Rieu is not so much a musician as a baroque-uniformed salesman selling candy-coated sound and a fake luxury tourist experience. Look at the Rieuworld costumes, the covers, the frosted cream cheese, the frilly, hollow prettiness, the artificial prince-and-princess settings, very much in the tradition of the seediest, mushiest MfP, lacking only the young girls on the covers in wide, forced smiles meant to denote pleasure, wearing little but transparent lace tunics. Actually, Music for Pleasure would have been too good for Rieu – he would have belonged on the Woolworth's even flakier Music for Pleasure knock-off, Pickwick, which was to MfP what Bjorn Again are to Abba.

Decently covered, decently talented, Nicola Benedetti and her Silver Violin tops both the Amazon classical chart and the *BBC Music Magazine* chart. Although she is presented with the correct amount of seriousness, and the intention of bringing proper, permanent classical music to a wider audience without appearing too compromised, it is essentially a moderately mature extension of the cheery MfP spirit, resulting in the type of cautiously tasteful easy-listening album, classical music broken down and cleaned up for non-classical fans, best described by an Amazon customer as 'a lovely relaxing disc especially half asleep in front of the fire'.

Catrin Finch and her adorable, moisturising harp at number two, Einaudi's airy, oversweet cupcake minimalism at three, John Wilson's jaunty nerdcore *A Celebration of the MGM Film Musical* at four, gleaming Lang Lang's expensive piano, Miloš Karadaglić's guitar, Alison Balsom's trumpet, the *Fifty Shades of Grey* compilation all seem like twenty-first-century Music for Pleasure albums, where the cheerfully vulgar, cut-price packaging has been replaced with something shrewdly planned by marketing departments to be restrained and consciously cultured. And possibly for, in the nicest sense, the half-asleep.

Lower down the chart, on Amazon, in the twenties, we get to some familiar Beethoven, Tchaikovsky and Mozart, and among the Alfie Boes, Piano Guys, *Downton Abbey* collections and the *Only Classical Chillout Album You'll Ever Need/Most Relaxing Classical Album in the World... Ever*, some Fauré, and at thirty-two, a glint of the highbrow bullying its way into the cocktail and scaring the children, the quixotic Glenn Gould's magisterial and quite simply must-be-heard – in conjunction with his 1981 re-recording – 1955 *Goldberg Variations*.

This is where we might be breaking away from the warm, cuddly MfP, into the 1970s' Classics for Pleasure, even approaching the definitely permanent, even if we aren't really, and after Gould, the more modern MfP-type albums keep coming: the celebrities, the waltzes, the packaging, the favourites, the masters, the collections, the onlys, the evers, the carols, the box sets, the soundtracks, the Previns, the courteous, the remains, the unthreatening covers, the dolled-up, presentable instrumentalists often staring wistfully at their own glazed accessibility, or holding their instruments to show us what it is they do as though it is some sort of mystery.

Max Richter's *Recomposition* of Vivaldi's *The Four Seasons* is at number seven in the *BBC Music Magazine* classical chart, and is a shiny, beckoning example of the new well-intentioned attempts to relocate classical music, drag it out of the stuffy sonic museum, refresh the stale and overfamiliar and invite in a new audience who resist the cluttered cultural orthodoxy of classical presentation but generally enjoy musical adventure. In fact, Richter's adaptation, or 'improvement', giving an ultimate favourite a methodical electronic polish, places it squarely in the world of the frisky, kitsch Music for Pleasure hybrids, updated into the post-Aphex world, but still essentially the equivalent, for all the carefully cool disguise, of a funky version of Bach or a bossa nova Brahms. A neat little exercise, to an extent, turning a John Lewis tea towel into one from Ikea, highly irritating if you think about it too much, and hardly in the intellectual, analytical sphere of Luciano Berio's arrangements of Monteverdi, Purcell, Mozart, Brahms and Mahler, or his handsome completion of Schubert's provisionally sketched out but abandoned Tenth Symphony. In the Music for Pleasure charts, despite the names and reputations of the composers Berio pays homage to, I imagine his album of transcriptions would be about 7,945 in the classical chart – it is 110,760 in the overall bestseller ratings – but if there was such a thing as a permanent chart, a collection of transcendent classical pieces that is some heavenly equivalent of a hit parade, a chart where the newcomer can go to find some of the greatest classical pieces, it is in the top thirty. In those charts, Rieu is 1,456,657, just above Rolf Harris, and just below Paloma Faith.

Max Richter defined the music on his debut album *Memoryhouse* (2002) as 'post-classical', something he almost immediately regretted. It too specifically suggested a new form of novelty fusion music, mostly never a good thing, rather than an attempt to move what had happened to music in the twentieth century – as technology, chance and machinery became as great a factor in the composition and production of music as scored notes, harmony and acoustic sound – into the twenty-first century, where memory and reality itself was to be challenged, reinforced and even assaulted by hyper-evolving technology and accelerating randomness.

When Richter came up with the term post-classical, he was also thinking of post-rock, the invented genre of a new kind of guitar group infected by studio experiments, electronic invention, improvisatory approaches, sustained tones and the fluid, multidimensional zones where Pink Floyd, King Crimson, Soft Machine, Can, Miles, dub reggae, trip hop and the twelve-inch remix had glanced, sometimes collided, against symphonic and conceptual classical dynamics and a whole other, higher world of looping, tuning, vibration, ambience and timing. Perhaps, the hope was, there was something emerging after 'classical', after all that had happened between, say, Schoenberg and Cage, and between Debussy and Eno, let alone between Bach and Birtwistle. There was still somewhere to go, new borders to cross.

He was only trying to be helpful – he might have preferred to say that his music could be called 'tender' or 'mood' or 'film' – or, considering how his music developed over the next eighteen years, 'soundtrack' or, in the best sense of the word, 'incidental', or even, in an ideal world, just 'music', but he didn't want to alienate anyone looking for a convenient description of this expressive mix of classical craft and electronic filtering. In fact, memoryhouse was probably the actual genre *Memoryhouse* occupied, in the way that there was house, an original, darker, computer-generated extension of disco that then itself splintered into deeper, less rhythmical, more suspended-in-space, abstract sub-houses – and the memoryhouse was in fact the mind, the imagination, the whole interior world of the individual, and music is made in this memoryhouse, for this memoryhouse, a room where memories, of things that actually happened or only seemed to have happened, can be stored, explored and replayed.

Richter is not quite on the verge of entering the serious classical lineage, one or two discreetly disordered, radical moves on from the great and not-so-great minimalists, using art as a way of giving us clues about how to live, brilliantly extending centuries of continuity as if things are only just beginning, not drifting to the edge of one long, fragmented end. He's not quite on the verge of inheriting the avant-pop classical presence of Eno, proactively reshaping musical minds and fortunes, keen on there being a pragmatic use for his music. He's not quite on the verge of becoming the kind of classical personality that suavely slips into Classic FM loafers, using the events of the past as a necessary security blanket. Perhaps he is simply a smart, refreshing alternative to bludgeoning soundtrack composers like Hans Zimmer; a nice, dreamy thing to put on a playlist in a world of playlists courteously announcing 'you might like this', between Cluster and Stars of the Lid, or between This Heat and Sun Ra, between Murcof and Messiaen, where one thing continues to lead to another, without any real direction, towards a disappearing future, simply because it can, and will, making the sort of patterns that at best gently expand our ideological, emotional, existential and intellectual comfort zones.

Max Richter's music all emerges from his particular response to the profound instruction of experimental electronic pioneer Luciano Berio, his ingenious teacher, when suggesting to Richter that he make his once dense, convoluted, more determinedly modernist music simpler, and simpler, and even more simple. He recommended that Richter set himself and his music in motion by ejecting the complex and showy, by pulling back from the overacting and the peacock displays. Intensity, virtuosity, energy, nerve, theatre, personal destiny, narrative pulse and conceptual insight could still exist inside sparer structures, subdued tempo, reduced volume, softer explosions and minimal, repeated gesture – amidst a noisy, cluttered, broken-up world, delicacy, and a withdrawal from overpopulated territories, was a bolder direction to take.

THE BEGINNING — TO *THE PLANETS* AND BEYOND

4. WHERE THE A IS FOR AWARE, ARDENT, ABSURD, ASTONISHING, ANALYTICAL, ALARMING, ATONAL, APESHIT, AND THE Z IS STILL, BUT NEVER STILL, FOR ZAPPA

The death in 1993 of Frank Zappa is perhaps the point where Max Richter can imagine a post-classical music began. The death of Zappa is one way of marking the end of a classical lineage that began in the sixteenth and seventeenth centuries, and there can then plausibly be a post-classical era for those born after the cut-off period, who were classically educated but found it difficult to ignore the sensuous lure of pop, rock and electronic music.

It could be said that classical music, if we fancy a nice tidy A to Z, goes from Jacques Arcadelt, one of the most famous and influential early composers of madrigals and secular vocal music, born in 1507, active during the Renaissance in both Italy and France, to Frank Zappa, a very different kind of Renaissance genius, active in and around American rock 'n' roll and European intellectualism, who brought it all — what began with madrigals and various invented forms of secular music — to a hell of a climax. Echoes and subsequent ripples were destined to last for decades, one way or another.

Musician, cultural critic, technician, self-publicist, libertarian social commentator, arranger, satirist, parent, stunt guitarist whose solos were spontaneous compositions, paranoid historian, educator, genre mutilator, inventor-ish of the pop album that wasn't just a collection of singles, Zappa was always the fire-in-his-eyes leader of a cult inspiring proto-geek loyalty, but at the turn of the 1970s, when American rock went mad with influences, the cult was more on the inside of (counter) culture than it is now.

His name alone was glamorous, something to be instantly curious about, and when I first started paying attention to Zappa, with the zany hair and the zanier facial hair, in the early 1970s, the albums you immediately wanted to buy had gonzo excitement and ambition written all over their covers and in their titles. Musically, from big-headed, big-minded *Freak Out!* in 1966, and then *Absolutely Free, We're Only in It for the Money, Uncle Meat, Hot Rats* — a top-ten UK album — and *Weasels Ripped My Flesh*, the records seemed as packed with pun, texture, self-reference, connective tissue, buried, seething meaning as a James

Joyce novel, with song titles and an overall spirit that had a literary dimension, as well as far-out, far-fetched suggestions that here was a logic-challenging surrealist as much as a composer, an offensive, deeply black comedian as much as a very white, guitar-neurotic rock star.

Some of this music sounded more or less exactly like you would imagine from someone inspired by the self-creating noises of Varèse, Webern, serialism and Stravinsky from a twentieth-century classical world, as well as breezy, smooth-tipped doo-wop, freedom-seeking free jazz, and, as a guitarist teaching himself, the haywire blues.

He was drawn to avant-garde classical music through a review he read of Varèse's percussion-propelled *Ionisation*, written between 1929 and 1931, which promised a 'weird jumble of drums and other unpleasant sounds', and he never lost that love of the weird and aggravating, whatever music he invented, insulted, honoured, parodied, regenerated, seriously composed through the fifty, sixty albums he made before his death at fifty-three; being born in 1940 meant that he just made it inside an apparent cut-off point, because it seems that those born before 1940 generally missed being swept up into pop and rock, and were in many ways the final generation of classical musicians, mostly emerging as names and players during minimalism and post-minimalism, and those born after 1940 tended to be diverted by rock 'n' roll and had names like John Lennon, David Bowie, Brian Wilson, Patti Smith and Lou Reed.

In the same way that Varèse being born when he was, ready to be enveloped by the twentieth century, was not so much influenced by other composers as by natural objects and physical phenomena, Zappa's music was similarly influenced by much more than music, by the random noise and oddball energy of American television, utopian desires, the complexity of thought, a loathing of bigotry, and the filthy, emancipating might of smut.

Where do you begin making some kind of way through the knotty, never-ending music of Zappa, what albums should you try? Well, sometimes I think it's best to take them one by one as they came, as if they were in order, progressing as they go along – which they sort of do, if sometimes sideways with flashbacks, like the episodes in some epic *Wire*-like television series – ignoring compilations, swimming through the mass, mania and mire from the conceptually demented Mothers of Invention (1965–70); the weirdo jazz-rock *Hot Rats* hinge in 1970; to the Flo and Eddie post-Turtles period, where the catalogue gets scatological on *Fillmore East – June 1971*, and then with *200 Motels*, where psychedelic ambition imploded and/or exploded into deranged mock opera because, as Frank says, 'touring makes you crazy'; leading to the stewed, dropout big band of 1972 including *The Grand Wazoo*; the most mainstream he more or less got, with *Apostrophe* and *Overnight Sensation* between 1973 and 1975; the reunion with sibylline sidekick Captain Beefheart in 1975, *Bongo Fury*, six years after they mapped out the skin of the universe with *Trout Mask Replica*, both playing straight man and funny man; the fertile solo work to the end of the seventies, including *Sheik Yerbouti* and the naturally cryptic and complex triple-album psycho-rock opera *Joe's Garage*, peaking with one of his greatest guitar performances 'Watermelon in Easter Hay'; the eighties that were as tricky for Zappa as they were for Dylan and Bowie, starting with the pure exploratory guitar of *Shut Up 'n Play Yer Guitar*, leading to his acquiring a Synclavier synthesiser that brought out the uncontrollable control freak in Zappa, fiddling while America dumbs down, and then I just haven't got the time and space to explain how by his death he was closer musically to Pierre Boulez than the Fugs, to composing music for chamber ensemble and orchestra rather than rock band.

You want ten Zappa songs to sample from the murky, moving mountain – that's as tough as learning Latin in a day, but for the sake of this list, I'm choosing ones where the titles open doors to Zappa's mentality: 'Stink Foot', 'Who are the Brain Police', 'The Duke of Prunes', 'Eat That Question', 'The Ocean is the Ultimate Solution', 'Don't You Ever Wash That Thing', 'Call Any Vegetable', 'The Torture Never Stops', 'You're Probably Wondering Why I'm Here' and 'Cosmik Debris' – 'what kind of guru was he anyway?'

But as the whole point of Zappa music was how the mind changes, and to change minds, in a minute I'll change my mind. Actually, don't listen to Zappa at all if you are not in the mood for the apparently unlistenable: it will only lead to confusion. Just track down his writing/ interviews/political rants that inspired playwright, dissident and eventual last president of Czechoslovakia Václav Havel, and place Zappa as philosopher-performer between Antonin Artaud and Slavoj Žižek.

He lived in his own world, and followed his own agenda, and was uncomfortable outside it. In that sense he is the missing link between Ornette Coleman and who cares? It's why whenever a Zappa festival is mooted or achieved, and it comes to imagining bands directly or indirectly influenced by Zappa, it's very difficult to think of any. Phish, perhaps, as a sort of tribute act; Mars Volta maybe and contemporary composers like Philip Cashian, who orchestrates Zappa's guitar solos as though they were blueprints for radiant concertos. You can list musicians and groups who admire or even adore his attitude, his subversive smartness, his playing and savage playfulness, his sarcasm, how prolific he was, from Hawkwind, Kevin Ayers and Faust to Panda Bear, John Zorn and Tenacious D, but you will not come up with anyone making sound as ecstatically eccentric, defiantly difficult and structurally adventurous that links dead on with Zappa's. Unless you could reform the Bonzo Dog Doo-Dah Band with Harrison Birtwistle, Henry Cowell, David Foster Wallace, Yoko Ono, Lightnin' Hopkins and David Letterman.

I once asked the artist-music producer Brian Eno about Zappa, who seemed to share a similar craving to create an experimental collage of influences from pop culture and the avant-garde, and he said, well, he was a big influence, but in reverse – 'He'd showed me exactly what I should not be doing. He fused together all the *wrong* things. I did not like his music, but I am very grateful that he did it. Sometimes you learn as much from the things you don't like as from the things you do like. The rejection side is as important as the endorsement part. You define who you are and where you are by the things that you know you are not. Sometimes that's all the information you have to go on. I'm not *that* kind of person. You don't quite know where you are, but you find yourself in the space left behind by the things you've rejected.' As an artist once said about Jackson Pollock – 'I'm glad he did what he did. Now I can go and do something else.'

In the wide-open early 1970s, when what had been set up in the 1960s could go anywhere, Zappa the extremist fitted, while having sonic, (a)moral and narcissistic fits, among all of the crazy, revelatory counterculture greats, Hendrix, the Velvets, Janis, Joni, Lennon and co., but perhaps in some eventual history of twentieth-century culture he will fit into a story that also includes the Italian Futurists, Cage, Stockhausen, Ligeti, Duchamp and Joseph Beuys more than the Grateful Dead or Bob Dylan, or perhaps he'll be squeezed in, a little lonely, between Gertrude Stein, Groucho Marx, Lenny Bruce and Olivier Messiaen.

5. TEN 1970S CLASSICS FOR PLEASURE ALBUMS THAT SHOULD BE RELEASED AS A BUDGET BOX SET, PRICED TEN TIMES THE ORIGINAL PRICE OF TEN SHILLINGS AND SIXPENCE, THE EQUIVALENT NOW OF £5.25

- Igor Stravinsky: *Firebird* and *Petrushka* Ballet Suites (Berlin Philharmonic conducted by Leopold Stokowski)
- Edward Elgar: *Enigma Variations* and *Introduction and Allegro for Strings* (London Philharmonic Orchestra conducted by Sir Adrian Boult)
- Jean Sibelius: *Finlandia/The Swan of Tuonela/Karelia Suite/ En Saga* (Vienna Philharmonic Orchestra conducted by Sir Malcom Sargent)
- Edvard Grieg: Piano Concerto in A minor/*Peer Gynt* Suite (London Philharmonic Orchestra conducted by John Pritchard, soloist Peter Katin)
- Michael Tippett/Ralph Vaughan Williams: *Fantasia on a Theme by Thomas Tallis/Fantasia on Greensleeves*/Concerto for Double String Orchestra (London Philharmonic Orchestra conducted by Vernon Handley)
- Johannes Brahms: Symphony No. 3/*Hungarian Dances* (Hallé Orchestra conducted by James Loughran)
- Ludwig van Beethoven: Piano Sonatas: *Moonlight, Pathétique, Appassionata* (Daniel Chorzempa)
- Henry Purcell: Ceremonial, Theatre and Chamber Music (Virtuosi of England conducted by Arthur Davison)
- Frederick Delius: Orchestral Works (London Philharmonic Orchestra conducted by Vernon Handley)
- Wolfgang Amadeus Mozart: Piano Concerto No. 21/*Eine Kleine Nachtmusik* (Virtuosi of England conducted by Arthur Davison, featuring Moura Lympany)

The Playlist – A Few of My Favourite Things

Claude Achille Debussy *circa 1905: 'I want music to seem to rise from the shadows and indeed sometimes to return to them.'*

1. THE AGE OF STORAGE

One of the more beneficial facilities of the streaming sites is how quickly it is possible to gather together a vast library of music, from the obvious to the obscure. To work out what you have in your library, which if you're in the mood or professionally looking for clues can grow by the minute, it helps to make playlists, your very own organised compilations of music. It is one way of cataloguing and controlling an amount of music that can appear to stretch throughout eternity.

There is no shape to it all, so producing personal playlists can create some shape if you need it, and a feeling all this music is moving in one direction, not fractured into millions of directions or basically just piled up in a dark corner, or many dark corners. I started to make playlists of the music from across time that I was finding, to sort it out for myself. To see if it meant anything. To relax into it… or the exact opposite.

Coming up with playlists and ideas for recommendations, even if just for myself, rapidly enriched my listening experiences and expanded my discoveries: one thing would lead to another and another, and one composer would lead to another, one century to another genre to another treasure, another piece of amazing luck. I was essentially looking for a way to make the streaming availability work as a resource, more than what, on the surface, it was, a placing of all music into one easily accessed station, or warehouse, or storage facility.

If you happen to be making a map of the music you are interested in, or studying certain genres of music, or contemplating the number of musical canons that seem to exist, or writing a book, then this new world of storage is extremely useful. If you have any sort of need to track down music as quickly as possible, not necessarily for pleasure, or because you are on the hunt for something in particular, but because you are learning about a certain history of music, it is a revelation.

An interest in classical music has emerged, as much as any other reason, because I can now find everything I am looking for or don't even know I am looking for, whereas before streaming, the task of tracking down music and making connections was difficult and expensive. I liked the idea that in these playlists you could break free of genre settings and fixed histories and move things around, even as it contradicted how the sites were increasingly designed and arranged into very particular, separated and very predictable settlements.

Making playlists became a kind of new creative venture, as though it was the creation of a playlist that was the one new format or genre that streaming sites had introduced. It was a democratised creative act, and it could be said that it was the new album in an era when certainly the making of most music, popular or otherwise, was itself part of a curatorial process – the locating, sifting and sorting of influences to make the sort of music you grew up liking or studying, because it was easier to do it than it once was, not least because there were so many preferences. The production of a playlist, the placing together of memories, music, favourites based around personal taste and life experiences, was itself an act of the imagination.

Everyone had the potential to become a critic, to be a self-styled creative, to be a curator – and therefore, everyone had the potential to be their own artist. There was no real place for me to write about classical music and explore and explain my new interest, but I could make playlists, which to some extent is the purest form of modern criticism. The selection process is a display of your discrimination: this is what you like, and this is the order you would like to hear it played. Who needs anything else? Who needs writing, or interpretation, or myth-making?

Pop writers needed to find something else to do now that mostly they had been replaced, made redundant or their value completely reduced. As a rock critic who appeared also to have some sort of eccentric interest in classical music, I was invited onto numerous public panels, as though I might have the answer to a question I wasn't particularly interested in – how do you make classical music of interest to a wider, more diverse audience, including the young, many of whom treated music in general as simply a resource, something to search, and use in the background of their lives, and the curation of those lives?

The desire for classical music to reach a wider audience implied it was somehow good for you, which suggested a worthiness that meant it would never be of interest to a wider audience, because those were exactly the sort of people who wanted to find things for themselves and make their own minds up. There was a reluctance to face up to the inevitable, that we were going through such a dramatic shift in the nature and appearance of reality, and this came with an increasing number of well-intentioned attempts to try and deal with associated tension and confusion through public debates and community discussions.

There were many things that seemed permanent in the latter decades of the twentieth century that are now reaching their natural end because of the internet and its new equivalent of a remote control, the mobile phone, which helped you constantly change channels – which were effectively realities – minute by minute and put yourself at the centre of all broadcasts. There was a need among those with a more threatened late twentieth-century approach to try and cancel, or postpone, or perhaps just delay the inevitable, and as part of this, the question of how to interest the young and the usually uninterested in classical music seemed to be one way of dealing with the end of things and maintaining collective cultural memory.

I wasn't necessarily interested in finding marketing methods to make a more diverse audience discover classical music, which seemed as futile a gesture as protecting the dodo, but I had developed my own personal interest in the past, present and future of classical music as a creative energy flowing through history, and a developing belief that there was something about it that seemed better prepared to survive into the future.

As pure energy, classical music fitted well onto streaming sites, and because to some extent it had long lost an immediate, fashionable context in a world increasingly distracted by the quick fixes and uncomplicated, accessible pleasures of entertainment, it had become almost accidentally inserted inside the body of streaming, where it would be carried forward, possibly more successfully than pop and rock. Pop and rock had developed so emphatically inside the world of records and CDs, which seemed more disconnected when packed and processed onto the streaming sites. Classical music had never been made for particular formats, and so streaming was just the latest arena where it made itself at home, as it was passing through on its way to wherever, even for ever. Streaming, outside of the way the interfaces were designed, the emphasis placed on modern music, suited classical music, where the main thing had always been the music itself, not necessarily the record sleeves, or the innovation of the mix.

This was my theory, anyway, and I had been weaned, very much pre-social media, very much from the time when the rock critic apparently had some powers, on the idea that you sent these Marshall McLuhan-like probes out into the world to see where they landed, if at all. And if they did land, what would happen to them? How would their messages be interpreted? Sometimes you'd send out a contradictory probe, to see where that might land, and what the response might be to that theory. You weren't demanding that everyone agree with you or follow your principles. You weren't making rules. The rules were what troubled you.

If anything, you were just trying to break away from the limiting rules that had been established, often in response to a probe someone had once sent out containing certain ideas and propositions that were not intended to end up as dogma. But social media had wrecked – or evolved beyond – that form of abstract, now increasingly sweet, naive debate. Now, and I wasn't quite ready for this as it seemed more rooted in business and warfare than in the distribution and investigation of ideas, things were much more specifically, even fundamentally oppositional. It was also much more a world looking for information, recipes, lists, guides, tips, certainty, data and summaries, and not so much the incidental, provisional and tentative, the glancing against reality leaving traces that may or may not resolve into something. It had become a world of fixed, futile arguments, and a world vainly looking for help, for advice on how to bake, travel, learn a new skill, make yourself up and fix a minor – or major – problem.

The mechanics and motives of radicalism, which should never settle into one direction, were being replaced by a fixity of thinking that encouraged a general conservatism. This was my theory, anyway, or the beginning of a theory, and on various panels and debates I could improvise an argument about what I was thinking, although what I was thinking was not necessarily a definitive position. It was a working-out in very turbulent and divisive times what was actually happening to us, and to reality, and therefore, because this is where I started and where I would finish, to music. Perhaps I was just expressing these feelings as part of my quest to decide on a final piece of music I would listen to; advising myself.

One probe I sent out, considering that the streaming era had changed things in terms of the presence and context of music, was that there needed to be a change in approach to how music was defined, classified and written about. When writing about pop music, and the virtual viral sounds, processed emotions, constructed sound effects and mechanised celebrities representing the mechanical sounds, it increasingly seemed, as the twenty-first century got closer to being twenty years old, that new categories needed to be introduced.

It seems strange to be reviewing the new musical world of constant stimulation, synthetic fantasy, curated eclecticism, mild appropriation and raging self-promotion in much the same way, with the same terms and more or less the same expectations as music was reviewed thirty and forty years ago; to review a piece of pop that was not so much simply music but an engineered and/or ingenious series of signals, rhythms, ideas and poses, without paying attention to the most important aspects — its qualities as a special effect, designed to thrill, as erotic distraction, branding opportunity, advert for the self, as a demand for attention, as a form of energy that can blast through and compete with all the technologically channelled commercial noise. Songs were being reviewed as pieces of art or entertainment as if they were still emerging and featuring in a world that was now forty years old, still linked to a music business and culture that does not exist any more.

Ultimately, it is missing the point not to review the most important element in the making and distributing of modern post-music — the machines, and their operators, manipulating what's left of pop from behind the scenes, or behind their DJ/creative-mogul masks and pseudonyms.

This is beyond music; it's about a form of presence, and pretence, of appearance, and make-believe that has a continual soundtrack, but there needs to be a whole new review category in which to place it, and make connections, if anyone still cares. As I talked, it would seem like I was the only one who did still care, or at least the only one who still cared about what I cared about, especially if I expressed annoyance over how the names of the genres and musical alcoves of Spotify were so dull and unimaginative; to those in the audience it seemed to be about as important as complaining about the colour of the shelves in a supermarket. To the marketing people, I was missing the point about what was essentially branding, about using new strategies to reach subscribers in a world where content, which music had become, was all about market share, influencers and commercial consistency.

The content must contain elements of 'cool' and 'hipness' because this new world was based on the fashions and styles of pop culture, where those things were prized as commercial devices. I was out of date worrying about how the music was presented and what labels were used. The point was, it was all there, and the sites had found convenient ways to transmit what they now contained – which was, more or less, everything. What else did I want? I wouldn't stop probing, although the anxiety I would feel after one of these presentations or debates would always cause me, safely settled back home, to say to my partner Elizabeth, 'Please remind me never to do this again.'

I would continue working out my position, how classical was not only worth listening to for emotional and intellectual stimulation but was actually a new thing; classical music doesn't sound modern – not in the way, until recently, we have thought about the sound of modern – but as thinking goes, about what it is to be alive, about what music is, there is so much it achieved and proposed that has yet to be understood and properly assimilated. If, in a popular-culture sense, classical music has been old-fashioned, or on the outside of market forces and radical trends, it is now something else, its modern essence more contemporary-seeming now that pop and rock is just everyday and everywhere.

I used to think classical music was old-fashioned and out of date, but I now realise it was just too modern. By modern, I mean it was concerned with all the workings of the mind, and how that reflected and created reality around it. By modern, I mean a kind of energy that both grounds us in the here and now and sends signals of intent out into the future. Rhythmically, too, it was often way ahead of rock and pop, pressing all kinds of agitation and animation into its rhythms that made rock rhythms – if not the electronics of pop and hip-hop – seem increasingly tepid and obvious.

It didn't *sound* modern, because pop music made much better use of the recording studio, had composers that thrived as performers and advertisements of their own music, and as a technology-based entertainment, as a modern entertainment experience, it was light years ahead of classical, even at the tacky, hyper-commercial end.

This was always pop music's greatest weapon in its taking over of the main musical landscape in the twentieth century – that technology and machines were essential in the making of the music, centred around the great, pleasure-seeking, sound-altering magic of the recording studio, and it went through its accelerated changes inside forty, fifty years as new equipment was discovered and exploited, whereas classical music did not seem to change or be about to change, having already gone through its great accelerated progressions. If it was changing, those changes were more or less invisible, or inaudible, so far removed from most people's everyday experience of music that it was in its own way as dead as music that was centuries old.

Classical music was either too new, and wilfully weird-sounding, or too old and elaborately cocooned inside dreary establishment-coded rules and regulations, or it belonged, in a middle-class sense, to your parents, or even grandparents; either way, it didn't sound electrically or even acoustically modern, not like a great pop record, because it didn't use special effects and electronic extras to spice it up and articulate the very essence of seduction and perception.

At best it had what Anthony Burgess called, when writing about Mozart and his representation of the nature of the Austro-Hungarian Empire, 'static tranquillity'. The music that emerged roughly within the orbit of the serious instrumental music that could be labelled 'classical' and that had some of rock and pop's initial speculative spirit and unorthodox elasticity tended to be so far into the experimental, conceptual margins, that in many ways it was closer to, say, John Foxx, Pink Floyd and Brian Eno than Mozart, Sibelius and Mahler.

In its heyday, leading to the compact-disc era and a few years beyond, pop music sounded sensational, on the move, inventing and distributing new heroes and superstars by the year, while conventional classical music sounded bloated and dead, and seemed to be definitively old-fashioned. But – and you could go back into the eighteenth century when the idea of a 'classical' music started to take shape, all the way through the overlapping eras of renewing action and reaction in the next 250 years – the ideas, the deeper meaning, the philosophical, romantic, even political thinking was in an abstract form, always contemporary and exciting, if only you could break through the coating and prejudices that made it seem too distant and aloof.

For years I was convinced it was decadent, convoluted and over-formalised, turned into a cultural irrelevance by those using classical music for their own purpose as a bland, futile and protectionist symbol of the 'high arts' and their position in the establishment. It never occurred to me that actually it was simply too rich and active with suppressed, volatile energy and rhythms that were not anachronistic but actually more advanced and convoluted than anything in pop or rock.

As long as humans live, songs won't die, just as telling stories never will, but the basic structure of pop has collapsed, leaving just fragmented blasts of slippery assembled energy relying on increasingly present history to maintain the illusion that there is such a thing as a scene or a collection of scenes, containing new trends, leading to the next set of new trends. The initial energy that made pop music happen so instantly and persuasively – the charts, the sleeves, the photography, the record labels, the two-sided vinyl album and single, the way that one thing developed into the next thing, mostly leaving the last thing behind, other than something to fold back into the new thing, but in a new form – has become defunct. This isn't necessarily a bad thing, just what has happened after all that movement, now that there is such a glut, of all the music happening now, and all the music that ever happened, all of it available to pluck out of the air, as the world becomes one big mobile playground, combined with one big ideological battleground.

The pop stars of today are the machines that the music is made on and then played through; the groups and singers that represent the machines and computers are like travelling salesmen, demonstrating the wares, acting out the necessary human-ish element of engagement, going through the motions of dressing up and performance. Pop stars are an impaired, occasionally inspired community of manipulated, manipulating commercial travellers, which has its attractions, but has less and less to do with music and more to do with a kind of dazed re-tuning of ancient show-business conventions. The next generation may well find all of this as stale and moribund as we do Vera Lynn and Cliff Richard.

Essentially, nothing now changes in pop but the technology; it used to be that way, but there was also an attached level of purpose and drama, of stylistic audacity, and even subversive, discriminatory focus, of exciting new forms of glamour and presentation that didn't seem mere anagrams of previous glamorous presentations.

Technology has taken over and carries pop music all over the place, and even beyond all over the place. It's not, as such, music any more; it's either a sentimental wallowing in the past, for older people — just like classical music once seemed — or basic adolescent urges reframed using the new machines, so that today's pop and rock is essentially about what it was about in the fifties and sixties, with different coverings, body shakes and street noises used to ensure it sounds like today, for standard as-cynical-as-ever commercial reasons. Music that was all about change has become music that is all about nothing changing, or changing so quickly it cannot be detected outside its own circuit.

I was thinking about this one day when the *Observer* got in touch, and for once they didn't want me to write something about what had happened in the 1980s, about the rebirth of Duran Duran, the race for the Christmas number one, the death of another rock star, the latest post by Cardi B or the latest Rolling Stones tour, but to see if I wanted to write about the new interest I had in classical music, with perhaps a short accompanying playlist — that being the key, really.

I knew that it was a novelty piece — old-school, near-extinct rock critic with fancy, if not downright pretentious interest in classical music — and I knew exactly what they wanted. A late-life confession piece written as though it was the equivalent of a change in diet, and the playlist was essentially the recipe at the end of the emotional reason for the new diet. How could I turn it down: a first chance to write about classical music in a national newspaper! My entire 'career' had come to this!

They possibly wanted a nice, positive answer to the question — can classical music cross over to a pop and rock audience? There is no 'yes' answer, and there isn't a 'no' either, but any real shift can only happen once those finding new music are born outside the span of rock, all the remaining anniversaries, song deconstructions on podcasts and nostalgic reboots. All you can do for now is make a playlist, and, if you're lucky, get to write an intro…

2. AN INTRODUCTION BY A ROCK CRITIC TO SOME CLASSICAL MUSIC PLAYLISTS

I was asked by a friend, aware of a big recent shift in my listening habits, if I would compile a playlist of some pieces by the late nineteenth/ early twentieth-century French composers Maurice Ravel and Claude

Debussy. I was happy to be asked, because at least I wasn't being asked to comment on the latest scrubbed-up set of finely tuned songs by Taylor Swift or this week's contrived multi-named collaboration featuring Ed Sheeran, as if I might have something new to say, even though I have been saying that sort of stuff for nearly forty years.

It doesn't seem to matter that what I say might be completely out of date, or that in a way I am overqualified, if not simply over-aged, to comment on post-Cowell, post-Insta, internet-era pop that is less about music than a coldly – or warmly – formulaic combination of product design, market research, branding, publicity and social-media-generated gossip. To write about much modern pop you need to be an expert, not in how pop was in the 1960s–1980s or even 2000s, but in a very different set of systems, sweeteners and strategies, and have an understanding about the role and skills of a new breed of creative moguls like Wyclef Jean, Will.i.am, Kanye West, Cardi B, Drake, Beyoncé and Jay Z. Their music is a small part of what they are, the rest made up of their image as directed and refracted by social media, whereas in the last few decades of the twentieth century a pop star was all that you heard and saw, through a very minimal framework. You got everything all at once, without having to piece it together from other less fixed elements of their performance. Mostly you pieced it together in your imagination.

I didn't really see many write about this new world of pop music in ways that understood this fluid, post-musical operational style, and I didn't think it was my place to even try. I wouldn't necessarily be writing about music, but a form of creative image-making, curational management style, and I would need much more understanding of the nature of hashtags, Instastories and micro-influencers. And if I ever did try, any response to what I wrote was usually blank. What was I talking about? This was one reason why I was feeling more comfortable thinking about Ravel than Kanye and his mad-mouth theories about being a creative coordinating an ever-evolving entertainment brand.

And if I was thinking about anyone relatively new and musically more pure, less cluttered with the marketing and the social-media-cultivated mannerisms, it would be someone like Kamasi Washington, who, for all his bold, discriminating blending of style and sensibility, is still embedded in a sentimental yearning for a time when it seemed decent, even dignified, to imagine and subsequently conceive musical progressiveness.

I also don't want to keep writing the same things about the music I wrote about in the 1970s, as though that is all I am good for, keeping some sort of flame alive for the sake of recapturing and reliving youth and therefore unrealistically deferring the 'D' word, the biggest 'D' of them all. I don't want to keep remembering the 1980s in a bleary haze of nostalgia, somewhere between sentimental and senile. What excited me about music when I was younger was how it kept introducing me to new experiences and helped me adjust to new sensations and life stages. I haven't lost that desire for the new, the next, the unexpected, the rare and wondrous, but I now find that you don't necessarily have to wait for what is apparently new to find the new.

Classical music seems old and irrelevant to non-believers because it is mostly from the past, proudly as old as time, but look and listen a little deeper and you can find that it is filled with a constant flow of newness. Its whole history is based on the idea of composers finding something new in reaction to what has gone before, building on technique, breaking away from precedent, rejecting the existing canon, responding to new environmental pressures and opportunities and their own mental appetites, searching for new ways to create a surrogate world, a unique beyondness, through which to read this world and all other energetic parallel worlds. There are thousands of neglected, ignored, misplaced 'news' from previous times, and now that the world has been profoundly rearranged by the internet and the constant presence of information, judgement and conversation, much of it from the past, the excitement is in finding these new 'news' and making them come alive.

I reached the stage where I decided, if I was listening to pop and rock that was up to and over fifty years old, not because I was being nostalgic but for the enduring thrill of hearing intensity, greatness, ravishing novelty, I might as well listen to music that was up to and over a hundred, 200, 300 years old. Rock and pop are now sinking back into that past, especially to those born in the twenty-first century, many of whom could reach their early teens with as little knowledge of the Beatles as of Beethoven. Great music was about, and responding to, the same things — being alive, seeking pleasure, falling in love, feeling happy, feeling sad, defining truth, articulating faith, fearing death, repelling demons, a total immersion in mystery – whenever it was written and whatever the circumstances.

Discovering classical music recreates that feeling of wanting to know new things, find new music, and discover unknown places and experience wonderment and a general sense of difference. It's nostalgic for that curious and restless feeling I once had, but also it contains an intense hunger for the unexpected, and for the fresh. It's a way of updating an interest in music, to remind myself – surrounded, hounded, by pop music on TV ads, talent shows, Netflix series, nerdy podcasts, games and cinema soundtracks, bombarding us with the same riffs, rhythms and rhymes, the same sugar rushes, the same outlaw, out-of-it, out-of-time way with cool and edge – that there is always something new under the sun, especially when you go on the hunt for it.

I can also hunt for all the rock and pop that I missed, or that missed me, but now that I am aware of all this other music, I feel its pull as much, if not more, than the music I have traditionally been interested in. It's also a language that will continue to make its way into the future, for as long as there are people who love space to think, in order to work themselves out, and understand and appreciate the minds of others.

My recent move into the classical sphere superficially seems like the classic, clichéd middle-aged move from rock and pop – until the last decade or two, traditionally meant for the young and lusty, of no use to those above thirty: a late-life drift into a conservative, grown-up and absolutely uncool and square world, leading, perhaps preparing the way, soothing the expanding existential pain, for death, that permanent irrelevance, the ultimate way of being out of touch with the latest trends.

For me, though, it has been more a move to where the provocative, thrilling, actually adaptive ideas are, where deep and determined critical thinking is, more because rock music and pop culture have themselves settled down and become the status quo.

It seemed pop music had become a form of skilfully engineered, instantly distributed product design, the performers little but smoothly delivered entertainment goods, and that is how they should be reviewed and categorised. New categories desperately need to be invented to deal with new circumstances. The current pop singers are geniuses of self-promotion, but not, as such, musicians expressing radically glamorous ideas, and most rock is now best termed 'trad'. I like a bit of product design, even the odd slab of trad, and have not turned my back completely on entertainment goods, and am constantly fascinated by the antics, scandals and occasionally the shrewdly and expensively sourced beats of the creative moguls and their offshoots, but when it comes to music and working out what music is for, when it comes to thinking about music as a metaphor for life itself, what tends to be described as classical music seems more relevant to the future. Well, my future.

Pop — and rock, and associated subgenres, all the way to the most superficially radical and experimental — is now trapped inside its own engorged, ebbing, over-the-top and largely subservient obviousness, a conservative, straight-faced compilation of inherited, rehashed, barely twisted poses, chords, images, beats, melodies, expressions and subject matter, packed into friendly, neutered festivals, living most of its actual life inside the dead hot and cold zones of machines, television commercials, sponsored venues and nightclubs.

What once seemed to be connected to a form of resistance to the establishment and to standard ways of thinking is now embedded in the mainstream, and any alternative urges are completely compromised by the fact that all music, however rebellious or challenging, has to be transmitted through the generous, if shady, surveilling corporate channels of Amazon, Apple, Google, Facebook and Spotify. Pop and rock have basically bought up, and bought into, a set of restrictive systems that they once, trivially or profoundly, opposed.

The music hall, vaudeville, show-business side of pop music has taken over, ejecting the militant, provocative and genuinely experimental side, and I find myself in my disturbing later years bored and frustrated with all this glittery orthodoxy, these old-fashioned values crudely and simplistically disguised as virtuous-seeming rebellion. Not because it's too noisy, risky, controversial and alienating, but because it's too timid and ultimately reserved, stuck in its ways, however superficially psyched up, sexy and mischievous. There is also more and more of the same, and there is such a glut of low- to medium-quality, quite plausible but deeply boring pop music, there needs to be more a regular cull than more talent shows discovering new talent for the sake of it, or in a last-ditch attempt to keep things going.

I've turned towards classical music, and the tumultuous mental energy of its great composers, and all its massed, turbulent history, because it seemed this was where I was more likely to find the radical and experimental, and music that was about difference, and ideas, and how surprising and provocative they can be, and how necessary, when reality is experimenting on itself. It is about music that puts you in touch with – or at least close to – what could be called magical, placing you back into the world after you have visited this other world feeling stronger, saner and more vigilant. It is also, refreshingly – because it appears old, difficult, intellectual, intimidating, boring – outside of the constant neurotic need to create an apparent new zeitgeist, and hip daily gossip, and perpetuate a stale oversubscribed idea of cool.

Classical music suffered during the vinyl age, as music accelerated incredibly quickly because of technology and consumerism. The packaging, the overall image, was never as cryptic, artistic and exciting as the packaging of pop and rock, as though really it didn't want to come down so much that it ended up merely as product, or it was so worried about being intimidating that the works were presented softly, accessibly, banally. Now that the packaging has been removed, and music is no longer as much about being an object, music is more in the air, in the spaces around us, not so rooted in the solid. This seems to suit classical music more, because in essence it is about the spaces around us; it is never rooted in the solid. It reflects the way we communicate with each other...

Classical music is readily available on Apple, Google, Spotify and Tidal, but somehow, in these new spaces and zones, it takes on the quality of an enigmatic, shadowy and glamorous underground, subverting these rootless techno-territories with its complex, alluring representation of strangeness, melancholy, beauty, loneliness, memory, space, fantasy, love, death, and, it turns out, sex, drugs and revolution, its true meaning destined to be revealed over time, its secrets released slowly. It's like finding genuine works of art on your local supermarket shelf.

For me, my relationship with classical music profoundly changed when I began to think of the music as devious, unclassifiable mental energy, as transcendent data flowing through space and creating special breathing space in a crowded, competitive world. Before then, the harps, flutes, violins, brass, clarinets and percussion could sound flimsy, whimsical, dated, occupied with making mere patterns, stuck in time, adrift from sassy contemporary currents. Suddenly, using new twenty-first-century gadgets and devices to find and play the music, hearing the music come down from wherever – somewhere out there – through my phone into my headphones, or through my tablet and then wirelessly to my portable speakers, seems as though I am having the thoughts, fantasies and dreams of great minds beamed straight into my mind. Classical music suits this new, abstract situation, whereas most pop and rock rely on other elements – the solid object, a social context, a tangible community of those who are the same age, a raging scene, a rigid sense of time and place, an accelerating form of nostalgia. Classical music can supply a pure, direct injection of the imagination, unfiltered by commercial or institutional distractions, unhindered by trivialised, ruptured notions of contemporary relevance. Once you make it through the formalities of classical music, the still-standing intimidating barriers of entry, there is the underestimated raw power of its acoustic sound, and an endless supply of glorious, revolutionary music now easily accessed as if it is all happening now, not in a pointless past.

As I worked my way into the history of classical music, and became more aware of how it had emerged, evolved, interbred, probed, rebooted and adapted, I realised that here was music made up by active, agitated minds dealing with extraordinary revolutionary changes in human behaviour, perception and circumstances. Suddenly it seemed alive in the now, appropriate to what was happening now, the mass changing of physical and mental shape, geography, society, perception, mentality, history – more so than the recent rock-and-pop-styled music that meekly followed decades-old fashion, and now just mostly follows itself, much like classical music seemed to forty years ago. For all the noise it makes, pop is in danger of falling into the background, something that is taken for granted, just another way of persuading people to buy things, subscribe to services, make playlists and act obediently as the world is ordered around them. The potency of the drug is wearing off.

Now that, to an extent, all music is about the past, and a curation of sampling and taste into playlists and knowing revivalist music, now that fashions and musical progress have collapsed, discernment wiped out, classical music takes a new place in time, not old or defunct, but part of the current choice, as relevant as any music, now that it is one big gathering of sound perpetually streaming into the world, up in the clouds, in the air, given mind-expanding meaning and purpose by how we engage with it. If you are interested in music that helps us adapt to new ideas, to fundamental change, that broadcasts different, special ways of thinking and warns us about those who loathe forms of thinking that are not the same as theirs, if you are thinking of making a move – that pseudo-radical Mercury Prize list coming around like a Yo Sushi conveyor belt one more time driving you over the edge, or perhaps because of that fifth Maximo Park album, yet one more slice of R&B-infused pop, one more posting about the greatest live album of all time, the pop singers who also write cookbooks, the mock drama of the latest announcement of who's headlining at Glastonbury, of pop groups from the past piling up on endless reunion tours, annually rewinding their forty-, fifty-, sixty-year-old novelty hits – here are eight ways of beginning, eight different doors into what is best thought of as life-enhancing, mind-bending outer space rather than the scary, once-and-for-all end of your pop-loving youth.

3. EIGHT STEPS BEYOND

1. Mozart – Masonic Funeral Music *in C minor*

Until recently, the big, marbled names like Mozart, Brahms and Beethoven seemed far away from urgent, modern life, and were all about death, dying and mourning. They were also co-opted and corrupted by an establishment coldly buying up culture to protect their narrow values, as though beauty could be owned, and radicalism necessarily neutralised. Because it is now possible to get to music that once seemed the other side of the universe, and gain unfiltered understanding, I can enjoy Mozart as a great, powerfully active mind moving across the uncanny, insanely absurd vastness of the cosmos, revealing and inventing itself, and therefore reality around it, through the uncompromising ongoing strangeness of music. Once you appreciate that the otherness of Mozart is as transcendent and stimulating as anyone living, as startling as any surrealist, you could spend all of your time patrolling his compositions and finding new places to start. To find a sense of brand-newness, I started with some of the less over-exposed and starry comfort pieces, like the austerely lovely, low and deliberately slow K. 477, the supernaturally solemn *Masonic Funeral Music*, written in 1785, digging deep into Gregorian chant and an unspecified, subtly twisted future mood. From there you can head in a thousand different Mozart directions, and a million other directions that are as likely to lead you to Alice Coltrane and Nina Simone as Iannis Xenakis and John Luther Adams.

2. Debussy – Sonata for Cello and Piano

The great thing about the way music is now accessed is how quickly you can move from one time and place to another, which really suits the hundreds of years of classical music and the way it moves in all directions at once — all of the time and activity, all those composers, conductors, orchestras, ensembles, versions, repertories, programmes, voices, connections can now be held more or less in one place, and, astonishingly, inside your phone, which increasingly means inside your mind. You can call Schubert, Stravinsky, Bartók, Lutosławski, Birtwistle, and they get right back to you. The one-sided conversations you can have are out of this world.

Pop and rock seemed much more tethered to the idea of the record, the packaging, to the social and cultural contexts unfolding around it, whereas classical music was always less fixed, and neurotically over-obsessed with protecting its purity, and seems especially liberated now that music is increasingly one single mass. It kept its distance, and that has proved an advantage now that the commercial music business has collapsed.

If you find one piece of classical music you like, and you are interested in the essential adventure, pleasure and smartness of classical music as opposed to the facile tricks and shallow illusions of show business, you can very quickly move out and about into a world that once seemed hermetically sealed off and controlled by mean, dismal and/or arcane forces. You can make your own way into a world that is new because it is new to you, a collection of responsive, connected and mutinous individuals in their own amazing world inside their own spaces and rooms and locations, making sense of who we are and where we have been, a vital representation of spontaneous thought.

The Mozart *Funeral Music* randomly turns up in numerous settings, including vast streamed compilations dedicated to the 'dark side' of classical music that take you to Verdi, Holst, Messiaen, Górecki, Glass and more doors into space — and there it is on a Decca compilation of over thirty hours of Benjamin Britten as performer and conductor that flows from Purcell and Byrd to the very different English fields of Vaughan Williams and Tippett. Among an entire personal history of music psychedelically whispering and fabulously blasting inside one musician's immense turbulent imagination — and now inside Google Play — there is Debussy's unearthly, defiantly beautiful, end-of-life Sonata for Cello and Piano. Concentrated into twelve intensely powerful, subtly volatile minutes, once heard they will haunt you for ever. It was written in 1915, but still sounds like it is just being thought of, like it's post-jazz, and post-Cage, simultaneously coalescing and disintegrating.

Classical music is not all big, mighty orchestras and epic, overpowering, bloody-minded symphonies, or tarted-up operatic fussiness; it is also filled with ravishing and sometimes deliciously haywire intimacy, the small, constantly varied combinations of instruments and exquisite, ever-surprising solo recitals. You can follow a truly fantastic trail of mental solo cello from J. S. Bach and Britten's suites to Sofia Gubaidulina's 1974 *Ten Preludes*, which forms some of the most radiant, breathtaking and poetic of all music and which is the purest sound of what it is to be human on the edge of something beyond at this weird, stomach-churning moment in time.

3. Berio – Sequenza V

One solo trail will always lead to another. You can quickly discover new stars operating as rebels interested in making the world a freer, fairer, wonderfully odder world, discover the very different things that make them tick, and their own ways of ordering and reordering the universe. Luciano Berio's *Sequenza*s are fourteen exploratory pieces written for solo instruments between 1958 and 2002 – while all that pop and rock fuss was going on in a very different kitchen. Imagine if occasionally they both found themselves in the same kitchen, or even on the same stage.

Think of the *Sequenza*s as a kind of box set, a mysterious, untamed, ancient and modern world to explore in enforced isolation like a great novel or HBO series. My favourite at the moment is *V*, for solo trombone, and, even more madly, for clown, and also for vivacious and a little vicious. It was written in 1966, the same year as Dylan's *Blonde on Blonde*, Cecil Taylor's *Unit Structures* and Coltrane's *Ascension*, and I'm happy to slip this gem into that company – classical history freshly released into the new world refreshes jazz and rock history, and vice versa. These minds were all at play at the same time, thinking the same way from differently stoned points of view.

Students of the innovative, analytical electronic music pioneer, theorist, composer, conductor and teacher Luciano Berio included arch-minimalist Steve Reich, whose phase-shifting tape-editing he influenced, agit-minimalist Louis Andriessen, pop minimalist Ludovico Einaudi and postmodern impressionist composer Max Richter. Berio's own love and endless curiosity about music would take in Italian opera, early twentieth-century modernism, the Beatles, jazz, international folk music and the epic romantic symphonists. His post-serial music would often blur the boundaries between language and sound — text and music being equal in his mind — and his 1958 *Thema (Omaggio a Joyce)* — an electro-acoustic elaboration of Cathy Berberian's recorded voice — is one of the classic early works of electronic music, composed onto tape using prerecorded and manipulated natural and electronic sounds. 'If the experience of electronic music is important,' he wrote in an author's note to accompany the piece, 'and I believe it is, its meaning lies not in the discovery of new sounds but in the possibility it gives the composer of integrating a larger area of sound phenomena into musical thought, thus overcoming a dualistic conception of musical material. Just as language is not words on one side and concepts on the other but is rather a system of arbitrary symbols through which we give a certain form to our way of being in the world, so music is not made of notes and conventional relations among them, but rather identifies with our way of choosing, shaping and structuring certain aspects of the sound continuum.'

4. Shostakovich – Symphony No. 10

I have lately developed a crush on the formidable Dmitri Shostakovich, where once the name alone suggested I would not be at all interested. Such music tends to be presented as though it is too aloof to be of interest, or too static and uninvolving, something talked about as if it is in the world of Mary Berry and Fiona Bruce, not John Berger and Susan Sontag. I first found Shostakovich through his Second String Quartet, because I had fallen deeply for the idea of the string quartet, in the same way as I became addicted to power trios in rock, and quartets and quintets in jazz. After hearing Schoenberg's dramatic Second String Quartet, I decided to hear as many second quartets as I could find. I was devouring every quartet composition I could track down, by all the performing quartets who had their own areas of concern and ways of presenting the music. This would have been impossible to do before the cloud, this relatively inexpensive, fluent way to access such astounding performance and continuity, as if it is a dream you can simply conjure up out of the blue. For £10 a month you can now travel anywhere you want to go – and limiting yourself to pop and rock, which is all over reality TV, compilations and ads anyway, seems a complete waste of this unlikely, unexpected and admittedly ridiculously unrealistic resource.

There are histories within histories inside classical music, unfolding in a variety of directions over complicated, fast-changing centuries, as genres and styles shift in and out of position, as one composer takes over from another, accepting and rejecting what happened previously, looking for new ways to preserve and extend – sometimes by tearing it apart – a certain form, exploring how four instruments can do the same thing so differently, so that Haydn and Mozart leads to Cage and Ligeti, and it is as exciting to see how that happens as it is to note how Elizabeth Cotten became Beyoncé or Thelonious Monk became Autechre. Once I had got to Shostakovich's string quartets, I then moved to his symphonies, and experienced how he developed from his menacing, mischievous and momentous First as a teenager in the mid-1920s, still studying at the Petrograd Conservatory, to his final one, his Fifteenth, before he died in 1975 at sixty-nine, so that a whole life of learning, perception and reaction to his Stalin-soaked time and place is contained within this one collection of works. In his earth-shattering Tenth, from 1953, an 'optimistic tragedy' fully immersed in life and chaos, some see as an intense, defiantly gorgeous expression of the pain and pressure he felt living during the recently ended Stalin years. A subversive blast of liberation, making most of the history of prog rock sound pretty quaint, it sounds like he believes he is immortal. When the music plays, he is.

5. *Webern* – Langsamer Satz

Shostakovich's complete, history-encompassing symphonies alone run for over thirteen hours; call them up on your phone, you have the number. A compilation of Anton Webern's complete works runs for just over six hours, a collection of intense, delirious and spooky short stories with startling endings more than a run of immense, sweeping novels. What took him forty years to complete can now be taken almost as a whole, listened to in one sitting, although the amount of ideas and thinking compressed into this brief musical output are hallucinatory. Experience, delight, fear and apprehension are distilled with dazzling precision and severity into smaller and smaller moments of contemplation, beginning during a time shared by the Debussy of the Cello Sonata, ending in a time shared with Charlie Parker and Edgard Varèse. *Langsamer Satz* (*Slow Movement*), written in 1905 when he was in his early twenties, was an unusual early fragment of an unfinished string quartet, a condensed symphony, reluctant romanticism lusciously blistering into the mind-altering atonality to come, sounds that left sighs in the dust of history, prettiness radiating into something stranger, the sound of a new world opening up, and still, even now, the sound of a new world opening up. He was born the same year as Franz Kafka; one plots an escape from Wagner, the other from Victor Hugo.

6. *Earle Brown* – Times Five

Earle Brown's exploration of form and formlessness, time and timelessness, sound and silence, old and new, works brilliantly in this new world of listening to music as though it is streamed directly from one mind to another with no barriers or mediation in between. You look for it, you find it, you work out its meaning according to your own taste. Part of the so-called New York School with John Cage, Morton Feldman and Christian Wolff, and the famous post-war avant-garde including Boulez and Stockhausen, his fractured, tender *Times Five* from 1963 is wilder than anything that has happened since, conceptually, if not in aggression and volume. For those looking for the missing link between Mozart and Madlib – and aren't we all? – it's abstract (classical) music for an abstract, phantom, post-real Space Age that is yet to happen, but seems scheduled to happen soon, and where most pop and rock will seem very dull and dated, like it came from another century, one from the past. Earle Brown tends to sounds like he comes from another century, one from the future.

7. *Sofia Gubaidulina* – Sonata for Double Bass and Piano

I read a review of the four compositions focusing on the double bass that Sofia Gubaidulina wrote, which noted that the demand for music that was both composed for the double bass and written by the great, uncompromising and deeply spiritual post-Stalin Soviet composer was minimal. The implication was, so few cared for such obscurity that such art and craft, or such cerebral dabbling, was heading for extinction.

There would be no campaigns to save such activity from crashing out of existence.

Then again, there might be some micro-influencers, perhaps in groups of three or four, who do launch a campaign, lamenting how such extreme, fragile exotica is disappearing, as though a rare, delightful creature exists in only a few, very threatened numbers. It is not perhaps important that such music exists, even if some of the campaigners could make a case for the way it celebrates the moral imagination, but it does seem depressing that there is a likelihood that such music melts away, precisely because of how it stands up for the moral imagination. If this sort of thing can disappear as though it never even existed, then not long after, other more popular but equally vital art and entertainment might follow it, leading, more or less, to the collapse of civilisation. These sort of fastidiously organised, almost illusory fragile fibres keep things going much more than seems immediately apparent.

For those out there who do stubbornly crave the combination of Gubaidulina and double bass on four pieces written between 1966 and 2007, including the stately Sonata, the music is important and heavenly, not least because it is such an unusual, occasional thing – low, earthy and exotic notes, set in and around certain highly organised, misty and exquisitely balanced spatial environments, the bass existing inside and outside the piano and a Russian variant of the accordion, and deeply, darkly out on its own, conjuring up a feeling of the sublime and the desolate, the expressive and the secret, lyrical and abrasive, east and west, gutsy and cerebral, the ancient and the contemporary, as though Bach jammed with Webern and Pärt.

If music was given the equivalent of Michelin stars, instead of Amazon marks (no offence), Gubaidulina would have had three stars for years, and be featured in lovingly shot Netflix documentaries that marvel at her commitment to something that sometimes seems to be purely her essential commitment to making such sound. Hear the double bass sonata played by Daniele Roccato, one of those heroes of the oversized, under-used double bass, lugging the instrument around the world and searching out extremely rare, specialised pieces for his instrument among the likes of Berio, Alfred Schnittke and Hans Werner Henze. He strolls, wanders, plunges through these pieces as though he has just discovered a new, unexplored island, eyes and ears wide open, nimbly mapping out new feelings, new territory and unique, hidden coastlines.

Gubaidulina simply adores the mystery found in the sounds and noises the bass can make, and of course the spaces in between, as if without it the universe is incomplete. With her energetic, fundamental understanding of what a powerful soloist is able and wanting to play, giving them freedom to interpret her specific instructions, she gives the instrument the kind of devoted attention bass-mad Roccato naturally relishes – she thinks the instrument has a soul, she locates it, Roccato completely agrees, adds his own sense of devotion, and the sound of this meeting of souls – composer, player, instrument – allows the bass to speak its mind, and once released, once understood, it's got a lot more to say than anyone ever guessed. This going to the limits and beyond of what an instrument can traditionally produce, the combination of structure and accretion, discretion and strength, theatre and contemplation is directly linked to the instrumental *Sequenza*s of Berio, where whole worlds of sound are introduced.

The focused Roccato is sure on his feet, matching the undimmed confidence of the composer, always making sense of the mood shifts and sliding scale, the bracing stillness surging into urgent action, the hints of inexplicable transcendence, the dramatic awareness. Trembling at the edge of (commercial) extinction, confessing fears and pouring out the heart, releasing tension, this fierce, anomalous dedication to confronting the dangerously stultifying status quo, however few notice, is worth championing. You might not be one of those who thought the world lacked studious Daniele Roccato playing philosophical Gubaidulina, but if you are searching for music as an elevating, evocative experience you've never had before, find this remote, isolated island where the last of their kind make their survival some kind of miracle.

8. *John Cage* – Organ^2/ASLSP

With all its stops, pipes, multiple locations and spatial presence, and the way that sound can emerge from a variety of discrete locations, the church organ, the ancient king of instruments, is the ultimate prepared instrument, as well an acoustic representation of an electronic synthesiser. Sounds can be manipulated, you can look through them, not at them, silence is just another sound, echoed and layered, duration and tempo constantly adjusted, and acoustic space itself can be controlled. It sounds an ideal instrument for John Cage – the High

Lama of the prepared piano, always pursuing pure sound, conceptual flexibility, disordering exercises, unrelated juxtapositions, magical transformation and ambient suggestions rather than musical specifics – but he produced little music for the organ. Perhaps, though, enough to comprehensively demonstrate his own interest in the instrument's possibilities, his fascination with its architecture, without having to live there for too long.

He visited the organ, or found it lying somewhere near where he was passing, and used it sparingly to exploit his own interests in the noise of sound and the sound of noise and a general sense of purposeful purposelessness or purposeless play. Cage dedicated himself to locating and enhancing mystery and spiritual freedom through music as a succession of sounds that was perhaps in some far opposite direction to the weighed-down, ritualistic atmosphere of worship that the organ represents; both approaches, though, linger patiently and with elusive purpose in separate, purified spaces far removed from the idea of music as mere harmony-addicted entertainment and basic consumer product.

In 1985 Cage wrote a piano piece, *ASLSP* – as slow (or softly) as possible – referring both to the first exclamation in the final paragraph of James Joyce's *Finnegan's Wake* – 'soft morning city! Lsp!' – and also to the suggested tempo for the piece, as slow as possible, which, naturally, had no set duration. Performances subsequently ranged from twenty minutes to seventy, with one or two more literal or light-headed explorers heading off towards the all-day.

It was commissioned by a music competition where listeners and a jury were more used to hearing the familiar pianistic likes of Beethoven and Chopin, and the original brief was for a piece between five and ten minutes long. Cage wrote something in eight sections where he suggested that any one of these could be omitted, and any one of them repeated – and if each section happened to be a minute long in how it was played, the piece would last eight minutes. On the other hand...

The compositional strategy of *ASLSP* led to Cage's final organ work, *Organ²/ASLSP*, in 1987, where it was better suited, because a pipe organ can theoretically hold a tone for ever, and as a piece for organ it became one of Cage's most famous pieces. It reflects that side of contemporary Caginess that hovers in the spirit of comedy and the divine, between the gimmicky and the defiantly profound, the religious and the rebellious, between the sentimental and the conceptual, sound art and tourist attraction, the absurd and the sublime, the cosmic and clownish, conman and philanthropist, whimsy and eternity, nothing and its echo.

The vague, and yet entirely precise, Cageian instruction, or advice, of 'as slow as possible' led, among those with plenty of thinking time on their hands, to consider exactly how slow that could be. Various musicians, scientists and philosophers attending a 1999 symposium on organs in Trossingen, Germany, excited by passing through Cage into the mechanics of musical time, and time itself, concluded that the only way to answer the question was actually to answer the question and not just talk about it at conferences, and really play it as slow as possible, even if that took centuries rather than minutes or hours.

The piece is currently being played, permanently, in a manner of speaking, in a former Cistercian convent — and at various stages barn, distillery, pigsty and hovel — in the small town of Halberstadt, Germany, home of the world's first great organ with a modern keyboard arrangement, finished in 1361, 639 years before the project began. Because of this achievement, and the original organ's design, the convent also sometimes used as a stable could be said to be the birth of modern music.

The ultimate performance, a second coming, began on 5 September 2001, Cage's eighty-ninth birthday, nine years after his death. Foolishly, or fantastically, following the instruction 'as slow as possible' to the limit, it will take 639 years to complete, in 2640, so that a piece of organ music could end up lasting as long as a constantly maintained organ itself sometimes does.

It has been described as the planting of a 'musical apple tree'. The first year and a half passed by in total silence; so Cage's greatest hit, one of the twentieth century's greatest works of art, the endlessly entertaining $4'33''$ of silence — the epitome of his chaos embracing theatrical presence as part showman, part Zen master, part dice-throwing shaman and part Dada barracuda — was remixed to last seventeen months. In its own way, $4'33''$ is also passing through time continuously, always there to listen to as long as you decide to pay attention to it, even if only for a moment. Whenever there is silence, relatively complete, or filled with the random noises of the day or night, you can consider that you are listening to $4'33''$.

For Cage, silence had become the equal of sound in music, and if music was made of blocks of time, these blocks could contain either silence or sound. The silence that entered his music in the late 1940s was a response to the incessant noise of mid-century American culture, a commitment to the beauty that came out of quietness, and therefore stillness. Depending on your definition of what music is and what it is for, the same musical effect could be achieved by silence, or the silence that music can reflect, parody, imagine and continually feature as part of its structure and energy.

Cage was aware, before it became so obvious, how loud the planet is – the noise that spills out from the constant grip technology has on the planet, from mobile phones, TV and radio stations, power lines, electrical fences, wind and lightning, the oceans, GPS satellites, planes, trains, cars and wi-fi. To escape the non-stop noise of the earth you have to get to the far side of the moon. You have to find some sort of otherworldly void, or perhaps a dream. Cage's framing of silence was his attempt to produce this void, a dream abyss, among all the noise; in the middle of the noise of time, which music illuminates, decorates and connects with, a lack of sound, even if that still makes a sound, contains it and prepares for it. His 'silence' was in effect a dreamlike version of music. Without silence, there was no music.

The first movement of the organ *ASLSP* is scheduled to last for seventy-one years. There was a dramatic note change in 2013, the first for seven years, made on Cage's birthday, as all changes will be, greeted with a celebration by an audience not entirely made up of theologists, musicologists, philosophers and Cage obsessives. The word was spreading.

Individual chords will last months or years, and weights will be used on pedals and keys to maintain the sound. Moments of change become the object of pilgrimages, to hear the poignant moment when something happens, and a new note, a new chord, appears and everything changes, for now. At other times, visitors can drift in and out, staying for as long as they want, noting the nothing that is happening, and returning if and when they want to renew acquaintance. If you want to contribute to the funding – because it cannot simply run of its own accord – you can choose a year to sponsor between now and the proposed end of the piece.

It is both a sign of friendly madness, and of hope, that there will be a future around for interested parties and possible audiences to inherit and complete, and even understand, the task, which over time will seem quaint, heroic, barmy, annoying, mesmerising, or yet another confirmation that Cage, by then a kind of Christ, was the twentieth century's greatest artistic prophet. The response to it as a conceptual endeavour and spiritual experiment includes numerous other projects and works, including films, sculptures, installations, compositions and writing, keeping the work company, feeding it some nourishment, leading it forward.

If it all works out and it remains tended and attended, it could be the one piece of music from the last few hundred years that will still be around in a few hundred years, possibly because it cannot be Spotified, and surrounding its slow, considered presence will perhaps emerge, slowly, an entire new civilisation based on a new religion with a first commandment of: You shall not rush. (Impatience was the sin that drove us out of paradise. Patience is our route back.) The fifth commandment: Begin anywhere.

The tenth commandment: Listen to *ASLSP* as though it is the last piece of music you will ever hear. Take that, Time.

4. FOLLOW-UP TO THE ABOVE: TWO PLAYLISTS WITH NOTES AND RECOMMENDATIONS, CONSIDERING THE TIME RAVEL AND DEBUSSY SPENT COMPOSING MORE OR LESS AT THE SAME TIME

A Maurice Ravel (born 7 March 1875) playlist

...that does not include what tends to be called his greatest hit, *Boléro* (1928), which threatened to relegate his music to the status of kitsch; Ravel was originally certain that no orchestra would want to play it, this guarded exercise or experiment in creating a masterpiece, or at least a complete, engaging composition, using the least possible material... although a *Boléro* playlist could include:

1. Orchestral versions moving it away from camp, cut-down Torvill and Dean/*Dancing on Ice* and campier Dudley Moore/Bo Derek in Blake Edward's romp-com *10* towards the mystical, the compelling scrutiny of a detail given devastating, possibly neurotic grandeur, one long very gradual crescendo, until nobody can breathe any more, with underlying tragic intensity, best when conducted by Boulez, Rattle or Marriner.

2. A 1970s Tomita synthesiser rendition paying tribute to it as fancy novelty piece on the edge between tasteful and tasteless, and explicitly honouring Ravel's fascination with automation. (Stravinsky famously labelled him a 'Swiss clockmaker').

3. A Django Reinhardt translation, *Troublant Boléro*, which giddily illuminates the romanticised, artificially created Latin rhythms.

4. Echoes of it coursing through numerous volatile prog-ish pieces, including King Crimson, Genesis and Jeff Beck ('Beck's Bolero', from a 1966 session containing an early sketch of Led Zeppelin with Keith Moon on drums, John Paul Jones on bass and Jimmy Page on guitar, failing to recruit the Small Faces white soul terrier Steve Marriott as singer for this prototype supergroup).

5. The themes and scores of a number of Akiro Kurosawa films, including the innovative and influential psychological thriller *Rashōmon*, a notorious distraction for non-Japanese watchers, because the director instructed his composer Fumio Hayasaka to 'write something like Ravel's *Boléro*,' one of his favourite pieces – possibly because it is, to some minds, completely, enthrallingly nerve-racking, and it dwells on something for longer than seems normal, the act of someone who goes on looking even when he has found what he wants – and never as clichéd and kitschy in Japan as in the West.

6. A jaunty Benny Goodman treatment of it as a wonky theatrical confection that jams it all in under less than three minutes and which would gladden any lonely-feeling clarinettist's heart.

7. A nice, frilly Larry Coryell early 1980s improvisation with unashamed jazz-funk wings based on the piece that needs plenty of sunshine and possibly a drug of choice to hear sympathetically.

8. Large traces of the rhythm marching through 'Running Scared' by Roy Orbison, and

9. 'Kicking Horse on Brokenhill' by Godspeed You! Black Emperor, and

10. They might be stoned, but there are those who claim to hear a blast of its rhythm lurking inside Lynyrd Skynyrd's 'Freebird'.

There was another Ravel 'hit' – this one more ghostwritten – with his particularly personal, lush orchestral arrangement of Modest Mussorgsky's piano suite *Pictures at an Exhibition* produced in 1922 and becoming the most performed and recorded version, and its radiant intensity and elegance an influence on all subsequent orchestrations. Orchestration for Ravel was something other than composition, and few can rival him when it comes to orchestral colour. Debussy said that Ravel possessed the finest ear in the history of music. He was squeezed out as a major figure between Debussy and Stravinsky by that damned *Boléro*, and being French didn't help in terms of reputation, nor did the ratings that put the Germanic at the top, as if it was somehow universal, above and beyond, and everything else was provincially nationalistic.

For a less idealised – or perhaps more idealised – version of a Spain he was born near but hadn't yet visited (he didn't until 1924), with the sultry rhythms and intensity of his Basque mother's country impressed indirectly into his memory, there's the forceful, supple *Rapsodie espagnole* (1907–8), based on pieces for two pianos, and his first published piece written for orchestra. There are luxury versions from orchestras led by Claudio Abbado, Bernard Haitink and Leonard Bernstein, but to really feel the imagined Spain, go for Fritz Reiner and the Chicago Symphony Orchestra. Arranged for two pianos, try Vladimir and Vovka Ashkenazy.

In a more sensible world – or perhaps a less sensible world – the Ravel hit would be the verdant and demented fantasy *Daphnis et Chloé*, written as a ballet, but symphony-like and, as with *Boléro*, not based on an original piano composition. At fifty to fifty-five minutes it's his longest work, made up of multiple pieces, using his largest orchestra. Most of his work was less than half an hour, for theoretical, aesthetic reasons, and also because this was about the amount of music he could hold in his head when mentally developing a composition. Half-crazed, inspired like much of his work by sorcery, pumped up with passion, blazing somewhere deliciously odd between sexy and chaste, swooning and cerebral, definitely the work of a dandy who championed beauty above all else, opening the lush red-velvet curtains on what would become the picturesque Technicolor sound of a classic 'golden age of Hollywood' score, it was overshadowed by Stravinsky's *Rite of Spring* the following year, also commissioned by Sergei Diaghilev of the newly formed Ballets Russes, based in Paris. The battle for best version of *Daphnis* is traditionally between the Boston Symphony under Charles Munch versus the London Symphony Orchestra in the early 1960s under Pierre Monteux – who conducted the original performance about fifty years earlier in 1912, and also the world premiere of *Rite of Spring* – but I swing for the hardcore Berlin Philharmonic conducted by Pierre Boulez, matching his aloof intellectual rigour to Ravel's flaming metaphysical rigour. The knowable embraces the unknowable. It obliterates all possibility of Hollywood glitter and seriously confirms Ravel was as much magician as musician and craftsman. *Boléro* was a fantastic, spellbinding trick; *Daphnis et Chloé* really does make the world disappear and reappear somewhere entirely different. Elsewhere, there was more magic, and less conjuring, and constant examples of his single-minded dedication to artistic perfection, to a musical innovation that was more poetic than technical.

Ravel-gazing: the playlist without Boléro

i. Piano Concerto in G major (1929–31)
Berlin Philharmonic conducted by Claudio Abbado, featuring soloist Martha Argerich, and/or Royal Concertgebouw Orchestra conducted by Eduard van Beinum, featuring soloist Cor de Groot, and/or New York Philharmonic Orchestra directed from the piano by Leonard Bernstein.

Ravel liked to travel, not least in his music. In this concerto he's putting together inspiration he received from Mozart and his Clarinet Quintet with a love for American jazz he had encountered on a trip to New York in 1928, where he heard George Gershwin's 1924 *Rhapsody in Blue* for jazz piano and orchestra. Beginning with one of music's most famous glissandos, it's clear that Gershwin had been paying attention to Ravel and Debussy. (Gershwin was also taken with Lizst, Tchaikovsky, Chopin and Gilbert and Sullivan of the nineteenth century, intrigued by Berg and Stravinsky of the early twentieth, and he played tennis with Schoenberg, who he asked for lessons.) Gershwin took Ravel to the jazz clubs of Harlem, where he embraced a whole new array of marvels that seemed to share a Parisian edge.

The concerto's trombones alone give away how much Ravel was attracted to the power of jazz, albeit filtered through an intellectual fascination with the baroque, and his intention is to match the virtuosity of jazz improvisation with the virtuosity of a concerto and combine sounds he could hear in both the blues and early twentieth-century modernists.

It's a short jump from the Bernstein version to Herbie Hancock's jazz-hands version of the eloquently serene second movement of

Ravel's concerto, which he placed on his great Gershwin tribute album *Gershwin's World*, suggesting that Ravel's influence on jazz came about because of the jazz influence on him.

You hear Ravel – a certain propulsive swing caught up in the spirit of Mozart, Satie, Stravinsky, Prokofiev and Saint-Saëns – in Art Tatum, Bud Powell, George Gershwin, Duke Ellington, Billy Strayhorn, Gil Evans, and, following how the swing of jazz leaked into musicals alongside the opera and pop, all the way to the opposite extremes of Sondheim and Lloyd Webber.

Ravel's astonishingly prescient atmospheric experimental masterpiece 'Le Gibet', the proto-minimalist/ambient middle piece of the piano triptych *Gaspard de la nuit* from 1909, which distils in one glacial place the piano writing of Mozart, Liszt and Satie, seems to suggest many of those jazz-musical ideas were simmering long before he actually experienced American jazz. In fact, he seems to be hearing ahead to Ahmad Jamal, Bill Evans, Keith Jarrett, Chick Corea, Paul Bley and Jason Moran – he infuses the strictness of a Bach fugue with the sense of the music sounding improvised. Try it by Jean-Yves Thibaudet and/ or, as dark as dark gets, as melting as melting gets, as slow as slower gets, Sviatoslav Richter, and the rarely played but glorious orchestral version, by the Philharmonia Orchestra conducted by Geoffrey Simon. You can hear the formation of Ravel's relish for obsessively repeated notes, reflecting a fascination with machines and mechanisms inspired by his civil-engineer father, and the materialisation of a pre-jazz swing space and time in 1898's *Sites auriculaires* – 'place which can be sensed by the ear' – for two pianos, the first piece, *Habañera* (which was orchestrated to become part of *Rapsodie espagnole*), sounding like something from a twenty-first-century Vijay Iyer or Jason Moran solo piano album, and the second piece, *Entre cloches*, preshadowing the inspired dissonance of Thelonious Monk.

ii. *Tzigane*, **Rhapsody for Violin and Piano (1924)**
Fanaticism in motion, with soloist Anne-Sophie Mutter, from the *Back to the Future* album, in a programme alongside Bartók, Lutosławski and Wolfgang Rihm, and/or Arthur Grumiaux, alongside Paganini and Mendelssohn, making you wish Hendrix had attacked this mesmerising celebration of show.

iii. Violin Sonata No. 2 (1923–7)

Ravel once said that *Boléro* might be his masterpiece, but it unfortunately contained no music. In a way, by then his music was all behind him, leaving only the sheer structural ingenuity, the meticulous thoroughness, the disciplined bravado to wash up into *Boléro*, as though the piece was a stripped-down, motorised version of his entire musical imagination, a highly logical representation of the fantastical, the ultimate celebration of his idea that music was a kind of gala separate from reality, a delightful game. A fine Philips record introduces the playful, brainy, emotional, intensely curious, restrained, eccentric, entertaining and innovative non-*Boléro* musical Ravel, with solo violinist Arthur Grumiaux's Sonata sandwiched between Ravel's single string quartet masterpiece in F major (1903) played as a cosmically sure thing by, among many others, Quartetto Italiano – usually predictably combined on albums with Debussy's equally ravishing single quartet, which Ravel's echoes and enhances, the two continually influencing each other, driven by the same passions, Ravel chasing the elder, sometimes stepping ahead, both championing the underestimated power of reticence, recharging the mystery of and in music – and Ravel's sensual psychedelic chamber masterpiece, perhaps his masterpiece among masterpieces, Trio in A minor (1914), smartly played by the Beaux Arts Trio.

The second movement of the Violin Sonata, entitled 'Blues' – Ravel deliriously exploring the structural innards of the recently cooked-up American blues – supports Bob Dylan's outlandish but entirely reasonable theory that the blues started in the feverish late eighteenth-century dreams of Africans stolen to become slaves as they heard exotic-sounding, yearning, pretty spooky classical instrumental music wafting out of venues in European ports while they were waiting to be shipped into a horrible future. Their attempts using voice and cheap, broken instruments to recall the barely remembered, barely believable melancholy sounds, mixed with their own imperishable musical instincts, stoical toughness, ancestral subconscious, heartbeat rhthyms and nightmarish experiences, became the blues.

iv. La valse, a Choreographic Poem for Orchestra (1920)

Another study in crescendo. Hear it by the London Symphony Orchestra conducted by Claudio Abbado, capturing how intoxicated magic can turn to anguish, and of course there's the inevitable, edgily romantic wide-screen drama Leonard Bernstein brings to Ravel's fascination with the scary, over-the-top drama of the waltz and its mournful post-First World War acceptance of the end of the old world, 'dearly held ideas crashing to earth in chaos'. There was definitely a place for this understanding and scrutiny of unimaginable changes in circumstances exactly one hundred years later.

v. **Folk songs, sad songs, beyond songs, sensual allure, the risk-taking of emotional exposure, and a taste for the marvellous**
Deux mélodies hébraïques (1914), *Tripatos* (1909) and *Chants populaires* (1910) sung by Cecilia Bartoli, *Trois poèmes de Stéphane Mallarmé* (1913) sung by Suzanne Danco, *Sainte* (1896) — one of his first published compositions — 'L'indifférent' (1903) sung by Jessye Norman or Janet Baker, and 'Sur l'herbe' (1907) sung by Gérard Souzay.

vi. **Introduction and Allegro for Harp, Flute, Clarinet and String Quartet (1905)**
Two rival harp companies commissioned Debussy and Ravel to write pieces for their hi-tech new harps – Debussy delivers *Danse sacrée et danse profane* to Pleyel and Ravel delivers – in a rush, to counter Debussy's efforts – *Introduction and Allegro*, a miniature concerto, to Erard, principal makers of the conventional pedal harp. Hear it, if you aren't disturbed by spectacular, rushing lashings of highly strung harp, by the Nash Ensemble and/or as if played in a feverish dream by the Chamber Music Society of Amsterdam. It's also one of the few pieces of his own music that Ravel himself recorded, or at least supervised, and hearing him 'play' one of his own pieces on the piano as if he is doing it right now, say, *Pavane pour une infante défunte (1899)*, seventeenth-century dance music directed towards the jazz age, the work of someone with a pleasure loving ear, or the audaciously modern 'Le Gibet', sounding like he had somehow heard Cage's piano music, Harold Budd and Morton Feldman, treating musical moments as objects to move around and place in space, is to appreciate how he used music to understand memory, the perception of change and the sensation of time collapsing in on itself.

Joe Walsh, once of the James Gang and the Eagles, who had a very different sense of unfastening from time, uses primitive synthesisers to briefly interpret *Pavane* on his 1974 solo album *So What* – his daughter was killed in a road accident that year – and a song 'The Lamp is Low' based on the Ravel piece was recorded by the Harry James Orchestra in 1939 featuring a young, not-quite-yet-himself Frank Sinatra.

vii. 'Oiseaux tristes' (1905)

I love hearing Pierre-Laurent Aimard play 'Oiseaux tristes', the tender then raucous then solemn second piano movement of Ravel's five-part piano suite *Miroirs* (1905), each movement dedicated to a member of the diverse, all-male French avant-garde artists' collective les Apaches, named after a vicious, stylish Parisian street gang in turn named after the Native American tribe, and Ravel's reflections of what each member was thinking when they looked in a mirror. Ravel helped found the ever-evolving collective; Debussy was never a member, more a spiritual influence, and the group acted in some ways like a devoted Debussy fan club. Ravel wrote the suite responding to something Debussy had said about wanting to compose music that sounded so free it seemed improvised, and the weird thing is hearing someone as fastidious as Ravel write something so spontaneous-sounding. He doesn't want to leave anything to chance, but he's not afraid of improvisation. Stranger, though, is hearing Ravel play it himself in 1922, or he was in the room as it is prepared, through a piano-roll recording. It still sounds like he is making it up as he goes along, but according to a long-term plan, and doesn't sound quaintly, distantly '1922' but closer to now, because the space, movement and feeling in it are timeless.

For further strangeness, hear *Boléro* with Ravel in charge, long before it had become tamed by overexposure, giving it a languid bohemian edge, treating dance as a kind of stagnation, and a sense that he was using music to describe a sturdy but boneless sea creature going around in circles, possibly until the end of time, or in this case until the spell is broken or the mechanism snaps. The early recording era is having an impact on his music, and *Boléro*, as much as anything, is like a national anthem for this new nation of technology, ideally to be played every time you open Spotify, and Ravel self-consciously builds it as a container for music that is itself made up of music and which can now be stored for all time, give or take the breakdown of civilisation. Ravel, as he often did to his piano pieces, gracefully orchestrated two of the *Miroirs* movements, 'Une barque sur l'océan' and 'Alborada del gracioso'.

viii. Schéhérazade, ouverture de féerie (1899)

It says a lot about Ravel's predilection for the exotic and for idealising faraway lands and the fabled East, assumed utopian land of sexual liberation, that he became so infatuated with *One Thousand and One Nights* (*The Arabian Nights*) he attempted an opera on the subject.[1]

Later, he wrote a song cycle with the same name based on poetry written by fellow Apache Léon Leclère, writing as Tristan Klingsor, paying homage to Rimsky-Korsakov's symphonic suite also called *Scheherazade*. Both Ravel *Schéhérazades* are classic, geographically vague, turn-of-the-century Western fantasies of pseudo-oriental-sounding music and occult urges — as if the mysterious distant horizon of the Far East is just over the coast from the south of France, easily reached on a musical magic carpet.

You're not hearing authentic otherness, but thoughts about otherness — this is Ravel the well-turned-out illusionist preoccupied with the suspicious, irresistible power of music to move us, the ironic cartoonist skilfully representing fantasy Arab air, further refining his understanding of how to use orchestral colour to articulate transcendence. It's the mobile work of an intelligence capable of assuming different roles and entering new characters to experience the adventures of others, of adopting new disguises and seeing beautiful scenes in his mind.

It can sound a bit Disney, after decades of Hollywood soaking up this kind of melodious fairy-tale resonance, but he is really analysing how music works and therefore how the mind works. He moves as a tourist through this caricature of Eastern otherness, rooted, however tenuously, in a real place, in order to reach his own true sense of otherness, and a replacement of even a remote sense of reality with something else altogether. The Stuttgart Radio Orchestra under Stéphane Denève takes it very seriously indeed as an abstract analysis of using musical colour as a way of rearranging reality, as a way of pretending to pretend, and this solemnity actually suits the glowing, shifting hyper-drama.

ix. **Sonatine pour piano (1903–5)**
This is Ravel the historian advancing backwards into luxurious eighteenth-century musical elegance without completely retreating from less traditional, perversely ghostlier, turn-of-the-twentieth-century

---

[1]The first European version of the twelve volumes, a composite work derived from the oral traditions of India, Persia, Iraq and Egypt, had been translated into French in the early eighteenth century, drifting into the vagabond exoticism of Baudelaire, Valéry and Mallarmé.

techniques – as if with very early postmodern instincts he is discreetly decorating a neat and tidy classical building with some abstract, austere modern shapes. Neoclassical Lisztian precision is bruised by some of those radical textural elements and unprecedented compositional techniques that Ravel was freshly utilising, which became known first of all abusively and eventually generally as 'impressionist', where Liszt's formality and tonal boundaries dissolve into liquid without sacrificing the sparkling virtuosity.

It's a soft distortion of classical order, unlike the firmer modifications of Stravinsky and Schoenberg happening elsewhere. Ravel had recently beautifully expressed this 'impressionism', a misty lack of definite lines, in *Jeux d'eau* (1903) (hear it by An-Ting Chang or Martha Argerich in 1960). Being inspired by the sound of water and the amorphous musical sounds of fountains, streams and waterfalls liberated Ravel from following a classic key scheme. The colour and manipulation of sound was subverting previously unchallenged systems of form, structure and tonality. A new music was emerging to represent new, disorientating, blurred, fragmented feelings now that the speed of the twentieth century was quickly picking up. There's no immediate breakdown of order, but there are a lot of new forms of stress. It's not far from here to the sublimely organised nervous tension of 'Le Gibet'.

x. **Menuet antique (1895)**

His first published work (hear it by Monique Haas), after a couple of years composing, was relatively conventional, but there are already signs of everything he would become as a composer and thinker over the next thirty-five years: appreciating the power of the piano, its use as a technologically detailed sketchpad for orchestra – hear it orchestrated in full Ravel regalia by the Academy of St Martin-in-the-Fields – but also the eloquence of reticence; exaggerated, and refined; impassive and sonorous; rhapsodic and ultra-modern; cheerful and serene; whimsical and suggestive; humorous and melancholy; strategic and impulsive; in almost shy hiding, but self-confidently in full sight, exhibiting magnificent technique and ambition; the stationary agitation; the repressed ardour; the French extremism; the puzzle maker with the magic hands; the looking at something new in the style of another era, so aware of the past and so full of the future; ultimately a nostalgia for the unreal that sends us somewhere between being simply charmed and the edge of the divine. A century or so later, it still seems to be music growing into the moment.

5. CLAUDE AND MAURICE: TOGETHER, FOR EVER AND NEVER

The fastidious, self-conscious Ravel and the dishevelled, bohemian Debussy, thirteen years older, are very different as personalities, but in the imagination always placed side by side, wrapped around each other, and in their own worlds at the same time, when France, and Paris, was at the centre of the art universe, where it existed between the middle of the nineteenth century and the end of First World War. Somewhere near, and somewhere far away, completing a supreme, sublime piano trio, there was the immensely sentient prototype conceptualist Satie, scanning ahead to the silence of Cage and the minimalism of Glass (especially on *Embryons desséchés* from 1913), but the double act was really Debussy and Ravel, building their works up from the piano, where they began their thinking, and creating their landscapes that face each other across a border, and yet exist on other sides of the universe. They were in tune with the work being done in painting, poetry and drama – with, as ethereal influence, the flickering ghost of Edgar Allan Poe never completely extinguished – and couldn't help but be aware of the new thinking, their antennae constantly picking up movement in all of the arts that in turn motivated them to be constantly sending out their own signals, unnamed feelings and impressions.

They respected and admired each other, finding themselves working at the same time and place, both highly sensitive to music, although Ravel was known to criticise some of Debussy's orchestrations – 'If I had the time, I would re-orchestrate *La Mer*.' There were constant debates among their peers about who influenced who, but what upset the pair the most was any claim that their music sounded similar, harnessed together under the label 'impressionism'.

The similarities were that they both only wrote a single string quartet, almost mirrored each other's moves in terms of subject matter and the creation of piano suites, and were both committed to escaping the force field of Wagner using weapons of delicacy and discretion. They both responded to 'ragging', the playing of piano from listening to ragtime at the turn of the twentieth century, adding enough of this tangy clarity to their more formal classical playing that they would then feed back into the jazz bloodstream.

As total believers in essential beauty, they were both also committed to the idea of 'charming' music, to being charming in and with their music, so that their radicalism, their transformation of musical language, never became as ascetic, as unforgiving, as Schoenberg. They both, in different ways, possessed a female energy that flowed into their music, which in a man's world, one continually made and remade into a man's world, broke up some of those solid classical dogmas and orthodoxies and introduced a new kind of sensitivity into music – it wasn't about their gentleness or sensitivity but about other powerful, tenacious ways of perceiving and capturing the complexities, emotions and rhythms of the world. Women were locked out of the main classical stream, but Debussy and Ravel, in some form, had the key, at least to redirect musical texture and atmosphere, if not actually to free female composers.

They found their own ways of breaking through, which shared sentiments because of time and place, and the influence of other arts, and a sense of wonderment from the arts bustling and battling around them, but there were few actual musical similarities. Later they could be linked because of their harmonic impact as pianists and orchestrators on post-bebop jazz. And here I am placing them together as though that's how it always should be, but that is more because of how, with different skills and temperaments, if shared artistic energies, they both set up the twentieth century.

Whoever influenced whom – and perhaps mentor Debussy, the first to plot a route away from Wagner, later became mentee, perhaps not – you get the feeling that even if the other had never existed, at least so nearby, with a shared set of colleagues and friends, they would still have created the same music. They were in the mood and didn't need the other to induce that mood. But it makes a great story that they were around at the same time, and although no legitimate double act, they cannot be separated in the imagination because of how their distinctive representations of the tempo and stresses of the time do, in the end, interlock.

Their friendship petered out in the early years of the twentieth century, and Debussy was annoyed when Ravel ignored his plea to make absolutely no changes to his string quartet – 'In the name of the gods of music, do not touch a single note' – instead incorporating suggestions offered by his music teacher Gabriel Fauré. They were not as close as is assumed, but when Debussy died in 1918 Ravel was one of the few lingering friends who turned up at his forlorn, under-attended funeral, even as the Germans were bombarding the city in a last-ditch attack on Paris.

They were the first classical composers I really got to know after the early rocky relationship with *The Planets* and even after I experienced many more composers, those that came before and after, including others of this alleged 'impressionist' period such as Delius, Bax, Respighi, Martinů and, at the English end, Vaughan Williams, they remain two of my favourites. No new knowledge could sink them. Of the two, when I listen to Ravel, except perhaps *Boléro*, he is my favourite, and when I listen to Debussy, he is my favourite. It's not a competition, except when it is, except when you are thinking of a piece of music you want to hear next, or even a piece of music you wanted to play because something important has happened in your life or is about to happen, something that will change everything. Their music is perfect to listen to when everything is changing and you need emotional assistance, even ultimate protection from disaster.

6. A DEBUSSY DOZEN WITH EXTRAS; BECAUSE THE IDEAL FRENCH MUSIC 'GENERATED EMOTION WITHOUT EPILEPSY'

'Art is the most beautiful deception of all. And although people try to incorporate the everyday events of life into it, we must hope that it will remain a deception lest it become a utilitarian thing, sad as a factory.' Claude Debussy (August 1862–March 1918)

'Debussy said quite some time ago, "Any sounds in any combination and in any succession are henceforth free to be used in a musical continuity." ' – John Cage (September 1912–August 1992), who goes where Debussy might have gone if he had been born decades later or lived decades longer *i. Piano Trio in G major, II. Moderato con allegro (1880), performed by the Arensky Trio/ Fantaisie for Piano and Orchestra; I, Andante ma non troppo (1889–90), performed by the Sofia Symphony Orchestra*

Play the Piano Trio in G major to hear where Debussy comes from. An early supporter of Debussy, the wealthy benefactor Nadezhda von Meck, who had hired him as a piano teacher, proudly sent a Debussy piano piece written when he was in his late teens to her friend, the Russian romantic composer Pyotr Tchaikovsky, whom she would also sponsor. He judged the piece to be nice, but too short. Anticipating much of the criticism that would stick to Debussy as he matured, Tchaikovsky complained that its vagueness means it 'never gets anywhere'. He described it as terribly shrivelled.

In his late teens, still a student, never remotely showing infant signs of musical genius, still awaiting his first formal instruction, Debussy formed a piano trio under the guidance of Madame von Meck that would regularly play the works of Beethoven and Schubert. He wrote an undeniably attractive piece for piano trio that made clear that his response to what he saw as the heaviness and opaqueness of German music was to compose with an almost hesitant, free-flowing lightness and clarity. It was written with confidence, but at this early stage containing an insecurity and erraticism that would eventually become a strength. This probing delicacy and an apparent persistent lack of orthodox completion – the music never finished, it simply reached an end – were early, playful, if inexperienced signs of a new style, where he would become obsessed with the sound of sound, often allowing his love of the wonders of its purity to be more important than following the musical rules. It is his love of sound itself that makes him so modern, anticipating the recording era, which, as exploited by pop and rock, was as much about how sounds, textures, pulses, effects were compiled in one place as about the basic musical structure.

As a lost composition possibly destroyed by Debussy and discovered a century after its composition, it needed considerable reconstruction, and it becomes an early sign of a believer in music as a kind of enchantment.

Debussy was always extremely self-critical, relentlessly pursuing throughout the 1880s the establishment of a sound style that was his alone. The *Fantaisie* for Piano and Orchestra was another work that he disowned, feeling that his breakthrough into large-scale orchestral music still showed too many signs of unprocessed influences, and a Germanic structural firmness he was determined to transcend. He remained frustrated that he was still hemmed inside bars – needing to find a way of unlocking rhythms so that they didn't sit inside the bars but flowed through them. 'It is necessary to abandon yourself completely and let the music do as it will with you – to be a vessel through which it passes.' But how practically to achieve this?

The later, voluptuous weightlessness, the coming gorgeous otherness was still forming. A still-young composer who became famous for his works for piano, the *Fantaisie* was the closest he came to a piano concerto, writing the piece during 1889 and 1890 but withdrawing it as soon as the score was completed. It wasn't performed until after his death in 1918, after regular attempts to adapt the work to keep up with his developments elsewhere as a composer and thinker, always understanding more about how to combine piano and orchestra in a new way. Like Schubert, Debussy never wrote a conventional piano concerto; he did not possess, or want, the kind of show-off, extrovert character best suited to writing concertos and was worried about displaying a 'slightly ridiculous contest between two characters' – another reason for his reluctance to engage with the concerto form. His temperamental unflashiness, a depressed ego, an edge of wonder, a sense of irony, even sarcasm was what made his music move into a future where the invention and manipulation of sound would become more important than the obedient following of rules and musical conventions.

ii. *Rêverie (1890)*

Original version for solo piano performed by Noriko Ogawa; arranged for string quartet by the Brodsky Quartet; song 'My Reverie' (1938) with lyrics by Larry Clinton, sung by Sarah Vaughan, reimagined for cello by Julian Lloyd Webber, and also used as a recurring theme in the first *Westworld* series, among much inevitable Radiohead, to suggest at the very least that all was not what it seemed and never could be and that the whole dreamworld of the TV *Westworld* and its dreamy fictional creator Dr Robert Ford was constructed around the enigmatic musical contemplations of Debussy.

The title alone of this brief solo piano piece, referring to a state of being pleasantly lost in one's thoughts, wandering through whatever came to mind, suggests the twenty-eight-year-old Debussy is finally fully finding himself, by finding his music, which belongs only to him, and which, for some, fails to resolve, to become something – even though it is itself completely something, somewhere between a dream within a dream and a thought about a thought. He is beginning to achieve the natural flow he was striving for, the resistance of the mechanical-sounding, of the predictably ingenious.

Rêverie's lack of fireworks becomes the fireworks, and over time it has been turned into other works, and also in 1938 a song, which led to some seeing the piece as muzak, as Debussy's techniques enter the mainstream and become more familiar. When imaginatively transformed into a string quartet by the Brodsky Quartet, it becomes a plausibly intoxicating partner to an acknowledged masterpiece, Debussy's one authentic string quartet. Debussy himself was still not entirely convinced by what quickly became one of his hits, and was appalled and embarrassed when his publisher later cashed in on his fame and issued the piece from a manuscript he found lying around, without Debussy's knowledge. 'It is a work of no significance and, frankly, I consider it absolutely no good.'

He thought it far too commercial, a mere exercise when he was needing to attract attention and land paid commissions, and a betrayal of his uncompromising quest for uncorrupted musical magic. Perhaps listeners could see/hear that what he was creating was an illusion, or combining various tricks he had learned or discovered for himself – the real magic was yet to come, magic colliding with space, where the unknown is made to materialise out of nowhere, all his influences, the more Germanic intellectual ideals and aesthetics of his teachers shaken off, or masterfully veiled, and replaced with only his intentions, where the desert is turned into a beautiful sea, the sky is alive with motion, and music should, above all, exist to give pleasure. When he was young, Debussy adored Wagner, but once a real sense of musical mission started to shape his thinking he turned against his one-time idol, and he would write appalled but lyrical anti-Wagner diatribes.

Before Debussy, among the French, only Hector Berlioz rivalled the achievements of the German and Austrian music primarily represented by Mozart, Beethoven, Schubert, Wagner and Brahms. Debussy looked to cultivating and accentuating a sense of Frenchness, the rhythm of the language – not forgetting the food and weather – and a certain subsequent vividness in matters of form and instrumentation, in order not necessarily to dismiss those composers but to discover a new music, for a new time of intense change and of necessarily radical individual expression. Always fascinated by music from around the world and by exotic cultures, Debussy committed himself to finding a new music that took its basic energy from French traditions and ideas but reconsidered and deepened what it was to be French.

iii. *String Quartet in G minor (1893), as performed by Quatuor Ébène*

The only time Debussy specified a key, and with for him an unusual lack of a poetic title, as though he was acknowledging or mocking the formal tradition of the string quartet.

A couple of years after *Rêverie*, where he is still experimenting with the motion of music and being musically in the moment, which instantly makes it sound modern to this day, on his completely non-academic quest to 'free music from the barren traditions that stifle it', Debussy is now a long way along the bridge connecting the classic eighteenth- and nineteenth-century romantic era approaches to form, melody and harmony, and the freer, looser, less orthodox, more exotic and aurally pleasing, tonally challenging tendencies of twentieth-century music. With his uncannily beautiful quartet, Debussy of course insists there is no bridge, he is simply floating between one place and another, and you believe him. At the time there were those who were a little baffled – charmed, yes, and accepting that something original had happened, but wondering why there had to be a bridge at all and anxiously questioning what strangeness, even chaos, it was leading to. We have entered Debussy's middle period, a series of what have become historical turning points, on the border of modern music, where Debussy has found Debussy, in between serene stillness and the heavens above the moon, at one with the mysterious forces he knew were helping him cross the bridge, even if he didn't need one to reach where he was going. Already on the drawing board was...

iv. Prélude a l'après-midi d'un faune *(1894), performed by Berlin Philharmonic conducted by Claudio Abbado/*Syrinx *for Flute (1913), performed by Vincent Lucas/*Rapsodie pour saxophone *(1901–11), performed by Nicolas Prost*

In Stéphane Mallarmé's fragmentary, wilfully obscure but popular poem 'The Afternoon of a Faun', it might be that nothing happens, give or take a drowsy, dreaming faun's wooing fancy for two wandering nymphs and his feeling at one with nature. It was an attempt to make language take on the effect of music, where there can be no explicit meaning, and yet it can move the listener as though they have been let in on revelatory private moments and secret feelings. The sound of the words is perhaps as important as the music, something that would have appealed to Debussy, who had his own literary talents. Also, for Mallarmé, there was a conviction that words needed their meaning pulled from inside. Ideas should not be presented in a straightforward way or they cease to be ideas, merely instructions. This was Debussy's idea of poetry, which only hints at what is to be said and which is always finding abstract ways to deal with the dark and raid the unconscious, to keep the senses sharp and clear.

Debussy met the difficult Mallarmé in 1890 and regularly attended the poet's weekly salons. Soon they were discussing some form of collaboration, a theatrical project inspired by the poem featuring incidental music, which eventually became Debussy's improvisational-seeming but intricately constructed symphonic tone poem. The minder of modernism, Pierre Boulez, suggests that it is exactly here, as a fluttering suggestive flute ushers the piece into position, that modern music really begins. 'The flute of the faun brought new breath to the art of music.'

Anthony Burgess wrote that hearing *L'après-midi* on the radio as a twelve-year-old in 1929 Manchester was the moment he really discovered music after some uncomfortable childhood violin lessons. He'd been searching for the BBC Dance Orchestra on a radio he had managed to build himself, and somehow tuned in the 'sinuous, exotic, erotic' flute solo. 'I was spellbound. The velvet strings, the striking clarinets, the harps, the muted horns, the antique cymbals, the flute, above all the flute.' It was, he said, a psychedelic moment. 'An instant of recognition of verbally inexpressible spiritual realities…'

Music was Burgess's first love. The 'inexplicable magic' the flute introduced into his life led to a determination to become a composer, and within a few years, self-taught, he was writing his First Symphony, featuring orchestration that he described as being 'Elgarian with Holstian condiments'. His music was never as shrewd and scintillating, or audaciously convoluted, as his writing. In a way he was more Debussyian in his novels than in his music; his literary structures, learned in many ways from Debussy and other quiet radicals, were always more provocative than his music. In that sense his books were more musical than his writing, and often written in response to music, even about the effect of music and the nature of that inexplicable magic. Despite writing over 250 pieces, never shaking off a mild, lightly appealing early twentieth-century Englishness, and being unable to plunge into the depths like Debussy, he failed to become, as he wished, 'the musician who writes novels rather than the novelist who writes music on the side'.

As in the poem, Debussy finds a way to make time itself stop and something else take over, somewhere between losing touch with reality and seeing things all too clearly. Mallarmé himself is reported to have considered that the music of the poem was enough, and that somehow it was criminally wrong to merge poetry with music. On the other hand, while casually noting a 'dissonance' with the text, he wrote a letter to Debussy calling him 'a marvel!'. He expressed admiration for its 'sensuality, its richness'. Ravel once admitted he would like the piece played at his funeral, and he transcribed it for piano, articulating yet another order of movement.

A version for a ballet, premiered in 1912, is acclaimed as the moment where abstract, modern dance begins, eloquently remaking the music's forward-looking narrative, taking both the fantasy of the poem and the fantasy of the music still further into the future, although Debussy considered there to be another 'dissonance', this time between his carefully created fluidity and the dance's sharp, almost expressionist, edges. He was also not so keen on the faun using one of the nymphs' scarves for a little sexual relief.

He felt that one form of physicality clashed with another, but if it did, that was because art, responding to the speed and turbulence of the times and making similar decisions, was heading out and coming in from all sorts of new directions. The faun's flute had previewed this activity and action.

Choreographed by the twenty-two-year-old Vaslav Nijinsky, working on a new language of movement, who took the leading role of the horny faun chasing the tantalising nymphs, the ballet dislocated tradition with a more dramatic revolutionary emphasis, making more explicit the sense of orgasmic dynamics Mallarmé embedded in his poem, which the typically more cryptic Debussy sensuously glanced against. Reviews condemned 'vile movements of erotic bestiality' and the police were summoned for a second sold-out performance. Rudolf Nureyev once said that the faun was his favourite ever role.

The flute, this time in the mouth of Pan, his last melody before death, continues all by itself in the three-minute *Syrinx* – which means 'Pan pipes' – originally written as incidental music for *Psyche*, a play written by Debussy's friend, the poet and dramatist Gabriel Mouray. Debussy intended to give the player as much freedom as possible, to the extent of avoiding bar lines or breath marks and keeping the central key a mystery – anticipating John Cage's post-musical dreams of freedom, where ideas, suggestions and instructions were more important than notation.

The solo flute, exploiting the modernising updates to the instrument since 1777, when Mozart wrote his Flute Concerto in G major, will continue into the stricter tempo of *Density 21.5*, written by Debussy's friend Edgard Varèse in 1936, and revised a decade later. It was to be played on a platinum flute, platinum having a density of 21.5g per cubic centimetre. *Syrinx* was considered the first major piece for solo flute since C. P. E. Bach's Sonata in A minor written a century and a half before, and can also be connected to Luciano Berio's 1958 piece for unaccompanied flute, *Sequenza I*, creating a distinct, overlapping twentieth-century trio for flute that shared attitude, material and technique.

Rapsodie for Orchestra and Saxophone had been commissioned in 1901 by American arts patron and amateur musician Elise Hall who played, before its jazz-inspired popularity, the relatively new alto saxophone, and wanted additions to the very sparse repertoire. The disorganised, undisciplined Debussy, never good at fulfilling such commissions, preferring to take his composition by surprise, teasing out ideas, and unfamiliar with the instrument, spent the money to get rid of ever-present debts and moved on to other more personal deadlines. To Debussy's amazement, a few years later she turned up in Paris, tracked him down and asked where the piece was. He called her the 'saxophone lady' and, less kindly, an 'old bat', complained she dressed like an umbrella, and remarked on her American tenacity, but set to work imagining how to make it work and how to showcase what he called 'this aquatic instrument' – it took him seven years to complete.

Debussy's solution was naturally not to celebrate the instrument through virtuoso playing but to investigate the sound and personality of this alien new instrument. He wrote it for saxophone and piano, and a few years later, a year after Debussy's death, it was orchestrated, or at least prepared for publication based on Debussy's instructions for an ethereal orchestral tableau, by the composer Jean Roger-Ducasse, adding a more conventionally minded sax solo radiantly echoing parts of the String Quartet, so that it becomes another unintended Debussy version of a concerto. In this case, a forlorn, yearning saxophone doesn't compete with, share the stage with or provoke the orchestra; it begs to become part of it, as if to be taken seriously as an instrument. As a textural impression of sound it is halfway across a bridge – one that does not exist – between *Prélude à l'après-midi d'un faune* and one of his accepted, abstractly descriptive classics, *La Mer*, as if he needed to complete this initially 'disagreeable', even puzzling task in order for his mind to make yet another leap into using notes, sounds and colours to conceive a new music.

By the time the *Rapsodie* was ready for a premiere, not only was the composer dead, but Hall had become completely deaf and never got to hear the unlikely piece she had commissioned.

v. Pelléas et Mélisande (1902), Act I, Scene III: 'In front of the castle', performed by the orchestra and chorus of the Royal Opera House, conducted by Pierre Boulez

Debussy's only completed opera – he long toyed with turning Shakespeare's *As You like It* into an opera – presenting a tragic love triangle based on poet and philosopher Maurice Maeterlinck's eponymous play set in an imaginary kingdom is, as he said, not inspired by Wagner but by an idea of what comes after Wagner. Blood and thunder are replaced by mood and atmosphere, and it somehow seems right that, after Wagner extravagantly reaches the pinnacle of the idea of the opera as established between Mozart and Puccini, Debussy elegantly brings the whole idea down to earth, without sacrificing unearthly cosmic glory. It points towards the eclectic twentieth-century operas of Strauss, Stravinsky and Britten, where a heady combination of symbolism and realism was added to the essential formalised combination of words and music. It also signals a disconnected end-of-century nervousness that would leak throughout the twentieth century, climaxing with its own disconnected end-of-century nervousness, when the work seemed more relevant, and more performed, than ever. The characters, in a state of high awareness, feeling intensely all the time, are self-consciously doomed to exist where they are placed; everything is predetermined, and it is a feeling that is growing in the twenty-first century – there is no way out and what happens next happens next. The only ways of disturbing this unsettling set of conditions: dreams, music and art.

It's opera not as monstrous display but as a dream that the translucent music is part of, and the music doesn't undermine any of the necessary drama with its intense Debussy-created stillness and timelessness, and also creates the character and the wonders of the kingdom and the passions and despair of the story, as though its buildings and scenery, the gloom and menace, the castles and moonlight, as well as the characters and emotions and what exist as near human beings, and their sexual attraction to each other – and even the language of the singers – were made of music. There was no need for Debussy to write another opera; he had created a perfect one, which works as a piece of music whether you believe in the fantasy of operas or not.

As conducted by Boulez – his first production of the opera was in in London in 1969 – it leans towards the abstract and even seething, with much made of its early links with modernism. In notes written for his London production, Boulez talks of the opera as 'a theatre of fear and cruelty'. Debussy's music wasn't 'impressionistic' in the way it was described, as if directly connected to the evocative painterly shimmer of French impressionist painting, but Boulez was the perfect conductor for imagining and maintaining a form of discreetly suggestive and vivacious sonic impressionism, to confirm Debussy's instincts, where literal precision is somehow relieved of its duties and technical terms are useful only as far as they go. Also, Boulez was the perfect conductor, on the quiet, inside this musical dream, for the way in which, at the very beginning of the century, it astutely previewed the sound of the twentieth century.

vi. Danse sacrée et danse profane, *version for harp and strings (1904), performed by the Los Angeles Chamber Orchestra, conducted by Gerard Schwarz, harp soloist Nancy Allen*

This was Debussy's answer to a call from the Pleyel instrument builders to write a piece that would feature its newly designed chromatic harp, featuring two intersecting rows of strings – and this is another small-scale Debussy version of a concerto, with, ambitiously, the harp as the featured instrument. Written as Debussy was writing *La Mer*, and a short while after *Pelléas et Mélisande*, it is definitely an aside to the opera, part of the same dream, the same intense worship of where the known world touches the unknown.

(Debussy's piece was playable on the pedal harp made by Erard, the company that commissioned Ravel, but Ravel's piece was not playable on the Pleyel harp. This ultimately meant that the chromatic harp was doomed, and the pedal harp won out in this random war of the harps.)

vii. La cathédrale engloutie (The Sunken Cathedral) *(1910), Preludes Book I. No. 10, performed by Arturo Benedetti Michelangeli, as well as 'The Snow is Dancing' from* Children's Corner *(1908).*

Also *Canope* from Preludes Book II No. 13 (1912–13), performed by Sviatoslav Richter; *Étude 10 pour les sonorités opposées* from Études (1915), performed by Mitsuko Uchida.

La cathédrale engloutie is one of the twenty-four preludes for solo piano, split into two books of twelve, where the titles were given at the end of the piece, enabling the listener to make up their own mind what was being pictured in the music, and to create an uncompromisingly pure listening experience, in between what you thought you were hearing and what Debussy intended.

Prelude No. 10 describes the rise from the depths of the sea of a submerged cathedral and is based on an old Breton legend. A city has been drowned, and at certain times of the year its cathedral would eerily rise above the water. The piece tells the story by effectively drowning sound, or making it seem as though sound can appear to be dissolving, or shifting into a new shape, a new texture. Debussy achieves the effect he was looking for – not 'impressionism', which he said only imbeciles called it – using only the piano, which is one of his greatest illusions, or magical achievements. He is composing with sound, as many electronic musicians would do a century later – not writing music by placing one note next to another and so on, but by layering, editing and placing sounds in close proximity to each other. New kinds of patterns, shapes and forms can be invented, related to instinct, the imagination and emotion, which are musical but not hemmed in by purely practical musical technique. In doing so he extended the range of the piano.

The twelve piano *Études* – each one features a name suggesting the technical motivation for its composition – make it clear that Debussy's piano technique began with Chopin: they are dedicated to him. Chopin extended the piano's potential in a way that set Debussy up to take further the whole idea of what you could do with the keyboard. The piano could take in all of human life with Chopin and Liszt, but somehow Debussy found more life, and more humanity, if only by being himself, with all that meant in terms of what he wanted the piano to sound like. Liszt was perhaps more of an influence on Debussy in terms of the effect of sound, certainly the use of pedals – where the piano could be made to breathe – the keyboard registers and the variety of ways you could attack the keyboard. Liszt was interested in pure piano sound itself outside of music, and this made it through to Debussy. It made Debussy realise how, in writing music, you could go over and above the notes while entering an ambiguous world of the indeterminate.

The *Études* emerged in an intensely energetic and audacious blast of creative vitality after time spent editing the works of Chopin, typifying how, for Debussy, the creation of music was the most important thing in his life, and his greatest music therefore contained his life. The *Études* reflected his musical soul but also his rigorous but often veiled technique, a summary of his research into the limits of what playing the piano could achieve, which went beyond his usual elemental fascination with sound.

They were Debussy's final significant work for solo piano, pointing the way to a change in his thinking, and a connection with atonalism, and were music about music connected to nothing outside of music and, in that sense, are the absolute distillation of the Debussyness of Debussy, his abilities as a self-styled, self-taught musician with an extraordinary technical ability. They also express his skills and progressions as a composer in the last fifteen years of the nineteenth century and the first fifteen of the twentieth. Here is the essence of the spiritual Debussy and the composer who now relished action as much as he revelled in the static.

viii. Images pour orchestre, I. Gigues (1909–12), performed by the Royal Concertgebouw Orchestra, conducted by Bernard Haitink

Debussy wrote three pieces called *Images*, the first two sets for piano, extending his control of a new kind of abstraction, which he fancied entered the literature of piano 'to the left of Schumann and to the right of Chopin'. *Images* seems an obvious title now, with his attempt to produce musical imagery, but at the time appeared a little strange and unsettling. The second piece in Book 2, the intently mystical *Et la lune descend sur la temple qui fut* (*And the Moon Descends Upon the Temple That is No More*) is still, slow, beautiful, moving, quiet, a place to go to explore the source of modal jazz piano — hear Bill Evans at the beginning and end of 'Blue in Green' from Miles Davis's *Kind of Blue* — with a mysterious opening chord lifted from the early French harpsichordists who framed his own modern thinking, a kind of formal freedom, and also a place to visit to begin your time with Debussy, and his skill at musically moving forwards at the slowest possible pulse while moving the history of music forwards. (The early French harpsichord stylists Debussy was influenced by meant even as he was as technically up to speed as a more obvious iconoclast like Stravinsky, he retains that distinct but non-nationalist French quality that was so important to him.) The third iteration of *Images* took seven years to complete, is for orchestra and contains three movements, each one reflecting his sense of three different countries' music. This final major orchestral work by Debussy originally began as a work for two pianos.

The first movement, *Gigues*, and last to be completed, was intended as a tribute to English music, but this is an English music entirely in the imagination of Debussy — an imagined or dreamed Englishness, with a perhaps extremely accurate undercurrent of melancholy and borrowed hints of the possible reality of high-spirited English jigs. The second movement, *Iberia*, for and from Spain, itself in three parts — Debussy loved doing things in threes – is more literal, possibly given a little more national authenticity because Debussy once nipped over the border for a short day visit to San Sebastián to watch a bullfight. He seemed to know enough about the colours and rhythms of Spain, and perhaps, unashamedly, some of the less refined and more nostalgic components of Spanish music, to produce an uncanny, irresistible representation of its bright brilliance. Its more specific sense, a more realistic dream of Spain, a Spain of the imagination that somehow comes close to an exuberant, sensual reality, and the physical agitation that is in its music, makes it by far the most popular of the three countries Debussy 'coloured in'.

Hear *Iberia* and hear not just Debussy's insinuating imagining of Spain but a sound that can confidently be described as 'Spanish' – some might say an impression of Spain, but Debussy would resist such a label, preferring to think of these pieces as 'an effect of reality'. The picturing of Spain, on the streets, through the sultry night, the sunlight and bright light of a morning, as though a series of visual images, suggests why Debussy's music became of such use to those composers who would originate and develop incidental music for films.

Debussy slipped through an ancient Italian May Day song and two French children's folk songs for the third piece, the naturally effervescent *Rondes de Printemps* (*Spring Rounds*), and although he expressed distaste for the idea of 'impressionism' in music, a programme for the first performance in Paris, conducted by Debussy, contained a note, which presumably he approved, that said: 'The musician attempts to translate for the ear impressions received by the eye. Just as the painter takes pleasure in the contrasts of tonality, the play of light and shadow, so the musician plays with the shock of unexpected dissonances, with the fusion of rare musical timbre… This is a musical impressionism of particular nuance and rare quality.'

ix. Le Martyre de saint Sébastien (Fragments Symphoniques) (1911), III. La Passion, *performed by the London Symphony Orchestra, conducted by Pierre Monteux*

A little-known major work by Debussy, originally written in two months as the incidental music for a vast, over-the-top, five-hour, five-act mystery play by poet, novelist, socialite and soldier Gabriele

D'Annunzio telling, somewhere between the kitsch and the cosmic, the legend of a twice-martyred saint. D'Annunzio wanted a production drenched in music. 'There is music between every syllable, between every verse,' he announced. 'There is music in every individual gesture, in every movement of the crowd.' D'Annunzio called each act a 'mansion'. The Third Mansion is entitled 'The Counsel of False Gods'. Not to everyone's taste, he was Debussy's kind of strung-out poet, reflecting the erratic, impulsive artistic taste of an autodidact in everything but music — Debussy admitted that the mere thought of working with him gave him a sort of fever, which is probably why he was able to finish the music in eight manic weeks.

The enigmatic, or batty, immensity effectively blocked the light from ever reaching some of Debussy's loveliest music. The fragment is a short version, not edited by the composer, of a strangely opulent complete version featuring songs, spoken word and choir, and which showed that as much as he had escaped the shadows and ecstasies of Wagner into his own sense of drama, he was still fascinated by them, even as he was imagining a future for musical theatre, some enigmatic multi-sensed place beyond opera, that never went any further, possibly because it couldn't. If Debussy had musically imagined the spirit of nations in his *Images*, here he imagined paradise as a kind of theatrical genre, an exquisite, idiosyncratic extension of *Pelléas* that exists once and only in this form.

X Jeux *(1912–13), performed by the Vienna Philharmonic, conducted by Lorin Maazel/*La Mer, trois esquisses symphoniques pour orchestre *(1903–5): 2.* Jeux de vagues (Play of the Waves), *performed by the Berlin Philharmonic, conducted by Herbert Von Karajan*

If you can't quite take the above sonic spectacle, then begin with the obvious Debussy on the way to the freakier one… 'The sea has been very good to me,' Debussy admitted as he was completing *La Mer*, three symphonic sketches. 'She has shown me all her moods.' He claimed he once thought of becoming a sailor, and even though 'only the chances of life led me away from it', he never lost his passion for the sea. And this being Debussy, *La Mer* isn't about the sea, it *is* the sea.

As with Holst's *The Planets*, it helps that there is a title for the piece — as opposed to Three Symphonic Sketches for piccolo, two flutes, two oboes, cor anglais, two clarinets, three bassoons, four horns, three trumpets, three trombones, tuba, kettledrum, cymbals, tam-tam, two harps, and the traditional strings. Then again, within seconds, even if it was called *The Sky* or *Untitled*, you would so clearly be presented with the sea, as unavoidably as if it is a film, and you don't necessarily need the titles of each 'sketch' to know that Debussy is examining, celebrating, holding in musical time an immense sea at rest, a sea waking itself up and lashing itself into a pure fury, and how the wind makes waves as if each one is itself a sculpture, a work of art, even a manifestation of consciousness. What is achieved is a way of describing and in turn creating the reality of an experience, or an object or a phenomenon that isn't a painting, or a photo, or a poem, or a drama, or even to some extent in the context of the time a piece of music – it is a completely unknown form of presentation, and it can also work in articulating a dream, a memory, a life, or a fleeing, intangible feeling. Again, as with *The Planets* – and as with many great pieces of classical music – it is written about something that exists without humanity, which can make the music inexplicably moving and often deeply, strangely sad, by placing within this momentous, mysterious non-human existence a vivid, thinking, transient human presence. The greatest classical music articulates the astonishing lonely human presence that has found itself in the centre of an otherwise fathomless void: it represents the human mind in a way that fits into the form and formlessness of the universe, and detects its shape, its dark power and even its reason. Classical music at its most modern, restlessly contemplative best is the purest concentration of a feeling of 'what the hell are we doing here' at this time, in the middle of all this unmeasurable space, surrounded by what we have made up to make it all seem acceptable and understandable.

It is one of many pieces Debussy wrote about water – the first piece of the first set of piano *Images* is *Reflets dans l'eau* – and this also is not simply about attempting literally to recreate water sounds but reflects on the idea of water, how it moves, speeds up, slows down, but also its strangeness and ultimate, mute, esoteric otherness, where the sounds it makes are not necessarily what it is, or even, if you think further, what water might itself be thinking about, considering that, in its own way, it is alive.

Debussy expresses a first impression of the magic and miracle as though he is seeing it for the very first time – and his water pieces are more about what he sees, and thinks about, than what he hears, and follow the principle that there is magic contained in water and the way it embraces the whole planet. He was never interested in merely describing an experience but in taking it to another level – articulating how an experience alters or affects our soul and our memories. His music remembers the impact of an experience on our imagination rather than experience itself.

He finished *La Mer* in Eastbourne on the south coast of England, but it might as well be an Eastbourne on Saturn.

The helpful light of attention failed to fully reach Debussy's music for ballet, *Jeux*, because of the notorious premiere two weeks later of Stravinsky's more raucous and controversial ballet *The Rite of Spring* – Debussy presented his radical, daring changes in a quieter, more discreet way, so that there is no knotty, needling noise to knock you out or over, or infuriate you, but a kind of fluid, eddying musical lightness that is somehow made of light.

The ballet itself, choreographed by Nijinsky, was nothing too dramatic, let alone shocking, even though it was one of the first ever to be danced in contemporary dress. The 'play' or 'games' in the title referred to its setting on a tennis court at dusk, where what ensues among the three characters, two females and a male (Nijinsky) is a bit of symbolically to-and-fro tennis, a little flirtation, some sulking, and always a simmering eroticism. In some ways it's a sequel to the faun action, and inaction, flickering fantastically on what Debussy could make the border between dream and reality like very few others.

Debussy's middle-period ideas were liberating for the twenty-years-younger Stravinsky of the famously disorientating *The Rite of Spring*, and Debussy is still experimenting on *Jeux* but without it seeming that there is anything radical happening. The experiments and extreme changes in tempo lead to a sense of coherence, a gently deformed waltz, rather than worked-up, relentless disconnection, and it becomes influential on future music, from Stockhausen to Messiaen and Ligeti, in how it creates a tensile collage of mood and effect.

It wasn't just his obsession with sound that made Debussy sound relevant, however remotely, throughout the twentieth century, but also his awareness of what you could do with form by imagining music as sculpture – a floating sculpture – as much as simply a matter of carefully learned, organised sound. To some extent, he made the sort of sculpture where there is no sense of a beginning or ending, other than what there has to be so that it can at least be performed. The endings and beginnings of a Debussy piece were what made him sound more end of twentieth century than beginning of twentieth century, the equivalent of the difference between Charles Dickens and Virginia Woolf.

Without making a fractured, fragmenting meal of it – although he was producing something made up of many shifting, coalescing, dissolving fragments and shapes, with a clear awareness of Schoenberg and his modernist transformation of the romanticism of Brahms – Debussy is previewing the development of serialism, certainly according to Pierre Boulez, who enthusiastically promoted Debussy in the 1950s as a godfather of serialism. The composer in Boulez was almost envious of the way *Jeux* renewed itself moment to moment, the conductor in him relishing its definitive Debussy combination of composure and spontaneity.

It would be the last orchestral score Debussy finished before his death in 1918, as usual completing it on the piano first of all and then building it up, thinking, as he noted, 'of that orchestral colour which seems to be lit from behind'. Debussy had musical influences but seemed to separate himself from them more than the more heralded radicals like Schoenberg and Stravinsky – he pushed himself elsewhere, determined not to sound like anything else without sounding like he was forcing his originality, his artistic independence, without ever sounding 'difficult to understand'. He was one of the first to argue that tonality should be got rid of, or least reorganised, but he never fully dismissed it; his tonality was intensified, illuminated, by his awareness of the possibility of atonality.

xi. Berceuse héroïque (A Lullaby for a Hero) *(1914)*, *piano version performed by Walter Gieseking, orchestral version performed by the Royal Concertgebouw Orchestra*

During the war, while Ravel was driving an ambulance on the front after being judged too old and too short to take part as an aviator, Debussy was fighting colon cancer. 'My age and fitness,' he reported, 'allows me at most to guard a fence. But, if to assure victory, they are absolutely in need of another face to be bashed in, I'll offer mine without question.'

Always hopeful the war would end quickly, almost allergic to his piano as the war started, feeling that music was inappropriate in such a hellish time, he would be drawn into a campaign protesting against the rejection of Belgian neutrality by the Germans, and he contributed to *King Albert's Book*, sponsored and published during the winter of 1914 by the *Daily Telegraph*, subtitled 'A Tribute to the Belgian King and People from Representative Men and Women'. Other contributors among a list of allied artists and intellectuals included Edward Elgar, Jack London, Saint-Saëns, Edith Wharton and Maurice Maeterlinck. Debussy's contribution was this 'lullaby' for a hero, a brief, tranquil, ultimately solemnly unheroic and deliberately elegiac improvised piano piece incorporating the Belgian national anthem. 'It has no pretensions other than to offer an homage to so much patient suffering. It's the best that I can do…'

The 'héroïque' in the title was Debussy irony – war was too bleak and miserable for him to consider anything literally heroic, dwelling as only he could on something mysterious, even mystical, to honour the dead. It was the only piece he wrote during the first year of the war, with lingering echoes of influences on his life of Chopin, who pioneered the lullaby form of the berceuse, and the late piano miniatures of Liszt, amidst echoes of the war and its bringing of death. (Other berceuses that seem to drift into and extend Debussy's include Brahms's *Lullaby*, *Berceuse* by Frank Bridge for cello and piano, Ferruccio Busoni's *Berceuse élégiaque*, Gabriel Fauré's *Berceuse*, Op. 16, 'Berceuse' from *114 Songs* by Charles Ives, *Berceuse sur le nom de Gabriel Fauré* by Ravel, Berceuse in A-flat major for solo piano, from *18 Pieces*, Op. 72, No. 2 by Tchaikovsky, and *Berceuse for the Infant Jesus* by George Crumb.)

As if relearning music, giving it another layer of intense, born-again beauty, Debussy found the strength to write more than he had for a while during the hard war years, when it was difficult to earn a living, even as he felt beaten and depressed by the senseless war, the oppressive Germans and his state of health, experiencing a painful operation, radiation treatment and aggressive drugs. It was his artistic way of declaring war on the Germans, and to find a way, however small, to ensure 'that French thought will not be destroyed. I think of the youth of France, senselessly mowed down. What I am writing will be a secret homage to them.'

xii. *Sonata for Cello and Piano in D minor (1915), performed by Matt Haimovitz/Sonata for Flute, Viola and Harp: III. Finale (1915), performed by Ensemble Wien-Berlin/Sonata for Violin and Piano (1916–17)*

Debussy's 'role' in the war was as a protector of French culture, which became an exaggerated end-of-life enhancement of his existing desire to resist the Germanic influence on music and assert a less direct, more abstract sense of attack. Because of this indirectness and abstraction, he avoided a sense of dogma in his protection of French tradition in art – taking it forward and allowing in modern, and foreign, influences and his own untethered creative energy rather than celebrating some imaginary French purity or inflexible French identity. Any French purity for Debussy had to involve change and improvement.

He always embraced French tradition in his ambitions for something new, often looking back to the clarity and plaintive reserve of the neglected French baroque for inspiration. In 1915, turning to classical models and the German masters of the forms he was usually indifferent to, such as Beethoven and Brahms – not perhaps his idea of German 'barbarism' – he had the idea to write a series of six sonatas for different instrumental combinations, with the final one combining all the instruments he had used in the series.

He died before the project was completed, but the three he did complete offer a forceful suggestion of where his musical thinking would have moved if he had lived longer than just fifty-six. For all its baroque influences and incorporated sonata formality, the cello sonata emerges from his aggressive experimental sensibility, and rather than merely settle into mild updating, especially considering the circumstances of his disintegrating life and a world falling apart around him, he reimagines classical form with modernist purpose, and creates instrumental effects that come across like a ghostly preview of recording techniques. He's looking back into time, towards a more formal music, but also looking ahead, to then-unimaginable novelty.

Debussy wrote the cello sonata in the seaside town of Pourville, near Dieppe in Normandy, reacting, he said, to cellists who had been asking him for some time to add to a limited repertoire. Beethoven wrote five sonatas for cello and piano, next to thirty-two for piano. By the time he wrote his fifth for cello, in 1815, he was on the verge of entering his late period, with all that that means in terms of innovation in form, content and the advancement of instrumental technique.

Debussy never reached an equivalent late period into which his Sonata for Cello and Piano could have been a portal: it was appropriate that he left behind a mysterious space after his death, a 'what if-ness' that then drifts back over the work he does complete.

The cello sonata, like the other sonatas some kind of sequel to his string quartet, aches with where Debussy is in his life, demoralised by the war, fighting his own war against cancer, so exhausted that even dressing seemed too demanding a task, and he would write: 'Try as I may, I can't regard the sadness of my existence with caustic detachment. Sometimes my days are dark, dull, and soundless, like those of a hero from Edgar Allan Poe, and my soul is as romantic as a Chopin ballade.' The sonata is relatively short, at under eleven minutes, but Debussy compresses a fantastic amount of contrasting musical insight and emotion into the piece, and perfectly achieves a musical, autobiographical balance between romantic and modern music, opening the space beyond.

The Sonata for Violin and Piano was his final finished composition; he still retained his sense of humour and noted that it sounded exactly like an 'example of what a sick man would write in a time of war', which is, in the best sense, true, in the way an extremely sensitive artist responded to the war, and battles his personal predicament, alternating between delicate contemplation and a weirdly joyful energy. (Play it as part of an unofficial series of extraordinary violin and piano sonatas alongside Leoš Janáček's, Bela Bartók's No. 1 from 1921, Shostakovich's in G major from 1968, Beethoven's Violin Sonata No. 9, Franz Schubert's Fantasy in C major and Ravel's Sonata for Violin and Piano No. 2.)

Debussy played the piano at what turned out to be his last public appearance in September 1917, six months before his death. In the original published edition, given the original title of *Six Sonatas for Diverse Instruments*, he signs it as 'Claude Debussy – musicien français'. He had gone his own way. He found a new direction. It was French; it was individual. It was not French; it was universal.

7. BONUS: 'THE HOLY EGOISM OF GENIUS'/'LA FLÛTE DE PAN'/'METAFORCE'/'OUT OF THIS WORLD (VERSION 138)' (1999) BY ART OF NOISE FROM *THE SEDUCTION OF CLAUDE DEBUSSY*

I was a member of the avant-pop collective Art of Noise in the early 1980s, a group whose image I designed to be the 'house band' of the Zang

Tuum Tumb record label I had formed with the record producer Trevor Horn and his wife and manager Jill Sinclair. Although a journalist, I was hired as a combination of A & R man, conceptualist and general provocateur by Trevor to dream up a record label, and then with Art of Noise to dream up a band. My part in the group was influenced by the invisible role Joseph Beuys's student Emil Schult had performed in Kraftwerk during the 1970s, contributing ideas, images, reference points, titles, lyrics, album-cover concepts and in general making Art of Noise as much performance art as pop. It seemed obvious after Schult that a member of a pop group didn't necessarily have to play an instrument or sing, but could operate in the shadows, sometimes as a shadow, but one with lots to say.

I decided to make the Art of Noise masked and anonymous, and for them to be what I perceived as the exact opposite to Trevor's previous band, the Buggles. As an unforgiving rock critic immersed in the ideological, deconstructed force of post-punk, at the time I had viewed the Buggles, certainly their image, as tacky, almost Eurovision, and their number one hit 'Video Killed the Radio Star' a pretty annoying novelty hit that was somewhere between Chicory Tip and Abba; over time, this has proved a kind of winning, even credible pop formula, and combined with it being the first song played on the pop-changing video channel MTV, it was turned into a meta-novelty hit.

At the time I wanted to see if I could make Trevor Horn of the Buggles someone mysteriously of a band where it was difficult to work out where in the world they came from – in the end they came from the recording studio, a country all of its own – or what they looked like. The first publicity photos consisted of a spanner, a rose, an engine, and later a statue of Sigmund Freud represented the group.

Horn possibly offered me the job at his record label because when I interviewed him as a Buggle I thought his music was rubbish, but when I interviewed him later as the producer of ABC's really romantic *Lexicon of Love* and Malcolm McLaren's surreally romantic *Duck Rock* – not to mention the weirdly pleasing easy listening of well-flossed pop fluffians Dollar – I thought his music was fabulous, making innovative use of the accelerating potential of the recording studio and increasingly sophisticated computer technology.

He needed to know, perhaps, why I thought there was such a difference between one and the other, not necessarily because he disagreed with me, but because he wondered if I knew something about pop music that he didn't. I didn't, of course, but he was intrigued by the difference between how and why a critic wrote about music, and how and why a musician wrote and performed it. Could I perhaps explain to him why some rock and pop music was instantly credible, and some rock and pop never would be? Being an *NME* critic I could, of course, easily explain why Yes were reviled and Johnny Rotten was as important as Elvis Presley, and to some extent it had more to do with the clothing worn, the language used, the faces pulled, and the social history being made than the actual songs.

Trevor and I often had long talks about the idea of pop music as, for me, an important statement about life, death and sex best experienced when it was subversive and strange, and, for him, a commercial combination of sound, melody and rhythm concerned with love and meant for the dance floor, best when it was fresh, catchy and disposable. For a while, although I might have been dreaming this, the spirit of those animated conversations about the purpose of pop spilled into the studio, where Trevor and his team of workers were intently cutting and pasting together pop songs, using electronics to disguise their electronic structure, one of which, under the band name Frankie Goes to Hollywood, included an explosive ode to orgasm that became the biggest selling single of the 1980s.

Fancying the future, where I believed all pop should be heading, I raided the manifestos of the early twentieth-century Futurists for the name of both the label and its house band. I'd been reading the Thames and Hudson guide to Futurism, part of a series of art books, and possibly took at least 75 per cent of my thoughts about the label from its pages, when ideas found through this kind of pre-search research seemed more mysterious than they would post-Google.

A key influence on the sublime, subversive nonsense and haywire analytical precision of Dada, the Italian Futurists furiously proposed that a new world of machines — cars, aeroplanes, factories, lights and the cities they illuminated and connected — and a world at war, on the verge of self-destruction, required a whole new, aggressive mental attitude, and a whole new, provocative vocabulary. They could see how early twentieth-century reality was being torn apart by new forms of power, and transport, and communication, and nation-building, and that this astonishing historical rupture needed an equally disruptive form of art, music and literature to represent it and diagnose it. In the early pre-Google 1980s, such thinking could easily be absorbed by pop groups who themselves became a way for listeners to be bounced off into obscure corners of history that hadn't yet been made part of a readily available index of everything

Zang Tuum Tumb was taken from a concrete poem intended to create a sense of the sound of a firing machine gun by Italian futurist leader Filippo Marinetti relishing, or reviling, the assault on human sensibility by the noise of war. I made the name stand for the sound of Trevor Horn's painstakingly achieved drum sound, generated by the new sampling computers, which were producing synthetically infectious sounds that replicated, recreated, approximated, imagined the sounds of traditional instruments, including drums, and invented a few new instrumental and vocal sounds from scratch – indeed, from scratching, as the basic collaged soundscape of Art of Noise emerged from a trip Trevor Horn had made with ex-Sex Pistols manager Malcolm McLaren into the ghettos and side streets of New York. They discovered in the open air, on the streets, a new breed of ingenious non-musical disc jockeys who were creating new sounds and an edgy, energetic, post-funk music by scratching the needle across sections of vinyl records and splicing the made-up rhythms together in an invented, randomly fixed and danceable structure. Vinyl and the needle that scratched sound from the record's grooves through bass-friendly speakers was their instrument, and the Art of Noise used a new computer sampler called the Fairlight to extend the principle.

The Art of Noises were an Italian Futurist ensemble from the early years of the twentieth century, organised by Luigi Russolo, who generated their noise and rhythm as though they too were sampling – imagined music, industrial noise, street sounds, overheard voices, ghostly interference, resulting in a musical equivalent of cubism. Russolo and his colleagues wanted all sound to be possible for music; they were frustrated that it was difficult to capture the noise of the new world using the limited variety of orchestral instruments, and dreamed of an infinite variety of tones and noises being produced by the appropriate mechanisms. In 1913 Russolo wrote: 'Ancient life was all silence. In the nineteenth century, with the invention of the machine, noise was born. Today, noise triumphs and reigns supreme over the sensibilities of men.' The Art of Noises romanticised motion wherever they found it.

We knocked off the 's' and the 'the' — although that was negotiable — to become Art of Noise, who would use electronic instruments and rhythm generators to fuse a similar repertoire of found sounds, and on the noisy quiet, steal music and sounds from other places before the legal and business music world caught up with this radical technological method of processing and reconfiguring influences.

Sounds could be found in other music, from any sort of sound and vocal, to create imagined instruments and novel percussion sounds, and these sounds could in turn be reshaped in any numbers of ways after a process perfected through progressive early disco to isolate, connect and repeat the instrumental rhythmical parts of a soul or funk song. The vocals — as with Jamaican dub, where a similar studio process was running in parallel, opening up sound as though with a tool found on Mars — were turned into echoes of meaning, or disregarded altogether, allowing pure sonic momentum to lift and redirect the listener.

The twelve-inch remix was a relatively new art form at the time — the first commercial twelve-inch release, invented to satisfy disco music's insatiable desire for repeated, rhythmical highs and constant climaxes, was sometime around the mid-1970s, and ZTT started life in 1983. The art of mixing, embellishing, abstracting, distorting, clarifying, exaggerating a song and turning it into something else was very much an exciting, experimental way of testing and challenging the limits of sound recording, and the early life of ZTT also coincided with an accelerated use of the process of sampling in order to conceive, treat and remodel a song.

Collage was the greatest artistic innovation of the twentieth century; the twelve-inch remix was confirmation that music is itself a collage, and pop songs are composed more as layers, bits and pieces of information, emotion and sensation than as conventional musical structures. Pop songs are sculptures in time and space that combine solid pressure with liquid determination, and the twelve-inch remix became a chance to experiment with how a pop song is created, so that the techniques used in the making of a twelve-inch mix infected and influenced how pop songs are made.

There was a vast change in what a pop song turned into after the twelve-inch remix became a part of the pop system, which increasingly became a hip-hop system — pop songs became much more a compilation and interconnecting of rhythms, hooks and special effects, and any rock group that wanted to sound contemporary had to incorporate elements that originated in the more experimental, structurally audacious dance and electronic music. The existence of the twelve-inch helped to remix pop music itself, so that it still exists today, even though in many ways – because there is no vinyl, no solid object, no charts, no recording studios – there is no pop music. The twelve-inch remix gave pop music more time; what was invented to extend a piece of music extended pop culture deep into the twenty-first century.

Reality itself was being remixed – repeated, reprised, reorganised, realigned, regurgitated, replayed, repeated, repeated, repeated, and repeated, and rebeated – and the twelve-inch anticipated and amplified this notion of the remixing of reality, and the way that the machines we use in our daily lives that help perform this remixing – phones, tablets, computers using an array of apps – are versions of the recording studio, drum machines and samplers that were used in the construction of the twelve-inch mix.

We designed Art of Noise as a band and as a brand to be the soundtrack to this intensifying remixing of reality, even as we existed in what now seems a prehistoric version of reality, coming as it did before the likes of Google, Facebook, Twitter, Netflix, Spotify, Instagram and TikTok. MTV had to stand in for all of that.

The musicians and technicians who formed the band that Trevor used to produce Malcolm McLaren, and create a prototype hip-hop band, became Art of Noise, with me as the lead singer in a band that didn't have a lead singer, replacing the ideas and energies of excitable cultural tourist McLaren. We were an abstract pop group built out of a combination of musicians, writers – thinkers – and technicians; the madcap Fairlight operator J. J. Jeczalik, the thorough recording engineer and mixer Gary Langan, the perfectionist record producer Trevor Horn, the elegant, classically trained pianist Anne Dudley, and, on theory and representation, me, also responsible for manifestos where I would announce things such as 'nothing has remained safe from the virus of entertainment', 'art exists because reality is neither real nor significant' and 'as soon as a mystery is explained, it loses its energy'.

This type of mixed ensemble, in the tradition of early twentieth-century artists such as Les Apaches as much as any pop group, seemed the way forward, reflecting how enterprising electronic music groups, exploring the new possibilities of synthesisers, were already making the idea of bass, guitar, drums and voice outmoded. For a while, before hip-hop and electropop in all its forms officially took over in the twenty-first century, at a time when Kraftwerk seemed to be replacing the Beatles as the most important pop group of all time, the future seemed guitarless, and the central instrument of popular music had become the recording studio, with its electric embrace of machines – and eventually the portable versions of the recording studio that would be reduced to the size of a laptop.

I like to think I correctly diagnosed, through the Art of Noise of 1983–4, that the future of pop music would be increasingly about sampling, image, remixing, studio manipulation, guest vocalists, events, anonymity, pseudo-identities and the computer generating, splintering and overlapping of beats that reflected and energised a fractured, fracturing world. I could describe Art of Noise in a number of ways – that was part of my job – and right now I am thinking we were a mutant, masked, non-existent, genre-chopping pop quartet, resisting classification but making an animated montage music that remixed impressionism, modernism, *musique concrète*, minimalism and the pop song, the missing link between Claude Debussy and Daft Punk.

The Debussy element in Art of Noise was not necessarily a fanciful claim, a throwaway part of the many manifestos I liked to issue as part of any release we made, claiming the group as a cryptic missing link between the Shadows and Steve Reich, between Stockhausen and Booker T and the MGs. Anne Dudley, from the very beginning, made sure that a certain eloquent musical dynamic was part of the playful, extremely nerdy collection and collision of sampled and found sounds, and her detailed, romantic, lyrical and spaced-out playing, rooted in early twentieth-century France, emphasised that there was indeed striking contemplative and rousing female energy in Debussy, and his neo-partner Ravel.

The group looked back, as part of a futuristic 'raiding of the twentieth century', which was the title of a central group manifesto, to the clear unfiltered beauty of the piano of Claude Debussy, while looking forward to a time when pop music was all about the programming and processing of sounds made on machines and then listened to on machines. This was a little like the way Debussy would look back to the clarity and rigour of the baroque era and forward to what actually turned out to be the other side of modernism and would be known as postmodernism. Being self-consciously postmodern – blame the metaphorical lead singer – Art of Noise constructed music behind a carefully designed image of a group that then wondered, and hopefully anticipated, what lay beyond the postmodern, where certainly pop music was effectively one mass congregation of electronically conceived, endlessly recycled special effects.

The original group broke down by 1984, in laughter and tears, and Anne, Gary and J. J., as an Art of Noise without masks and without theory, had some hits with featured musicians such as Duane Eddy and Tom Jones, who replaced, some would say sensibly, the far-fetched claims and counterclaims of the lead singer who couldn't and didn't sing. The lead singer in a group that didn't have a lead singer also – as a form of role playing, honestly – turned out to have the ego of an actual lead singer.

Sixteen years later, a new version of Art of Noise, including Anne, Trevor and me, recorded an album with Lol Creme of 10cc that paid direct homage to Claude Debussy's veiled but significant sound-loving influence on the group, mirroring his end-of-century music at the end of the nineteenth century with our end-of-century music at the end of the twentieth century.

We also examined how in his compositions Debussy imaginatively foreshadowed techniques and effects that could eventually be produced using machines and multitrack recording and essentially, for our purposes, was indeed the sound of the beginning of modern music. At the time, I was immersed in Debussy as a spectral preview of electronica, not feeling, it seemed, a hundred years old, but not yet interested in other classical or non-rock/non-jazz instrumental music from before, say, the 1950s. I was yet to make the move backwards from Debussy towards Beethoven and Mozart, and sideways to others adventuring into modernism.

Art of Noise's Debussy album certainly sounded enriched and at times, even though I say so myself, incandescent, expensively doing things with the sound of sound and the rituals of rhythms that might have made Debussy swoon, and we thought we had made it clear, as if in a dream, how Debussy at the beginning of the twentieth century made it all the way through to the jazz, ambient, electronic and – in some of the spaces and sensual swagger – hip-hop end of the century.

I was particularly pleased with 'Metaforce', a song featuring influential American MC Rakim, where he intellectually rapped about

Baudelaire as a kindred spirit of Debussy – and in turn as an ancestor of the intoxicating rhythmical language of hip-hop – based on some notes on Baudelaire I sent him. 'Out of This World' was the purest example of synthesisers and recording techniques reflecting how Debussy, with just his imagination and skill on the piano, could simultaneously produce motion and stillness in music; our greatest hit from the early years, 'Moments in Love', love turned into longing sound, was saturated with this movingly static Debussy, as he might have composed if he'd lived after Kraftwerk and the 10cc of 'I'm Not in Love'.

Alas, the idea of a group called Art of Noise producing a neo-concept album that balanced electropop, meta-jazz, drum and bass, opera, Debussy and speculation about the musical narrative between the so-called French impressionism of the early 1900s and the enchanting French easy-listening electronic pop of Air did not turn on the outside world.

I thought the combination of Rakim, Art of Noise and Baudelaire conjured up a few new delightful answers to the question 'What is beauty?', but in the week of its release, no one could believe their ears, in a bad way, and made their excuses and turned to something else. This Debussy version of the Art of Noise played live, the only recorded example of an ex-*NME* rock writer finding themselves in a pop group with an ex-member of the Buggles and the progressive supergroup Yes, an ex-member of 10cc (Lol Creme) and the winner of an Oscar for the soundtrack to *The Full Monty* (Anne Dudley). When people ask me what I did when the group were on stage, I explain that mostly I recited, unsteadily, in an outfit that might have been what late Elvis would have worn as a member of the Baader-Meinhof, a poem written by Charles Baudelaire called 'Get Drunk', while Trevor in a Savile Row three-piece suit played the double bass over a wonderfully woozy Ronnie Size remix of the track we did with Rakim. And that, for Art of Noise, was the end of the twentieth century, and the end of proceedings; we finished in a lonely place, which seemed appropriately Debussyesque.

PART FIVE

The Writing – Finding the Right Words

Anna Thorvaldsdottir with the New York Philharmonic Orchestra 2018: 'An orchestra could be other than an orchestra.'

1. ON BECOMING AN INSIDER

As the rock critic who had attended the Royal Academy of Music in the search for modern, evolving classical value, I was asked by an online magazine called *Sinfini* to write some pieces about classical music, obviously as an awkward but keen outsider that others not sure of the classical rules could identify with. 'Awkward outsiderness' was perhaps, after all, the true superpower of the rock critic now threatened with extinction, if not more or less all wiped out by amateurs (no offence) and algorithms. Their knowledge wasn't required any more, but maybe their experience and attitude was, their determination to transmit enthusiasm as though it was the most important thing on earth.

Sinfini was produced in-house by one of the last surviving of the twentieth-century-style major record labels, Universal Music, putting up a determined business fight in the face of streaming, and stacked with classical music archives that needed a new, younger audience to reach to give their classical arm some contemporary energy and make it more marketable. They didn't cover purely Universal artists, but the general intention was to create a new context for classical music, where it could seem to be for the under... fifties, or whatever the new youth now was. The alleged 'funkiness' of eclectic-minded but non-classical critics was required so that *Sinfini* didn't seem like any other classical magazine essentially targeted at those already in the know, complete with inside knowledge, extremely happy with their marginalised but extremely well-tended lot.

Courtesy of *Sinfini*, I received some temporary credentials that enabled me to enter this other world. My first move into the classical establishment was designed to not be too intimidating; in many ways, it wasn't even a move into classical music at all, but what was now called 'classic', thanks to others in the music industry also working out how to market classical music – all that music, all those musicians, all that potential product and, you never know, money – to a wider, more diverse audience. One solution was to 'disguise' it. This was the Classic FM approach, as though 'classical' made it seem like attending a double period in chemistry, but 'classic' made it seem very approachable and nicely upmarket. Join the classic club; you know you deserve it. From there, you will soon be looking down on everyone else, even though they don't even know you exist. Possibly because you are so relaxed.

Slowly, I was moving deeper into the forest, knowing more and hearing more, and even if only to myself trying out my thoughts on the music... but first, I showed up at the place, or palace, where the mainstream world had taken classical music, a consequence of a series of marketing strategies that confirms how marketing and commercial persuasion is a type of violence. No shadows, absolutely no darkness and, please, no long words and no theories allowed. Classic indeed.

2. CROSSING OVER WITH THE CLASSICAL TV SET

Handing out or receiving awards, or just hanging out, at the 2012 Classic BRIT Awards at the the Royal Albert Hall, was ITV's idea of a dream team – snowboy Aled Jones, singing dreamboat Andrea Bocelli, cyclist Victoria Pendleton, recyclist Andrew Lloyd Webber, Salford popera singer Russell Watson, cherubic choirmaster Gareth Malone, manband millionaire Gary Barlow, reality TV singer Joe McElderry, self-loving interior designer Lawrence Llewellyn-Bowen and highly sensible broadcaster John Suchet. I thought I'd died and lost the remote control. And then, the Presley of proceedings, the ultimate name to explain the essential bow-tied, twinkly-eyed, Middle England, express-delivery, Thornton's cosiness of what was taking place, which could only happen in this country, with its complex blend of smug arrogance and self-deprecating insecurity, of Empire heritage and brittle island defensiveness, of the plainly sensible and the slightly dotty, of polish and melancholy, of prurience and gardening...

gardener-slash-TV-presenter-slash-novelist-slash-safe-pair-of-hands Alan Titchmarsh! creeping onto the stage, making a smarmy crack about the evening's host, Myleene Klass, and being applauded as though he alone was responsible for everything ever written by Ludwig van Beethoven and Agatha Christie.

Titchmarsh! confirmed that this was a ceremony that had more to do with what in the twentieth century was safely known as light entertainment, patrolled by sweet-smiling, desperately pleasant-seeming middle-of-the-road titans such as Val Doonican, Harry Secombe, Des O'Connor and Hughie Green, some more naturally soothing than others. Titchmarsh! was one of many weapons used to sell to a mass audience a polite, unthreatening idea of classical music during an evening that had as much to do with classical music as the carrots witless Titchmarsh! talked about in his reference to the shape and general presence of Myleene, who was draped in silky, or sickly, orange and reading one of those scripts clearly written by no one, which favours words such as 'incomparable', 'legendary' or 'stunning'.

There was an icing-sugary whisper of a classical-music element to the ceremony, in that the music used to form the soundtrack to this shrill 'classic' exhibition of celebrity gossip, daytime television perkiness, Hollywood films, TV commercials and puffed-up West End musicals carried with it powdery hints and occasionally more concrete examples of the grace, beauty and drama of orchestral music. For those that have come to music through pop or rock, the way 'classical music' was dressed up in candelabra kitsch and shopworn corn would not have persuaded them that there was anything here for them. This was a marshmallow hybrid of the gentlest easy listening and soft, airbrushed classical that back in the twentieth century, when there were still solidly maintained and progressively idealistic critical standards, would have been viewed as at best ersatz and at worst moderately sinister. It was, for something intending to update and modernise a world viewed as over-formal, antique and elitist, extremely old-fashioned, with an allergic resistance to anything original, genuinely sensual and surprising.

For ITV, this is The Arts. For the sane rest of us, it is the pimped end of the pier. The ceremony was the bewildered if sparkly love child of the Eurovision Song Contest and the last night of the Proms, with somehow a dash of the 1970s' Miss World, Brucie's *Strictly Come Dancing*, and Harry and Meghan's wedding. The awards won by 'legendary'

John Williams for his ferociously attractive Spielberg and Harry Potter scores, leading to a rousing medley of his melodic highlights, regurgitating romantic classical music history with groomed, hammy panache, added luxurious levels of loaded entertainment energy. To some extent, as a laden buffet of the far-fetched and frivolous, it was not at all unentertaining. At times, especially when the male and hearty, lush-haired dude of waltz André Rieu went for the nerves with a style of waltz that implied it had been invented by Walt Disney, Angela Rippon and a kitten once owned by Salvador Dalí, the whole circus was like a psychedelic variety show that might have existed on the *Titanic* in the 1960s, had it not actually sunk fifty years before. Priceless indeed, as Brit Classic sponsors Mastercard like to make clear.

The ultimate commercial contemporary brilliance of the event, a ruthless brilliance inherited from the cruel tabloid world and the even crueller Simon Cowell, intended to deflect the sort of critical perspective that might question its motives, and indeed its tenuous relationship to classical music, or to any music at all, was to position various human bodies representing the imperial, valued and cherished around the budget pomp, clichéd choreography, glossy theatrics and Botoxed jolliness. As Russell Watson, with his very own brave-comeback-from-personal-disaster story, heartily boomed the boom of pure Brit boom, a slow-motion slurry of images played out behind him, sympathetically blending queenly primness, emotional flag-waving and Olympic heroism. Tears were intended to be jerked, and the stacked-up Albert Hall audience was encouraged to swell with pride, and along the way, as a bit of a bonus for those looking to capitalise on the persuasive power of pretty melodies, middlebrow classical music was saved, or at least given a patriotic purpose very useful in uncertain times.

To appear suspiciously resistant to this scheming nationalistic reduction of music to a sticky, manipulative meringue would be to question the virtues and valiant efforts of the Team GB athletes and their constant Queen. Who would want to do that, to suggest that commercially mocked-up, middle-of-the-road melodrama and an occasional pleasing burst of bright, efficient playing was being given a fine coating of synthetic sophistication and undiluted emotional power courtesy of royal jewels and sporting champions? Only the really churlish would suggest that a force field of protection, using an unlikely combination of Olympic gold medallist Bradley Wiggins's beloved pumping thighs and the Queen's candy-coloured begloved royal fingers, had been constructed to repel the feeling that what was going on was deeply unseemly.

The throwing of well-regarded, even sovereign human bodies around the mediocre, the maudlin and the meekly nostalgic, around the distillation of music into an under-baked pudding of sentiment, was perfected in the event's stunning, incomparable, instantly legendary finale. For me, and this is an entirely personal opinion that I understand is traitorous enough to see me hanged, it seemed like a burial ceremony for music itself, if only the formal putting into the ground of fifty-ish years of popular music that began with an urgent, horny Beatles bang and ended with limp, lifeless Gary Barlow OBE presenting their official jubilee anthem 'Sing' with all the dignity of three not particularly close friends assembling a set of Ikea shelves: cherub Malone, bland Barlow and allochthonous — honestly — Lord Andrew Lloyd Webber were surrounded by the Military Wives. The Wives formed a decorous, sacrosanct barrier around what, if positive discriminating critical values were still thriving and permitted, would be swiftly dismissed as on the deadly side of dreary.

Using the Wives, and elsewhere using Olympic medal winners and so-called national treasures, and various young, attractive virtuoso players glad of the attention they receive playing an instrumental non-pop music that is not the usual recipient of publicity, is a way of establishing some sort of exemption from a critical world where mediocrity and the damned obvious is properly dismissed, in a very human way, for the wider benefit of culture and society. You cannot argue with it — the general Barlowering of musical standards — for fear of offending the courageous, the imperial, the beloved and those that are gold, or upsetting those sold to us as above suspicion.

Those of you that possibly spotted me during the television broadcast, an accidental VIP sitting among the great and good of the post-reality-TV classical set, might have detected on my face a look of shock or awe, which was either because I had overdosed on Titchmarsh!, or because if this was a hint of the commercial future of the classical musical industry in this country, I realised that the end result was that the music and its spectacular history would be used only as a backdrop to show-biz shenanigans, the baking of cupcakes, the slow-motion running of Dulux dogs, the special-effect hurling of film fantasy, the knighting of

Barlow, the winning of medals, the mummifying of Katherine Jenkins and the deification of Lloyd Webber.

Or, perhaps, I sensed that the Albert Hall had hit an iceberg in the shape of the fluffy gothic set used for two songs from *Phantom of the Opera* and was slowly sinking, with the only survivors, in a cruel twist of fate, likely to be Barlow and Lloyd Webber, who would then turn the whole tragedy into a musical. And then, as if the evening hadn't already been enough of a trip that it could be bottled and sold as a hallucinogenic, André Rieu thanked Anthony Hopkins for having written him a waltz. And Anthony Hopkins himself, wearing his best Hannibal Lecter-goes-to-the-opera clothing, taking a sip of Chianti, stood up and waved.

You had to be there. Well, not necessarily.

I was not invited back, and the Classic BRIT public relations company were horrified at the application of actual criticism – or at least a surely healthy splash of suspicion – to their wedding-style ceremony, which they felt was stunning enough to surely be above such misery-guts pettiness. They complained with some force to Sinfini *for allowing the 'wrong sort' into their fantasy. I imagined I was considered the wrong sort because I worried what kind of life it would be if it was one where the last piece of music you ever heard in your life was conducted by André Rieu and written by Anthony Hopkins.*

The next ceremony I attended, on my Sinfini *mission to learn more about the rituals and habits of classical music, had at least not knocked the 'al' off 'classical': the awards handed out by a magazine very much for those in the know, for those who would have been horrified by the lack of 'al'.*

3. THE ART OF PERSEVERANCE

A few days later, the more professionally sedate and carefully modulated Gramophone Classical Music Awards, despite being held at the Dorchester, seemed set on a barely decorated desert island that the gaudy Classic BRIT vessel would steam past without having any idea that anything was happening there, give or take a couple of earnest oddballs trying to make fire by rubbing sticks together. This was the quiet, dignified approach to classical music, a modest, almost mute celebration of the music as something ghostly, intense and moving for those in the know, with their very own refined tastes, and knowledge, and understanding, with standards miraculously unspoiled by commercial pressure, fickle popular culture or temporary music fads and fashions.

This was the unhurried, apparently unworried, almost blissfully – and/or complacently – serene classical of Radio 3, as far away from the ITV/Classic FM of the BRITs as the sun is from the moon. Few outside the PR world and Decca Records seemed to belong to both the sun *and* the moon, although twenty-year-old pianist Benjamin Grosvenor crossed from one to the other, winning at the Classic BRITs because he is a quirkily cute young prodigy surrounded by a sweetened halo of hype, winning at the Gramophone because of the uncanny clarity of his playing, which seems to zip through the centuries and to the edge of the galaxy.

This is the classical world that those weaned on pop and rock would consider lacks anything sensual, spectacular or sonically adventurous enough to ever interest them. It's a remote, even cobwebbed world made up more of mysterious rules and regulations, a whole series of almost cultish and quite airless routines and habits, rather than of sound and content that reflects and makes sense of a conflicted world, ever-changing around us. Even young Benjamin, as formidably sensitive as he is, seems to have been tamed, prematurely matured, in the name of mundane commercial positioning, or poisoning, of the sort of wildness and unpredictability that might make him actually timeless enough to interest outsiders and generate genuine cultural momentum.

Oddly enough, in its quiet, studious commitment to quality of performance, and recording, and hierarchical order, despite the meticulous, almost neurotic historical breakdown of music into very specific and uncontroversial shapes, eras and genres, the Gramophone Awards are closer to the current holy grail of classical 'cool' than the Classic BRITs – because in the end, any 'cool' that classical music can carry will come not from softening, lightening, sanitising the idea of great minds using sound to reflect personal feelings about life, death, love, memory and thought, or decoratively wrapping it in trite, uplifting entertainment, or adding dance beats, rock rhythms, light shows or electronic pop static, but from the essential integrity, insight and intelligence of the music, the players, the composers and the hardcore fans. It will come from innovation, not dilution, from absorbing and replenishing avant-garde twenty-first-century impulses, not blanking them out.

It will come from the fact that what has continually driven the music forward, even as much of it has been set in stone, co-opted by the establishment and dressed in uniform, is an experimental spirit, a quest to make things different, to search out and reflect new worlds and new environments through unprecedented sounds and concepts. This experimental vision means a music that started its history before the Industrial Revolution was still alive, for all its cultural, commercial and creative distortions, in the dissolving post-industrial era, and more capable than pop and rock of extending that history into the twenty-first century.

Pop and rock have lost the formats and most of the industry that helped shove classical music into the past, and now that it is floating free of context it is threatened with losing its own unique momentum and meaning. The technology, playfulness and sonic freshness of pop may end up feeding the next period of classical development, influencing the language and, more importantly, the context without creating ugly, contrived hybrids. Pop and rock fades away as a music still developing and influencing mainstream manners, stuck forever inside a ravishing, racy fifty-year period, and becoming the past, which it can do nothing but repeat, recycle and reconsider. Classical music, meanwhile, has already spent years facing up to its apparent decline and extinction, and appears better suited to the adaptations required now that objects are being replaced by abstract experiences and the making of memories.

This liquid, experimental classical energy was inevitably far better expressed at the Gramophone Awards, even though the music it fetishises has centuries of complicated, overlapping history, and apparently belongs only to the privileged, specifically educated and middle class, while its major heroes are long dead and turned into stern, forbidding statues, its new heroes invisible and even incomprehensible, where it seems you have to dress up in the right clothing and time your applause, and it all seems to require explaining and defining in ways that feel dry, educational and over-detailed. The stubborn intelligence of Gramophone was something that might yet fight back against the glitter-ball Classic BRIT dumbness, an intelligence that is ultimately more glamorous than the shrivelling, soul-destroying small talk.

Then again, the serious, airless Gramophone method of maintaining interest in the music for a select few, and fastidiously consolidating aesthetic patterns, can be just as alienating and lacking those new necessities 'diversity' and 'inclusivity' as the bloated Classic BRIT cruise-ship approach, and it does not have loud, familiar cheerleaders like Hopkins, Titchmarsh! and Barlow on its side. As its leading critics were shown on a huge screen sensibly talking about each of the winners, demonstrating such fussy, religious care and devotion to the pieces and the performers, you just wished sometimes they would tell us what the music made them feel, why it matters so much to them, and why it actually matters in any wider cultural sense, and why anyone else outside their particular club should actually care. But of course, in this world, being seen too clearly to sell your wares is too vulgar, and too distracting.

The Classic BRIT awards were very much about a pretence of 'wish you were here' in terms of creepily making 'classic' music friendly to a popular audience; the Gramophone awards were not even pretending when they made it clear they 'did not wish you were here'. Unless, of course, you learned the language and passed various initiation ceremonies. I had a different language in mind.

I would not be invited back, which I admit says much more about me than Gramophone *magazine. I had enough time left on my* Sinfini *credentials – before I was totally found out – for one more ceremony...*

4. THE ODD ONES OUT ON TABLE 29

... another one held at the Dorchester. This is one the Royal Philharmonic Society has held since 1989 for live music-making. Some might say that my recent interest in classical music was simply so that I could gain entrance to these ceremonies which always, however thoughtful and idealistic, have the quality of relatively grand parties with added decadent elements. Drink flows, fine-ish food is served, mundanely otherworldly politicians taking an interest in the arts are entertained, senior male Radio 3 presenters host with ossified élan, much younger female assistant presenters must treat the wry, jaunty seniors as though they are as wise as Doctor Who – no senior female time-lord presenters in this particular universe – and those on the inside of the community seem in an end-of-term mood whatever the time of year, and between the lines, or between the tables, mischief is on the cards.

For a while, after I take my seat at table 29, I am given little bits of coded slang and protected inside information concerning various leading lights – the night's giver of the awards, Dame Janet Baker, with a speaking voice that makes the Queen seem common, is given the nickname Dame Granite Brown and, despite attending an event committed to new music, I'm told she loathes anything new, which is approximately anything in the last hundred years. Later, someone else will indignantly contradict this view, celebrate her style and appetite for the new, but tell me that the very fine Britten Ensemble is apparently affectionately known as the Britney. My supply of gossip about how the classical community pricks possible internal pomposity runs dry when it becomes clear I am something of an outsider – not from round these parts – worse than that, a journalist, who might pass on this information to the outside world. As if.

Generally, the RPS Awards are, on the grading table of seriousness and good intentions, ranked pretty high – this is not for the classical music as promoted by the Classic BRIT Awards in a style that makes Baz Luhrmann appear demure – and at times it grazes an even higher brow than the Gramophone awards. The RPS Awards reflect the belief system of a society that has been in existence since 1813, and that has aged without losing its conscientious faith in music as definitely a romantic, enlightening force that, without making it too scarily blatant, fights ugliness with beauty and ordinariness with the uncanny.

They prefer to give awards and prizes to community endeavour and pioneering ventures, rather than mocked-up and Botoxed virtuosos and scrubbed-up pop acts looking for a little attention because they can't get any in their own world. Classic FM – a sort of pop act – does win an RPS award, which disconcerts me, as their method of shining light onto classical music appears to be to drain it of all meaning, mystery and intricacy, and carefully position it close to the current beige and cushioned cultural space occupied by the Chelsea Flower Show, baking and sewing programmes, and dreamy crime programmes sponsored by Viking River Cruises.

Classic FM forensically removes the guts of classical music, transforming it into a kind of fragrant security blanket, rips great pieces of music out of context and history, and utilises presenters oozing with courtesy who are like dentists, soothingly telling you that there will be no pain, and everything will be all right. Perhaps the fact they won an award for creative communication — 'for broadening the reach of classical music' — is a little ambiguous, as they are indeed very creative in successfully establishing a recognisable contemporary brand while playing music that the popular audience is mostly indifferent towards. Their award, though, did look a little 'pop' next to other awards, but that, again, is probably part of their creativity, that they can serenely flow between the manipulative vulgarity of the Classic BRITs and the more cultivated RPS, at ease with both.

The RPS was conceived to promote performance of what was once almost too practically simply called 'instrumental music' in the years before the term became problematically fixed as 'classical' and before there were permanent London orchestras or any regular series of instrumental performances. Its first concert featured performances of symphonies by Haydn and Beethoven. Four years later, it requested a new symphony from Beethoven after ill health forced him to turn down an invitation to come to London and visit the society. Completed in 1824, the symphony turned out to be his Ninth, the Choral, his final one, initially thought of by some critics to be cryptic and inelegant, in time so loved, well known and packed with generalised uplifting glory it would become adopted as an anthem by national, ideological and commercial brands wanting some inspiring sophisticated gloss. On the stage as the awards are handed out, there is a very white bust of the stern and immortal Beethoven in prime position, just to remind everyone that the RPS was founded on the ability to spot and nurture the very best.

A society that more or less begins with such a legendary hit inevitably gains the kind of momentum that means that 200 years later, it is still operating, commissioning, handing out awards, encouraging adventurous projects, searching out unlikely ambition and negotiating its place in a world that is now very definitely 'classical', to the extent of being both firmly established and highly polished, and fraught with aesthetic, cultural and economic problems. In a world that now has so much weighty past, it is not clear what its future actually is, other than more of the same.

Sometimes that more of the same might be given a twist of difference by being from unexpected areas of the world — the RPS handed out five International Awards to organisations and orchestras from around the world committed to the idea of classical music as vital and life-changing, including Rosemary Nalden, creator of the Buskaid Soweto String Project, Armand Diagenda, who has built out of nothing and nowhere a symphony orchestra in Kinshasha, and Dr Ahmad Sarmast, who has created the Afghanistan National Institute of Music. Seeing Wagner played in Africa and J. S. Bach in Kabul is a little like finding the apple on the moon Stockhausen once talked about while describing his *Gesang der Jünglinge*, although it's a shame these orchestras inherit the idea that to perform classical music means to dress up in starched evening clothes. True forward momentum might occur when music originally composed in these places adds uncorrupted local atmosphere to European formality and produces a new, potentially startling dynamic; at the moment it seems to be faintly patronising, with traces even of old-fashioned imperialism, to suggest that salvation in these parts of the world might emerge through the canonical sounds of Western privilege.

I found myself – perhaps viewed under the circumstances as some sort of maverick – sitting at a table that contained the composers Thomas Adès, Gerald Barry and Oliver Knussen, one of the greatest of the great under-cherished modern British composers, sacrificing a lot of potential visibility for his music through his conducting, curating and generous teaching. His giant presence at the table made me even more ashamed than usual of an idiotic modern media landscape that pays constant attention to the lacklustre entertainment contrivances of Simon Cowell rather than the lively mind and musical language of Knussen, who should be definitively sealed into the cultural landscape as a modern master, constantly called upon to guide us, and disturb us, with his thoughts and memories about music, life, love – anything, really.

If you know no Knussen, and need to know where to start, as is often the case with such an amount of music, challenging but always sublimely melody-conscious, start as I did, with his mercurial *Scriabin Settings*, and then move among everything to his *Ophelia Dances*, written when he was twenty-three, to *Songs Without Voices*, to *Sonya's Lullaby*, Cantata for Oboe and String Trio, *Two Organa*, the *Whitman Settings*, his Second and Third Symphonies, and to his Violin Concerto, which is on an album, *Autumnal*, also featuring the exquisitely heartbroken yet rousing *Requiem: Songs for Sue*, written after the death of his wife.

For me, still tentatively venturing, fairly blinkered, into the vast, dense forest of classical music, with that epic, mysterious expanse of deep, deep still water at the centre of the woods, and a horizon viewed through the trees that is constantly changing shape, sitting at this table was even more intimidating to me than other awards events, where I have sat next to Helen Mirren – and was told to entertain her so that she did not leave the ceremony after twenty minutes, because she usually got bored – and Doris Lessing – for whom a discussion of suicide was small talk.

Adès was in playful, explicitly off-duty mood on the other side of the table from me, joshing with favourite chum Barry, who won an award for large-scale composition with his delectably demented opera *The Importance of Being Earnest*. Other awards included Rebecca Scales winning for Chamber-Scale Composition, New Music 20x12 for Concert Series, the Heath Quartet winning for Young Artists, Sarah Connolly for Singer, and the Proper Job Theatre Company and Scunthorpe Co-operative Junior Choir for Learning and Participation, their deliriously received award somehow even further away from Classic FM than the one the Birmingham Opera Company deservedly won for their cosmically madcap performance of Stockhausen's *Mittwoch aus Licht*, with its notorious *Helicopter Quartet* scene.

Adès would occasionally and abruptly lock on to a piece of music as it was played before or after an award was handed out in a way that was more electrically focused than anything I have ever seen, as though he was seeing, tasting and feeling music as much as hearing it, and in just a second would work out its value and precision, or lack of value and precision. His connection to music was highly charged, as though he was on high alert that the difference between pain and pleasure was tiny, and at any moment he might slip from feeling bliss to feeling agony. His mentor Knussen was less bothered, almost acting as though he was not present at anything to do with music, more some sort of duty, a form of detention that he could just about deal with as long as he didn't have to write out a hundred times the line: 'It is one of the great weaknesses of criticism that it tends to treat everything as of equal importance and is obliged to use the same language for both the trivial and the significant.'

Knussen, in sweater and slacks, broke the so-called elegant evening dress code on every single level imaginable, plumping for comfort rather than formality, looking every massive, bearded Game of Thrones inch the inspired odd one out – a knight in rusty armour – on a night when everyone tried to look comfortable hiding behind the general stuffy respectability of the occasion, and he seemed to be just about holding in check sheer outrage with the bow-tied unnaturalness of everything and its disconnection from the ultimate greater point of the music.

At one stage, a glass of red wine was knocked over in front of him, and the wine stain that Pollock-splattered the white tablecloth seemed to represent the explosive state of his brain that for the moment, being as reluctantly polite as possible, he was keeping under control. Although he might be termed a revolutionary with possibly abusive intent, to the point of extreme rapturous grace, he seemed in the mood to deny such an allegiance, at least until he was outside the heavy polished doors of the damned Dorchester.

In my defence, as much as I confess I enjoyed the hospitality – and in the interests of openness admit I had four glasses of red wine – I viewed that year's ceremony as not so much pleasure and occasional pain, but further research into the eternal enigma of where classical music begins and ends, so that perhaps one day I could have a conversation with Ollie, as I now knew him, about other things than the wait for food and the need for a drink. I could one day communicate with Adès above and beyond a few half-hearted grins and bored shrugs across the table and tell you more about him than that he seemed very pleased with his goody bag stuffed with the BBC guide to the Proms and various shampoos, lotions and moisturisers, and particularly cheered when a winner thanked their mum. He left in the company of those who had given me a little insider's insight into the quirks of the classical community, and naturally, not being from these parts, I was not invited. I remained on my own.

The society's history does help supply one way of forming an elevated history of classical music. Other works the society has commissioned during its 200 years, apart from Beethoven's Ninth, can be helpful tunnels into classical musical history for anyone looking for unexpected ways in.

MY TOP ELEVEN OF WORKS COMMISSIONED BY OR DEDICATED TO THE RPS WOULD BE:

1. Neglected romantic Louis Spohr's 1819 Grand Concert Overture in F major, which has taken me to Hilary Hahn's performance of one of his eighteen violin concertos, No. 8, his intensely graceful piano sonatas, which somehow sound less anachronistic than many

young contemporary composers angered or frustrated by the idea of melody, to the violin chinrest, which he invented, and to the notion of the conductor's baton, which he was one of the first to use.

2. Philharmonic Society member Vincent Novello's dramatic cantata *Rosalba*. Novello followed and established many of the society's basic tenets, single-mindedly pursuing musical knowledge as a teacher, editor and music publisher.

3. Saint-Saëns' 1886 Symphony No. 3, dedicated to Liszt, which he wrote as a summary of his career, combining orchestra and pipe organ, in a good way as merrily and sometimes murderously mad as a symphony can get, a big part of the *Babe* film, and possibly the missing link, because there has to be one, and someone has to say there is, between Beethoven and Pink Floyd's *Atom Heart Mother*.

4. Dvořák's 1896 five *Biblical Songs* with orchestra – virtually his last set of songs, the sound of grief, written over a three-week period while in America on hearing about the death of a friend and also of Tchaikovsky and the mortal illness of his seventy-nine-year-old father. He was perhaps feeling homesick and constructing a new American music by reimagining Negro spirituals and Native American rhythm, so that solemn, sometimes apocalyptic Catholic churchiness inherited from Europe and his swept-up melancholy Czech folksiness is fused with his freshly coalescing New World discoveries, introducing warmth into austere ritual.

5. Alan Rawsthorne's First Symphony in 1950 – the romantic tradition of symphony arriving later in Britain than anywhere else – for fans of the red, white and blue Britain of Elgar, Vaughan Williams and Walton, but also taking you to the more shadowy, monochrome Britain of Maxwell Davies and Tippett, and wherever next, faced with whatever next.

6. Vaughan Williams's final symphony, his ninth, joining Beethoven, Mahler and Bruckner on that number, dedicated to the RPS, definitely for lovers of the flugelhorn, first performed at an RPS concert in 1958 conducted by Malcolm Sargent, four months before Vaughan Williams's death at eighty-five, an ominous, powerful symphony that confidently, even cosmically, resists any approaching darkness. The London Philharmonic, conducted by Adrian Boult, were scheduled to record it on what turned out to be the day Vaughan Williams died, and went ahead with the session six hours after his death.

7. William Walton's *Variations on a Theme by Hindemith*, based on a rarely heard cello concerto by Paul Hindemith, commissioned to celebrate the RPS's 150th anniversary in March 1963, a lovely, loving tribute by Walton to his friend and colleague, who played the first performance of Walton's 1929 Viola Concerto.

8. Lutosławski's 1970 epic, extraordinary Cello Concerto, where the traditional concerto relationship between featured instrument and orchestra is channelled via controlled Cageian intervention into specific Cold War-era tension between the heroic cello as freedom-seeking individual and the orchestra and conductor as a strict, authoritarian society troubled by their own secret doubts.

9. Malcolm Arnold's 1988 (Shakespearean) Cello Concerto, written for Julian Lloyd Webber, uneasy easy listening, terse yet congenial.

10. Robert Saxton's 1991 *Paraphrase on Mozart's Idomeneo*, sixteen uncompromising miniature movements for wind octet distantly ghosting Mozart's first mature opera, an experimentally dramatic refraction of experimental drama.

11. Mark-Anthony Turnage's *Two Baudelaire Songs* for soprano and seven instruments, written in 2003–4, with singer Sally Matthews, bittersweetly dipping back into Baudelaire's time, filtered through Turnage's interpretation of all that has happened in subsequent modern adjustments to Baudelaire's time. Looking backwards, but also looking in the mirror, within a hall of mirrors.

The RPS does reflect, without it seeming unwieldy and overwhelming, a classical history that has moved from the unstable passions of Beethoven to the unstable passions of Turnage, via the breaking down of tonality at the beginning of the twentieth century, and the worship, concussion, hangover, resistance and general reconditioning that followed, and also a world veering away from the imagined and unimaginable future, where history is now as much present – through museums, anniversaries, worship, memorial series, revivals, nostalgia, internet babble – as the present; in fact, is really the essence of the present. The current trend to plunder history in case it all goes missing in a future constantly receding before us as computers take over reality definitely helps the history of classical music, which has always survived radical historical changes, often being the key expression of those changes, with a role now of connecting with the greatness of the past, and reinvigorating it without being overwhelmed.

After the ceremony was all over, with photos taken, cliques formed and reformed ready to head off into the inviting London night, Ollie admitted to me he never usually attended such events – maybe if he won something he'd turn up, and it says something about the RPS that he has won one of their awards, but he felt awkward and out of place in the surroundings. 'Although,' he reflected on this particular ceremony – fronted by this particular society, dedicated to resist, where possible, the insidious colonising magnetism of the miserable middle-of-the-road – with something sad, lonely, but defiant and wise on his mind that might well make it into a composition, 'on the whole, it is a good thing.' With that he sauntered off, presumably back deep into the boundless forest, a long way from Park Lane, and to his house near Ravel's, Britten's and Webern's on the very edge of the dark, still waters.

My appearance in public debates as the token 'youngish' representative of the 'rock' world continued, with various appearances on radio and at conferences whenever there was a need to explore a wider, more inclusive social role and a possible wider and, of course, younger audience for classical music and its component parts. It seemed to be taken for granted there was a reason why classical music needed to reach a younger, more diverse audience – to keep the form and the history alive, to give marginalised communities access to something that was ungenerously monopolised by the middle and upper classes, to open up opportunities for those that felt, quite rightly, that they didn't belong. More talk seemed to be one way for a solution to be reached about how to achieve this crossover. This usually skirted around the edges, or plunged right into the deep end, which can actually be very shallow, of marketing speak.

There was also, as far as I could see, a real chance, however positive and optimistic – even desperate – the intentions, that this crossover was never going to happen. It never could happen; the world doesn't work like that, as much as the chatter of social media has made such changes seem easy enough. As though all it takes is one fine podcast and a dashing hashtag.

The good intentions, the fact these debates were happening, occasional attempts to mix one world with another, mostly seemed to draw attention to the chasm between one world and the other, with the only real attempts to bridge it involving the loss of the 'al' and the presentation of classical music as some kind of equivalent of a diet that was good for your soul in the way that a high-fibre, low-sugar diet was good for your heart. In the middle of this there was an occasional pained, or simply puzzled, cry of 'what the hell were we going to do about opera?', which was, depending on your point of view, either one of the wonders of the world or as eccentrically outdated as a penny-farthing.

With opera it appeared that any crossover was all going in one direction – the classical music media and institutions reaching out to those who usually expressed no interest, permanently searching for ways to make it more accessible to them. I could see another way that the form might be kept alive, how it might still exist, even thrive, in the future, but not necessarily because it was good for you or because it was packed with fancy, to the point of holy, melodies. The way to widen its appeal was for it to seem part of everything, not set somewhere else, and my approach to this was not to talk about it as something esoteric that needed protection or as something warped that needed straightening, and certainly not as something old-fashioned that needed new branding. I wasn't necessarily bringing the expected rock 'n' roll to the discussions I was being invited to – I was bringing rock 'n' roll writing, which, no longer in its heyday, was also needing a little helping hand. If opera needed saving, so did my kind of writing and thinking about music, which to the non-believer would seem as far-fetched, eccentric and irrelevant as opera.

Now that reality had been shaken to the core by the Pandora's box of the internet, by a general attack on the nature of truth and the value of anything, everyone was living in crazy town, with their own territory to defend, and their own issues to question. I had my way of getting through. Sometimes I could talk about it live on the radio, as though there actually was a solution and one way to find it was to take part in debates, which started to have their own dangers.

5. THE CRITIC AS OPERA DIVA

Opera. Radio 3. Glyndebourne. Debate: does opera matter? What is the future for opera? Still there?

The problem with the word 'opera' is that even if you have never seen or heard one – and in fact have only come across it through the tatty realm of Simon Cowell and his camp, rich-man's fascination with its sensual glamour and mystique – you will have a very definite opinion about what it is, and why it is not for you. Expensive, stuffy, kitsch, snobby, bloated, fancy... old. We're fifty years after aesthetic autocrat Pierre Boulez proposed that the correct response to the perceived ossification of opera was to 'blow the opera houses up', but then he didn't quite mean that, only that he too, with his usual irreverence, was trying to work out what to do with it, how to modernise it, keeping the usual repertoire, but developing new ways to present new forms. Nothing changes, including the desire to change.

Opera is one of those words that contains so much historical and symbolic weight and prejudice that you have to clamber through dense, thorny tangles before you even get to what it might actually be, and if there is anything really left, other than it being a segregated leisure pursuit for the entitled.

First of all, on my Glyndebourne day, a trip to the world-famous annual opera festival in a fine, unhurried part of England, which is part work, part dream, part detour into how the other half, well, 1 per cent live, I take part in a live mid-morning Radio 3 debate on the programme *Music Matters* about the relevance of opera. Relevance to whom? may well be the question – for those to whom it is relevant, it is extremely relevant; for others, it is as relevant as needlepoint.

For the debate, I am surrounded by believers on the panel and believers in the audience, and I am worried that if I bring with me the full dynamics of my wariness about the current state of opera – as an evolving art form, if not a business, an epic token of civic pride, or a backdrop for architecture and morality – I will be more or less strolling into a church during Sunday service and shouting at the top of my voice that God does not exist. Or I will be telling wide-eyed young children on Christmas morning that there is no such thing as Santa. Worse, I will be attending a meeting of blinkered extremists clinging to their psyched-up, fucked-up fairy tales for meaning and purpose, and pulling apart the fragile basis of existence for those who consider opera the sublime, sacrosanct peak of all musical and artistic enterprise.

The angry cult followers carrying torches and expressing utter contempt for my thuggish monstrosity will perhaps turn on me, and send me into cold, dark exile where I will be forced to appreciate the enduring wonders of their faith. I can only return when I can sing

something fiendishly difficult that requires me to rattle off nine high
Cs and a couple of two-octave leaps while wearing heavy headgear the
size of a small car and walking a flaming tightrope. It could be the
beginning of an opera.

Or the beginning of a reality show. On the panel of articulate, defiant
opera guardians slickly hosted by the always publicly confident Petroc
Trelawny there is the hearty and venerable northern knighted bass (Sir
John Tomlinson); the open-minded artistic director of the Danish
National Opera (Annilese Miskimmon), committed to promoting
opera as a modern, democratic and thriving artistic endeavour; the
measured, eminently reasonable representative of the Glyndebourne
management (David Pickard); the feisty, challenging founder of
a country-house opera season that is perhaps dreamier and more
luxurious than Glyndebourne (Wasfi Kani); and austere, unoperatic
me, the awkward, ignorant tin-eared outsider, representing the voice
of the suspicious, indifferent people who see opera as an indulgence
for the wealthy, and/or a minority sport with arcane rules, and/or pure
escapism for spoilt snobs and posh nerds, and/or sanctioned acid trips
for the establishment, and/or a form of psychotherapy for those in the
middle of a family feud or perhaps requiring lessons in fidelity, and/or
an ornate embodiment of the ever-rigid class system keen on protecting
its privilege. If this is a reality show, I am the favourite to be voted out
first, complete with 'Poisonous Paul' nickname, and there is a hum of
suspicious nervousness about my position from the others. What nasty
things am I going to say?

I am not actually against opera. I don't think of it as being dead,
any more or less than traditional politics, twentieth-century cinema,
scheduled television, department stores, print journalism or pop music
is dead. There are problems, but only the kind of problems all of us face
as the essential structure of reality changes to accommodate the new
spaces and circumstances being injected into our minds and packed into
regularly delivered gift boxes by the technological and communication
consequences of the computer and its damaged soul, the internet.

Opera is, perhaps, undead, and this is something that is making me
appreciate its twisted, decayed, ultimately perplexing beauty. It wasted
away years ago in terms of where the rest of the world was, technologically,
artistically and culturally, and the more accessible, crowd-pleasing
parts fell off and grew into The Musical, ripe melody and unabashed

sentiment in over-friendly hyperdrive, and the most melodramatic and raunchy storylines escaped into the extreme caricatures of everyday life that are television soap operas. But it kept going, in a weirdly shaped afterlife, where it was given financial and critical life support by those who consider it the clearest symbol of a civilised society and by those who think that inside the exquisitely layered fairy tales, dazzling showpieces, tongue-twisting language, acrobatic arias, heartbreaking laments and metaphorically deliberate over-the-top-ness there is the most exquisite theatrical balance of music's heady abstractions and the power of the visual imagination.

I was once a devout atheist, but now I am more leaving behind an agnostic state and heading optimistically into the misty, Delphic opera country, where there be daft and divine stories so lavishly told and so clearly indestructible that in a Shakespearean sense — with complex life stories being packed into three-minute songs, moments of mischief transformed into explosive excess — there must be something to it other than it being a protected privilege for the accursed self-serving high and mighty. Perhaps I am battering past the word, the image, the offensive luxury status because I have decided that opera is one of those things so much in opposition to a world squeezed into the sense and moral fibre-shredding shape of Twitter and the light-headed, picture-book world of Instagram that it must actually be, behind the bow ties, picnics, costumes and nineteenth-century rituals, a lonesome, lingering sign of intellectual life.

I am beginning to fancy the insular extremist elements, the convoluted belief system, the array of secret lovers, silver-tongued heroes, dark, brooding anti-heroes and untameable, spirited heroines, perhaps because I am reaching the correct stage in life. The abyss can be spotted a little too closely at the edge of my vision, and sometimes right in the damned centre, and great opera never fails to take into account that for all the life and love, wit and whimsy, dexterity and transcendence, always there is death, and more death, and dreams beyond death, transformed into the most perfectly played death scenes, featuring a considerable expression of deep sadness, moist memories and drawn-out tender reflection on the lover being left behind. Opera is a golden, temporary production straining to the limit to suggest there is a light at the end of the tunnel of life's miseries even as it knows there is no such thing; even when there is no hope, the sheer virtuoso of the performers and performances demonstrates how there must always be hope. Out of such intentions bizarre legends are created.

The panel quickly make their case, which as usual involves the believers becoming very defensive, and amazed that their world, which they love and cherish because it is so full of life, conflict and history and ingenious, intensely felt ways of explaining the fun and games of existence, the abuse of power and the power of love, is considered on the outside so eccentric, impractical and unhinged. The outside actually dwarfs their country, which is really a small island on the edges of the world that is perhaps about to fall off the planet altogether, and every so often make spectacular, ghostly reappearances. This also sounds like the beginning of an opera.

Just in case I'm challenged, and look a little off the pace, I've done some research. I'm ready to express an outline of some knowledge about the late sixteenth-century Renaissance, Italian beginnings of the opera concept as part of a general return to classical values. It travelled to other countries via the mind of Mozart, to the grand opera of France and the Wagner music dramas from a chest-pumping dream of Germany, but it would essentially remain an Italian concept, from the early inventions of Monteverdi via Rossini and Verdi to the peak romantic virtues of Puccini, the majority of the mainstream repertoire from the 1780s of Mozart to the 1924 death of Puccini hitting grandiose heights with the ultimate might of Wagner.

I can talk at length about Debussy's *Pelléas et Mélisande*, the perfect opera for the non-opera lover, how it exists within itself as a great unclassified musical fantasy that just happens to tell a story using words and extreme emotion, and which exists both as an extension of the spectacular marvels of Wagner and as an indirect antidote to its theatrical grandiosity, but which finally occupies a place all of its own. The Debussy opera suggested a future for the form, as opposed to it staying where it reached with Mozart, Wagner and Puccini, and then cruising into a succession of nostalgic or contemporary settings of pretty much the same beloved works.

There's no time for history, or any sort of knowledge, deeply felt or lightly learned. After an inevitably rushed forty-five minutes of live talk radio, where the panel and host evaluate the position of opera in a cruel, indifferent world, the conclusions are pretty much the conclusions that would have been reached before our discussion. Opera is in itself a fantastic way of manifesting the fantastic and features the finest works by some of the finest composers, but it has an image problem. The industry is in crisis. The halls, boards, institutions and management structures are falling in battle, many fatally wounded. There are millions of people who love it. Any new season premiering at La Scala in Milan will make CNN as though it is a close show-business relation of Hollywood. On the other hand, subscribers are dwindling. But then cinema showings to enthusiastic packed audiences seem to suggest it is more popular than ever, and there are plenty of podcasts that appear to bring the idea up to date, if only because anything that has a podcast devoted to it must therefore be of interest to the modern world – as opposed to it being a sign that it is actually a hobby that diehards love to tell others must be the centre of the universe because it is the centre of their universe.

It is too expensive. It is not as elitist as it seems. The media get it wrong and always paint it as being only for the wealthy and/or cognisant. It needs to get a younger audience, and yet, like fine wine, luxury cruises, Agatha Christie, double glazing and financially planning for death, it is not something the young necessarily want or need, especially now that they have so many distractions, many of which supply the senses with as much pleasure, philosophy, visual enchantment, opulence and opportunities to dress up and hang out in the open air as opera. Fans of the HBO psychodrama *True Detective* will suggest it was more seriously operatic than any opera, and then there's *Game of Thrones*, the fall of Neymar and Katie Price, the news coverage of Pistorius, Savile and Putin, the madness of Trump, the madness of his triumph, and the marriages of Kim and Kanye and Harry and Meghan. Anyone who has attended a synthetically deranged, mechanically precise neo-operatic Deadmau5 performance where the relentless, history-splitting beat goes higher and higher, louder and louder, featuring climax after climax, might wonder if that is what a modern Mozart might be actually doing. Everyday seems as preposterous and melodramatic as opera, so who needs the unreal thing.

For me, the amount of commitment to designing the sets has not been replicated by the attention paid to the sound and performance of the music itself, and the setting and style of the voices, which are often a barrier to entry for those who love voices but are used to them being amplified. As with most classical music, the insider anxiety that modernisation will warp the essence of the form into something unrecognisable means that it is an authoritarian, historical authenticity that is deemed more important than intelligent, sensitive adaptation.

Opera became the most popular form of musical theatre when watered down and renamed as The Musical, inheriting many of the same impulses and narrative eccentricities. The Musical achieved its popular success by accepting that singers who sound like they are from the eighteenth century sound unappealing and hammy, if not actually scary, to music listeners who are used to hearing the voice treated, controlled and electrified. Recorded music perversely created a natural, human sound; to the outsider, the unfiltered, microphone-free opera singer can sound totally unnatural, somewhere between a neutered monster and a distressed fairy. Surely no human beings should be capable of making such a sound that is either a supreme, miraculous thing, or a creepy, extremely dated one. The sensational, or deeply strange, sound, the immense repositioning of vocal potential, takes the sort of getting used to, of understanding and fully appreciating, that few potential fans have the time for.

Opera uses high-tech sets, flash scenery and ostentatious design in attempts to keep it up to date, which can often swamp the protected authentic art and organic singing and contributes to the notion that opera is a plush, over-garnished folly. Avant-garde design, experimental concepts and innovative, minimalist settings have created the illusion that opera can have a contemporary energy, but ultimately it remains inside a bubble; of the world, but, however powerful and sophisticated the meaning and message, set apart from it, like first-class air travel, red-carpet events and royal boxes.

Any musical modernisation of the form does not appeal to the hardcore loyalists. A mention of amplification, or a replacement of all those willing, skilful bodies in the orchestra with backing tracks, is the equivalent of showing a crucifix to a vampire. The loyalists adore the sacred texts, the magical, canonical classics, the supernatural escapades, the endless prevailing, the tearful reconciliations, the living for art, the living for love, the singing for dear life, the familiar fables, myths and yarns, the mental and sentimental plots, the psychological struggles, the suspense and dread, the battle between good and evil, the old-as-time moral pronouncements. They consider the glittery, singsong musical, however serious and historical, or even however *Hamilton* and historical, too much a thick, tarted-up betrayal, and the cryptic postmodern opera too much an ordeal, possibly mocking the tradition rather than honouring it.

I am, though, prepared to accept the panel's view that it is definitely not an archaic sport for the few, a premium art for the pampered, and it has a rich, spellbinding repertoire that can change its shape to suit whatever time and situation it finds itself in. I accept their complaints that if opera was as closed off, cold-blooded and exclusive as it is generally perceived, they would not feel comfortable working there. Then I head off for an afternoon at Glyndebourne that will culminate in an opera, Tchaikovsky's highly favoured, and highly flavoured, late nineteenth-century *Eugene Onegin*. This is where things get really weird. The plot thickens. The haunting begins. Reality bends. I fall asleep a thousand times and always wake up somewhere else from where I fell asleep.

Slowly, the audience, like ghosts, descend on the gorgeous grounds, set among classic, timeless English hills, themselves apparently murmuring private melodies, and arrange themselves around the theatre itself, which seems sealed off from the effects of weather and decay. They carry picnic baskets, champagne bottles and blankets, and are dressed as though for a high-society wedding. I am one of very few males not wearing a bow tie and my shoes, though from the deluxe part of a shoe shop, look suspiciously like the sort of trainers that not so long ago barred my entry from certain nightclubs, despite their provenance. I don't know what I was thinking. I am making it too clear that I am not from round here.

The opera is the centre of a very pleasant day out, somewhere between the Ascot races and a drive to a nice country pub, but perhaps also here is a world where what is being created are the rare conditions required to engage with the extraordinary entertainment that an opera is. Here is an imaginary kingdom being created, however full of cliché, in order to produce the tunnel through which you fall in order to reach the imaginary sphere of the opera.

This is why the buildings in which operas are mostly played out are either radically new, requiring immense patronage and experimental architectural play, or extremely, solidly old and grand, the illustrious and/or floating surroundings emphasised through outlandish costume and even more outlandish wealth, the rituals and a hallucinatory remoteness stubbornly maintained. All this is what protects and sustains the illusory quality – it is a virtual reality, in fact, which is, as I try to say during my little solo moment in the *Music Matters* debate, where the future of opera might lie, its innate virtual reality merging with the virtual reality that will increasingly transmit entertainment and pleasure directly into an individual's personal space, even directly into their mind.

Opera is old, established, impenetrable, but it is also made up of ravishing, flexible components that can easily translate into a shape-shifting, streaming, post-reality world craving exceptional image-based novelty. (In the reality-show version of the panel, this is where I was voted off the show.) At one panel debate discussing similar issues at the Royal Opera House – the heart of matters – I extended my 'future of opera!' solo a little too enthusiastically. This audience was largely made up of ROH subscribers possibly imagining they were in for a pleasant evening uncritically revelling in the delights of their favourite pastime, despite the panel title making it clear this was a debate about, yes, 'relevance'.

I entered the realms of talking about plugging the essence of opera's captivating titillations into the brain itself, thus bypassing the whole expensive, controversial, increasingly impractical rigmarole of theatre, sponsorship, etiquette, costume, stage sets and so on. I pushed forward further into what, for me, were proposals not necessarily meant to be grounded in current realities but exploring the frontiers of where opera might be in a century, after surviving against the odds for at least a couple of centuries. I imagined the use of new entertainment technology becoming an additional part of the basic multimedia opera synthesis of drama, voice, orchestral music, dance, light and design, extending its lifespan and rewiring the traditions and the classics, taking the experience deep into the twenty-first century.

I am riffing off something that maverick broadcaster, critic, musician, genius, philosopher and tremendous pianist Glenn Gould said not long after his scandalous retirement from public performance in 1964 – predicting that 'the public concert as we know it today would no longer exist a century hence' and that it would be entirely taken over by electronic media. As his Canadian friend and ally Marshall McLuhan had established, the electronic media would increasingly convey the message – all messages, including opera.

Out of the dark of the audience I became aware of someone slow handclapping. Feeling more provocative than usual, being inside the British home of opera, with the outrage of a great tenor having a problem with an incestuous troublemaking member of his family, I asked if that slow handclap was for me? A voice boomed back at me with a baritone contempt, 'Why don't you just shut up?' It was not the first time I had heard these words.

I defended myself with considerable vigour, as did the man with the voice, and we argued for a few minutes, to the point where it was almost time to set the date for a duel. I swear the women in the audience started to sing some sort of war cry. Some other audience members, faced with my villainous double-dealing, clearly felt that God had abandoned them in their hour of need. Dry ice swirled. Special effects were switched on.

Eventually the dispute spluttered to an end, not least because my opponent started to cough a little too excessively, as if he was preparing for his solo. It was only at the end of the talk, when the lights came on and the dry ice dwindled, that I realised I had been arguing with a frail older man, possibly in his late eighties, who was definitely in a wheelchair.

He was wheeled out by his stoical wife, also in her eighties, still smarting at my dragon-breathing contemplations of a virtual future for opera – all he wanted for that future was the same classic operas, the same great singing, the same pantomime costumes, the same torment and delight, the same frivolities and intoxications, the sort of no-nonsense sets he was used to and of course The Tunes. The Tunes! He still seemed quite animated, with quite a few operas left in him, so luckily our disagreement had not turned into a death scene and a journey to heaven straight out of Wagner.

At Glyndebourne, as is the tradition, the opera will start around five in the afternoon, so that even with long intervals it is still finished in time for those who need to get the last train back to London. It is all very civilised, and people are certainly looked after better than they are at a rock concert, where how you get there and get home is entirely your business, and your hard, plastic seats are at least an improvement on sitting on the floor. One of the Glyndebourne intervals is long enough – ninety minutes – for dinner, or in my case recovery from shock, so that there is a long, long break after the famous duel scene. I had a Kit-Kat. When we come back to the opera, many years have passed in the story, and it feels like they actually have.

I have been given my ticket free, and only notice when I take it out to enter the theatre that it would have cost me over £200. The price does not matter, to some extent, in a world where, as someone in the *Music Matters* audience pointed out, it costs that kind of money to see Monty Python or the Rolling Stones – with plastic seats – with their own raging against the dying of the light. That's a simple matter of the world as it is, where some have, and many do not, but that does not mean things grind to a halt as though that alone would equalise matters. Combined with everything else, the ticket price does make the experience take on the quality of something non-musical and definitely non-artistic. It puts proceedings into another zone of luxury.

It makes me realise that in any properly established new world there should be different sorts of categories, and something like this should not really be reviewed or covered as 'music' but something else. The Glyndebourne experience perhaps comes under the heading 'escape' or 'relief' or 'trip'. A massage for the soul. Mourning, perhaps. Stimulation as a relaxation. In the middle of all the ossification and regimentation, there is a lightly deep and transfixing tragi-manic romantic opera featuring vivid star turns, an elegant, clear-cut production, a powerful orchestra, a scrupulous, masterful conductor, masses of alert, skilled singers, mannered choreography, dancers, set designs, lights, a great use of the opening and shutting of curtains, so that mere material has personality, all of which combines to become a spellbinding and often preposterous work of art that is both from the freakishly freaky past and the psychedelically other.

There is no sense of the knife edge that the singing and the music is balanced on because it is presented so flawlessly; the fact that at any given moment it might all collapse is never apparent, which is part of the appeal of these huge spectacles that are like seeing the Eiffel Tower actually being built in front of your eyes and then somehow that being done in collaboration with the writing of a great novel.

Because it is Tchaikovsky, there is a lot of sweetness and whipped cream, and occasional enlivening tartness, and a delirious reflection of the delights, disasters and queerness of love. There is also the way that this sort of seductive, momentous musical theatre expresses thoughts about how sinuously the mind works and deals with the circuitous pressures and preciousness of reality. It is as though the invention of opera was, in part, imagining what heaven might be like, as an almost hysterical abstraction of our reality, as an illumination of the light of life amidst all the surrounding cosmic darkness, and obviously what is consoling, inspiring heaven for some is hell and hogwash for others.

If you find it heaven, you are very lucky. During the famous Letter Scene, Tatiana, the lover callously rejected by the selfish Eugene, pours her feelings of love into a letter as only a soprano in such a situation can, which of course becomes an aria from the verge of death: 'Let me die, but first...' Around me, it seems, worryingly, that many of the audience have stopped breathing themselves. It is a combination of a sweet little death, tears and emotional satisfaction that perhaps only opera can provide, certainly so sumptuously.

But the opera is only part of the event, and the rest of the proceedings, the hanging out, the eating, the country air, the coach parties, the chauffeured cars, the dinner jackets, the gowns, the Marks & Spencer food, the weather — cloudy, with sunny intervals and light rain — the eighty-year history of Glyndebourne, the superlative ease of everything, make it all whole, and complete the dream/nightmare.

What does happen to me, after it is all over, always happens when I see an opera as romantically luscious and death-accepting/defying as this one: they stay in my mind, infecting my memory and imagination in all sorts of ways, and will do for ever. So that's what life — and death — is all about!

At the hard centre of all the palaver, and all the distractions, all the things that have preserved the tradition — the costume parade, the money involved, the sedate setting, the re-creation of nineteenth-century gaiety and grimness, the apparent utter lack of anything subversive or mind-altering, the apparent minimum-wage secondary importance of the hard-working musicians tucked under the stage in the creation of the illusion, the flouncing and sometimes preposterous pantomime quality of the production, even as it flirts with emotional chaos and betrayal and fear and loathing — there is mesmerising, ineffable truth.

I don't want to dress up; I don't want to have to spend a lot of money; I don't want to feel that it is only for those receiving corporate gifts; I don't want to feel that it relies too much on its past splendours; I don't want to feel that it is all about maintaining a wonky status quo. I don't want to be slow handclapped for suggesting it might be a little selfish of its obsessed fans to presume the whole tradition will survive for much longer in its current form. I don't want to think it is only an age thing, a way of spending time inside a protected fantasy that is itself inside a protected fantasy and using it to postpone death through the most ridiculous but captivating representation of the extremes of life. But I find myself falling more and more for the damned thing, knowing and accepting that the more I fall, the more I become an undead member of the cult.

It might, more than anything else, be a near-death experience for the near-dead, but it can also make you feel more alive than ever, and readier for life...

As illogical as this might be, considering how, for many, Mozart's most impressive achievements are the operas, I have decided as I make my way around Mozart to leave them until last – at least as whole pieces to be taken in one go, as apart from the occasional glancing against fragments of the story that happens during a marathon Spotify listening session. I make a rough estimate of how long that will take – moving through everything else first – and there is a real danger I will run out of time, out of life. Mozart stopped writing his piano concertos at his usual rate in 1786, concentrating that dramatic energy on the building of the operas, and perhaps it is the better place for me to go after establishing a certain understanding of the piano concertos, even just the knowledge that there are twenty-seven, and they go in order, and in any order.

I'm still afraid of Mozart's operas, the first one appearing when he was fourteen, *Mitridate, re di Ponto*, which is enough on its own to make anyone afraid – that he was already so able in his early teens to absorb technique, style, rules, expectation and filter it through his own energies to produce a coherent event. It's packed with impressively garnished crowd-pleasing arias full of vocal heroics, showing he was musically, if not psychologically, already aware of what an opera could and must be. Begin there, as Mozart did, before he was the Shakespeare, or actually the Mozart of the canonical operas.

I'm apprehensive about all of those beasts and beauties, as if they might abduct me, similar to how I was afraid of taking acid when I was a teenager. I might not return as myself. One of the things that happens, though, when you go mad for Mozart is that you start to follow the works and extreme commitment of, among others, various conductors, and trailing Otto Klemperer's Mozart ventures eventually led me to this recording of *Die Zauberflöte* from 1964, the 1964 of *My Fair Lady* rather than *A Hard Day's Night*. It features a cast that I am led to believe is the 1964 opera-world equivalent of, say, a retro-camp crime caper featuring Michael Fassbender, Brad Pitt, Penelope Cruz, Tom Hardy, Florence Pugh and Javier Bardem. Once I have got used to the Klemperer and understood more fully where the fun and the philosophy, the glamour and the spirit, meet, and worked out why Ferenc Fricsay's 1954 production sounds closer to Mozart's time than now, I will gravitate to Claudio Abbado's no doubt more priestly and demanding 2005 version.

I have decided the operas are the final Mozart place to go, so that when I get there, experienced in listening to his music, understanding how he evoked his own world, elevating it above his time and place, I have a better Mozart in my mind, and therefore a better understanding of what the creation of the operas involved — and if it does indeed 'throw open the gates of heaven', then I want to have the right set of experiences to fully appreciate such an event.

English locations cover wild extremes, from Glyndebourne in a cushioned, privileged South to Huddersfield in a stoical neglected North in the same way that English music, as part of an overall display as a land of performance and performers, travels from the national spirit, the elegantly, evocatively captured, unthreatening and elevating time of Elgar to the post-national spirit, the dismantled, disturbed and demanding time of Birtwistle.

Following Glyndebourne I had enough remaining Sinfini *credits to be given the job of visiting the sturdy, steady West Yorkshire town that, oddly enough, was the birthplace of both the first female Doctor Who — Jodie Whittaker — and the second captain of the Starship Enterprise — Patrick Stewart — as well as being the unlikely home of an internationally famous festival of experimental music. In Huddersfield there is the permanent past laid out in strong stone amidst dark and secret hills, a hard, uncompromising present that never seems to let go, and, in between the lines, between the steadfast lives of the locals, conjured up between the relentless years, strange bewitching sounds emerging from a future that never quite takes hold.*

6. WHAT PLAYS IN HUDDERSFIELD PLAYS IN HUDDERSFIELD

There is no doubt that the Huddersfield Contemporary Music Festival is in itself a kind of work of art. The 2013 season is the thirty-sixth, and it is a consistent marvel in terms of what it has covered since the first festival in 1978 – when creeping fog nearly forced a cancellation of a modestly budgeted weekend event – and what it presents each year, a dense, marauding daily combination tumbling over ten days of around fifty performances, talks, workshops, installations, featured composers, premieres and sundry gatherings, with national and international music circling and recycling those areas where improvisation, jazz, electroacoustic, sound art, choral, film, theatre and orchestral circle and recycle each other and sometimes cancel each other out. It's all sponsored and supported by councils, institutions, groups, companies and educational concerns looking to align themselves with the visibly civilised and instructive. Anyone interested in studying where experimental, so-called cutting-edge music has moved since the 1970s, and how it develops and refines modernist, post-serialist/minimalist traditions and innovations established since the 1950s, in learning who the leading exponents, heroes, villains, adventurers and newcomers are, has to attend, and keep up with all the action.

Each 'hcmf' occasion, however tricky and difficult the music, or solemn, detailed and academic the conversation, tends to be sold out, giving a slightly distorted picture of the amount of interest in this country for music so obscure its presence in the depthless, pleasure-seeking modern world is about as loud as a butterfly's whisper next to a road drill. Even, or especially, if the music being played would sound for many people like a road drill. People seek comfort and security in whatever works for them; well-drilled entertainment, or the sound of drilling into concrete.

A book written about the festival by its founder and original director and professor of music at Huddersfield University, Richard Steinitz – 1,104,407 in the Amazon charts, no reviews – is called *Explosions in November*, and for those who regularly attend the Festival, and attend as many of the five-a-day events as they can, it does contain explosions, of pleasure, surprise and occasionally authentic musical history. Many of the modern giants of post-war contemporary music have attended – Cage, Stockhausen, Boulez, Berio, Xenakis, Harvey, Carter, Pärt, Reich – helping create the special momentum that gives the festival its fine-spun international reputation.

The legendary reconciliation between the patiently argumentative Cage and the impatiently argumentative Boulez after the friends fell out in the mid-1960s over some arcane and/or crucial musical dispute – the composer must be in control of their material versus the composer letting go of control through the throw of a dice, Satie rules versus Satie sucks – happened in Huddersfield, where the pair were photographed in a local pub with Olivier Messiaen. The trio, alas, were not captured grouped around the salad buffet bar loading up weeping tomatoes and forlorn olives in the town-centre Pizza Hut, where they apparently dined.

Those explosions in November, of innovation, or would-be innovation, of ideological clashes, are increasingly self-contained, and even though the festival's reputation is also because of its location, the imposing, distinctive Huddersfield, filled with striking industrial and sporting history set into glorious windswept West Yorkshire country, it is less and less of that Huddersfield, and more and more of the Huddersfield that is purely of the festival, a spectral Huddersfield that annually presents an imaginatively selected, extraordinarily disciplined array of sonically challenging music and associated discussion inside the town, but is somewhere else altogether. While the music festival does its busy, probing and self-possessed subterrestrial thing, spread around its university centre in church halls, studios, mills, theatres, town halls and creative arts buildings, most of the locals are entirely oblivious to the amount of thinking and skill occurring out of harm's way. It might as well be on another planet.

This might not matter; the festival belongs there and nowhere else, breathtaking manipulation of sound and breathtaking landscape are within sight and sound of each other, and it gives Huddersfield a necessary if unobtrusive presence in the wider world, along with a plucky football team that sometimes rides high and sometimes sinks low. There is, though, something particularly disturbing about emerging into a battered, peeling town centre sagging into vacant Saturday-night squalor from an exquisitely performed hour of atmospheric and mysterious chamber music brilliantly played inside a creamily elegant, brightly lit church hall – the only signs of nightlife in damp, depleted Huddersfield town centre being either a series of intense bursts of concentration from musicians and listeners as something very severely sub-Berio or repetitively post-Feldman happens, or a carnival of chaotic, flesh-toned revelry fuelled by blue 99p cocktails, haywire party time glued to a strip-hop or trash-step soundtrack inside pubs and clubs holed up between decaying betting, pound, coffee and charity shops, protected by surly-looking bouncers. Glimpses of dated desires for utopia as attained through glistening, unorthodox musical structures exist alongside mini-skirted and tattooed explosions of urgent escapist frenzy generally accompanied by the sound of 'Things Can Only Get Better' or Thicke's corny, horny, rapaciously rotten-to-the-core 'Blurred Lines'.

The Pizza Hut where, perhaps, music history was once made, still exists, the salad bar still containing the same unchosen olives and weeping tomatoes, but the idea of Cage, Boulez and Messiaen wandering after dark around the shuttered, heartbroken, sloped and cobbled shopping streets of twenty-first-century Huddersfield with the aura of mystics floating a couple of centimetres off the ground, surrounded by the constant drummed-up dance sounds spilling out of the pubs and clubs makes the mind spin, and yearn for an operatic interpretation.

My experience over the opening weekend took in four concerts, three on the Saturday night, one midday Sunday. This makes me something of a weak-willed part-timer compared to the true obsessives immersing themselves in the whole ten days, and already looking forward to next year. A hardcore, discriminating audience for new music, many of them from West Yorkshire, has been built in the area because of the festival, and they demand a constant, uncompromising parade of the experimental and progressive, of fresh discoveries of instrumental and structural possibilities.

Because the disruptive, ground-breaking energy of music whose ideas were established in a rage of tradition-trashing purpose fifty years ago is running out of steam, the festival itself can seem more charmingly eccentric than aesthetically provocative and confrontational. Perversely, the festival becomes increasingly decorative, even, in its own way, escapist, a close cousin of the friendly, middlebrow literary festival, of the fascination with antiques and baking, a sign of where interest in culture is more of a convivial time-passing hobby than a cause. The music would still be strange and uncomfortable, even totally ridiculous and offensively fussy to a mass audience, filled with the surely non-musical, ugly and painfully ear-splitting, but to the loyal audience, it is an oddly consoling, comforting demonstration of the lovingly curated and moderately edifying, not necessarily there positively to change the world, but mildly to keep alive the idea that believing in such a thing still matters.

Watching the BBC Singers conducted by Nicholas Kok in St Paul's Hall summed up how there is such a fear of apparent frivolity or, at the opposite extreme, of anarchic, mind-bending urgency that the presentation of challenging new music can come across as a hybrid of the strictly organised cultish and the cordial supper club. *Haut terrain*, a searching, cerebral choral piece by Charlotte Seither, was at times so lusciously spare it didn't particularly matter — as it really shouldn't — that the singers were dressed as though they were serenading customers searching for posh puddings at Marks & Spencer, with expressions suggesting some of them were seconds from a panic attack, but once they took on Cecilie Ore's more politically engaged celebration of freedom of speech, *Come to the Edge!*, the combination of the radical sentiments and the stuffy presentation was extremely awkward.

Ore's piece features quotes from George Washington, Abraham Lincoln, Lenny Bruce, Che Guevara, Shakespeare, Harry Belafonte and the Russian trial of the Pussy Riot members, and is an attempt to make an intricately structured piece of modern music actually be about something, rather than just inspired by a vague feeling, or an ancient, bewitching Latin term, or a latent conceptual intention, or, ultimately, its own despairing, or triumphant, battle with structure and musical history. It's not just the sight of the twenty or so singers being in front of us in their characterless black clothing but also being mere empty vessels to pass the sound through that made this piece so frustrating. It is sung in such a dainty, plaintive way by the Nicely Dressed and Faceless, you feel if there was a revolution it is the equivalent of making a protest banner out of fine lace. It satisfies the guilty need of the composer to do something with technique other than just demonstrate it, but as a composition it lands in the real world like a cashmere cardigan in a muddy field.

Georg Freidrich Haas's hour-long 2000 *in vain* for twenty-four instruments has been described by Simon Rattle as the first great masterpiece of the twenty-first century, and received its highly anticipated UK premiere at the town hall in the fine hands of the London Sinfonietta conducted by Emilio Pomarico. Painstakingly constructed in the image of something ethereally monumental, a spectacular demonstration of how to blend dazed movement with dazzling stillness, and layer presence over absence over presence, one step forward, two steps back from Debussy, Ligeti, Krzysztof Penderecki and Reich, featuring two mildly disorientating sections where the hall is completely blacked out while the hyper-alert orchestra feel their way forward into the billowing darkness of the music, it was as though Haas was attempting to score *Meddle*-period Pink Floyd and *Phaedra*-era Tangerine Dream, and achieve fidgety, mesmerising psychedelic opulence through orchestral ingenuity. Beautiful, but for all the intricate technique and intrigue, it looked and sounded older rather than newer – avant-trad, or trad-garde.

The lights-out element often favoured by Haas to sharpen the senses teeters on the gimmicky in the context of a performance where the orchestra is still all in cocktail-party black and wiped out of intrusive expression and feeling, and the aloof conductor still acts like a slightly impatient tyrant who's on his way to something much more important. This enhances a general feeling that what is missing from the piece – which no amount of careful scoring or scene-setting can compensate for – is spontaneous drama, and a dynamic sense of real risk-taking; the orchestral performance takes a snapshot of the idea of compositional audacity, an enticing sketch of the revelatory, but does not unveil it as if for the first time.

in vain's massed static might also demonstrate why it would mean next to nothing for those frolicking and freaking out in the nearby beat-pounded clubs and pubs, experiencing their own monumental assault on time, their own sense of the needle sticking in a record's grooves, and why most everyday music listeners will feel repelled by the tones, silences, structures, length, complexity, technicality, abstraction and expressed spiritual basis to much of this music. Melodies are a form of happy ending, constantly resolving into satisfying, optimistic conclusions, whereas whatever melodies there are in music showcased at the Huddersfield Contemporary Music Festival are buried, compressed, implied, masked, questioned, stretched out into unexpected shapes or blasted into spinning fragments, and the intention to reject cliché, and therefore corrupting sentimentality, means sacrificing the constant, relieving and expected supply of happy endings and their sugar-coating of a cruel world.

In many ways, the Huddersfield music is more optimistic and hopeful than the cynical mainstream music crammed with the glib happy endings of well-crafted but simple-minded melody, but its harsh, considered realism, or defiant, playful surrealism, and its stubborn rejection of easy options and tranquillising familiarity means it can seem hopelessly pessimistic, even nihilistic. Idealism and philosophical good intentions disintegrate among all the confined, inward-looking and perfectionist detail.

The final concert on the first Saturday of the ten-day festival was the twelve-piece Ensemble Linea plus guest, the Arditti Quartet founder Irvine Arditti, playing four pieces in St Paul's Hall – the very square, formal, dressed-up musicians taking bows, the conductor playing the firm, no-nonsense leader of some benign cult, while they performed pieces written in the last two years by Brian Ferneyhough – seventy that year – Raphaël Cendo and James Clarke that precisely, festively shredded melody, texture and potential happy endings into spectral confetti.

The pieces made clear how oddly regimented and square much of this stern, convoluted, bright and brutal music can sound, and the clash there is between the limited sounds that can emerge from the instruments and the unlimited theoretical appetite of the composer. The Ferneyhough and Clarke pieces in particular felt like counterintuitive attempts to score free music, resulting in an unsavoury struggle between cramping rigidity and fantastical freedom. Without the bravery and stunning instantaneousness of improvised music, they lacked the miracle of hearing the music simply appear out of the minds and instincts of the players – watching the ensemble copy what had been fastidiously prepared for them, however agile and powerful the communal timing, seemed as empty as though they were miming. And then again, outside the church hall, as the stricken Huddersfield town centre approached a boozy, bombed midnight mayhem of truth-skinning reality-TV-inspired fun, there was this savage break between the almost mythological, reverential analysis of sound and the gruelling need to smash the face into dignity-pummelling boredom-escaping self-gratification; two different ways of losing your mind, or trying very hard to find it, of achieving blissful lift-off and being utterly consumed by something outside of the human.

Sunday, midday, back at St Paul's Hall in the university, the Quatuor Diotima, and four quartet pieces plus occasional oboe, exceptionally transmitted. Plenty of energetic, agitated clusters of sound, technical studies of string sonorities and extended effects, X-rays of the uncanny, tiny worlds caught in constant movement, abrupt nuance changes, uneasy calm, close-ups and zooms out, loosening and tightening, fierce and tender, gentle and violent, the imagination transformed into sound, including the world premiere of another furiously self-conscious and sensitively berserk Ferneyhough piece, *Schatten aus Wasser und Stein*.

Ligeti's Second String Quartet from 1968 was the time lord of all the pieces played, because he is a master of contemplative twentieth-century experimental techniques, in this instance honouring and elaborating upon Bartók's formidable Fourth and Fifth String Quartets, immaculately articulating the imaginative sounds, questioning stamina and introspective brilliance that are still being echoed, followed, referenced and reinforced forty-five years later. This combination of players, composer, piece, venue and attentive audience is Huddersfield at its very best, which now does mean a perverse sense of nostalgia for when this kind of new music was actually new, and part of a more influential, urgent-seeming and still evolving research and development department, not anxiously circling what the new can now be, and who and what it is for, and for heaven's sake what happens next? The new that in effect is more or less old, because it turned out that what came after modern and then postmodern was more, much more, of the same, much of it curated at fastidious annual festivals.

It used to be that the clear-cut mission was to break away from the past, or completely reshape it, to enter a brave new world where Bach was no longer listened to, and nothing of the sort happened, except for the lack of Bach, but not quite how the rebels imagined it – where it would be replaced by their lessons, not simply shoved aside by an onslaught of entertainment. The question of what these old, new sounds are for becomes increasingly pointed. Has the avant-garde done its job in keeping something going, even if that just perversely meant refreshing tradition, or is it now the past – and a music that was so much against the past becoming the past is even more useless than music that wasn't made with such forward-thinking commitment?

Outside, damp, chilly early-afternoon Huddersfield town centre has a hangover after the throbbing excesses of the night before, not from desperately attempting to work out the meaning of an avant-garde artistic impulse in the twenty-first century. Families and shoppers tentatively regain control over the streets that a few hours before were the location of an orgy of buzzing bad taste; a hybrid of the pound shop and Greggs, Poundbake — pies, sarnies and cakes for a quid — is doing great business. What would the Sunday shoppers have made of the sounds being carved out of and into eternity in church-y, school-y hidden venues around the hills and winding lanes of Huddersfield? What would have seemed more terrifying, or self-indulgent, or in a way more lonely — the drunken revellers noisily slaughtering themselves, or the festival obsessives relishing noisy and/or noiseless sounds that seemed both frozen in time and smashed into moving pieces?

Despite the messy conflict between realities, between local tribes and their faiths, between high-street desolation and composed self-regard, and the technical problems of form, function, repetition, insularity and presentation, it would be mad not to hope that the Festival reaches edition number fifty, and beyond. Even if by then only fifty people are actively engaged in this sort of enterprise, this belief in music not as an easily ordered and stored consumer item, or a form of easy-going pleasure, a congenial hobby, but as something closer to religion, containing answers to the damned meaning of the universe.

For all its eddying around, and dwelling in the same haunted spaces, the music remains ahead of its time, too modern for now, too fast, too slow, too everything at the same time, at its best making the more serious, extreme glitch genre seem square, written and played by musicians thinking too much about life, about death, about their own isolation and technique, but perhaps destined to make more sense to more people as the century develops and time and place mutates into something else altogether. Maybe Huddersfield's role is to freeze the new music it specialises in — in the suspended animation that a lot of the compositions resemble, in a secluded moment of time — while all around it reality and twentieth-century time changes shape.

Inside a protective bubble, cut off from the rest of the town but completely part of it, in the way it is embedded in reality but on the outside attempting to make new rules, the music waits for when there is a demand for it, possibly when the town of Huddersfield itself doesn't exist any more. Waits for when the miraculous happy ending — to the relationship between music and society, between brain and time, between noise and silence, between life and death, between technology and thought, between intellect and pleasure, as predicted by Cage, possibly while eating in Huddersfield Pizza Hut — will finally happen.

A few articles for Sinfini *appeared to seal my reputation as someone from outside the realm who might be able to offer fresh, realistic insights into the state of classical music, where it was as a business and industry, and also where it was creatively and historically and how it might connect to the rest of the musical world. At the peak of my tentative presence as, nearly, a writer about classical music I received an invitation to give the keynote speech to the Association of British Orchestras, which represents the interests of professional orchestras, youth orchestras and the wider UK classical industry, with a brief to describe how I saw the role and future of the orchestra. This was how I found myself – as if someone was telling lies about me, or perhaps the truth – shaking hands with the very limp fingers of the blank-eyed Minister for Culture (who shall remain nameless because he didn't seem to possess enough personality to have a name) before delivering the following in front of representatives of esteemed orchestras such as the BBC Concert Orchestra, the Britten Sinfonia, the Hallé Orchestra, the London Sinfonietta, the Royal Liverpool Philharmonic, the Royal Opera House and the London Symphony Orchestra.*

I didn't really know what they were expecting, except there was this general sense of how to reach outside the usual audience, their usual subscribers, but I did know that I had a lot of words to read. After all, I had written them. What motivated me to deliver my speech was some vague notion that what I was about to say was going to change their world.

I was also at the peak of my excitement about the unique function and uncanny power of the orchestra as a highly skilled collection of musicians committing their lives and imagination to music. I was even beginning to fall in love with how much power the orchestra could generate, and the distinct styles of each one, although I still found it odd that, for instance, when a great orchestra performed the musicians all wore the same clothes, and the lights stayed on, and there was a noiseless formality about when you were meant to applaud and indeed not applaud – as though this wasn't about pleasure, and bliss, and altered states of mind, it was about a dismal sort of obedience.

It was about a form of knowledge and understanding it was assumed everyone possessed. It was difficult to work out the way in, unless you were already in the know. How did you ever get to know, unless you already knew? Schemes to help introduce outsiders seemed underwhelming and unimaginative, and not so much about music and musical history, but a kind of warming community spirit that ultimately was simply about maintaining audiences and trying to act fashionable, not changing the world. But what was the alternative?

I suppose that was the reason I had been asked to give a speech; someone somewhere must have a solution to how the orchestra didn't come across as a remote, complicated endeavour, and, perversely, considering the amount of humanity and creative verve, apparently an ordeal? Maybe I knew what that solution, the alternative, was.

7. THE CRITIC AS UNLIKELY MOTIVATIONAL SPEAKER

I am aware of, but nowhere near an expert in, the challenges facing the cultural positioning of classical music and the institutional side of the orchestra in the age of media histrionics, joyless content crafting and relentless self-promotion. I am alert to the speedy changes in means of production and consumption, instrumentation, venues, programming, vaguely hopeful that classical music is reaching a stage in its history where it ceases to be known as classical and simply becomes music, but mostly I see the orchestra not as something in crisis but as something with so much experience at dealing with various problems, it seems capable of dealing with this collapsing, expanding new world, and finding a way of yet again reinventing itself. Which it obviously has to do.

Like steam trains – and lately recording studios, banks, high-street shops, newspapers, TV channels, political parties, educational systems – the orchestra is from another time, and it does not seem to work, financially, structurally, socially, in the fluid, shape-shifting, miniaturised new world, which is now always on the verge of becoming another new world, which is intent on making the twentieth century seem as distant as the seventeenth, while turning us all into targeted consumers whose desires are being inexorably whittled down to only reflect what it is we are being sold, and told by those doing the selling.

Like other systems, institutions, genres, societies, organisations, religions, foundations and values that are threatened by a complete, digital and self-styled smart overhaul of what it is to be human and relate to each other, and what reality is and could be, classical music and the orchestra gets most attention in articles, programmes and debates that generally wonder whether it is dead, or if it isn't, how long it has left, and in what form it can survive. What on earth will be the sustainable business model that will see it still around in fifty years' time? It is always put on the back foot, cornered, having to defend its right to exist as a business, as a musical philosophy, as somehow an organisation that has meetings about how to cultivate innovative practices, when, it's said, very few really care, just a small community of connoisseurs. One of the difficulties the orchestra faces is always being treated as though it is in unstoppable decline, a simplistic, prejudiced twisting of the debate that overwhelms what it is the orchestra should really be doing – making sure that the vast diversity of serious music composed over many centuries doesn't get wiped out in some insidious techno-equivalent of the Kindle-inspired burning of the book. And what those who understand the need for the orchestra must do is establish very firmly, and without it sounding sad, defeatist and wishy-washy, what the actual value of great music and art really is at a time when, for the purpose of creating an obedient mass of customers accepting only what is on offer, the questioning, probing intelligentsia itself is being shrivelled into an easily bullied and discarded, and slightly dotty minority.

With the orchestra, words like 'dodo' get used. Elitism. Victorian. Pomposity. And it's undeniably true – the orchestra, in many ways, can be viewed as an ancient, outmoded thing, a toy for the rich, for the sentimental and nostalgic, an expensive, overprotected indulgence for the narrow-minded obsessives and the casual cultural tourist. It suffers from nervous, frivolous, sometimes well-intentioned attempts to modernise itself, to locate relevance, to appear cool, or it just suffers because it was not built for the atmosphere as it is now. It is forced to compromise, to perpetuate tired but popular rituals, to make embarrassing audience-courting deals with pop, light entertainment and rock, with annual anniversary-laden festivals, to take on menial community tasks and appear to perform musical healing – as if they should become a worthy social service rather than abstract, driven custodians of a momentous, genuinely psychedelic, reality-shaking musical tradition – to set up fun, creative learning programmes, to become public educational institutions, all of which ultimately increase its dry, haughty and weary irrelevance to a world trained to seek the smashing, consoling instant, and which force the orchestra to move away from its purer, loftier, more mind-expanding principles. Attempting to look as though it is a gentle, friendly, even adorable thing, content sincerely to serve the local community, it ends up seeming even more aloof and stiff, worried so much about its purpose and future that it comes across as already accepting an inevitable demise and merely arranging the last will and testament and trying to do a bit of end-of-life charitable good.

It isn't, as such, merely a dinosaur, it's like it is from another planet, an alien species, speaking in tongues, articulating a reality that seems as foreign to the world we're sold and limited to as ancient Egyptians or future Martians – precisely the thing that now excites me as a fanatical music lover, always on the lookout for the fresh, the enlightening, the delightfully disturbed. Perversely, what seemed stale and static in the middle of rock and pop's rise to glory now seems fresh and unsullied, and as we are breaking free, for better or worse, from traditional, modernist notions of distinct, easily measured progress, of one thing leading to the next thing in conventional linear order, the orchestra is freed from the museum – or everything else has joined it in the museum, otherwise known as the internet – and can become a new thing, a new force, a new way of seeing, hearing and making sense of things.

So I come to the idea of the orchestra knowing all about the sense of crisis – the fear and anxiety, or acceptance and resignation, or ingenuity, negotiating and campaigning – that there is from those on the inside, who make their living from them, who believe in them, who spend their time working out how to make them viable, or more viable, or useful, or accessible, or simply functional. I've read years and years, even decades, even a century, of doom and gloom, or slightly deranged, enforced optimism, of stories of struggles to survive, of ways to deal with a ruthless, uncaring, money-minded changing world that seems to be leaving them behind.

But I also come to the idea of the orchestra as though it is a new thing, new to me and therefore truly new – always releasing astonishing information about the history and present of music, and art, and possibility, and I am not so much hindered by reality, by practical problems of funding, governance and sustenance bogged down with fixed costs, audience share, subscription models, worries about the need to democratise the concert experience, the monetisation of the virtual experience, the dreary white-male dominance of proceedings, the elusive younger audience, as mythical as elves and goblins – I come to the orchestra at a time when everything is changing so much that we are in many ways beginning from scratch in terms of what the new is, and what the new categories are, and so I arrive here blissfully ignorant of the essential bureaucratic, political, financial and repertoire problems that can lumber those involved with a sense of despair and confusion.

I think – perhaps I dream – of the orchestra as a great example of how art and the arts have constantly justified themselves by helping individuals to adapt to new ideas, to fundamental change, supplying clues about how to protect ourselves as humans from the damaging consequences of those environmental changes that result from technological economic advancements or mutations. Art tells us about beauty, and broadcasts different, special ways of thinking, but it also warns us about the perils of the type of people who tend to crave power and influence, who don't care really about beauty, unless it is worth millions, and who loathe ways of thinking that are different from theirs, especially when that thinking questions their right to possess any sort of power.

Change and progress is part of being human, but it also historically threatens what it is to be human – and art is ultimately what helps us deal with the force of change; it explains it, predicts it, contains it, is a necessary antidote to the rampaging forces of those claiming power. It is the most vital corrective alternative to the entrepreneurial energy that generally exploits technological change, mostly to make money and take control of our interests, and it is a mysterious form of opposition to those who, especially at the moment, use the development in technology to herd us into obedient, pacified communities whose sole function is ultimately to consume and download and disappear into a kind of censored, gated territory of lifestyle ease, merciless entertainment and moral indifference.

At this point, in the middle of the sort of changes that will either end us or profoundly transform us, even replace us, there is an extraordinary need for the orchestra as an unclassifiable symbol of otherness and artistic endeavour, as a method of communicating thought about the vastness of the cosmos, the glory of love, the wonder of existence, the drama of history, the nature of our minds, which music is a mirror of, a maker of, beyond words, and logic, and temporary societal pressure.

I say this as a newborn fan, falling in love with what those who have worked for, in and around the orchestra all their lives already appreciate: the uncanny, civilising, even absurd nature of the thing.

I say this as someone that wants to avoid as much as possible the usual language that reduces the existence of the orchestra to a political problem, or a cultural inconvenience. For it to survive, how it is discussed and regarded needs to shift away from it being in its last stages, too clanky and clunky to survive in a streamlined digital world, too demanding to work in spaces that can't cope with intricacy and genuine intimacy. It needs to invent a new context for itself, not by responding to the pressure put on it by cynical business, superficial media and indifferent technology, all quite happy to see it shrink to next to nothing, but by grasping the argument on its own terms, making a case for its existence that is not about revenue, fame or tech strategy, but that is about why there needs to be the orchestra, because the alternative is quite simply desolate.

It's easy for me to say this, completely oblivious to the details of how it is funded and functions, the internal and external battles with each other and with outside sceptics, but then, at the moment, I am in control of what is being said, and sometimes, what is being said needs to be less about the mundane, everyday practical details and more about a truth that is actually fantastic, about believing in something else, in other ways of thinking and being, to such an extent that it becomes true. At this moment in time, we can make up new rules, we need to make up new rules, and to some extent that means a world where classical music barely resembles what we mean by classical music at the moment, in the way it is currently presented through the traditional radio channels and concert venues, and the orchestra is only related to a nineteenth-century orchestra in the way a bebop quartet was related to a 1920s trad-jazz group and an anonymous electronic duo tinkering with the history of disco are related to four boys from Liverpool inventing a new kind of British empire in the early 1960s. The orchestra and the classical music it represents has missed out on so much technological and cultural change this past hundred years – fearful of losing its identity – that it is now struggling with what it is in relation to the rest of the world. Now is the time to catch up with change, and even overtake those things around it that did keep up while it was preserving itself, and yet really losing its momentum.

It needs to be about helping to invent new categories to deal with the new circumstances, responding to a world that undeniably contains sinister elements intent on restricting individual freedom and creepily using entertainment and pleasure, ensuring that the true complexity of being alive and organising cities, societies, media to reflect positive thinking are still represented through developing forms of art and music.

If the orchestra is of worth, and had worth, then surely the aim must be to ensure it survives in some form, in some way, into the next era, and one way to guarantee this is to not weaken and soften its power when presenting the idea of the orchestra, but to toughen it, exaggerate its more radiant, poetic and breathtaking elements, sell it not as a local community service, or mere pleasant, attractively ornamental decoration, which is then easily absorbed into the world as it is, even if that means it dissolves completely, but as a brilliant, ground-breaking example of unique artistic endeavour. It should not play sweet, it should not stubbornly carry on as it has been doing until the buildings it appears in are no more, or the sponsors it relies on have moved elsewhere; it should act like it knows it is on a crusade to oppose soft thinking, banal interaction and weak minds.

If I made the rules, I would demand a world where the orchestra doesn't chase audiences or try and make friends with them, hunting down a specifically targeted audience or sticking with the one they have by perpetuating outdated modes of presentation, but makes up a new world for audiences to find and decode, an update of the spirit of the music at the heart of its core repertoire that came out of the blue; the newest, most miraculous thing on the planet alongside electricity. Realists might point out that being so pure and uncompromising would render them redundant within a matter of months; for me, a strain of truth in how an orchestra positions itself in the new world related to the actual depth and power of the music, which is rarely as smiley, fake-welcoming and polite as the marketing indicates, would give it a better chance of an extended and influential life. In the end, the greater point is not reaching a wider audience, because to do so means sacrificing every single thing that you do that means anything, but ensuring that music as something more than entertainment survives by ensuring that it still evolves, by marketing the music played by orchestras not as some sort of spa therapy, or teaching aid, or social welfare, but as something that contributes to our knowledge of music and therefore of what it is to be human, here in space, at this weird moment in time.

For me, the future of the orchestra, even beyond the problems of funding or structural replenishment, involves committing itself to the idea that what it is about may be problematical, difficult, severe, even obscure, but that's what it is, and it's ridiculous to pretend otherwise. It doesn't mean it cannot be enchanting, inspiring, poignant, erotic, hair-raising, spine-tingling, glamorous... in fact, it's more likely to mean that it can be, and can be to more than its relatively satisfied hardcore audience.

The ways the orchestra announces itself to the world should be stranger, not nicer; it should let itself be intriguing to those that still want the different because it is so uncompromising, not because it pretends it is in the same basically pleasing world as the entertainers, and it should be unashamed in reconnecting our musical tradition with its primary source of inspiration, the inner spiritual life of its citizens, accepting that one of its jobs is to reawaken this, not contribute to how it is being deadened by those pleased that an inner, questing life is being removed, because that makes the consumer easier to harness, even hoodwink. The orchestra must conceive of a role that accepts there is a kind of ideological battle going on, and set itself up as a confident, compelling alternative to commercial standardisation and the online reduction of possibilities, not try to find inoffensive ways to compete with their ingratiating, weightless delights.

If the orchestra survives in a neutered, reduced, exiled form in the new world, because it was so worried about losing its audience, becoming just another dutiful element in a controlled entertainment landscape, merely another stored, tamed choice, a mere subservient component, it might as well not exist at all — its future must be as the most extreme, challenging version of what it is and was, a streaming, cloud-era reinvention of a perhaps over-romanticised nineteenth-century idea of the orchestra, a ravishing development of the essence of the orchestra as a combination of brains that becomes one brain that presents the ideas of another brain that is better than all other brains put together. It must not be put off by the fact that classical music and the orchestra clashes with prevailing cultural norms, but make a virtue of it, connect with those increasing numbers of people unconvinced, even repelled, by Google, Apple and bossy, controlling companies and their designing and dominance of reality, their self-serving manipulation of our minds and lives.

In a machine-ordered, and disordered, world, the orchestra should exist as a glorious reminder of a staggering, largely untapped and unexplored musical heritage – become a rival machine, hand-made and cosmic, imaginatively connected to other serious-minded rejections of trivia and sensationalism, to literature, cinema, politics, architecture, design, a whole world outside, and put so much concerted pressure on the media to take it seriously as a going concern, not something to pity or just plain ignore under pressure, on the verge of becoming obsolete, that it begins to take control of its own destiny. In my dream, it does this by acting and appearing more resolute and cerebral, not less.

The orchestra is just as likely to be a part of what comes next as anything, and just as likely to disappear as all those other things that once seemed to be permanent and constant – churches, newspapers, books, record labels, TV channels, office hours, Test cricket – and from my position, dreamy and unrealistic, utterly unmoved by the dreadful, complex realities of patronage, management, governance, what will make it survive is a greater emphasis from those that are involved on what it is as art, on the fact it is transmitting art and therefore the important thinking and judgement of great minds keen on making the world a better, fairer, freer, wonderfully odder and radically safer world.

At the end of my talk, there was what can only be described as applause, which politely lingered for up to a few seconds. The audience had either heard it all before, or never heard anything quite like it. I felt a strange calmness, as if I now understood that I was in no position to save classical music or offer clues about how it might become more accessible, or visible. I was looking to classical music to save me, and there was enough of it for me to keep listening to it for as long as I needed to. It wasn't about reality; it was about fantasy.

I decided that perhaps this was the end of my period as performer, panellist and public speaker, at least when it came to unravelling the mysteries and the practical problems and cultural reputation of classical music as an industry and as an art form. No more appearances on radio or television acting like I had something important to say about the past, present and future of classical music, hiding the fact I felt out of my depth, or just out of breath.

I thought that I should perhaps, like the great Glenn Gould, a man of the north beyond the north, with something on my mind I needed to work out for myself, withdraw from public appearances and pursue a more private, even lonely exploration of the story, meaning and modern potential

of classical music. I would keep my ideas to myself, or turn them into a
book, a kind of relation of the orchestra, where I didn't have to wonder
whether the reader was applauding for more than a few seconds or giving
me the standing ovation I felt I deserved. And of course I could safely ignore
the Amazon response (no offence), especially when it was the equivalent of
no applause at all, of 'why don't you just shut up'. In private, alone with my
music, with my subscriptions, I could happily make plans, and imagine an
ideal future, which mostly consisted of me discovering more fantastic music
to listen to until the final piece, going nowhere but travelling everywhere.

8. ABOVE AND BEYOND: THE VIEW FROM ICELAND

A couple of years after I gave the speech, I talked about the orchestra, as a very modern resource, with the poised, quietly spoken, tough-minded Icelandic composer Anna Thorvaldsdottir, who makes amazing vaporous music that is within reach of classical structures and post-rock meditation. With a desire to capture the tremendous power of natural phenomena — on earth, especially the extremes, above and below the surface, of Iceland, and out in space, imagining what exists on the other side of black holes — she demonstrates complete faith in the vast potential of the orchestra, how it can span the delicate and nervy to the thunderous and absolute, from the slow thawing of icicles to a violently erupting volcano.

She uses the formal, massed symphonic assertiveness of the orchestra to articulate intimate, oblique ideas that are influenced by the methods of making atmospherically mindful sound art, handling the unwieldy orchestra as though it is one intimate instrument that she can use calmly, or fiercely, to make the most personal, dreamlike and dramatic of sounds.

She writes beautifully for smaller, more mobile chamber ensembles — the clouded *Into − Second Self* for four horns, three trombones and four percussionists, the shivering, shifting *Tactility* for harp and percussion, the broken, thrumming *Ró* performed by the CAPUT Ensemble, the drifting space drama of *Trajectories* for prepared piano and electronics — pieces that are like dissections or X-rays of mysterious subterranean masses, sonic textures put together that place an emphasis on the sounds they make. But it is her spectacularly evocative, even exultant, large-scale compositions — the churning, inexorable *Aeriality*, and

Metacosmos, where the orchestra as great shards of ice seems to orbit Saturn – obeying no order but their own, finding sounds that are hidden inside other sounds, that prove how writing in an orchestral language can still be as much a measureless twenty-first century adventure as a worn-out nineteenth-century one. She uses what she hadn't invented in order to invent what she wants to invents, falling in love with her materials.

She lived until she was sixteen in Borgarnes, a small town founded in the late nineteenth century surrounded by blackened mountains and churning ocean on the south-west coast of Iceland about seventy kilometres from Reykjavík. The population was around 3,000, and she grew up thinking everyone in the world was growing up in similar, remote circumstances, surrounded by wild, momentous and untouched natural elements, by uncertainty, wondering what was on the other side of the ominous mountains, through the dense forests of birch trees or across the endless dark water. Her mother was a music teacher, but there was never any pressure on her to play an instrument 'which would, I think, have put me off'.

As a child she tried plenty of instruments, innocently searching for one that she could connect with, that meant more to her than simply making noise for fun, including piano, flute and trumpet, but at thirteen she settled on the insinuating warmth of the cello, for the theatrical appearance as much as anything, which became the love of her life. 'I would practise six, seven hours a day. I was taking it very seriously. It seemed to be something that could take me somewhere.'

Gradually the idea of being a composer, a maker of things, perhaps just for the sake of it, became more important to her than becoming a cellist. Being a composer was a way of making sense of the natural and community sounds that people living in a small, disconnected town were immersed in, of closely examining the isolation of which the Icelanders have a hypersensitive, near-mystical understanding.

'We were always singing in our family. My mother grew up in a home where there was nightly singing. Whenever the family got together they would sing together, Icelandic folk songs about the great local sagas and legends, and I think that's how my first music was made. I was not writing it down, I was making it up. And there was always the wind making noises, the ice cracking and the houses creaking, and I very quickly started to hear these noises as musical.' The whistles, roars and hums of her isolated homeland became as much an influence as Ligeti, Penderecki, György Kurtág and Crumb, metaphysical collaborators who eventually helped her discover how much precious, exotic movement and noise could be found inside the everyday strings, wind and percussion of the orchestra.

Shy, secretive, unsure of herself, she had an almost nervous sense of ambition, which even now that she works with major orchestras as a lauded and awarded composer still seems to drift through her otherwise completely assured, meticulously assembled pieces. As international, as public as she becomes — recording for the revered Deutsche Grammophon label, with its vast catalogue of classical achievements, mixing her own records, promoted as a serious contemporary voice, dressing the enigmatic, impish part, elegantly taking care of social duties — there is still a sense she remains inside her small, obscure town close to the middle of nowhere, making up stories using sound, wondering what is outside where she lives, and what is inside. Her music means she can take memories and myths of Iceland with her wherever she travels or lives.

In her teens, most of the composing role models she was listening to being inevitably male, living at what could seem the far edge of the world, the prospect of becoming a composer seemed particularly far-fetched. 'But I was very stubborn. I just wanted to be where the men were, perhaps to say, well, there are women as well who can do this, and go to concerts, and parties, and be involved. And make things. It wasn't particularly what was driving me; it was more subconscious than that. I wasn't thinking as much as I might do now about where were all the female composers. The drive for me was just wanting to discover things and move towards some destination. It's like learning a language that is then a pleasure to use, and it's an adventure when you start speaking it and using it. Composing was something I loved doing, and something that seemed as natural to me as the landscape all around me. They seemed part of the same thing.'

In her late teens, after studying a largely conventional repertoire, a sympathetic music teacher noticing her intellectual curiosity introduced her to contemporary music, which liberated a whole new series of musical wishes. 'Hearing this new music gave me a different sense of the textures and tones you could achieve on the cello, much more than with the more traditional classical cello playing. Playing contemporary music on the cello blew my mind. It made me realise what you could achieve with an instrument that wasn't only about making the sound that tradition dictated this one instrument was meant to make. A cello could be other than a cello. The sound could be stretched, adjusted, extended. And then I started to imagine what could happen if every instrument in the orchestra was also manipulated in such a way, sometimes all at the same time. An orchestra could be other than an orchestra.'

Her determination to get things done, to make music for her own pleasure, and to hear on combinations of instruments the sounds she had heard emerging from strange, desolate surroundings and a restless, lively imagination – certainly triggered by experiencing her first hallucinatory opera in Reykjavík at five years old – meant that she was writing a piece for orchestra before she had even started formally studying composition.

'It sounds ridiculous, and of course many people told me that I was wasting my time, there was no future in it. It seemed impractical to be writing for an orchestra, not a smaller, more accessible ensemble. Even that would have seemed fanciful. For some reason I wasn't put off. It was something I wanted to do. I wanted to explore, perhaps in the same way that as I grew up I wanted to explore what there was out there beyond the small place where I lived. My passion was for discovering how far you could go, from a small thing to a large thing, and from a small soft sound to a big loud sound. I was such a tiny little person surrounded by all this history, all this music, all this snow and desolation, and I didn't really have a plan about where I was going, but I trusted that I was going somewhere. If I made a contribution, I passionately believed it would lead me somewhere new.

'I honestly didn't even think my orchestral piece would ever be played, and for a while that was fine, as I was so anxious about anyone hearing what I had written, but a couple of years later the Iceland Symphony Orchestra heard about this crazy young lady who had written a big piece for orchestra, and they played it. I was lucky they paid attention to me. I didn't expect it – I always thought I would only ever hear it in my head – but once I heard it played that made me more sure that this was going to lead me somewhere.

'What was amazing was it sounded just as I had heard it in my head. And it did lead me somewhere, to new people, new environments, new inspirations, and a way of learning all sorts of things, about my music, and about who I was.' A decade later she would become the director of the Iceland Symphony Orchestra, bringing the worlds she had found beyond and the new self she had created back to Iceland.

A musician her age, in the early twenty-first century, in Iceland, where Björk, Valgeir Sigurðsson, Sigur Rós and Múm came from, with their own protean methods of fusing instruments, histories and genres, would surely usually have been turning to electronics and the cracks and crackles of glitch to transmit the shadows and reflections of the Icelandic spirit. Electronics seemed a more accessible, portable musical method of scratching below the surface, of conjuring up intrigue and physical reality, to tap into secrets and the unconscious. Instead, or as well as, she became transfixed by the absurd, unfeasible, many-handed and -headed orchestra — was this a madly romantic, gloriously impractical desire that represented her wildest young dreams, or more realistic and practical, and appropriate to her immediate ambitions?

'I loved the energy of the orchestra. I was interested in untranslatable-seeming energy: the ocean, the volcanoes, the cold, the wind, how everything coalesces and disperses, like a piece of music, and it seemed obvious to me that the orchestra was how you could fully capture that kind of momentous energy. There are things you can do with electronics to reflect this, and I love and use electronics, but there was something about the organic nature of the orchestra that made more sense to me. Acoustic music could actually be stranger, when you have so many people on stage working in unity, the array of instruments each with their own unlimited potential, and all of the different players with their own unique tactile qualities. I made it a passion of mine to get to know each instrument and their capabilities and resonances.

'You learn how you can make a multitude of different sounds using many different configurations of instruments, and when you have a sound in your head that you want to reproduce, you get experience in working out what combination of instruments can help you achieve it. You gain experience in how to capture the sound in your head. And even though I do have natural influences in terms of sound, it is never about simply recreating those sounds. It's as much about the proportion of the wind as the sound, building up different perspectives of what the wind is, and does, and makes us feel. Where does it come from? Where does it go? I'm not wanting to create merely the sound of the wind, but the energy of the wind. The orchestra can do this in thousands of ways.'

Coming from Iceland, somehow above the rest of the world, separated from its trends, prejudices and styles, means that she comes to the orchestra – like some of her close contemporaries such as Johan Johannson, Víkingur Ólafsson and Hildur Guðnadóttir – with a kind of radiant naivety. Inexperience could encourage fabulous boldness, a mixture of reticence and youthful bravado. She does not come to the orchestra burdened by centuries of precedent, obstructed by its overuse and its negative connotations. It never occurred to her that using the most traditional of instruments would interrupt her quest for the monumental and the uncanny. It is almost as though it is a new toy.

'Absolutely. We do our studying, but the history we study has not had the same direct impact on Icelandic music. We are new to all of this. It isn't that long since our first major classical composer, Jón Leifs, passed away, in 1968, only nine years before I was born. There are not centuries behind us, just decades. We are only just starting. I don't begin with this sense that everything has already been done. If I did, I would need some oxygen. We're a small country, everybody seems to know everybody else, especially if we are working in music. Musicians are used to working across genres. Someone who plays in an orchestra in the day might play in a death metal group at night. It's no big deal, like it might be elsewhere.'

Coming to the orchestra fresh and with a more fluid, less institutionalised sensibility meant there seemed to be so much about its potential that felt unrealised.

'There seems a tremendous amount more to explore through the orchestra than it might seem to those used to the standard repertoire. That also means that you become aware of what the orchestra cannot do, which itself becomes the kind of challenge that can lead to being inspired, having to work around it. It also seems important that the orchestral repertoire is extended, that unusual, less obvious pieces from history are featured, and also that new composers use it not as an old-fashioned model, almost as though it is compulsory, but as something that remains completely new. It's fantastic when you see an orchestra used to playing a certain sort of more obvious symphonic music having to adapt and play something they're not used to playing. It's here things can happen that have never previously happened and a whole new world appears out of nowhere.'

Not only playing the music of the dead keeps the very idea of the orchestra alive. Mixing up assorted timelines, reasons and energies, and a range of sounds that stretch across centuries, can make the orchestra, as a precise organising machine and a mind made out of minds, ghostly and futuristic.

PART SIX

1973, the Year When – A Playlist With Information; The Persistence of Memory

Lee 'Scratch' Perry *1970: 'There is nothing music can't do.'*

As I gave talks and appeared on panels examining the state of classical music, and what was to become of it, I became more aware of the enormous, effectively unbridgeable separation between the classical and non-classical music worlds. The general view was that somehow classical music needed to be democratised by either becoming an approachable form of ever-so-slightly-demanding easy listening, or by incorporating certain elements that might make it trendy – the venues where it was played, a certain informality, the beats and rhythms of modern music.

My conclusion was to find ways of bringing the classical and the non-classical together without really making it any sort of issue or drawing attention to it. I was thinking more of how John Peel would often include something from the so-called classical side of things in a radio show that otherwise featured dub, weird, wandering, underground and eccentric, and the way Brian Eno moved fluently between experimental classical and experimental pop as though there was no difference between the two approaches, and therefore demonstrating that there was no difference.

I imagined what it would have been like if, as I grew into music listening as a teenager, barriers between the two worlds didn't exist, and now, in the streaming world, there wasn't still a feeling that even as they now existed in the same space, the access to either exactly the same, they were not for the same listener. I imagined a world where the divisions between the two never existed, and history had been written in a different way.

With the new information I had found as my interest in classical music increased and I heard more music, I imagined what my listening history would have been like if I had been aware of classical music in my teens. Streaming puts all music together in one place, but all music was in one place before; it was just not so clear. While rock, pop, soul and jazz was making its presence felt after the Second World War and increasingly drawing all the attention, classical music was still in action, and still working forward, and one answer to the question of how to make classical cool, or more relevant, if you felt that was relevant, appropriate or possible, was to imagine a world where classical music was part of music, not somehow set to one side.

I wanted to put together the music that I had been aware of during the pop era that dominated cultural attention with the music that was happening elsewhere outside of where I was concentrating, to produce a different kind of history that imagined a world where music wasn't so separated into genres and alcoves but belonged in the same space.

For my initial example, I could have chosen any year after recording music began, to demonstrate how popular music, from early jazz, blues and country, was immediately separate from classical, which eventually meant there was a huge gap between one world and the other that could never be connected. It might not matter that there is this division, but I became interested in terms of my own construction of a classical history and what I had been missing. I was also interested in what would happen to the pop music that was dominant for fifty years now that its imperial phase was over, and it enters history, and becomes more about its past than any future. It was a way of outlining an alternative history, and also of discovering what was happening at the same time in a way that begins to make sense now.

I chose 1973 because it was the year when I bought my first classical album – which could easily have been my last – and when as a bedroom teenager my fascination with rock was rapidly intensifying, producing the kind of enthusiasm and knowledge that meant within three years I was a professional music journalist. I was finding out about music by the day, but I now realise there was energy and momentum happening in the other place, the classical realm, and in the world of streaming, where music is now all placed together and the cultural reasons for the separation have disappeared, it made sense to put all this music together in one playlist. The separation into zones and genres seemed counterintuitive; not a way of discovering music and expanding interest and possibility but dwelling inside your own alcove.

This is 1973 – you could do a similar thing with every year since music recording began. It wasn't a way of making classical music the in-thing, or more diverse, or more accessible, but it was a way of saying: 'If I had a radio show, I would put music from different times and spaces together in one place, because it sounds best that way, and opens up more inspiring connections, instead of it being split into demarcated genres and zones that mostly only contain other things that are like it.' Perhaps the idea wasn't going to make classical music fashionable or even friendly, but then again, it was a better idea than classical music either keeping itself to itself on Radio 3 or being some kind of agreeable social club hosted by Classic FM and its less nannyish rival, Scala.

1973 was the year when the United Kingdom entered the European Economic Union, the year when Watergate helped us with a name for all future scandals, Carly Simon began the year at number one with 'You're So Vain', John Tavener premiered his Variations on 'Three Blind Mice' for orchestra, the year when *The Godfather* won Best Picture Oscar, when the Bond film was *Live and Let Die*, when Perry Henzell's film *The Harder They Come*, starring Jimmy Cliff, opened, when Sofia Gubaidulina's *Roses* for piano and soprano premiered in Moscow, when David Bowie was Aladdin Sane, Lou Reed walked on the wild side and made up a 'Berlin', Slade were feeling the noize, Dobie Gray was drifting away, Bruce Springsteen was 'Blinded by the Light', Tom Waits was calling 'Closing Time', Bob Dylan was 'Knocking on Heaven's Door', Sly and the Family Stone were 'Fresh', Queen recorded their first radio session for John Peel, when Marvin Gaye sang 'What's Going On' and Ann Peebles's 'I Can't Stand the Rain', when Morton Feldman's *Voices and Instruments II* for three female voices, flute, two cellos and bass, Alfred Schnittke's *Suite in the Old Style* for violin and piano and Iannis Xenakis's *Eridanos* for brass and strings premiered, when Ian Carr's Nucleus released two albums refining their tangy English survey of the current jazz-rock mind of Miles Davis, when Ornette Coleman started recording again after a five-year pause, making a field recording in Morocco with the Master Musicians of Joujouka, when Stevie Wonder reached No. 1 with 'Superstition' and 'You Are the Sunshine of My Life', when Free, Family and the Byrds played their last show, 10cc played their first, the Everly Brothers split up,

Gram Parsons died, and DJ Kool Herc DJed his first block party for his sister's birthday in the Bronx, New York, where he mixed instrumental sections of two copies of the same record using two turntables. His friend Coke La Rock rapped, taking cues from Jamaican DJs like U-Roy to put together speaking and spontaneous thinking with ghosted and ghostly beats to create a kind of rhythmical autobiography.

It was the year when the first album was released on Virgin Records, helping to set up Richard Branson's business empire, the rock symphony *Tubular Bells* by nineteen-year-old multi-instrumentalist prodigy Mike Oldfield, a floral hybrid coming out of his fascination with the patterns and reveries of both Johann Sebastian Bach and Terry Riley, inspired by the intrepid, lyrical prog-jazz of avant-bop pianist Keith Tippett's glorious big-band orchestra Centipede, the missing link between Count Basie and agitating Dutch minimalist Louis Andriessen, something of a glorious folly, which *Tubular Bells* initially seemed to be as well, if more modestly, until its hypnotic opening piano theme surprisingly slithered into the demonic-possession horror film *The Exorcist*, released the same year. Richard O'Brien's goth, frilled musical *The Rocky Horror Show* opened in London, starring Tim Curry, Julie Covington and Richard O'Brien, Norman Jewison's musical film *Jesus Christ Superstar* opened, starring Ted Neeley, Carl Anderson and Yvonne Elliman, based on the rock opera – which was in fact neither rock nor opera – by Andrew Lloyd Webber and Tim Rice.

It was the year when the magician David Blaine, singer Andrew Bird and Josh Homme of Queens of the Stone Age were born, when the first mobile phone call was made, when Open University students received their degree at home for the first time, when the IRA bombed Manchester and London, the year when John Cleese (temporarily) left Monty Python's Flying Circus, the year when Virago Press was established, when J. G. Ballard's *Crash* was published, Thomas Pynchon's *Gravity's Rainbow*, and Kurt Vonnegut's *Breakfast of Champions*.

It was also the year *M: Writings '67–'72* by John Cage was published, described as mainly mesostics making sense or no sense at all, inspired by music, mushrooms, Marcel Duchamp, Merce Cunningham, Mao and Marshall McLuhan – Cage once said mushrooms vied for his attention because, like Marcel Duchamp and music, they begin with the letter 'm' – although the 'm' was chosen, of course, by chance operations. (Cheerfully perplexing sceptics, cynics or non-believers prone to scorn such deviant artistic play was part of the effect he was after.) Much of the book consists of his fascination with irrationality and with the nineteenth-century American transcendentalist Henry David Thoreau, filtered through his belief in the artistic beauty of the everyday ordinary.

Cage himself invented the mesostic, writing as a kind of game, performance works using language, a way of organising your thoughts, where a prose poem grew like a tree, sprouting branches from a central word. This book is set in over 700 different typefaces and can be read forwards or backwards, and is part of a series of five books in which Cage tries, as he says, to find a way of writing that comes through from ideas and is not about them. Writing as a way of producing ideas. He was always hunting for ideas.

Meanwhile, Cage's partner in time, but little else, Karlheinz Stockhausen, was giving the final lecture at Imperial College in London in a series on electronic music and his serial shaping of space, which he had begun in 1972 at the Institute of Contemporary Arts. The last lecture was on the meaning and structure of his epic 1970 piece *Mantra*, a piano duo with ring modulation,[1] where one mantra of thirteen notes is developed into 153 parts. *Mantra* is basically a giant crystal created from a small snowflake. In other words, this something like seventy-minute work is a melodic and thematic explosion, derived from a one-minute tune.

Mantra was the first conventionally notated piece Stockhausen wrote following a long period of investigation into improvisation and alternative notations, including text scores. Stockhausen said the work is like an imagined constellation of stars. He spent time in Japan and India and had begun to absorb aspects of spiritual thought and practice that culminated in his vision that he was a visitor from the star Sirius, where 'everything is music, or the art of coordination and harmony of vibrations ... The art is very highly developed there, and

[1] A way of synthetically processing live sounds from acoustic musical instruments, everyday noises and electronic instruments to produce a different, often metallic or robotic spectral profile. It was one of the most recognisable effects used by the BBC Radiophonic Workshop. If you have heard the Daleks say, 'Exterminate!' or a Cyberman say, 'Delete, delete!', you have heard a ring-modulator effect pushed to an extreme setting. More subtle settings would produce a beautiful, trembling shimmer. The Radiophonic Workshop and Stockhausen were using the same relatively primitive Space Age effects units to explore different galaxies.

every composition on Sirius is related to the rhythms of nature ... the seasons, the rhythms of the stars.' Stockhausen gave lectures on his theories because he believed that learning the techniques involved gave the listener an opportunity to expand their consciousness on some level (musically and otherwise) and would enrich the listening experience.

Mantra is an important turning point, or perhaps starting point would be more appropriate. From the composition of *Mantra*, with its 'formulaic mantra', an intricate design of material spread across musical (and extra-musical) parameters, which became prototypical of almost every composition written subsequently. 1973 was the year when Stockhausen was at the height of his powers, if you believed in Stockhausen as a musician, and in a sense *Mantra* is still a piano piece, embellished with electronic effects, full of attractive textures and enthralling energy, for all the shape of the galaxy, tree-of-life theories that surround it. It is very much in a musical tradition of Mahler and Stravinsky, the sort of music and musicians he ignored when he started composing in the 1950s.

1973 was the year when Stockhausen delivered his lecture as a combination of charming, eccentric TV presenter enthusiastically presenting some marvellous new scientific theory that explains the movement of the earth, an absurdist comedian trapped somewhere between Jacques Tati and Monty Python's Eric Idle perpetually on the verge of delivering a hilarious punch line, and a self-certified prophet who took the process of amplifying a piano using two microphones with such unabashed seriousness, he clearly believed the resulting sound might help definitively explain whether God exists or not.

A 1973 PLAYLIST WITH EXPLANATIONS

1. Prelude and Fugue No. 3 in C-sharp major, BWV 848, by J. S. Bach. 1973 was the year when the great and virtuous Russian pianist Sviatoslav Richter released a recording of Bach's *Well-Tempered Clavier Book I,* so that a musical collection of intricately patterned solo keyboard music composed as a combination of exercise, meditation and commissioned job in 1722 was investigated in 1973, and it belonged there, even if it sounded at the time distant from where the world was, and even further away from where the lively, fast-changing popular music of the day was. Richter brought the *Well-Tempered Clavier* into the then modern world, where it discreetly mixed with other music even though it is only now, through the computer making all music available in one space, that we can really understand how his Bach recital was as much 1973 as it was 1722, and in a way all the years in between, and those after Richter recorded it. It can be heard more clearly how this was as modern, if not more so, than all the fashionable activity that was drowning it out at the time. There were artificial boundaries between different forms of music then that have now been demolished, and you get a better sense now how, at any given time, all sorts of different things are happening at the same time, some new, some old, some visible, some invisible, but all creating the evolving, spiralling energy and texture of a particular period. History is always travelling in different directions. The modern is being made by things from the past as well as the present. Listening to Richter play now, we are hearing 1973 as much as anything, a part of the atmosphere, because the music of other eras and ages was still being played, and refreshed, and repositioned, and was still passing through time, bringing other music with it. Think of this as being from 1973, because in many ways it was, and you begin to think of the year in a different way.

2. *Music for Pieces of Wood* by Steve Reich, written in 1973, rooted in his desire to make music, and patterns that Bach would have appreciated, with the simplest possible instruments, in this case five pairs of tuned wooden claves. One of the loudest pieces he ever wrote, using no amplification whatsoever. Pierre-Laurent Aimard's version of it from *African Rhythms* is played on the piano. Slowly, in phases, looping around, quietly, then a little louder, Reich's once obscure, tricky music moved further into the mainstream. In 1973 this sounded too uncanny ever to make it as famous and as familiar as it became.

3. Beethoven's Piano Concerto No. 4 in G major, Op. 58, II: Andante composed in 1805–6 and premiered in 1807 – the last time Beethoven appeared as a soloist with an orchestra – and performed by Vladimir Ashkenazy and the Chicago Symphony Orchestra conducted by Sir Georg Solti, released in 1973. Hungarian conductor Georg Solti considered the Chicago one of the three best orchestras in the world. On 7 May 1973 Solti was on the cover of *Time* magazine with the tag line 'The Fastest Baton in the West'. Director of the Royal Opera House between 1961 and 1971, responsible for possibly the greatest recording of Wagner's massive *Ring* cycle, with early stereo effects used to create a 'theatre of the mind', he had become a British subject the year before and was also knighted. He was once asked whether he was optimistic about the future of music: 'I have always been optimistic about the future of music and always will be. This leads to the question of what will happen if nobody writes any music today that will last through the twenty-first century. The answer is that we have enough good music from the last 400 years that will last at least another 400 years. Why should I bother with what happens in 2420?'

4. 'To Roger Waters Wherever You Are' by Ron Geesin from *As He Stands*, released in 1973. It was the year when *Dark Side of the Moon* was released, in March, beginning a run in the charts that would last for years, but one-time collaborator Ron Geesin, who orchestrated and arranged the 1970 Pink Floyd album *Atom Heart Mother*, helping them to finish it, released *As He Stands*, which featured a plaintive request to an old hippy colleague who was now fast becoming an international superstar. Music that began in the same place had split in two, one side of it becoming iconic and international, the other side disappearing into the gloomy, magical undergrowth.

5. *Makrokosmos* **Vol. 1** by George Crumb, twelve short 'fantasy pieces', each based on a different sign of the zodiac and dedicated to a person born then, where an amplified piano is used as a theatrical object to make sound somewhere between the prepared piano of John Cage, with various objects placed on the strings inside the instrument to alter their sound, and the way Jimi Hendrix used his guitar, performer fused with instrument into spellbinding madness, especially in how the player leans inside the instrument to get direct access to the strings. The piano is turned into something else by being amplified, and the pianist becomes much more of an extroverted, physical performer than usual, as they are expected to speak, sing, chant, whisper and whistle and make various noises while playing and effectively exploring themselves, sound and the usually passive-seeming piano.

As well as the references to Cage – and also how his prepared predecessor Henry Cowell would get inside the piano itself – the belief in the abilities of the piano comes directly out of Bartók and also Debussy, via his *Preludes*, in the amount of orchestral colour and sonic extreme a single pianist extracts from a piano. The idea of composing piano music that tests the technical and musical resources of an instrument and the virtuosity of a musician stretches all the way back to Bach's *Well-Tempered Clavier*, and from there through Chopin, Liszt, Schumann and Shostakovich.

Crumb has specific instructions for how each movement should be played, which help to describe the range of sounds and emotions the work covers – darkly mysterious, very fast, whimsical and volatile, moderately with incisive rhythm, eerily with a sense of malignant evil, poised, expectantly, gracefully with an elastic rhythm, joyously like a cosmic clockwork, with mechanically precise rhythm, breathlessly with élan, musingly, with the gentle caress of a faintly remembered music, vast, lonely, timeless. The first volume was in memory of Bartók, a second volume following soon after was in memory of Mahler, and the various examples of people born under a certain sign included Brahms. Crumb was openly revealing about how much the music belonged with and to other music and musicians, part of an epic extended web of sounds and ideas connecting centuries and a whole collective of geniuses, technicians and listeners. If I had heard this at the time it wouldn't have seemed 'classical' but connected to the electronic German music I was listening to, and to esoteric early Virgin avant-rock collectives such as Henry Cow and Hatfield and the North. As monumental as it is, there was no clear route to it in 1973; there is a route now, via Spotify, and just one listen of this masterpiece is easily worth a month's subscription, whether you play anything else or not. Also largely hidden from view…

6. 'Life Study 1' from the astounding, ridiculously under-cherished and uncannily beautiful *Life Studies* for fifteen solo strings by Nicholas Maw: jazz from Jupiter, classical from 2420, premiered in Cheltenham on 9 July 1973, performed by the Academy of St Martin-in-the-Fields. More than most, Maw proves that sadness is more interesting than happiness, that it often makes for a more beautiful music, which can make the listener happy hearing it. At the time, if I had been made aware of it, I could easily have played Fripp & Eno's *No Pussyfooting* and then the *Life Studies* and then:

7. 'Heimatklänge' by Kraftwerk from their 1973 third album, *Ralf and Florian*, the one before *Autobahn*, that eventually they would more or less disown, rewriting history to establish their starting point elsewhere, when the patiently conceived rhythm kicked in, working out how as classical musicians they would make pop music that wasn't a clumsy fusion of the two but a radical new methodology; the pop they produced with classical rigour and technique ended up influencing black music instead of only being influenced by it.

They took the exploratory electronic production of sound out of the enclosed music academies, research departments, science labs and television workshops, and the mysterious, ideologically arrhythmical, star-counting hands of their spiritual German step-forefather Karlheinz Stockhausen, and into the more active rock world, which was up to then mostly played with the woody, traditional instruments used to play the blues and rock 'n' roll. They became influenced by the pop they considered to be as progressive as modern classical music – their frail, android singing, seemingly drained of emotion, yet strangely poignant, was actually a tender tribute to the (to them) deeply alien, sunshine harmonies of the Beach Boys, and their poetic approach to accumulating and manipulating repetition was taken from the languid, sinister rock of the Velvet Underground and where they had absorbed it from early minimalism.

They loved the lovely patterns of Bach that sounded artless but weren't, the simple but stupendous, heartbreaking melodies of Brahms, and, experimenting with machines and various modular synthesisers, and bit by bit, they worked out how to make music using electronics that gave a new dimension to the idea of sounding beautifully, sadly, a little madly, human. They were artists who happened to turn their ideas not into painting or sculpture or photography, but into being a pop group. This pop group was an inter-media comment on the idea of what a pop group could be, and how it could explore subjects and themes outside the usual childish list of sex, drugs, parties and adolescent angst.

They identified how all pop music, even the very best, is a form of novelty music, a sonic representation of the fresh and surprising information we are constantly drawn to as a species. Their better-known songs, wistful, cryptic commentaries on telephones, calculators, neon, motorways, radios, trains, bicycles, models, transport, European civilisation, replication, ones that *2001*'s Hal might speak-sing in partnership with the speaking clock or the satnav lady, anticipating curt text-speak, sneaked sideways into the pop charts as if they were one-hit wonders, a gimmicky act where books about the group happened to quote Theodor Adorno, Walter Benjamin and Jean Baudrillard.

They created most of the blueprint for all electronic pop and sound-track music, and we are as compromised and polluted by technology, distracted by entertainment and controlled by communication as they prudently predicted. The computer, announced Kraftwerk, long before there were smartphones, would soon directly connect us to the world, and we would perceive everything through a ghostly glow of pixels to a soundtrack of regulated, machine-generated noise. Funnily enough, I now realise they were not far from the following, in terms of their loveliness, loneliness and enigmatic way of coming to terms with how the world is created each and every day, and understanding the mystery of timing in their own good time.

8. *Grimethorpe Aria* by Harrison Birtwistle, commissioned by Elgar Howarth, the conductor of the Grimethorpe Colliery Brass Band of South Yorkshire. After Howarth became the band's professional conductor and music adviser in 1972, moving away from the London Philharmonic Orchestra and the solid, unthreatened establishment, he immediately changed the reputation of the band and brass band music in general by generating new kinds of repertoire, not least by encouraging modern composers to write for the band.

Birtwistle, of the industrial North, born in Accrington, Lancashire, relished the plaintive uniqueness of the British brass bands, and within that the performative uniqueness of the Grimethorpe Band. He barely missed a beat between the dark sound and weatherbeaten immensity of the piece he had written for Howarth and the London Philharmonic Orchestra the year before, *The Triumph of Time*, and the piece he wrote for what was considered a weaker vessel, a brass band. Howarth had been a member of Birtwistle's circle of ambitious young modernists in Manchester in the 1950s, along with Peter Maxwell Davies and Alexander Goehr, and would regularly work with Birtwistle during the next few decades. His role in both commissions undoubtedly made one commission appear naturally to follow from the other.

For the brass band Birtwistle in effect, still in the mood, wrote a kind of sequel to *The Triumph of Time*, not for a moment considering he needed to write something light and playful – quite the opposite. He heard the sound of a northern brass band with its own striking history and committed players as a method of achieving the driving, desolate intensity he previously achieved using the allegedly more formal and professional London Philharmonic.

He was not interested in treating the brass band as a conservative ensemble that used the instruments traditionally and generally clung to the obvious, but as simply another flexible, intriguing multi-instrumental way of pursuing his meticulous, tumultuous ideas. His melancholy memories and mesmerising honesty flowed seamlessly from the orchestra to the brass band, whether the music was played by full-time experts in their world or skilled part-time miners. The two works are a supreme demonstration of intense pessimism that becomes somehow positive. A weird kind of optimism materialises simply because the sound exists. Ultimately, it's music beyond such things – in the way that a piece of coal, or a grey cloud, or an ominous atmosphere is neither optimistic nor pessimistic, it just *is*.

However magnificent it was, high and mighty classical snobbery and dismal northern stereotyping greeted its appearance at the Proms in 1974, when the Grimethorpe and another great northern brass band, the Black Dyke, played, after eighty years of neglect, part of the determined drive of Grimethorpe's transplanted leader Elgar Howarth. The idea, to those stuck in their classical ways, suggested a definite lowering of tone, as if blunt-speaking, coal-dust-covered working-class hobbyists were intruding on their precious, previously unsullied festival.

Howarth conducted the evening's performance in a midnight-blue velvet suit, to be greeted by a heckle from the audience of 'Where's thi flat cap then?' Howarth briefly touched the back of his head. The sceptical audience was gradually won over, especially after the bleakly majestic *Grimethorpe Aria*, and complementary pieces by Holst and Elgar, and enthusiastic applause would have suggested that British brass bands playing with such dedicated precision, grace and insight would become a regular feature at the main British festival of music.

They didn't. The North, in this case a grand Yorkshire portion, didn't belong, not really, even as they resolutely got stuck into Birtwistle's no-nonsense fantasia, which imagined a very different kind of inexplicable Britishness, somewhere between merry and menacing. It was just another one of those slightly patronising, ultimately gimmicky curatorial gestures the Proms still makes, as though it is as democratic and open-minded as it likes to think it is and keeping up to speed with changes in fashions and styles, but which, in the end, never allows anything in that might upset the well-guarded apple cart.

9. Overture No. 4 in F major, composed by Thomas Arne, performed by the Academy of Ancient Music. The Academy of Ancient Music was formed in Cambridge in 1973 by harpsichordist and scholar Christopher Hogwood as a period-instrument orchestra, with the intention of getting instrumentally closer to how music composed centuries ago was originally performed, and rediscovering ancient music. In September of 1973, under Hogwood's direction, the AAM made their first recording: *Arne – Eight Overtures*. Eccentric eighteenth-century theatrical composer Thomas Arne wrote 'Rule Britannia', and his 1745 arrangement of the national anthem, with a melody dating from the time James II was defeated by William of Orange, has since changed little. The eight overtures, following very distinctive, plaintive and jaunty English lines and written at the very beginning of British symphonism, were taken from a variety of his stage works and first performed as a complete collection in 1751.

10. Piano Sonata No. 3 composed by Michael Tippett in 1973, the year after his Beethoven-infused Third Symphony, with signs of that influence still lingering here in the formidable amount of rigorous attack and thought. It was first performed by Paul Crossley and described as 'the most pianistic' of his four sonatas, which were written over a time period of forty-eight years, monitoring his changes as a composer. Here, his more experimental sixties drifting off, he is in full-blooded classical mode.

11. Bremen, July 12, 1973, Part II (extract) by Keith Jarrett, released on the beautiful box-set triple album of over two hours of intense, joyous piano improvisations, *Solo Concerts Bremen/Lausanne*, released on the then four-year-old ECM label of Manfred Eicher. It was the first of Jarrett's solo concerts to be released on ECM, after his driving, emphatic studio-recorded ECM debut *Facing You* and before the distillation of this improvised style into *The Köln Concert* double album, which sold enough copies to ensure the future of the most adventurous and purist of record labels, one that mostly recorded and released endlessly travelling, trans-genre instrumental music. I was distracted a little by Eno, Bolan, Bowie, Sparks and Mott at the time, but on the hypnotic, epic quiet this was in the vicinity of being my favourite album of the year.

12. 'Entry in a Diary' by Ralph Towner from the exquisite *Diary*, released in 1973 on the ECM label. By now, thanks to the Jarrett masterpiece, I was already an avid collector of the relatively young ECM label, already sounding like it had its own sound, never considering I would be one for the rest of my life, drawn to musicians and instrumental music that could make you feel all at once more lonely and less lonely, and which seemed to emerge into space through space as though from space, always finding new space. It was already becoming one of the greatest contemporary record labels, committed to mostly abstract, impressionistic instrumental and improvised music, to a predominantly European abstraction of post-bop modern jazz, to the most exceptional and experimental, iconic and inventive classical sounds of the past few centuries, from the old-time sacred to the postmodern avant-garde.

Towner, founder member of world-music-minded improvisers Oregon, favouring unamplified six- and twelve-string acoustic guitar, is as much an integral part of the free-flowing ECM spirit as the more renowned Jarrett, and the year before had guested on Weather Report's 'I Sing the Body Electric'. His music might be called world, New Age, ambient, jazz, classical, but I always thought of it as elsewhere, and here it was, lost in wonderful thought, in 1973, the year glam rock called its own. 1973 was a good year to begin discovering – and to carry on discovering – ECM. ECM's output since its first release in 1969, as a total musical and conceptual statement of intent, as a complete work of art, is in itself a momentous endorsement of the idea that without music we would not be fully human, there would be something missing, a palpable hole in time and space, in our collective imagination. Nearly fifty years later both Towner and Jarrett are still recording for ECM, in many ways as though they're still in 1973. Or 1673. Or 2073.

13. 'Now Here (Nowhere)' by the Dave Holland Quartet from the 1973 ECM album *Conference of the Birds*, featuring Dave Holland, Sam Rivers, Anthony Braxton and Barry Altschul. An avant-garde masterpiece, gorgeous as much as it is abrasive, fragile and feisty, apparently strange, but really incredibly logical, and on its own giving lie to the imperishable idea that ECM music is slick, posh and frictionless muzak. This is on fire, and any film of the turbulent uneasy events of 1973 should really feature what was as much the sound of the year as the records of Led Zeppelin, the Who and Pink Floyd, which are the ones usually used.

ECM had already begun to specialise in transcendent manifestations of spiritual music as inspired by musicians across centuries from Johns Dowland and Coltrane, from Webern to Pärt. Jazz, as modern and elegiac as any, but connected to ancient music, as earthy and eerie as any. The 'E' stood for Editions – Editions of Contemporary Music – but it could easily have stood for 'European', and so ECM was also a jazz music that erupted out of the more experimental cerebral elements of Coltrane, and the places where Bill Evans had blurred and ecstatically sedated the sound of Miles Davis, and then his own, because he listened to and came from Debussy, Ravel and Satie, adding a tincture of sonic surrealism to jazz's own take on reality.

There were other albums released in 1973 helping to pick up the label's independent-minded momentum, which will continue as long as its founder and central creative light Manfred Eicher – producing the majority of their recordings – is alive. A few from that year are as worth finding and absorbing as the Towner, the Holland and the Jarrett, some the best the label has ever released, showing how far the label had come in just four years, and already suggesting how many tributaries of sound and possible direction were splitting off from its original starting place: in 1973 alone Stanley Cowell's *Illusion Suite*; Paul Motian's *Conception Vessel*; Dave Liebman's *Lookout Farm*; Jan Garbarek and Bobo Stenson's *Witchi-Tai-To*; Eberhard Weber's *The Colours of Chloë*.

The ECM albums of music are Eicher's life's work, never particularly part of any mainstream, never particularly critical darlings, always embedded in his deeply philosophical, intensely idealistic sense of musical history, a world view that mixes up music, sounds and musicians from around the world and across time according to his probing, eclectic taste, which tends to be biased towards meditative representations of the sublime, the serene and the introspective. Once described as the most beautiful sound next to silence, ECM's motto could be 'Keep calm – and touch the face of God'.

With ECM, and Eicher, there is a consistent commitment to the enduring mystery of music revealed through enlightened, ambitious and serious works, often themselves shrouded in mystery, hidden behind cryptic, always faceless, inevitably beautiful and poetic cover art and framed inside a sumptuous, spatial recorded sound that some see as cold and decadent, or offensively New Agey and bland, and others worship as an endlessly questioning reflection of the divine universal balances and connections calculated and cultivated by musicians from J. S. Bach to Miles Davis, from Mozart to Hendrix.

There have been around 1,600 ECM albums released, a number of them undisputed masterpieces, most of them worth hearing at least once, in total an extraordinary celebration of and inquiry into the very idea and purpose of music, and musicians, and composition, the ancient and modern power of structured sound, of manipulated noise that carries with it meaning and insight, that compensates for the vagueness of language, and a celebration of the album itself, which is now, for all the lamenting nostalgia, a thing of the past, like transistor radios, pipes and *Carry On* films.

ECM and ECM New Series were born in the vinyl age and resisted being part of the streaming system until 2017, concerned they would just disappear into the ocean of sound, effort and beauty dissolving into the wherever, but the fact that you can now find these ECM albums on Spotify, Tidal, YouTube Music and so on is an unbelievable piece of luck, and might even mean the music doesn't actually disappear but lasts much longer. It just needs to be found, and it can be found, almost all of it, with just one subscription service. Streaming might be in one sense the end of the world for music, but it also might be where the world of music is held in place and given certain protection as reality changes shape and, to some extent, moves heaven and earth into a very different dimension.

14. 'In Every Dream Home a Heartache' by Roxy Music from their ultra-glamorous hyper-eroticised second album *For Your Pleasure*, released in 1973. It was the year when my favourite album was possibly this dark, topsy-turvy and ironically sincere pop, elevated by the pop-art studies of singer Bryan Ferry, and the last Roxy record featuring cavalier sound artist Brian Eno, bringing along into intense song-forms his own research into the chance operations of John Cage and the art of making connections.

What was Bryan Ferry thinking as he crooned his dark infatuation with skin that was like vinyl, accompanied by a glowering gothic drone? And what was Brian Eno thinking when he enigmatically, or sulkily, or just plain distractedly exited stage left, fleeing Roxy, and swiftly releasing a 1973 album of very slow, electronically treated Robert Fripp guitar, aware of the phasing of Steve Reich, the temper of Morton Feldman and the looping of Terry Riley, which went on for approximately ever and which was somehow even lovelier when played at half speed and which, ultimately, seems as captivating and erotic – especially when played in the dark – as its naughty if not downright baleful step-cousin *For Your Pleasure*. The budget price of Fripp & Eno's *No Pussyfooting* album and glowing multi-mirrored cover – more glam than classical – made it especially seductive. *No Pussyfooting* was cerebral ritualistic novelty music blending the academic with the playful, the meandering with the mischievous, which ended up, incidentally, helping invent the whole ambient genre, and for me it became a portal into instrumental music that could just as much be classical as anything else.

15. Symphony No. 1 by Krzysztof Penderecki, premiered in Peterborough in 1973 and performed by the London Symphony Orchestra. It comes at the end of an avant-garde period for the Polish composer, who began composing at the end of the 1950s as an unknown assistant professor in the composition department of the Krakow Academy of Music. At the time, he said that his interest was 'in liberating sound beyond all tradition', and on his early masterpiece in 1960, *Threnody for the Victims of Hiroshima*, for fifty-two string instruments, he was balancing on a pinhead between chance and serialism, the great monuments of twentieth-century modernism; the emotional power achieved in the piece took Penderecki by surprise, and the title arrived only after he had heard it being played. A year later, he was extending his obsessive commitment to extending the range and power of strings with *Polymorphia*, to the point of imagining what the thoughts and dreams of ghosts would sound like.

On the 1962 *Fluorescence* he combined a traditional symphony orchestra – although each instrument played unconventionally, all part of a collage rather than a composition – with an experimental percussion section that includes sheets of metal, glass, electric bell, saw, typewriter and siren. The result is a number of people playing with one distinct voice, essentially channelling the subconscious of the composer in the purest way imaginable.

After twenty years of searching for ways to intensify and deform traditionalism with avant-garde techniques, in 1973 the forty-year-old Penderecki wrote his First Symphony in a deliberate attempt to summarise his experimental years and his pressurised quest for new sounds, which would lead to new structures and new textures. Through four movements, Penderecki perfects his ability to feature sound more than harmony and melody and yet, because of his intrinsic musicality, produce striking coherence that sounds as much conventional as wilfully innovative. The symphony was effectively the climax of his time as a sound artist who used mostly natural instruments, a clear contemporary of Ligeti and his static, star-gazing sound-spaces, and liberated a very different composer, relinquishing his sonoristic passions, closer to Bruckner and Dvořák. His music became more the kind of music you would imagine being played by traditional instruments.

For Penderecki, being avant-garde, and working in a country at the time under a repressive communist regime, had meant reconstructing the world from scratch, confronting profoundly disappointing and unsettling surroundings by imagining truer, stranger other places where the imagination is not hemmed in.

After his First Symphony he withdrew from the avant-garde spirit of his youth and the collaging of sound and effect, and began exploring the idea of the symphony itself, and he remodelled himself less as an *enfant terrible* extremist and more as a deep-thinking romantic guardian of tradition, keen on experimenting within the orchestra's limits rather than disrupting it. Anxious that what he had been doing was founded on nothing, and had little impact beyond a small clique, he decided his 1960s speculation was in the end more destructive than constructive, and the First Symphony is where he is balancing on a pinhead between revolution and evolution. It's like John Coltrane going backwards from the transcendent sheets of sound to the early, elegantly enriched standards.

It was the Penderecki equivalent of the sheets of sound that established his originality. His early sonic and existential balancing acts, his ability to coolly, provocatively generate tension and suspense, fear and release, sound and noise, music shifting between this world and unknown others, of the quiet and the loud, soft and hard, high and low, made him a favourite of the most purely cinematic film directors, especially those working on horror films, wanting inscrutable, closed, chilling sound more than open, explanatory words.

These directors were especially interested in the stressed, startling music he made before the First Symphony, all those glissandi, clusters, sharp contrasts, his exploration of purely sonic phenomena, and his methods of articulating, among much else, the dark side of the (Polish) soul. David Lynch turned to the composer for *Twin Peaks*, *Wild at Heart* and *Inland Empire*, as did Martin Scorsese needing nerve-racking atmosphere for *Shutter Island*, Alfonso Cuaron wanting something apocalyptic for *Children of Men*, and you can hear his music significantly contributing to the absolute else-whereness of *The Shining* and the disturbing near-else-whereness of *The Exorcist*. Penderecki's music powerfully finished off the two most notorious horror films of all time, helping the images and stories get under the skin and deep into memory, perhaps scaring him onto the more or less straight and narrow.

16. 'Ah, Serenissima!' from Benjamin Britten's *Death in Venice* performed by Peter Pears and the English Chamber Orchestra. At the time a long way from the consideration of a sixteen-year-old obsessed with the droning instrumental music of a highbrow glam-rock star, Benjamin Britten was in fact being as alluring, eccentric and clearly as erotic, alien and intoxicating as Roxy, Sparks and Bowie, composing his austere, heartbreaking final opera, *Death in Venice*. It was based on the haunting Thomas Mann novel about an ageing writer obsessed with a boy's beauty, featuring Gustav von Aschenbach, who was based on Mann and Mahler. Britten wrote the tortured role of Aschenbach for his long-time partner Peter Pears, dedicating it to him, and portrayed the protagonist's aesthetic and existential crisis over seventeen scenes. He had been thinking about writing it for a long time, postponed it once, and was in poor health while he wrote it. He managed to finish it before entering hospital in May 1973 for open-heart surgery. He suffered a stroke immediately after and was unable to attend the opera's premiere on 16 June at the Aldeburgh Festival.

17. 'Chocolate Field' from *Coxhill/Miller–Miller/Coxhill*. The subdued Albion music of 1973, much of it rooted in the dreamy and gentlemanly experimental Canterbury scene of Soft Machine – made touchingly and not a little touched by the fluctuant, slippery likes of Hatfield and the North, Egg, Gong, Kevin Ayers and Hugh Hopper, incongruously exploding into the chart mainstream through the one-boy band Mike Oldfield, who therefore helps Richard Branson set up Virgin Records and, beyond that, hippy corporatism – has ended up being the rock music from that year that grows and grows in actual timeless intensity.

1973 was the year when Robert Wyatt, once of psych-pop jazz freaks Soft Machine, had the nasty accident that paralysed him, postponing his radiantly introspective, desperately soulful record *Rock Bottom* until the next year. But amidst the horror of the year, he did collaborate with the sublime subdued duo of avant-garde saxophonist and busker Lol Coxhill – a free-jazz Spike Milligan – and Steve Miller, of light prog-cavaliers Caravan. Their sound was a mischievous relation, slyer and less, shall we say, hygienic, of the ECM one being developed at the time, with Britten, Vaughan Williams and Frank Bridge as influences in place of the radical Europeanism of Webern, Varèse and a pastoral take on the intellectual swing of Coltrane.

A roguish English eccentricity was expressed with extreme, uncompromising elegance and I can never think of 1973 without thinking of their alert, lovely method of relishing and realising the essential disorientating madness of music. Elsewhere, as a growing part of Branson's initially mail-order Virgin Records, on the way to trains, airlines, islands, space travel and bankruptcy, there was what could be called, and was, a Canterbury supergroup, Hatfield and the North, who were already gearing up for their debut 1974 album on Virgin by recording a 1973 session for John Peel, which was where you heard most of the music you ended up buying and living with for the first time. Radical new musicians would use the beautiful broadcasting symbol of the subdued Peel and his subversive use of the BBC to help work out and discreetly promote their style and sound.

18. String Quartet No. 3, Duo II: Largo tranquillo by Elliott Carter was completed in 1971, consistently divided into two duos, but not premiered until 1973, played by the Juilliard String Quartet, which it was dedicated to. Not for the faint-hearted, the Third was perhaps the most complicated of his quartets, but probably the most exhilarating, a special example of art conceived with scientific precision so that the real and the unreal are always circling each other, combining, and separating, and recombining. That year it earned Carter, then sixty-five, his second Pulitzer Prize for music. He received the prize in 1960 for his Second Quartet. The Pulitzer could seem like a daft, compromised token of some sort of affection, but it got this right.

19. 'Gimme Danger' by Iggy and the Stooges from *Raw Power*. Another great, relentless American with something of the European thinker about him, Iggy Pop was in 1973 still a Stooge singer, making the third Stooges album with some help from David Bowie, who together, under a certain sort of personal and artistic pressure intentionally or not mixed the sound of guitars, bass and drums – and the corrupt crooning and perverse poetry of Iggy – into something blurred around heavy metal, pop and accidental noise that would influence the sound of punk and post-punk as much as anything else. It was the obscure side of culty at the time, but over the years it's become considered a grown-up classic, Sinatra for surrealists. Record-company executives at Iggy's Columbia label wanted a couple of ballads to soften the savagery, and in Iggy-land 'Gimme Danger' is a ballad. If there's beauty in there, put some of that down to the input of Bowie, adding some imperial radiance to the guitar that Iggy originally wanted to be scraggier and sleazier. Iggy's yet to win a Pulitzer Prize.

20. Sonata No. 2 for Piano, III: Sehr langsam by Paul Hindemith, performed by Glenn Gould, who in many ways was more Iggy than Iggy when it came to self-belief, self-indulgence, provocation and extreme image building. Glenn Gould, remarkably, won only one Grammy during his lifetime, and that was not for his playing, even of Bach's *Goldberg Variations*, but for Best Liner Notes of 1973 for an essay he wrote about the composer Paul Hindemith, one of Gould's favourites, to accompany a recording that included his version of Hindemith's Piano Sonata No. 2. (Forty years later, he won a posthumous Grammy Lifetime Achievement Award.)

In the notes, full of wonderful thoughts and strong opinions, prose as bold as his playing, Gould credits Hindemith with waking him up to the merits of contemporary music, having previously hated all music, as a naturally precocious fifteen-year-old, that came after Wagner. Gould wrote that Hindemith found 'the true amalgam of reason and ecstasy: repose'. He always said he would have wanted to have been a writer if he hadn't been the challenging and argumentative star pianist. His thinking about music was as original as his playing. He was the Bach man, but Hindemith was the perfect composer for him to channel his love for Bach into modern music, approaching him as he would Bach, relishing the awareness of tradition, the precision and elegance, and playing it with as much vivid intensity and cerebral swing as he would Bach.

21. Concerto for Two Pianos and Orchestra by Luciano Berio, who had in all seriousness definitively decided by 1973 that writing a traditional concerto had no meaning – it wasn't like the baroque, classical and romantic eras, where there was some meaning in analysing, or celebrating, or reconfiguring the classic competitive relationship between soloist and orchestra, between a self-determining individual and the masses. For Berio, a new composition was often founded in the idea of solving a problem, even if that problem had been created in the first place as an intellectual challenge, a creative springboard. A new temporary problem of how to use and manipulate a combination of instruments would produce a new composition, which as part of its existence comments on its own existence.

For him the problem of the relationship between soloist and orchestra had been long solved, but he conceived a new set of problems and relationships with his two-piano concertos, where the two pianists were having to work out their position between themselves, and their relationship with the orchestra, while the orchestra itself, in order to deal with the new threat of two soloists, split into a set of smaller ensembles negotiating their relationship to each other, and then to the pianists as soloists and as a connected duo.

A multitude of differences are created, and the hope of the utopian, of the academic, of the artistic searcher, of the teacher and philosopher is to conceive of a situation, constantly in motion, where a unifying harmony is achieved amidst all the conflict. The war, and peace, is on as the pianists go hell for leather and the orchestra, in the heat of battle, keeps changing its mind about who and where the enemy is, or indeed if it is even the enemy.

The correct conductor was in place for the premiere of this wonderfully tangled and tempestuous piece in March 1973 – released that month, '20th

Century Boy' by T. Rex, 'Frankenstein' by Edgar Winter, and albums by the three-year-old Swedish Mamas and Papas Abba (*Ring Ring*), the Mahavishnu Orchestra (*Birds of Fire*) and Todd Rundgren (*A Wizard, a True Star*) – Pierre Boulez, adding his own threat, experience and analysis, his own understanding of the everyday realities of human thought, to the jumble of energies. If you want somewhere to start with Berio before you make your way through his epic, important *Sequenza*s this is as good a place as any, and his approach to combining and recombining instruments in the concerto is directly related to the intimate examination of an instrument's distinct properties that he was exploring in the solo pieces.

The concerto was commissioned by the New York Philharmonic, which Berio had developed a relationship with in the 1960s; his 1968 learned, proto-sampling voyage through the history of music, *Sinfonia*, a masterpiece of colliding meanings, eras and sounds, was commissioned by the orchestra for its 125th anniversary and dedicated to Bernstein, then the orchestra's music director.

One everyday reality for the composer five years after completing one of music's greatest biographical adventures was how hard up he was. Genius and vision alone did not pay the bills, especially when he was the kind of composer writing music, however compelling, that commented on itself and a history it may or may not belong to. He needed to write a financially embarrassed letter to the orchestra's managing director asking for a little extra money in advance. 'I don't have to tell you of the enormous changes in the world in the last two years and I'm sure you are aware that the price of bread (and caviar) has gone up,' he joked. 'Which is a pretty subtle way of asking if you can augment the commission fee – before I have to send my children out on the streets to beg for a little caviar (with chopped onion on the side).' He managed to elicit $1,500.

22. 'Future Days' by Can from the album of the same name – another candidate at the time for my favourite album of 1973... and another album that would not have sounded the way it did if it hadn't been made by musicians taken by the instrumental line-ups and amplification of rock but using a classical, and jazz, approach to the abstract editing of sound, space and tempo, and they were as much descendants of Stockhausen, *musique concrète*, La Monte Young and Terry Riley as of the Velvet Underground, Miles Davis, Frank Zappa, MC5, Sly and the Family Stone and James Brown. Once Can was opened, they in turn flow as hallucinatory minimalists with their fingers on a multi-verse of pulses directly into the Berlin of David Bowie, the punk and post-punk of the Buzzcocks and the Fall, zigzagged into This Heat and Cabaret Voltaire, right through into the e-swing of the Stone Roses and the mesmerising repetitions of rave, and beyond into electronica and beyond that.

23. Symphony No. 7, II: Andante con moto–Molto vivace–Lento by Malcolm Arnold, premiered in 1973, each movement a portrait of one of his children, to whom it is dedicated, which disconcerted some, as it is one of his fiercest, bleakest and most unsettling symphonies. The brooding Andante second movement is about his son Robert. He wrote the soundtracks for films such *Bridge on the River Kwai* and the St Trinian's films, but turned down a request to write the score for Kubrick's *2001: A Space Odyssey*, where outer space was lined with music, which might have enhanced his reputation, which was always as someone light and compliant rather than as powerfully eclectic and inventive.

24. 'Hamlet's dialogue with conscience' from *Six Poems of Marina Tsvetaeva* by Dmitri Shostakovich. In 1973, Dmitri Shostakovich was sixty-seven, and still composing, if not quite at the speed he once had. He was considered by William Walton the greatest composer of the twentieth century, and by Pierre Boulez a third-hand Mahler. He lived for all but the first eleven years of his life under the communist system of the Soviet Union, and to some he was the system's obedient musical laureate, to others, critical of Stalin and communism, his music consistently contained symbols of dissidence, and was full of pain and shame, and a constant dread.

This searingly introverted song cycle is based on the poems of 'the eternal rebel' Marina Tsvetaeva, who committed suicide in 1941 after a tragic, restless life filled with death and poverty. The music could only have been written by someone who identified with her loneliness and confusion about the chaotic changes in her country, who responded to the themes of love, art and death scattered through her poetry. This is the 1973 where history and the present weighed heavily on the free world and the Iron Curtain seemed unbreakable. Towards the end of his life Shostakovich's music was more and more considering death, more and more metaphysical – like Mahler's music at the same stage of life – so this is the 1973 where life was fading away, producing an otherworldly intellectual response, and a belief in the importance of song, whatever hell the world suffered. 'Tie A Yellow Ribbon' was the most popular song in 1973, for a battered world demanding the happy endings of pop melody, and perhaps these songs were the least popular, being largely about despair, and not easy to sing along with, but they were the most emotionally devastating, and will last far longer.

25. It has been said that work backwards, or sideways, from everything you know about hip-hop, post-punk, electronica, trip hop and post-rock and you end up at Black Ark. This was the four-track studio in the ragged suburbs of Kingston, Jamaica, where in the early to mid-1970s, after some pivotal early ska in the 1960s and the inspired mentoring of the internationalist reggae stars Bob Marley and the Wailers, Lee 'Scratch' Perry technically, mischievously and metaphysically remade reggae – and therefore all adventurous forms of music made, dubbed, remixed, sampled and programmed inside recording studios that followed. Work backwards, and forwards, from the very first, more or less almost cubist dub album in 1973, *Upsetters 14 Dub Blackboard Jungle*, which broke inside multitrack recording to explore the space between rhythm, and between ancient African sources and radical Jamaican play. The acceleration that happened in Jamaican music between the early 1960s and the early 1970s, as it zigzagged from ska and rock-steady via toasting and reggae to futuristic dub, was an aspect of a nation rapidly discovering a new identity once it had been released from the British colonial presence. The pent-up musical inventions and varieties of showmanship tumbling on top of each other as liberated locals made up for lost time, a version of how the German electronic musicians were using music, imagination, intoxicants, machines and recording studios to create a new national sound that repaired considerable psychic, cultural and environmental damage. Positive new myths emerged out of a period of ruined, ruinous myths.

Perry's experimental dub was one source for hip-hop, ensuring it would at its best always be an experimental music, but also, as contemporary music, it was a fabulously irregular elaboration of what Stockhausen and Milton Babbitt were doing with the power of electricity, the information of sound and the structure of dynamics. Perry was also a Jamaican Phil Spector, a reggae Brian Wilson, pioneering the use of the recording studio as a musical instrument/dream machine/idea processor – or perhaps, with his expedient manipulation of more primitive technology, the anti-Spector, with a wall of sound made of mud, straw and cosmic dust.

Perry's extreme, tricky auteur style might all have been sacred, clownish visions fuelled by weed, rum and Rastafari, it might have been sheer bloody-mindedness, it might have been the ravings of a lunatic always at the end of his tether, it might have been an early sign of some of the crazier rituals he indulged in at the end of the 1970s once his mind started to get knocked out of shape by all the sonic and mental shape-shifting he'd been doing. Maybe he was just having premonitions and turning them into sound.

But let's put it down to musical genius that connects mathematics to mysticism like some avant-roots techno-guru mixing Bach and Stockhausen, a shattered, shattering, surrealist genius that harnesses a fluid cast of musicians, contributors, show-offs, toasters and singers with a precise, delirious understanding of how to use electricity, rhythm, frequencies and technical wiliness to marshal Space Age shenanigans, deranged motion and perfect drama in a song.

As a metaphor for Perry's own nervous breakdown – as though his mind had been remixed and ruptured by the pressure of technically realigning the atoms and molecules of music, by trying to blend production, performance, composition, curation and entrepreneurship decades ahead of Kanye, Dre and Jay Z – Black Ark burned down at the end of the 1970s, taking with it the mysteries about how he found his sound. Perry said he did it himself. He didn't burn the evidence of his work, though; there's still the sound, still making space in between space and time.

26. Perfect to play after the scratch dub, *...explosante-fixe...* by the intimidating, outspoken and brilliantly analytical Pierre Boulez, with a title taken from a poem by surrealist André Breton – 'convulsive beauty will be veiled-erotic, fixed-explosive, magic-circumstantial, or it will not be' – reflecting the piece's fragmented, fitful momentum, which began in 1971 with the death of Igor Stravinsky after *Tempo* magazine asked various composers for some short pieces for a commemorative edition. Boulez declined, but the thought process led two years later to a provisional piece for three instruments, which was soon replaced by a more enhanced version, chasing evanescent shapes and full of inquisitive movement in classic Boulez manner, for flute, clarinet, trumpet, vibraphone, three strings and harp, with electronics intending to manipulate the overall sound, which didn't satisfy Boulez, not least because of the primitive, erratic state of the electronics. (If only he had called in Lee Perry as his electronic consultant.) Apart from anything else, and no doubt not intended as such, it is an ecstatically emotional and strangely elegant flute concerto, surprisingly landing in history after C. P. E. Bach's Flute Concerto in G Major, Haydn's 1780 Flute Concerto, Mozart's two flute concertos, Carl Reinecke's Flute Concerto, Malcolm Arnold's Concerto No. 1 for Flute and Strings and the place where it all started for Boulez – the future in a flute – Debussy's *Prélude à l'après-midi d'un faune*. Bouleze noted that ...*explosante-fixe*... was in the end written in memory of Stravinsky in the way that Stravinsky's *Symphonies of Wind Instruments* was composed in memory of Debussy – 'by being extremely different in their tone colour, form and musical ideas'.

For Boulez, who once described himself as an interrupted composer, revision was part of the compositional process, and after further attention, much more than mere minor improvements, and a more successful technological system enabling a better balance of fidgety chamber orchestra, a trio of flutes and graceful electronics, it became in 1985, *Memorial*, in memory of a flute player, and is at the centre of a nexus of pieces based on the same material and the original sketches. While the attention on the accelerating progress of electronic music since the 1960s often tends to concentrate on its use in popular music, Boulez spent decades extending and refining his use of electronics and perfecting how they could be delicate, nuanced and precise, and under the control of the composer, both an extension and a replacement of conventional orchestral instruments.

27. *Paris 1919* by John Cale, its title inspired by the Paris peace talks in 1919, which led to the Versailles treaty, is superficially a philosophical musical abstraction of an obliquely self-examining, melancholy Graham Greene novella, full of cryptic characters, travel, art history, the Spanish Civil War, Shakespeare, fellow Welshman Dylan Thomas, Greene himself, the spirit of Dada-surrealism. It was also a subtle but confident and intelligent version of a romantically anti-romantic synthesis of rock and classical, as if there might have been something of Britten in the Beatles and Ives in Gram Parsons – and somehow it was the missing link between the *Hunky Dory* of 1971 David Bowie and the *Low* of a very different David Bowie six years later.

Cale had co-founded the Velvet Underground, worked with La Monte Young and Tony Conrad, recorded with Terry Riley and produced albums for Nico and the Stooges, and all this meant that by 1973 he was to create what was packaged and promoted as rock music as though it should be played by a shadowy but flamboyant avant-garde ensemble with a taste for the baroque, surf rock and minimalism.

Paris 1919's unique, lucid fusion didn't go anywhere, either commercially or as a genre, and Cale never really followed through its hyper-literate ambitions, although wherever Cale went over the next forty-five years, as performer or producer, however far away, or just around the corner, the idea of this ultimately impossible hybrid of dreamy pop immediacy and erudite classical grandeur always shadowed him.

It was the tubular bells Cale had been using on a session for this album at Richard Branson's Manor Studios in Oxford that Mike Oldfield spotted being wheeled out of the studio he was about to use to record music for his Virgin Records debut. He figured he might be able to use them in some way and asked if he could borrow them for his session. They were wheeled back into the studio. He thought of a way of using them.

28. 'Synphära' from *Cyborg* by Klaus Schulze, briefly an original member of Tangerine Dream and then Ash Ra Tempel, whose early imaginative and introspective use of the rudimentary new synthesisers and sequencers to create a then rare, pulse-driven drone music that was chronologically and aesthetically midway between Stockhausen's far-flung atmospheric cosmic tuning and Kraftwerk's self-conscious machine beauty, purposeless flow fused with random impulses and profound asides. It seems inevitably other-worldly because of the machines and the spacey sounds, non-melodic but strangely soothing, and points from psychedelia rather than minimalism – although it shares an interest in the static and the spatial – towards ambient and New Age. It is travelling at the same speed, if in another part of the galaxy, as:

29. *Persian Surgery Dervishes* by Terry Riley. Leaving the score behind, and his first instrument, the piano, following his instincts, two live performances with Riley on portable electric organ and tape delay in Paris and Los Angeles were recorded, and so we get to hear exactly what he was thinking – about who he was and how music could reveal it to him – on 18 April 1971 and 24 May 1972. The tape delays allow him to react to his own thoughts, to echo his own instinct, and get deeper into his feelings.

Superficially, he's thinking: where do I end up if I follow a route that began with the modalities of North Indian classical music, the trance-inducing repetitions of North African Sufi devotional music and the spiritual improvisation of John Coltrane's *Ascension* and Anthony Braxton's *Ghost Trance* pieces? It was released on the French avant-garde label Shandar, in the margins of the margins, and not as well known as the Riley works that were interesting psychedelic rock audiences getting used to the extended jams of Grateful Dead and, through another mirror, Soft Machine – *In C* and *A Rainbow in Curved Air* – and how they found unprecedented links between the sonics of rock and pop, the methods, durations and tones of minimalism and the less visible, less audible, music from then far less familiar and more distant – and ancient – parts of the world. It is music that tends to be talked about in reference to other music and performers, but which really belongs to its own genre, which threaded through other music to come – you can already hear it the same year in *No Pussyfooting*, where Riley's looping methods of time-lag music, the calming of space, were being pop-tuned by fine-art rock conceptualists Fripp and Eno.

30. Serenade No. 11 for Winds in E-flat major, I. Allegro maestoso by Mozart, conducted by Otto Klemperer. 1973 was the year when J. R. R. Tolkien, Pablo Picasso and Noël Coward died, the year when, on the very last day, the three-day week was introduced as a result of coal shortages caused by industrial action, the year when Maria Callas sang her last concert in Paris on 8 December. Afterwards, holed up in her Paris apartment, she would spend many a sleepless night with her old recordings, listening to the voice that had now left her, and she died a loner four years later, unable to forgive the world that had forgotten her... 1973 was also the year when the mighty German conductor Otto Klemperer died, aged eighty-eight, on 6 July. Klemperer was from a time, before pop culture took over imperial powers, when the orchestra was, for better or worse, considered culturally consequential.

Unfairly regarded as ponderous and old-fashioned, he started out as a protégé of Mahler, a student of Schoenberg and, despite anger from the Nazi regime that he was neglecting their version of German tradition, a young, lively and daring modernist, partial to the avant-garde, an attitude he took with him when he moved to conducting Beethoven, Bruckner and Brahms, twisting time so that it seemed as though the older music came after the later music. His last recording and the last time he led an orchestra was two years before his death, a devoted performance of Mozart's Serenade in E-flat, K. 375, written in 1781... but the man born in 1885, the year Brahms wrote his Symphony No. 4 and Gilbert and Sullivan's *The Mikado* premiered, lived to 1973, helping to bring Mozart with him, with Mozart sounding like he always knew his music would make sense whatever the year, whatever the occasion, and whatever the company. A story is told that when Klemperer was asked for a list of his favourite composers, Mozart was not on it. When he was asked why, he replied, 'Oh, I thought you meant my favourite of the *other* composers.'

PART SEVEN

The String Quartet – In Four Parts

The Danish String Quartet 2019: *feeling air from another planet.*

After my televised Royal Academy time, my radio report on the first classical album I had ever bought, the making of playlists, the panel appearances arguing for something when I really didn't want to argue, the simultaneous passionate attack and defence of opera, a few quasi-investigative commissions for *Sinfini*, somewhere between dazed and daring, the perhaps overzealous speeches to the insiders and professionals, I felt ready for what I had been building ever since I had composed a string quartet... a history I was beginning to think I could now write, bar the sort of mistakes of fact and taste where those in the know would have their view confirmed that I wasn't as classical as I hoped, that I was still pop, that I should stay where I was. That was the British thing to do: stay where you are and never imagine you can change the shape and depth of your life. In fact, mostly, never imagine, full stop.

I didn't care about that; I needed to generate a history, however rough, a sense of structure, a place to start, for my own sake, if only to help me in the search for that last piece on the playlist it would have taken my whole life to compile. I had a feeling there would be lots of string quartets on that list, many of them coming towards the end of my life, as the quartet became increasingly familiar and what I started to listen to more than most other music.

Here they come; four black figures, carrying instruments, and seat themselves facing the white squares under the downpour of light; rest the tips of their bows on the music stand; with a simultaneous movement lift them; lightly poise them, and, looking across at the player opposite, the first violin counts one, two, three – Flourish, spring, burgeon, burst!

Virginia Woolf, 'The String Quartet'

1. FIRST MOVEMENT: SONATA FORM, ALLEGRO, IN THE TONIC KEY

When I was being filmed by BBC Four studying music at the Royal Academy of Music I was extremely worried I would end up as one of those very minor near-celebrities learning or going through the motions of learning how to bake/paint/sew/parachute/play the trumpet. I was taking it a little more seriously than that, and hoping that after years of being obsessed by pop music and therefore, as far as I was concerned, music, the experience would help me in what was increasingly becoming a mission – to delve inside classical music, make sense of it, and learn to appreciate and enjoy it while establishing my favourite composers, genres, pieces, musicians and eras, and being able to write about all of this as fluently and occasionally persuasively as I like to think I did about pop and rock. There would be for me new things to write about, starting from scratch, so it would create the equivalent of a brand-new scene for me to investigate. To some extent I would be writing for those who were also new to this world, so I would be the first to discover it, opening up something not just for me but also for whoever read my writing. It would be new for me and the reader. To those who knew where they were and what they were doing, it would be best perhaps if they turned their back, or at least allowed a little leeway between the detail in their map of the territory and the alleged irregularity of mine.

It was a substantial early part of my own attempt to work out where to start discovering classical music while being completely outside a whole new language, a complete, elusive history, another planet, filled with other species, very different landscapes, massive mountains, forbidding valleys, weird mists, complicated coastlines, scary swamps, varied atmospheres and unknown colours.

On and off, I was filmed over a few months, beating out crude rhythms in an attempt to learn metre, trying to get bewildered young tuba players to play solo versions of Fripp & Eno's slow-motion meta-drone *No Pussyfooting* and falling in love with the score as a kind of quasi-literary object that was able to transfer mental activity, complex information and artistic structure into a universal language through dense, built-up, often interrupted time.

I was interested what impact having even a small amount of technical and historical knowledge would have on how and why I wrote about music, for some an absurd, unreasonable, even impossible task. Up to then, my understanding of how music was conceived and written, in terms of the nuts and bolts, the functional, technical aspects, was limited to working inside recording studios, and watching music largely being built up and pieced together from various elements of electronically generated, found and manipulated sound material and occasional instrumental and vocal performances randomly gathered across weeks and months. If there was any score to this music, it would make more sense for it to be created after the work was finished, a bit like making a script after an improvised piece of theatre was completed. A recorded pop song, however pre-planned and even pre-composed, mostly materialises out of improvisation, accidental and spontaneous moments, and becomes itself, a coherent, arranged piece, through mixing and mastering, none of which can be initially notated.

The recording studio, even though it had largely been designed and developed around the recording of the large orchestra — hence their churchlike size and acoustic quality; sometimes they were converted churches — had by the end of the twentieth century become the home of pop music, but was on the verge of being replaced, as large buildings containing specialist rooms, by laptop computers, the real pop stars of the twenty-first century. All of the elaborate technology that had been developed since the 1950s to create increasingly sophisticated pop and rock records could now be compressed into a small machine, which enabled plausible recreations of music that once took complex and expensive technology to produce.

A classical music composition was done and dusted by the time it entered a recording studio, and just needed to be recorded, and then balanced; a pop song was mostly made up inside the studio, a basic structure and dynamic brought to unreal life by increasingly multifaceted, engineered attention to detail. Practical reality leading to that energised unreality, that assembly of a multitude of details, which then feeds back into reality. The sound of the song, of each individual part, and how those parts were systematically mixed together as a fluent, mobile sum of separate parts, was ultimately the most important factor in the production, what separated it from other songs, and what made it sound like the year, the month, in the 1960s and 1970s, almost even the very week it was released.

The production company exhaustively filming me at the Royal Academy for the BBC were perhaps looking for more of an obvious reality-television climax, hoping that I would arrange an overfamiliar pop song using whatever pseudo-classical skills and techniques I had scraped together during my months at the Academy. Pop music with a classical twist, the holy grail for a decaying record industry looking for new commercial possibilities, often to cater for an ageing, or maturing, audience, as though the classical element upgraded the pop side with a topping of accessible posh, and the pop part brought classical a little down to earth and made it more user-friendly.

Unfortunately for my producers, the thought of this hybrid was horrible to me, always suspicious of anything that tries to find solutions to reaching a wider audience with a mutant product that is never going to reach a popular market unless it is so corrupted it ceases to be anything resembling its original state, the very thing that is meant to be reaching a wider audience.

Also, I had become obsessed with the score, with the making of marks on a piece of paper that would eventually be played and interpreted by a group of musicians focused on nothing but those notes and instructions. It seemed a way of establishing control over a piece of music, so that you were as much the performer as the composer, and the very act of creating a score was as much theatrical as it was creative. It seemed the whole point of what I was studying; that I could make music effectively by thinking about what I wanted it to be and then using a pencil and piece of paper. Arranging a pop song in an apparent 'classical' style seemed grubby and ordinary next to this demonstration of style – or at least, this attempt to capture a demonstration of style. This, for me, was where the mystery was, in how the classical composer conjures up order and structure, organises emotion, creates a graphic, revelatory entertainment, a view inside the imagination, inside pure thought, all produced by making these marks and being in complete imaginative control of the end result.

My dream was to write close to a proper score that when played would sound like a plausible piece of what could be taken, even by relative connoisseurs, as close enough to a classical composition for me to feel I had avoided producing a hybrid of pop and classical features that ended up being neither one thing nor the other. That ended up being a pointless, vulgar, even deeply offensive mutant.

There were many barriers to this possibility, even apart from the fact that I was learning less than one-tenth of 1 per cent of what you would need in order to be as original and sophisticated as my ego wanted me to be. In reality-television terms, I didn't fancy producing the equivalent of a burnt cake or a botched sweater, or of getting only three questions right in my specialist questions on *Mastermind*, with seven passes on the bleeding obvious. Feeling so embarrassed would mean never being able to write again. And the idea of creating an original melody, something that didn't copy anything else, that came completely out of my head, my experience, that represented my feelings, seemed about as likely as being able to swim to the moon.

Melody remained the great mystery, as it does for most musicians, however skilled, the abstract intuitive technique of somehow making real and permanent the essence of memory; the catchier, the stickier the melody, the more permanent the memory, miraculously made, abstractly, into something solid. I had an absurd ambition to be in technical and emotional control of a piece of music that possessed its own radical melodic strength that somehow indicated how I was listening to the likes of Debussy, Webern and Shostakovich, understanding it, and learning how to process the thinking behind the music and do something vaguely similar myself.

As I was studying a mass of necessary rules and regulations, the actual form and history, harmony and counterpoint, of what a concerto, or a sonata, a symphony actually was continued to elude me, as if there was almost a mathematical formula involved, a scientific background required that I could never achieve, because I didn't have the time, the patience and/or the skill. What I did have, as a writer — and as someone who had spent time in the recording studio as pop songs were imagined, improvised and invented, a composition gradually evolving into its finished state — was a sense of structure, a love of rhythm, and a fascination with arranging themes, movement and momentum, which could hopefully enable me to piece together narrative from a combination of repetition and revelation, whether in an essay, or a mix.

I eventually discovered that a concerto, sonata or symphony was nothing other than a decision a composer had made about the length, complexity and sonic intention of a piece; it was a way based on training, instinct and confidence of classifying various sections of serious instrumental music, and of commercially clarifying the basic style of presentation. They were all just pieces of music, some more elaborate than others, in formal and informal competition with various precedents, and originals that never existed in the first place, but possibly should have. The formats, the formulae, the combination of instruments and aesthetic intentions could become carriers for technical ingenuity, deeper feelings, dreamlike states, innovative dynamics and complex insights, but what came first, more often than not, was the choice of sounds, the palette of textures, the rhythmical framework, and into which category the composition would fit.

I learned that classical compositions were essentially based around a particular choice of instruments, from the one to the many, all wind, or all strings, or a mix of wind and strings, with added percussion, or not, and consisted of a series of moments that became movements, featuring a carefully organised sequence of manipulated textures and tones that effectively told a story, created an atmosphere, expressed a pattern and shape, and/or made some sort of confession, and unfolded in an order that suggested that even though there were no words, what was happening was a reflection of an evolving narrative or self-revelation, a specific personal position in life and music. There were numerous other technical decisions that needed to be made or accidentally arrived at – the key, the tempo, the length – but the most important thing of all, after the initial motivation to write something, anything, the chosen combination of instruments, and the tonal pattern, was that living order was transferred from an abstract one, something substantial emerging out of a period of thinking.

For not much more than one second, I thought: *I will write a symphony.* That seemed undeniably classical, and suitably epic, if not downright insane, like suddenly deciding I was going to design and build a house. I live in one, and have read a couple of books about architecture, so surely I could make one. I had started to listen to symphonies, and learn a little about them, so perhaps the next stage was to compose one of my own. Or to learn more about their nature by failing to write one.

What I needed to do, give or take, was select the conventional combination of instruments that could create enough grandeur, work out some dramatic themes, organise the relationship between instruments and get the hell as plausibly as possible from A to B. Or Z. Or a letter that doesn't even exist. I'd learned enough to realise that it would be the equivalent of writing a novel, and not one by Jackie Collins; more Joycean in its scope and scale. (A chamber piece being more Kafkaesque, a solo piece occupying the land of Beckett.) There was no end in sight of that particular task, packing so much language and shape into a period of time that felt suitably symphonic, and so therefore no beginning. I was intrigued enough to consider it for that one ludicrous second.

Any thoughts about writing a concerto were wrecked by the fundamental fact that I cannot play an instrument — one of the great revelations for me at the Academy was when the head of composition, Philip Cashian, explained that it was quite possible to study composition and compose music without being able to play an instrument. But the instrumental virtuosity required when writing a concerto — essentially, writing for a soloist, representing the composer's own struggles and breakthroughs, who is in mortal combat, or a romantic, even erotic connection, with the orchestra — meant there was no chance of writing this other great example of the classical form. The same really in terms of writing a solo sonata, which would require a lot of notes aggregated into a pleasing coherence requiring serious playing ability on at least one instrument.

Clearly the most practical possibility was a chamber piece. A little light night music moving into and out of the shadows. Eventually, failing badly in trying something persuasively ethereal based around harp, percussion and piano, ending up with something unravelling in limbo between atonal and aimless, I arrived at the notion of writing a string quartet. This seemed, actually, the most classical thing of all, as the string quartet is the thread that runs constantly through the entire mainstream history of classical music, from the very beginning, as the idea of a classical form consisting of certain rules and regulations took shape, to be consequently adjusted, refined and on occasions rejected, even assaulted, all the way to right now and beyond.

It's combining four instruments into one, one voice into four minds, which is where some of its magic lies, and the level of ability I had in terms of narrative structure and basic sense of rhythm, plus primitive knowledge of understanding how a score was put together and making music as a collage of shapes and momentum, could help in the assembly of one. It might be like being able to wire a plug; I don't know how it all works, but I have an idea how to put it all together, given the basic tools and elements, so that it fulfils its immediate function.

The string quartet has been approached by all the great composers many times, or on occasion – whether obediently or subversively – as the most intimately challenging and exposed way to express and concentrate not only their melodic and structural skill, their dramatic purpose, their sensitivity to symmetry and internal order, their appetite for fighting for musical territory, their ability to surprise and to sustain logical development without sounding obvious and repetitive, to be original – even though it would appear, after centuries of string quartets, that there is nowhere new to go – but also their own personality, drive, desire, soul, philosophy, contemporary thinking and temperament. The quartet, I concluded, was the most direct and personal route into the mind and world, and intriguing, beguiling, desolate madness and astounding sanity, of a composer. It is, for me, more thought-provoking than the grandest, most complex symphonies. This was the one for me, because, of course, however cerebral and introspective the composer, the string quartet also required some amount of showing off and innate self-referencing, which I understood as a writer. Before it becomes clear what the style, attitude and meaning of the piece is, a string quartet says: look at me, and listen to me, a self and a personality transformed into the most transparent and bewitching of musical constructions, the most explicit example of how meaning is made and directly communicated through purely instrumental, always wordless music.

Following the history of the string quartet as a series of works of art and solutions to compositional problems was also a useful way of roughly tracking the history of classical music itself, from the very first composers who developed the ideas, and made up the abstract rules and regulations, moving away from thick, dense and demanding textures and establishing a more accessible melodic approach with a much lighter atmosphere, through the adjustments in economic and artistic context between the end of the eighteenth century and the beginning of the twentieth century, and every important, innovative, ambitious composer since. The quartet developed at the very centre of this eloquent, refined new form of music, one that was being made with artistic impulse as much as audience-pleasing motives, the ultimate example of the chamber music that was distilling increasingly ambitious and grand orchestral music to its fluid, expressive essence.

It was at the heart of the emergent classical experience, because a composer experiences the writing of a string quartet both as a technical exercise, enfolded inside a relatively fixed set of parameters, a fundamental inherited framework, however elastic and esoteric, and also as a chance to dream of the marvellous, to add to the vocabulary and the style without straying so far that it ceases to be a string quartet. The string quartet boxes a musician into its history and its overall formula, as a writer and player, but offers paradoxical opportunities to break free, to be both inside and outside the box at the same time, earthbound and floating, praying and gossiping, seeing and hearing. It's made for pleasure, for emotional release, for a sponsor and/or mentor, but it was beginning to require artistic commitment as much as professional integrity in order constantly to generate new material.

For the sake of a tidy history, a tidy beginning, Haydn, a prolific composer in all musical genres, is the generally accepted central starting point for the cerebral, sensuous and intensely articulate use of two violins, viola and cello, which it turned out went together like mouth and mouth, body and body, earth and sun, although there were earlier versions of this line-up. He was definitely not the first to write what we would recognise as a string quartet.

Henry Purcell, in the last few decades of the seventeenth century, and before him a number of Elizabethan lutenists, wrote quartets for 'viols', the precursor of the violin family. Sometimes for two viols, sometimes for six, but the use of four anticipates what's to come, as if the whole idea was being rehearsed, with no sense of it necessarily going anywhere particular or blossoming like it did. There wasn't much sense of 'the future', and no sense of music being something that would last, in some cases, for centuries.

You were passing through time, with few, elusive methods of collectively remembering what had just happened – which would lead to the initial speed of thought and invention, the satisfying of the demand for something new and something else, that would eventually lead to the momentum of what became known as classical music. As new forms of culture progressed with increasing speed to satisfy increasingly sophisticated and civilised needs and desires, music inevitably responded, keeping up to speed, reacting to all the changes with its own changes. It would be the last thing to be left behind; the changes in human life, the changes to reality happening through the next centuries wouldn't be complete without a musical accompaniment, a clarification, a metaphysical mirroring of the changes, inventions, progress and, of course, negative factors being introduced to society. Music followed and scrutinised, sometimes celebrated or abstracted, condemned or transcended, a world that was constantly in flux.

There would increasingly be music that wasn't reacting to change, content to settle, to cosy up to itself, and this would sound old-fashioned, as though it was looking back into the dark, fearing progress and the light that there must be ahead; the best, most stimulating music became a symbol of progress, a rehearsal and reflection of all the changes going on in the world. By its very nature it was an active art of change, where patterns constantly lead to new patterns, and minds are continually being opened in order to understand and appreciate what was happening next.

Music becoming an authoritative way of providing abstract authenticity to cultural drives and developments was also where certain problems began in terms of the reputation and wider reception of classical music, even the fact it was known as 'classical'; it became a symbol of elite, establishment power, of its practice of wanting to own and supervise everything, even the arts. Perversely, considering the methods and intentions of the composers and their music, it became a way of protecting the status quo and adding an artistic dimension to mainstream institutions and ideologies, and of giving a kind of secular glory to newly formed capitalist ventures. It became a way of announcing that one sort of taste was superior to other forms, and it was the taste of those who could afford to control and organise the existence of the music, and build the buildings that contained and taught it, that became enshrined as objectively definitive.

Early music is often a source of positive inspiration for modern and even postmodern composers, not least because it functioned and regulated itself before classical music became so entwined and identified with social forces of order and control, and business. Before the certified, institutionalised and/or fairyland classical era, there are fewer unappealing or even suspicious associations, and there was a little more anarchy, populism and idiosyncrasy in any connection with power, religion or the aristocracy. The late seventeenth-century music of pre-Enlightenment, pre-industrialised, pre-urbanised Purcell had not been purged of nourishing, off-kilter connections with energetic, vivid, even zany folk tradition. He was still having the sort of lively, engaged and unstuffy fun and games with his music and audiences that became unwelcome when classical music was appropriated and supervised by the elite and executive 'higher forces', and a sense it was music for the rich and powerful monopolising versions of 'good taste' and nothing to do with magic, or mystery, or even subversion, even if the great composers still worked that way. Institutionally, during the eighteenth and nineteenth centuries, classical music lost looseness and directness and certainly any deviant roughness, as if this alleged pre-eminence was a natural fundamental state, not a recent set of contrived inventions and decorations.

Purcell is on the edge of a great change, before such working composers and their compositions were landed with a whole different set of formalised conditions and cultural responsibilities, not because of their often still wayward, provocative creativity and imagination, but because they would become possessions, and their elusive, sophisticated art become a calcified, stifling symbol of wealth and status and, ultimately, straitlaced cultural smugness.

Purcell was still writing fantasias for his trusty old-fashioned viol even as it was being usurped by the violin, the speculator anticipating in his writing the quartet as a way of transforming four diffuse voices into one. Purcell remained loyal to the viol consort – a Renaissance-period term for any chamber-group combination of instrument or voices – as a method of achieving some of his bolder, more unorthodox ideas, suggesting he would have been comfortable with the string quartets to come, and even with what was to come after the form was fully realised.

There were others apart from Purcell trying out isolated examples of this as yet informal quartet style with its roots in the baroque trio sonata, where two solo instruments played with a cello or keyboard. The adding of a fourth instrument to the common trio was a quiet revolution. There were quartets written during the baroque period for different line-ups, including, at baroque's zenith, the forward-looking, prototypically conversational *Paris* Quartets, composed in 1730 and 1738 by the ingenious, self-educated, incredibly productive and popular

German Francophile and Italian expert Georg Telemann. A master self-promoter, a musical sophisticate with a cosmopolitan flair, he was better regarded than Bach and Handel, and was a Bach-like devotee of adventurously combining then very separate national styles.

The rise of a German-centric musical tradition began in the early eighteenth century with a combination of the Italian preference for exuberant voice and virtuoso violin, as championed by Vivaldi, and the French taste for flute and oboe and a tendency towards a variety of dance rhythms. A few French composers concluded that a single piece of music could combine the different styles, but a distinctive German style emerged from the 'mixed style' of Italian concertos and sonatas and French dance suites with local Germanic folk elements. The concerto elaborating elements of the suite was the first stirrings of the idea of a symphony, and in the suite, particular instruments being given a solo role was an early hint of a more grand, extensive concerto style. Telemann was one of the more energised and ingenious proponents of this hybrid – a master of 'mixed taste' – as baroque pleasantries mutated into something with more sophistication and potential.

In 1733 he poured all his learning into the discreet-seeming *Musique de table* (*Table Music*), to be played at banquets, festivals and feasts while people are eating. Philosopher Immanuel Kant, responding to the *Table Music* of Telemann and other composers who were designing music for eating to, imagined it at its idealised best as a sublime form of muzak that could open the gates to heaven, but at another extreme merely a light, agreeable sound lacking expressive purpose, which encouraged guests to talk intelligently to each other at banquets and other social gatherings. Music was a changing play of auditory sensations, what Kant described as a 'play of tunes', which produces enjoyment and appealing emotion, but which is essentially simply part of general, undemanding social intercourse.

Table Music was to some extent intended as pleasing, unobtrusive background music, but Telemann used the task to smuggle in his new ideas about a different form of instrumental music, which is as much about individual instrumental prowess, structural complexity, the fusing of traditions and melodic invention as it is about moderate musical skill and low-level atmospheric decoration. He wanted it to be more than Kant's mere 'pleasant art'. It sold well, but Telemann also wanted it to be more than simply popular because it was so light and inoffensive.

Table Music was not only for the players to enjoy playing and for listeners to not be too disturbed or distracted by the music; there was now, more authoritatively, a third element: the expressive qualities of the music, which can become sublime in their own way. Telemann was exploring earlier than most the idea of art in music, as low in the arts as it was rated, of beauty without particular context, how 'through harmonic compositions, one can instil all sorts of feelings into the soul of men while at the same time pleasing the mind of an expert with the ordered and ingenious structures of these works'.

His *Table Music* was a late-baroque tour de force, a comprehensive collection of styles, genres and instruments escaping baroque rigour and detecting a new musical age fast approaching that helps prepare the way for the Viennese classical composers to come. His was the most up-to-date music of its time, and it was deliberately composed to be fashionable, to be the music that would appeal to an enlightened Parisian elite who wanted the best and most modern experiences.

The existence of music with an abstract artistic and intellectual purpose becomes a separate entity from one that was dedicated simply to the joy of playing and the gentle, uncomplicated act of listening. Out of functional music composed for very specific purposes, a new kind of indefinable artistry materialises that transcends previous expectations of what music was for and what it could achieve. It could be something in itself. A German philosophy of music was beginning to be defined, one that codified a confident national sense of its own musical, intellectual and artistic talents, and which created the passage from the cloistered baroque to the unbound and dominant classical.

In his *Table Music* Telemann was already relishing a freer, fuller and more distinct musical dialogue between instruments, initially especially between two violins. His *Paris* Quartets were two sets of six works further refining essentially artistic discoveries made with *Table Music*, specifically written for four virtuosi, scored for flute, violin, viola da gamba, with cello or harpsichord as the bass – the flute having the role of what was to become in the early string quartets the first violin. A multi-instrumentalist's exact knowledge of the availability and potential of instruments was becoming particularly important for new compositions; like Bach and Vivaldi, the self-taught Telemann recognised the solo potential and gorgeous liquid power of the cello decades before it was fully released from basic, lowly duties.

Who wrote a very first 'string quartet', if there was such a singular breakthrough, is naturally a lost-in-time mystery, although some credit Gregorio Allegri as being responsible for a definite prototype. He lived between 1582 and 1652 and wrote the mesmeric *Miserere* for nine voices, a setting of Psalm 51, which has been used ever since during Holy Week in Rome's Sistine Chapel. Visiting Rome, a rebellious fourteen-year-old Mozart copied it from memory – writing the music down was punishable by excommunication, because it violated the Vatican's autocratic commitment to preserving the music's mystery and maintaining control over the collective imagination. Mozart's illegal copying ended up being published in London, a kind of bootlegging, but the Pope was in awe of Mozart's astonishing feat in memorising the entire thing more or less perfectly, and excused him.

Alessandro Scarlatti, known for his sacred and secular vocal music and an astonishing, inexhaustible 555 harpsichord sonatas that were perfectly made to cross over to the piano, wrote a set of works somewhere between 1715 and 1725 that some consider among the earliest recognisable string quartets. These works were called *Sonata à Quattro per due iolini, violetta e violoncello senza cembalo* – sonatas for four instruments: two violins, viola and cello.

A master of structure and idiom, his scoring significantly left open a range of performance possibilities, something that passed into the principle, once settled, of the string quartet in terms of the collaborative relationship between composer and performer. The performers adhere the given instructions, but there is room for them to follow their own instincts and impress their own personality and style within very tight and ordered precepts.

Haydn stumbled upon the combination perhaps by accident in the mid-1750s when he was asked by a patron to play some music at a country estate fifty miles from Vienna, and the only available players were two violinists, a violist and a cellist, all local musicians, including the cellist who later tutored Beethoven. Haydn, in his early twenties, made good, lively use of the four instrumentalists, giving all the best lines to the first violin with the other, lesser voices following and supporting. What he came up with was much liked by its audience, not really fully appreciating what kind of birth they were witnessing. Their warm approval encouraged Haydn to take the idea further, relishing rather than rejecting the fact they were all string instruments, excited by how this generated a liberating unity of sound, one voice with four accents, four sensibilities with one purpose, and enabled him to project so purely his own personality and musical intentions.

It was a time when the disappearance of words from pieces of music like the string quartet was being treated with suspicion, even resentment, as if music without words couldn't possibly mean anything or be profound. By its very nature, without grounding text or an illuminating religious context, the music could be about anything. For those unconvinced by this new trend, there was no sense of it being anything other than just four instruments dancing around each other for the sake of it, a kind of fancy superficial lark with no redeeming qualities. It was merely sound, a temporary pleasure, not capable of achieving the evocative, articulate richness of fine art or the sound of reaching out to a higher form. Pop music, if you like.

Haydn persisted, in some sort of anticipation of the early nineteenth-century theory that music without words or officially assigned higher meaning contained innate spiritual power, as though the very nature of his persistence was proof that this was serious music, not purely an exercise, a bit of fun or a mere demonstration of hard-won technique. This persistence, his obsessive belief in his composing, played an important role in establishing instrumental music as a genre equal, if not more, to vocal music. He kept going because there was this new need constantly to replenish musical stock, because a growing audience demanded something innovative, not a constant set of repeats.

Throughout the 1760s, he wrote a few quartets in five movements from fast opening to fast finale, working towards defining certain commandments for the fundamental style of a string quartet not properly established in earlier workings by Scarlatti and Allegri. Those didn't inspire any followers, and Haydn rejected them and other earlier provisional practitioners, such as the pioneering Milanese symphony composer Giovanni Battista Sammartini, as any influence on his approach, citing C. P. E. Bach's idiosyncratic, stream-of-consciousness keyboard innovations as a more direct inspiration. Carl Bach, the second surviving son of Johann Sebastian, found himself in the hinterland between the old-fashioned baroque period of his father and the new freedoms of the classical era for which Haydn and Mozart helped to create the foundations.

This was a period where things we now take for granted were falling into position. Before the idea of the conductor had been clarified, when it would be the keyboardist or lead violinist who led the orchestra, often the composer and/or administrator of the ensemble, it was C. P. E. Bach who introduced the idea of emphatically lifting his hands off the keys to mark the beat. Elsewhere, elected leaders would use their neck or a bending at the waist, a crude form of 'body conducting'. Eventually the first violinist became the more natural leader, with a better insight into how to advise string players about bowing and general style. They would be placed on a raised platform to be seen, gesturing with their bow, which became the beginning of the baton.

Carl Bach was also caught between the era of the harpsichord, with its limited register and range, and the arrival of the newly invented, more flexible sound-stretching pianoforte, and this also seemed to instil a then typical pattern, making sense of decorum and orderly precision with a certain unexpected and stimulating expressive wildness. It wasn't so much a reaction against father Johann – who taught him innovative fingering principles and who obviously gave him quite a start in music and provided Telemann as a godfather – as a rejection of stiffening baroque conventions, and a red-blooded fascination with fast-arriving modern fashions.

As if explicitly reflecting this position between the old and the new, living on the verge of massive changes in music and society, C. P. E. Bach's music would switch abruptly and often randomly from the manic to the lovely, the tense to the soothing, keeping listeners wondering more than usual where the music would go next. It was an abstract sign of the kind of editing in art and entertainment that would become so prevalent in the twentieth century, when electricity enabled form and time to be shifted and layered into different shapes and flow through music, film, television and radio. We would become more used to the idea of being moved abruptly from one state of mind, one view of reality, to another, a constant shift in perspective, in a way that for centuries could only happen inside literature, stories and dreams, or the music of the bolder, more inventive minds.

The exhilarating, surprising, mood-switching raw emotion Bach ploughed into his playing, the juxtaposition of ideas and feelings, was of more interest to Haydn in how he imagined the quartet than simply following those that had also fortuitously or fairly naturally alighted on the quartet line-up. It was this restless, sometimes reckless collision of sounds and emotions, textures and dynamics as an abstract suggestion of musical propulsion that would help the string quartet achieve its long life, able to absorb the new styles and fashions of the time and survive as a kind of indestructible machine for thinking and expressing pure feeling, a true blank canvas where anything was possible.

The virtuoso cellist and composer Luigi Boccherini, born in Italy, living in Spain, is an example of a composer fatefully slipping from history, a contemporary of Haydn who was exploring this new line-up at the same time as, if not before, Haydn, and was the first to put on a public string quartet performance. There is no evidence of any awareness between them of each other's work, as though they were having the same thoughts independently, like two research scientists making similar breakthroughs and discoveries in different places at the same time. (Two hundred years later, Milton Babbitt in America and Pierre Boulez in France, as part of a ruthless purification of what seemed, after a monstrous war, oppressive tradition, are simultaneously coming to ways and means of developing Schoenberg's twelve notes and challenging the role of the composer in terms of their direct and possibly tainted control over a composition. At the same time John Cage, from another direction, is using indeterminate methods to remove, or in other ways enhance, the total involvement of the composer. The Boccherini in this story is Ruth Crawford Seeger who, ten years before Babbitt and Boulez established musical manifestos for an absolute form of serialism, was expanding the limits of Schoenberg's early strategies.)

Boccherini was as popular as Haydn at the time, but he receives only marginal credit for his quartets, even for his existence, outside a few indignant specialist defences of his role in the history. He becomes more of an isolated figure in the story either because he was nine years younger than Haydn or because his quartets never advanced technically beyond an obliging, engaging lightness. He was also outside the Austro-Germanic culture that was quickly dominating the history of classical music and eventually the classical repertoire of major performance organisations. This Austro-Germanic dominance created the self-belief in a nation's superiority as an act of pride, innocently set into motion by Telemann's *Table Music*, breaking away from French and Italian styles, on its way to Beethoven's belief in his country as an act of psychic protection and Wagner's as an act of triumphant dogmatism. The

Austro-Germanic influence came to an end with the proto-modernist romantic Mahler, born in 1860. His ten boundary-stretching symphonies were a kind of final flourish to the great Viennese symphonists (Haydn, Mozart, Beethoven, Schubert and Bruckner), acting as a link between classical Germany and the modernism of the early twentieth century.

During Haydn and Mozart's time, this burgeoning nationalist self-belief deflected attention away from other countries and composers as if by the very fact that they were not based in Vienna – a major cultural and educational centre for most of the pre-modern era – they were of lesser worth. The adaptations, inventions and/or styles of the Viennese composers were increasingly not considered local but universal.

The perception was that with his quartets Boccherini never developed a deeper, more evocative style, or broke away from a basic functional template. Defenders refute his reputation as more moderate and limited and less learned than Haydn, because he was clearly an important founder, and his extensive other writings, including symphonies, also written in parallel with Haydn, were versatile and inventive. He has a greater claim on the development of the string quintet, but it is Haydn who is regarded as the sole architect of the more classic and ultimately more compelling quartet.

Between 1769 and 1772, finessing the internal order and prospective design that becomes a major contribution to the more sophisticated classical constitution, Haydn wrote eighteen string quartets, settling on a four-movement structure, each following a set tempo that became standard for Haydn, and then for others taking his lead. He placed an emphasis on lively, sinuous melodic lines, initially for the first violin, but eventually allowing other parts, including the cello, the chance to soar. It is Boccherini as a superb cellist who does get credited – as some kind of compensation – with being the first to provide all four instruments with a great deal of freedom and of course to push the cello into the higher ranges, so that there can be more at play than just the assertive collaboration between violins and viola. Haydn, though, is as likely instinctively realising the undeniable potential of the cello to become part of the democracy, and vastly extending possible permutations in the four-way relationship.

This was where the string quartet was being invented: four equal partners, all with something to say, accompanying, leading, scheming, racing, calming, chatting, philosophising, dreaming, fleeing, retreating, confessing, loving. Even as his descendants would vary and deconstruct the form and structure, they remained faithful to the spirit — to the extent that for Beethoven's momentous final quartet, the last one of his legendary late quartets, where he had extended structural possibilities to the point of breaking through into another genre, he returned to Haydn's classical frame as an act of deliberate sentimental nostalgia inside the overall revolutionary process, and a distinct homage to the composer who first definitively showed the way. Haydn's approach directly inspired followers, believers in what became a kind of trans-historical cult of composers committed to creating a conceptual continuity that has lasted until today.

Haydn's flow stopped in 1772 as his energies were directed elsewhere while he worked in near-isolation, contracted to another patron with very specific demands on his composer. Released in 1781 from this contract, which also stopped him from marketing his works, he returned to writing quartets with extra appetite, now he was more in control of his own destiny and finances. Having immersed himself during the previous nine years in other styles of music, radically extending his range and ambition, his wit and judgement, his next series of quartets, a set of six numbered twenty-nine to thirty-four, nicknamed the *Russian* Quartets and collected as Op. 33, were a vivid clarification of recently acquired new compositional skills and of how he had imagined a coherent string quartet form by revitalising his primary early ideas.

After rudimentary hints in his early 1770s quartets, the cello is fully released from its unspectacular, mostly supporting chores, becoming as fully active, even as silver-tongued as the other instruments. It is now much more than a mere accompaniment, generating a multitude of textural possibilities, which becomes a key moment of revelation; obvious now, but at the time a complete shift in musical reality. The string quartet has been fully invented.

Elsewhere, as Haydn makes it his own, and takes the credit, other subsequently neglected composers long snuffed out of history are hitting their stride with this new idea: the French François-Joseph Gossec, the violinist Carl Ditters von Dittersdorf, two Czech composers, Jan Křtitel Vaňhal and Paul Wranitzky, and the illegitimate son of wealthy planter and Nanon, a black slave mother of Senegalese origin, Joseph Bologne, whose stage name was Chevalier de Saint-Georges. At a time when interracial marriages were forbidden, slaves were regarded as movable, unthinking objects and the belief in African genetic inferiority was rife, he became one of the most famous men in France.

Even as he was establishing a major reputation as musician, orchestral leader and composer and playing duets with Marie Antoinette, he was being treated as a freak, a half-man, sealed off from overwhelming white privilege. He fought back through sheer skill, self-confidence and charisma, and his champion-level flair with a sword earned certain respect. He was as flash on the violin as he was as a fencer, led the premieres of many Haydn symphonies, and went on to command the first unit of black soldiers in European history. Born a decade before Mozart, a 1770s star before Mozart was a star, and more at ease in the role, he was said to have dazzled Parisian society with his talents and presence, which some say led to an envious Mozart using him as an inspiration for the villain in *The Magic Flute*. He's quickly written into the wider story as 'Le noir Mozart' – even though he came first, so Mozart was 'the white Bologne' – the first classical composer of African descent, and an early campaigner for the abolition of slavery. But that's another story...

Between the 1760s and 1806, three years before his death, Haydn wrote sixty-eight string quartets, a panorama of his entire compositional output. (Boccherini disciples point out he was just as prolific, if not more so. Wranitzky wrote over seventy, as did one of Haydn's most famous pupils, the composer, conductor and publisher Ignace Pleyel, works described by Mozart as 'very well written and very pleasant', but which never rose above the brightly imitative, as if there was no reaching past Haydn. Bologne wrote at least eighteen, with who knows how many whitewashed from view.) Haydn's quartets provide a constant commentary on their own evolving status and the evolving nature of music in the eighteenth century, establishing the basic quartet model, the combination of surprise, silence, grace, precision, tonality, coordination and proportion that would inspire Mozart, always on high alert, living on the edge of his nerves at a time of great transition, miraculously quick to spot and instantly comprehend a new direction and allow himself to be carried away. Whatever else Mozart was – special one, freak, filthy-minded merry prankster, travelling virtuoso, permanent adolescent, hard worker, needy neurotic, the pragmatic craftsman, the musical Descartes, disconnected from reality, force of nature, a clear eye on the world, death-haunted, concealed behind his work, celebrating the ecstatic act of being – he was a listener beyond compare.

And any serious contemporary musician of the time needed to be aware of what Haydn was doing, perfectly timed in Mozart's case, as he reached maturity as a self-reliant artist rather than a prodigy with an over-eager showbiz papa. It was his other 'papa', Haydn, who inspired him to 'make experiments' and 'become original'. Absorbing and retaining anything imaginative, cultural and open-minded that he encountered, paying attention to new ideas and intellectual currents, Mozart was making a new music before the concept of 'new music' really existed.

When he needed some kind of propulsive launch pad, someone close by who had already made considerable moves into the future of music, making progress after J. S. Bach and already creating an extensive body of work that needed studying, and then surpassing, there was Haydn. Mozart's genius begins with how he integrates the previous insights of Bach and Haydn, receiving vivid clues about how to project spiritual content through a sensuous form. Bach and Haydn enable him to take charge of the world.

On the other hand, for the sake of balance, resisting the hijacking of historical reality – the control of what is taught and believed about music by a Mozart-dominated musicology, the shaping of our education by those who use a Mozart as manufactured deity expressly for the purpose of representing untouchable genius, to embody 'pure order' with the deliberate intention of exiling and warding off the institutionally and culturally marginalised, disenfranchised, impeded, destroyed – Mozart was derivative, because he copied, stole, imitated, paraphrased, passed off transcriptions of Bach and Handel after minor tweaking as his own and slickly absorbed the creative impulses of others; he took from the very best the musical world had to offer at the time, and added crowd-pleasing cream and sugar, or at least large doses of saccharine. His history of multifarious borrowings is in itself unequivocally indicative of a lack of originality and true creativity. He is not worthy of all the adulation; the myth begins to crumble before our very eyes. As John Cage said, there are many ways to hate Mozart, without actually listing the ways. It is understandable resistance in the face of the cult and the acceptance of godlike genius that is being expressed, not necessarily rejection of the music.

Cage may also have been reacting against one of his teachers, Arnold Schoenberg, who once wrote: 'I owe very, very much to Mozart;

and if one studies, for instance, the way in which I write for string quartet, then one cannot deny that I have learned this directly from Mozart. And I am proud of it!' He valued what he called the 'prose-like' quality of Mozart, acknowledged his bravery in fighting for the virtues of dissonance when that could have seemed the work of the devil. I mention this because, speaking as a music snob through and through, I wonder what difference it would have made to my views on Mozart, as the blank, plaster-cast antique-shop bust, dusted with icing sugar, the rococo legend, dead to the modern world, if I had been aware of Schoenberg's knowledge and appreciation of him as, if not a direct influence, an ancestor practising a similar form of magical thinking. From Mozart, he said, he learned:

1. Inequality of phrase length.
2. Coordination of heterogeneous characters to form a thematic unity.
3. Deviation from even-numbered construction in the theme and its component parts.
4. The art of forming subsidiary ideas.
5. The art of introduction and transition.

And then put Mozart together with an unlikely musical partner: Edgard Varèse, living between 1883 and 1965, the son of a non-musical and abusive father, who dreamed of a music set free and who viewed sound as a 'living matter'. Like Mozart, he did not set out to tear down, but to find new means. Against the backdrop of the insular originality of Varèse, and his self-styled 'organised sound', which Stravinsky, as usual, brilliantly observed 'has dated in the right way', Mozart sounds a little different, bringing out the 'dynamic asymmetries', the tension and anguish, and this is another way to approach Mozart. Think of him in a different place and time, in unexpected company, thinking about how every work of art alters and charges its predecessors, so that what might not be immediately obvious in the music of Mozart abruptly turns up, liberated by more abrasive and confrontational, less established company.

Think of him in the secluded, purifying deserts of radical humanist Varèse, desperate to produce 'the epic impact of our epoch', to generate music that sounded like 'voices in the sky, as though magic, invisible hands were turning on and off the knobs of fantastic radios'. He also wrote that the title of his apocalyptically soulful early 1950s piece *Deserts*, combining acoustic instruments and electronic sounds, refers to: 'all physical deserts (of sand, sea, snow, of outer space, of empty city streets), but also the deserts in the mind of man; not only those stripped aspects of nature that suggest bareness, aloofness and timelessness, but also that remote inner space no telescope can reach where man is alone, a world of mystery and essential loneliness'.

At its premiere in Paris on 2 December 1954, with *musique concrète* specialist Pierre Henry in control of the electronics, *Deserts* materialised between pieces by Mozart and Tchaikovsky, its dissonant evocation of aloneness deeply unsettling a conservative audience, but put together as some kind of mental montage, the eighteenth-century melodies of Mozart seeming darker, his exploration of form more dramatic, and the insistent, moody, mid-twentieth-century noise mechanics of Varèse not necessarily that distant from Mozart's sublime sense of order.

For all the turning of Mozart into something nice, pleasant, pretty, seemly, his music teems with all the disorder of the human condition. And even if the following quote is a forgery, part of some unreliable fantasy about his life, the fact it needed to exist and be attributed to him is a clue to what is expected from the idea of Mozart: 'When I am completely myself, entirely alone, or during the night when I cannot sleep, it is on such occasions that my ideas flow best and most abundantly. Whence and how these ideas come I know not, nor can I force them.'

The philosopher Arthur Schopenhauer was a flute-playing Mozart fan who considered our lives of blind men willing 'to be doomed to misery' but that temporary relief could be found in the contemplation of art. He noted: 'Every genius is already a big child, since he looks out into the world as out into something strange and foreign, a drama, and thus with purely object interest... He who through his life does not, to a certain extent, remain a big child, but becomes an earnest, sober, thoroughly composed and rational man can be a very useful and capable citizen of this world; but he will never be a genius.' Schopenhauer didn't consider genius to be a matter of the imagination, but a pursuit of earthly virtues, a quest based on their own circumstances and surroundings, experiences and knowledge.

Schopenhauer once responded to a definition of music by the sublimely eloquent German polymath Gottfried Wilhelm Leibniz, one of the great thinkers of the seventeenth and eighteenth centuries and inventor of calculus, and the binary system that became the basic code of virtually all modern computers. He was worth paying attention to, and Leibniz said that music is a hidden arithmetical activity of a mind that does not know it is counting. Schopenhauer took this to another level – that music is a hidden metaphysical activity of a mind that does not know it is philosophising. In that sense, the philosophically untrained Mozart, only ever working and thinking in sound, is one of the greatest philosophical minds that ever lived, at a time when philosophy was beginning to supplant the role of religion.

The inspirational impact of Haydn on Mozart is probably another reason why Boccherini begins to fade away from the main story that would be told for generations to come until it seemed the absolute truth. In this story, Mozart directly takes over from Haydn, which is difficult to dispute, and this unambiguous seal of approval helps promote Haydn to 'father' role. Any others in the hunt fall off a cliff. As far as Mozart is concerned, and he becomes the story's central character, Haydn wrote the source manifesto. He came up with the commandments. Boccherini, to add insult to injury, becomes branded with the nickname 'the wife of Haydn', for the way, despite the hundreds of rigorously organised compositions, he seems to be operating in the shadow of Haydn.

Haydn's sensitivity and playfulness, his easy-going poise and sense of the absurd, a wild relish for human eccentricity, his embracing of deep feelings, his exhaustive fund of melodies, found a swift pupil in Mozart, who identified with Haydn's quick-thinking methods of binding revolutionary verve with lively, earthy accessibility. History and style could be radically altered and redirected, new rules proposed and rapidly refined, without any immediate unsettling sense of threat or danger. The music was still very much an entertainment even as it was in a way experimenting with its own existence. It was something crazed and incandescent being tamed by hard-earned technique, or that technique, which could be emptied of emotion, is freed from restraints and too much reason by an inner craziness, an impulsive striving to transcend the mundane, to make actual changes to reality.

The personality of Haydn, his commitment to relishing and yet resisting traditional forms, pointed forward to the approaches future quartet composers could take; to continuing the line in a straightforward manner, or to deviating from established continuity, or in Haydn style, simultaneously accepting and subverting convention, elegance framing militant elements and vice versa.

Haydn had surely done all that could be done with the structure and line-up of the quartet in his sixty-eight, definitively articulating his sophistication and subtlety with the final two, the works of someone who fully understood he had climbed some sort of summit and was both triumphant and in awe of his own achievement. Mozart could see how high Haydn climbed, as high as prim and primal overlord Bach, enough to kiss the sky, but already could see a way to go higher, as Beethoven could later. Always new continents, new mountain peaks, remote islands to discover. Always the same, always different, must move on, must do better, to keep the spirit alive, got to give it another try; perhaps tomorrow perfection is grasped.

Haydn made it part of the venture that it required the vision and bravado of the heroic composer, establishing how a key part of setting out to write a sequence of quartets involved finding a place to go where no one had gone before, even though it seemed the idea had gone as far as it could. Find a corner of space and time that no one had explored before. And the great romantic quartets pour through a composer's life, sometimes regularly, sometimes erratically, and end with some sort of climax, some grand, or shattered, very intentional gesture of completion – as with Schubert, who knew he had during his lifetime the mighty Beethoven in his way, let alone in the recent past the absurdly sure Mozart, who like Bach could do no wrong because he said so. But amidst illness and despair, Schubert came to the end of his fifteen completed quartets with three indisputable masterpieces that fuse together innocence and deep knowing, delicacy and power, anger and acceptance.

Those three long, intense, sometimes sinister-seeming, ultimately end-of-life works were written after a break in his quartet writing of eight years; he'd written the twelve earlier quartets as a teenager between 1811 and 1816. As it should, the unnerving, aggressive fifty-one-minute final quartet sees Schubert reach his peak, moving heaven and earth to break free of the shadow of Beethoven and the comprehensive achievements of Haydn to get there. He turns all his effort and willpower into ferocious, innovative, if still soothing music, even as he appears to be changing stylistic direction, still processing self-discovery, and somehow still confidently heading towards a mysterious new place he wouldn't live to find.

These late-life creative acts of defiance and acceptance, of earned wisdom and fully firing and intact instinct, are not so common in rock and pop music. Youthful early creativity is usually quickly drained, as that early defiant instinct gets smothered, sometimes by learning technique, which is not necessarily an advantage in rock and can obstruct the original vitality of unhindered intuition, or because there is no more to say once the directed rage of youth has dimmed. The maintenance of early creative fire, modified by time and experience, by success and/ or failure, by changes in life and circumstance, has equivalents in jazz, where ideas and energy can still develop and intensify into old age, but is particularly present in classical music, which creates another level of intrigue as a listener and as a historian examining its continuing presence.

Most rock acts spend the decades after their twenties, and lately possibly their thirties, merely either directly repeating their early hits and presence as a simple act of audience-pleasing nostalgia, or they repeat themes and motifs, responding to few, if any, new influences, and there is no sense of creative development, or the feeling there have been any sequential changes in life and sensibility. Where there are signs that the ageing rock musician has managed to transfer and translate early instincts and appetites into a confrontation of mortality and impending doom, and their music evolves with artistic power and avoids basic rehashing of their old days, then this music seems to take on an enduring classical quality. It turns the whole of a life into something artistic, as happened with Beethoven and Schubert, a brave commitment to trying new things, moving away from their past glories and seeing forward into time, even as death approaches. It gets lifted out of being rock into a new place that hasn't yet been defined, but where it belongs, alongside the historic works of art that survive long after the time of their making.

Looking within rock music for those also using their music to articulate where they are in life, as they move towards death, and how this can be an influence on their work, does not take you to many places. The greatest late-life creative thinking in rock tends to be the work of those who died young, and were facing up to the abyss, to an inevitable climax, whether they knew it or not, or sometimes when they really did know it – Ian Curtis, Jimi Hendrix, Marvin Gaye, Jim Morrison,

Janis Joplin, Kurt Cobain, Gram Parsons, Laura Nyro, Otis Redding, John Lennon, Bob Marley, Sandy Denny, Tupac Shakur, Tim Hardin, Donny Hathaway, Nick Drake. Their end-of-life work is often done before they reach thirty. The late-lifeness in classic rock groups, say, the Beach Boys, the Beatles, the Rolling Stones and Led Zeppelin generally emerged at the end of a specific period of creative vitality – obviously so with the Beatles, who deliberately finished off their existence after a few years at the end of the 1960s, their last and therefore vivid, straining, acceptant and resonant late-life works being contained inside *The White Album* and *Abbey Road*.

Some, increasingly most, groups continue into a lengthy afterlife, muscle memory forcing them on as performers and, of course, sponsored troupers fighting to see another day. The Stones drag on for forty years after they have completed their most urgent and focused work, becoming zombie entertainers sponsored by corporations in a kind of cultural limbo, with its own thrills and electric nostalgia but little that is as new, as irresistible as they were in their first decade, when they were seeing ahead to the light, not looking back to recreate their youthful appetites, and when there was such a hungry purpose to what they did. Rock groups tend to enter a commercially curated period of anniversaries, farewell tours and box sets where their vital signs have effectively stopped and all that's left is the memory of when they were seeking money, adventure and love, and it all comes down to the circus of greatest hits, however entertaining to watch. As artists, innovating through form and content, they have left behind their most original sense of personal expression and have nothing actually new to say, other than yet another announcement of yet another world tour, and yet another affecting, occasionally admirable reminder of what's left of their powers.

The act of performing, where the performance by a great performer is central to their life, can create an aesthetic equivalent of late-life expression, a building up to a particular, defiant presence at the end of life where the bravery, and openness, of the performance itself creates an enthralling sense of tension and excitement. The sheer presence of the performer, and their agility, or fragility, becomes the enthralling personal element, the main, spellbinding ingredient, a holding on to the vitality of life even as it comes to an end and their energy starts to diminish.

What it doesn't have is the direct, articulate commentary on reaching a certain stage and state of life, the acceptance, or defiance, of the inconceivable inevitable, and a working out of how new artistic impulses relate to original impulses with repeating them, and a creation of something inventive and insightful that could only be created by someone in their later years. The performer and their performance are still rooted in the idea of an eternal youth, the marvel is in the re-creation and maintenance of marvellous early energies, ultimately a kind of illusion, as though time can be held in place, and mocked and outwitted, until the very end. The idea of the performer, in the long arc of history, means that ultimately Iggy Pop and Barbra Streisand, Paul McCartney and Dolly Parton, Cher and Steve Tyler, Mick Jagger and Barry Manilow are in the same subset, closer than seemed apparent at the time, marvels of perpetual emotion living in a dual state between then and now.

The performer resists time in the miracle of them turning out to sing the same songs as if they are still as fresh as ever. The artist expresses how time is still moving but about to break down completely, while still feeling alive with ideas and attitudes, with the energy still to advance and experiment as an artist. All of that is still racing forward even with the dead knowledge that time itself, exactly that which allowed you the freedom and space to think and be, is collapsing in on you. There is no time, and still you play with time, test it out, stretch it as far as you can, beyond your own limits, your own burnt-out chronology. To the very end, you are paying attention to detail. Time passes; events occur; old age approaches. But humanity remains always the same.

For those that lived and live longer, Bob Dylan, Marianne Faithfull, Leonard Cohen, Johnny Cash, Nina Simone, Scott Walker, Tom Waits, David Byrne and Joni Mitchell certainly continually evolved artistically and individually in ways that can be compared to the great classical composers – and elsewhere compared to the great novelists, still charged enough and determined enough, and bravely, generously confessional enough, to continue experimenting with their craft in late life, for a world they will not live to see, a time, often just a few months ahead, they will never get to know.

Dylan, being Dylan, functions in late life as both the penetrating artist and the great performer, mysteriously wandering the edge of time one more time, turning death down for one more show, before time crumbles away completely and takes with it the path he's on. Perhaps Nick Cave, Jarvis Cocker, Fiona Apple and Polly Harvey will still be observing and negotiating where they are in life and what death feels like as they come to the end, lifting themselves up above being mere performance sideshow, however riveting, committed to one day being from the past but never seeming old-fashioned.

David Bowie's final album *Black Star*, continuing a trajectory he had begun a few years earlier with *The Next Day*, produces an anomalous sort of self-contained, experimental rock record that seems to fit more next to Beethoven, Schubert, Dvořák and Shostakovich, and in jazz Ornette Coleman, Paul Motian, Cecil Taylor and Anthony Braxton, in terms of late-life emotional impulse and intellectual stamina, and a powerful, poignant need still to be probing how far music, and his own music, and his life, can go.

The themes ultimately are about the very mystery of living, conceived at a time when there is a greater mystery fast approaching, and the aloneness of everything. Life is turned into original structures above and beyond the genres Bowie might have worked in, which were a quirk of the time he found himself alive in. Even in centuries to come, the meaning, the life force, the temperate, perversely aroused energy he directed into his music means, like the late Beethoven, with the final recordings of his existence, it will never seem old-fashioned. It will simply be from the past, where we once were, but it's about the pulse of what it is to be human that passes through time, whatever changes there are in the world itself. Things happen, reality replaces itself with more reality, but in spite of all the commotion, the currents and pressure, everything human remains the same.

He found a place in his final weeks where his music was alive as it was when he was in his twenties and at the very centre of fashionable attention, but it's very much about what it is to be almost all of the way through your life. The light has all but diminished, your time has passed, but your music has the most power it has ever had.

The artist, in this mode, acts in their final days as though they have all the time in the world, at least in terms of what they create as shapers of reality and makers of myth. They inhabit a peculiar shrouded form of sped-up slow motion, where they are so behind and so ahead, knowing there is no miracle to come, no authenticated reports of a magical mystery tour to which this life leads.

The planet is falling to bits around you and your own personal reality is shrinking and disappearing. It's everything that surrounds you that is being annihilated, because you have less and less use for it, and the annihilation gradually moves nearer because soon you will disappear too. As the annihilation gets closer and parts of the world fall away, the great artist is still working out life and deciphering its mysteries, their existence reaching a psychedelic intensity that the best artists can turn into great art, into immortal music.

There is effectively no audience any more, no one to think about in that sense. What lies ahead becomes your audience, where you are placing your music, in an eternity, a nothing. The absurdity that you must die when you have arrived at the height of your creative powers must not get in the way of what you are wanting to express. Your attention must not fall backwards into the softness of where you once were when death seemed so far away. It must stay focused on the task at hand: to continue bringing light and lightness to proceedings, however low you feel, or lost, or acutely self-aware of the solidity of time disappearing. Reality reduces itself to the act of creation, of composition; it is the only reality that makes sense as everything else becomes erased. It is something that keeps you alive; the impression of human-ness itself into the music, so that in many ways it is not just about being human, an examination or celebration or final, accepting resignation: it is human.

Mozart writes his quartets as a young man and does not know that he will never become an old man or even a middle-aged man. God knows where he would have gone in the extra forty years he might have lived; by the end, perhaps hinting at a real understanding of the various spaces, speed and extremes of what became serialism, bebop, dub and minimalism, or even of genres and textures that never got invented, sounds that have yet to be created or found. He had to be taken away – by the inexorable energy of the universe, if not, as such, a higher being – because although he was born at exactly the right time to become Mozart, he was also born too far ahead of when and where he should have been, and a longer life might have genuinely distorted the space-time continuum in terms of what he released through his music. As he went about his business, he had no idea that his life would be so short – surely he had done enough to get a ticket to a longer life, adding, after all, the dimension of unlimited imagination to our lives?

But his work, for all its delightfulness and determination, always has a sense that this might be it, the end, always balancing on the edge of what might be, never quite making it. Underneath the surface shine, the antic precision, there was a firm, even sense of something already dealing with death. Beneath the emblazoned precision, the exquisite capturing of the softness of his sensations and a beauty deeper than light, he's shivering with fear, acutely aware of how much disease and decay there is in the world, in his time, for all time, death never far away.

He was always at the beginning of life at the same time as being acutely aware of the end of life; every single one of his compositions ends with a real sense of how life ends; all that thinking and feeling, all those defiant, fantastic melodies, just stopping with a devastating, striking abruptness it's hard to ignore. 'I never lie down in bed,' he once wrote, 'without considering that, young as I am, perhaps I may on the morrow be no more.'

This pull between being consumed by alive-ness and losing himself in the moment, which is somehow separate from time, and has immediate connection to it, contributes to the alien quality of a music that is otherwise so airy and embedded in lively, enterprising human energy. It is really strange, the fact this music exists, and emerged at such a time with such complexity and preparedness, such awareness of its own position in history as it would develop over centuries, sounding relevant now, in terms of an individual's relationship to life and death, if not directly as part of a post-truth reality, but sounding like it belongs in the time it was written.

In 1785, almost thirty, Mozart dedicated six of his twenty-nine quartets to Haydn, responding in particular to the *Russian* Quartets, written when Haydn reapplied himself to the concept after time spent otherwise engaged. Mozart had himself taken a break of almost ten years from composing quartets, many of them written as intriguing teenage exercises when quartets were still an unfamiliar format and there were no clear models to follow. Besides, as he approached his twenties, there were other ways to be as Mozart as he wanted to be, but he immediately began writing his response to Haydn in 1782, soon after he had first heard the *Russian* Quartets, instantly hearing a multitude of stimulating clues about the quartet's infinite possibilities.

He took, for him, an unusual amount of time to complete them. He engaged in this particular artistic challenge, this animating, multidimensional endeavour, very seriously, calling their gestation 'a long and laborious study'.

In these six, acknowledging the debt and inspiration, the sound was as light and effortless, as dramatic and varied as Haydn, a kaleidoscope of musical ciphers, anagrams, games, frolics, data, illusions, build-ups, leaps forward and associations, but accepting the deeper, near-messianic motivation to push as far as possible into the unknown, he pressed inside the music the personal intensity, melancholy, joy, terror, relief, regret, ecstasy, that blend of misfortune and intoxication, mischief and perception that elsewhere he needed whole operas to achieve.

As much as they were directly inspired by how Haydn had imagined something 'new and special', they were also a way of passing through Haydn on the way to becoming even more Mozart. He does not imitate Haydn but inhabits the essential idea of making musical breakthroughs and achieves that in his own way – he breathes in the air of Haydn and breathes out his own. It's almost a religious act, an act of faith, of transformation, absorbing the spirit of another in order to nourish his own. It's not so much the music he believes in but the fact that such music can be made. That all this potential lies ahead.

Haydn is in his blood, but the sound and complexity and astounding self-possession of these six quartets is all Mozart. And by the very nature of setting out to be as new as Haydn, imaginatively to acknowledge his originality by being himself original, he moved beyond Haydn, and took the quartet principle to another level.

In the audacious slow opening to the last one of these six, nicknamed the *Dissonance* Quartet, a spirited essay in what can be read as both comedy and tragedy, containing happiness and suffering, truly the missing link between Haydn and Beethoven, between Bach and Bartók, something so eerie, apparently unfocused and dissonant happens that those reading the score at the time assumed it was a printing mistake, emphasised in a couple of bars where the violins and viola are silent; perhaps a sly celebration of the cello's new freedom as certified on the surface by Haydn – and, stuck in the next room, the historically mute Boccherini – certainly some sort of hidden acknowledgement.

This is where centuries-old classical music, previously for me locked into its fixed historical setting, of no use in modern times other than as part of a nostalgic, repressive desire for the familiar, becomes untethered from time and space, simultaneously incorporating different time periods, alive in the moment. The composer ventured forward into the world at a particular time, but the ideas being considered and the sound that is made means the composer is always venturing into the future, however much the presentation of the music gets wrapped in the past, in sentiment, catalogue, repertoire and specialised academia.

Mozart might become a combination of what time and analysis, and institutional necessity, the power of the establishment, of academic contemplation decides he is, becoming a strange combination of the visible and the invisible, of seer and servant, but the music flows on, fluid and elegant but always discreetly and sometimes not so discreetly cryptic, powering through temporary, fashionable adjustments and translations of who and what he was, always responsive to the situation where it exists again. Performance, concert, records, cassettes, compact discs, radio, and now streaming and gaming, where cultural momentum is disrupted once more; the music never runs out of energy: it always finds its place, or a place is found for it, belonging to no one time, no one medium, no one self-governing, self-centred membership of listeners. Some music might not be able to jump so readily from raft to raft so that it finds a way to cross the merciless oceans of time.

Even ears accustomed to the stark, disorientating early twentieth-century string quartet miniatures of Anton Webern, the smarting late twentieth-century hyper-expressionism of Brian Ferneyhough or the blasted poetic evocations of Helmut Lachenmann will feel agitated hearing the *Dissonance* Quartet, as Mozart anticipates musical abstractions and austere Beckett landscapes lying over a hundred years ahead. There is even a flickering glimpse of minimalism, with its own sense of reaching back into time to create its hybrid of the contemporary and the romantic, of the Dark Ages and the postmodern light fantastic. Time floats rather than flows. A new type of beauty is revealed. In anxious, troubled times, passing music through a Mozart prism, after experiencing the mistake and/or intentional leap into otherness of *Dissonance*, it becomes clear how music helps us tolerate cognitive dissonances — especially useful as we're tossed on the perpetually screened and shared ruins of post-truth and apocalyptic decay — and aids protective accumulation of knowledge and idealistic, progressive cultural evolution. In other words, when things get bad, play your favourite music, with some Mozart mixed in.

Haydn's not entirely convinced response to possible errors in the printed score of the *Dissonance* Quartet was: 'If Mozart wrote it, he must have meant it.' It was now Mozart that Haydn would be responding to as the innovator in his subsequent quartets. Mozart becomes the teacher.

This was where the formulated ideal of a classical music transcended the earlier idea of music being functional, for domestic recreation, social gatherings or organised worship; the string quartet was also rooted in the decorative madrigals of the fifteenth century, but Haydn and Mozart, amidst their other stylistic and genre innovations, precisely because they were driven to solve problems, make discoveries and test possibilities, provided this form of chamber music with deliberate artistic strength. It wasn't music necessarily for purely functional use, either relaxation or in church, but music that existed because the composer was trying new things out and extending their intellectual and emotional range. It didn't mean it wasn't attractive enough for distraction or solemn enough for worship, but now there was increasingly an added element: personal aspiration, and an accelerated need to explore the self and the power of your imagination, which is where the free-thinking dynamic of personal freedom – absolute free time, beyond the interference of the mundane – exists.

Haydn's quartets, and Mozart's, especially the ones dedicated to Haydn, were the beginning of all the variations and developments that were to come, the intricate, reflective four-way conversation, the combination of the self-absorbed and the altruistic, wit and allusion, the battle of wills, the distillation of music itself and a composer's mind into a very specific organism, challenging to play, pleasurable, or pleasurably demanding, to hear.

Whatever has come since has its source in the first stirrings of Haydn, alertly reacting to the first stirrings happening around him, and the subsequent enriched refinements of Mozart; this discovery of a new way of representing energy, and mental activity, and then the enhancement, redirection and regeneration, and occasional dip in energy and lack of interest.

The quartet thrived in the established classical era, where Mozart and then Beethoven and Schubert relished the challenge issued by Haydn of dealing with a restricted palette of sounds and repeatedly investigating how to generate contrast and unexpected texture writing for four equal instruments. The string quartet became established as the prime, prestigious and dominant chamber music unit, existing in its very own world, in unbreakable apartness.

There was less concentration on the format in the nineteenth century, and Tchaikovsky, Brahms and Schumann, for instance, limit themselves to three, as though bowing to the inevitable sealed-off presence of history, and Haydn's sixty-eight, Mozart's twenty-six, and Beethoven and Schubert's late, free-falling monuments and treasures, music as a justification of our existence, where everything is measured, watched and in a sense revealed. The quartet era seemed to be over, pressed back into history like the madrigals, fugues and consorts. There was enough already made, surely.

Wagner, playing the role of his own god, only left some partial sketches for a potential quartet, but he hinted at what the musical architecture might have sounded like in a private piece he wrote as a birthday surprise in 1870 for his wife of four months, Cosima, the daughter of Franz Liszt. It was a year when the fifty-seven-year-old was reaching his own summit, including completing the philosophically and psychologically complex *Ring* cycle, his central artistic statement, but love for his wife brought out of him this unlikely ethereal gem.

The original title was *Triebschen Idyll with Fidi's birdsong and the orange sunrise, as symphonic birthday greeting, presented to his Cosima by her Richard*, but it was eventually titled after his recently born third son, Siegfried. A tender, loving, liquid-slow chamber piece, essentially a love letter never meant to be heard publicly, very much a sensitive, doting Wagner for those who don't like the idea of empire-building Wagner, *Siegfried Idyll* developed themes from some of his quartet sketches and was initially scored for a thirteen-piece chamber orchestra, small enough to be grouped on the stairs outside Cosima's bedroom so she would be woken by its playing, and eventually for a larger orchestra.

A year later, devoted fan and friend Friedrich Nietzsche, whose *The Birth of Tragedy* was dedicated to Wagner and celebrated his music as a force for good, sent his own gift to Cosima, a whimsical composition for piano with four hands that liberally quoted *Siegfried Idyll*. It wasn't particularly Apollonian or Dionysian, let alone a holy or unholy fusion of both. It didn't sound like the music of someone who once wrote 'music can exalt us, divert us, cheer us up, or break the hardest of hearts with the softest of its melancholy tones. But its principal task is to lead our thoughts to higher things, to elevate, even make us tremble.' Wagner did not tremble and was not at all impressed at this tremulous amateur offering. Nietzsche seemingly never knew of Wagner's dismissive reaction, but by the end of the 1880s he had grown disgusted with his former idol and influence, jealous at his success and power. He now saw Wagner as a diseased symbol of the cultural decadence eating into contemporary society, a fake musician.

Siegfried Idyll was a particular favourite of intense Canadian pianist Glenn Gould, and in the 1970s he recorded a piano transcript he made himself. A version of this was also his final recording, in the autumn of 1982, when he conducted a chamber orchestra he had assembled himself, his debut recording as a conductor. He had planned for the next stage in his life to be as a conductor, especially on records, which he felt gave him control over the music.

Unusually for a classical musician, appreciating how the recording process offered new creative possibilities, he far preferred recording to playing live, having given up public performance in 1964. He suffered a stroke three months after the recording session for *Siegfried Idyll* and died one week after turning fifty. His rendition of the *Idyll* does not fully communicate why he was so drawn to the piece, as if he was using the session to work out why it is so beautiful and not particularly allowing the musicians under his control to help him find out.

It might have been that the new role he was actually looking for was to be a producer and use the studio as his new instrument, applying his vaulting, interpretive brilliance to illuminating music through multitrack recording. He seemed to have the singular talent, and the control-freakiness and crazy determination, to be a Brian Wilson or a Phil Spector rather than a Bernstein or a Boulez; in pop, the producer takes on the role of a kind of conductor. A Toscanini recording of *Siegfried Idyll* from 1936 with the New York Philharmonic just lets it be beautiful, by letting everyone play beautifully.

The string quartet form didn't fit into Wagner's ferocious belief in music as 'the total work of art', or he felt its peak of creativity had already been attained and he was concentrating on more explicitly dramatic representations and cloud-skimming peaks he could conquer before anyone else. He studied throughout his life the next to last piece Beethoven wrote before he died, the very last he composed of the infamous final ground-breaking six string quartets, where he was coming to terms with his fate. For Wagner, in the concentrated form of a string quartet, here were vital clues and recommendations about how to structure a coherent but expansive form of highly charged musical drama.

Beethoven's ideas about what music could do and be and sound like, and how far it could see, were so advanced, it was as though part of him was already penetrating the afterlife and he was reporting back, having already reported back from surveying the tangled, tantalising mysteries of the mind. T. S. Eliot, talking of his own artistic purpose, said he was striving to get beyond poetry in the way that Beethoven was striving to get beyond music.

Beethoven's Op. 131 String Quartet No. 14 in C-sharp minor evolved from his demanding original final movement to quartet No. 13, which took on a life of its own as the daunting *Grosse Fuge*, Op. 133, coherence emerging from obscure beginnings, described by Stravinsky as 'an absolutely contemporary piece of music which will be contemporary for ever', which in turn was inspired by the spirit of Bach and his elevating exploration of the complex art of fugal counterpoint.

Fugues — literally meaning 'flight' — were Bach's natural language, a baroque form of composition using two or more instrumental voices, which demonstrated the basic skill of the composer. They evolved from earlier types of contrapuntal compositions such as imitative ricercars, capriccios, canzonas and fantasias with a history rooted in the Middle Ages, where everyone would be singing or playing a melody, but at different points at the same time.

Bach was the most sophisticated, disciplined and accomplished of fugue writers, lifting these stylistic combinations of exercise and expression, mathematics and musicality to the status of art, a merging of feeling and philosophy, before they faded out of fashion with the eighteenth-century rise of the sonata and the symphony. Mozart and Beethoven — and 200 years later Shostakovich — would reach back and flex their mental muscles and solve self-imposed problems with their own versions and models, resplendent combinations of study, resourcefulness and flights of the imagination.

Bach, who died in 1750 at sixty-five, nine years after the death of Vivaldi, was alive too early to have written a string quartet, the line-up not yet formally fashioned, his life ending as the concept began, but his fugues and their energies and lines, unity and economy, the ingenious combining of voices and themes, ornament and complexity, the elegant juxtaposition of melodies that don't fight with each other, became embedded in the form, part of the quartet's propulsive, interactive, intimate and emotional nature. Plenty of his ideas were ready to be assimilated into the string quartet tradition.

His mysterious, unfinished *The Art of Fugue* – the last of his monothematic cycles, which included the *Goldberg Variations* and *The Musical Offering* – is a fantastic intellectual challenge, one of the truly great creations of the human mind, quixotic and partly abstract. It was perhaps deliberately unfinished, allowing fugue fanatics to work out an ending, and one of Bach's last works, published the year after he died, and sometimes thought of as a 'last will and testament', where the mathematics was mixed with the mystical, the clinical with the divine. Fourteen fugues and four canons, all in D minor, all based on the same melody, possibly an abstract exercise not necessarily written for any particular instrument or line-up – no instruments were marked in the score – basically never to be performed or realised in sound, have in the end been interpreted by everything from solo piano, organ and harpsichord to string quartets and full and chamber orchestras.

I love it played by Gustav Leonhardt on harpsichord, Helmut Walcha on organ, Joanna MacGregor on piano, Fretwork for consort of viols, Academy of St Martin-in-the-Fields for orchestra, and sublimely reimagined by Harrison Birtwistle for string quartet. There is an inevitably, elatedly idiosyncratic interpretation by Glenn Gould from 1962 on his only album of organ music, recorded in an Anglican church in Toronto, ruggedly relishing its undefined shape, its sublime incompleteness and its heady reputation as a cerebral, intellectual work, as a sonic puzzle. Consisting of the first nine fugues (the first nine clues) he sped, a little things-to-do, people-to-see madly through the task, taking on its growing complexity, and was all done in just over half an hour; others took nearly forty minutes for the same nine fugues. The brevity and pace, the sense sometimes he might be on the verge of crash landing, perversely seem to amplify the melancholic, mesmerising grandeur of the music.

It has also been taken on by string quartets, defying the argument that this inappropriately applies post-Haydn developmental style to a pre-Haydn concept. Quartet versions of *The Art of Fugue* are a clear intimation of what an intended Bach string quartet would have sounded like, amplifying the tenacious brilliance of his fugue writing, which can be logically be placed in a quartet setting, and supplying evidence of how much Bach's indestructible and impeccable music reached into the limber mind of Mozart and provided psychic previews of the guts and glory of Beethoven.

Beethoven's Op. 131 is music as an articulation of a state of consciousness that is a glimpse of where humans evolve, centuries before we have become so pure, so elementally other. Nietzsche observed that Beethoven's gaze had become so strong he could make out the bottom of the dark well of being and the distant constellation of future civilisations. The poet Ted Hughes wove his thoughts on the quartet into everyday, and not-so-everyday, details of a hotel stay with his doomed lover and future wife Sylvia Plath in his poem 'Opus 131', where different dimensions of reality begin to clash.

He contemplates in anguish how not even his musical superhero Beethoven will be able to cancel out her tragically manipulated mortality or somehow even postpone through his brilliance her inevitable fate. The music, for all its sacred properties, which romantics love to exaggerate, is no lifeline. For all its tumultuous artistic power, thought stretched out on the horizon of a mighty mind, it cannot protect their relationship, and maintain its fierce heat. Despite Beethoven, winter is coming, in this case bringing with it the unique endless loneliness of suicide. Hughes describes the musicians as being like insects crawling through his lover's inert naked body. The notes, with their sharp faces, carry her torso off into different corners of the universe.

The music opens a 'great door' in the air, in this case to 'horror', and he talks of how Beethoven, the greatest influence on his artistic imagination, is trying to resolve the cosmic finality, the weird destiny, of his silence.

Beethoven's loss of hearing began in 1818 and had developed into total deafness when he wrote Op. 131 eight years later, a year before his death in 1827. His deafness is the loudest way there is in the world of previewing his death and an eternity spent hearing nothing. His being starts to break down in preparation for death and he can do nothing in the face of this except fight with and for his music, his determination to make himself heard, distilled into his string quartets, which remain to him unheard outside of his imagination, where, it seemed, in the black hole of himself, he was beginning to hear everything.

For Hughes, it was necessary for the great artist, the intrepid, super-conscious explorer patrolling the dangerous borders between the real and the unreal, the Beethovens and the Blakes – both dying in 1827, the year Edgar Allan Poe's first book of poems, influenced by Shelley, Coleridge and Byron, was published, a very good year for the life and afterlife of romanticism – to go deep into horror. Deep into, in Hughes's words, 'an echoless cosmic horror' – and deep into despair and danger, deeper and deeper, with an absurd sense of duty into what chaos and desolation has collected at the 'grisly' bottom of human existence. The artist emerges from their unfathomable black adventures into hopelessness with a new form of creative energy, so that the messages and insights scattered through their work have an uncanny, unprecedented and perversely inspiring freshness.

Hughes was obsessed with Beethoven from youth to death, loving how he composed 'singing and roaring and walking very fast', how the music could sink its claws into your skull and 'digest you into its horrible joys'. He once wrote: 'I have only ever felt that sensation of being drawn deeper & deeper into some holy beautiful, holy terrifying & utterly concentrated state of awareness by Beethoven's late quartets.'

Beethoven wrote on the title page that Op. 131 was 'put together from pilfering from one thing and another', but even though he might be stealing fragments or absorbing certain influences, how he puts it all together belongs completely to him. Influences are always a mysterious thing, ranging from a few words here and there to an artist's whole life's work, and, for a musician, influences that are not necessarily musical at all. And, for a writer, influences that are not necessarily literary. As Bob Dylan once said, possibly meaning it, he learned as much writing his early songs from the painter Cézanne as he did from the more obvious candidate Woody Guthrie, and it's the Cézanne parts that made his songs timeless, that turned smartly inherited but ultimately secure, dead-end folk tradition into volatile experiments with voice and song. The fact he can even think of referencing Cézanne means that he is the kind of artist who can take a song from somewhere else and copy it almost note for note, with a little change in emphasis and a little shift in language, a few new words, and when it becomes, say, 'Don't Think

Twice', all his, however much he borrowed, it is not simply a catchy, likeable folky pop song but an absolute work of art — and a work of life — where meaning constantly slips and slides into other dimensions.

In his Fourteenth String Quartet, Op. 131, Beethoven used a non-stop mood-contrasting seven movements concentrated into thirty-five sense-distorting minutes, which, apart from anything else, demonstrated how much the form could achieve as an artwork and as actual experience. He had moved far beyond the more genteel, Haydnesque notion that the quartet is a lively, learned, agreeable interpretation of experience or an argumentative conversation between friends or enemies, or forces of nature, or indeed in the sense that sometimes a cigar is just a cigar, a simple lucid, decorative musical conversation between two violins, a viola and a cello. Beethoven was doing so much more than a literate arrangement of sounds and themes; he was creating life. He could see no other way.

Beethoven, mad with livid reason, at the end of an all-consuming journey made for the sake of art, dragging something sublime up from the depths of his disability, isolated from society because of his deafness and an uncompromising artistic need to do things his way, music burning away his suffering and fanaticism, presents the quartet as a ritualistic clash between the different dimensions of reality Hughes refers to in his poem 'Opus 131'.

If there is a conversation, it is himself with Bach, Haydn and Mozart, who have already turned into the same dead-and-alive being he is turning into, but there's much more than talking going on, however profound — it becomes a clash between civilisations, between flesh and blood, memory and forgetfulness, being and non-being, sound and silence. The string quartet becomes the ultimate way to unleash the imagination. Beethoven's imagination is at its most untamed when he is completely deaf. He was plunging through his music into a deeper, spiritual world, and ultimately plunging outside himself. The mind and body go away, but the soul is left behind in the music — his new mind and body.

Wagner wrote an operatic, book-length essay in 1870 commemorating the one-hundredth anniversary of Beethoven's birth, loving himself and the new German empire along the way. A deaf musician! he marvelled. 'Can you imagine a blind painter?' He said of Beethoven's Op. 131, as though this was enough in terms of his contribution to the art of the string quartet, in awe of its biting beauty and ultimate serenity, its raging fury:

> 'Tis the dance of the whole world itself: wild joy, the wail of pain, love's transport, utmost bliss, grief, frenzy, riot, suffering, the lightning flickers, thunders growl: and above it the stupendous fiddler who bears and bounds it all, who leads it haughtily from whirlwind into whirlwind, to the brink of the abyss – he smiles at himself, for to him this sorcery was the merest play – and night beckons him. His day is done.

Some composers in this late nineteenth-century era only wrote one quartet, as a kind of intellectual and/or emotional exercise, a brief learned sample of ability, love and understanding, a temporary excursion into another apparently almost closed-off land – the eighteen-year-old Richard Strauss, still with a crush on Haydn and Liszt, writing a very pleasing one in 1882, Puccini making a brief, concentrated contribution, with the meditative 1890 elegy *Crisantemi*, and, in the middle of all that Italian-opera drama, which made chamber music next to invisible, Verdi, almost thinking to himself while the premiere of *Aida* is postponed, makes extremely skilful use of all the last-thing-at-night study he did of the quartets of Haydn, Mozart and Beethoven, with his String Quartet in E minor, his only purely instrumental piece, which, inevitably, is very easy to sing along with. It was just a little off-duty dabble for Verdi, who remarked that he didn't know whether it was ugly or beautiful. 'But I do know that it's a quartet!'

Ravel and Debussy, connected as ever, each compressed their interest, curiosity and respect as well as their unsinkable musicality into one intense, swirling model, where they use sound like paint and replace the idea of the quartet dialogue with a sense of a four-way relationship between different lengths of time, between imaginative shapes, weird fibres and shadows of feeling.

A contemporary of Marx and Wagner, Bedřich Smetana's connection is typically with fellow Czech Dvořák. Most known for opera and orchestral music, including his tone poem *Ma Vlast* (*My Country*), his acutely autobiographical, earthy and tragic First String Quartet, *From My Life*, was written in 1876, two years after he had become deaf in both ears, one way of matching Beethoven. An insistent, anguished note in the finale signified the ringing in his ears, which led to his hearing loss, and Smetana used the four instruments to represent four people talking about what had oppressed him in his life. The music fades away into silence in the final movement. His less-familiar, more terse and fierce Second String Quartet was finished seven years later, a few months before he died at sixty after years of mental anguish, another desperate way of attempting to match Beethoven's unstoppable creative drive and the tempestuous other-worldliness of his late quartets.

Smetana's melody-mad adventure-seeking national partner Dvořák, with a touch of late eighteenth-century yearning, completed fifteen string quartets towards the end of the nineteenth century, and his String Quartet No. 12 in F major, known as the *American* Quartet, is his famous impression, almost a deliberate fictional construct, of an emergent American identity. He had a sort of job to do that inspired in him an equivalent sense of pioneering quest to Haydn and Mozart, providing him with the necessary sense of optimism and courage, or foolhardiness, to imagine what this young nation's music would sound like.

Asked in 1892 during a three-year stay to help imagine a national sound for a still young and unformed America, Dvořák controversially combined his curious-outsider, even tourist take on the resilient indigenous music of black slaves and the haunting reflections of Native Americans he'd experienced on his travels cross-country with the endless otherness of the vast, lonely, awe-inspiring way-out-west landscape. The rough, folksy and provisional sources of what became jazz and blues, still wet with the sweat of Africa, still bittersweet with despair and devastated hope, were eccentrically and lavishly redirected. Gutsy, freedom-seeking spirituals and mysterious, arcane Native American atmospheres were elegantly strained through delectable Czech melancholia, generous melodies that confidently faced up to Mozart and the ornate European gestures of Haydn, Brahms and Wagner, this grand melange of home-grown and immigrant styles eventually filtering back into American music.

Pupils of Dvořák during his time in New York became mentors to Ellington, Copland and Gershwin, all of them receiving some deflected Dvořákian glow, and his audacious blend of the fragile and the monumental swept into maturing cinematic Americana through classic westerns and eventually the John Williams of Steven Spielberg.

The *American* Quartet's volatile combination of pioneering optimism and world-weary acceptance, jaunty melody and haunted history, an intimate relation to his famous *New World* Symphony, comes from the verge of the American twentieth century, when Eurocentric classical music was, perversely, seen as a solution to the troublesome construction of a distinct American musical voice.

It was just in time to be of use before the technologies that enabled recording, cinema and radio sent American appetites for entertainment way beyond the realm of the classical music tradition; the connections Dvořák made between ancient and modern, between races and traditions, between his homeland and appropriated temporary homeland ensured that classical music had a presence, however diluted or corrupted, however unofficial or abridged, in the American twentieth century. Without directly knowing it, film lovers were receiving an adapted history of classical music, sometimes straight from the source, because of how mainstream movies used classical styles and their technical sophistication to add grandeur and elevating emotional power to their stories. Serious classical music, otherwise thrust to the margins by the purposefully distracting post-industrial procession of the popular arts, was smuggled into the heart of American culture through its greatest cultural invention, cinema. For example, see how easily Mozart as a presence, as much as through music, slipped into film, and often films about the future: there he is in *Alien*, Ridley Scott's original film, a coda and kind of continuation to Stanley Kubrick's *2001: A Space Odyssey*, where the flawed, brave captain of the doomed spaceship *Nostromo*, Dallas, frustrated by the abnormal happenings interrupting a routine flight back to earth that aggressively threaten his authority, seeking vital solace from danger and tension on a claustrophobic and deeply troubled spaceship, retreats to an escape shuttle for some necessary contemplation. He thinks about the evil that has invaded his vessel, wonders if abandoning ship is too cowardly, stares out at the endless silent stars, into the heart of the mystery of creation, and the second movement of Mozart's *Eine Kleine Nachtmusik* is heard exquisitely harmonising with all the shattering quietness out there, oddly because we are far out in the future, and yet obviously because Mozart will survive, as a form of enlightening, enriching entertainment always adapting to circumstances, impervious to shifts in fashion, technology, human capacity, shrinking attention spans, environmental and medical crises, violated imaginations and capability. He has become one of those who will not be forgotten, because eternity recollects them. He understood what the rest of us will not see until the end of time.

Dallas, the alienated captain, *Enterprise*'s Kirk with complications, is portrayed as a committed Mozart listener to make the watcher think he must be intelligent, responsible and sure where truth can be found in a chaotic, disappointing cosmos. (Kirk would have listened to Elvis, a descendant in some ways of the youthful perfection of Mozart, although the perfection was all in the voice, presence and ultimate assigned universality.)

The music is both in tune with the fact that the spaceship is suspended in, and sweeping through, the eternal unnerving night of space where, the more you think about it, nothing makes sense, where humans, however advanced, remain small and insignificant and inappropriate, because we are listening to the eighteenth century while surrounded by the technically, futuristically adventurous — but then, Kubrick and *2001: A Space Odyssey* has already made it clear that spaceships and classical music seamlessly fit together as if somehow they are related to each other, as ways of travelling through space and time, and deep into the mind, extending the idea, the very being, of humanity into new places of otherness. Great classical music is a kind of spaceship built to explore the vast unknown.

In space, as close to the middle of nowhere as you can get, as close to our idea of eternity, Mozart's music becomes the incalculable sound of God, Himself in the middle of creation, in the middle of creating all that we experience and imagine. The implication is that when it comes to aliens, we might not be able to teach the most advanced civilisation anything about science or technology, but our music will be unique to us, the essence of who we are, and endlessly fascinating to those from other worlds looking for clues about who and what we are/were. And, of course, there is the suggestion that Mozart — picked out by the rest of us, certainly those who tend to have a say, as special hero, their virtues exaggerated, promoted beyond ordinary mortality, the offspring of an archangel, the other, deviant side of the universe from being standard, a demigod, if not the sound of God thinking — was himself some kind of alien, as outrageously otherworldly as an octopus, a being whose natural environment is as much timeless outer space as it is eighteenth-century Vienna.

The same piece is also used, less majestically, for a variety of reasons that include the kitsch and commercial as well as the creative, in *Batman*, *The Bonfire of the Vanities*, *Charlie's Angels: Full Throttle*, *La Femme Nikita*, *There's Something About Mary*, because it's Mozart, because it does things, sometimes dead obvious, sometimes a little strangely, to the world the film inhabits.

Dvořák's *American* Quartet was at the same time a rousing act of melody-soaked nostalgia for the assumed heyday of the string quartet even as it was proposing the indigenous, anomalous sound of an energetic, hybridised new world. Dvořák believed in the string quartet enough to use its formalities and traditions, and endless scope, to transmit a novel, exuberant pulse into American music, one that referred to a tradition before there was ever really an actual tradition.

Back in Europe, the string quartet received a new lease of life in the modernist early twentieth-century era of Schoenberg, Bartók and Shostakovich, when there was enough distance between them and the early classical masters, as part of a wider need to renew and initiate, to begin again, but using previous procedures as a way of finding paths to cover new ground. The modernists needed to know about the old kingdom in order to advance towards a new unknown. In an era breaking into abstraction, the string quartet could still be a relevant vehicle, with its own proven ability to be more than merely representative and rigidly classical.

There was also a enduring subversive quality to the string quartet, and over time it had become a form of outsider music, of most interest to outsider composers, a purist pursuit for composers searching for the most direct, extendable means of expressing ideas; the opulent, formidable, fixed symphony orchestra reduced down to a compact collection of endlessly movable cells.

Another era of indifference followed in the immediate, stern post-war years of Boulez and Messiaen, as though there was nothing more to be done, not so much because of the early giants, or monsters, but because of pre-war Webern and Bartók stacking up apparent deathless end points – it didn't seem possible for things to get any more string quartet than what had happened with Beethoven and Bartók, and then with the monumental reductions, the epic concentration, of Webern – before another boundless renewal of energy ranging from the dislocated and atomised to the blissful and analytical after the 1960s, with Kurtág, Lachenmann, Ferneyhough and Rihm.

However much new music rebels against the classical tradition, however much it blows it apart or rejects its traditions and savages its sense of elitism, it can never escape its pull. The sounds made in an extreme aleatory composition – a piece of music deliberately dependent on chance, luck or an uncertain outcome – still follow each other like the notes in a Mozart composition.

Even at its most deranged, indefinite, harrowing, flexible, complex, asymmetrical, even aggressively unmusical and dependent on chance, a piece of classical music still exists within the frame, inextricably connected to the centuries of ebb and flow; if it leaves the frame, it immediately becomes something else, however serious, whether it is jazz or rock, and of no interest to the purists, conservative or extreme radicals. If you say there are no rules, then that is a rule, and however extreme the new music, it does become the latest in a series of conventions. The history is always made up of a strictly organic chain, and innovation paradoxically becomes the only way of remaining on the rails of tradition.

John Cage, however far he strayed, going deep, not so much into the mind but the mind of the mind, where accidents happen, and which has a life of its own, working with time and nature more than notes and harmony, only really makes sense in the context of classical history and his resistant, idiosyncratic relationship to it – even if his influence can and does extend elsewhere – and John Adams, as successful as he is as a classical composer with his grand, public intellectualism and populist minimalism, is relatively obscure outside the frame, and if he tipped out of it, he would be exiled from the tradition and therefore the associated institutions and need to construct an entirely different context for himself.

The battle between classical stability and constant change, between establishment order and the breaking of order, between tradition and innovation, form and formlessness, between the consoling and the disturbing, between consensus and resistance, between a craving for progress and an acceptance of the status quo and a comforting 'high musical art', between live performance and recorded performance, is symbolised through the string quartet, and the route, leading to more routes, and detours, and digressions, and sagas, and pauses for thought, momentum building up over centuries, travelling from Haydn and Mozart, Beethoven and Schubert, unbroken, and beautifully broken, with an eventual, fairly general abandonment, or deft realignment, or sometimes unashamed embrace, of the strict Haydnesque structure, to Britten and Schoenberg, Cage and Stockhausen, Xenakis and Feldman, Ligeti and Hilda Paredes, Glass, Maxwell Davies and Birtwistle. And, I had to hope, me, Morley – ish.

With those early eighteenth-century works setting up the deliberately testing, contained conditions, you can hear the very beginning of something that has carried on ever since, always changing, and yet somehow never changing, for better or worse – the decorum and self-obsession, the purity of form drifting into effete elegance, contradicting the original raw spirit of inventive curiosity, but elsewhere, the constant craving inside this small space to discover new forms of insight and expression, and to keep the origins of the format alive inside subsequent manifestations of originality, havoc and audacity.

It all traces the move from over 250 years from 1750s Haydn to twenty-first-century Matthias Pintscher, music going backwards and forwards at the same time, dust in the wind that somehow you can keep track of, wherever it blows, so that Cage's 1950 quartets written almost as an acknowledgment of a 200-year anniversary can sound medieval and pretty, and Schubert's, written in the 1820s, tense and raging. Hindemith's protean, elemental third of seven quartets, written in 1920, sounds as though it could have been written during the life of Brahms, but also during the life of Berio.

The history of the quartet is a history of a particular language that will always reveal itself in different permutations, a language that is both instantly familiar, a form of prose that makes clear sense, but is also elusive and alien. Through clues, signals, tension, relief, innovation, consolidation, liberation, an organisation of matter and material, occasionally pure blasts of pleasure, and sometimes outright nightmare, it provides a history of feeling, fear, love, lust, anxiety, despair, joy, determination, discovery, retreat, triumph. The composers create sonic self-portraits, portraits, landscapes, still lives, abstractions, situations, impressions, sculptures, exhibitions, diaries, theoretical statements, visions, essays. And from limited means, and limited possibility, emerges the unlimited, and a perpetual discovery of new possibilities.

2. SECOND MOVEMENT: SLOW, IN THE SUBDOMINANT KEY

If you were asking me to give you a playlist of my favourite string quartets, well, now you're talking...

At first, the story now goes, in terms of looking for a place to start, if you fancy beginning at the pinnacle, you absolutely have to get to know the resplendent five late Beethoven quartets, Nos. 14–18 – turning four instruments, four players and a compilation of notes and instructions into a single being conscious of its own consciousness, completing the journey from quartets being fancy 'amusements', entertaining distractions, to full-blooded existential attack, profoundly extending the limits, achieving holy artistic authenticity.

Joining Beethoven at the deep, resonant centre, and simultaneously the edge of this universe, of the mind's awareness of being, the dense, coiled and uncoiling Bartók, his hypnotic, thrilling, relentlessly inquisitive investigations, all done and dusted and driven forward after six quartet masterpieces between 1909 and 1939, doors opened one at a time again and again, each impression, each note possessing its own distinct existence, the series tunnelling through the rest of his prodigious work, leaving many moments that will haunt you for ever, each quartet revealing more of itself every time you listen, because you can just keep going deeper.

Milton Babbitt meticulously analysed how much they confronted contemporary music problems of the time and, without rejecting the 'hazards and connotations of tonalism', noted how even though they were written over a period of thirty years, there is crucially a basic unity of purpose that 'invests all six with the character of a single, self-contained creative act'. To start, try numbers 4 and 6 first, or, actually, just try them in whatever order you fancy, but hear them.

The Shostakovich cycle, the first appearing in 1938, is a highly personal and stirring fifteen-part crusade from a composer who passed through a revolution, two world wars and political oppression, through personal and artistic hardships and sorrows, filled with fierce longing, a profound sense of fear and secret transmissions, giving voice to the silenced. It's a constant source of study – don't let that put you off – and wonder as his thoughts turn increasingly inward and he perfects the same uncanny ability Beethoven possessed to attain the most intense feelings during the quietest moments.

By the end of the cycle, in his cryptic, death-soaked six-movement Fifteenth, from Elegy to Epilogue, written in hospital in 1974 in the last year of his life, the music gets slower and slower, marching towards the inevitable darkness; the end is in sight, energy diminishing, life and music breaking down, fate accepted to a point, deeper and deeper into the hidden inside, where time becomes unmeasured, space flutters outside itself, no resurrection possible. Meanwhile, the learning, the finding out, never stops.

Crying grief and agony so that we can hear beauty, he's still maintaining the point of his existence and the immutable, profound essence of the string quartet, its enduring continuity, by writing music that is unlike any he's written before, even as he summarises his musical ideas, casting a final backward glance – basically, his final quartet purely, courageously, indignantly, affectionately expresses his love for music, which has carried him through a turbulent, even brutalised life and, like life, kept him apart from oblivion, but which for him must come to an end. Music is unstoppable, even if the composer is not. The composer dies; the music does not.

Death had also been the inevitable subject of his Fourteenth Symphony, finished in 1969 shortly before his fiercely sombre and still innovative Thirteenth Quartet, and therefore a definite partner – a deeply felt, appalled complaint about what, at the end of a life, seems to be the absurd shortness of life. Death awaits us all. There is no other way, even if at the end you are still thinking so much, have so much to say, and so much to create. Shostakovich remarked: 'I do not see anything good about such an end to our lives, and this is what I am trying to convey...'

This is where music without words can say so much more than music with words, where the words limit the necessary complexity and strangeness of expression. By the stoical, fatalistic Fifteenth String Quartet we are hearing his final 'words', and in some ways the final screams, the final beats of consciousness, the end pulses, the ultimate depletion of passion and purpose, all the time it took for him to take all that time with him, as previewed in his mighty, melancholy Thirteenth String Quartet.

Some would add the imposing, volatile Elliott Carter series of five composed between 1950 and 1995, at an average of one a decade, to this celebrated, even formalised mountaintop, the Carter cycle to the late twentieth century what Bartók's were to the early twentieth and Beethoven's to the early nineteenth. They are the ultimate example of how a series of quartets become a form of autobiography, marking out the changes in the life and music of the composer, recording critical and passionate moments in a life and work.

Carter's 1950 forty-minute leap-to-freedom First is a gloriously intense, berserkly lovely analysis of the very idea of attempting to rewire and thrust forward the structure of the quartet following the achievements of Beethoven and Bartók, written 'largely for my own satisfaction growing out of an effort to understand myself', somehow persuading the listener there were more than four instruments, and time was turning a few corners, bebop was happening nearby, and planets sound like this at their core; the intense, lucid, 1959 Second — after the vast First the rest become more compact, about twenty to twenty-five minutes long — fully aware of Xenakis and Boulez elsewhere rampantly staking out the post-war avant-garde as a matter of life or death, and Carter makes the idea of the four-way conversation seem as though each instrument is speaking a different language, but each instrument responds to the other with complete, spontaneous understanding; the notorious 1971 Third, the 'double duo' working in different elusive realities where their respective movements exist separately, an ecstatic, collapsing blitz of change and contrast, a flaming alternative to the chilled minimalist mix of medievalism, conceptual music and postmodernism happening nearby, and sounding a little cowardly next to this; the 1985–6 Fourth almost a sigh of relief, a frantic, fretting calm after the storm; the intricately constructed 1995 Fifth written at eighty-seven, a final feisty confirmation of Carter's methods of combining a deep understanding of the formal essence of the quartet, featuring four protagonists, each possessing an independent nature with the adventurous, experimental and abstract propulsion that extended time and time again the parameters, because, for all the limitations, there are no limits.

The Fifth ethereally eases to a quiet dissolution either because there was no more to come, and Carter had decided to finish his series here, with calm, the sun setting, or because, perhaps, there was more to come from this intrepid voyager constantly drawn to the gleam – after all Carter lived on for seventeen years – both for Carter and the idea of the string quartet, which had evolved since the eighteenth century into these beautiful, ugly, dramatic, voluptuous mythical beasts. Living creatures that could now fly and breathe fire, spin the darkest of webs, be a detective on an adventure to solve a mystery, reveal perfect dustless light, sing hymns to time, orbit planets, swim under water and touch the bottom of the ocean.

Carter's quartets were the zenith of modernism in the way Telemann's *Paris* Quartets were the ultimate distillation of baroque styles, so that those who came afterwards and wanted to sound fresh were compelled to conceive new angles of approach; play the Carter and Telemann next to each other and they clearly come from the same space in the universe, if not quite at the same time, although in centuries to come they would seem chronologically near to each other and fit fantastically together, from a pre-digital time when humans were really human and didn't they know it.

Climbing closer and closer to the mountaintop, almost invisibly, certainly taking his own, lonely route but with immense purpose and a cycle of thirteen numbered quartets written between the early 1980s and 2011, Wolfgang Rihm, the post-avant-garde, post-Stockhausen German romantic, relishing his role in extending – exaggerating and erasing at the same time – the Austro-German traditions from Beethoven to Berg, Mahler to Lachenmann.

A sort of lover of laws who's fascinated with lawlessness, Rihm works in an awkward and unusual place between the sentimental and conventional and the indelicate and unconventional. He is an elusive, elevated musical neo-conservative with radical impulses or vice versa, a traditionalist partial to Schumann who is excited by a modern idea of music 'that renews itself at each instant'. Feeling it expresses 'the secret nature of art', he is committed, like Stravinsky, more to the idea of the string quartet as a fertile ensemble to work with than the prescribed musical form; a perfect flexible setting for intellectual and impassioned experimenting – and simultaneously the resetting of limits – with structure, noise, tension, history, duration, tempo, symbols, stasis.

His string quartets, as is often the case with composers, form the primary core of his vast output and a continuing, renewable diagram of his interests, restlessness and rigorous craftsmanship. The single-movement non-numbered requiem *Grave* from 2005 is a quieter, cooler way in, which makes you realise classical music as a cultural organism always seemed to be dying because it is often about dying, and the formidable one-movement thirty-minute Eleventh exists at another extreme, and is full of extremes, from the coherent to the fragmented, the reserved to the exuberant, the soft to the violent, and from rupture to rapture.

Webern is at the very top of the mountain, but set self-contained inside a dimly lit, eerily illustrated cave, which is quite small, as his music — what Stravinsky called 'his dazzling diamonds' — doesn't take up much space. He was freakishly shot at sixty-two by an American soldier during the Allied occupation of Vienna, right at the end of the Second World War, in the last minutes before a curfew would have taken hold. We don't know how far he might have gone with his music, and how much more there would have been and in what styles, and indeed what effect the war years might have had on his sensibility and concerns. Webern became a martyr for the hardcore avant-garde ideologists; the soldier that accidentally killed him was so consumed by guilt he committed suicide.

Two pieces for string quartet that Webern wrote as a twenty-two-year-old in 1905 taking, at the suggestion of Mahler, lessons from Schoenberg — 'a real genius of a composer', Schoenberg said after his pupil's death — seem to present him looking two ways almost simultaneously, producing a cross-section of two musical eras. They represent the moment a musician moves from tentatively embracing the conventional and the traditional to inventing with rigorous intellectual order a brand-new set of conventions and traditions. He writes them the same year as the first group of German expressionists was formed in Dresden, with their own regeneration of romanticism and mysticism.

The exquisite in-love *Langsamer Satz* — Wagner's *Siegfried Idyll* is definitely an ancestor — reflects where musical sound and style has moved from Mozart and Beethoven through Brahms, Wagner and Mahler, the melodrama and full romantic force of the nineteenth century gradually burning out, tonality still lingering, realistic images still being represented as tonal structures, but stretched even further than Debussy took it, while the plainly titled, more directly energetic, exquisitely crafted single-movement 1905 String Quartet drizzles a little with dissonance, setting out from the darkest shadows of Beethoven's darkest moments, tonality now almost completely deteriorated, a ghostly anticipation of how strange, intense, fragmented, unyielding, untethered and controversial music, often seen as an anti-music, would become, and how much attention it required as whole worlds passed by in seconds.

Langsamer Satz is beautiful and elegant and reveals a warm, Mahler-activated Webern who could have quite convincingly continued and developed the music of the past 150 years, and even have become a popular, beloved favourite, a reliable source of enduring, even weeping loveliness. The String Quartet – no need as the freshly christened modernist to use suggestive or surreal titles to presume poetic depth – is an exacting Webern drifting towards the enigmatic, beginning to think about the methods and meaning of music and rework them, as if to deliberately pull it away from what has become the obvious and the standard. Lessons with Schoenberg and his post-tonal organisational techniques had definitely made a difference.

To get to its soul, and his soul, he already begins sacrificing the features that made *Langsamer Satz* so delicate and attractive; he purifies his music, melts down the melody, breaking everything down to its cryptic essence. The beauty remains, if often bitterly so, but it is extremely abstracted, and needs concentration to detect it within the concentrated form it now takes. The music moves from being accessibly lovely but verging on the transiently decorative to becoming a series of massive enigmas folded into small vessels. Other variations of *Langsamer Satz* he might have gone on to compose could only at their best be as lovely, but they would never be as good, so he moves on. Or the source of the love there is at the centre dries up, and the rest of his musical life is spent searching for new love, and a new way of expressing love that acknowledges its true, elemental force by rejecting to the point of mania, if not glacial aggression, any sign of cliché.

His mother dies the year after, which directly or not becomes a catalyst for a more psychologically and technically sophisticated, and ultimately more beautiful music, if we accept that true beauty contains a weirdness beyond compare. The romance doesn't so much disappear as become something else entirely; romance that doesn't so much warm the heart as celebrate the miracle of its beating existence.

At sixteen minutes, the String Quartet is the most 'monumental' of Webern's string quartets, which together easily fit onto one CD but which for me find their best home in the world of streaming, where these examinations of scale and silence, shape and essence have no solid borders and can almost be conjured up by using the mind. Webern's music suits the underestimated, unadorned strangeness of music-streaming sites, and seem to have been composed in readiness for such an abstract and contextless method of transmitting music – the assertive brevity of his early twentieth-century pieces finds weirdo descendants a century later musically using the brevity of TikTok clips to catch feelings, show off themselves and share entertainment with strangers.

By Webern's middle period, between 1909 and 1913, his music now enriched by atonality, he's writing string quartets that were so outside the tradition they needed another name. The *Five Movements* is completed inside eleven minutes – the middle movement saying everything it needs to say about scale and refashioned identity in its forty seconds – and the longest movement of the *Six Bagatelles* is about seventy-five seconds. The shortest was over in a matter of moments, somewhere between unfathomably graceful and non-existent, marking out a slender, entrancing musical space existing in between molecules – small units of mass – and a Mozart masterpiece. Each movement needs just a single page of score; sometimes it can seem as though those scores were printed with invisible ink.

His possibly biased friend and tutor Schoenberg, part of a system of encouragement that had prompted Webern to experiment with new techniques, was given the responsibility of explaining such challenging early twentieth-century concision. He wrote in an introduction to the score, a little inappropriately hyping up the fiercely reticent Webern: 'One has to realise what restraint it requires to express oneself with such brevity. You can stretch every glance into a poem, every sigh into a novel – such concentration can only be presented in proportion to the absence of self-pity. These pieces will only be understood by those who share the faith that music can say things which can only be expressed by music.'

Webern's delicately intricate, pared-down but lush late-period pieces, now centred in the by-the-numbers organisational alchemy of post-twelve-tone serialism, including his last completed chamber work, the 1938 String Quartet, Op. 28, when he was in his mid-fifties, complete the journey from conventionally evocative Brahmsian sweetness to his own remote, sublime modern readjustment of the heavenly Bach balance of poetry and calculus. It's what he himself called 'not epic breadth but lyrical compression' but which, even as the sound circles a multitude of sonic and intellectual twentieth-century future directions, feels connected to the final vibrations of Beethoven and the nebulous reveries of *Langsamer Satz*.

Webern does not make it as easy any more, Stravinsky noting that he doesn't place a lot of premium on the listener's sense of involvement, but the rewards are immense – in a way, more melody, more pleasure, but achieved in an oblique, hermetic way, as though there are multiple, fleeting glimpses of what he achieved so directly with *Langsamer Satz* but which would become bland and everyday if he repeated himself.

Webern arises out of the past with no intention of smashing it apart but also with no sentimentality for its anniversaries, systems and formalities, and his ascetic, detached desire to understand and articulate what the meaning and value of music is produces a new music not for the sake of it but purely to work out why as much as what and how. New music as a way of throwing light into the darkness of the future; new music, new art that makes the future happen, because it will exist there, and it will belong there. It is one of the things that will certainly exist in whatever the future is. New music is a form of confidence that life will go on, whatever strangeness and horrors get in the way, and this will be a part of its reality. There will be people around to listen to this, to think about it, work it out, enjoy it, dismiss it, analyse it. Eventually, they will 'get' it. It will sound part of the everyday, music to enjoy, not analyse, or simply ignore. If you don't have this kind of confidence in the future, in progress, in fundamental survival, in carrying forward the kind of contemplation and beauty held inside the music, then what else is there?

It is through Webern – as much as Debussy, Strauss, Satie or Ravel – that you can find the missing link between Mozart, what he and his Viennese peers inspired and imposed throughout the nineteenth century, and the more modern post-war, post-electricity, post-atonal, post-jazz, post-minimalist, post-laptop music of the late twentieth century and early twenty-first century.

Webern was in many ways more a minimalist than the so-called minimalists in terms of exploiting minimal means, his use of silence and space and short duration. The central 1960s 'minimalists' were veering away from the astringent, possibly tuneless post-war consequences of

Webern's experiments with the audacious, dissonant and deliberately distorting twelve notes of Schoenberg – feeling that by finding a radical method of restoring classical music's structural discipline he had assured the next hundred years of German musical supremacy – and its next step the even more unhinged serialism hatched in post-war laboratories. At the same time, the minimalists, and their neo-romantic progeny, were picking up where Webern left off in terms of what you could do with tension and release by using the repetition of the same note in the same octave register; time seems to stand still or lose track of itself.

Debussy, Strauss and Ravel pulled away from where Beethoven and Wagner, needing to outdo the originators, Bach, Haydn, Mozart, set course for the heavens; to escape the gravitational pull of those that invented and refined formats, rules, systems and standards, they needed to become gods. Their way of becoming gods was as artists, as heroic as possible, as though that was the only way humans could attain superpowers and become myths, almost beyond belief, and outside of time. After such efforts, such achievements, those that came after them with their own intentions to keep progressing withdrew or mutated into subtlety, organised a different set of codes of conduct, broke free of the genius of the originators and the volume and vanity of the artist gods.

There is an invention of tradition where the past is transformed, not merely imitated. Those that authentically inherit any style do not simply repeat the rules and regulations as they begin to rearrange and then completely destroy the musical language they initially seemed faithful to.

Debussy, Satie and Ravel established enigmatic new territory, music as a less grandiose, less over-styled series of regions, bringing sound down to earth while still aiming for the exquisite and uncanny. By the time Webern was composing, following the eighteenth-century beginnings, the nineteenth-century transcendences and then the late nineteenth-century retreat, the one way he could keep going, a form of progress, was by imagining a new process of originating; along with Schoenberg and Berg, without losing memory of what had come before – and what had come before the originators, from darkness, mysteries and worship – he found the nerve and vision, and the scientific system, to begin again.

With Webern especially, this involved whispering more than shouting, and intense, self-scrutinising, almost encrypted condensation rather than epic, demonstrative longevity. However jagged, angular and apparently deviant, some say ugly his music – even the short length of some of the movements and overall structures was a jolt to the system – he still retained the lyricism and sensuality of Schubert and Debussy.

His avant-garde post-Second World War disciples and idolisers – the needling, cocksure administrator Boulez and the deceptively mild-mannered mad scientist Babbitt especially – concentrated on more explicit Webern breakthroughs, his presentation of new dimensions in sound, as though it was all detached calculation, detailed theory and no sensation. Serialism suggested a fresh start after the war, its auditing, analytic processes and procedures unattached to any ruinous nationalist ideas. Serialism championed the mind, not a particular country or tradition.

Eventually the raid on the oppression of tonality, the rejection of the spectacle, led to its own obstructive and over-academic restrictions. It hardened into music, some of it apparently made of concrete and engine sounds, that for some broke away from music to listen to, becoming instead music to think about, and therefore mostly ignore, almost a strand of philosophy where thoughts were expressed in sound, but this was long after Webern's astringent but still profoundly spiritual realignment of classical basics.

This was where the minimalists came to life, inspired by the soul of Webern rather than the later data processing, although there was a little of that as well. Minimalism – still very much a process music – was an emotional, intuitive and open-minded form of serialism after the unforgiving, intellectually exact style of Boulez and Babbitt had crashed on a particularly difficult corner, leaving Stockhausen with the wreckage, the cosmic debris. (Serialism was killed as much by those who invented it as the next generation; it had its uses, and then it had none at all.) It needed a new name, though, because the 'serial' label had run into formulaic trouble; and then, indeed, a similar thing happened to the 'minimal' term.

Webern's radically economic but still emotive reaction to the bulging grandeur and late-romantic excess of Wagner anticipates Buzzcocks' mid-1970s punk-rock backlash against the torturous, ostentatious meanderings and overripeness of Emerson, Lake & Palmer, bringing music out of the backward-looking, future-fearing, pre-industrial woods and forward into the urgent realities, and unprecedented hallucinations, of the modern world. Some musicians adore the grandiose, as if they fancy living in castles and dallying with mythical creatures, and some, in appalled, ideological opposition, rip away the excess.

The music didn't start from absolutely nowhere: influences, the correct influences, were carefully selected and reprogrammed for the needs of different times. With Buzzcocks, rock-guitar solos that had gone 'Freebird' hysterical — the overexcited, nationalistically confident solos of Lynyrd Skynyrd — are distilled down to the incandescent repetition of a single, resolute note, much better suited to austere, chaotic mid-1970s social and cultural conditions; with Webern adventures in sound seem more thrilling when they last for seconds, not hours, the sort of seconds that contain so much intensity and insight.

It's the familiar history: the spring of spring replacing the organic decay of autumn with a confusing, bracing chill in between. One thing leads to another, the new, the modernist and the punk cannot exist without their severely articulate rejection of the old, the vainglorious and the undesirable. Thank you, Wagner, and thank you, Emerson, Lake & Palmer.

Who says thank you to devout serialist and very early electronic pioneer Milton Babbitt, whose music became so demanding it eluded human application and needed to be reproduced by computer? Here was a mathematician, teacher and writer who was acquainted with Albert Einstein while teaching at Princeton and who carefully studied the original Twelve-Tone Three, Berg, Webern and Schoenberg — and taught Stephen Sondheim, who was a little better at channelling intellect into more accessible feeling. Babbitt considered Schoenberg's compositions to be one of the most profound intellectual achievements of the time, and the influence was significant in turning him towards music, where he could still consider mathematics but with a wider remit.

During and after the Second World War he developed his own advanced system for creating music, devising rules for melodic, rhythmic and textural methods of organising musical material. It was on paper, on the blackboard, in theory, a logical progression from the twelve-note achievements and dead ends of Schoenberg, but produced difficult, dense music that seemed entirely illogical — to non-believers in this world, probably outnumbering the believers by a million to one, it sounded completely random and absurdly, infuriatingly jumpy. It can make the most extreme experiments of Webern seem very nineteenth century, although none of it would have happened without the precedents of the Second Viennese School.

The idea of avant-garde turned into the joke 'haven't garde a clue', but the problem, or the genius, as with avant-garde jazz guru Ornette Coleman, was that Babbitt was in possession of far too many clues. There is perhaps too much care for music, too much desire to protect its force and beauty, which sometimes requires a kind of conceptual and theoretical armour, to keep music from being totally worn down to the ordinary and easily taken for granted. Babbitt the mathematician is looking for hard musical facts and seeking certain truths, which seems to get in the way of actually just pleasing and moving people.

Babbitt could see that the twelve notes weren't simply something to be generated using mathematical permutations that would result in a sort of instant music; you still required taste, style, imagination, personality, experience and an awareness of tradition in order to shape and structure your material. And within the history of serial music there are as many extremes as there are in tonal music; you can go from a stimulating intellectual beauty to a form of serial easy listening where there are flashing moments of the weirdly familiar and oddly bland. Cage would consider Babbitt too much a 'musicologist' to be totally freed from the past, even if for most people there seemed more relentless equations than musical emotions.

Like Cage, who was otherwise engaged at the time, making his less sceptical, less organised and ultimately more charming mind up in a more metaphysical way, Babbitt's music was as much inside his thinking and writing, and his undermining of ordinary aesthetic judgements, as inside his actual musical pieces. His philosophy wasn't an extension or demonstration of his music, it was his music, or at least completed it, helped give it the context it otherwise lacked so that it was often just treated as cold, calculating and possibly irredeemably crazy.

He wasn't particularly concerned about giving audiences their usual diet; he wanted to see what the effect would be on listeners, and music itself, if he invented a completely new diet. This diet might not make nutritional sense, or necessarily taste good, but that wasn't the point. The point was to go to extremes to work out what happens next, in music, in a musical piece, and what effect does that have on listeners, and what does that actually mean? Cage and Babbitt were both, from their own locations, examining what it means to say: this is a good piece of music, and this is a bad piece, and what is the actual effect of either? To do that often meant making music that at the same time could be 'good' and 'bad' – music that simultaneously sounded like music and sounded like no music at all. Like Satie before them, they were uncertainly groping their lonely way amid conflicting ideals – deeply committed to a fantastic idea, joking in a ponderous way, pursuing a fragile, subtle idea that needed protecting with layers of irony. Consequently much of the music is not easy to take seriously.

The point – one of a multitude all happening at the same time – is to take an extreme single-minded position, and then stubbornly, slyly defend it, as though music itself is ultimately a matter of composers being single-minded and possessing complete conviction that what they are doing in the time they are doing it is absolutely what is necessary. For the hyper-cerebral, oddly genial Babbitt, music in that pressurised, ruined post-war period needed a passionate form of defence to maintain its importance and place in the modern world, which had other things on its mind. At the time, when everything was in flux, that didn't necessarily mean writing lovely show tunes or singing the rocked-up blues. Exciting, outlaw, even apparently irrational thinking about music and its purpose was just as important, at a time when everything was changing because of war, politics, technology and media.

Babbitt wrote brilliantly and sensitively about music and, most controversially, he wrote an essay about the demanding but conceptual necessity of avant-garde music and the idea of the contemporary composer as a specialist comfortable with their obscurity that was given the aggressive, scandal-grabbing title 'Who Cares if You Listen?'. There was never a problem, as far as he was concerned, that he was more interested in his music than an audience. He thought it ridiculous that the layperson would be anything other than bored and puzzled by what they couldn't understand. They couldn't understand advanced work in mathematics, physics and philosophy, so why the latest advances in music, which, in his eyes, should be as advanced as the most radical scientific research? By its very nature, in the modern world, musical research and development should take place in private, educational establishments providing a home for the complex, difficult and problematical in music.

This music was not initially for sale, or for purposes of show – it was for testing the far limits of what music could become, which in turn fed into music that was for sale and show – and in terms of his experiments with electronics on the RCA Mark II Sound Synthesiser, particularly in new rhythmical potential, this came true.

The Mark II, installed at Columbia University in 1957, was the first programmable electronic synthesiser combining sound generation with a music sequencer. Babbitt said that it could take six or seven hours of work to create one minute's worth of something that sounded like music, but it enabled him to produce sounds and structures that were impossible to play. He issued an early defence of the idea that machine-made music was soulless and inhuman by countering that it was in fact more human, as the composer was now in control of every detail of the music. And not all mistakes and randomness would be corrected, in terms of the actual idea and intention.

It was how serialism as a virtual machine, conceived mechanically to produce music with various degrees of human input, turned into technological reality, all of which confirms a personal theory that pop music is a branch of minimalism, which itself is a branch of serialism. Music produced on machines is a technical manifestation of the ideas and calculations of serialism, which was a way of programming music, or arranging novel, near-impossible-seeming structures before computers. Therefore serialism, the most unlistenable and least listened-to music of the twentieth century, was closely related to the most listenable and listened-to music of the era, pop music.

QED.

Babbitt's work with primitive music technology meant that even as he was at the leading edge of where electronics then was, in terms of turning computer-generated sound into music, he was essentially at the stage of a computer equivalent of early music. The capability of computers at the time compared to now was, relatively speaking, medieval.

Time moves quicker, not least because of technology, so sixty years later, as we reach the overthrow – or completion – of reality by computers, Babbitt can seem as far removed from where electronics is now as Bach was from Webern; that early work, though, exists as a kind of sacred text, part of the DNA of where all electronic music, therefore all pop, now is. The year 1957 is Elvis, and it is also the RCA Mark II, and Spotify, that damned abundant pleasure machine, is their love child.

QED.

Even as Babbitt explored the abstractions of sound in the far, far margins of any sort of music industry or conventional music history, he still composed, and his music occasionally came in from the cold, including the superficially conventional production of string quartets.

He didn't quite match Bartók's six quartets — there were six in total, but the first failed, never quite coalescing into a finished piece. As a series, they explain Babbitt as much as the Bartók six explained Bartók. You don't, after all that, necessarily need to know the procedures, philosophies and processes, the compelling speculations, the monstrous intricacies and equations that led to their composition. You don't need to appreciate the complexity of the non-repetitive arrangement of the key twelve notes and how as well as aggregating the notes he was also aggregating, according to fixed predetermined sequences, rhythm, dynamics, range, volume and pitch, which became known as 'total serialism'.

It remains difficult for the imagination to grip onto his ideas of a multidimensional musical matrix, but the musical residue contained in his scores has intrinsic power even if you have no idea what he was talking about. Babbitt once said, as if he had anticipated the 1980s drum sound of Phil Collins, that 'nothing gets old faster than a new sound', and he proves in his music how much it is ideas that matter, the strength of the world that is created, not the actual sound. But in his world, contemporary composition, new technique was necessary to get to the ideas.

The music can be listened to as music, especially if you think of it as being what happened to jazz music made by someone who as a young boy in the late twenties was listening to Webern as well as Louis Armstrong, Bartók and also King Oliver. Around 1927, what Armstrong and Webern were packing into potential musical form was so far apart, and yet in the neighbourhood of the same neighbourhood, coinciding with a general reappraisal of social, moral and aesthetic values developing after the end of the First World War — in many ways, both were pushing thinking to the musical foreground as much as James Joyce had with language in the novel throughout *Ulysses*.

Babbitt's string quartets are, as they should be, all things considered, closer to Ornette Coleman and the Art Ensemble of Chicago — where musical movement and transformation happens sometimes faster than the ear can tell, there are astonishing dances of similarity, a perfect storm of data, and random-seeming patterns are completely intended – than they are to Haydn and Schubert.

There is always Ornette Coleman in the air whenever a shocking, unconventional and investigative new music comes along that breaks with the past and proposes a whole new way of thinking about, and playing, and making sound. This new sound arrives, apparently out of nowhere, and the response is often panic, or derision, or actually just depthless indifference and ignorant insults, because the sound seems wrong, off, primitive, strange, alien, annoying, aggressively formless, wilfully anti-commercial, frighteningly cerebral, just plain peculiar. It offers no obvious consolations, it doesn't sound like anything that's come before, except in ways that seem to mock precedent and tradition. A music that has so much going on in any given moment doesn't need to actually get anywhere, which confuses those expecting music to tell some kind of linear story.

In the end, this new sound, always a sound influenced by the way Coleman twisted his own particular youthful influences – big band, swing, blues, bebop, church – into truly something else, is the sound that changes music, and musicians, and confirms that great, exciting new music, from Beefheart to the Necks, is always about the unknown, the unexplored, the unexplained.

Coleman's story is to some extent simply a jazz story, the enigmatic, provocative and stubborn outsider who followed the pre-war rules of Louis Armstrong and the new post-war rules of Charlie Parker with the daring, scary idea of no rules at all. Or 'there is a law in what I'm playing, but the law is a law that when you get tired of it, you can change it'. He responds to the freedom he hears in Parker, who inspires him to play the alto sax, and he resolves to take it further. (In his novel *V*, Thomas Pynchon refers to a character based on Coleman – and Charlie Mingus – and the way 'he played all the notes Bird missed'.)

The moment you fall in love with the actual music of Milton Babbitt rather than merely investigate his ideas about music, which I did while listening to his thirteen-minute Second String Quartet, is one of the great musical experiences, very like the moment that free jazz leaps in your mind from total chaos to delicious, delirious and completely logical precision. One can become the key to understanding the other. Babbitt might be pseudo-jazz and Ornette might be pseudo-classical, but ultimately the energy, splintering from a kind of Creole serialism, relates one to the other.

It's as though a foreign language suddenly makes sense — Babbitt did once say, 'Don't worry about whether or not the music sounds coherent to you the first time you hear it. What about the first time you hear a sentence in Hungarian? — Assuming you're interested in listening to and learning Hungarian' — and you appreciate what you are hearing is the equivalent of circling an object and continually seeing it from many different directions all at the same time. It's not all changing, zigzagging, and moving here there and everywhere for the damned wind-up sake of it, a moving wall of random tones; once you stop being sent dizzy by it all, the piece stops spinning around, and settles into shapes and moments and textures that are most definitely musical, and mostly definitely dramatic and captivating in a way that can be described as entertaining, which many would consider a bizarre thought.

In an ideal world you would want to hear it produced and mixed by a studio master, in the way that Jimi Hendrix or Kanye West are produced. Increasingly, as a way of mapping and diagnosing the amount of information everyone attached to a computer or smartphone now experiences every day, the music of Babbitt makes more sense — this is what that swapping, sharing, circulating, cross-referencing, searching, Instagramming, Snapchatting, Zooming, playlisting, buying, selling, booking, TikTok-ing world actually sounds like.

That Babbitt is achieving this dazzling interaction between uncertainty and certainty, noise and meaning through a string quartet, the truest projection of the maths and magic in music, is yet more proof of what you can do and how far you can go inside an eighteenth-century model. After all, Rembrandt used a canvas and so did Pollock. In between the two — centuries of sensation, invention and speculation, of certain alterations in the nature of life itself.

This isn't necessarily a recommendation of where to begin listening to string quartets, or indeed to hear the piece for pure, instant pleasure, because you might listen to it and decide to seek me out and firmly question my sanity, or worse. But it is a recommendation to delight in a world where someone can be so individual and so committed to their own ideas that such a thing with such a heightened and unique sense of gorgeous form exists.

Before you make it to Babbitt, one way to get to know the string quartet is to make your way to the acknowledged mountaintop greats and official treats from other centres and examples, one where the less obvious, less prolific chamber-music writers felt the need to write a quartet, like William Walton's highly traditional but deeply felt and elegantly formed post-war No. 2 in A minor. Following the disastrous debut of his first self-described 'immature', atonal, Schoenberg-lite quartet, written as a twenty-one-year-old in 1923, he withdrew it from public performance. He tried a second quartet twenty-two years later, after a time writing mainstream film scores, which he was worried had erased some of the skills and instincts required to express something serious and personal. A certain fastidious civility, even fussy anti-atonal conservatism, had eased out much of the youthful fascination with the contemporary modernity being hatched in Vienna, an ageing reserve that contributed to his unfashionable post-war reputation, but tantalising traces remain as the younger man battles with his older, more settled version.

Walton described the quartet, during its two-year composition, as a 'suicidal struggle' and on completion, for all its lyrical grace, romantic devotion and mature playfulness, he felt that he had overcome some barbed-wire entanglements. This elevating fight for territory, for completion, can be heard in the nervous energy and occasional sense that he needs to run for the hills, as though away from himself and the bloody idea of a string quartet. He could leave the form behind because to some extent he had won his fight and created a realistic version of a perfect quartet, as much a companion piece to the intoxicating, enchanting loveliness of Debussy's own sole effort as the Ravel it's usually coupled with.

Stravinsky only wrote three quartets, also often logically programmed with the Ravel and the Debussy, each one a shadowy but key component in his overall canon. These near anti-quartets included the vividly speculative and discreetly libertine *Concertino* written in 1920 and orchestrated for twelve instruments over thirty years later, and *Double Canon* from 1959, a sonorous seventy-five second snapshot of infinity. The most specific of this cryptic trio was the miniature abstract *Three Pieces* – his very first chamber piece, a Webern-brief seven minute encore, retreat or tentative step forwards written in the months following the riotous, jarring *Rite of Spring*, a hinge between his idiosyncratic extension of late-nineteenth-century romanticism climaxing with the controversial ballet and his post-war, post-revolution neoclassical middle period.

There's a lot of imaginative information and provisional thinking — foreshadowing ideas about repetition and continuity, stasis and movement materialising half a century later in minimalism — condensed into short, almost incidental seeming episodes. He didn't consider that he was writing within the quartet genre and its traditional singing voices, simply that on this occasion he had decided to write almost by the way for these particular stringed instruments, with a fairly casual attitude to what the instruments were and their usual blended relationship to each other. They really are three separate pieces, not movements, from very different dreams, with their own subject matter — dancing, clowning, contemplation — that fall somewhere between exercises and exquisite. At first they didn't even have titles, as though they were merely nebulous think-pieces. Stravinsky gave them titles fourteen years later — *Danse, Eccentrique, Cantique* — when he adapted them as part of his Four Etudes for Orchestra. Three Pieces becomes a kind of spectacular x-ray of his protean compositional thinking at the time.

From the lesser-known parts of a composer's repertoire there are two Vaughan Williams quartets, the first from 1908 and revised thirteen years later, deftly materialising out of his liberating studies with Ravel and his feelings for Debussy, with Dvořák hovering at the edge of vision; the more adventurous, riveting second over thirty-five years later, appearing during the Second World War, coming out of the dark of Bartók and the tension of Shostakovich but also the viols of Purcell, with, of course, a very English accent.

I sometimes use Benjamin Britten's First, Second and Third, some mildly alternative musical history, to see off Beethoven after too much of all that, some of Britten's most personal and allusive music naturally appearing through his quartets. Britten remained loyal to the traditional tonal system at a time it was being dismissed by the new Webern-infatuated radicals and aesthetic autocrats. He was convinced that originality emerged from the imagination rather than systems or techniques.

The Second String Quartet is firmly conventional, which turns out to be a brave act considering the apparently conservative nature of such an approach, but its traces of Purcell and its uncompromising faith in tonality actually gives it strange, immutable power certain serialists would secretly swoon over.

It was the English modernism of Frank Bridge that was of more interest to Britten — his pupil — than the regenerative, transnational modernism of Webern. Bridge's level-headed modernism was still rooted in the rivers, bridges, hills, skies, villages, steam trains, hedgerows and meadows of home even as the First World War, pushing things to the dark side, turned his early, polished post-romanticism into something sharper, edgier and more speculative. His changes are more reserved than the changes of Webern during a similar time, but it does mean he leaves behind, if not as exceptionally as Webern, an earlier pastoral friendliness.

Two of Bridge's four gorgeous, gripping quartets come before this world war chasm and two after, all four of much appeal if you happen to like both the early idiosyncratic Viennese style of Schoenberg and the uplifting Edwardian nostalgia of Elgar and can imagine one becoming the other. At a nexus where Vaughan Williams becomes Messiaen, Michael Tippett's anxious, transcendent Second – one of three he wrote in the 1940s before a thirty-year gap and then two more – becomes another way of knowing, and going beyond knowing, the timeless Bartók and the late Beethoven, still connected to the nineteenth century but aware of the twenty-first coming soon.

After studying with Vaughan Williams for a year in her teens in the early 1920s – he remained a lifelong friend – Irish-born Elizabeth Maconchy came across the Central European modernism of Janáček, Berg and Bartók, a terrific revelation after the polite, rigid Edwardian music it was assumed she would be inspired by, leading to the simple, plain little pastoral piano pieces she'd surely be writing – until, in the eyes of the music establishment, she would presumably get married and stop composing. Confounding expectations, she fell in love with the torrid psychological energy of the string quartet, what she called an intellectual art, 'an intense but disciplined expression of emotion', for her 'perhaps the most satisfying medium of them all'.

She wrote her first quartet in 1931 – the beginning of a cycle of thirteen, almost Shostakovich-sized, completed in 1984, coursing through the rest of her orchestral and ensemble work and her three operas, the one thing she would keep returning to. They were never particularly celebrated, never allowed into the English company of Britten, Frank Bridge and Vaughan Williams, and as a composer she was never fashionable or part of any movement, but it never stopped her working out again and again what could be done technically, emotionally, viscerally, with a quartet.

It was the one musical place she felt she belonged, even if few outside a small circle ever noticed.

Her first youthful quartet exists as a concentrated blast of almost forbidden self-confidence, powerfully resisting the idea that she is somehow not allowed to enter the quartet club, edgy, liberated modernist toughness cracking open the Little England conservatism that had been instilled in her; the final one, in her late seventies, just eight minutes long but containing echoes of all her rigorous, independent quartet thinking, her strength and delicacy, an emphatic conclusion to her lifelong commitment to the form.

Her contemporary, the more radical, provocative, contrary Elisabeth Lutyens was a pioneering English neo-serialist — sometimes judged Britain's 'first serialist', she was nicknamed Twelve-Note Lizzie — inspired by the miniaturism of Webern, also accused at an early age of liking Debussy, which was viewed as 'not quite nice'. She wasn't a particularly devout serialist, but adapted some of the strategies so that she could write fast and avoid clichéd harmonies, and her music was bravely sparse, exotic and odd-seeming, especially in the 1930s and 1940s, when most British music around her was more richly coloured and obviously romantic. She was always out on her own, too far out in the thirties and forties, and then apparently outflanked as a enquiring modernist in the fifties and sixties even as she never relented from experimenting with form, and orchestral and instrumental force.

Like Maconchy, also inspired by Bartók's striking quartets of the late twenties, Lutyens wrote thirteen quartets between 1937 and 1982 — from their point of view, the string quartet was a new idea, a new ideal, something they could use to get their bearings. Lutyens' quartets were separate journeys that were part of an overall adventure, and also a struggle for rights, an insight into how making music her own way helped her develop an uncompromising imagination, open to surrealism as much as serialism, with an unflinching attraction to the unconventional. Through music, with the volatility of the string quartet at its centre, she finds out for herself what matters to her. The thirteen quartets, an achievement in themselves, were a core part of her continuous investigation into dramatic structure and organisational rigour, essentially a summary of her esoteric musical philosophy, a constant, evolving framing of questions rather than an attempt to find answers.

Some composers felt, like Debussy and Ravel – and Strauss, Verdi and Puccini – that writing more or less just the one quartet was enough; everything could be said in one solitary creation. Sole quartets to relish include Delius's poignant single quartet written in the middle of the First World War, often paired with Elgar's luminously post-romantic quartet written at the end of the war.

Ruth Crawford Seeger's single, heady, prophetic, structurally audacious twelve-minute quartet from 1931 – when she was just Crawford, before her reinvention as folk-song collector and transcriber – is one of the great works of post-twelve-tone American modernism, and one of the great quartets. An infectious, enigmatic marvel of complexity, of loud and quiet, ebb and flow, smooth and agitated, tension and resolution, it beat Babbitt and company to the very first total serial punch.

She had travelled to Europe in 1930 on a Guggenheim grant, intending to write a symphony. In the end it was a radiant string quartet that irresistibly asserted itself in her imagination, allowing her to actually be more sonically and structurally ambitious than a larger work, but despite a torrent of ideas and theories, and the new, simpler influence of her folk transcriptions, a second never appeared.

Seeger was a contemporary of Cowell, Copland and Varèse, influencing Carter, anticipating Xenakis, Lutosławski, Penderecki, Ligeti, Henri Dutilleux and Braxton, and arranged the quartet's ingeniously assembled third movement for string orchestra as Andante, a discordant relative of Samuel Barber's 1938 Adagio for Strings. This itself emerged from his one string quartet, an irresistible response to Beethoven, which featured a sombre melody from the slow, sad second movement that was transformed via the recommendation of conductor Arturo Toscanini into the processional, instantly recognisable Adagio. Appearing while America was still reeling from the Great Depression, just before the beginning of the Second World War, it became a regularly used symbol of American sorrow and public mourning. Decades later, as a manipulated ingredient in a series of mood-shifting trance anthems, the amorphous sadness would be flipped and sped up into joy, listeners swept up in a completely different way by its stately simplicity, mourning bursting into spirit-raising ecstasy.

There was an intriguing thirty-minute one-movement one-off quartet from piano performer immortal Glenn Gould in 1955, a few months before the twenty-two-year-old recorded a mercurial set of Bach's

Goldberg Variations that caused almost a rock 'n' roll sensation. His quartet was one of the last signs of his unexceptional, early ambitions to be a composer, his incandescent *Variations* establishing him as stormy, genius interpreter with little time left for straightforward personal expression, unless you count his 'contrapuntal' radio documentaries – and also his playing of Bach, Beethoven and Schoenberg, which contained compositional intelligence, individuality and insight that the quartet keenly hints at, mostly when it in fact intellectually quotes Beethoven, toys with Schoenberg and romantically celebrates Strauss.

Witold Lutosławski's only quartet, in two movements, from 1964, is a great example of his intellectual emotionalism, dramatic intensity and controlled aleatorism, one that plays with chance by not fixing the tempo of each individual part, even as pitch and harmony are specified. Each musician is in their own world, playing with relative freedom, close but apart, and the classic string quartet 'conversation' is an interrogation coming from different time zones, no two performances ever the same, sometimes lush, sometimes sinister, a way of claiming John Cage as an unlikely ally of his enemy, the ever-present Beethoven. The musicians take their chances with the score, but they eventually end up back together, a collective after all, one that has just had a weirdly shared experience in isolation from each other.

Henri Dutilleux's lone quartet is a cosmic compression of his subtle orchestral clarity, written between 1973 and 1976 after close study of Beethoven, Webern's *Six Bagatelles*, Berg and Bartók, a twentieth-century masterpiece often programmed as a rare post-war part of the Ravel and Debussy French family, connected to the same textural, temporal flow but with a more labyrinthine psychedelic complexion. An ode to the back and forth of memory, or, more accurately perhaps, déjà vu, the seventeen-minute, seven-movement *Ainsi la nuit* slices up time, predicting what is about to happen and checking back on its own progress, in seven short, connected movements and eleven sections. Boulez initially disapproved of his more conservative, certainly kinder French contemporary – whose atonality was more accessible, his serialism more gentle, his love of Brahms less censored – possibly because Dutilleux objected to his post-war 'authoritarianism' concerning what Boulez saw as the frivolity of Satie and Poulenc.

Pierre Boulez's own isolated quartet was the truly thwarted *Livre pour quatuor*, written in the late 1940s as the twenty-three-year-old was embarking on a nervously intense and ideological policy-forming period of compositional research and development, enthusiastically fusing the rhythms of Stravinsky with the harmonies of Schoenberg – because who else was going to? – even as he was sarcastically booing Stravinsky's music and spitting fire at twelve-tone cliché in a 1952 obituary of Schoenberg.

He had been introduced to serialism at the Paris Conservatoire by Olivier Messiaen, just before an intellectual relationship with John Cage began, starting while Cage was in Paris to study Erik Satie, for Cage the start of the twentieth century, if only for the way he avoided sonatas, études, impromptus and any other conservatively settled piano forms, but who Boulez hated. Despite various disagreements like this they became pen pals until 1954, keeping each other informed about developments in avant-garde music either side of the Atlantic.

A couple of years after his friendship with Cage began, Boulez met Stockhausen, three years younger and with a perfectionist determination to make everything new. Boulez is angry with music of the past, Stockhausen not at all bothered, and cannot muster up any feelings at all – it is dead, of no use or concern to what he is doing or the future space he is imagining, and he listens to what his teacher Messiaen plays him to know what had already happened and what he doesn't need to repeat or revive.

Cage and Stockhausen as sacrilegious pre-hippy free thinkers, inventing themselves as artists and even myths, made Boulez feel a little conventional and buttoned up, despite the furious way he redirected tradition into something he felt was totally new. On the night at the Maverick Concert Hall in Woodstock, New York in 1952, when David Tudor legendarily premiered John Cage's *4' 33''* of silence, provoking much analytical, emotional and historical noise, part of the night's programme included the First Piano Sonata by twenty-seven-year-old Boulez, an intense, zesty work by someone convinced a recalculation of the twelve-tone procedure was the most modern, and actually most flexible, way of making music.

The piece sounded oddly archaic in its unabashed, if bashed-in musicality next to Cage's immortal gesture, where he decided that whatever noise you make, however modern, angry, smashed, rigorous or unpretty, will still effectively be music and connected to the traditions you are rejecting. The Boulez form of verve and virtuosity, the risk and effort involved, what he called 'the danger', seemed ordinary, even stuffy – and certainly stuffed with music – next to the meditative philosophical methods of Cage, which drew a serene blank, a true zero, a beautiful secret, Godless and gorgeous. Boulez merely organised his frustrations and furies into a piece of music full of numbers, still using sound; Cage went back to a beginning, to an absence, in order for everything to begin again.

Cage and Stockhausen proposed a complete and necessary break with the past, musically and artistically, Stockhausen dealing in information, calculation and signals, Cage suggesting music was merely where noise communed with silence. The serialists were not so much breaking with history as organising an idiosyncratic, if argumentative refinement of it. Both embraced Dada-inspired chance and randomness as part of the musical process, motivating an impressionable, keen Boulez to try and match his undeniable connection and identification with musical tradition with the hermeneutical, begin-again philosophies of his two new mentors.

This was when classical music's response to the catastrophe, destruction and emotional and intellectual challenge of two world wars was to become bad-tempered, even vicious with the idea of music, because it was useless at saving the world; you wouldn't say it was pessimistic music, but when other responses to the devastation of the wars materialised in the 1950s as either Little Richard and Elvis Presley or Miles Davis and John Coltrane, that did seem a little more positive, probably because they weren't weighed down by centuries of precedents, strictures, breakthroughs and breakdowns.

Feeling the weight, the challenge, or perhaps just seeing the light too many times a day, Boulez's quartet was abandoned after some revision in 1959, then typically revised later, for a larger orchestra in 1968, and once more in 1989, before a final edit nearly sixty years after its composition. 'The string quartet remains an ordeal in the initiatory sense of the term,' he once said, as though it was that sentiment he was putting to music, and in honour of this he had worked hard on this one quartet, at the time and over time.

It is Boulez-appropriate that it was never definitively completed and remained in flux, and that he never returned to the quartet challenge, confidently declaring them dead – naturally imagining that because they were to him, they were for everyone. To process more comfortably a very personal, almost possessive selection of the modernist music that had an impact on him as a precocious teenager – Debussy, Ravel, Bartók, Messiaen, Berg, Webern – distracted and out-conceptualised by the philosophical, amusical music of Cage and Stockhausen, he became a creative conductor, fluid collaborator and aesthetic mogul, an all-round avant-garde mover and shaker, the modernist showman par excellence.

The change he had demanded since the Second World War led to plenty of change for him, and to some extent, as much as he raged, and then middle-raged, and old-raged, for progress and the new, he more or less stayed as he was, a kind of stationary contrarian, as others caught up and the world around him took on its own unexpected, endlessly transmitted postmodern shape. The full-time composer, angry young man and zealous missionary turned into a more formal, if still intimidating ambassador and part-time celebrity composer, eventually adding to his judiciously chosen core repertoire intrepid contemporaries such as Ligeti, Birtwistle, Berio, Carter and Zappa, continuing to point out how all this pre-war and post-war modernism naturally connected to him. He made himself the common link; he died on 5 January 2016, five days before the death of David Bowie. The twentieth century had then well and truly ended; the twenty-first century would quickly make itself felt with a whole different series of alarms, assaults and infections that made the twentieth century seem very distant. (In many ways the twentieth century only really got going by the time of *The Rite of Spring*.)

With all its combative musical changes, the array of movements and post-movements, the twentieth century becomes the most varied century for the string quartet – even the century of the string quartet. Through the quartet you can follow in detail where classical music began and ended from early modernist experimenting to the postmodernists and hear significant samples of composers thinking as they negotiated their way through genres, dogmas, trends and various rejections of trends, exile and a rapid increase in stylistic and environmental influences. Even if you only listen to twentieth-century string quartets you can learn a considerable amount about the evolution and condition of twentieth-century classical music, from the explicitly, unashamedly pleasurable and consoling to the awkward, puzzling sounds emerging from conceptual art and revolutionary zeal and purpose.

Even in the last few decades of the twentieth century, when general musical attention is largely directed away from the progress of classical music, the string quartet is still being moved forward, somewhere else, by undaunted philosophical loners with their own problems to contend with, and their own desires to satisfy. Rock 'n' roll begins, and makes irresistible noise, but elsewhere, even after Carter's transcendence seems to bring Haydn's time to an end, and Cage's ultimate minimalist silence seems to erase history, the string quartet, sometimes noisier than rock, sometimes holding its breath, carries on as usual, even if in the hands of the unusual, guarding new marginal outposts.

La Monte Young's first twelve-tone composition, his five sparse, angular post-Webern miniatures for string quartet from 1956, *On Remembering A Naiad*, also branch out from the brainwork of Cage, the laconic, muted trumpets of Miles Davis, and a general sense of altered consciousness. Each section about a minute long, it was written a year before his Trio for Strings, where minimalism is often said to begin, the long goodbye to serialism, a few notes held for a very long time, because Young knew more than most how a single note — and the silence before and after — is (the beginning and end of) music. The movement that music represents through life from birth to death is replaced by an explicit stasis.

Rigorous romantic, scientific mystic, provocative modernist, deviant analyst Iannis Xenakis, with his background in engineering and architecture, his working relationship with le Corbusier and the influence of Bach, Debussy and Bartók, summarised the immense, involved mathematical dazzle of his often massive, cosmically pulsing music with his four quartets. The first was the inevitably visceral and spatial *ST/4-1,080262* from 1962, lifted directly from a spectacularly convoluted piece for a larger, ten-piece ensemble, 1956's *ST/10-1,080262* — his ST (stochastic) computer algorithm being his form of the fugue, where a set of rules, in his case a randomly determined process, could lead to any number of compositions. His music was all part of an investigation into the potential ways music corresponded to the basic laws of the measurable universe.

ST/4 derived from the same set of data as *ST/10*. This drew a fantastic link between the eighteenth-century salon of Haydn and the kaleidoscopic future of electronic music — Xenakis beat Boulez to the punch by being the first composer in France to use a computer to make music, to work out his visions.

Xenakis hadn't intended to enter what was by then the considerably populated quartet genre. The appearance of *ST/4* from *ST/10* was the result of experimenting with his algorithms, having gained access to the computer facilities at IBM France. His Second, twenty-one years later, the exhilarating, virtuosic, constantly evolving *Tetras* – Greek for four – was more deliberate, and his quartet masterpiece, which illustrates both the incandescent extent of his ciphered ideas and theories and also what can be achieved, inside and outside of time, within the formalities of the quartet form. It's the perfect entry into the unrelenting, ever-expanding space of his music. The slower, fluidly abstracted and more austere *Tetora* – another word for four – from 1990, narrowed his focus, and the even more distilled, even emaciated *Ergma* from 1994 completes the cycle, which moved from explosive to frail, from a cosmos forming to it falling apart into itself.

As a whole, spanning almost his entire career, the quartets demonstrate how at the centre, the blazing heart, of his uncompromising computer-generated compositions, the dense orchestral clusters and percussive power of his music, all its cascading flux, there is a musician whose genius was how he organised sonorities created with strings. He's as much a descendant of Vivaldi's string ingenuity – Vivaldi using the changing seasons as a conceptual trigger to produce musical pulse and patterns – as he is of Pythagoras' 'music of the spheres', totally controlled by numbers.

Hungarian student of Messiaen, close observer of Webern, Gyorgy Kurtág's nervy, shattering First from 1959, just in case Webern and Bartók's early twentieth-century applications were being rubbed out by the dogmatic selection processes of serialism and *musique concrète*, proves he's a master at demonstrating how much can be expressed through containment, concentration and concision. Here, the 'conversation', the question-and-answer routine abstractly absorbed from the history of the quartet, is made up of few words, but a lot of facial expressions, tics and hand gestures, and the string quartet is used as a route to get closer to the bracing unknown rather than to any conclusion or comforting sense of release, as shown forty years later with his tense, sinuous *Aus der Ferne III*, the string quartet carefully breaking into calm, anxious Beckettian silence. His works for string quartet are simultaneously epic and secretive, liberated and obsessive, full of ambient quartet history with sudden detours down uncharted paths.

Luciano Berio's three quartets, all in one movement, supply an advanced history of the quartet, and of Berio's restless, ever curious mind, and how he was both connected to and disconnected from music happening elsewhere at the same time. The First, *Quartetto*, in 1956 overhears Webern, the Second in 1964, *Sincrone*, overhears four voices stubbornly saying the same thing, and then in 1993 *Notturno*, after one of these gaps where a composer is occupied with other aspects of their work, in Berio's case extensively experimenting on vocal range, instrumental capacity and acoustic space, incorporates elements of pop and theatre, basically the drama of the song that had by now travelled both rationally and irrationally from Schubert to the Beatles.

The cerebral but soulful, innovative and analytical Berio effortlessly compresses all his progressive thirty-year experiments and research into his Third Quartet, and if you hear it sandwiched between a couple of classic four-movement Haydn quartets, you can appreciate how its mentality and historical awareness is both far ahead of where Haydn was but also right beside him, as if this is where Haydn could have been if he had composed after Webern, Stravinsky and jazz. For Berio, tradition is a memory, even an illusion, to tap into more than a solid, objectified reality.

Solemn slapstick anarchist Mauricio Kagel's typically weightless and compassionately deconstructed First and Second Quartets, made into one piece in the mid-1960s, is a philosophical play on the ultimately enigmatic, even absurd nature of the string quartet, music blurring into theatre, combining the piercing self-consciousness of Beckett with Cageian prepared manipulation of the four instruments. Kagel imagines a contemporary music that exists in all its avant-garde, even post-Dada fervour, as though there has been no electricity or machinery.

Twenty years later, still looking to break out from what he considered a conservative art, vainly looking for the hidden places composers never reached, his loaded, lavish, almost collaged Third and Fourth Quartets are sensitively demented, dense and light-hearted, precise and scatter-brained, majestic and mocking soundtracks for early twentieth-century silent movies directed by Jean-Luc Godard.

George Crumb's abrasive ritualistic protest in sound, the amplified 1970 *Black Angels – Thirteen Images from the Dark Land* is a singular, electrically surrealist response to the horror of the Vietnam War, using the quartet to represent a battle between good and evil – 'Things were turned upside down,' explained Crumb. 'There were terrifying things in the air... they found their way into *Black Angels*.' The piece contributed to the formation of the Kronos Quartet and is the perfect place for Hendrix fans to enter the quartet cosmos.

The intensely austere provocateur Sofia Gubaidulina's first of five single-movement quartets appeared in 1971. The four players begin relatively connected to each other, possibly on the same wavelength, but each end up isolated, in a world of their own, lost to themselves, the traditional, overheard quartet conversation completely fragmented into savage privacy. Almost a quarter of a century later, after a genre-shifting sequence of theatrical, conceptual and philosophical experiments with the quartet form, her Fifth, *Reflections on the Theme BACH*, a spiritual conversation with her youthful inspiration, and conversations between body and soul, skin and string, time and place, plants and ghosts, where she summarises the adventures, inner tensions and atmospheres of the strangeness of her previous four quartets and weaves that with an uncanny futurist plunge into the baroque traditions that continue to fascinate her, the seriously soulful student of sound and its fugitive shadows.

Reviewing and rewiring the string quartet as an object, a language, a convention 'forbidden by its own familiarity', Hermann Lachenmann's hyper-unreal 1972 String Quartet No. 1, *Gran Torso*, is an act of love for the quartet form and simultaneously a withdrawal from it, where radically new ideas were being examined through a genre with a 220-year history. It was running parallel to theories of 'intertextuality' fashionable at the time, where history was seen as a text to be read, and the meaning of the text determined by its relationship to other texts.

Gran Torso was an erasure and an intensification of the tradition, a haunting resurrection of its very early life, a postmodern redirection of the expected dialogue to a combination of troubling blankness and intense articulation, a quietening of the usual conversation to something softer than silence, an extrasensory stripping of all the flesh and blood of a traditional quartet, leaving some kind of skeleton that has enough breath left to form words.

Lachenmann's three quartets, written between 1972 and 2001, grew from the techniques, philosophies and investigations applied to a 1969 solo work for cello, *Pression*, a connection between the sonatas of

Beethoven and Brahms and the solo saxophone of free-jazz musician Evan Parker and the free guitar of Derek Bailey, where sound gives birth to sound, and space gives birth to time. It's music as a form of physical and metaphysical energy that is transferred from the bodies of the cello and the cellist to the body of the listener.

In 1983 some of my favourite ever pop songs were released – 'Blue Monday' by New Order, 'This Charming Man' by the Smiths, 'This is Not a Love Song' by Public Image Ltd, 'Song to the Siren' by This Mortal Coil – and I was busy conceiving the pop-futurist Zang Tuum Tumb label that would release Frankie Goes To Hollywood's 'Relax'.

I was art-directing the visuals and the conceptual outline of Art of Noise, whose post-minimalist romance 'Moments in Love', released that year – a 1983 classic, I can confidently claim as critic, if not co-composer – came from the first Art of Noise record *Into Battle* (titled that way because pop music was much more a matter of life and death back then). It was somewhere between a maxi-single and an album, which I had edited together with producer Trevor Horn from hours of sampled and often improvised material as though it was a kind of song cycle about the revelations of audio collage. With all this going on, let alone everything else attracting my attention, I failed to notice that 1983 was a great year for string quartets.

Russian Alfred Schnittke's astounding Third Quartet – of four, written between 1966 and 1989 – liberally borrows from, or pays allusive homage to, or lovingly subverts influential late Renaissance Orlando di Lasso, Shostakovich and Beethoven, becoming a classic work of art about classical music, or a classic piece of classical music about a work of art. It is also an immensely knowing string quartet about a string quartet, analysing and revelling in, obsessing over how a single quartet can contain such beauty, harshness, tentativeness, certainty, confusion, invention… and how, at the end of a classic quartet, after all the spiralling, soaring, calming despair, delight, melancholy, lostness, harshness, brooding, transcendence, after all the life it reflects, there is a sense of simply giving up the ghost, of all this energy, and reflection, coming to nothing. Until you play it again.

In 1983, Terry Riley's thirty-seven-minute *Cadenza on the Night Plain* in thirteen episodic sections was an example of how he finally fell for the medium of the string quartet, which could be as therapeutic, and as lovely, and as open to experiment as anything. Its adventurous sound was a long way from his oblique First String Quartet, but clearly linked.

As a graduate student in 1960, Terry Riley had written a spare, moody eighteen-minute single-movement string quartet. (His first instrument as a child had been the violin.) At the time, he was under the influence of La Monte Young, especially the long, sustained tones and random silences of *Trio of Strings*, and John Cage's *String Quartet in Four Parts*, rather than his early spiritual guide Karlheinz Stockhausen – which actually moved him away from atonality in the direction of Western classical music, especially Debussy and his promotion of timbre above melody, even as another important, *concrète* influence on the piece was the foghorns he would hear in the misty distance as he walked along the San Francisco coast.

The quartet was an early emerging hint of the juxtapositions, the simplicity of the elements, the textures and repetitions, the stasis and action, the Eastern-style drones that seeped and pulsed into a variety of meditative, musical compositions that would end up being grouped together as minimalism. Riley's quartet was written four years before his 'greatest hit' in 1964, *In C*, the hypnotic, passionate anti-serial trance piece, one of the great left-field musical artefacts of the 1960s, which helped fix him with the misleading minimalist label.

After his obscure, primitive first attempt at a quartet, moving further and further away from formal composition, working more as a soloist, the idea of writing string quartets, however experimental, seemed irrelevant. Twenty years after his first he was ready again.

Cadenza panoramically rises up out of John Coltrane and Indian raga; at times improvisational passages play hide-and-seek with parts where it seems he is blurring and slurring the strings to produce sitar-like tones. His unexpected return to the string quartet genre was inspired by the Kronos Quartet, which urged him to overcome his lone explorer's resistance to writing for ensembles. They knew a quartet composer – magic meets music, motion meets emotion, late baroque meets postmodern, a specialist in subtle tuning systems, rhythmic flow plus modal organisation, keen on encountering resonating sonic possibilities – when they heard one. In turn influencing the Kronos Quartet, encouraging them as a unit to think like a composer, introducing them to an array of non-Western musicians, especially from

India, over the next thirty-five years Riley wrote twenty-seven quartets for Kronos. In many ways, they were his Band and he was their Dylan.

Morton Feldman's subtle, slow, still, ecstatically unemphatic six-hour 1983 Second String Quartet requires incredible physical strength and spiritual energy to play, one way of expressing his impatience with what Feldman called the 'bourgeois audience' and his hatred of the conventional duration of a classical music piece, with an average of approximately twenty-five minutes. Perhaps here is the answer to the question: how long is a piece of string?

If you ever get the chance to hear a rare live flowering, Feldman's Second String Quartet is best heard where you can imagine that you have no idea what music is, so that it does not necessarily occur to you that its length is any kind of anomaly, or that you can believe that all music is contained in this one piece. If Schubert had lived to the age of 150, he would have been writing quartets like this. I sometimes wonder if you do attend one of the very rare performances, whether you can still claim you were there, and experiencing everything, even if you slept all the way through it.

Transcendent isolationist, one-time rock musician, Darmstadt teacher between 1982 and 1992, fiercely cerebral, formidably prolific and disruptive romantic James Dillon's first string quartet in 1983 was simply called String Quartet. It is as though that was basic enough and yet also abstract enough for someone who makes music that comes from pragmatic investigative impulses as much as euphoric magical thinking. The quartet symbolised how Dillon writes music that defends something that shouldn't be lost, a fundamental European culture, even as he is surprised there are still people around wanting to defend it at all – including, of course, the very idea of the string quartet, and who the hell he is writing for and why.

To some extent he is writing his string quartets – eight would follow over the next thirty-five years, independent of each other but connected by some kind of relentless intellectual force – for himself, as a test of certain thought patterns and technical processes that are rehearsals for, or intimations of, his sensual, severe, larger-scale orchestral and solo works. The quartets are like intense research departments where he experiments with ideas that help him create extraordinarily detailed, densely compelling, delicate and immense worlds. They are, as he has said, spread 'journal-like throughout his work', as Bartók's, Lutyens' and Carter's were.

His energetic avant-garde spirit revels in the historic, endlessly inspiring string-quartet tradition, even as part of him rejects it, somehow defiantly summoning up the willpower to push the possibly obsolete medium even further into the future. The deep radicalism of his personality suggests he shouldn't keep adding to the tradition, but he just can't help himself; he's got no choice because, in the end, he's part of a certain musical history, passing through like Beethoven and Varèse, leaving monumental or hidden traces whether he likes it or not.

John Cage was fascinated by the intellectual give and take of the form, even as he was fascinated by theatrically deforming it. In the 1950 *String Quartet in Four Parts*, describing seasons and places, he ended up – by chance – advancing beyond modernism by refracting the melodic simplicity of medieval music. In his 1983 *Thirty Pieces for String Quartet*, arranging time and space more than notes and sounds, he has his players rehearse alone, and in performance sit far apart from each other around the audience.

Made out of a series of coincidental solos, played whenever and however the players want within a specific time frame, the soft, delicately fierce music that appears from the decisions and interpretations made by the performers needs a certain patience, and preparation, from the listeners to complete the circuit. If you have the patience, and are prepared for thirty minutes of flexibly structured, randomly materialising solos, some rhythmical, some active, some sustained, it is a dream of the string quartet at another extreme to the contrasts and engaged commotion of Carter. Marvel that there is still structure, that there is coherence, and it actually ends in a way that even the most cautious of listeners would have to agree, even though it is by John Cage, is like a piece of music.

Six years afterwards Cage's *Four* – one of his late-life number pieces, where the name of the pieces comes from the number of players – is his most extreme abstraction of the quartet model, even as the four players are more together than in *Thirty Pieces*, flowing through each other's awareness of the music, rather than soloing. It's a clarification of ideals, even an un-Cage-like musical resolution, an illumination, at the end of his life.

Two hundred years after Mozart was working on his momentous Haydn quartets, the first great works to take the baton from Haydn, written between 1782 and 1783, it seems neat enough that the history of the string quartet had come to some sort of conclusion; surely nothing could come after Riley's *Cadenza*, filtering the string quartet through the circuitous experiments in repetition and variation of the 1960s; Feldman's confidential transformation of the string quartet into symbolic event; Dillon's gracious, inimical use of it as a kind of private sketchbook for future, more substantial works, a basic postmodern compositional strategy; Cage's surreptitious reduction of the format to nothing but the divine mysteries of time; and Schnittke's solemn, sensual testimonial to the glories of the string quartet through an elevated postmodern remix of Renaissance, romantic and twentieth-century techniques.

But, probably because of how Mozart had sent Haydn into so many different directions, directions that were multiplied over centuries by the efforts and insights of subsequent composers, there were too many routes the quartet had taken and too much momentum for there to be such any neat, conclusive ending, a cool, resigned fading away or a dramatic finale. It had all been done before, but there was still more to be done.

The quartet kept coming.

Harrison Birtwistle's *Nine Movements for String Quartet*, written between 1991 and 1996, imagined an entirely different history of the string quartet from Schnittke, perhaps bouncing off some model idea of Stravinsky, offering a glimpse of how, in a wider sense, his entire music orbits classical history, but never lands, existing in its own sector, or diabolical neck of the woods. Birtwistle uses the four instruments you must use but entirely for his own purposes, so that whenever he creates a string quartet — the twenty-nine-minute disruptive, dismantled, despairing *Tree of Strings* from 2007, 2015's intimately intricate *The Silk House Sequences* — he does not break the rules, the essential relationship between the 4 x 4 strings, which would mean it is not a string quartet, but he comes up with some other rules as well, so that his quartets are familiar enough, and entirely unfamiliar, at times as if all other string quartets are mere ghosts and echoes of his, and they attempt to make contact, and fail, in frustration, and a kind of mordant celebration.

The extreme perfectionist Georg Haas's 1998 Second String Quartet solemnly balances the explicitly tonal with organic microtonal interference – demonstrating his fascination with quarter-tones and miscellaneous outsider sonorities. It hovers between an impression of the implacably ancient and something ghostly at the other extreme, so the traditional – from Bach to Shostakovich and to some extent even Cage – occasionally penetrates through an unattached, otherworldly atmosphere, which is, as Haas notes, 'something distant, lost and clouded'. Amazingly, this and his other quartets – including the vaporous, orgasmic seventy-minute Third, to be played in complete, sense-sharpening darkness – are played on the same instruments that Haydn used for his string quartets.

John Adams charged, agile 1994 *John's Book of Alleged Dances* for electrified string quartet, taped percussion and recorded prepared piano, 'alleged' because the steps for these ten 'dances', which can be played in any order, have not yet been invented, although there were choreographers who naturally took the bait. Inspired by an early enthusiasm for John Cage, which he found completely refreshing after a time spent reluctantly studying high serialism in the hushed composition department at Harvard, the quartet deftly targets and exploits the quirkier, cheekier side of Cage.

Adams has unclassical fun mingling jazz, minimalism, folk and the jaunty side of experimental, demonstrating why he is one of the most popular of modern composers. He has an ability to distil the theoretical qualities of Cage, the fidgety repetitive pressure of minimalism and the theories and challenges of the avant-garde into a highly appealing and extremely tuneful musical performance – selecting the more entertaining elements, matching them with his virtuosic knowledge of music history, from Monteverdi to Messiaen, and ejecting the more austere, difficult and disconcerting aspects. Even those with stubborn prejudices against more difficult music find something to enjoy in Adams, who mixes the genial with the scholarly.

Karlheinz Stockhausen had the ego and instincts to perform for his public, and extend his brand, in a way that resembled Adams, but he could never bring himself to ignore his insistent mystical inner voice and create the accessible soundtrack that would have made him an international treasure.

His *Helicopter String Quartet* from 1993 is where *musique concrète*, sound installation and arcane philosophy gets a Hollywood budget. In between gimmick and cosmic, the kitsch and the magical, the extremely daft and the highly technical, the four players each play the piece independently in a separate helicopter, so that the string quartet and the whirring helicopter rotor blades are mixed down for an audience who are gathered somewhere nearby and Stockhausen, in a manner of speaking, at least through his music, gets to fly, or not...

Centuries of quartet action and reaction give us this spinning mix of clarity and complexity, austerity and joy, absurdity and deep seriousness, pure drama and supernatural atmosphere, acceptance and rejection, battles of will and battles of wit. And after all that immense, titillating, glorious, exhausting, intertwining, hot-blooded, heart-warming, ancient, modern, cooling, brief, calculating, seething, prodigious, postmodern, post-beyond endeavour and fulfilment, a vast intimidating set of precedents, revelations, meditations, connections, detours, examinations, detachments, confrontations and refinements that are often themselves genius, musical movements coexisting and overlapping and merging into each other, a sacrosanct history that intimidates and/or inspires the boldest, bravest of composers.

There's the internal dynamic, the intimate integration, the combination of precision and propulsion, elegance and energy, vigour and melody, fury and fragility, introspection and extroversion, the organising and refining of concentrated private space, the pared-down reduction of larger groups of instruments to a compressed, enterprising centre, the intoxicating, endlessly diverse combination of hues, textures, tones and timbres, and the basic idea of the space that there is in between and around the musicians and instruments, space representing the resounding stillness of truth, against and inside which all the drama, argument, questioning and contemplation happens.

I thought, in a reckless state I can only put down to my madness, the sort of lunging, veering madness that often leaps to the surface of a great quartet, and then buries its head, I want to have a go, and not make a complete fool of myself, or, what the hell, make a complete fool of myself.

3. THIRD MOVEMENT: MINUET AND TRIO, IN THE TONIC KEY

Once I had made the decision that I was going to compose a string quartet, I returned to a story written by Virginia Woolf. Her extraordinary experimental short fiction, 'The String Quartet' (1921), explores the pleasures and frustrations of 'capturing' music in language.

In the early 1920s, at the beginning of the recorded-music era, with the newly invented gramophone and the arrival of the wireless, she was a knowledgeable, almost daily, listener to 'classical' music, writing while music was playing in the background, which would encourage the appearance of a certain momentum in what she was writing, the prose mirroring or matching the energy and structure of what she was listening to. Woolf once gave some details of her daily routine: 'We'll play bowls; then I shall read Sévigné; then have grilled ham and cheese for dinner; then Mozart.'

She considered that 'music is nearest to truth', certainly considered that it diagnosed, reflected and described modern changes first – then art, then words – and was constantly fascinated by the cultural practice of music and by the relationships between music and writing. This was particularly seen in the rhythmic sound of the sea she wanted to communicate throughout her novel *The Waves*. Many of her most striking stylistic innovations were often inspired by music, and she considered that music was a more direct method of communication than language. She once imagined a colony where marrying was not allowed – unless you happened to fall in love with a Beethoven symphony. Before her death in 1941 she was planning a book on the influence of music on literature.

This connection was always of interest to me, the idea of how you wrote about music, and transformed a piece of music into words about that piece of music when particularly a great piece of music was its own best description and explanation. Woolf once wrote that all descriptions of music are worthless, actually 'rather unpleasant', and her way of reporting on a piece of music was to come to the music as it is filtered through consciousness, connected to how Debussy's impressions of reality were from inside experience rather than some literal copy – reacting to music in another state, at another stage, one more accurate in terms of a listener absorbing a piece of music into their own life, where it becomes totally unique and personal.

Consciousness as impacted by music is what she responds to. Music as a catalyst for thought, and how different sorts of music provoke different levels of thinking. What is your state of mind after you have heard some music? How does music actually make meaning? How does the listener make meaning out of music, and will that be the same meaning for everyone?

She is concerned with how, as a listener, music makes you think other things, and how those things are the ones worth writing about and bring you into the soul of the music. It's a better truth than a much more local, quasi-objective response, a report or review that doesn't really extend beyond mere summary or extend to a verbal imaginative brilliance that is truly in keeping with what inspired the thinking in the first place. Her writing, from an early stage, to the annoyance of some of my editors at the *New Musical Express*, and possibly a good 50 per cent of the readers, no offence, had an impact on my writing about music and made me wonder even when I was reviewing Suicide or the Clash: what can you say about a piece of music that adds to the pleasure and vitality of that music, and how best do you say it?

One conclusion I had, which also fed into the idea of wanting to write music and which was one of the main influences on how I wrote prose, was that writing about music was like performing it, or at least, a powerful piece of writing can become part of the performance, something that promotes it but also celebrates it and profoundly complements it.

The most useful piece of writing about music becomes its own performance, and also a contribution to the subject, helping to take it to another level, even to some extent helping to complete it, to finalise its intention and meaning, or what over time it will come to be about. The writer is a metaphor for the actions of a potential audience, completing a circuit, making the music whole because it is being heard and responded to, contributing to its meaning. The best writing about music should be as a result of great listening.

The writing can add to the value and vitality of a piece of music by placing it in a necessary historical and emotional context so that it doesn't merely exist as a series of patterns and noises that drift through nowhere in particular. And for me, when I wrote about music, it wasn't necessarily the task to 'review' the music, to grade it, describe it, even attempt to explain it. There was plenty of that already existing, so why add to all of that particular noise? As Woolf thought, it is often the conventional, prosaic writing about music 'that leads us astray', taking us away from the actual purpose and pleasure of music and undermining, even neutralising its existence.

I was more interested in a response to the music that would be made up, like music itself, of energy and rhythm and even mystery, and itself be a way of implying the beauty, or not, of the music without attempting to reduce it down to mere description and mere opinion. I wanted to react to a composition with a composition that sometimes might not even be referring directly to the music, but which became a part of the music, an evocative enhancement, a sympathetic accompaniment. Writing about music at its best should make the music something else, send it somewhere else, change it into another state.

Towards the end of her life Woolf famously remarked, 'I always think of my books as music before I write them.' She was jealous of how a musician could write, in a string quartet, four lines at a time, because if she could somehow write this way, layering and shaping her prose in a fluid, magical harmony, it would better reflect how in life 'there are always things going on at different levels simultaneously'. Her writing would inspire composers who have set her words to music, or responded more obliquely to her work, recognising its innate musicality, and therefore its way of commenting on and investigating the practical and abstract purpose of music.

On 7 March 1920, Woolf attended a concert that included a Schubert quintet 'to take notes for my story'. Several other works have been proposed as contenders as a 'source' for her string-quartet short story – from a listener's exclamation in the story, 'That's an early Mozart, of course,' to Schubert's *Trout* Quintet, and even Schoenberg's anxiously futuristic, wild to tranquil and everything in between Second String Quartet from 1908, standing right on the edge between old and new.

Schoenberg's Second String Quartet received its London premiere in 1914 following several years of circling interest from the British press in Schoenberg's music and the definitively post-romantic and post-industrial emergence of atonality, appearing at the same time as abstraction in art – and the atom-splitting calculations of modern science – and a desire radically to transform representations of how people experience and understand an increasingly chaotic, unstable world.

Schoenberg's formidable future in music is opened up, and in its setting of a Stefan George poem, a line appears that magically proclaims this future: 'I feel air from another planet.'[1] The Second String Quartet demonstrated Schoenberg's fascination with how form – in art and music – materialised out of a compulsion for self-expression. It also existed as a kind of brief but epic translation of the history of the string quartet, looking back to work out a way forward, this endlessly varied way of wrestling with ideas, intimately exposing creative tension, with hints and echoes and distortions of visionary quartets by Brahms and Beethoven as if he was reverse-engineering the puzzle of how they constructed their quartets, hiding their workings as they made their way through.

Woolf writes of someone attending a performance, possibly of a Mozart string quartet. In between the narrator's thoughts and bits of overheard conversation, each movement of the piece became words that attempt to imitate and represent in images the sound of the music, rather than plainly describe it. Juxtaposing the banal remarks that frame the performance with the exuberant flights of fancy that unfold during the playing, Woolf's work celebrates music's capacity to stimulate memories and associations, from the routine to the ecstatic. And it celebrates in its making of shapes and rhythms music's own 'weaving' into a formal 'pattern' and 'consummation'.

'The String Quartet' seems more interested in exploring music's capacity to stimulate imagination than in representing a particular musical work in language. There are no technical terms used, little about the actual playing, and we never find out what is being played. This writing about music influenced the way I wrote about music – to respond to music as an act of the imagination, as a compound of sensations, and elaborate on the consequences of that, on individuals and the world itself, rather than limiting the response to merely the sound and its immediate context. The job of writing about music actually seemed to me to be about building a bigger context inside which the music existed, a cultural, social, personal, historical, visual, commercial, intellectual and emotional history.

Without the context, its place in time, its position in relation to the fashion and style of the time, music, especially pop and rock, floats

---

[1] A wonderful description of all great pieces of music. By the late 1950s, running out of twelve-tone, serial steam around about Stockhausen's 1957 Gruppen, this particular planetary air would become suffocating, restricting creative fantasies rather than unleashing them.

free of meaning. It becomes connected to nothing outside its own place inside an enclosed system that feeds back into itself. It can sound remarkable, completely original, a stunning way of generating a new kind of musical hybrid, but if no appropriate myths can be spun around it, no sustained shades of hyperbole extending its cultural shape, no estimation of where it fits into a history of music, then it will remain a mere vibration in the margins, a form of discreet interference, at best of cult interest, good for some, bad for others, a mere matter of taste, its only hope that a random, unpredictable context reveals itself over time. The world catches up and finally gets it, sometimes long after its original intensity has drained away.

I would often end up being guilty of what Woolf didn't like in writing about music – vague formulas, comparisons and adjectives – but usually this was either because of commercial pressure, because the abstraction I tended towards was of no use in mainstream journalism, or because I couldn't come up with the right words to explain and explore how what I was writing about was 'beyond words'. There had to be words, at least when reviewing for money, with the purpose of simply guiding listeners towards something they might not have considered, and this will inevitably involve a formula – which often leads to the naming of a genre, and yet another rigid box to lock music inside – some comparisons and, when all else fails, a chain link of handy adjectives that can make wild stabs at attempting to convey what the music sounds like.

The Woolf-like stream of consciousness, very derided in the increasingly conservative world of post-1970s rock writing, was in many ways a better way of responding and describing how music itself is structured and moves from one state to another, how one image gives way to another. It didn't bring the music down to earth, sorted and summed up, where it could be practically graded, filed, and safely transformed into a consumer object or a curated list, placed inside a specific genre rather than a fluid, unfixed, forever-shifting symbol of mystery, of human emotion and human expression. Conventional rock critics, acting like amateur musicologists rather than writing in the adventurous, even experimental, tradition of the first rock critics who were influenced by literary stylists, artists' manifestos and exploratory theory, were not fans of this approach. They liked the boxes, and the lists; they liked performing thorough autopsies on old albums, being obedient to the standard hierarchies, filing things more or less in alphabetical order, determined to solve mysteries and over-explain where really the mystery should be maintained.

Often the very act of choosing the music to write about, either as a positive or negative thing, is the most important and instructive act of criticism – the selection is the recommendation or condemnation, the drawing of attention to something worth knowing or not – and everything else is merely a dance around the music and associated information in order to communicate enthusiasm and excitement, or disappointment and disgust.

Ideas and impressions float away from the music, to the extent that often you might not seem to be referring to music, but to dreams, images and memories that the music inspired. The listener finds out for themselves what the music actually sounds like, which will often be different for everyone – certainly the 'better' and more interesting music is, the more it will sound different to different people. More ordinary popular music, organised to appeal to the masses, will sound the same to more people, because there must be a common agreement about what it sounds like for it to be popular. It must reinforce beliefs, expectations and biases, not challenge or overturn them – even if it now exists because it is connected in some form to music that originally did question the status quo and took a new direction. Music that generates a multitude of interpretations and sounds different to each individual, and challenges settled belief systems, will mostly be unpopular or at least less likely to be a commercial success.

A great music critic aims to make the right choices, ones that fit fluently but also unexpectedly into history, and that send history off on new tangents. The choice, their musical taste, is their aesthetic breakthrough, and the writing then becomes an elaboration, expressive and impressionistic, of that choice; from 'The String Quartet', Woolf's 'Flourish, spring, burgeon, burst!' or 'Tramp and trumpeting. Clang and clangour. Firm establishment. Fast foundations. March of myriads. Confusion and chaos trod to earth' or 'soar, sob, sink to rest, sorrow and joy' is tremendous writing about music, about understanding the world: it could be about Ornette Coleman, the Fall, Harrison Birtwistle or J Dilla. It anticipates Ted Hughes's fiercely loving writing about Beethoven – 'On the glassy limits of ghost', the brilliant idea of music as a scalpel – and makes way for the innovative American rock writers of the 1960s and 1970s, splintering from the revved-up, unbalanced, reality-cracking New Journalism of Tom Wolfe, Joan Didion and Norman Mailer. These few Woolf words about music are better than all the content of a million reviews on Amazon. (No offence.)

She writes in *The Common Reader*:

> Let us record the atoms as they fall upon the mind in the order in which they fall, let us trace the pattern, however disconnected and incoherent in appearance, which each sight or incident scores upon the consciousness. Let us not take it for granted that life exists more fully in what is commonly thought big than in what is commonly thought small.

This isn't about music, but it is another great piece of writing about music and how it works, as pattern, as mystery, and as a stimulator of emotion, a method of organising, disorganising, reorganising time. Woolf, both in her prose, even when she is not necessarily writing about music – I can apply the above to much fractured, exploratory contemporary music fantastically scattered in the margins, say, by Evan Parker, Tyshawn Sorey, Mary Halvorson and Henry Threadgill – and in her musical choices, is a fantastic music critic.

And then one of her stories became an influence on how I approached the idea of actually composing a string quartet. As 'The String Quartet' shows, Woolf was fascinated by the radiant intimacy of the ensemble format, the formal constraints governing composition for four parts that needed dedicated negotiation, and, above all, the discursive character of string quartets as a quartet of people thinking aloud in each other's company. Thinking the thoughts of others, but also contributing thoughts of their own. In that sense, not so much a conversation, but an aural X-ray of their fleeting thoughts, floating memories and passing impressions, an insight into how much they know and respond to each other's moods.

If the symphony is an equivalent of the great novel, then the string quartet is a slim volume of poems, the compression of all that commingled thinking and harmonic adventure into smaller, but equally as rich and startling shapes, with a particular purity about the relationship between the sound of the four instruments, four minds, four lives, and the infinite glimmering structural possibilities.

In order to actually write a quartet I listened to as many as I could, piling into the vast amount that materialised on the streaming sites, encouraging everyone to become an expert. I am still listening to as many as I can and realise more and more that I will run out of time before I have listened to them all, and I show no sign of being bored and losing interest. My favourites, the ones I ached to get close to in my own composition, in my dream of the fantastic, were by Shostakovich, Debussy, Ravel, Webern, Schoenberg, Britten, Babbitt, Smetana, Crawford, Ligeti, Xenakis, Cage, Maxwell Davies...

I did for the TV programme and for my own needs write a few minutes of something for a string quartet, selecting a tempo, a key signature, moving notes around on a page, stacking them up, turning them backwards, randomly reorganising them, chasing elusive melody, glimpsing the far, far edges of one, looking for some Woolfian spring and burst, some Hughesian insectoid gnawing, getting a little insight in using a compositional computer program into some of the more facile elements of constructing a minimalist piece. The cut-and-paste technique and various automatic settings that have changed writing and often turned it into flat word-processing or soulless content farming can be used in the writing of music when you use one of these programs; convincing facsimiles of a certain sort of repetitive intensity can effortlessly be achieved, easily giving the illusion of following in the slow slow quick quick slow foot foot foot step step ( ) foot footsteps of Steve Reich and Philip Glass.

The elite, ludicrous advantage of working inside the Royal Academy of Music, stocked up with scores of some of the best young musicians in the world, is that it was easy to try out a provisional composition using a personally assembled quartet of musicians attacking my loose assembly of notes, pauses and phrases as though they might be actual musical treasure. Even if I required a harp, it wouldn't be long before someone turned up to the room we were working in and rolled a harp through the door, just dropping in from heaven or a study room on another floor.

Hearing something you have put together yourself, however primitively, as it emerges from nowhere and becomes a certain sort of organised sound was deliciously unfamiliar and moving. And it certainly satisfied the ego, all that power to build a reality in your image. It was definitely something you could become addicted to, where your very private thoughts that you had not even worked out for yourself were becoming the tangible shape of an actually quite good idea that others could objectively experience.

My string quartet appeared, or at least an extract of one, one movement pretty much to pop-song length, but a piece that I had notated myself and that could be read by Royal Academy musicians and transformed through their expertise and quite unexpected enthusiasm into exactly the shape I wanted. What was I thinking? It definitely sounded, with its distinctive bittersweet tension, as if I had been influenced by Debussy, Britten and Shostakovich, and Nick Drake, Robert Wyatt and New Order – there even appeared to be a combination of restless zest, flickering melancholy and a little edge that reminded me of what I see when I look in the mirror. Fear! The best quartets definitely feature a little fear, for the end of life, for the sense you will never rise to the challenge, and never finish even one quartet.

It had my fingerprints and sounded like it could be a soundtrack to something I once dreamed. In a funny sort of way, it was embarrassing that I had revealed so much about myself, for all the millions of words I have written about myself, even though it would remain, once it had been broadcast, completely obscure and take its place once again at the back of my mind. Just that little burst of personal solo musical activity was strangely disorientating.

Even though I say so myself, it wasn't too soggy, or burnt at the edges, or poorly seasoned, and the paint more or less dried. It wouldn't get me voted off in week one. Compared, though, to the real thing, it was, after all, a little reality television. It was in the style of something, but you couldn't quite tell what.

I am still working on my 'second' quartet, on extending that first attempt into a more authentic multi-movement structure, still dreaming of the fantastic, a task made much more difficult by now not having luxury access to my own personal string quartet laid on by the Royal Academy of Music. If I ever finish it, I'll let you know. As long as I don't finish it, it still exists, at least there is life in the fact that I still think about it, and meanwhile, the same impulses go into writing about the phenomenon of the string quartet. I am writing a string quartet at the same time as I write about their history.

4. FOURTH MOVEMENT: RONDO OR SONATA RONDO FORM, IN THE TONIC KEY

A way into the history of the string quartet is either through a composer – and the connections that open up with other composers, following, influencing or breaking away – or through the lens of a particular ensemble, the string quartet that plays the string quartets – some protecting an elitist version of the canon, some concentrating on the purely contemporary, some acting as academics and historians, some mixing and matching ancient past and modern past, some searching obscure, precious corners for pieces that had never made the canon and probably never would.

Paralleling the rise of rock 'n' roll after the Second World War there was an emergence of great professional string quartets – the Amadeus, the Hollywood, the Juilliard, the Beethoven, the Quartetto Italiano, the Czech pair Smetana and Janáček, both playing their pieces from memory. In an alternative zone, tidily, conscientiously parked to the outside of the greedy, dominant and demanding popular culture, the string quartet developed its own glamour and intrigue, each group possessing their own virtues and values, specialising in their own particular area of concern within the repertoire. Composers would write for a particular ensemble. Relationships were established. A core central canon was created, digging into over two centuries of movement, and movements.

The Alban Berg Quartett formed in 1970, a Vienna-based ensemble choosing the name of the 'moderate modernist' Second Viennese School composer whose two quartet masterpieces, Op. 3 and the *Lyric Suite*, definitively replace tonality with the thematic. They felt the composer, ushered beyond romanticism by his teacher Schoenberg, best expressed their intention to honour both the romantic and the contemporary. Their repertoire stretched across from the beginning of string quartet time – when Mozart took over from Haydn – through Beethoven, Brahms and Bartók, to Stravinsky, Berio and beyond.

Digital-era ensembles appeared – Emerson, Takács, Tokyo, Pacifica, Ethel, Brodsky, Jack, Balanescu, Arditti, Esmé – each one a portal to enter familiar territory or marginalised brilliance. The constant replenishment of string quartets reaching from the known and traditional to the very new and obscure is the one area of classical music that seems to find a way to escape the exclusive, closed-in nature of the institutionalised classical scene. The quartet's intimate belief in the enduring, evolving values and virtues of the quartet composition, often their promotion and commissioning creation of additions, enhancements and revisions creates a sense of mobile contemporary energy often lacking in classical music, afraid to dilute its assumed purity by engaging with the whims and fashions of the turning modern world.

The Arditti Quartet, formed in London in 1974, exemplifies the art of interpretation, notation transformed into performance, becoming experts in twentieth- and twenty-first-century music by playing it, understanding it and distributing it to a wider audience than avant-garde music usually reaches. They perform as a combination of installation, education, exhibition, declaration, communication, collaboration, translation, investigation and exploration. Playing the work of others, the music they select, that they commission, what they put together and how, and the introspective, intellectual agility of their playing is where they become themselves even as they follow notes and instructions. Essentially, they receive a telegram with a few curt words, or a cryptic series of codes, often containing much compositional micro-management leaving very little room for subjective interpretation, and they must turn these messages into fantastic performances, individually distinctive but still faithful to the original prose.

They were the quartet trusted and charged with the premiere of Stockhausen's high-risk high jinks *Helicopter String Quartet* and, roughly speaking, they concentrate on the European post-war avant-garde with cerebral and monumental commitment and never stray into the muddying, to them completely irrelevant, waters of pop, rock, jazz, folk or non-Western world. Other contemporary composers who completely trust – or trusted – the Arditti to premiere their quartets include James Dillon, Thomas Adès, Harrison Birtwistle, John Cage, Elliott Carter, Brian Ferneyhough, Fred Frith, Jonathan Harvey, Mauricio Kagel, György Kurtág, Helmut Lachenmann, Conlon Nancarrow and Wolfgang Rihm – because the quartet exists, and has become their own comprehensive library of modernism and beyond, the ongoing momentum of the quartet can exist, unexpectedly flourishing after post-war Boulez more or less sternly resisted its charms after his early youthful dabble. Avant-garde composers can express solidarity with the overall tradition but operate inside an active and fertile subsection where perhaps the quartet can be conceived as beginning with Cage and Carter — or even composers that didn't write one, like Varèse — rather than Haydn and Mozart, ghosts in this particular machine that you don't quite believe really exist.

The Arditti's American theatrical step-cousins the Kronos Quartet, sharing certain parts of the experimental repertoire, are constantly crossing what some might consider illegal borders and sneaking back into their world with some previously forbidden bounty, from Jimi Hendrix to Thelonious Monk, from Africa to the Middle East, India to South America. The Kronos, in classical terms, are a bit pop, unashamed American entertainers, even as they are as likely as the Arditti to play Feldman, Cage and Berg. You can tell that a great part of their DNA was supplied by their initial inspiration, the musical and often visual art-drama of Crumb's *Black Angels*. Morton Feldman wrote his long, long and very very long Second String Quartet for them, because he liked a bit of drama, and there's no drama like a piece that does so much while doing so little for six hours.

They steered Terry Riley and John Zorn into the quartet channel and would have done the same with a still-living Jimi Hendrix, on their own mission to widen the repertoire, which seemed very Viennese in the early 1970s when both quartets formed, and to much of the outside world still is. The Kronos Quartet, though, plays shows and even uses amplification. The Arditti Quartet is more like the reading of poetry, the senses folding thick and dark, and a lot of it doesn't rhyme.

The Arditti keeps a very straight face, and their commitment to opening up the repertoire and matter-of-factly celebrating the obscure and difficult takes them to many different and often awkward places, and as long as there are modernist traces, to Mexico and China, but they have no fear about being considered the quartet that plays the complex, challenging music, sealed inside what can seem an austere mausoleum of modernism, which might actually turn out to be a spaceship. After all, they preserve the spellbinding, spiky, ascetic, flamboyant quartets of Schoenberg, Luigi Nono, Dillon, Ferneyhough, Dutilleux and Lachenmann, carrying them forward; there they all are on Spotify and Tidal, next to everything, including Taylor Swift and Cardi B, if you know where to look and have the inclination, because, quite simply, someone has to. The Arditti's mission is more spiritual than the spirited

Kronos, but both have their own glamour – with Kronos, the glamour of an indie rock group, with Arditti, the glamour of intrepid explorers discovering virgin territory. It was to Arditti founder Irvine Arditti that Pierre Boulez once snapped that the string quartet was dead; he eventually apologised.

If the Kronos Quartet spread themselves too thin and the Arditti live inside a monastery, or on the dark side of the moon, there are other less extreme examples who will more conveniently guide you through a rock-steady quartet history, until you feel ready for some cerebral Arditti rigour or some exotic Kronos tourism.

In the last few years, Quatuor Ébène, with power-trio directness, jazz-quartet élan and mainstream-label support, but without getting too tarted up, will smartly and not a little cockily take you to Debussy and Ravel, to Brahms and Mendelssohn, into the wicked forest of Beethoven, all the way back to the origin stories of Haydn and the curling eternity of Mozart, and they've recently set off through Bartók. The Belcea Quartet started in 2001 with the sublime Debussy and Ravel quartets, so often paired they can seem connected like twins, and have since recorded Schubert, Brahms, Britten, Mozart and a religiously complete Bartók.

Many of these performing string quartets are still promoted and packaged as though it is important that they are seen in their publicity photographs holding their instruments, as if to prove something, and wearing dark, formal clothes and a look of handsome, inviting openness. They will appear in venues in formal settings that seem to contradict the mysterious, addictive appeal and verve I am assigning the form. I'm not sure what the answer is, how the string quartet, all that sonic possibility drawing with it the depth and daring from such an astonishing, undimmed repertoire, that dazzling articulation of charisma, is often hidden behind the musicians performing as if they are merely channelling, not expressing their own complicated, driven psychology. Sometimes the most intense, explosive quartet can perform the music as if they are the equivalent of newsreaders, mere mouthpieces delivering prepared news – even if sometimes these bulletins are dreams of the fantastic – with little room for adding their own personality and soul.

One of the fascinating, and to outsiders troubling, elements of the working string ensemble is their regular readiness to spend so much of their time and effort at the service of another composer, sacrificing themselves as conventional creative bodies with turbulent, personal urges to express and invent in order to act as hosts for their favoured ones. They must act as mediums, calling up ghosts, or at best inventive interpreters, giving a local spin to foreign insights. The active string quartet consumes the works of other musicians and is consumed by those works.

It's as if there must be a distance between appearance and playing, or the whole world collapses. This is at the heart of a wider problem, for those who are concerned about such things: that the image of the string quartet remains stuck in a formal limbo, however much some might like to concentrate on the spectacular, often truly otherworldly nature of the repertoire, and the connections that can be made between one extreme and another, between eras and styles, or the stupendous, highly charged nature of the sound, when the balance, interaction and perception is exquisitely maintained.

The Brooklyn Rider, perhaps, suggests a glimpse of a glimpse of a solution to the problem of communicating all this ravishing, reflective brilliance to a wider audience without sacrificing the integrity of music, history and interpretation. They are not the string quartet turned into something daytime, made over and glossy, pumped up with dance beats and hair, but even though their route is through a conventional indie channel, with the bearded, hung-over look and image of a group you might imagine playing at rock festivals, they're on the edge between being taken seriously, for experimenting with context and form, or being dismissed as trivialising the important, for experimenting with context and form.

They emphasise the dangers of appearing 'crossover' and 'cross-cultural' even when the intentions are completely honourable, the playing effervescent and the overall conceptual approach done with sensitivity and enthusiasm. They are a string quartet, but they do not follow the formula as established from the Hollywood String Quartet of the 1930s to current darlings the Ébène, by concentrating on the core repertoire, mainstream and/or obscure, and establishing themselves as the latest cultivated ensemble to weigh up the great and the good and develop their own specialist expertise. They are instrumental, but with more of a pop-group dynamic; for some, this already smacks of gimmick, of being as much middle-of-the-road as the latest major-label, whizz-kid virtuoso, Euro-styled-as-accessible classical hero. They recorded the complete quartet works of Philip Glass, their version of the Takacs making their way through Beethoven as a key part of their life's work, but don't necessarily fancy consistently immersing themselves so thoroughly in the mind and total musical span of another composer.

Brooklyn Rider's template is more the Kronos Quartet one of cultural curation than Ébène's polishing up of the stricter, almost professorial Alban Berg model. Each of their albums, concerts and sundry events is programmed to represent their interest in collaboration, in placing different periods, voices and styles together, and detecting potentially new musical patterns. They're interested in the intermingling of the relatively normal canon with other, secret canons, and various furtive experiments, in an attempt to conjure up another way of presenting serious music, some of it, awkwardly, over 200 years old, to an audience more comfortable paying attention to current technologically based trends.

Brooklyn Rider will play a Mozart quartet, but as part of a set that includes their own music. They'll play Beethoven, and then conceive a group response, a form of remix, a sampling of Beethoven, if I am allowed to say such a thing. This could immediately kill them for purists, allergic to any disruptive detail that might suggest there is a jaunty jazz-ness, or a loud-mouthed rock-ness, an experimental urge about proceedings, and not necessarily something that charms those for whom Mozart still resides at the very opposite of whatever the current rock 'n' roll spirit might be.

Imagining what a Mozart or a Beethoven would prefer as musicians in the twenty-first century – the splendid but sterile concert halls or some curatorial mixing and matching – is futile, because there is no way you can lay one era over another to produce a realistic equivalence in an age where the romantic idea of genius has been shattered into millions of pieces by the hammer of Twitter, the pummel of Snapchat and the brainwashing mirror of Instagram; a Mozart alive today might be a film composer, a new version of Beethoven writing music for games, or they might simply be completely lost in how things are, adrift among all the abundance... if anything, I would like to think they would be downtown rather than uptown, marginalised rather than mainstream, TikTok more than André Rieu, and definitely underground more than crossover.

Brooklyn Rider included a Bartók piece, his String Quartet No. 2, on one of their albums, *A Walking Fire*, using it as a way of amplifying Bartók's probing ethnographic interest in non-Western musical traditions, his borrowing from East European folk and African rhythms, placing it among music drawn from Romania, Russia and Iran, including a piece written by group violinist Colin Jacobsen — and perhaps this is at the centre of their aesthetic, the dislocation of time and place, the collapse of arbitrary barriers between regions and eras, the melting of any kind of stiff, alienating hierarchy, so that they can play their own music after playing the holy Bartók without it seeming peculiar or superficial in the patient pursuit of a refreshing, accessible new system. Bartók is perhaps made new, or at least is able to maintain time-travelling flexibility, by being placed among a new kind of post-pop world; it's dangerous, but better to try it than not, as long as it does not involve glitter balls, laser beams and dry ice.

Brooklyn Rider will flirt with gimmickry if it helps them move towards their ideal performance setting, a music that represents all manner of travel — to find their music, to play and sell their music, to go from the beginning of one piece to the end, following a specific journey originally written by a master, and then reporting on that journey by making a journey of their own.

Perhaps the most dramatic sign of their intention to find a new way of being as a string quartet, as an eclectic music ensemble fusing different forms and modes without sounding limply fusion, is the cover to their *A Walking Fire* album. It does not feature the four members uncomfortably arranged around some antique chairs or garden furniture, each of them in open-neck black shirts or over-pressed casual, holding their instruments with a gawky sort of pride. It's an album cover that does not look like it's been designed by a committee dedicated to hiding the possibly stern, intricate, even gothic instrumental content behind highly contrived pleasantness, like that's one way to crack the problem of getting non-pop music to a pop audience, like they might even care. It's a small thing, but it gives me hope that one day the history and future of the string quartet will not be presented as though it is still in the eighteenth-century tradition of being an amusement, a diversion for a reserved, self-appointed intelligentsia. It will blast out of the parlour, out of the suits and ties, the ballgowns and the inward-looking chat rooms, and invade planets, including this one, as a truly and eternally amazing force for good, spectacular energy that must always find ways to fight extinction.

If Ébène inherits Berg, and the Brooklyn Rider is more Kronos, the Danish String Quartet, formed in the early twenty-first century by four students at the Copenhagen Academy of Music, all born in the 1980s, emerges from a gallant, cerebral but still passionate Arditti sensibility. They are already planning for the time in 2060 when they will beat the record for the longest-running string quartet, and hearing their confident, compelling recordings of the complete string quartets of Carl Nielsen and Paul Hindemith, you believe they will make it, one way or another. In 2016 they moved to the ECM label, for those who favour a certain kind of resonant, untethered and immaculately recorded instrumental music the best label in the world – although new circumstances need a new label for 'record label'. As things stand, signing to the label certifies the Danish String Quartet as one of the world's great contemporary chamber groups.

The Danish Quartet recorded for ECM one of the most fantastic modern quartets, Thomas Adès's ultra-smart mutantly traditional First String Quartet, *Arcadiana*, written in 1994 when he was in his early twenties as a series of seven short movements, each one a fantasy of a lost idyll and dream places, which abstractly, unsentimentally dances around hints and shadows of Mozart, Schubert, Debussy and Elgar, Adès fearlessly aiming to compete with such genius, imaginatively interlacing and deftly twisting the timelines of musical and quartet history.

The Danish String Quartet makes *Arcadiana* seem deeply up to date and yet something that owes its existence to centuries-old quartet ideas, essentially excavating glistening, optimistic futures from the past as the best recent quartets do. They make it seem as though the idea of the string quartet is not retrospective at all, even when they play music written a long time ago, but a form that still has plenty of places to go and plenty of time to do it, as long as there are the right kind of obsessives prepared to deal with the challenges. They play the music as though it is the best way of making sense of the world.

The Danish String Quartet clarify their energetic, confident curatorial commitment to the history and future of the string quartet – and to themselves as a long-term quartet – with their *Prism* project, on ECM New Series, where the group plans a series of five albums that may well become the best way of beginning a relationship with the beginning, middle and beginning of the end of string quartet music. It's an intelligent, inspiring sign – at last – of a fresh, contemplative and artistic way of approaching and illuminating the repertoire and making a modern sense of how the quartet travelled from when there was no such thing to where there is now an immense, moving history. Beethoven is to be the 'prism' through which they move between an early quartet and a later one.

The first in the series, *Prism I*, brilliantly introduced the concept, where they match, intellectually and pleasurably, one of Beethoven's dazzling, deathless late quartets with one of the fugues from Bach's *Well-Tempered Clavier* for harpsichord or organ – and eventually for Glenn Gould – that influenced Beethoven. It is in the same key as the Beethoven Quartet No. 12, E-flat major, and it was arranged – or re-composed – for four strings by Mozart, letting Bach pass through him, as he passed through Bach, learning how his mind worked, and learning about basic form, the science of composition, and the deep secrets of transferring feeling into music.

This close encounter with Bach occurred at about the same time Mozart was being motivated by Haydn to take a new approach to the format of the string quartet, the two things combining to revolutionise his thinking about the potential of the quartet. After that revolution, the revolution of Beethoven, taking the four-piece choral ideas of Bach – the very special arrangement of the harmony that changed so much for Mozart – as a basis for his idea of how the four quartet instruments could be felt to be singing, expressing much more than if there were mere words.

The third piece on each *Prism* will be a masterpiece chosen by the group that emerges out of the imaginative presence of the late Beethoven quartets – whether directly connected and inspired by, or radically disconnected – and these need to have some significant presence themselves to take their place between Bach and Beethoven. On *Prism I* the place is taken, with no weakening of magnificence, poetic intensity, doom or glamour, by Shostakovich's bleak, determined, ultimately profoundly silent final quartet, No. 15, the one he wrote in hospital as he was dying.

Putting the composers and their quartets in this new dramatic context, as part of one world, one setting, brings them alive, together in time; Bach elegantly sets up Shostakovich with a brief, knowing nod, seamlessly flowing into the late twentieth century, because of the many doors he opened and paths he created, and Beethoven celebrates the life and death of Shostakovich, his angry, tender quartet abruptly charging into view as soon as Shostakovich has uttered his final 'words', as though, come to think of it, he has the answer to the question Shostakovich was asking as he faded away, an answer he found while paying attention to Bach, who asked the very best questions.

The second *Prism* features another of the resplendent Bach fugues from *The Well-Tempered Clavier* and one more of Beethoven's secluded, late-period string quartets, the multi-movement No. 13, constantly shifting, sometimes abruptly, through wild moods, concluding with the immense, radical Great Fugue, which sets up the Fourteenth Quartet. The Great Fugue was originally separated from the work because of its unyielding complexity, its bizarre, revolutionary drive, the way it seemed to be literally breaking up the assumed coherence of classical language, which initially seemed to unbalance the whole quartet.

Beethoven pragmatically, if reluctantly, replaced it with something more cheerful, lighter and more down to earth, which can unbalance the quartet in a different way – leaving behind a sense of anticlimax, as the cryptic clues Beethoven leaves during the first five movements about the searing finale to come are not resolved. Played on its own as a complete piece, which the Great Fugue often is, means that it lacks the build-up that makes sense of all the transformative meta-drama that Beethoven fits into what was always meant to be a last movement, not so much as any sort of farewell, but as a gesture of the belief he now had in his own powers.

The DSQ naturally finish the Thirteenth with the Great Fugue, putting it in its rightful place, relishing its formidable technical challenges, responding effortlessly to Beethoven's instructions to play it 'somewhat free, somewhat scholarly'. They attack it with such grace and precision you can hear how some have considered the Great Fugue to be Beethoven's response to Bach's *The Art of Fugue*, the abstract creation of a grand puzzle that he leaves to others to clear up at a later date.

These pieces lead into and out of Schnittke's Third, his 1983 quartet, which quotes the Great Fugue as part of his summary of the art of the string quartet, and of art itself. Surrounded by masterpieces by Bach and Beethoven, it becomes clear, as it settles into the same magnificent space, how much an equivalent masterpiece his Third String Quartet is, in its own world, but with strange awareness of others. And also what an outstanding, revelatory album the Danish String Quartet have made, as though there can still be a point to the concept of the album, as a way of telling stories through collecting music material in a particular shape and passing it into the future. As is their intention with their *Prism*s, part of their art of discovery, reaching back in time and envisaging a way forward, Schnittke is elevated to the heights of Bach and Beethoven, and he in turn illuminates their subversive, intangible greatness with his.

On later *Prism*s the quartets that emerged from the helix of Bach and Beethoven and sharing the same tonal centre will be by Bartók, Mendelssohn and Webern. I hope, as they head towards 2060, and a very different, twenty-first-century normal, they make more than five of their *Prism*s, finding replacements for Beethoven as their prism, and at the moment they are the ensemble I dream of playing my lonely, brief string quartet, even if they see it as something that at best only really connects reality television with a promotional gimmick for this book.

If anyone asks me now what my favourite group is, I am likely to reply the Danish String Quartet, or maybe the German-based all-female Korean Esmé Quartet, formed in 2016. In early 2020, in a similar exploratory spirit to the DSQ, making their own history, discovering worlds within worlds, the Esmé Quartet put together on an album Beethoven's explosive and ethereal 1800 String Quartet No. 1 – the second he wrote, purposefully setting out from the shadows of Mozart and Haydn, ready to go all the way – with Frank Bridge's exquisitely contemplative 1904 *3 Novelletten for String Quartet*, Edwardian reserve already beginning to tip over into enigmatic otherness, and Unsuk Chin's febrile, inquisitive 1996 *ParaMetaString*, for string quartet with magnetic tape/sampler. One from the early nineteenth century, one from the early twentieth century, one from the verge of the twenty-first century, placed into a new abstract time, circling each other, interrogating each other, the form in endless transition.

A string quartet as my favourite group is a little disorientating for those expecting me to say retro-indie darlings Fontaines D.C., based on my youthful taste in post-punk from forty years ago, rather than my taste around the same time for Brian Eno's Obscure Record label, with its considered, tentative approach to a world that is never what it seems, where reality itself is often clearly one long wondrous, devious experiment.

PART EIGHT

The Obscure – Changing Direction

Cornelius Cardew *1964: 'Bear in mind that parts of the score may be devoid of direct musical relevance.'*

A couple of years after I had finished making the BBC documentary at the Royal Academy of Music, I started occasionally teaching students from the Academy composition department. Not in any way 'how to be a composer', but perhaps more 'how to be a listener', and even 'how to use music'. I did some talks about my listening experience on the border between classical and pop, where the likes of Yoko Ono, Brian Eno, John Cale and Terry Riley operated, simultaneously belonging to both the classical history and the pop history, making replenishing connections between the one and the other.

There was an ease with which certain musicians weaned on experimental music from classical or rock inhabited the two worlds, and introducing a new repertoire to the students was also a way for me to continue my learning about how music had moved from the historic sound of Mozart to the intermedia noise of Masami Akita's *Merzbow* – there was a definite map to be drawn that could connect the two across time, and the fact that the map needed to be continually updated and redrawn made it more fascinating.

I decided in one talk that I gave to concentrate on a composer who was becoming one of my favourites for how modern and out-of-the-blue original he was in the ways he merged sound, structure, emotion and instrumentation. For his strangeness, as well, and his influence, which, as is often the case, became way out of proportion to his direct impact on the mainstream.

I needed to see if having put Mozart and Webern together in one paragraph I could now put Mozart and Cornelius Cardew together in a book. Cardew had always been near the border of classical and pop, if only because he was working extensively during the 1960s, when genres were mutating, rock was progressing, classical was recovering from its serial and concrete outbursts, but it was those he influenced who explored territory the other side of the border more than he did. He was more underground, as a theorist, as a classical musician, and as a non-classical musician whose musical styles were the consequences of his political choices imagining a new form of radical folk music.

Before my time at the Academy I would have considered the musical beginnings of Cardew to have been the late 1950s, Cage, Stockhausen, the new New York sound artists, when he was one of the first English composers to seriously engage with the fast-developing post-war European avant-garde, but I could now begin my history of Cardew from at least 200 years before.

I had learned what happened to music between the death of Mozart of the First Viennese School (Haydn, Mozart, Beethoven and Schubert) and the birth of Webern of the Second Viennese School (Schoenberg, Webern and Berg) ninety-two years later in 1883, and then what happened to music between the birth of Anton Webern – beginning as a teenager at the turn of the century, full of yearning, post-romantic nineteenth-century Brahms, and then refining his music after the First World War into a concentrated essence of twentieth-century avant-garde spirit, serenely, radiantly inhabiting its own space, a completely different application of detail and intensity from Mozart, far less motivated than his one-time teacher Schoenberg to feel the need to compete in history with Beethoven – and the life of Cornelius Cardew, born in 1936, around the same time as Pauline Oliveros (1932), Yoko Ono (1933), Arvo Pärt, La Monte Young and Terry Riley (1935), Steve Reich and Harold Budd (1936), Jon Hassell and Philip Glass (1937) and Louis Andriessen (1939).

Cardew's life was short: he died in 1981, after classical music had entered and left its post-war, end-of-twentieth-century experimental phases, the acceptance, rejection, modification, alteration, diversion and extension of the pre-war serialism, *musique concrète*, event music, electroacoustic and minimalism, which flows into ambience, and at the same time, from other directions, pop and rock.

I numbered my talk, and structured it like a piece of music, turning it into a collage of information and interpretation that explained, if only to me, how certain changes had been made in music around the edges of classical music – and therefore to the history of classical music – before, during, and after the minimalism that pulsed, probed and patterned through the 1960s, and its abstract, sonic impact on what was essentially a very British combination of cerebral art, music, extreme, self-conscious whimsy and experimental tendencies emerging from the underground rock scene.

The following is based on a talk given to a composition class at the Royal Academy of Music using a soundtrack of music that played along with my presentation, materialising in no particular order, adding emphasis, irony or coincidence to the talk, presented as much as though it was performance art as a lecture.

- *Treatise* – Cornelius Cardew
- *The King of Denmark* – Morton Feldman
- *Fontana Mix* – John Cage
- *Sound Patterns* – Pauline Oliveros
- *Cyclotron* – Luc Ferrari
- 'European Son' – The Velvet Underground
- *Anthem for Keyboard Solo* – Wendy Carlos
- 'Fullness of Wind' – Brian Eno
- *Memories of You* – Cornelius Cardew
- *Autumn 60* – Cornelius Cardew
- 'Mind Holes' – Yoko Ono
- *The Well-Tuned Piano* (by La Monte Young, arranged for guitar) – Noël Akchoté
- *Half Past France* – John Cale
- *Christian Wolff in Cambridge* (by Morton Feldman) – Alvin Lucier
- *A Rainbow in Curved Air* – Terry Riley
- *Petra* – Maryanne Amacher
- 'A Thousand Ways' – Cabaret Voltaire
- *Swimming With the Stone Book* – Andrew Poppy
- *Furor* – Philip Cashian
- *Rhythmic Variations* – Daphne Oram
- *In a Landscape* – Peter Broderick
- *A Sky of Cloudless Sulphur* – Morton Subotnick
- '7:42' – Cluster
- 'Tanith' – Throbbing Gristle
- *For Aaron Copland* – Morton Feldman
- *Music for Strings and Interference* – Andrea Mazzariello

- *Toccata* – Sofia Gubaidulina
- 'The Robots' – The Bad Plus
- 'Chemistry' – Jon Hassell, Brian Eno
- *Harmonien* – Karlheinz Stockhausen
- *Aeolian Harp*; *The Banshee* – Henry Cowell
- *The Letter* – Harry Partch
- *Vision and Prayer* – Milton Babbitt
- 'I'm Glad' (1966 demo) – Captain Beefheart
- *Hill Runes* – Peter Maxwell Davies
- *Gougalon (Scenes from a Street Theater), VI. The Hunt for the Quack's Plait* – Unsuk Chin
- *Quest* – George Crumb
- *Afternoon of a Georgia Faun* – Anthony Braxton
- *Rain Dance Pt 1* – Derek Bailey
- *Forest Murmurs* – Franz Liszt
- *Atlas Ellipticals With Winter Music*, Electronic Version – John Cage
- *Awakening of a City* – Luigi Russolo
- *1, 2, 1-2-3-4* – Gavin Bryars
- Chaconne from Partita in D minor – Ferruccio Busoni/ J. S. Bach
- *Mahler Remixed 1* – Fennesz
- 'Flower' – Spontaneous Music Ensemble
- 'curvcaten' – Autechre
- *The Tides of Time* – Elisabeth Lutyens
- *Nothing is Real* ('Strawberry Fields Forever') – Alvin Lucier
- *For Morty* – Christian Wolff
- *Spectral Canon for Conlon Nancarrow* – James Tenney
- *December 1952* – Earle Brown
- *Scenario* – Helmut Lachenmann
- *Rrrrrr…*; *Ragtime-Waltz* – Mauricio Kagel
- *Dream* – John Cage
- *Ellis Island* – Meredith Monk
- *Seven Organism Study* – Charlemagne Palestine
- *Tilbury Pieces* – Christian Wolff
- *Water Gong* – Anna Lockwood
- 'N + R (Love is Friends)' – Cecil Taylor

All of this music is available on Spotify; perhaps this was my main point. Find this music. Listen to it, and to what the algorithms of

Spotify suggest you listen to next – who needs critics, experts, dreamers, researchers when you've got algorithms! Work out what happens next. What can you compose without repeating anything other than what cannot be anything other than a repeat that is an extension of this music?

The music, though, if only so the likes of me still have a function, needed some sort of introduction, a form of non-fiction romance, possibly along the lines of:

1. Morton Feldman said in 1967 that what was going on in England at that time was not a return to the past or a rebellion against it. He said it was a way of getting out of history.

2. A few thoughts on when musical transgression was being increasingly used as a form of protest...

3. Experimentalism as I am going to think of it in a period, say between 1965 and 1975, or between the late 1950s and the early 1970s, which was a compression of between the early twentieth century and three-quarters of the way through the century, was a messy series of encounters and performances, a shifting configuration of borderlines made and remade piece by piece, moment by moment. Borders and genres have been drawn and described to explore this period of music making in the margins, away from the mainstream, by scholars and writers, to organise it enough so that it can be controlled and to some extent explained. Here was a classic example of something that could not be controlled and did not want to be controlled, art and music that was fighting all sorts of control from within and without, being labelled as something. In this sense, at this time, the music I am going to call experimental was music that didn't, as such, belong anywhere – it was not rock or pop or jazz or classical or incidental – and to some extent became known as experimental even though some of it became labelled as rock or jazz or classical, for the sake of argument, for the sake of control.

4. Really, experimental music does not exist but is perversely – this music did not want to be named, did not exist to belong in the usual spaces and places – the name that has been passed onto certain sections of certain networks, associations that are so sparse and fragile that they would have escaped attention altogether if something had not been attributed to them.

5. One way of describing where this music we call experimental was at this moment in time of spontaneous music that was post-Cage and post-Coleman, and it could be heard in venues at the time, such as the very

formal Purcell Room, the rock-bound Roundhouse, the avant-garde ICA and the plush and posh Royal Albert Hall. This anarchic combination of places where the music would turn up shows how mixed-up this music was, able to fit anywhere, not yet sorted out and unmixed by those needing to put things in their place. It shows how things were moving in their own way, able to change shape to fit wherever, in the way that the music changed shape to fit wherever. There was no specific grouping. It was a time when the passing back and forwards between the so-called popular world and the so-called serious world was at its most vibrant and fluid. The results of this were all around – the idea that a pop group as well known as the Beatles absorbed avant-garde elements was a symbol of this state. The Beatles' most experimental songs came from their willingness to appropriate 1960s avant-garde traits, however. It's possible that the famous string glissandos linking the two parts of 'A Day in the Life' came from the opening of Xenakis's *Metastaséis* rather than the more obvious *Threnody to the Victims of Hiroshima* by Penderecki. Alex Ross definitely thought so. The other two major influences were Stockhausen – whose image appears on the cover of the *Sgt. Pepper* album – and Cage, whose chance methods inspired Lennon's *Revolution 9*. The influence worked both ways, of course. Cage later returned the favour. He based one of his pieces entirely around Beatles songs, confirming the idea that the fixed divisions between low and high culture were mutating and melting down. The best thinkers in music were committed by instinct to breaking down borders and responding to changes happening in all music, whether it was in soul or jazz or pop or classical, whether it was where Coltrane, Coleman and Davis were going, or where classical was, whether that was Stockhausen, Cage, La Monte Young, Terry Riley or Steve Reich. Low and high culture were merging inside the recording studio, the home of pop, where electronic instruments were also making novel connections between art and entertainment, spirit and flesh, and albums were evolving as original art works as much as commercially convenient collections of songs. During these years the lapping and overlapping and general curious interference between one area and another to create new areas of interest was intense and constant.

To some extent this was because of the urgent, general, myth-building peace-seeking opening of minds to possibility; a new level of intrigue about other states of mind and being, because of drugs; because of freedom-seeking post-war informality; because of a desire for change and action; and because of the effervescent convergence of scenes and minds. The mixing of high and low could have been a mere superficial, short-term flirtation, like third-stream jazz in the 1950s, or crossover classical at all times; but this was a progressive period of compulsive creative productivity – as though untethered, unclassifiable art and music could genuinely be a way of fighting chaos, violence, bigotry, sexism, racism, conservative conformism and mindless consumerism. Numerous factors contributed to this sudden outburst of new ideas which shared similar attitudes and approaches, whether they were notionally academic or commercial, black or white, American or European, ancient or modern, pop or classical, amplified or acoustic, serious or escapist. This combination of electronics and imagination, the emphasis on performance and on sheer sound and the philosophical idea of music making emerged as a positive social activity as the earth shifted under people's feet. Around this time you could look at La Monte Young, Terry Riley, Cornelius Cardew, Andrew Cyrille, the Mothers of Invention, the Art Ensemble of Chicago, Soft Machine, Sun-Ra, the Who, the Velvet Underground, King Crimson, and see like-minded musicians who were producing what could be called experimental music, music that did seem to be outside of history, even as it was embedded in the turmoil and acceleration of the 1960s, because of its combination of amplification, freedom, energy, the sung and the unsung, the need for explosive self-expression during a turbulent, challenging period. It might feature electric guitars, ensemble instruments, synthesisers or jazz instruments, a traditional score, or a new kind of graphic score, or a complete lack of a score. Essentially it was a mixed, mobile category of adventurous music and perhaps adventurous music is as good a label as experimental, or maybe it could be called expectant, or nebulous, or quite simply something else. A playlist of music from across this interweaving border-crossing period would include:

6. *In C* by Terry Riley, *In the Court of the Crimson King* by King Crimson, *The Marble Index* by Nico, *Soft Machine* by Soft Machine, *Variations IV* by John Cage, *The Black Saint and the Sinner Lady* by Charles Mingus, *Who's Next* by the Who – Terry Riley generously leaking into classic rock staples 'Baba O'Riley' and 'Won't Get Fooled Again' – *Sound Patterns* by Pauline Oliveros, *Monster Movie* by Can, *The Piper at the Gates of Dawn* by Pink Floyd, *Ascension* by John Coltrane, *Moondog* by Moondog, *Faust IV* by Faust, *Deluxe* by

Harmonia, *Silver Apples* by Silver Apples, Max Neuhaus's realisation of music by Cage, Stockhausen, Earle Brown and Morton Feldman on electronics and percussion, *The Parable of Arable Land* by Red Krayola – a free-form freak-out where psychedelia met tape manipulation – *Fixed Elsewhere* by Evan Parker, Derek Bailey and Han Bennink – each listen increasingly resolving into something closer to a musical composition those tempestuously brittle, battling slivers of sound that otherwise arrive pre-fractured in a thousand sizes, shapes and velocities (Bailey once said: 'Recording's fine if it wasn't for fucking records') – *Joy of a Toy* by Kevin Ayers and *White Light/White Heat* by the Velvet Underground.

7. John Cale studied with Cardew, became a member of La Monte Young's Theatre of Eternal Music, and was one of the founding members of the Velvet Underground. At the time it was noted that what was described as the pounding choral music of the Who and the Velvet Underground was called rock and was not just linked with but actually belonged in the same sound world as Terry Riley and La Monte Young.

8. John Cale's gestures towards early minimalism's experiments with sustained intonation featured in the amplified viola drones that propelled 'Heroin' and 'Venus in Furs' on the Velvet Underground's first album, and the startling crashing noise that interrupts the opening rhythmic pulse of 'European Son' (a straight 'borrowing' from La Monte Young's 1960 Fluxus piece *Poem for Table, Chairs, Benches, Etc.*), are certainly a direct transference of techniques from the contemporary 'avant-garde'. But at the heart of the five studio recordings and five live records making up the original group's legacy is, above all, an intensification, elaboration and amplification of rock's *own* most basic elements of repetitious pulse, overwhelming volume and electronic timbral affect. Repetition, and the formal possibilities of the loop or 'riff' was of course the ragged line joining together minimalism, Warholian pop, structural film and early rock in the mid-1960s.

9. *The Velvet Underground & Nico* and *White Light/White Heat* also asserted the potential for the mass-produced sounds of a Bo Diddley or the Crickets to drastically reconfigure the very sense of what an avant-garde in the latter half of the 1960s might actually be. Cale is a classical musician who warps the rock 'n' roll timeline, and it is with

the Velvet Underground, as with Kraftwerk, that you see a thriving hybrid of the formalities and training of classical – incorporating the very latest experiments – and the already existing new traditions of rock 'n' roll.

10. The categories were being jumbled up. At that time, and I am reducing a few years into one paragraph, within touching distance of each other, more apparently than now, if only to a very small minority of interests, there were Satie, Ives, Varèse, Schoenberg, alongside newer figures such as Babbitt, Berio, Cage, Ligeti and Cardew. The minimalists Reich, Young and Riley were materialising, leading to a rock zone that included Can, Velvet Underground, Faust, Gong, and there was Robert Wyatt, Henry Cow, Caravan, Spontaneous Music Ensemble and King Crimson. The disc jockey John Peel would play some Webern in the middle of all this, within reach of some early studio experiments, with the shape and hollowed-out density of reggae's rhythms, where the voice was replaced by the echo of time, stretching back to the beginning of time, a surreal Jamaican sound called dub, as if there was no doubt it all fitted together, if only by not fitting. There was Jimi Hendrix, rock but beyond rock, as in beyond borders, and Frank Zappa, whose debut album in 1966 was called *Freak Out* and although filed under rock, it came from Stravinsky and Varèse as much as doo-wop and political satire – tightly ordered, carefully orchestrated, with an anarchic playfulness that made it sound packed with creative and personal freedom.

11. The British free jazz was a European distillation of the American free jazz, some of which was rooted in civil-rights protest, where striving for political freedoms directly led to striving for musical freedom, some of it in revitalising charismatic religious worshipping, and some in the unfettered pursuit of sheer spontaneous beauty, the sort that composed music could dilute by being so prepared. The British political dimension was rooted in a very different sense of liberation, but still instilled the music, the energy, with a similar sense of charged, probing urgency. John Coltrane had said: 'I want to produce beautiful music, music that does things to people that they need. Music that will uplift and make them happy ... what music is to me – it's just another way of saying this is a big, beautiful universe we live in, that's been given to us, and here's an

example of just how magnificent and encompassing it is.' He said, 'I must keep experimenting,' and his experiments in generating pure musical originality were closer to where the British improvisers were – breaking free of abstract traditions and conventions for the sake of discovering new sound and new ways of collaborating. The free jazz of Evan Parker, Derek Bailey, Keith Tippett and John Stevens all the way across to the freedom-seeking avant-pop of Bowie and company via the extreme rock that defied standard British traditionalism and conservatism, where there was a general suspicion of the internationalism of modernism from the point of view of nationalism... in previous decades this sort of experimentation and absorption of other otherness was considered un-English, but in this new progressive climate, this did not matter; different sorts of musicians were enthusiastic about newness in whatever form it took, whatever their style was, so that a pop or jazz or folk or rock or classical musician was taking things from the outside world of art, music, literature, film, theatre and applying it to their music, creating unprecedented connections between styles that had never happened before – there was difference but also a sense of something being shared. The internationalism of neoclassicism was never a problem, of course, to the conservative critics, only the internationalism of the avant-garde and experimentation, because it threatened not only national spirit but also assumed order and hierarchy. It bent the rules, which could only lead to the destruction of standards.

12. The contact area among most of this new music was improvisation, from that place that was both post-Cage and post-Coleman, committed for a number of intellectual, emotional and creative reasons to a course of action where the outcome is unknown, discarding the composer in favour of sounds alone, even if the music was still composed, or rooted in music that had been composed. This move towards freedom meant that music that previously had been very much in one tradition or another was now in a new space – avant-garde classical music that highlighted performer freedom and improvisation met somewhere with the experimental jazz that has catapulted out of bebop into the wildest imaginings of Ornette Coleman... as though this was a clue to the new world, not just in music but in how to live, a whole new set of meanings could emerge, and also, as though the whole point

of making new music was to reinvent music from its very source, constantly somersaulting musical history, no tradition, no goals, no expectations... anything else was lazy, banal, useless... and if music represents who we are as human beings, it needs these subtle, difficult, neglected, awkward elements to be represented, otherwise music is a lie and a distortion.

13. Born in Gloucestershire in 1936 to a radical, bohemian and impoverished middle-class family, moving a few years later to Cornwall, where art and music flourished, Cornelius Cardew had a precocious musical talent. It was first nurtured as a chorister at Canterbury Cathedral, and later at King's School, Canterbury, which had evacuated to Cornwall during the Second World War. He learned to play the piano and the cello, took lessons in composition, became interested in the music of Schoenberg, and soon seemed destined for the Royal Academy of Music. His headmaster couldn't wait to get rid of him, describing him as 'one of the most difficult boys I ever knew – shy, reticent, introverted, self-centred, obnoxious to most people; lacking graciousness and humility ... everyone was glad when he left.' Some would say this approach to life never really changed – he could be playful, but very stern, even cold, these things a cover for a deeply melancholic temperament. He was also undeniably charismatic, and had the fluid, dominating characteristics of a cult leader, able to motivate people to enter areas of enterprise and exploration in ways very few others could have done. He, strangely, made strange things make complete sense, even if they involved a kind of craziness.

14. The Royal Academy in the 1950s was hardly a place for progressive spirits, and although Cardew proved an exceptional interpreter of Bach and Schubert, his natural dissidence soon led him to the European avant-garde – Webern, Boulez and Stockhausen – to which his contemporaries Susan Bradshaw and Richard Rodney Bennett were also drawn. Later, as a fellow and then a professor of composition at the Royal Academy, he put on the first UK performance of Boulez's *Structures* for two pianos at the Royal Academy and concerts by the leading avant-garde composers, including Terry Riley and Christian Woolf as well as Stockhausen and Cage. The mecca for music students in those days was Stockhausen's headquarters at the Darmstadt School, near Frankfurt in south-west Germany. The summer courses for new music started in 1946, a determined correction to the rejection of modern music by the Third Reich – initially concentrating on composers, including Stravinsky, Schoenberg and Bartók, who had been suppressed by the Nazis. By the early 1950s, a younger generation of post-war composers started to exert control, led by Boulez and Stockhausen with links to others through Europe including Berio, Henze, Kagel, Ligeti and Xenakis, Babbitt and Carter in America, as well as the New York School of Cage, Feldman, Earle Brown and Wolff. The consistent view among an otherwise disparate group of musicians and thinkers mythologised as the world centre of the avant-garde was that tonality was obsolete, and Stockhausen in particular dismissed the notion of regular beat because of its connection with the marching music favoured by the Nazis. Britten and Shostakovich were treated with derision and critic Tom Lubbock described the core members as the 'Darmstadt Headbangers'. In some ways the Darmstadt School, aggressively letting the past go, created its own marching music.

15. In 1957 Cardew won a scholarship to study at the electronic studio of Westdeutscher Rundfunk in Cologne, the public broadcasting institution, the first such studio in the world, with a reputation as 'the mother of all studios'. Initially, he threw himself into the machinery of electronic music with enthusiasm, becoming Stockhausen's protégé, lodging at his home, helping him with his musical production, creating works entirely for electronics, using a sine-wave generator to produce individual tones and recording them onto multichannel magnetic tapes. It was the beginning of music being opened up to all sounds – just as Babbitt was doing in America.

Stockhausen was only eight years older than Cardew, and together they visited the Brussels International Exhibition of 1958, and listened to the mysterious mathematical music composed by Varèse and Xenakis for the Philips stand that Le Corbusier had designed.

Cardew quickly became aware of what he saw as the Darmstadt School's inadequacies. He disliked Stockhausen's 'religious mania' and complained about having to say grace before meals – not at all the habit of an irreligious former choirboy. He came to see Stockhausen as a purveyor of gimmickry, and his pursuit, as he strived to reclaim German myths after they had been poisoned by the Nazis, of what could seem yet another form of nationalism. Cardew was ready for something new, and when a fresh wave of American composers, influenced by John Cage, arrived at Darmstadt to sample the European experience – and find it wanting – Cardew was excited by the more human alternative that they appeared to offer. In 1958, meeting David Tudor, Cage's pianist and pupil, was an important new influence, as well as Feldman, Wolff, Brown and Young. He would pay close attention to what these composers were doing in association with the pianist John Tilbury, and their connection meant that Tilbury would be playing Cage, Feldman, Wolff and also Cardew, which would make sense next to what the Americans were doing.

16. 'I like an auditorium,' Cage once said, 'where the audience do not sit tight together in straight rows, but are free to move around, and leave without embarrassment.'

17. If Schoenberg had freed the composer from composing tradition, John Cage, a pupil of Henry Cowell as well as Schoenberg, freed the composition from the composer. Cage blurred the distinction between what is music and what is not music, which inspired the English experimentalism that developed through Cardew and his associates. Cage promoted silence, altered instruments (1940), sounds of nature (1941), found sounds (1951), the very movements of the performer (1952), the collage of random noises (1952), and even the background noise of the auditorium (1952) to the status of music, preferring the narrow range of percussion instruments while pioneering electronic music in *Imaginary Landscape No. 1* (1939), and composing *Sonatas and Interludes* (1948) for 'prepared piano'. Still not content with his research into music and listening, in 1951 Cage also introduced indeterminacy and randomness into the process of making music, as demonstrated in *Concert for Piano and Orchestra* (1958). Cage's music could therefore be the random ('aleatoric') outcome of 'events' that were foreign to traditional music-making (in which the only events are the musicians playing their instruments based on the composer's score).

As in Zen meditation, Cage's pieces highlighted a higher dimension, which was not to be found in the minute details of the piece but in the experience of it. While Cage did not attempt to bridge the gap between performer and listener, he downplayed the composer (who specifies only the actions, not the music itself), increased the degrees of freedom of the performer (who produces the music), and, indirectly, demanded that the listener began to 'listen' in a different way, more integrated with the act of making music.

18. The composer Gavin Bryars considers the time he spent with John Cage to be one of the five most life-changing things that happened to him musically. In an interview I conducted with him at the Royal Academy, he told me:

'I met Cage first in 1966, around the time that I stopped playing improvised music. I was more and more interested in especially the work of people like Cage, Feldman and Wolff, that area of American composition which, certainly in Cage's case, removed all messages of taste and was trying to be as free as possible from ego. Now, that was completely the opposite of free music, where you're completely engaged in the moment and it's all about you.

'It's entirely subjective in the sense that it's you reacting at high speed. There's no time for reflection. You're working instinctively. I felt that, ultimately, the instincts that you have are some of the product of the various things that you already know, and you bring to that situation. To a certain extent, they're triggered and take different directions by the people you play with. But ultimately, it's constrained by its environment.

'By contrast, if I was sitting at home thinking about writing something, I could have ideas which would never occur to me in the heat of playing. I could think completely outside the framework of that little world. It seems to me that was one of the reasons why eventually I gave up playing improvised music. It was a philosophical debate. It was subjective versus objective, hot versus cool and so on and I chose the considered moment, not the chance decision. I gave myself time to think. Patience and time became the most important thing in my music.

'I was teaching at the time and I took a bunch of students with me to see the Merce Cunningham Dance Company with Cage in London. It was a place called the Saville Theatre, which I think is now the Odeon Shaftesbury Avenue. I went there and what I saw that night probably changed my life. Because what I saw and heard was just so staggeringly beautiful and so staggeringly extraordinary. The first thing was very simple. It was a piece called *Nocturne*, which is an ensemble piece. The music was from the five *Nocturnes* of Erik Satie, written in 1919, played by Cage on the piano.

'I remember one section, which is a dance solo. The choreography was by Merce. The design by Robert Rauschenberg. Merce was wearing a completely bright white outfit. The light was brightly white. There was a kind of screen at the front in which light was projected. Everything was just dazzlingly white.

'Beautiful, absolutely quiet music caught in limbo between being strange and wonderful. I thought it was just perfection. The second half was a piece called *Variations V*, where the stage was a kind of massive display — all sorts of objects, of plants, all kinds of things. In the pit there were three people, David Tudor and John Cage and Gordon Mumma, all operating electronic stuff.

'As the dancers moved there were all kinds of beats and sound going, very different kinds of groove, and as they moved across the stage, they went through photoelectric beams which would trigger things in the pit. They would touch all the objects on the stage, were hooked up to contact microphones. It was anarchy and I thought it was just absolutely sensational. These two things, this perfect order and the chaos were in the same world. I thought, *Well, that's what I want to do.*

'A friend and I went backstage. We met Cage, who was absolutely charming even though my friend was terribly pushy, and he just expressed interest in what we were doing. He took a couple of pieces of mine, which would actually appear in a collection of his, and then that was it while he was in London. But then in 1968 I went to Illinois because I'd been working in London accompanying dance classes, and I worked with an American dancer who was completing a postgraduate degree at the University of Illinois. I had done some music for him, and he said that if I could get out there and be with him I could do the piece.

'My aunt paid for my airfare. I flew to New York. I went to a concert and I bumped into Cage, who remembered me. I said I was going to the University of Illinois. It turned out that he was on a fellowship there for two years, so we'd see each other. When I was there, I was on a tourist visa, so I wasn't allowed to work. Cage knew I was running out of money, so he hired me as an assistant to work on the project he was working on out of his own pocket. He was incredibly generous.

'So I found myself in his company for a long period, working with him directly and indirectly. Being in his company or around him is extraordinarily special. One of the things I've always admired about Cage is that, even as students, people don't study with Cage. He doesn't really give lessons. You're in his company and you learn through him and what he does, rather like the kind of atelier system in Renaissance painting. You work in there as part of a process, and you're contributing some stuff and you know what's going on through that. You learn through doing.

'One of the great things about Cage is that nobody at all who has worked with Cage writes music sounds like him. There are no copycats, because he's not teaching music, he's teaching thinking, which can be applied to music, but also to many other things. If I had gone to mainland Europe and studied with Stockhausen or Boulez, there would be a right and a wrong way to write music, and it would have been their way. There wasn't that sense of dogma with Cage and that's a measure for me of his greatness as a teacher. He allowed you and encouraged you to be yourself, not to follow an established model. Once you've done that Cage thing, in a sense it is a Zen experience, moving through something and coming out the other side as a different person. You can go back and do whatever you like, and it will be very different from what it would have been without contact with Cage. Your mind is in a different place, that's the difference. Nothing can be the same again once Cage has shown you a kind of enlightenment, a different way of being, really. That's where having philosophy in the background made me appreciate that. If you're a copycat, you're not being yourself. Cage teaches you to be like him but to not be like him. If you truly copy his sensibility you cannot make music that is anything like his. It can only be like yours.'

19. Cornelius Cardew was, inevitably, soon questioning Cage as well as Stockhausen – not being a copycat at all, coming out of Cage into his own freedom. He took very literally the fact that to learn from him was to not be like him. No set text, so to speak, no new system, however flexible and unhindered, was going to satisfy him. As soon as he seemed comfortable with a new situation, he changed his mind. However free it wanted to make the composer, it introduced new rules. It was perhaps his way of maintaining necessary innocence, and never becoming settled, and he would

also incorporate and develop the sort of games, plans, ideas, systems, strategies, disruption, self-questioning and play he learned from Cage and Stockhausen – and the Dada-infused thoughts of disparate art collective Fluxus – in order to sustain a fresh approach. He turned his back on the sounds and noises and preparations of Cage and Stockhausen, but carried on their ideas about ideas, or at least the idea that the best art came about by having ideas about ideas. He started to have his own ideas about ideas.

20. Modern music, said Cardew, and he was talking about Cage and Stockhausen, as one of the few that got close to both, has become precious, isolated, restricted, leading socially, emotionally and musically to a kind of desert, where there is no life, and it has to be changed. To some extent he appeared to be agreeing with how conservative critics had reacted to the experimentalism of Cage and, indeed, Cardew.

21a. 'As a musician Cardew was outstanding because he was not only a good pianist but also a good improviser and I hired him to become my assistant in the late fifties and he worked with me for over three years. I gave him work to do, which I have never given to any other musician, which means to work with me on the score I was composing. He was one of the best examples that you can find among musicians because he was well informed about the latest theories of composition as well as being a performer.' (Stockhausen)

21b. 'I had been part of the "school of Stockhausen" from about 1956–60, working as Stockhausen's assistant and collaborating with him on a giant choral and orchestral work. From 1958–68 I was also part of the "school of Cage" and throughout the sixties I had energetically propagated, through broadcasts, concerts and articles in the press, the work of both composers. This was a bad thing and I will not offer excuses for it...' (Cornelius Cardew)

22. The role of popular music is capable of giving voice to radical political views, the plight of the oppressed, and the desire for social change. Avant-garde music, by contrast, is often thought to prioritise the pursuit of new technical or conceptual territory over issues of human and social concern. Yet throughout the activist 1960s many avant-garde musicians were convinced to a fault that aesthetic experiment and social progressiveness made natural bedfellows.

23. Fascinated with music as sound, with the human response to different sounds, and with the difficulty of exactly notating their production, Cardew explained, circa 1960, when taxed with his lack of interest in politics, that he was really interested only in 'noise'. This would change.

24. Cardew came to believe, John Tilbury says, that it was only 'through the spontaneous generation of sounds in freely improvised music' that music could aspire to a sourceless and transient autonomy, the ambition of his friend Morton Feldman. As a result, the manuscript of his first major work, *Treatise*, looks more like an artwork than sheet music – a 'graphic score' – with wavy lines and exuberant diagrams providing only the most approximate guide to what needs to be played. Based on Cardew's reading of Ludwig Wittgenstein's one book-length philosophical work *Tractatus Logico-Philosophicus*, it was composed between 1963 and 1967, and some parts of it were broadcast without much heat or immediate consequence on the Third Programme, which would be replaced by Radio 3 in 1967. People tended to puzzle about music that seemed to be a puzzle and seemed to lack the one thing music should contain: music. Cardew later described it as 'an attempt to escape from the performance rigidities of serial music and to encourage improvisation among avant-garde musicians'. He'd had an idea about an idea.

25. In 1968 a young critic and early music specialist Michael Nyman was sent out by the *New Statesman* to review a new work by Cornelius Cardew, an obscure British maverick. He did hear music as much as an idea.

26. What struck Nyman about Cardew's latest piece, *The Great Learning*, was how different the musical language was from that of the complex, fretting and angsty European avant-garde. 'It was very gentle, it was very modest, it wasn't trying to make a huge technical statement,' Nyman once explained. 'It wasn't threatening, the musical material was limited, modest, minimal. It certainly was a new land of music that should be given a title.'

27. This title itself – and a new set of borders, alas – was coined by Nyman in 1968, in his review of Cardew and his minimal musical material. Minimalism, as he described it, not perhaps thinking it would stick, and become sticky, and stickier, re-examined melody and functional harmony and after the rootless severity of serialism and the irregular interference of *musique concrète* re-established pitch as a primary structural element in music. But this wasn't simply a direct, sentimental return to an eighteenth- or nineteenth-century sound world – the composer John White, a colleague of Cardew and Nyman, observed: 'The analogy that comes to mind is very much that Zen thing about people who acquire enlightenment leading a perfectly normal life again, but a couple of millimetres off the ground, and so it's possible to listen to Rimsky-Korsakov's *Scheherazade* now with absolute delight, because I listen to it as though it had no prehistory. Whereas before Cardew there was an obsessive toffee-like consistency in musical history that glued everything into place in a rather soggy, unadventurous way.'

28. In the late 1960s and early 1970s British experimental composers were embracing compositional techniques that lay beyond the boundaries of modernism and broke the avant-garde thread that could be traced back to the Renaissance. One of those techniques, now an archetypal characteristic of postmodernism, and then hip-hop, was that of appropriation. Composers, one way or another, looked to the established repertoire for source material and made pre-existing material their own, often through experimental processes like chance operations, multiplicity and repetition. The devotion to repetition was something shared across all these borders, and some say that the new experimental German rock groups' appreciation of repetition inspired by the pioneering post-war avant-gardists was as much motivated by an American group of GIs called the Monks, who in the mid-1960s, as a kind of anti-Beatles blast, performed in Germany a viciously rhythmic, brutally stripped-back proto-punk music that could sound as bespoke and abstract as any *musique concrète*. *Musique concrète* is one of the original sources of the ideas of sampling and of electronic music, and one of the innovators, Pierre Schaeffer, was a pioneer not only in the way he technologically created loops using microphones, record players and tape recorders, and assembled found sounds, but also, like many electronic-music practitioners, he was not as such a musician.

29. Inspired by his interest in jazz (he was never a jazz performer), Cardew moved ever further in the late 1960s towards free improvisation, joining the guitarist Keith Rowe and the drummer Eddie Prévost in the post-jazz post-everything ensemble AMM (what that stands for – it stood for something – was a secret). Their sounds were ever evolving, members came and went. Cardew stayed for a few years. Using electronic and acoustic instruments AMM pushed the limits of sound and collective creativity. Collectivity was crucial for AMM, and in everything Cardew did. This was music that was composed on the spot, with equal input from all participants. AMM was an experiment not just in musical improvisation but also in radical democracy, in the spontaneous articulation of collective determination. For any of these projects to work, the artists essentially had to approach music composition with a socialist attitude. Scratch Orchestra built on this radical democratic perspective, and also began to include Cardew's inventive visual scores and an open-door policy to membership. The group grew out of one of Cardew's teaching jobs, although the ethos was to challenge the role of the teacher. His philosophy on band leadership was sometimes described as 'reverse seniority'. It was a time when in the art schools and progressive music schools the role of teacher and pupil was more one of interplay and collaboration than a one-sided ordering of events and tasks.

30. Founding member Eddie Prévost wrote about the astonishingly non-referential AMM: 'The prevalent notions of musical theory, practice, hierarchy and structure (thematic reference, jumping-off points – for example the "head" arrangements from which improvisation lifted off – and even the relatively informal criteria of the then "free jazz" movement) were replaced by the creation of, and engagement with, a sound world in which there was not even a formal beginning and ending. And, from its first raucous explosions, it knew too that it was not only speaking in a new language but that it was talking about things not perceived in any music the member-musicians had heard elsewhere.'

31. AMM did find a small niche at the time at the quirky, zonked fringes of the 1960s UK rock scene, playing shows with the Syd Barrett-led Pink Floyd and often seen, in a total misunderstanding, as a psychedelic curiosity, enough so that even Paul McCartney attended a 1966 show. He sat quietly throughout and afterwards when asked his opinion said, 'It went on too long.'

32. AMM took improvisation into very abstract realms, consisting of long, dense shifting drones with unusual sounds competing for space and time. It was music that said: we are here, these are our traditions, the decisions we are making; we know what to do next. Sometimes it refers to this or that modern classical sound or this or that avant-garde jazz style, but mostly it comes from entirely within the movement of their own mind, imagining that there is no music elsewhere to refer to, let alone music that is labelled and stuck into genres. Therefore they were not a free-jazz ensemble or a contemporary classical group or actually any sort of hybrid, which caused confusion among audience and to some extent themselves. Their debut album, *AMMMMusic*, was released in America on Elektra – home of the Doors and Love – in an attempt to reach the new psychedelic youth market; if nothing else it was fucking weird, and therefore surely it could blow your mind. In the same spirit, at about the same time, Island released 1968's six-movement *Karyōbin* by the loose-limbed free-music collective Spontaneous Music Ensemble in the UK. The music was full of life, but the sort of life most people wouldn't recognise as life: it didn't seem to have a heart, or perhaps actually had too many hearts. SME were drummer John Stevens's fascinated response to AMM, but with a more identifiable jazz rhythm section – soon the lingering traces of jazz would dissolve, replaced by one of those musical inventions that has never been titled, so as adventurously spectacular as it was, it remained on the outside of the outside. One of its main concepts was an extremely open, leaderless aspect where a premium was placed on careful and considered listening on the part of the musicians. Saxophonist Evan Parker observed that SME's leader John Stevens had two basic rules: (1) if you can't hear another musician, you're playing too loud, and (2) if the music you're producing doesn't regularly relate to what you're hearing others create, why be in the group? This led to the development of what would jocularly become known as 'insect improv' – music that tended to be very quiet, very intense, arrhythmic, and by and large atonal. Much of it was static at the same time as it feverishly circled itself and headed out in new directions before tracking back.

At its best, the performances achieved a telepathic unity that was both an intense, emotional comment on the imaginative energy of American free jazz, and a series of answers, or questions, inspired by AMM.

Titles on the AMM debut included 'In the Realm of Nothing Whatsoever', 'Silence' and 'What is there in uselessness to cause you distress'. It still sounds vibrant and strange.

33. Prévost wrote the thirteen aphorisms that constituted the original AMM sleeve text. Examples: 'III: The reason for playing is to find out what I want to play' and 'V: Every noise has a note'. As Prévost acknowledged, you can go only so far in explaining with words something that goes beyond the rational.

34. In 1968, as revolutionary ideas spread through institutions of higher education, notably art schools, Cardew was asked to set up an experimental music workshop at Morley College, an adult-education centre in south London where Gustav Holst had taught fifty years before. His class attracted eager musical amateurs, curious students from the Royal Academy and avant-garde enthusiasts from the visual arts, many of whom came together in the large experimental group Scratch Orchestra, created under Cardew's inspiration and leadership in 1969 along with Howard Skempton and Michael Parsons. Scratch, really, because here was an orchestra starting from scratch every time they performed – always beginning in innocence of what had come before and what was about to come, and even what music actually is. Among those who passed through the orchestra were Brian Eno, Michael Nyman and David Bedford, who in 1974 would fastidiously orchestrate his friend Mike Oldfield's *Tubular Bells*, as though hunting down its classical sources – and worked in the late 1960s and early 1970s with pop artists such as Kevin Ayers, who as a combination of showman, storyteller and vagrant virtuoso was like a shadowy, sadder, and in other ways jollier David Bowie.

35. The Scratch Orchestra, as with many pop groups of the late 1960s where art school met rock music, and art met pop, attracted people who wanted to 'do their own thing' and were an explicit example of how a new kind of music was benefiting from being part of art colleges and their concentration on the visual arts. There was a greater sense of play in fine art, which started to influence the making and performance of music. While some Scratch members concentrated hard to perform challenging large-scale works such as *The Great Learning*, others showed up and crawled around the performing space dressed in Christmas-tree lights.

36. Some of the group played carefully worked-out modern classical pieces, while others, the non-musical, would play along, but play whatever they wanted, either as a sincere if crude attempt to play music and eagerly join in or just to disrupt proceedings as part of an assault on elitism. This freedom eventually led to divisions among the members, in terms of working out what piece they were playing, the music they were starting from even as they were starting from scratch: musicians wanted to use their musical training, non-musicians wanted to retain unorthodox notation, where the scores could be read, as plain non-musical instructions, by non-musicians. The poetic scores Cardew developed contained suggestions, recommendations, images, prompts, visuals, and could be interpreted imaginatively, adding to the possibilities of what music was.

37. Internally, Scratch members turned on each other, not just in musical combat but also as an ideological cell. Anarchic subgroups wanted more freedom in musical performance, older members were tired of waiting for their chance to organise 'proper' concerts, and most of the orchestra resented the common outside assumption that the Scratch Orchestra was Cardew's group, which seemed to contradict its central leaderless premise and be in opposition to the democratic, socially harmonious thinking that initially drove the group forward.

38. It is true that, as the orchestra's 'name' composer, Cardew brought BBC recordings and other exposure that would not have been offered even to other known composers associated with the orchestra. Cardew wore this role lightly, wanting to be colleague rather than guru, and when he ran into trouble, it was as an ordinary member of the orchestra. At one performance sponsored by the Arts Council he interpreted a text piece that read 'Act as obscenely as possible until the authorities intervene', by drawing nudes and four-letter words on toilet paper. Cardew was successful: he was arrested, the concert closed, and the event became national news. The avant-garde generally makes the mainstream news for some

perceived act of mischief, of naughtiness, as if any ideological sting could be removed from this very un-British pursuit by turning the participants into village idiots or basic fools. Daft rather than dangerous. Silly rather than subversive. Spike Milligan rather than John Cage.

39. Morton Feldman referred to AMM as being the moral centre of new music in England.

40. The International Carnival of Experimental Sound, which occurred at London's Roundhouse in August 1972, was a product of this time, somewhere between hippy happening and academic conference, both dedicated to wondering, and wandering, aloud. It was intended by its promoter, the idealistic American Harvey Matusow, to convene anti-establishment musicians, performance artists, film makers and dancers under the theme 'Myth, Magic, Madness and Mysticism'. John Cage participated, and AMM were one of around 300 billed artists including David Bedford and Lol Coxhill, naked cellist Charlotte Moorman, composers David Rosenboom, Michel Waisvisz, John White and Christopher Hobbs, Sweden's Fylkingen collective, Spontaneous Music Ensemble, the Taj Mahal Travellers and the Portsmouth Sinfonia – another grand, ecstatically eccentric experimental folly, a tickle rather than a scratch, somewhere between art and nonsense, where non-musicians or less-than-competent musicians playing an instrument they were not familiar with enthusiastically tackled classical classics, demolishing, or perhaps honouring Beethoven with a woozy combination of affection, aggression and exultation.

41. Cardew was a deeply moral thinker, intensely, even belligerently engaged in a constant struggle for truth in art, life, the political world and himself. In face of all criticism and mockery, he stood with his personal, political and aesthetic beliefs against British musical conservatism, the avant-garde establishment, and finally, the experimentalism he himself had created. In 1974, after his Marxist passions had spun off into severe Maoism, he turned against, or outgrew, his radical period, concerned that the music was too difficult or unattractive to be listened to by a working-class audience, and that ultimately it was perceived as being silly, ugly and pointless. He didn't want to feel detached from everyday people's lives and aspirations, and he rejected his earlier modernist style, deciding it was a distraction. Modern music seemed elitist, opaque, even violent, and often an unfunny joke, and Cardew started to struggle with how to reach the 'masses' with a socially valuable music committed to creating a better society.

42. 'I have discontinued composing music in an avant-garde idiom for a number of reasons; the exclusiveness of the avant-garde, its fragmentation, its indifference to the real situation in the world today, its individualistic outlook and not least its class character (the other characteristics are virtually products of this).' (Cornelius Cardew)

43. His early musical training as a pianist and his days as a star performer of Bach spiralled back into his next music. Searching for a setting that helped him understand the purpose of music as something useful and enlightening for a potentially wider audience, he distilled complex ideas into simple, accessible, almost innocent piano pieces that were laced with motifs and methods inherited from Bach, Poulenc, Debussy, Bartók, Satie, Stravinsky and Gershwin. He turned to the past to find a new music, to recover a naivety before idealistic overthinking had ruptured it, where music was not explicitly packed inside capricious ideological intentions. Those looking for absolute confirmation of the link between Debussy and Bill Evans can find it on a 1975 album, *Four Principles on Northern Ireland and other pieces*. This features compositions based on the revolutionary songs of different countries as one way to achieve music that was both universal and populist, even as it stayed firmly in the margins. Even without knowing the motivation for the music, it is moving, soulful music. The music – as was always the case with Cardew's expressive piano performances – was beautiful and Arcadian, whatever the political thinking behind it. The political thinking perhaps gave what was at this point almost conventional-sounding music a radiant honesty that lifts it above being simply decorative, but what was making the music so compelling was perhaps more his amorphous munificent instincts as a musician and human being.

44. '. . . if the word "romantic" should be rescued from the whimsical sentimentalists, it is so that we could then apply it, properly, to Cornelius Cardew: a real fountain of breathtakingly adventurous music. Immense skill and moral discipline, yes, but at the heart of the matter is simply the actual beauty of these hauntingly evocative soundscapes.' (Robert Wyatt)

45. Cardew was killed at the age of forty-five by a hit-and-run driver in Leyton, east London, not far from his home. He was not the type to trigger a revolution, however revolutionary his thinking, but his political engagement and public displays of disaffection with the establishment elite led to him being monitored by MI5, to the extent of perhaps having his phone tapped, and there were dark conspiratorial rumours about the absurd, violent suddenness of his death.

His later, demure, less experimentally fired work might have been his final decision on the purpose and processes of music, and his music, or he might have been in transition to another, unknown approach, or even been on the verge of returning with less rigid expectations to some of the inspiring avant-garde enterprise, which had a greater, more generous reach than he might have realised.

46. One sign of how English experimental music had become so active and activist in this period, with Cardew as central, commanding – but genial and/or stand-offish – curator and catalyst, was a week-long festival in 1973 showcasing its developing, if secretive presence during the month-long Europalia international arts festival, which celebrated Britain's entry into the European Economic Community, presenting a comprehensive survey of British culture. This uncompromising outsider music was a shock to those expecting 'serious', more familiar English music to involve the grand symphony orchestra and the normal uplifting nationalism of Elgar, Britten and Vaughan Williams, or even to show off the alternative home glories of the Beatles and the Kinks, and certainly nothing that seemed to be a cerebral soundtrack to philosophical questions about the nature of music, an abnormal nationalism. By the time Britain was heading to an inglorious exit from the European Union in 2020 there was little sign of this peculiarly English experimental music, possibly because beyond this surprise exhibition of a peculiarly English experimentalism that was intellectually challenging but often charming and attractive – generally excused, or redirected and tamed, as being a matter of good old-fashioned English eccentricity – there was very little sign of it ever moving into the mainstream classical organisations and media. The loss of Cardew himself contributed to a dissolving of momentum. The experimental sensibility he personified and championed, giving it an English charge and a humanist boldness, which was somewhere between ideological and magical, had to find other routes where it could materialise.

47. Those that passed through Cardew's idiosyncratic, determined, ultimately amiable and obliging thinking, exposed to his ideas, which were social, philosophical and political as well as musical, were encouraged to be musical participants and performers even if they were not musicians. Morton Feldman, when he was a believer, said that anything that happens in English music will happen because of Cardew, and it sort of came true. Brian Eno was one of his most visible students, or listeners, or converts, an obsessive, bustling artist-musician who would make music using artistic techniques, and definitely those techniques in terms of structuring music using grids, technology, numbers, chance, instructions, whimsy and even fantasy. Ideas that were defined or refined in the mind of Cardew, after his eventually reluctant exposure to the thinking of Cage and Stockhausen, passed through Eno into a wider world that Cardew never managed to reach.

48. Eno became a very public manifestation of one of the many directions that could be taken from how Cardew thought about music, made it, questioned it, and then started over again. This direction was based around how ideas, reasoning, values and mood were as important in music as any musical technique and knowledge, and also a consideration about what music is for, and why it is needed, and what happens to it once it is made. These ideas and tenets didn't belong in any particular musical genre or history but could be used to refresh and extend the range of music that was both classical and popular.

49. Eno was first sighted by most people in feathery glam drag attending to various silver machines, apparently stripped of any artistic dignity, as a part of the hyper-dramatic pop collective Roxy Music – the artist very definitely not wanting to put a distance between himself and a potential audience. It very soon became apparent that here was a conceptualist as much as an instrumentalist and even though he acted in performance as though he was some sort of eccentric

keyboard player, his main instrument was the recording studio and the machines connected inside it. And having been involved in the sort of art colleges where to study was to work in collaboration with other interesting artistic thinkers, he wanted to make things happen, and this involved organising things, making connections and essentially inventing possibilities. British experimentalism, which seemed a by-product of classic island-incubated, single-minded eccentricity, was also linked to the idea of the zealous inventor, sizing up certain problems that needed sorting out, many of which few others would notice, and dreaming up ways to find a solution.

50. Brian Eno's Obscure Records – a series of experimental works that because of Eno, with authentic, seductive pop-star credentials, soon to be working in Berlin with David Bowie on lusciously idiosyncratic rock music that started from scratch, and as an invisible member of the weird world music of Talking Heads, seemed connected to playful pop glam as much as they did to the avant-garde frontiers of classical music. Eno used the label he described as 'a research and development department' to distribute information and manifestos about the kind of music that had intrigued and inspired him as an artist as much as a (non) musician and, basically, fan. It was music, and thinking about music that existed in some fluid, provisional and alluring zone between what elsewhere was easily filed as either pop or classical. It literally set out to save intangible, problematic music from obscurity, and although this music, and the musicians involved, came from the English and American experimental scenes that had been running in parallel during the 1960s and early 1970s, it was packaged and presented as though it was somewhere between pop music and progressive rock. You would be interested in it if you were interested in John Cale, Can, Robert Wyatt, King Crimson and Lou Reed, and a certain sort of stripped-back and noisy music turning up in downtown New York, where bands with art on their minds as much as noise had names like Television and poetically minded singers christened themselves Richard Hell.

51. Obscure Records had an independent attitude embedded in the paradoxically traditional and utopian commitment of avant-garde

and/or experimental musicians to the music itself, not any commercial potential, and it was definitely an influence on the punk independent labels that would soon be starting – labels such as New Hormones and Factory of Manchester, Fast Product of Edinburgh, Zoo Records of Liverpool and Rough Trade of London. It wasn't obvious at the time, but the spirit of do-it-yourself, of a playful, experimental and often artistic attitude to rock and pop that was part of the original punk spirit and would be more obviously expressed in the more adventurously structured and eclectic post-punk, and its close cousin electronic music, emerges from what in a classical sense could be claimed as the three major post-serial musical developments after the Second World War – John Cage, American minimalism and English experimentalism. One of the portals that this spirit passed through – elsewhere you could say it passed through Kraftwerk, the Velvet Underground, Iggy and the Stooges and the playful, ruffled glam intellectualism of Sparks, Roxy Music and David Bowie – was Obscure Records.

52. In this story, which in some ways began with Mozart, Satie, Webern and Miles Davis, from Cornelius Cardew we move to Obscure, a label dedicated to apprehensive, disjointed experimental music founded by a pop star known by one name. This is one of the things that happened to and because of Cornelius Cardew.

53. The Obscure label in full consisted of ten albums, which someone somewhere should be making available once more in an extraordinary container designed by a descendant of Marcel Duchamp. The label was manufactured and distributed by Island Records, and it makes sense that the music almost didn't appear. It still had to go through various music-industry processes and filters, with music so in a world of its own that there was absolutely no business logic in releasing it. Island Records specialised in hard-to-sell, trend-setting Jamaican music, the increasingly internationalist reggae of Bob Marley, evocative, off-balance folk from Fairport Convention to John Martyn and Nick Drake, and a certain kind of wayward but exciting progressive English rock music from Traffic and King Crimson to Roxy Music – it missed out on punk, and early post-punk, more or less making up for that lapse by signing the Slits. Later, along with the eventual motivational involvement of producer Brian Eno, it encouraged to accidental and/or inevitable international glory a rough and eager Irish post-punk band called U2.

The label's head Chris Blackwell only half listened to the music on the potential first Obscure album while he was on a phone call. He was the kind of show-running record-company boss who placed his trust in others – if they believed enough, he gave them a chance, and Eno had sold the idea as if he more than believed – but he was also the kind of record-company boss who could dismiss a project if you betrayed that trust or he thought you'd strayed too far from reason. He supported the most adventurous music, but there were limits even to his receptive, wide-ranging, sometimes gambling philanthropy.

The piece being played was by Gavin Bryars: *Jesus' Blood Never Failed Me Yet*. As he talked on the phone he became vaguely aware of a piece of music that didn't seem to be going anywhere; just some rough-sounding old guy sadly singing to himself. The needle might even have been stuck. He stayed with it, paying a little more attention just in case the music was too far out even for a rock label that favoured the far out, and eventually something changed, some recognisable, almost soothing strings arrived – when he was growing up he had listened to classical music with his parents, and enough stirred in him to know that everything was okay, this wasn't Brian Eno being too weird to be true. It was Brian Eno being exactly weird enough to perhaps be on to something. Ultimately, without Island sponsoring these ten records, and letting them be like this, in this order, featuring this thinking, even if they had appeared in some form in other settings, there would be a huge hole in the history of experimental music.

Obscure No. 1
Gavin Bryars, *The Sinking of the Titanic/Jesus' Blood Never Failed Me Yet*, 1975
Obscure No. 2
Christopher Hobbs, John Adams and Gavin Bryars, *Ensemble Pieces*, 1975
Obscure No. 3
Brian Eno, *Discreet Music*, 1975

Obscure No. 4
David Toop and Max Eastley, *New and Rediscovered Musical Instruments*, 1975
Obscure No. 5
Jan Steele and John Cage, *Voices and Instruments*, 1976
Obscure No. 6
Michael Nyman, *Decay Music*, 1976
Obscure No. 7
Penguin Café Orchestra, *Music from the Penguin Café*, 1976.
Obscure No. 8
John White and Gavin Bryars, *Machine Music*, 1978
Obscure No. 9
Tom Phillips, Gavin Bryars and Fred Orton, *Irma* – an opera, 1978
Obscure No. 10
Harold Budd, *The Pavilion of Dreams*, 1978

54. Gavin Bryars of Obscure No. 1 also worked in corridors, halls, rooms, bars, studios, cupboards and ghost spaces near to and often very close to Cornelius Cardew, and is another direction that the music and thinking of Cardew took, even though it had nothing directly to do with him. Bryars could start to think about how different a piece of music could be to some extent, because Cardew had clarified in a musical way Cage's proposal that music could be anything. The 'could be anything' didn't necessarily mean it needed to be random, chaotic, extremely repetitive, theoretical, absurd, playful, soundless, soulless. It could be astonishingly, uniquely beautiful and soulful, and tell a story in a most direct, and simultaneously indirect, way. It could be wildly weird and, somehow, in its own world, where it went along with the rules that had been made up, however unlikely, completely conventional.

55. Gavin Bryars was born in Goole, a small, extremely unassuming town in East Yorkshire nineteen miles south of York, in between Huddersfield and Hull, forty-five miles from the North Sea – a place, he told me in an interview I conducted one afternoon in front of some students from the composition department of the Royal Academy, 'Where nothing happens. Everything bypasses Goole. You never go there, you only pass through it. Time stands still. Like in my music, so you can see an influence there.'

His mother was an amateur cellist, his father a baritone singer who sang in the local church and in amateur operatic societies and died when he was nine. 'Singing and death. Another influence on my temperament. Apart from that, I had a very happy childhood.' His uncle was the church organist, 'Quite a decent pianist. Hearing music in church from an early age is another influence.' He was the fourth of five children, none of the others doing anything musical.

'I never planned to be a musician, that's the first thing. Although I did start to play the piano when I was about four or five. My mother gave me lessons initially, then I went to a piano teacher in the town and eventually to the music teacher at the grammar school where I went, who was a very good pianist. I would play the piano at my mother's Sunday school, so lots of sight-reading of hymns and making things up as kids marched in the playground. I got interested in jazz by the time I was in my teens. The reality of life in Goole was there was no real big musical life, and you start seeking it out. You made things happen, one way or another, even if just through music and books. At my school, when I started doing my A levels, I didn't do music. Originally I was doing geography, French, English and general studies. At the end of my first term, by Christmas, I had got no marks at all in any geography assignment and the geography teacher sent me to the headmaster with the idea that it was probably a good idea if I didn't spend the next year and a half wasting my time, and I agreed. I thought, *Great, I've now only got three subjects, the rest have got four*, but the headmaster said, "Sorry, Bryars, but you're going to have to do another subject," so, "Okay, Sir, I suppose I'll do music then." I did music because I was lousy at geography. I had a lot of one-to-one time with a very interesting music teacher, a very interesting man with very liberal ideas. In the late 1950s he was telling me about John Cage's silent *4′ 33″* and Erik Satie's famously long piece *Vexations*, and you wouldn't have got that in many academies at the time, let alone local schools.'

Somehow, there was a logic in hearing about this experimental music after experiencing local playing and singing in a small, echoey church on slow-moving Sundays that seemed lost in time. Wherever his music goes, you can hear an elevating, abstracted intertwining of church and experiment, with a bracing rinse of Yorkshire stoicism and a constant sense of the broken time of 1950s trio jazz.

Bryars got decent grades at A level, enough to take him to Sheffield University, where he ended up studying philosophy, because to study music meant also having to study French, 'and I was by nature lazy.' At Sheffield he encountered the double bass, something he has loved the sound of since hearing jazz records, following the basslines on songs instead of the words.

'In the music department at Sheffield, there happened to be a battered old double bass in the corner, rather broken and the strings were loose and so on, but I asked if it was all right if I fixed it up.' He was drawn to the fact that the bass is the fundamental thing out of which, musically, everything else is built, and by the end of the 1950s had discovered Ornette Coleman, and therefore the bass playing of Charlie Haden, and Scott LaFaro, especially when he accompanied the pianist Bill Evans.

Bryars was totally fascinated by how in the Bill Evans trio, Evans, LaFaro and drummer Motian agreed so confidently on a time centre, they never needed to be slavish about it — they danced around it, toyed with it, embellished it, dismissed it, all the time maintaining dead-centre time, and never sacrificing swing. LaFaro's fundamentally beautiful sound, powerful but delicate, playing the foundation and yet finding the poetry, helping Evans and never hindering him, always knowing what his next thought was going to be, analytical and theoretical, was a huge influence on Bryars's bass playing, which in turn had an impact on his compositions. LaFaro himself was a fan of Webern — so that Webern's appreciation of tonality as someone breaking free of it passed through the bass outer space of LaFaro into Bryars.

'By the time I was in my second year, I was already working as a professional bass player, playing double bass in a nightclub in Chesterfield. I eventually played in a lot of local clubs, accompanying visiting light entertainers from the telly, like Des O'Connor, which was another good discipline. I was a very poor philosophy student, however much studying made me think, just about scraping a degree. I'm a really terrible role model when it comes to academic life. Although, strangely enough, much later I had a professorship. I've had three honorary doctorates and so on. I examine Ph.Ds. Yet my total music qualifications are A-level music — pass, grade eight piano — merit; that's it. You can get through life by being a total failure, but it takes a bit longer, that's all. Patience will get you there in the end.

'The people that I started working with as a bass player playing more seriously just happened to be two people who became very, very good and very famous in their own world in terms of jazz and improvised music, Derek Bailey the guitarist, almost *the* guitarist, one of the greatest free players of all time, and Tony Oxley, an extraordinary drummer, who would play with Georgie Fame, Kenny Wheeler, John Surman and eventually free-music giants like Anthony Braxton and Cecil Taylor. Tony and Derek were living in Sheffield playing in local pubs and they asked me to play with them because, of course, I happened to have a double bass. I played with them regularly and we developed a whole kind of language together by working constantly for a number of years, and so that became my life. I was essentially a jazz-improvising music player playing in the most remarkable company.'

With Bailey and Oxley he formed an almost mythical experimental trio called the Joseph Holbrooke Trio, playing incredibly complex, challenging music in a hidden North of England, so genuinely obscure at the time it was as if they never actually existed – especially considering how established in their own individual worlds the trio became. 'One of the advantages of being in the North, you're very isolated and consequently we developed techniques and ideas among ourselves without any reference to what was going on in the world outside us. It appears that, historically, this trio was one of the first groups in the UK to play free music, but we didn't know that. We were following our instincts and seeing where that led.'

What did you think you were doing?

'We just thought we're just playing together – and one thing led to another, as it often does. First, we started playing this kind of harmonic jazz related to Bill Evans, Coltrane, Eric Dolphy, Miles Davis, that kind of world, some modal jazz. I wasn't totally interested in modal jazz, more a kind of dramatic jazz. We moved into playing freer and so on because it seemed a natural thing to do. There's a transitional time when we did play sort of freely, but on established things, and then we completely freed ourselves. It was all about listening, really. You had to hear everything that was happening in order to make the next move.'

He stopped playing the double bass and improvised music in 1966 after one particular gig in London, putting his bass in his case and not getting it out for seventeen years. He turned from playing to composition.

56. Bryars's mysterious and yet matter-of-fact *The Sinking of the Titanic* is a hell of a place to start trying music that comes from a classical world even as it transcends conventions and imagines new forms of musical performance. It is one of the great musical events of the twentieth century.

It's a piece of imaginative documentary conceptual art presented as a beautifully evocative musical composition, as well as a kind of melancholy fantasy, conceived in 1969 as a provisional outline for improvisation within a certain framework, basically a series of written instructions and imaginings, and developed over the next few years. It was first recorded in 1975, scored for small orchestra and tape, fitting onto one twenty-something-minutes side of a vinyl album, with two additional versions featuring additional musical sources and choirs released in 1990 and 2007, eventually fitting onto one whole seventy-odd-minute compact disc.

57. 'I was working in an art college and there was a group of students who were not doing either painting or sculpture or printmaking. They were doing other things, or setting up events, different sorts of artistic things that didn't really have names. They were under attack by some of the more conservative element within the college because it seemed too vague. They put on an exhibition of this intangible work and they asked those members of staff who were sympathetic if they might put something in themselves.

'I filled in a single-page typescript, a written sketch for a possible musical piece called *Sinking of the Titanic*. The *Titanic*, among all maritime disasters, was the one for me that stood out. There was an aura about it, the idea it was a maiden voyage, the class distinction on the vessel between the poor and the privileged. And of course the musicians playing to the bitter end as it sank. When I first wrote it the *Titanic* had been a mysterious legendary object somewhere in the North Atlantic, about five and a half miles deep, several hundred miles from the coast of Nova Scotia. It wasn't yet a film, a large part of history. We've seen how it has become more famous, if you like. People go down there to examine the wreck. The whole idea of the *Titanic* has changed. It became a reality. Back then, it was less real. Almost mythical. It had to be imagined.

'The idea of putting writing on the wall, language-based artworks, the relationship of language to art, was something which was around at that time in the fine arts and in conceptual art with groups like Art and Language. There was Joseph Kosuth, who did these rigorous texts which you would read, and which were about questioning your perception of reality; it was words in place of image, and in my case words in place of music. Obviously, as someone who had studied philosophy, this appealed to me – a sense of asking not so much how you made art, but why? Could you just describe a work of art rather than actually make it, and have a similar effect on the senses? This way of working concerned itself with art's philosophical nature.

'They were not beautiful artworks; they were a way of producing meaning. And in my text, I described what a musical composition called *The Sinking of the Titanic* might be. My idea was that by reading the text, it could trigger your imagination to work out what the piece might sound like. Therefore in some ways the piece existed in your memory. I didn't envisage it going any further than that. It's rather like if you listen to a radio play, you can envisage the space in which things are happening. Your mind does more work; that's why radio is so great.

'Then eventually, about three years later, in 1972, there was a concert organiser who used to put on a lot of experimental music concerts who said he'd like to put on an evening of my work at the Queen Elizabeth Hall. "This thing of yours, this Titanic thing," "he said, "it's all very well what it might sound like in somebody's head. But what would it sound like if you played it in a public space?"

'Responding to this, I actually had to realise the idea and produce something which made audible sense, which was to make it a concrete version or project. The danger is that the version that I made, people think of it being the definitive piece. It is, but it's only a version of the piece. The record is a version of the piece. There are only ever versions of the piece. The text is a version, a live performance is a version, a recording is a version. By its very nature, because of what it is about, it must always be a mystery. It must never settle.'

58. Bryars was responding to stories that some of the working musicians on the doomed ocean liner *Titanic* were performing a hymn resembling 'Amazing Grace' – possibly the nineteenth-century 'Nearer, My God,

to Thee' – as the ship sank, and also to the details of the momentous voyage, other tunes the band had played during the journey, the initial collision, subsequent sinking, and the desperate, anguished search for survivors. He uses music to reflect on music being played in the face of imminent death by those precariously placed on a gigantic, solid mechanical structure noisily collapsing as it's swallowed by a raging, unforgiving ocean, forever submerged in 1912 and all the anniversaries, auctions, films, theories and documentaries to come.

59. 'The legend had it that the ship's musicians continued to play as the ship started to sink. There was no record of them having stopped playing. My imagination was they were still playing as they went under the water. My idea was the music then continues under the water. Of course it doesn't, but that's a minor detail. The idea of the music is somehow transformed by moving into this different acoustic space. Water is four times more efficient as a sound-production medium than air. Sound travels a long way: witness the songs of whales and dolphins. The sonic element within the sea is incredible. All those things, one thing led to another. The first thing I had to do was find out who were the musicians. It turned out there were eight of them.'

What did they play?

'There were two pianos, three violins, two cellos and a bass player. I even got pictures of them. I even knew their names. I worked out where on the ship they'd played, which rooms had pianos, and so on. When the ship was sinking, was it possible for the pianist to have played at the end? I worked out if they could have got pianos onto the top deck. There's a moment where electricity failed, so the service lifts couldn't do it. I thought it's very unlikely that they would have carried a piano at that moment onto the deck, very unlikely. I left pianos out of the initial instrumentation.'

60. Bryars wonders what happens to music if it was played under water, as it descends to the seabed, drifting through splintered debris and underwater denseness, imagining and generating new acoustic qualities and subterranean celestial sonic properties. It is a graceful, elegantly understated, powerfully down-to-earth, otherworldly work of art that turns sensation, experience, lost moments in time, the oceanic murkiness of history, the uncanny power of religious music, unbelievable terror and nobility, fear and bravery, violence and shock, faith and oblivion into a ghostly, extreme example of how sound itself has a ghostly, potentially immortal quality, either intensified or compromised when transformed into arranged music.

61. Bryars's eloquent composition, always intended to be open, to be unfinished, has never resolved since it was first thought of and written down, performed and recalibrated numerous times in a variety of settings, expanding and contracting in length and consistency over the years, as if it is always being lapped by icy waves, surrounded by submerged perils, at the mercy of surreal elements, but keeps travelling, through new realities, into different states of being. Bryars develops new ways and new sonic perspectives to reflect the big and small, private and intimate sounds of those final, frantic, eternal and sea-stunned, death-struck seconds, and process its disorientating historical immensity and desperate human strangeness. A final end is perpetually postponed, reflecting how the *Titanic* musicians played under the most demanding of conditions to keep hope alive, and embrace the inevitable in their own time. The last piece of music they ever hear – and the last piece many others hear, as they fight the most punishing and desperate of elements – is the one they play, as if it might lead them to safety, or at least keep them company as darkness takes them.

62. Bryars has reacted attentively and unsentimentally to the continuing commercial and cultural – and his own personal – interest in the sinking. Revelatory new pieces of research material and discoveries continually invest the piece with greater detail, more essential inner truth, keeping alive a piece about death and loss. Music about memory adapts as new memories are revealed and selected, and music reacting to history continues to unfold just as history unfolds, bursts of activity and speculation contrasting with periods of inactivity and consolidation. This way of changing a composition, of introducing new elements, seems a hint of the future of music, where compositions do not need to be fixed, but react to, or are altered, by new circumstances, forms of chance, communal mood and general environmental, technological and emotional distortion. Beginning as a piece of text about what a musical composition sounded like in your imagination meant the music could always adapt to new circumstances, as though even as a piece of music that could be played and heard, it was still an idea about what a piece of music sounded like in your imagination.

63. It was originally released in 1975 as Obscure No. 1, the opening example of the label's fluid, overlapping music, made where the cause and effect of minimalism and improvisation is intersected by thoughtful, serious composers and performers operating outside of the established classical systems.

'It was an advantage that as an unofficial group of like-minded thinkers and musicians we were outsiders, well beyond the pale as far as more conventional things like the BBC, the Arts Council and the established orchestras were concerned. It meant that we didn't get the usual institutional commissions and we never wrote for established organisations. We didn't write for standard orchestras, choirs, string quartets, because those worlds were not available within the pool of us experimental composers. What you had was the instruments that you each played in your group, a group that had come together quite informally, and that became your ensemble. You wrote for the instruments you had access to. You wrote for your group, your peers, those in league with your ideas. Then of course, the aim was to make that ensemble you ended up with, whatever accidental combination of instruments, sound like the most natural ensemble in the world, as though you had intended it all along. You invented your own musical history, your own musical language.'

The label set out to save fugitive, problematic music from obscurity, and indeed rescued *The Sinking of the Titanic* from sinking without trace. Bryars's record contained the *Titanic* work on one side, and another profound, haunted approach to the sound of memory, and the memory of sound, to darkness, and defiance, to litany, found sound and imagined consequences, on the other side, *Jesus' Blood Never Failed Me Yet*, featuring an anonymous rendition of a fragment of a song that Bryars came across looking through the rushes of a documentary about some tramps in London. This was the piece that convinced Island's Chris Blackwell to support Obscure — it would later be performed by one of Island's greatest signings, Tom Waits.

Jesus' Blood came from the mutable, accumulative repetition of minimalism, but it also incorporated traditional approaches to the making of music, so that it is a combination of the deeply unusual and hypnotic, and the strangely familiar and even comforting, the structurally idiosyncratic and the harmonically orthodox – an unhurried, unthreatening blend of the spiritual and the soothing that Bryars would develop as his music became formally connected to a more stable classical history.

'I remember all through this tape, the audio from a film about people living rough in Elephant and Castle, Waterloo and so on, it was just people talking, mostly drunk and sometimes singing folk songs, pop songs, all kinds of things, all a bit messy. Then right in the middle of this, it was just twenty-six seconds, a few frames, this particular person sang this little bit of a song, and I was just really struck by how he did it. It turned out that he was the only one out of all the down-and-outs they met who didn't drink. He was simply an old man, probably in his late seventies, really down on his luck. It's only the audio, so we don't know what he looked like. We know nothing about him. Once I started making the piece, we did go back to try and find him – to see if anyone remembered, and nobody did. The people who made the film on the camera remembered roughly what he looked like. He was very frail, had a bit of a beard. He thought he didn't have long to live. That's all that remains of him, just that fragment of him singing. What struck me was, (a), there was a musicality in his voice, and (b), he sang beautifully in tune and it happened to be in tune with the piano of my neighbour on the floor below, so I could use that and sketch out a simple harmonic accompaniment. The phrase ended by implication that it could begin again, and we were doing a lot of things in those days with tape and repetition. Listening to him, it seemed obvious to loop him, to extend it, so that he kept singing, whoever he was, wherever he was. Now in a way he has found a place to be. There's something about that old man singing that still touches me very much, and I must have heard that fragment thousands and thousands of times.'

64. This music, the sinking and the singing, the *Titanic* and the tramp, two extremes of loneliness, one paying attention to a momentous event in history, one to a truly obscure, ghostly moment, encouraged Eno to make his impractical label concept a reality, which it became for a dreamlike three years, a cultured, studious, uncategorisable counterpoint to the punk and post-punk music happening nearby, obliquely sharing a spirit of adventure and resistance. The label took its blissful leave with the gorgeous, profound prettiness of *The*

Pavilion of Dreams by Harold Budd, another place where Cardew, after, and resisting, where Cage and Stockhausen had travelled, influenced others who were making their own space and time without copying what he had done.

Of all the composers in the Obscure series, John Adams turned out to be one of the most famous — becoming one of the leading brand names of minimalism. Mostly known for his epic postmodern opera production, he filtered his perceptive sense of musical history, reaching back centuries through a processing sensibility that included the diligent English experimentalism and flowering American minimalism that had been collected by Obscure. This filtering of wider musical history through his knowledge of post-war experimentation became a system that enabled him to introduce a soft modernism to a wider audience. It was Gavin Bryars that introduced him to Eno and the label. Adams once told me in an interview, again in front of Royal Academy Composition students:

'You might wonder what the career choice of a composer would be whose first album comes out on a label called Obscure! I'd studied on the East Coast at Harvard, studying serialism as the rock revolution and flower power was in full flow. Webern and Boulez seemed very bloodless to me, and I needed to get away from all this very reductive, belligerent information, this severe seriousness. I'd been given John Cage's book *Silence* by my parents, and it all seemed very Californian, much more open and spiritual-seeming, so I drove all the way to San Francisco, seeking salvation from the serialists. My first job when I got to California was in a warehouse on the waterfront and I unloaded containers of clothes that were made in the Orient. I did that and it was nice and undemanding. I got a real dose of what it was like to be a blue-collar worker, and I was also beginning to ask serious questions about what I was going to do in life. Music, yes, but in what capacity?

'Then, by pure chance, I got a phone call from a friend who said he'd heard about a job opening at this very small school, the San Francisco Conservatory of Music, which at the time was housed in a former home for unwed mothers. It was a really charming building with little cupids above the doorway. The practice rooms had originally been little studio bedrooms for the mothers and their babies. I taught there for ten years, and one of my jobs was to run the contemporary music ensemble. I was always looking for music that was new and provocative and also could be played by these students who were not – they were not really able like Royal Academy of Music students. A lot of these kids could barely play their instruments. I knew about what Cornelius Cardew was doing in England and became interested in that whole area. Somebody, I think it was composer Robert Ashley, said, "Well, you should be in touch with this English composer Gavin Bryars." Of course I had never heard of him.

'He was about my age, maybe a couple of years older. I started a correspondence with him. This is in the days long before emails. They were letters that took a week to get to London, and a week to get back. He sent me what was called the Experimental Music Catalogue, which he edited, which was a publisher for this area of English music, and along with Brian Eno, they'd all gone to art school together and they had become part of the scandalous orchestra, the Portsmouth Sinfonia, one of the great events in Western culture. The rule was you could play in it as long as you didn't play an instrument that you knew. I felt a sort of kindred spirit and the bad-boy side of my personality was drawn to that idea.

'I invited Gavin over in 1974, and it was the first time he ever came to the United States, and we did a concert of English experimental music with the New Music Ensemble at the San Francisco Conservatory. I actually ended up conducting the American premiere of *Jesus' Blood Never Failed Me Yet* and *The Sinking of the Titanic*. Gavin introduced them himself. We also played pieces by John White and Christopher Hobbs, so it was very Obscure Records. We asked Cornelius Cardew to write a piece. I don't think I paid him any money because I couldn't. He was in his extremely intense Chinese communist phase, and he wrote us a piece and arranged it for the students called *Wild Lilies Bloom Red as Flame*, based on a Chinese melody.

'Cardew actually did come and visit the Conservatory. He was on a trip in the United States. I organised an event, and he was going to come and talk. He was two hours late because he had gone to an anti-war demonstration. Almost everybody was gone by the time he appeared. He was very serious, and it was very difficult to engage in casual conversation with him.

'I did this piece called *American Standard*, which was a reimagining of the hymn in the style of the English experimentalists. It was very simple and could be played by anybody, influenced by Cardew's anti-elitist idea with the Scratch Orchestra, of writing music that could be played by performers with limited technical abilities. It included a section called *Christian Zeal and Activity*, which had a tape recording of an evangelical minister telling the story of Jesus and the man with the withered hand. I looped the phrase, "Why would Jesus have been drawn to a withered hand?" There was quite a thing for building pieces around the voice of preachers — Steve Reich, obviously, with *It's Gonna Rain*, and later David Byrne and Brian Eno on *My Life in the Bush of Ghosts*.

Gavin sent a copy of the tape to Brian Eno and I ended up being on Obscure records, the second one, produced by Brian Eno.'

One thing led to another, including, for Eno, producing the biggest rock bands of the end of the twentieth century, and, for Adams, time spent first as the contemporary adviser to the San Francisco Symphony Orchestra, and then between 1979 and 1985 as their composer-in-residence, establishing his reputation with *Harmonium* and *Harmonielehre*, and in 2003 succeeding Pierre Boulez in the Richard and Barbara Debs Composer's Chair at New York's Carnegie Hall.

65. As an intellectually mobile loner, scene-setter, systems lover, obstinate rebel, techno-prophet, sensual philosopher, courteous progressive, close listener, gentle heretic, sound planner, adviser, explorer, oblique plagiarist, pedant and slick conceptual salesman, and as a devoted fan of the new, undrab and surprising, wherever it fell between John Cage and Little Richard, Duchamp and doo-wop, Mondrian and Moog, Brian Eno busily/bossily remade and remodelled pop music during the 1970s. He looked at and heard what the Velvet Underground, Holger Czukay of Can, Steve Reich, the Who had done, and went forth and multiplied. Eno created an atmosphere and helped determine what the history of electronic music was between the avant-garde laboratories of the 1950s and the laptop pop of the twenty-first century. He discovered that pop music was where you could be the kind of artist he wanted to be.

66. For listeners at the time, those curious about what was out there beyond rock and pop, Obscure was an amazing place from which to start searching other musical territories, inspiring a time-slip into thoughtful, probing music by composers and theorists such as Bryars, Michael Nyman, John Cage, John Adams and Budd. Once you made it that far and came across such inspiring and different approaches to composition and musical history, to what music was for, and how far it could go in rejecting cliché, creating surprise, and refreshing itself, it was easy to slip further and further out into wilder realms. It was an education, but was produced as though it was pleasure.

67. The title track of Brian Eno's own contribution to the series, *Discreet Music*, was a precise yet random, many-minuted sequence of treated, processed tones, seamless but blurred around the edges, rather than a strict, propulsive parade of traditional notes naturally performed. It took up one side of the album. It was instrumental, and displayed a strange knowledge, but was not inaccessible, and even as it could seem solemn, sombre, even unsexy, there was something completely enthralling about it. It referred to and refined techniques and immersive sounds from La Monte Young's non-developmental drone, Tony Conrad's reiteration, Terry Riley's ritualism, Miles's pared-back purity, where much of the action was in the pauses between phrases, and Steve Reich's layered, stalled minimalism, but was recorded with a rock producer's ear for dynamics and atmosphere and an enthusiast's knowledge of progressive-minded German electronic music. Eno stole a lot, and then brilliantly disguised it as his own, which in itself was a metaphor for the entire history of music since Bach, or, if you come from another direction, since the Velvet Underground.

68. *Discreet Music* became the unofficial first, insinuating stirrings of the suggestively slow, lingering ambient genre, so that what to some extent had risen out of classical music, and the tonal, speculative response of cerebral 1960s romantics to the abrasive confrontation of serialism and *musique concrète*, escaped such deadening classification, and generated new routes and positive hybrids.

The second side of the record was a three-part suite that helped propose baroque-era church musician Johann Pachelbel's Canon in D major as the original source of ambient music. It was written possibly for his mentee Johann Bach's (J. S. Bach's father) wedding in 1694, more likely for just the kind of ordinary domestic function Telemann's *Table Music* was designed for, and after being rediscovered in the 1920s, it became a wedding-ceremony favourite, a little less used than 'Here Comes the Bride'.

Numerous pop songs, including 'Let It Be', 'No Woman No Cry', 'I Should Be So Lucky', 'Go West', 'Streets of London', 'All Together Now' and 'Don't Look Back in Anger' were influenced by the structure, chord sequence and mood of the work, and pop artists from Procol Harum to Aerosmith, Coolio, Green Day, Spiritualised, Avril Lavigne, the Spice Girls and Maroon 5 have made good use of it. Pop producer Pete Waterman of Stock, Aitken and Waterman, whose biggest hits all appropriated the canon's magnetic two-bar bass pattern and repeated melody, called Pachelbel 'the godfather of pop'. Haydn borrowed it for his Second String Quartet, so it also takes a small part in the origins of the string quartet, and Mozart picks it up from Haydn, slipping the melody into his Twenty-Third Piano Concerto, on its way through to a wider musical history.

As an act of devotion to the concept of copying and adapting existing works – or vandalism, at least to how the canon's simplistically helpful musical codes was being abused – Eno mournfully transformed it, reshaped it, deviantly recovering its unsullied ancient beauty through the application of various algorithms, with Gavin Bryars arranging and conducting a musical accompaniment performed by what was called the Cockpit Ensemble. Eno randomly chose the titles for the first and third parts, 'Fullness of Wind' and 'Brutal Ardour', from the sleeve notes to his favourite recording of the piece – demonstrating his use of chance in all elements of a composition – and he encouraged his A&R man at Island, the writer Richard Williams, to do something similar for the untitled second piece. His choice was 'French Catalogues'.

69. In 1975, Eno, roaming through the limitless landscape of his idle thoughts, drifting backwards and forwards between foreground and background, between musicianship and non-musicianship, between listening and non-listening, between purpose and no purpose, minding his own business, happened to be putting on tape some atmospheric backdrops for film maker Malcolm Le Grice to work against as he created images for a Fripp & Eno live show. He slowed down the sound he was creating to half speed, just to see what it sounded like.

He liked it; he liked what was left of the sound; there seemed more and yet less; he left it as it was; he liked the way the music faded in and faded out, as if the listener had chanced upon an endless process, as if the listener had found a small part of something that was going on anyway, all the time, somewhere, somehow, and was hearing a small part of the small part, and other sounds were just out of earshot, but you felt that there was something else going on, so far away, so close, and in between the so far away and the so close was *Discreet Music*.

70. Erik Satie saw – or felt – a way that music could melt into pure natural sound, and his resolutely irresolute 'furniture music' – which extended the range of Telemann's baroque examination of how music might be used, his *Table Music* – also anticipated a world where music proudly, cloudily functioned in the background, behind life, under thought, around the back of action, making him the father of muzak. Satie's instructions, incidentally, as to how to play some of his lovely, lonely piano music have the ring of Eno's instructions, taken as much from art as from conventional notation – 'with amazement', 'don't leave', 'with great kindness', 'more intimately', 'don't be proud' – and make him the father of Fluxus, of ambient and of situationism.

71. It was as if Satie was gently liberating musicians from centuries of layered conventions regarding the formal and literal transferring of notation into music. Cage clarified structure, either with sounds or silence, time and motion, and in the 1940s he was making music that sounded as if it had been influenced by Eno. La Monte Young drew a straight line and followed it, absolutely as far as he absolutely could. Reich would stretch a single chord out for a matter of minutes. Glass was not so much a minimalist as a late-blooming romantic who could match diabolical patience with a remarkable sense of tonality. Eno pieced all these fragments together to create his own set of fragments, from the point of view of someone who could hear inside the Velvet Underground the way the guitars were down-tuned in deference to what Cale's viola was built to do, something that suited Reed's spare, unreadable voice, and which gave everything a squelched, slightly squashed sound with plenty of sustain.

72. As far as the pop fan was concerned, largely unaware of the classical and conceptual, droning precedents, Eno turned music down so

you could barely hear it, and he slowed music down so it barely moved. The turning the volume down happened when he was ill in bed and was unable to move and adjust the volume when some music was playing very softly, almost too softly to be heard. He had the choice of either concentrating hard so that he could make out the music, pushing everything else out of his mind, or just letting the music play almost out of reach in the background, as if in the distance, pushing the sound almost out of the way. Both reactions had their consolations. He made music that required close attention, or absolutely none at all, or somewhere in the middle.

He turned down the heat, reduced the tension, settled down, sort of stopped music up to the point where it would never appear to stop. The funny thing, although no one laughed, was that although the music seemed featureless, emptied, almost ruined, and it seemed to some bland and pointless, and it had been produced as drily and as scientifically as process music often is, it was quite beautiful. Actually, it was lovely. This perhaps is why the ambience of Eno, the music where he concentrated on concentrating a lack of concentration into a single musical universe, has travelled a lot further than you might have imagined it would at the time. Whatever happens to the world, there seems to be a place for it.

73. *Discreet Music* seemed like a kind of Enovelty, Eno being Eno, on the mad side of art and the self-satisfied clever-clever side of pop, and one that, if anything, came out of the past rather than the future, one that would never really take off. It never occurred to those of us loving this record, the sleeve it came in, the Obscure label Eno had released it on, that this shaped, shapeless music would permeate and saturate the future world. That it could really become the sound of the world around us. It seemed like a practical joke, or an indulgent doodle, or what Eno did on his holidays.

74. The glowing *Discreet* was the most explicitly glamorous of the radiant Obscure ten, not just because it was highbrow pin-up Eno, of Roxy, Bowie's modern mentor, but because it was clearly predicting with such force, considering how delicate and non-committal it seemed, a whole new set of possibly endless musical futures.

75. And then in 1978, Village People had a hit with 'YMCA', and punk
rock had made a lot of noise and advanced into post-punk, and the
self-trending Brian Eno deliberately elsewhere made an album that
was somewhere between documentary and dream, between rigid
and random, between quiet and quieter. Fans of 'YMCA' and/or
the Clash who heard the record might have complained that it
had no rhythm, no melody, that it was austere and unemotional,
cold and boring, and it wasn't clear where it began or ended. They
would not be able to choose a favourite track from '1/1', '2/1', '1/2',
'2/2', which all seemed to blur into each other.

76. *Music for Airports* was defined by Eno as *Ambient 1 – Discreet* must
have been Ambient zero, even less than zero – and to some extent it
was conceived as an aid for those with a fear of flying, or certainly a
fear of crashing, or perhaps just a feeling of anxiety about whether
they will ever see their luggage again, something to be piped over
the intercoms at airports. It was a simple, sophisticated opposition
to the traditional industrial idea of muzak, which seemed to ignore
or deflate the senses. Eno's muzak was a form of background music
that not only created a kind of aural cushion, an unfolding hint
of bliss in the day-to-day distance, but that also subtly lifted the
spirits.

77. Eno said that he was interested in the Borgesian idea that you could
invent a world in reverse by inventing the artefacts that ought to be
in it first. You think what kind of music would be in that world –
in this case, background music made as art – then you make the
music and the world forms itself around the music.

78. Eventually *Music for Airports* would actually be piped through
the intercom in various airports, and a few fans of 'YMCA' might
have found themselves tapping a toe or thinking something fresh
and amazing as they wandered through a terminal at LaGuardia
New York, aware but not aware that in the daydreaming distance
'2/2' is bringing the gift of music to holidaymakers.

79. The New York music ensemble Bang on a Can said of *Music for
Airports*:
      'The unique factor about Eno's work was that although it could
and can exist in the background of everyday life, it is music that
carries a potency and integrity that goes far beyond the incidental.

It's music that is carefully, beautifully, brilliantly constructed and its compositional techniques rival the most intricate of symphonies.'

80. Bang on a Can produced a live instrumental version of the four pieces, and Eno has humbly said that their interpretation moved him to tears. Husband-and-wife artists Lou Reed and Laurie Anderson heard it performed live and they said it was heartbreaking. Without thinking, or rather, with thinking, Eno had composed a piece of music that is all at once flat and multidimensional, barren and detailed, near and far, music and sound, feeling and unfeeling, spiritual and vacant, real and unreal, mundane and magical.

81. The music seems to have been around for ever, and yet to be appearing for the first time as you hear it — Eno's ambient music consistently creates this illusion that he has simply plucked sound out of the air, fully formed, fully shaped, like he has just captured a piece of nature and transformed it into sound. This is, say, a snowflake, that is a raindrop, a leaf, a feeling, a memory before there's anything to remember.

82. Somehow, for music that seems so static, so trapped in time, so framed, it seems different every time you hear it. It's as if, when the music is resting, stored away, it is still changing shape, changing texture. It is always on the move, before you hear it, as you hear it, after you hear it.

83. It's about Eno being down to earth and ridiculously exotic, extremely charming and rather strange. It's about the places you've been, the places you think you've been, the places you'll never get to go to. It's about time before time and time after time. It's classical music liberated by the pop idea that sound doesn't have to be so deliberately cut off from the natural and technological noises and commotion of the world. A music that had been devised as lacking narrative structure now had a kind of narrative structure — or not, depending how the listener felt at the time.

84. You are on your own. That's something you often feel with Eno's ambient work. Only you have ever heard this music, it was meant for you, it is up to you what you make of it, and there is no one around to help.

85. It is as though Eno resolved to draw the world in sound. In the course of his ambient years — which eventually became his 'app'

years in the twenty-first century, with his truly endless, and beginning-less, Reflection app, perpetual music reacting to the timing, attention and environment of the listener – he populated a space with images of provinces, kingdoms, mountain ranges, bays, ships, cathedrals, metal keys, swimming pools, invisible cars, trees, valleys, islands, fish, rooms, instruments, heavenly bodies, horses and people. Eventually, he starts to notice that this patient labyrinth of lines reproduces the image of his own face. Lurking in the shadows, the shadow of Cornelius Cardew.

86. Gavin Bryars's record contained elements that meant it could be classified as ambient, or electronic, or even experimental rock, and it can be seen as a continuation of work from the early, middle and later twentieth century, from Webern to Ligeti, but was really none of that. It was truly in a world of its own, and yet completely gripping, and for all its spectacular, spectral otherness, deeply accessible. It didn't obviously suggest ways forward like *Discreet Music*, but didn't shut down possibilities – it would just take longer to work out, and to absorb, in terms of what it proposed about how to write a piece of music as a response to feelings, history, consciousness, spirit, technique and technical knowledge. Much of the multimedia sound art, the immersive installations, the abstract musical theatre, which in the second decade of the twenty-first century is more likely to be nominated for the Turner Prize for contemporary art than the Mercury Prize for music – such as Elizabeth Price's video *The Woolworths Choir of 1979* – is rooted in Bryars, with his roots in Cage, Art and Language and Cornelius Cardew, with their roots in Duchamp and Satie, with their roots in the East, magic and the mind, and the focused darkness and aimless lightness beyond.

87. *Titanic* was so powerfully distinct, almost psychedelically anomalous, it instantly emphasised that the label was no gimmick, no trivial rock-star indulgence, and Obscure became a series of philosophical blueprints for much of what was to come in non-dance and even dance-linked electronic music. *Titanic* continues to sound how music should sound as the twenty-first century unfolds, a century technologically over-sure of itself, but surrounded by unprecedented pressures, unexpected dramas and vast, undulating darkness, requiring adaptive, indeterminate music that emerges out of and feeds back into the volatile transformation and fracturing of reality. (In this reality, the internet is either the ocean, or the iceberg, or both.) It examines the most extraordinary circumstances at the centre of a bewildering, world-shaking catastrophe as a way of understanding what it is about music that can make it such enthralling, consoling and necessary company, and a way of taking control in the middle of chaos and the unknown. To this day there remains so much space around it – and around *Jesus' Blood Never Failed Me Yet* – because nothing has come close to being anything like it as a sound piece, as documentary, as a ghost story, or as a work of art that began with a description, an estimation, and never ends.

88. I asked Bryars: where would you hope that *Titanic*, the piece *Titanic*, keeps going? Where would your imaginative version of it be in the future? 'I'd like to perform it on the ocean bed,' said Bryars. 'On three vessels. It would be very expensive, but then James Cameron's film was. It's a million dollars for each vessel, and you can only get one member of the public in the sub because there's three people: the driver, a communication person and one other person. If you get everybody down there, it's an awfully expensive thing. But yes, that would be fun. That would be the ultimate performance.' And still just another version.

Eventually the *Titanic* might return – in some kind of post-technological world, even post-disaster world, where the whole world was at death's door – to being a series of instructions and impressions about a piece of music that you read and imagine into existence, something you believe you have heard, even if you never have.

89. Five life-changing moments in the musical life of Gavin Bryars: 'The first one was when I first heard the Bill Evans Trio on record and it was the last recording of his great trio, which is the Village Vanguard album, recorded ten days before his brilliant young bass player Scott LaFaro was killed in a car crash at twenty-five. Evans was so stunned by the death he couldn't play in public for months. It was a ballad, "My Foolish Heart", which is one of the most exquisite pieces of music. They play it very slow, but so sure of what they are doing. The balance between all the players including the drums is fantastic; it isn't stating time, it's colouring it, weighing it up.

'Paul Motian uses a very beautiful little cymbal sustained throughout, which gives it a hardly perceptive pulse, and yet never loses the swing. The choice of notes LaFaro makes are earth-shattering, where he hits these notes is rock solid, right in the middle of the note and absolutely perfect in terms of the left-hand chord. Evans isn't using the root at all. You often hit the seventh, it would be the little finger on his left hand, and LaFaro would fill that out.

'There was one moment in it partway through where he makes a little adjustment as he was playing a note, and I can actually hear him make the decision about what to do. There's a sense of urgency about it, but also calm. It is in that moment where you actually witness someone's mind operating. You hear that. It's a mistake perhaps, but that makes it all even more perfect. It is so human.

'It's rather like when I was teaching art history. One of the things I found very interesting was Renaissance drawing, how when you see a drawing you may see some things which have been erased and something else would be put in its place. What do you see when you see that? You see someone's mind. You see a decision that someone has made. On the way to finishing. It isn't the art, it is the thinking behind it, a clue to how it came to be, which is as important as the finished piece itself.

'That's why when I write music, I use pencil and paper. I have never used a computer and never will. Ever since the first time, I always write with pencil and paper because when I rub something out, there's a trace left of that thought and I can see. I have not dragged it into the trash. I can also have the physical thing of having several pages in front of me at once; I don't have to scroll. So there is that physical thing where you can actually see your decisions. The first one. A very important one, leading to all the other decisions you make. You're building something up, and it seems important to have those moments still there somehow.

'The second is probably the Cage encounter. The third was working with Marcel Duchamp. One of the things I enjoyed about Duchamp was essentially that his work is an embodiment of ideas. It's not iconography. It's not the way something looks. If you look at a series of Duchamp pieces, there's very little resemblance between them. If you look at, say, a Bridget Riley painting, it will be lots of tessellations. Or, Frank Stella, there's a style. Francis Bacon, there's a style. As soon as you look at it, you know what it is. If you look at a Duchamp, you're not sure. You're not meant to be.

'Somebody looks at it, they're not even sure whether it's an artwork or not. But, whatever it is comes from the ideas behind it. He turns ideas into something without losing the ideas. The work doesn't take over and become something else. The ideas are still there. An encounter with the work of Duchamp became the third thing, which was life-changing for me because I then could see a way of making music which was not as it was before. A way of turning ideas into sound in a new way. In fact, 1972 to 1975, I wrote no music at all, and people say, "Oh, it must have been such a difficult period." It wasn't at all. It was just I was sorting my mind out because I was moving from this experimental world, that gave me *Titanic* and *Jesus' Blood*, into thinking something further, and what I came out with was my mind had changed. I wrote music in a different way because of those three years.

'The fourth: it was 1986 when I went to Japan for the first time and the night before I went, two days before I went, I heard on the radio a broadcast, a recorded performance of Wagner's *Parsifal* by Welsh National Opera, conducted by Reginald Goodall.

'I saw that the next night, which was Good Friday, Goodall was conducting ENO with more or less the same cast, but obviously in English. I was flying to Japan on the Saturday. I went to that performance and I was in a daze. It was the most astonishing thing I had ever experienced. In between the acts, where you have an hour-and-a-half interval, I was wandering around Soho in a dream. Afterwards I bought the boxed cassette set which Goodall had signed.

'I flew to Japan the next day. I flew on Aeroflot Airlines from Moscow, and the flight to Tokyo was fantastic. I had with me the cassette set of *Parsifal* and a miniature score. Goodall's tempo is very slow, it lasts about five and a half hours. I worked out in that thirteen-hour journey I could hear it twice in each direction, broken up by meals. I was flying over Siberia hearing *Parsifal* and the transition music in Act 1, Scene 1 to 2 is one of the most glorious moments of all time.

'The fifth was when I was working with the Latvian Radio Choir. About ten years ago, I was doing a concert with them and I think they're one of the finest choirs in the world, absolutely wonderful. They were doing a piece of mine that I had actually written when

I was a guest composer for the Hilliard Summer School in 1997, so I'm a fairly recent convert to writing choral music. It happens to be for about forty-eight or maybe fifty-one solo voices, a ridiculous thing to have done, but that's what I decided to do, in the one day I was given to write it.

'They were going to rehearse it, so I went and stood in my place. There were all these groups all the way around the building and I noticed there were three guys standing in the aisle and they were not in my piece, because they were three bassists. They were clearly rehearsing another piece and they started to sing, and it was the most beautiful music I had ever heard in my life. I didn't recognise it at all, couldn't work out where it had come from. It was so slow, truly ghostly, fading away as though into nothing but never quite getting there, and it completely held my attention.

'Later, I worked with the Estonian National Men's choir, and they were working on this same piece. This music started and it was like Arvo Pärt in a way, except the harmonies were closer to Richard Strauss, very stunning harmonies, with a very slow movement. Eventually, I found out it was by the Ukrainian composer Valentin Silvestrov, *Requiem for Larissa*, a piece written after the sudden death of his wife, one of his very few choral pieces, and it was the most beautiful, painfully private thing I have ever heard. It avoids the clichés that often come with writing this sort of moving memorial music. That was a life-changer for me in terms of understanding choral writing.

'I now write lots and lots for the human voice, including for the Estonian Male Voice Choir. I have a massive catalogue of vocal works. In an ideal world, that's what I prefer to be doing all the time, writing vocal music.'

90. 'Sinking of...' playlists.

FROM *THE SINKING OF THE TITANIC* AS A SUSTAINING AVANT-GARDE (CLASSICAL) MASTERPIECE

- Gavin Bryars and the Estonian National Male Voice Choir – *Farewell to St Petersburg/Memento/Silva Caledonia/O Oriens/The Summons/Ian in the Broch* (2009)
- Pauline Oliveros – *Tara's Room: Two Meditations on Transition and Change* (2004)

- Morton Feldman – *Durations I–V: Coptic Light*, performed by the Ensemble Avantgarde and the Deutsches Symphonie-Orchester Berlin, conducted by Michael Morgan (1997)
- Hans-Joachim Roedelius – *Sinfonia Contempora*, No 1: *Von Zeit zu Zeit* (1999)
- George Crumb – *Makrokosmos* Vols I & II (1999)
- Iannis Xenakis – *Electronic Music* (2000)
- Robert Ashley – *Automatic Writing* (1979)
- Evan Parker Electro-Acoustic Ensemble – *Memory/Vision* (2003)

OUT OF, AROUND AND UNDER *THE SINKING OF THE TITANIC* FROM OTHER DIRECTIONS

- The Joseph Holbrooke Trio (Derek Bailey, Gavin Bryars, Tony Oxley) – *The Moat Recordings* (2006)
- Alva Noto – *Transform* (2001)
- George Russell – *Electronic Sonata for Souls Loved by Nature* (1980)
- John Zorn – *Mysterium* (2005)
- Popol Vuh – *Einsjäger und Siebenjäge* (1974)
- Cluster and Brian Eno – *Cluster & Eno* (1977)
- John Foxx – *Cathedral Oceans* (1997)
- Coil – *Time Machines* (1998)
- Robert Wyatt – *Rock Bottom* (1974)
- This Mortal Coil – *It'll End in Tears* (1984)
- Stars of the Lid – *And Their Refinement of the Decline* (2007)
- David Bowie – *Low* (1977)
- Laurie Anderson, Kronos Quartet – *Landfall* (2018)
- Marconi Union – *Distance* (2006)
- Edward Vesala – *Invisible Storm* (1992)
- Robert Fripp – *Let the Power Fall* (1981)
- Taylor Deupree – *Northern* (2006)
- Fennesz + Sakamoto – *Cendre* (2007)
- Alva Noto, Ryuichi Sakamoto – *Glass* (2018)
- Andrea Parker – *Kiss My Arp* (2011)
- Ches Smith – *The Bell* (2016)
- Björk – *Biophilia* (2011)
- Chris Potter – *Imaginary Cities* (2015)

- Django Bates' Belovèd – *The Study of Touch* (2017)
- Julia Rovinsky – Dark (2012)
- Valentin Silvestrov – *Bagatellen und Serenaden* (2007)

92. I first heard the music of Michael Nyman in 1976 as one of the ten releases on Obscure's collection of experimental composers. Sounds were organised, sometimes found, noise was controlled, textures delicately emphasised, content erased, systems followed, bodies mimicked, voices imitated, quietness was an energy, discrepancies were juxtaposed, musical structures were open-ended and drifting, incidents were unidentifiable, random, subdued. The music was all about change, and often didn't seem to change. Somehow it was connected to the strategies of the punk and then post-punk that was emerging at around the same time. There was a similar rejection of orthodoxy, of rigidity, and both were radical ways of re-energising musical possibilities, and, perversely, of introducing a moral discipline into music.

93. Nyman's *Decay Music* was Obscure No. 6, set amidst the kind of composers and compositions he had been writing about as critic, theorist and conceptualist since the 1960s, after frustration with the boxed dogmas and dictatorial strictures of serialism and the narrowed, alienating fierceness of atonality. Because he was a part of Obscure, which was distributing to a slightly wider audience some of the terms of the recently conceived minimalism, he slipped outside true obscurity. Wherever he went next, Hollywood or concert hall, I always thought of Nyman as a key figure in this potent, mind-altering experimental movement.

94. Nyman, like the label itself, and like Eno, was operating under the practical, poetic influence of John Cage, for whom music was not necessarily what some would think of as being music. Some Cage music was contained on side two of Obscure No. 5, with a sleeve note by Nyman, who in 1974 had written the book *Experimental Music: Cage and Beyond*, featuring composers and activities largely ignored by mainstream critics. Nyman defined and described the origins and originality of the new music that interested him. He moved from Cage's game-changing role in the beginnings of the non-Stockhausen post-war experimental music, through the instructions, installations and impertinence of Fluxus, to the musicians layering, phasing and diligently repeating a sustained, cellular rhythmical music he had accidentally dubbed 'minimalist' – something he could trace back to twelfth-century composers Léonin and Pérotin, to Purcell's *An Evening Hymn*, to Charles Ives. He was anticipating the sort of music he would write once he returned fully to responding to music through composition: experimental, but open to romance and bliss; militant, but high on Mozart and the power that comes from a certain progression of chords. Instead of writing dry, insular, ethno-musical essays, he now turned his analysis and research into the action of music.

95. It was music that could just start anywhere, and end anywhere; music that remembers other music as though it was a dream; music that could be produced using different sorts of instruments, or no instruments at all, a combination of old instruments and electronics, or just electronics; music that might mix up techniques borrowed from the sixteenth, eighteenth and twentieth centuries, and of a time not yet marked; music that concerned itself with the perception, construction and progression of time itself. Music that took a basic set of ideas, decisions and doctrines – in Nyman's case set out in his writings on experimentation, on how the minimalists sequentially recovered tonality in a state of shock after twelve-tone music, his studies of pulse, his love of Handel, the music provisionally displayed in his Obscure release, an ambition to create a twentieth-century context for classical music – and that then set about creating permutations for as long as there could be permutations.

96. For Nyman, whose examination of musical possibilities across centuries, climaxing in the open-minded, increasingly cross-bred 1960s, was particularly complex and passionate, the permutations could last for ever, or at least, longer than a lifetime. It could certainly take him from the early 1980s to the second decade of the twenty-first century without his music ever sounding outmoded or exhausted, as much because of the charged, ghostly, ancient music he referenced as the emphatically modern pop music and classical classics he vigilantly revamped.

97. As a composer, loosely speaking still much closer to classical than rock, he became a combination of the critic, the historian, the musicologist, the thinker and the fan. Because of his collaboration

with provocative, theoretical director Peter Greenaway, who made scientifically organised, sound-conscious art films, he was also from the beginning a composer for film soundtracks, so that his music had a particular function, however abstract and challenging, and possessed another life. There was also as part of his presence the showman, and the show-off, which meant his music was just as likely to blast its way forward, even as it seemed to circle itself, and move without moving.

98. What separated him from the American minimalists he would inevitably be grouped with was his explicit eclectic enthusiasm for pop and rock, from Jerry Lee Lewis to the Velvet Underground, from Petula Clark to psychedelia. His music, seen as a continual commentary on the history of music – his history of music, his selection of sources, references and musical found objects, his craving to splice John Dowland with La Monte Young, with a gaunt big-band swing to generate a sort of unearthly medieval blues – would be less drawn to non-Western sources and neo-mystical properties.

99. In the early 1980s, his return to composing now in full flow, he was also connected to the rapidly developing concept of the remix in pop, which, after initial body-thrilling disco drama, was further experimenting with how a piece of music could be extended, edited and reorganised in ways that reflected the scenarios of Cage, the re-orchestrations of Berio and the tabulating methods of the minimalists. The greater popularity of the fluid, repetitive and evenly spaced twelve-inch mix and its way of amplifying and reinforcing a single musical phrase and creating a new coherence was shifting listening habits, encouraging audiences to adjust their expectations of what a piece of music could be. This ultimately meant the music as showcased on the ten Obscure releases would become increasingly accessible; those experimenting with tone, tempo and surface, in the orbit of Cage, stretching the very definition of music, inheriting his inheritance of Dada and Satie, were the sound of the future, where everything was taken from somewhere else, pieced together, repositioned, and repeated until it was ready for change, which was sometimes because of commercial pressure and sometimes just for the sake of it, or because something interesting occurred out of the blue to those in control of the music.

100. Nyman is committed to seeing things in a different light and anticipated from an early stage how modern culture would become an intellectual game, a puzzle made up of quotations, allusions and source material. He is in many ways a remixer of the past and present, of the adventures of others, of the musical world around him, of high and low culture, from the Renaissance to disco, a remixer of his own compositions, and his own image and self-consciousness. That he had an image, and seemed very aware of it, upset the purists, when such purists were a little more in control of cultural momentum than they are now. Such purists were of course further enraged by his popular success with once nicely esoteric music. It is a popularity that comes directly or not from his unabashed, often saucy fondness for instrumental lushness and an uncompromising weakness for the uplifting happy endings of melody that can seem very un-experimental, but utterly enchanting.

His particular approach to the thinking about and making of music, rooted in mathematics, philosophy, speculation, improvisation, archaeology and ultimately love, created a trans-historical template that he could adapt to any number of circumstances and settings. Instantly it is the sound of Nyman, because of his sensitivity to the importance of texture and tension, his loyalty to certain processes and procedures, so that there is a constant, classic balance between stability and surprise. It is much more a music of constant variety, and a variety of elements, than merely of minimalism's mesmerising patterns and deliberate targeting of the ecstatic. Even when a piece is made up of a mosaic of quotations, it is pure Nyman, a rigorous display of how he clears space for his very own thinking.

Whether writing, lyrically, enigmatically, for solo piano, for his raucous, jocular small band, for a chamber-sized orchestra or a larger one, whether writing song, opera or concerto, whether in period clothing, or postmodern quotes, sincerely solemn or deliberately self-parodying, Nyman analyses the structural challenges of music, how to manage time and sustain a composition, while presenting his analysis as gorgeous, ethereal structures. We hear calculation and study, but in the service of beauty and the unexpected. It is music, always changing, always the same, which, in Cornelius Cardew's words, 'Throws into high relief some of the mystery of being alive.'

PART NINE

The Piano – Light and Dark

John Cage *1949: 'As far as consistency of thought goes, I prefer inconsistency.'*

1. THE EIGHTY-EIGHT

Of all the instruments invented before the twentieth century, the piano can do the most – for the composer, the player and the listener. It was built in such a way that somehow it could cover every emotion, respond to every mood, anticipate every gesture, allow a mind to move across its eighty-eight keys from the beginning of time to the end of the road.

The piano travels the most, from the pub to the church, from drunken daylight to blissful dream, the honky-tonk to the poetic, the rowdy jam session to consoling New Age drift, the etude to boogie-woogie, hymn to nursery rhyme, crude to exotic, kitsch to cosmic, peaceful to violent, unbearable beauty to crazy mess, waves flowing forward and backward. It is the most intellectual of all instruments, and the most sleazy. There it goes, black and white and a million colours, a form of perpetual motion requiring brain power and finger strength, a whole history of music, of thought, of musical thought, as told through the piano: from Mozart to Monk, Schumann to Coldplay, Debussy to Dr John, Liszt to Little Richard, Cage to Liberace, Grieg to Joni, Victor Borge to Les Dawson, Arthur Rubinstein to Elton John, Tori Amos to Mitsuko Uchida, Vladimir Horowitz to Mrs Mills, Keith Jarrett to Billy Joel, Clara Schumann to Brad Mehldau, Glenn Gould to Lady Gaga, Queen to Ludovico Einaudi, Jane Austen's Jane Fairfax to Anthony Burgess's Ellen Henshaw, J. D. Salinger's piano player who is so good it's almost corny to Proust's memorable jumble of wrong notes, Kurt Vonnegut's *Player Piano* to D. H. Lawrence's 'Piano', battered stand-up to gleaming Steinway, sing-along cheerleaders to driven, despairing loners.

Beethoven's thirty-two sonatas breaking the walls of convention, Ravel's influence on Sondheim, Webern's symmetrical design, Chopin telling the piano all his secrets, the rhythm changes of George Gershwin, Errol Garner's rolling introductions, Bud Powell's solos, Nancarrow's whirlwind of notes, the strolling, swaggering ragtime of Scott Joplin, Jimmy Yancey, around 1915, shifting the ragtime left hand into the steady beat of the blues guitar, following the sound of the trains rolling underneath the Chicago clubs he was playing in, the dandy heat of Jelly Roll Morton, the boogie-woogie charge of Meade Lux Lewis, the pumping ego of Jerry Lee Lewis and what he called the 'brains in his fingers' telling him what to do, the dressed-up chords of Stevie Wonder, the rootless chords of Bill Evans, the left-hand chords of McCoy Tyner, the cluster chords of Cecil Taylor, the shifting chords of Ligeti, the dream chords of Ryuichi Sakamoto, the found lostness of the Necks' Chris Abrahams, the morale-boosting, wartime exuberance of Myra Hess, the wild stitches in time of Martha Argerich, the second sight of John Ogdon, the precise attack of Vladimir Horowitz, the velvety fury of Radu Lupu, the subtle power of Shostakovich, Sviatoslav Richter's spooky channelling of Bach, Handel, Schubert, Schumann and Lizst, the propulsion of Rachmaninov, the constant pulse of Philip Glass, the branded Lang Lang effect, the final note of 'A Day in the Life', one of many hints that pop music was in many ways a close relative of minimalism. For Dave Brubeck, the piano was the whole orchestra.

There it is, the piano: solo, leading, accompanying, at the striving heart of the solemn, streaming with melancholy, pumping up the vulgar, at the very shrieking birth, and all the breathing, heartbeating life, of classical, pop, jazz, rock, cinema, music hall, Broadway, and, as the synthesiser – which is modelled after the piano, a machine made from wood and wire and vibrating air, implying that sound is infinite – sending music everywhere. A familiar piece of everyday furniture, sometimes just there to support a photograph, at home in the living room, the nightclub and the concert hall, played by the barely competent and the seriously talented. There's also Dalí's obsession with the piano, growing up with one in the family home where his father kept a book detailing with some force the traumatising effects on the body of sexually transmitted diseases. The piano featured in many of

Dalí's paintings, including *Atmospheric Skull Sodomising a Grand Piano*, and 1931's *Partial Hallucination: Six Apparitions of Lenin on a Piano*, which neatly placed six miniature glowing Lenin busts along the keys of a piano, with swarming ants replacing notes on the sheet music.

In his *Piano of Mozart* a heraldic angel was painted onto the underside of the lid of a Steinway, and his *Surrealist Piano* celebrated the piano's glorious, shining shape, elaborate insides, and uncanny sound-shifting qualities, acknowledging it as a different species altogether, from a strange land, standing up for mystery.

With Michael Nyman, the fan and the theorist, the enthusiast and the academic, there is knowledge of all the above, and much more, so that his piano pieces are always searching essays in themselves on the astonishing, myriad possibilities – and limitations and illusions – of the piano, how lovely and how cruel it can be, how lyrical and revolutionary, passionate and controlled, pretty and unnerving, enigmatic and shameless, plain and fancy, friendly and reserved. He's fascinated by the feedback loop between the imagination, the configuration of the keyboard and the hands – left and right at odds with each other, simultaneously exploring different worlds, fingers producing endless patterns, making miles and miles of sound by being inches apart.

He knows the history of the piano's technological evolution, the rapid increase in its power and resonance between the 1750s and 1870s, creative ingenuity constantly demanding a better instrument, and how successive composers exploited its constant design innovations, and extended the repertoire. He follows a line from Bach's Christian Cross through the otherworldly mist of Debussy to Scriabin's mystic chord, to Cornelius Cardew's hypersensitive obsession with touch and note placement, which isn't that far from the obsessions of Count Basie and Cecil Taylor. He understands the reason the piano is so eternally popular – because it can be used for the flashy, irreverent, instantly satisfying highs of show business, but also for the severely, ideologically cerebral, for reading the mind and sensing musical ghosts, for answering the great questions of existence. It can go deep into the dark, troubling inside, and out, extravagantly, into the amazing, rushing, impatient world.

Nyman uses the piano, some notes, some chords, the spaces in between and all around, his melodic impulses and a natural percussive spirit, arranged around his experience of where the piano has been and will go, to criss-cross different cultural byways and tangents. Mostly he uses the piano to think, to display his thinking, about how and why music reaches and pleases the soul, and how and why music is the one way we can hear and feel what thinking is, the other side of language, of everyday, overused words. Nyman analyses the structural challenges of music, how to manage time and sustain a composition, while presenting his analysis as gorgeous, ethereal structures. We hear calculation, and study, but in the service of beauty and the unexpected.

Nyman most famously expressed his love for the piano in a film called *The Piano* (1993) directed by Jane Campion. In the film, Holly Hunter's mute Ada expresses herself not through words, but through the piano, symbolising how the composer translates unknown, unknowable thoughts from one world into another using unique powers of perception. She builds her world by composing music. Nyman builds this world inside his own world inside a film inside the world of the piano.

He gets inside the mind of someone else completely – a fictional character, and Hunter herself, an amateur musician who played the music written for her – without losing his own place, and knowing his place in piano history, among all that style, reflection and noise, all those moods, topics and experimental, utopian ideals. He pays a discreetly sensational tribute to the idea of the piano as a transcendent way of expressing and distilling capricious mental energy and a sense of place, as a way of travelling through time – imagining nineteenth-century music as if it is in the future. He relishes how the piano can complete the visual dynamic of film, how it can so exquisitely, tenderly represent love, hope and movement, but, importantly, also doubt, transience, pressure and a stunning, restorative stillness.

Michael Nyman knows how much there is contained inside the piano, so much melody, time and drama, so much ravishing space and feeling patiently waiting to be released, by someone else – the composer, the player, the listener, whoever is in control, whoever is craving order. With his own form of introspective glamour and unrestricted grace, Nyman makes you understand what Thelonious Monk meant when he profoundly reported that 'the piano ain't got no wrong notes'.

2. THE PIANIST

Joanna MacGregor is one of my favourite pianists, not just for the fearless vitality and vigour of her playing, but because of what she plays and why she chooses the music, and how in her eclectic recitals and on her albums she puts together music and musicians, eras and countries, genres and styles that no one else would think of doing. Taking great delight in making unexpected connection between different sorts of sound and energy, for her centuries of music can be assembled in endlessly imaginative ways.

As a concert pianist, just a small part of her large aesthetic portfolio as curator, festival director, composer, conductor and teacher — she is the scrupulous, highly conscientious and encouraging head of piano at the Royal Academy — she becomes a direct route into classical music. A route that will take you via the guidance of a flexible, flamboyant modern mind from Bach to Birtwistle, Scarlatti to Ives, Messiaen to Gershwin, Beethoven to Britten, Chopin to Satie, and in among that, Thelonious Monk to Moondog, John Cage to Chick Corea, the baroque to free jazz, Professor Longhair to Arvo Pärt and Mary Lou Williams to Lou Harrison. She zips across centuries, determined to get inside the scores and minds of the greatest composers, relishing how space and time between composers from different centuries seems to dissolve once the music is played.

For MacGregor, from a young age, Bach has been the centre of the universe, and everything circulates around him. With Bach, she sees a danger that never goes away. There is nothing before or after him; everything happens at the same time as Bach, who absorbs everything and reflects it back into the world. Bach moves everywhere, full of secrets, constantly calculating the movement between the mind and the world, his brilliance always reforming.

She talks about John Coltrane playing Bach to warm up. She will tell a story of how Shostakovich used to find Bach boring, until he played some selections from *The Well-Tempered Clavier* collection of preludes and fugues. He was inspired to write twenty-four of his own preludes and fugues, continuing, not copying the spirit of Bach, and one sound world seamlessly connects with another. MacGregor plays them both in one performance, and draws them into one place, where Bach and Shostakovich seem to inspire each other, and somehow have two minds – one a little jazzier, a little edgier, more shaken than the other – and share one voice. Her performance of *The Art of Fugue* – abstractly written for no particular ensemble or instrument – as a piano piece is an act of worship and enlightened ingenuity. She's mad about Chopin as well, how far he takes the piano, and then Debussy, another transcendent writer for the piano, and Bartók, and Ravel, and Britten, all of them approached in her piano playing with raw power and radiant control. It all comes back round to Bach, but from the viewpoint of also adoring the lucid, spellbinding etudes of Ligeti and the rhythmically complex, sublimely off-kilter piano-roll mash-ups of Nancarrow.

Hers is an iconoclastic virtuosity and a delirious, insatiable relish for all shapes and sizes of classical music that comes from an unorthodox childhood. She was always destined to see classical music in a different, excited way, a way that makes more sense as time passes and musical borders crumble. Born in 1959, she grew up in Willesden, north-west London and was taught at home until she was eleven by her Seventh-Day Adventist parents, who had a piano but not a television. She loved the piano, and her only teacher until she was eighteen was her mother, who made her believe you could play what you wanted; whether it was a hymn or Mozart, a pop song or a sonata, it all had the same worth. As a pop-music fan, MacGregor fell for T. Rex and Alice Cooper, which mingled with her mum's lively taste for jazz, which soon led her at fourteen to feel the genius of Thelonious Monk and Nina Simone, even as she was making her way into the cosmos of Bach. It all seemed to belong together, because there was no one to say it didn't.

She developed an uncompromising independence that meant she fought the grim expectation that a girl could play an instrument but not be considered a composer, and it also brought a creative exuberance and an unusual sense of freedom to her playing.

Formal teaching from when she was eighteen, first at Cambridge and then at the Royal Academy, didn't knock this independent thinking out of her, as much as there was a tendency to try and narrow her range, reduce her options, discourage her curiosity, tame her wildness, constantly question her individualism and criticise her appearance, as though that was more important to her future than her playing. Luckily she wasn't put off playing the piano in order to make discoveries, rather than winning competitions and doing what she was told. 'I just knew that if everyone played the same things, however brilliantly, it would be very boring. If I was told to concentrate on Tchaikovsky I would just think – but I know what else is out there!' She started recording in 1988, an album of American piano classics, and since then has made an array of albums that survey what she knows is out there, shifting naturally from Monk to Messiaen, Errol Garner to Rachmaninov, because nothing should stop you.

We talk in her office at the Academy, which is where she passes on her love and understanding of the piano as the source of all modern music.

I was always taken by how you would put unexpected things together in ways which seemed natural but, in terms of inside classical music, seemed to go against the grain. It was your 2002 album Neural Circuits *that was very important for me, in how it put Schnittke's* Concerto for Piano and Strings *with a movement from Messiaen's* Quartet for the End of Time *with Arvo Pärt, Nitin Sawhney and traditional Ghanaian melodies. It seemed important that the classical music was mixed with other styles, and it didn't seem twee or contrived, and all the music worked together. The connections naturally worked. There was a quote where you said that you juxtapose surprisingly, but in an obvious way, in a way because, if you think about it, the right choices will always fit together.*

I remember when I was in my mid-thirties I made a Bach and Nancarrow recording. I was recording for a label, Collins Classics, which was one of the big popular labels then. I wanted to do Bach's *The Art of Fugue*, which is one of those pieces that doesn't quite fill out two CDs. They said, 'What are you going to do to fill out the time?' I said, 'Well, I'll do Conlon Nancarrow,' who had written the quasi-Bach 'Prelude and Blues' before he went off to fight in the Spanish Civil War in 1936. It seemed a nice connection. They just went completely ballistic. They said, 'What are you thinking of?' I remember the distribution company actually said, 'You can't do that because no one will know where to put it in a record shop.' It was record shops then. You had to fit in the right section.

They said, 'The shops won't know whether to put it under baroque or under contemporary music.' These were the arguments you were faced with. But I did do it and it was seen as quite radical at the time. But of course it made a lot of sense musically, if not commercially. Doing *The Art of Fugue* on piano was also a bit controversial, because it wasn't written for any instrument in particular, not even the harpsichord. And we multitracked as well, which of course is not done in classical music, and it was all seen to break the silly rules, as if you were assaulting something sacred. I just felt these juxtapositions are meaningful as long as you've got an intellectual thread supporting why you are doing it. It's not for the sake of it, or to be fashionable, and certainly not as any commercial gimmick, which people sometimes assumed, or even just because I was female, and young, and doing something different – Bach with Nancarrow is no kind of cosy crossover.

You mention the way that there is often surprise from the institutions and the establishment about putting one thing with another that doesn't immediately seem to belong. It seems to confirm an outside view that the classical regime can be very rigid. You savour both Satie and Beethoven and can easily switch from one to the other, but somehow this doesn't seem allowed. On the other hand, there is a craving for some magic solution to make the apparently difficult music more accessible. For me, the way that you put things together as both a fan and an expert, listener and player, seems much more the way that might happen. Not by softening it or simplifying it, but by putting Johnny Cash next to, say, Frederic Rzewski and seeing the Berg in Gershwin. Do you approach what you do with a missionary zeal, to actively try and change things?

I think it's just a natural part of who I am, really. I think often people have thought that I've been doing things to take a stance or something, but it's actually much simpler than that. It just reflects the kind of the stuff I'm interested in and the beliefs that I have. I really do believe that late Beethoven is astonishingly adventurous and innovative. Beethoven sits really well with certain contemporary composers because they really do share revolutionary and adventurous values. They also are quite angular sometimes. He's quite fiery. Just last week, I played some late Liszt. Late Liszt is really weird stuff.

It's somebody who is right at the end of their life and they're thinking conceptually and it's so modern. It was considered so modern nobody wanted to play it at the time he wrote it. It was almost like he invented impressionism before impressionism came along. Of course, late Liszt goes really well with late Beethoven because the pair of them share this ability to just transcend any thinking of the time they're in and do something really new. I think, again, once you just take the composer seriously and do it through the composed thought, as it were, then all your juxtapositions make sense.

I have to say I'm not very keen on juxtaposing things just for the sake of it, or doing it in a – I don't know – Saturday-night-TV kind of way. Because I think, actually, audiences are quite heavyweight themselves. They quite like being challenged. They don't really want things to be soft, despite what it appears. They want to be taken somewhere – you get this in visual arts, don't you? The great blockbuster visual-art shows are things that are quite provocative and meaningful, and people respond in their thousands to that.

Again, from the outside, looking at the classical world, to generalise, there seems to be a constant defensiveness from insiders and institutions about ruining its purity by mixing things that apparently don't belong together.

There are those who want this music to be taken very seriously. I think one doesn't want to do things that are vacuous or anything. I have to be careful what I say here. I think classical music is often represented as a certain sort of high cultural watermark and some people can feel that their citadel is being stormed, which I don't think has ever been the case. I think there have been some easy-listening things released to try and reach a large audience. That's fine. But I don't think, in general, the more demanding-seeming classical music is going to go away, rather like Shakespeare. I don't think Shakespeare's ever going to go away. I think it's indestructible, actually, and I think there are certain composers that are absolutely indestructible. I think young people are very serious about who they are and what they want to play. All that's happening is that there may be new ways of programming the music and new venues. That might be the case. It's not going to destroy anything.

You talk about early patterns that developed because of playing with your mum at the same time, anything from Mozart to gospel hymns, so those patterns stick and create a fluid approach to both playing and repertoire.

I think so. I think fluidity comes as you move easily between genres when you're quite young. But I think you're trying to spot patterns as a youngster, aren't you? You're trying to spot the relationship between things, to make sense of the world. I remember when I discovered Charles Ives, as a teenager, I was just so thankful because he was a composer that made the link between gospel music, spirituals, Beethoven, American pop, brass bands, things I liked even though I was told they didn't really fit together. Ives absolutely laid it all out as it seemed to me it should be, with no barriers in between. Even now, his music is quite confrontational and quite complex, not easy listening at all, but he was someone I just almost wept with relief that it existed. It was all in my head, and here it was in someone else's.

How old were you when you made that discovery?
    I think I first heard of him when I was about thirteen or fourteen, and I didn't do anything about it until I was in my later teens, and then I really seriously started to play his stuff when I was twenty, even though it was very hard. Charles Ives is very difficult to play and even now, he's seen as a bit of a cult person you don't easily play. I started with short pieces, the very daring variations of *Three-Page Sonata*, which was wonderfully raucous, mixing up romanticism, impressionism and the avant-garde. I'm loving his faith in mixing things with no sense of it being wrong. Then there was *Some South-Paw Pitching*, and for all its complexity, it's extremely passionate. Then I progressed onto the First Piano Sonata, which has got this great central movement based on 'What a Friend We Have in Jesus', which was a hymn I'd sung as a kid. He does this absolutely rhapsodic, wild, atonal version of it, which to this day I think is a marvellous piece of composition.

What was the drive at that age; what was happening in your mind?
    Well, I was naturally quite curious about lots of things. I was curious about literature and architecture and I had a wide range of references. I love pop music obviously, and jazz, and gospel. Just because I happened to want to be a classical pianist, I was always going to be wanting to find ways to bring together a lot of things. I had a range of references, and, importantly, I liked composing music. I think the key actually is if you can write music, you're always going to be more exploratory as a performer. You don't have to be a good composer, or anything, but if you are any sort of composer it makes a difference. Somebody once came to see me play Beethoven and they said, 'You can tell that you write music because you have a slightly different take on everything.' You're working from inside. You don't just go: *This is a great piece of music, I must play it well.* You're trying to find out what makes it tick all the time. You're working with the composer as much as just following the notes.

When you say you wanted to be a pianist, when did this idea materialise?
Was it an unusual thing within your family?

Yes, it was a very unusual thing. Although my mother had trained as
a pianist, she gave everything up and she started a family quite young.
But obviously, from her, I got my interest in music. My father was a
lay preacher and worked in a black gospel church, so there was our
interest in gospel and hymns. Pop music you couldn't avoid when I was
a teenager. I grew up with a sense of being able to improvise at the
piano as well as playing Beethoven. In fact, I didn't want to be a pianist.
I wanted to be a composer. I didn't imagine I would be a pianist because
I didn't really have that background, and I didn't really know anybody
that did that. I think probably I wanted to write music more.

When did you realise where the piano could take you?

As I got older, I discovered I loved practising for hours and hours on
end, and I think the hunger to practise seriously is what you have to
have as a performer of any serious kind of music. You have to want to
sit at the piano and practise for six, seven or eight hours. It's perfectly
possible to be very skilful and gifted, but if you don't want to practise,
fine, don't do it. Because you have to not mind being very repetitive
and obsessional.

And on your own?

Yes, on your own, yes. I love being on my own.

Yet you are so gregarious and social...

I can be social, but it's not really me. I have a real need for lots
of my own time. Yes, I ended up curating festivals, teaching, working
alongside lots of musicians and doing many committees and panels.
But obviously, actually, the core of my being is to sit at a piano and
practise. With all my young pianists that I now mentor, I can see that's
what they need. They have to have that core of them being willing to
spend hours and hours on their own...

What about the composers you like to play, when does that happen in terms of
what become your favourites and the ones that don't? How does that change?

I think when you're young, you should try and play everything you
can because you need to find out who they are and what they've written.

What a good teacher would do for you is to try and make sure you're covering the basic range of what there is. You would learn a Mozart concerto. You'd certainly learn lots of Beethoven. You'd learn lots of Bach. You do Chopin, Liszt and Schumann, and then you make sure you do early twentieth-century music via the important twentieth-century composers like Prokofiev, Bartók and Shostakovich. Then, hopefully, you'll be introduced to contemporary music in some way, or even commission a piece. So by your late teens, you can actually with some truth say that you've got quite a varied diet. And then of course, you are going to be drawn towards certain things based on your personality and your reaction to music.

You will begin to discover what you love listening to and then what you love playing, and some students, they love playing Bach. They love Bach on the piano. Some find it rather trying, rather mysterious. Some people love playing Schumann. Some people love playing Latin American composers. You learn what the demands are technically and also emotionally. Just today, I examined a pianist here in this room. It was a very high-level exam where the student was playing late Schubert. Schubert is a complete mystery to us all, broke most of his life, and he died when he was really young, younger than Mozart. He had no idea that he would become very famous. Most of his work he didn't hear performed in his lifetime; he was definitely in the shadow of Beethoven. Even Rachmaninov didn't know any Schubert sonatas; he wasn't that known during his time. Gradually, by the end of the twentieth century, he had become better known. Of course now, we'll play a lot of late Schubert. We work on it. We can see his vision rather than what once seemed to be his flaws.

It's really interesting how young people now want to play his sonatas. They are really quite mysterious, heavy, philosophical, thoughtful, and in some ways, highly unusual – it doesn't quite hang together in a way that a normal sonata does. That becomes the attraction, the challenge. Composers go in and out of fashion. If a young person said to me, 'I hate Chopin and I'm not going to play any,' I always say, 'I think you need to play a bit more before you make that statement.' I think it's really important to have a literacy about what music is and what these cornerstones are and not be swayed by fashion.

It's important to you to bring other feelings and your own musical ideas to the playing?

One of the fantastic things about music is that it does have a provenance. There is a political and cultural provenance around a lot of composers, which enables you to then be quite free with them. All the great composers for piano were flexible and open, including Handel, and they recycled their music a lot. They themselves had a quite unsentimental vision of what you do with their music. Bach was a great improviser. He was able to keep reworking his material and moving things sideways, always rethinking it. There's always a lot of interpretive discretion because of how much of the composing was based on improvising. Knowing this gives you permission to have a quite imaginative approach to the notes, because you do have notes that you have to learn. It's an incredible discipline, classical music, because there it all is, it's written down and you must play what's written down. But at the same time, we know that they are quite complex creatures, these composers, and they do interesting things that can't necessarily be written into the score, and as a player you can too, within reason.

Up until quite recently, all these classical composers were great performers. They often premiered their own music and they often changed things and they often wrote their own cadenzas and improvised. It's a really useful thing to keep reminding yourself that they were practitioners too. We must view them as living, breathing, creative experiences, not just dry and dusty stuff. It is extremely modern and it's often psychologically very modern. Schubert is a very psychologically modern composer because his music is full of ambiguity and a lot of neurosis. There is so much heart-stoppingly beautiful music that's somehow deeply troubled, enigmatically anxious, so it's very, very modern in that sense. We can hear it now in a very modern way. There is ambiguity to a lot of this great, classic music, to Beethoven, to Brahms, to Schumann, which makes it modern, whatever the era.

I think classical pianists are very fortunate because they don't have to necessarily make their own music. They can do. They don't have to. They've got the most incredible reservoir to draw from, like a well that they can throw the bucket down deep and bring up this incredible stuff. It's amazing what's been written, and you can draw from that wherever you are in your life as a performer. I think if you're trying to create your own music all the time, then that's difficult. That's a different thing again. It could be difficult; it could be easy. Certainly, what you're not necessarily going to have as a pianist is a block, because you've got another Beethoven sonata you haven't learned yet. You've got more Mozart concertos. You've got Cage's sonatas and interludes, even his silence. You've got so much stuff you can do. I throw myself into really tough things like Messiaen's *Vingt Regards*, a twenty-piece suite for solo piano, a meditation on the infant Jesus, really huge, amazing stuff, physically so demanding. It becomes quite an ordeal.

Why do you do it then?

It's fantastic to lose yourself in something so difficult and epic and all-consuming. I always seem to want to do these epic things and I still do. I don't know why. I don't know where it's come from, but I always did take on these big complicated journeys, like the Charles Ives First Piano Concerto, which was very rarely recorded, very rarely played, because it's a huge thing to take on. I'm about to go into Chopin's Mazurkas, all fifty-nine, which people have done before, but it's an enormous thing to do. It's a hugely ambitious and tricky thing. I hope very much to play all the Beethoven sonatas eventually. I think it's a personal thing. You want to immerse yourself in these ventures, if only because they are there.

Also, I'm really interested in how composers develop. That's a gift for pianists, to follow the minds of great composers, to work out why they did what they did, as well as how. There's an intriguing chronology to follow in how composers write their big collections. The Chopin Mazurkas are total masterpieces and it's enough to just play some of them. They're fantastic and rich and deep. But by only playing some of them, you don't quite get this arc that exists, of a life and the life of a composer. The early ones are rather simply written when he was really young, in his mid-teens, the later ones were finished towards the end of his life a quarter of a century later. If you can play the whole lot, you get this unbelievable sense of how somebody developed intellectually and emotionally. It's almost keeping a diary, but also watching how he travelled forward.

You're raising your game by trying to do this particular cycle, and it's very, very difficult. Rubinstein wrote about recording the complete Chopin Mazurkas. He was the first pianist to ever record the complete Chopins and he did them in London in 1939, just before the war broke, and he's living on the edge of something profound and unsettling. He sounds intoxicated while he was playing. Fistfuls of wrong notes sometimes, but who cares, it doesn't matter. It's incredible playing, it's wild to hear, like he's having the time of his life, apprehensive and astonished all at once. Brendel recorded the complete Beethoven sonatas three times – for most of us to do it once would be unspeakable, and he did it again and again. Clearly, what these people are doing is immersing themselves and absolutely realising they're pitting themselves against something, against a great mind. If you're up to it, the challenge cannot be resisted. It's like climbing Everest all the time. It's there. It's calling you. You don't have to do it, nobody is asking you to do it, but it's a great and wonderful thing to do because it does change you and, hopefully, it changes the listener. This is what the piano can do.

SELECTED JOANNA MACGREGOR DISCOGRAPHY: MANY PLACES TO START DISCOVERING CLASSICAL MUSIC

- *American Piano Classics*: Ives, Copland, Nancarrow, Monk, Garner, 1989
- Benjamin Britten: Overture *Paul Bunyan*, Piano Concerto/ Robert Saxton: *Music to Celebrate*, 1990
- Benjamin Britten: Piano Concerto, Op. 13/Violin Concerto, Op. 15, 1991
- Charles Ives: Sonata No. 1/Samuel Barber: Sonata, Op. 26/*Four Excursions*, Op. 20, 1991
- *Gershwin Songbook*, featuring new arrangements by by Django Bates, Michael Finnissy, Gary Carpenter, Alasdair Nicolson, 1991
- *Joanna MacGregor on Broadway*, 1991
- Domenico Scarlatti: Keyboard Sonatas, 1992
- *The Music of Eric Satie*, 1992
- *The Music of George Gershwin*, 1992
- Johann Sebastian Bach: The Six French Suites, 1993
- Bartók/Debussy/Ravel: Piano Works, 1993
- Harrison Birtwistle: *Antiphonies for Piano and Orchestra/Nomos/ An Imaginary Landscape* 1994
- Olivier Messiaen: *Quatuor pour la fin du temps*/Zygmunt Krauze: *Quatuor pour la naissance*, 1994
- *Counterpoint*, Bach: *The Art of Fugue* and works by Conlon Nancarrow, 1996

- *Play*, 2001
- *Neural Circuits*, 2002
- Bach: *The Goldberg Variations*, recorded in Salzburg's Mozarteum, 2008
- Messiaen: *Vingt Regards/Quatuor pour la fin du temps/Harawi*, with soprano Charlotte Riedijk, 2010

Which can take you to:

- Messiaen – *Catalogue d'oiseaux* performed by Håkon Austbø
- Bach–Busoni – Complete Transcriptions performed by Sandro Ivo Bartoli
- Grieg – Complete Solo Piano Music performed by Gerhard Oppitz
- Beethoven – Late Piano Sonatas performed by Maurizio Pollini
- Beethoven – Fantasia, Op. 77, Sonata No. 11, Op. 22 and Sonata 29, Op. 106 played by Ursula Oppens
- Schubert – Impromptus for Piano, D 899 and D 935 performed by Murray Perahia
- Schumann – *Études symphoniques* and *Carnaval* performed by Pierre-Laurent Aimard
- Ives – *Concord* Sonata and *3 Quarter-tone Pieces* performed by Alexei Lubimov
- *Der Bote*: Elegies for Piano (C. P. E. Bach, Cage, Tigran Mansurian, Glinka, Lizst, Chopin, Valentyn Silvestrov, Debussy, Bartók) performed by Alexei Lubimov
- Debussy – Complete Works for Piano performed by Paul Crossley
- Carl Czerny – Nocturnes played by Isabelle Oehmichen
- Gian-Francesco Malipiero – Piano Music played by Sandro Ivo Bartoli
- John Field – Piano Music Vol. 1: Nocturnes and Sonatas played by Benjamin Frith
- John Field – Nocturnes played by John O'Conor
- Tavener – Piano Works played by Ralph van Raat
- Edward Macdowell – Piano Music Vol. 1 played by James Barbagallo
- Brahms – Works for Solo Piano performed by Julius Katchen

- *Horowitz Plays Scriabin* (box set)
- *Hommages* — to Ravel, Debussy, Milhaud, Poulenc and others, performed by Margaret Fingerhut
- Josef Suk — Piano Works played by Margaret Fingerhut
- Bartók — Complete Solo Piano works performed by Zoltán Kocsis
- Dmitri Kabalevsky — Complete Piano Sonatas performed by Alexandre Dossin
- Poulenc — Piano Works performed by Pascal Rogé
- Enrique Granados — Works for Piano performed by Daniel Ligorio
- Erwin Schulhoff — Complete Piano Works performed by Erwin Schulhoff
- Erwin Schulhoff — Solo Piano Works played by Margarete Babinsky
- *Bach Inspirations* — solo piano pieces by Liszt, Busoni, Rachmaninov, Bach and Franck, performed by Hannes Minnaar
- *Le Poème de l'extase* — works by Scriabin, Messiaen, Liszt, Manfred Kelkel and Harald Banter played by Maria Lettberg
- Scriabin — Complete Solo Piano Works played by Maria Lettberg
- Schoenberg, Berg and Webern — Piano Music performed by Peter Hill
- Feldman — Works for Piano performed by Marianne Schroeder
- Cage — Sonatas and Interludes for Prepared Piano performed by Boris Berman
- Cardew — Piano Album 1974 performed by John Tilbury
- Charles Koechlin — *Les heures persanes* played by Ralph van Raat
- Elliott Carter — Piano Music (Complete) played by Ursula Oppens
- Xenakis — Piano Works played by Stephanos Thomopoulos
- *Linkages* — Piano Music by Brahms, Wagner, Schoenberg and others, performed by Martin Tchiba
- Ligeti — Works for Piano played by Pierre-Laurent Aimard
- Busoni — *Fantasia Contrappuntistica* played by Hamish Milne
- *A Hundred Years of British Piano Miniatures* — including George Butterworth, Howard Skempton and Peter Reynolds, played by Duncan Honeybourne

- Earle Brown – abstract sound objects played by Sabine Liebner
- Luciano Berio – Piano Music played by Andrea Lucchesini
- Piano Recital; Boulez, Holliger, Berio, Bozay, Soproni, Messiaen – played by Klara Kormendi
- Brahms – Piano Pieces played by Radu Lupu
- Christiann Wolff – Piano Pieces played by Sabine Liebner
- Stravinsky – Music for Piano Solo performed by Victor Sangiorgio
- *Motherland* – performed by Khatia Buniatishvili, featuring solo piano works by Bach, Tchaikovsky, Mendelssohn, Debussy and others
- Brahms – Late Piano Pieces performed by Anna Gourari
- Brad Mehldau – Suite: April 2020
- Jacob Anderskov – Impressions of Bowie (Live)

3. THE ORGAN

The imposing, ancient cathedral organ is an unlovable and mostly unloved instrument, perhaps because it embodies with epic, ecstatic sadness the time and space that the cathedral contains and will ultimately be engulfed by. The many-piped, tooled, keyed and stopped organ opulently blasting through silence somehow records the unstoppable slippage of life into infinite abyss, and even when it celebrates life, drama and energy, it does so often sounding as if the effort of living can only lead to decline, decay and the inevitable diabolical end, which, the organ's necromantic sound implies, leads not necessarily to paradise.

Called the king of instruments, truly a monster, an esoteric ancestor of the electronic synthesiser, giving the player a chance to control a virtual orchestra, producing a combination of the showy and the solemn, the miraculously vast and the fussy, it's as out of place in the modern world as a suit of armour. For all the divine intention, sonic splendour, engineering glory, surprising physics and concentrated virtuosity, there is also an eccentric, comic phantom of the opera element, as if the ornate gothic architecture and the pushing of wind through pipes to produce sound is deeply absurd, even a little sometimes nightmarishly camp.

Olivier Latry, one of the three current chief organists inside Notre-Dame de Paris, sadly observes how the organ has fewer and fewer friends, even if those friends are extremely obsessive, making extreme trainspotters seem less than half-hearted. The pipe organ inspires the most exquisite geek intensity, but it is difficult to sex up the church organ like the violin, guitar or saxophone and give it friendly, middle-of-the-road appeal. Within the narrow band of commercial classical releases, organ music claims a tiny sliver, even if that sliver includes great, ungloomy works by J. S. Bach, Mahler and Strauss, and Messiaen's complete organ works, a six-disc sixty-six-piece work of art recorded in total by Latry on the Notre-Dame organ, which under his immense, judicious control, becomes — as well as a beast and a demented thingamajig — a ghost, a volcano, a firework display, an acid trip, a butterfly, a waterfall, a time tunnel, a dream, and a brain in tune with the brain of what might well be God.

Latry honours three centuries of his esteemed predecessors at the cathedral, including Daquin, Balbastre, Beauvarlet-Charpentier, Vierne, Cochereau, and their organising and enshrining of an exultant, meditative repertoire played since the 1860s on a regularly modernised Cavaillé-Coll.[1] Latry's timing and articulation is immaculate, a fluency easily taken for granted, and for him, the pipe organ is the sound of the soul, the sound of spirit, of permanence, the purest sound of all: if you want to believe, sample first the more tenderly other-worldly excerpts from Vierne's unsentimental 1927 *Pièces de fantaisie*, and Latry's own highly charged improvised finale for clues that he might enjoy the prog rock of Emerson, Lake & Palmer and the Moody Blues — where the Hammond and Mellotron stood in for the pipe — as much as Bach, and that playing the pipe organ requires a showman's single-minded swagger.

At the control of the Notre-Dame organ, as much a masterpiece of human ingenuity as it was 300 years ago, Latry powers on, convinced it contains the secrets of musical sound, and everything else is just temporary and plastic. As the world goes digital, synthetic, post-real, impatient, hyper-distracted, dipped deeper and deeper into a purée of data, it's the equivalent of trying to sail to Saturn in a sixteenth-century

---

[1] Aristide Cavaillé-Coll, a god to the organ geeks, was one of the major innovative mid-nineteenth-century organ builders exploiting problem-solving new technology, allowing a more gradual, frictionless creation of crescendo, a greater balance of contrasts and a richer range of shades: it is perhaps also this nineteenth-century romantic, pompous symphonic power of the organ, along with its conveying of austere contemplation that exiles it into the modern margins.

ship. For the non-believers, it sounds as though Latry and the organ are being slowly strangled by unforgiving time and space; for the believers, Latry and the organ are magnificently resisting the pointless flicks and ticks of fashion and the mundane pull of gravity.

4. THE INVENTION

Another place to start making your way through all the classical music that now surrounds you is to find one thing to be interested in and become your own expert in that one thing. It's a little like finding a designer, object or artist you like to collect from a particular period, and then obsessively building a collection, purely for your own benefit, to make sense of certain states of mind and, you never know, help organise your entire life.

If you choose the piano, that might be a little too general, and it would need breaking down into specific musicians, styles, eras, genres and instrumental groupings. Coming into classical music through the piano doesn't simplify things at all, as it still means negotiating your way around a few complicated centuries of endeavour and creativity and discovering what form of piano music interests you and which composers and players attract and intrigue you the most. Approaching classical music through the piano is as intimidating as working out where to begin working out where to begin making sense of the whole history and oceanic vastness of classical music.

You could begin at the beginning, deciding to follow those mysterious years during the eighteenth century, when we are on the brink of modern science and for a time it blurs with magic, with the family Bach at the inauguration and Haydn and Mozart not far behind, leading to the full-blooded engagement of Beethoven, through those decades when the architectural, sonic and conceptual idea of the piano as we know it today was being planned, nurtured and developed.

The balance and tone of the new sounds led to the early, expansive structural concept of the sonata and the concerto, and the definitive, liberating shift from the limited harpsichord. In 1700, the harpsichord would have been the instrument of choice, played at all the best parties. There are those, though, frustrated with how inflexible the sound was, and however hard or soft you hit the keys, the result was generally the same. It was not possible to vary the volume or sustain a note.

Mozart's relationship with the then new-fangled piano released new forms of reality-shifting virtuosity, and helped him articulate a craving for independence, fluency and flexibility, inspiring and accelerating the changes in the design and engineering of the instrument that led to the modern piano.

The piano, among all instruments that had their beginning in Mozart's time, went through an extreme and rapid technological transformation that would last until the nineteenth century. A musical instrument like the piano was at that point one of the most complex and astounding mechanisms in the world, and Mozart knew exactly what to do with it, had been waiting for such a combination of machinery and musicality. By the time he died just thirty-five years later the piano had started to kill off the harpsichord and clavichord.

Despite his legendarily early start as a composer, Mozart was not perceived as being a significant composer as a teenager in the way Mendelssohn was. The fame was more to do with his keyboard playing when little more than a toddler, and his father's over-eager entrepreneurial exploitation of his son's phenomenal talents. The intention for his father was to earn more money and find a better court position for himself, using his children as bait.

At age three Wolfgang could replicate what his talented older sister Nannerl was playing at the clavichord. He was permitted to begin to play instruments earlier than his sister, to play more of them, and to play them more flashily. He could show off in public the same 'tricks' on the harpsichord that for a woman would have been an impropriety. These flippant, precocious antics were enhanced a little by his own energetic compositions, which, apart from glimpses of an originality that only made real sense later, were not until his twenties particularly more accomplished than other composers of his time. You can now hear in those early glimpses the luminous emergence of a music yet to be properly processed.

Some suggest Mozart's first great unchallengeable masterpiece is his Ninth Piano Concerto in E-flat major, written as he turned twenty-one and familiarly known by the nickname *Jeunehomme* or, for the purists, *Jenamy*. Here are the first real signs of something out of the ordinary and unique to Mozart, an irregular challenging of form involving the unprecedented development of a complex way of arranging soloist and orchestra. The previous eight piano concertos are viewed as largely generic, if flawlessly constructed, the sound of many others at the time.

None of those eight seem to have his blood flowing through them, and then suddenly there is what Alfred Brendel described as an unbelievable leap in quality, as if at some obscure Austrian crossroads Mozart had sold his soul to the devil in return for an ultimate insight into the ritual and potential of composition that would render his music untouchable by time and criticism. He had moved into the future, which he never leaves.

In this future, when he is who he is, some suggest a major moment in the transition of Mozart from mere competence and efficiency to gilded genius was a year later, in 1778, when he was twenty-two and having a troubled stay in Paris with his mother while they were touring France. Art and real life fused tremendously. His mother fell ill, eventually dying, news he revealed gradually in letters to his father back in Salzburg, so slowly that he was still explaining her illness after she had died. His father would blame Mozart for the death of his mother, causing a new kind of tension between the father and son. Issues, always, even as the music took off and Leopold's dreams for his son started to come true.

It was during this difficult time shortly after she died that he wrote his Eighth Piano Sonata, the forceful, relentlessly rhythmic A-minor Piano Sonata, which featured an approach and technique barely hinted at previously, including an uneasy, edgy beginning, and was the first sonata he had written in a minor key – there would only be one other. He had previously only composed two pieces in a minor key, a string quartet and a symphony.

This was like sure, sensible crowd-pleaser Elton John suddenly playing like a vulnerable, searching, exquisite Bill Evans. Mozart uses his music not just to impress listeners with his skills and winged, dexterous style but to express his own emotional turbulence and press into the structure and textures of the music itself the unresolved tension he was feeling following his mother's death. The music wasn't just on the page, and then played; it was in his mind, and then transferred into the sound.

There is no direct proof it was written in response to his mother's death, and he may have started writing it before it happened. He was quite capable of writing deep, resonant and darkly emotional music without needing a specific trigger, but such a dramatic change in his life does seem to pass into the music. Thinking of this piece as a key moment of transformation doesn't seem to underestimate the achievement, as if it only happened because of his mother's death, but to appreciate Mozart's developing ability to combine the dynamism of pure feeling with his existing musical abilities. Then again, interpret it as confessional music of despair if you decide it contains an emotional, very human reaction to the loss of his mother, or as music of rebellion and anger if you consider that Mozart wrote his music in a place separate from whatever was happening around him, in a state of pure, isolated and almost inhuman sensitivity to the music of music, the potential of new sound mixtures.

Whatever the motivation, it was a striking stylistic departure from the previous eight sonatas, a powerful echo of the emergence the year before of a new insight into the concerto model; the revealing of a very different mind, the composer who was at once the most conventional and the most radical of composers, taking the existing rules and adding new ones that both broke with the past and extended it, accepting it but also rejecting or certainly redirecting it. So perhaps the moment he moves from potentially minor composer with celebrity childhood past perhaps beginning to overshadow his progress, on the way to exploring all of space and time and understanding how life began, is when he responds to an unexpected tragic event in his life and expresses despair, anger and a disorientated emotional anguish – the inexpressible – by intentionally conceiving something unorthodox and even experimental. It is 150 years later that Webern is as motivated by the death of his mother to accelerate into his new, unprecedented music.

Mozart is defying rules and veering away from some of the traditional guidelines of the sonata so that he can express these unfamiliar new feelings, the kind of feelings you will only experience when your mother dies, and when there are now unresolved feelings towards his father, the demanding taskmaster, thrown into sharper relief as he becomes the only surviving parent.

For those not so keen on biographically interpreting this creative breakthrough, because it would have happened anyway, it is true that at the time Mozart was testing out the new keyboard sounds of the pianoforte and was determined to impress an indifferent French audience and add to his childhood notoriety by coming up with something that was about who he was as a thinking, maturing twenty-two-year-old, not as a freakish seven-year-old show pony. He didn't want to be the former child star whose best years were behind him. Driven by whatever was driving him – the personal, the technical, the neurotic, the unknown, the nervous energy – he was already finding ways to use the newfangled piano to suggest embedded musical possibilities, as he realises that this one instrument can open up greater colours and dynamism than any other instrument is capable of.

In this story, his dramatic musical transformation from skilled, adaptive craftsman to enacting a large part of the very history of genius is represented by a work for newly conceived solo piano – the make-believe nature of his music, the epic holding forth in its purest state – that itself is about musical transformation and the piece's own paradigmatic quality, his genius in distilled form, his gift at switching from the idyllic to something else, something beyond, something much darker. His genius at moving in a moment from the otherness of a dream to the otherness of stark reality and then turning back to the dream, and so on.

Another good way of positively inhabiting the worlds of classical music is by reimagining classical composers who have over time, for various ideological and cultural reasons, been turned into fixed, banal and bewigged, almost inhuman historical figures, when they were once explosive innovators making sense of the turbulent times they lived in through startling, unprecedented musical expression. For Mozart, the piano was an equivalent of what the tape recorder, the microphone and the synthesiser would be during the twentieth century – a way of emancipating musical imagination, and producing an urgent, direct artistic reaction to the combination of technological inventiveness, brand new social settings and unprecedented cultural societal and political currents.

When he was born, the pianoforte was a relatively rare instrument, barely existing in Germany, new to Britain and unknown in France. The piano started to become, in Mozart's time, with Beethoven as a vital upcoming investigator of its truest capabilities, *the* instrument, an unbelievable neural link between a musical idea and its most profoundly flexible articulation, a remarkable way of translating ideas from the mind to an object. It became the ultimate connection between a machine and an operator, an artist, and this started to happen, not uncoincidentally, in Mozart's time.

The piano's flexible, dynamic potential developed alongside a historical shift in taste and sensibility, shifts largely instigated by Mozart, who was contributing more than most to the growing piano repertoire. He matured as a composer at just the moment the piano was invented, liberating him, and establishing the future of the instrument. He was writing music that was appropriate to the volatile nature of the world and reflecting the tension between the new and old worlds.

What Mozart relished about the new instrument, unachievable on the very one-dimensional harpsichord, was the way it could be played loudly and softly; its delicate extraordinary softness was as much an early selling point as its arresting, vigorous new loudness. One of the early pioneers of the piano, Bartolomeo Cristofori, replacing the limited plucking of harpsichord strings with more percussive hammers, originally clumsily christened his new instrument *gravicembalo col piano e forte* – harpsichord with soft and loud. Early pieces for the new instrument would be marked up by the composer as being written for 'the soft and loud harpsichord, commonly called the one with little hammers'.

The new 'soft and loud' instrument had a liberating variety, enabling someone who understood its new capabilities to more subtly manipulate volume and dynamics and drift between and through sounds – essentially, enabling the 'programmer' to enter a completely new sonic arena and deal with the nuances of experience, and the extraordinary distance made up of numerous colours and endless shadows between the mundane and the ethereal. Eventually, the 'soft and loud' – pianoforte – simply became 'soft' – piano. It could easily have been a forte, but that something so soft could be made by something that as an object was so solid captured the popular imagination.

In 1777 Mozart is excitedly reporting to his father about the possibilities of this new instrument. Within weeks he is writing the A-minor Piano Sonata, able to take from his mind the blasted angst he felt losing his mother, which could never have been as powerfully and accurately expressed on a harpsichord. Leopold described it as a 'strange composition', and it was not just because of its unusual open-hearted musical admissions, but also because it had been conceived on an instrument where the genius could not only prepare the notes and control the tempo, but one where he could play with sound, and extend range and dynamics. Being able to play with sound and extend range opens the door to another world, one that we are still living in. At the time, it would have added an extra dimension to reality and more than a few deeper, lighter new shades.

At precisely the moment his being is ripped apart by a torrent of emotions, or just filled with an unstoppable parade of ideas, which both require a new sort of instrument to properly process and decode, he finds himself gifted with a new sort of instrument. Here was an instrument that could keep up with the sophistication, adventure and technical expertise of his notation and the energy of his imagination, which was reacting in quick time to the world around him, which he saw more and more of on his travels. (The travels and musical tours, taking up a third of his life, may well have caused the wear and tear that led to a short life. He never really belonged anywhere, until the end, except inside his music.) If you've got the blues, it helps to have access to an instrument that has the subtlety, and the exuberance, to be able to reflect that. Previously a keyboard instrument existed sonically on the same tinkling level, whatever feeling you were wanting to recall and record. Suddenly the extremes of thinking and feeling could be turned into sound. A player, a composer, could get truly emotional.

It took a little time to get the instrument right; on early, erratic versions keys jammed and dampers didn't work. Eventually, the pianofortes built by Johann Andreas Stein suited Mozart's touch and flair and were mechanically capable of equalling on earth his epic, intimate musical dreams. His father, drily reacting to Mozart's exultant discovery, was a little annoyed at how expensive they were.

Almost exactly 200 years later, when European musicians such as Kraftwerk, Brian Eno and Giorgio Moroder were craving new sounds and greater possibilities in order to reflect troubling new times and necessary new moods, and the inevitability of change, they found what they needed with the synthesiser and the drum machine. The synthesiser also took some years to get right. At first synthesisers were built without keyboards, the sounds and noises produced using wires, touch, buttons and gauges. It was more about special effects, bleeps and buzzes than melody and harmony. A sense of rhythm was almost irrelevant. It needed Keith Emerson of Emerson, Lake & Palmer to ask Robert Moog, the inventor of the Moog synthesiser, to add a keyboard, so that it could be played like a musical instrument, not operated like a strange, static, noise-making vehicle that belonged in a laboratory, or was best used making creepy off-world noises for science-fiction TV shows. Thanks again, Keith.

The piano was Mozart's synthesiser, and as radically useful in communicating with an uncanny faithfulness pleasure, desire, loss, love and fear. The synthesiser was a descendant of the piano, and still didn't completely replace the piano in the way the piano replaced the harpsichord. Even the laptop, one place the synthesiser was heading, was connected to the piano, as an interface between thought and action, and contained the piano, as much as it contained everything. It could replace the piano, but it included the piano.

The idea of Mozart's music – now so solidly embedded into the comfortable and regimented view of classical music, lodged pretty solidly inside a deadening, marginalised protective bubble – actually expressing uncanny change and sensationally symbolising historical abruptness is, as the academics might say, counter-factual; the proposal is perhaps, in a scholarly sense, too unstable and romantic, and not very helpful in terms of understanding how and why he wrote his music, but it does seem to take those alienated by the routine myths of Mozart's life and music closer to the actual resonating brilliance and complex suggestiveness of his music and his ideas.

The piano during his time was not a polished, normalised symbol of the predictable, commonplace and even elitist; it was something that seemed of the future, and it became a way of taking you there, of thinking ahead and making claims on new ways of living and feeling. Mozart was not the Mozart we think of today, the powdered, sentimentally adored combination of boy genius, improvising hero, freak of nature, travelling showman and fantasy inventor of everything revealing the glories of the human spirit, whose hyped-up death made his life and established the legend.

This domestication of new ways of thinking is the end result, carefully coded, of the fact that Mozart, and of course 'Mozart', released from any original truth, represents, over time, a decent, reassuring sense of establishment order. Mozart has been tamed, turned into nothing but the agile, sweet and graceful, whatever inspiring wildness and revolutionary daring there was turned into caricature, and whatever great, enfolded mystery has been harnessed as something no more than lightly, crisply appealing. There can be no end to the explanations, but the wider cultural way of dealing with Mozart has been to try and bring the explanations to an end and a succession of culturally imperial claims to outright ownership. When Frederick Delius complained that, 'If someone tells me they like Mozart, I know in advance they are a bad musician,' it was out of dislike for the reputation rather than for the composer, the reputation that led a swooning Tchaikovsky to describe Mozart as 'the musical Christ, the culminating point of all beauty in the sphere of music'.

There have been many Mozart images that consolidated the idea of the Mozart effect, the apparent benefits of his music on the psychological welfare of growing children and troubled adults, Mozart as a spa treatment, an existential massage, a refreshing facial. There have been the images of Mozart that created and were created by the savagely appealing cartoon myth of Mozart the upstart prototype pop star as slammed into the last decades of the twentieth century by Miloš Forman's hysterical, Oscar-winning *Amadeus*.

The film was based on Peter Shaffer's play, relishing, through a mixture of shocking reality and madcap flights of fancy, the brattish burnt-out party boy, the maladjusted man-child, the amoral braying ass, the careless lout as accidental inspired artist, the assumed cockiness and lewd imperfections, the depraved, anarchic element of genius, and the murderous, sinister extremes of an operatically stacked life-and-death fable. Such perverting and yet illuminating theatrical and cinematic attention helped promote Mozart into end-of-century lists of top ten cultural figures of the millennium.

With rare, obscure exceptions, the late twentieth-century image of brand Mozart was increasingly fixed as the gay, rococo, china-doll eighteenth-century genius, protecting the presentable, commercial and highly fictionalised Mozart from any challenging, demythologising thoughts that the reality was very different, and much less romantic, miraculous and heroic.

There are hundreds of Mozart 'surfaces' and Forman only scratched one or two. Mozart was spectacularly, psychedelically strange, even dangerous, on a quest to revolutionise the idea of experience and knowledge and express his findings in the most amazing ways imaginable. The ubiquity of his influence means we can never know that shock of coming across and hearing him for the very first time, and to some extent our familiarity with the music and history undermines his inexplicability, unpredictability and inexhaustibility. So, begin with Mozart, with an open mind, as if you have no idea of who he was, when he was born, what he did, what happened to him, what happened to music, and just try to imagine him as being somehow not yet born, not yet available, and certainly not what he has been turned into.

I first came to Mozart as a listener without really thinking about it, and definitely without expecting it. I was in my early forties, and had previously given Mozart little thought, and if there was any thought, it would be based around the feeling that I would travel through my entire life without ever giving him much thought.

This changed because of one of my favourite piano players. Mozart was sometimes present in places I visited as I followed my usual interests — I didn't go to Mozart, I just found him, like an object that meant very little to me. As an unashamed Keith Jarrett completist, collecting everything he released, there he was when in 1999 I bought an album of Mozart concertos Jarrett recorded with conductor Dennis Russell Davies and the Stuttgart Chamber Orchestra. I was there for Jarrett, who played his part not as the improviser of flowing spontaneous piano pieces or as the clairvoyant interpreter of standards but, as far as I could tell, with an almost cautious and definitely not gimmicky faithfulness.

Being ECM, the music didn't sound like I had decided classical records sounded: smeary, bombastic, clenched, featuring soloists where it was difficult to work out what their character and personality was. It wasn't jazz, or Jarrett's jazz, which some would say wasn't jazz, not since the late 1960s, but it wasn't the Mozart I thought I'd find, drained of blood, ghostly, possibly quite incredible, but not much of a thrill. I remember feeling a bit funny listening to it, like I had come across an animal that I had been told was extinct, and then noticing that in fact it had kept evolving and had a fierceness about it, however timid it initially appeared.

Mozart's music was considered new and strange at the time it was written, thought too complex by his father to become as popular as he wanted it to be, featuring 'harmonic progressions which the majority of people cannot fathom', but in the new world of music, my music, that contained all of that Beefheart, Wire and Cabaret Voltaire, all that knotty, noisy post-punk and beyond, all that free jazz and electronic experimenting, which suited where my life and living was, Mozart's music seemed too familiar, and, I am ashamed to say, too old. It seemed to belong over there, in a far, far away past, not an ounce of it actually influencing the music I was mostly a fan of.

He seemed to be some sort of equivalent of the Beatles, in the sense that the paradox of Mozart is that music history would not be greatly different if he had never existed – though obviously music itself as a history, a passing-on of rumours and rituals, would be immeasurably the poorer. The line of succession leads around, rather than through, Mozart. His kind of perfection could be neither improved upon nor repeated, and most of the impact was about timing – the timing in the music, but also the time that it appeared, at just the time something like that simply had to appear, if only because subsequently it has been made to be that way in the hands and minds of musicologists and historians. It's all about patterns, in music, and in cultural history.

I didn't consider pursuing any interest, and my mind still slipped off the sound, the compression of the orchestra and Jarrett's verve into something tight, a miniaturised monumentality I wasn't used to. I realise now, having eventually made it into the world of the concerto, that I didn't know how to concentrate, and at the same time lose myself a little, throw away those prejudices, and translate the rhythm and details into an equivalent of the music I enjoyed for its persistent blend of familiarity and surprise.

I vaguely sensed but couldn't fully articulate that without Mozart, without everything that became Mozart and then became what followed, there would have been no Keith Jarrett, and the way he moved his fingers across the piano and applied certain levels of pressure in order to order his thinking. Mozart as an inventor, as much as anyone, of the piano. And then I played some Autechre, some Buffalo Springfield, some Sparklehorse – and stuck with the Jarrett jazz, set in my ways.

As a fan of Jarrett's label, ECM, and its sombre but often sensational contemporary classical music partner ECM New Series, and having warmed to Debussy by following back Jarrett to Bill Evans and his less obvious sources in late nineteenth-century France – even making the end-of-century musical biography of Debussy with Art of Noise, electronically commenting on the modern musical patterns that existed because of how Debussy thought and composed – I bought a New Series album in 2003 that paired Debussy with Mozart, Juliane Banse singing, with András Schiff playing piano. Mozart, again, was just there, not what I went for, which was the Debussy and his setting to music of poems by Verlaine and Mallarmé. Debussy would attend a weekly Tuesday meeting in Paris where a group of intellectuals, Les Mardistes, would exchange collaborative ideas about philosophy, art and literature. Mallarmé was in charge, and W. B. Yeats, Rainer Maria Rilke, Paul Valéry and Paul Verlaine would visit. Literary imagination influenced Debussy as much as anything else.

The combination of Mozart and Debussy was seen in many reviews as an unusual, slightly weird pairing, as though combining one century with another, one set of principles, theories and flavours with another, was all but forbidden in the classical world, a hint of the written and unwritten rules that bound classical music inside itself, sealed off from the turbulent, dislodging currents of modern reason, as the world around it changed. Mozart would mostly be paired with Haydn or Schubert, and Debussy with Ravel, and any other links or connections were very rare.

I immediately liked the pairing, the songs seemed to belong in the same sphere of existence, and the voices started to seem unearthly and haunting rather than brimming with a frilly, brittle prettiness, and something started to stir in me in terms of a different way of thinking about Mozart. Mozart not something owned and controlled by others, as the musician turned into a banal, oppressively opulent cultural mascot, as a relic from the dead past, but Mozart as something, someone, somewhere, some unfixed energy that was still able to move forward and change shape with the times, and function outside time, not become embedded in it. Here he was placed with Debussy, from a world and place over a century later, and sounding like that was where he belonged, because he belonged anywhere.

Jarrett said, *Here is this thing called the concerto, and don't worry about the genre and any associated rituals*; Schiff and Banse said, *There is no limit to what Mozart could do, considering when he was born and what music was at the time.* Debussy's music threw a different light on Mozart and blew away the cobwebs. Mozart presented through the shadowy, cryptic, severely discriminating ECM prism became glamorous and tantalising, not made of porcelain and lace, cake and flowers.

From the Jarrett, slowly — quicker once music streaming arrived — I moved towards more of the piano concertos, including the astonishing fifteen he wrote between 1782 and 1786, still being motivated as a composer by the newfangled piano, as well as everything else he composed in those years including *The Marriage of Figaro*, the quartets for strings in D minor and E-flat major, symphonies 35 to 38 and his Serenade in C minor for Winds.[2]

I started to understand how Mozart developed his concerto technique, and therefore actually worked out what a concerto is, what it meant to Mozart, and how that differed from what it meant to other composers, who mostly seemed to have different views on what it was, based around a few general, common and consistent elements.

I learned how from early in his life to much later he transformed the private play-at-home notion of the sonata into the more extrovert, public-display genre of the concerto, which would feature at its centre the starring role of the virtuoso, a role he could naturally play to dazzling perfection – and because he wrote most of these concertos very much for himself to play the soloist, the hero if you like, especially as pianist, making the grand entrances, the great displays of fluency and improvisational elegance, we perhaps can see into his mind, and what he thought of himself, or at least what he thought of himself as a musician, a pianist.

We can hear his breathing, and hear his heartbeat, his voice – even as he was making up his own 'Mozarts', hiding behind the music as much as opening up through it, playing himself, and playing another, concealing himself, and then revealing himself – as though these solo moments were his arias, where he could demonstrate the extent of his inspiration, and his calculating, intensely cunning and persuasive showmanship. In no other instrumental genre, whether symphonies or string quartets or sonatas, did he create as many accepted masterpieces. Here he was at his most curious, in terms of his own understanding that from his thinking, his decisions, often made up on the spot, a new form was developing, a whole new language, built around a completely new alphabet.

---

[2]Plus, inside these Vienna years, it should be said, just for the sake of boosting the marvel, of certifying the miracle, in traditional service of the ridiculousness of how much Mozart was packing in to his short lifespan, a glimpse into the accelerating highs and lows of his life: his marriage to Constanze in August, the June 1783 birth and death inside two months of his first child, Raimund, his second child, Karl, born in September 1784, his initiation into the Masonic lodge later that year, and his third child, Johann, born in October, 1786, dying a month later. He could be in at least two places at once, a sorry, sorrowful, prosaically churning real life, and an unstoppable, creative, musical life.

The thought of having to begin an engagement with the concerto, and how the idea evolved during through baroque, classical and romantic eras into the twentieth century, across countries, centuries, minds and histories, is definitely one of those barriers to entry to classical music as a whole, even if you are just hoping to be an enthusiastic amateur, let alone some sort of serious student. That ultimately 'concerto' means something as simple as placing one musical sound against another, alternating performing dynamics to produce vivid sonic contrast, initially to exploit the new sonorous possibilities grand architectural spaces offered for the massed and separated projection of sound, seems too simple a solution to what appears from the ignorant outside to be something of a grand, distancing mystery. But what began as a literal way to bracket a new form of composing for a multitude of organised instruments developed over time to become a complex layering of works and inventions where the amount of history overwhelms the word.

I could never really get to the word through that musical history it now contains and presents, and I think it was both correct and a mistake to be alienated by the word and the world it encloses and reveals. You do need to know something of what a concerto is and isn't, its original lower reputation as a flashy demonstration of excellence – emphasising artists and not art, the dubious proving ground of self-serving, self-dramatising virtuosity, probably what put some of us off about Keith Emerson and prog rock – next to the sonata, symphony or string quartet, about its history before and after Mozart, his innovative and liberating skill in balancing various conflicting elements and playfully, profoundly organising the dramatic tension and co-operation, or battle, between the two protagonists, the soloist and the orchestra. The soloist can represent the stressed idealist fighting against the power of orchestral might committed to crushing the freedom of the individual; the fleeing, rebellious soloist is resisting the overpowering expectations of social convention represented by the orchestra obeying the controlling conductor.

It helps to understand how it is both something very particular and also something that can be approached with great flexibility. It has definite rules, but they can be adjusted and adapted in all sorts of ways, and new rules can be continually added. It does help, listening to a concerto, to have some knowledge of the structural formality of a concerto, the development of themes, the scene-setting and arranging of sparkling virtuosic capabilities of the soloist within or rising up against the momentum of the orchestra. It helps to have even a crude knowledge that there is a blueprint, and blueprint phrases and sections, but within and outside that, the potential for varying density, shape, atmosphere and tone is unlimited, to a point. There is a rigid mould, a few necessary events and a certain predictable order, but within that, the mix, the procedure, the progress can be almost random – a rule-governed freedom, a freedom achieved through accepting limitations and breaking out while never straying from a set system. So loose, even frivolous, was the general nature of the concerto that in the late eighteenth century some critics considered that it had no fixed character, that its point was vague, and that at its most basic level it was simply a practice session for performers and composers. There were those who suggested it was amusing and artful but essentially nothing more than a titillating form of gossip.

It also doesn't matter whether you are aware of any of this, of, say, the fact that Mozart's concertos are among the most popular in the Western canon, that they emerged during the age of enlightenment, and the emergence of the idea of the relationship between the one and the many, the individual and society, and the importance of collaboration and co-operation, which the concerto so exuberantly symbolised. But perhaps only once you do know something of the history and formality, the importance of the dialogue that a concerto displays between an individual voice and a community of voices, can it be something you end up ignoring.

You might perhaps come to know a little about a few of the facts and controversies concerning the format, even appreciate the close connection between the concerto and the opera in terms of the placing of a soloist against an orchestra, and of how this gives something of a clue about the brilliance of Mozart's concertos reflecting his love of opera, and how the concertos were based around his own voice, which was his virtuosity, and his presentation of himself as a public performer where he would take on the role of 'Mozart' the composer, and, especially when he improvised, the genius.

It also is important, but not important, to have some knowledge of how Mozart's concertos had their roots in the circular patterns of baroque concerto form, but which were then opened out into something that moved more coherently through time, opening up time itself and the consciousness of time and how it comes from the past, into the present and then into the future unknown. His concertos told stories, which contained a certain order, that took the listener from the beginning of something to the end – they were sonic spiritual pilgrimages, musical initiation journeys, in which the hero – the central theme – undergoes various trials and tests on the way to integration and resolution. The cadenza point of a concerto is where the soloist is allowed to run completely free and demonstrate the extent of his virtuosity and improvisational skills, a final gesture of escape from the confines of the orchestra, a break from the social group before returning to it, co-operating with the collective but sure of their own independent voice. One of many, but with the rewarding, protective self-awareness of being a one-off.

Music captures, contains and coordinates the strangeness of the way time brings with it the past into the present, where there is a sense of the familiar and consoling, and then releases it into the future, where there is the less certain, and Mozart, and his unique take, often his origination of many of the historical musical rules and possibilities, is at his most magical in encapsulating this sense of time, and musical time, and the constantly surprising combination of tension and resolution, of the known and the unknown, and ultimately of giving a kind of shape to the future, which hasn't yet happened, but, to a point, is destined to, in some form or another. It is this 'some form or another' that Mozart seemed to formalise and elaborate on, without it being weird or chaotic.

When I knowingly heard my first Mozart piano concerto, which happened to be No. 23, K. 488 – I might initially have come across it in an Air France commercial – I had no real idea of what a concerto was, and only a very vague idea of how, along with the symphony, it was the central musical form of the romantic and classical tradition. I was ready to listen to the piece in a way I would not have been five and more years before, and then ready to find different versions, and find a favourite, settling on Richard Goode and the Orpheus Chamber Orchestra, and Hélène Grimaud and the Bavarian Radio Chamber Orchestra; I was curious enough to then extend beyond this one into the others, to see where it ranked, and fitted, into the series, a system in itself you could study, or just plain immerse yourself in, all your life.

Somewhere in the middle of my making-up of Mozart, paying attention to his music, after time spent at the Royal Academy of

Music, I felt confident enough to write a review of an album of Mozart music, without looking, I hoped, too much of a fool. What had I learned, if anything, about this music, which once seemed almost an unappetising gothic fantasy – and what kind of tone should I adopt, how much of my continuing ignorance was going to get in the way?

Thinking this would help me make my own Mozart, to stop, if just for me, the masterpieces sinking into the quicksand of all the music now Spotifyngly available, I went ahead: I tentatively ventured. I hoped I knew enough, even if just enough to have some sort of perception of what may or may not have been one person's comment on works of art that were part of a larger work of art, that I could understand in what I was hearing what was actually Mozart and what was merely interpretation, and at what point the complexity of Mozart met with the particular desires of the performer.

I knew enough to know that because I was reviewing something written by Mozart, there were many things to consider, and I was only aware of a very small number of those things, and of those things, I was only slightly aware. Could I detect if someone was just skating over the surface of the music, insipidly going through the motions, or achieving momentous aesthetic lift-off? But I had to begin somewhere. Because it was a review, I didn't have the number of words I wanted – in fact, I doubled the word length I had been handed, because what I was beginning to do was work out my Mozart, which needed enough words to fill a book, or part of one – but at least I didn't have to mark it out of ten.

ANGELA HEWITT/ MOZART PIANO CONCERTOS NOS. 17 AND 27 (HYPERION)

Getting to know the twenty-seven Mozart concertos, a spectacular solar system in themselves, is one sure way to go mad about the man and his mind, in a good way, even above the operas, sonatas, quartets and symphonies. Canadian crackerjack and former child prodigy Angela Hewitt, having tackled Bach's complete major keyboard works, has now, a little madly, set off to cover all the Mozart concertos. The first disc, released in 2011, featured three early concertos. Here she selects two later works, the intensely melodic, divinely self-possessed No. 17 in G major,

K. 453, and the final one, written in the last months of his life, the gently demented, intriguingly spare No. 27 in B-flat major, K. 595. But what in the end am I reviewing? The original compositions, the fact they were written in Vienna, in the middle of other classic compositions, satisfying, stretching, the expectations and desires of a certain sort of audience? The age and stage Mozart was as a composer, pianist, performer, thinker, mere man, self-made myth, historical illusionist? Hewitt's choice as she maps out the concertos, establishing her own sense of progress, of self-discovery, following the early ones with these particular Viennese examples, revealing her own thoughts about what Mozart was thinking about the direction of his music, or just her own thoughts about aesthetics, sound and self-confidence? Is there reason, or randomness, in the order she is following, an analysis of the source of his melodies, his regard for beauty, his intricate articulation of abstract inwardness, his creative energy, his apprehension, not about his own impending death, but death in general? Has she decided, by including the final concerto, the conclusion to this extraordinary series, with the unfathomable quality of a 'transfigured farewell', that she is not going to complete her original, ambitious task of covering all twenty-seven? Her chatty but knowledgeable notes about historical, biographical and musical context, which reflect her thoughtful reflection of the mysterious self-awareness that generated such fluency, fascination and drama? The actual performances – Hewitt's piano burnishing the wondrous, diaphanous continuity, framed by and framing the often wildly noble Orchestra da Camera di Mantova – which are unsurprising but inevitably stately, gracious and often gorgeous, helping me understand more and more about how Mozart folded the often deeply strange inside the familiar and soothing, the demonic inside the civil? The twee, scruffy cover which seriously undermines the idea that here is any kind of impression of works of art, any kind of emotional, determined refracting of emotional, determined compositions, of the idea that knowledge is power, which is fantastically glamorous? Or how Hewitt feels that Mozart understands her, that this uncanny relationship is at the heart of all such endeavours; an expression not of Mozart, but of Mozart's spooky possession of the performers. In the end, I am perhaps reviewing my own (late) bonding with Mozart, and the sense that, to cross the system of the twenty-seven concertos, let alone everything else, to make a map of my route, means building some sort of spaceship, out of words and memories, which will take more years than Mozart was alive.

I had found one way into Mozart through his concertos – there were a multitude of other ways in to the Mozart cosmos, through the string quartets, the sonatas, the symphonies, the operas, the trios, the religious music, the novelties – particularly persuaded by the sense that he more or less invented the genre, truly created something out of nothing, a new way of seeing the world, the equivalent of imagining into being the form of the novel and everything that can be. I could spend the rest of my life following and researching only the piano concertos, coming to all sorts of conclusions about who and what were the best, about how they stretch and replenish my imagination, possibly all the way to the very end.

He stopped the intense period of writing his piano concertos in 1786 – he had five years left and two more to write – concentrating certainly that portion of dramatic energy, the mesmerising relationship between story and orchestra, on the building of the operas, and perhaps it is the better place for me to go after establishing a certain understanding of the concertos, even just the knowledge that there are twenty-seven, and they go in order, and in any order, until the end.

Another way into Mozart was through the 'K' list; at first, I never paused to think what those incomprehensible seeming 'Ks' meant that were always attached to a piece of Mozart music. Once I had understood what all those K numbers were, I could then enter 'Mozart' through randomly selecting a K number and seeing where I ended up.

Each blind choice led to all sort of excitements, to a filling-in of the shadowy Mozart I had begun to create. It was like a roll of the dice, and there was another Mozart, another part of the story, another astonishing piece of fiction, another leap into the unknown, another sign that Mozart is made up of an awe-inspiring mountain range, and there is always another one to climb, so that you can see the view from the top, and even pluck up the courage to just leap out into the unknown, plunge into the clouds, swiftly sweep through the empty air.

The first time I ever seriously thought about the K numbers, where they didn't seem a cold, soulless, irrelevantly academic way of filing music, was through the Debussy and Mozart album on ECM Records. There was K. 307 and 308, K. 433, K. 472 and K. 476, K. 520 and K. 523. It previously felt naive to ask what the K numbers meant, and part of that classical thing where you feel, on the outside, ignorant of so much, and not actually made that welcome, apart from in a slightly sickly, patronising way. As always, I could ask Google without feeling embarrassed, unless there is a personal Google intern assigned only to me, passing on my ignorance and obvious searches for other Google staff members to have regular meetings about, involving much laughter and astonishment at my stupidity.

The K is for Köchel — Ludwig Alois Ferdinand Ritter von — a musicologist who had such a geeky crush on Mozart that he classified and numbered everything Mozart wrote, from a little harpsichord minuet written at age five (K. 1) all the way through to the Requiem he was composing thirty years later at the time of his death in 1791 (K. 626). It took Köchel about ten years to establish and compile his *Chronological Thematic Catalogue of the Collected Musical Works of Wolfgang Amadeus Mozart*, which finally appeared in 1862 and has passed through a number of revisions without losing the K-ness; where would Mozart be without Köchel! Not numbered, for sure.

Only recently have I become fully engaged with the catalogue and the K numbers, and begun to appreciate that here was a map, one of those great aids to discovery, one of those codebreakers that lets you work out where you are and what direction you could go in next. In Mozart's case, the map keeps changing shape, introducing new places to visit, new connections and combinations to make. And slowly, thrillingly, the changing mind of Mozart develops in my mind, and I am not put off by the sound, the sounds, the combination of instruments, which once sounded so prim and stiff — perhaps a bit suspiciously secretive — next to the agitated, agitating guitars and the shape-shifting electronics I grew up with, but now make me hear the thought processes, and the multi-directional multipurpose progression of an artist.

Now that history, and a history of music, has a new way of revealing itself to us, Mozart does not sound irrelevant or imperial and prehistoric, but part of the life of everything in the way such a thinker should be. If you can hear the music as power, as calculation, as a reflection of change, as an individual responding to his surroundings and his own intimate, complicated, restless and glorious thoughts, it is a very liberating moment.

If you are genuinely interested in how one thing leads to another, in Mozart, in music, there is no excuse not to simply start. Take a K number from the register — say, 451 — and see where you land. It happens to be his Piano Concerto No. 16 in D major, 22 March 1784.

Hear what else he was, astonishingly, writing at the time by going to K. 450 – his Piano Concerto No. 15, 15 March 1784, and K. 452, his Quintet for Piano and Winds in E-flat major. As well as writing some pieces of the same type in spurts, so that inside a month he would finish off a handful of concertos or sonatas, he also wrote very different pieces at more or less the same time, from small, very precise ensemble pieces to the historic, hallucinatory operas, from a sonata to a symphony, a concerto to a fugue, each form influencing, reflecting, reimagining the other.

His operas would be influenced by his experiences writing symphonies, concertos, chamber works, religious pieces, and his instrumental work would be influenced by his expressive work in theatre – one part of his musical mind educated another part, and new levels of surprise and originality would emerge as he tried something he had learned in one place in another place. Mozart's acute sensitivity to different instrumental and vocal timbres, and his virtuosity in juxtaposing and reconciling the most unlikely materials in an apparently effortless and natural way, place him supreme as creator of characters – whether that be in his operas, or when he personifies instruments themselves.

The characters, illusions, spectres, dramas and events happening more literally, if often excessively, in the operas had their equivalents in the music: his instrumental styles could generate such power that it felt as though pure music had taken on the shape of a person, or a god, or an identifiable emotional climax. He interacted with himself and made up new rules and established new possibilities for the structures and balance of music by pushing and rearranging limits previously assumed to be fixed and hallowed.

In September 1784 he wrote his Piano Concerto No. 18 in B-flat major – K. 456, a month later his Piano Sonata No. 14 in C minor – K. 457, a month later his String Quartet No. 17 in B-flat major – K. 458. They are all the same thing, but all completely different, at different stages in his development as a writer of concertos, or sonatas, or string quartets, or *notturnos*, but at the same stage of his life, as his mind luxuriates in itself. He is splitting into different Mozarts, simultaneously generating spectacular achievements in more or less brand-new form and content, splitting music into different styles, unprecedented genres, and you can see and hear this, and get a sense of the momentum and context because of the catalogue. It brings order to this thirty-year exploration of multi-layered order and kaleidoscopic disorder.

The K numbers make me realise how Mozart can keep coming to life in the internet age, because a few years ago it would not have been possible to gorge on his music, leaping through and across the K catalogue, into and all over his life, and his life's work, on binge sessions that can last, Netflix-style, for hours, making connections, noting development, experiencing how one thought led to another across numerous pieces and genres, and how, sometimes, somehow, later Mozart seemed to have influenced early Mozart, as though he knew where he was going all along, thought it all up in a moment, all that music came to him in a rush of emotion, and he then had to transfer the music and the structure into earth time, which took a few years, and sometimes it didn't necessarily emerge in any order, but one thing definitely led to another, until it didn't.

My own plan was to randomly collect K numbers, my own way of following an interest in a style of music, a performer, a conductor, an orchestra, an instrument, a period, all dealing with Mozart, from the five-year-old toddler god to the thirty-five-year-old legend, until one day I get to the point where I possess the whole catalogue, or as near as might be possible, considering that some seem more ghostly than others. Some K numbers I will inevitably have heard more than once, some only once. The catalogue more or less runs in chronological order, and you can go in any order you want, and each number itself releases numerous points of view that take you back into the catalogue, and the history of music and Mozart, from a new direction.

It's much easier to find Mozart now, because of the cloud and wi-fi, which make things more straightforward, if somehow always on the verge of abruptly vanishing. You can start simply by starting, and whereas once to experience Mozart, and all the connections, would have taken years and a lot of money, it now takes no time at all and a portion of a modest monthly subscription fee. I am not clear on the economics, and guiltily, lazily, refuse to face up to the problematic consequences of the faceless morass music is being turned into, but I can now speed through Mozart — the years he was alive, the years his music has been performed and recorded, by an endless supply of those who appreciate the sublime madness in the method — in a matter of days. He's at the other end of the phone. He's part of me.

Put into this unprecedented, largely inexplicable context, Mozart is more modern than anything. His way of thinking is brought to central contemporary life in this new setting, which needs to be explained, and thought through, because it is brand new, and which can make everything inside it brand new.

There he is, suddenly, everywhere, if you are in the right frame of mind, with the right account and the right number of hours available to spend moving from room to room, space to space, piece to piece, Bluetooth speaker to speaker, headphone to headphone, and if you don't stop, you can move through Mozart into all of classical music, so in terms of where to start, definitely go through the man whose name, after all, contains all of art and goes within six letters from A to Z, in some order. And in a world where people like to know and be introduced to new things through lists, there is absolutely nothing like a Mozart list, the first great playlist courtesy of Köchel – and it's a list of lists, because you can compile more lists based around Mozart than just about anything else, which in the end is why he is Mozart, and why he is having this continuing after-death presence.

There is a new Mozart, and previous models, which suited the desires and demands of the audiences of the time, are replaced by a different Mozart. This Mozart needs to be written about in a different way, because he materialises outside the usual places, outside the usual buildings and books, given a new life altogether because of the internet.

I roll the 'dice': K. 477, the *Maurerische Trauermusik*, *Masonic Funeral Music*, in C minor, the best known of his Masonic compositions, written when he was twenty-nine, rooted in Gregorian plainchant, featuring an instrumental line-up unique in his output – two violins, two violas, basset horns, two oboes, two horns and a bass – as dark as death, somehow as soothing, threatening and gentle, echoing his Mass in C minor, foreshadowing the Requiem. As soon as I play it, I feel a tug, I feel a welling-up, a sudden need to know more. Oddly enough, my research into this piece ends up with the myth that snow fell on the day of his funeral, but actually, it was a clear day.

Around the same time, Mozart also completes three piano concertos: 20 – K. 466, 21 – K. 467 and 22 – K. 482, the First Piano Quartet – K. 478, and the Thirty-Third Violin Sonata, K. 481, three still to come. There is also a brace of string quartets, the Eighteenth – K. 464, and the Nineteenth – K. 465, the one that was unusual and eventually infamous enough to be handed its nickname, *Dissonance*.

Another random selection takes me to K. 186, Divertimento No. 4 in B-flat major for wind instruments, composed in 1773 for a patron in Milan, his first original piece to feature the clarinet, as distinctive and fancy as a fingerprint. It features the kind of whimsy I would have dismissed if I did not know what else the composer had written, before and after, and once you hear the darker, deeper music, you sense where this delicate ensemble piece drifts closer to the edge, that it is paying attention, for all its jaunty precision, to the size and shape of the abyss. It's blowing nicely in the wind, because a storm has just passed, or one is on its way.

It makes me realise that early, badly advised thoughts regarding the K numbers, that perhaps it was best to begin at around 300, at a mature Mozart, was a naive mistake. It means, for instance, missing the G major Violin Concerto No. 3, K. 216, that he wrote at nineteen, among five he wrote in his teens, making a move from the lively K. 207 to this sparkling gem, where he makes the violin sing, and so it means missing one of those moments where an artist makes a mysterious move from the ordinary to the extraordinary, and we will never know why or how, from being nothing much beyond a slick organiser of received wisdom into something near-demonically special.

The five Mozart violin concertos emerge in one distinct part of his life, the First in 1773 when he was seventeen, the rest in 1775, unlike the piano concertos, which he cultivates throughout his life. A great pianist who also happened to play the violin – one of the few composer-performers who had mastered both instruments – it is as if he felt he had taken the form as far as he wanted to, or could do, with nothing more to say, or no more than their accepted inventor, Vivaldi.

Bob Dylan made such a move, a keen, ambitious and hard-working but ultimately derivative and imitative enthusiast disappearing into the downtown cobbles of 1961 Greenwich Village for a few months, gatecrashing parties, stealing a few records, experiencing a revelation, switching voices and faces, and then re-materialising as almost a different person, possessing or possessed by a different consciousness, with abruptly intact legendary qualities, ready to propel himself into the world as a version of himself, followed by more.

Somewhere around K. 216, Mozart, fancying himself as a chosen one, and therefore cockily acting out being just that, deciding that feeling he has is the throb of genius, comes to life. Mozart, Shakespearean to critic Wilfrid Mellers, is to me as much Dylanesque, the wandering through his own often self-generated myth, the wearing of different masks, the endless teasing of those that may or may not be wondering what he is doing, the constant need to explore deeper and deeper into what it is he is doing, leaving the resonant, provocative, mesmerising traces that the rest of us search through for clues, even as there is no one there, if there ever was.

Thinking of K. 216 makes me want to roll the dice again, hoping either to come up with something that has become a favourite, the String Quartet in D minor, K. 421, or something new that will become a new favourite: I roll... K. 397, Fantasia in D minor for solo piano, composed in 1782, which I like to hear Glenn Gould play, teasing it out as if it was by Bach, and I know he's the Bach man, the masked crusader, and sometimes you get the feeling he's playing the fantasias as though he thinks they are by Bach, and he is Thelonius Monk, and he strays and meddles and rethinks, and reminds you he also knows his way around Schoenberg, but in the end this dares to converse with Mozart, rather than merely obey, as though Boulez is channelling Oscar Peterson, which seems more in the spirit of Mozart than the more powdered, twee versions, even though Gould mocked Mozart for being far too right-handed and really soft on the left. (Charles Ives was particularly sniffy about what he called Mozart's 'lady fingers'.) Then again, it makes you wonder what he meant by that 'right hand', because he considered Mozart, ultimately, to be a 'hedonist'.

Which takes me to K. 475, the Fantasia in C minor, another piece from Mozart's 1785, where Gould is in his own slow world, which takes me to a room where it is being played by Maria Yudina, the great Soviet pianist who had a fierce intensity that could sometimes make even Gould seem a little safe and sound.

Mozart finishes the next year, 1786, with his Thirty-Eighth Symphony – K. 504, after a year of constant creation where his Fourth Horn Concerto – K. 495, twelve duos for Two Basset Horns – K. 487, a Trio for Piano, Clarinet and Viola – K. 498, and his Twentieth String Quartet – K. 499, are mere sideshows. K. 493, the Piano Quartet No. 2 in E-flat major, is then one of the rarer genres, a tense, reserved hybrid of showy concerto and yearning chamber music. He only wrote two piano quartets — the other was K. 478, the year before; the technically difficult concerto elements meant there wasn't much demand from less able, less demonstrative home pianists, the keen amateur ones from the professions contributing to the domestic, music-at-home scene in Vienna.

It makes me wonder about what was immediately before his Second Piano Quartet. K. 492 — which turns out to be all of *The Marriage of Figaro* — and on the other side of that, K. 491, Piano Concerto No. 24 in C minor, unrelenting and dramatic, streaming with melody, hinting at hundreds more, each of them suggesting even more, the penultimate one he wrote of the dozen in Vienna between 1784 and 1786, one of two he wrote in a minor key, writing it while he worked on all of *The Marriage of Figaro*, which makes sense as much as it seems beyond sense. He is inventing and refining a new sort of tragicomic opera, articulating how in an opera the poetry must always be the obedient child of the music, how opera's moral standards were always forming along with surrounding society.

I'm addicted to the hyper-sensitive Glenn Gould playing K. 491, as though he and the CBC Orchestra he's for and against are about to launch into space, and I love hearing the moment when Gould arrives, as if he has just leapt out of the mind of Mozart, pauses for thought, and then describes Mozart's mind, taking over a little, like he now knows Mozart inside out, or thinks he does, believing in this concerto more than any of the others. He's made up a Mozart; he's made up himself. Once or twice, by about the seventeenth minute, when the music seems capable of repairing a broken bone, I am about to cry, if not actually crying, because it has take me so long to get to and understand the compressed, fractal beauty of Gould's playing as much as Mozart's composing, of the interaction between orchestra and piano, one enabling the existence of the other, one dictating terms, the other asking some questions. I might never have made it, so also, I feel it so much more because I did find a way there. Maybe the last music I listen to will be the result of a randomly chosen K number, something by Mozart written when he was fifteen or twenty-five or thirty-five that, the likelihood is, will make incredible sense of the predicament I will find myself in, and make it seem as real or unreal as I want it to.

At twenty-five, in 1781, and we now know that means he is entering the last ten years of his life, his services at the court in his native Salzburg are no longer required, and he becomes a composer in Vienna, tied to no one, in modern terms a freelancer. Vienna becomes a musical mecca because the Austro-Hungarian Empire needed educated bureaucrats and music was an integral part of this education for lawyers, doctors and diplomats.

He earns money by teaching private pupils, from various commissions for operas, from music publishers, and from the pursuit of a superstar career as composer-pianist starring in concerts he arranges. The forty-nine-year-old Haydn is writing his Seventy-Fourth and Seventy-Fifth symphonies with thirty more to come – no mean feat, but the symphony was lighter fare at this point, an interlude between weightier matters, and not yet the composition pinnacle it would become by the time of Beethoven and, elbowed out by Ludwig but sure in his own way of his own mind, Schubert.

Mozart made it to forty-one symphonies, coming down from centurion Haydn's three figures, and then Beethoven got to nine, where each symphony was a great novel, not a short story or a well-told anecdote, and even that number in a lifetime for composers afterwards became a considerable task, let alone a hundred or even forty. Schubert completed seven, six of them by 1818, with later sketches remaining unfinished, for a number of reasons, including No. 8, which becomes known as the *Unfinished* Symphony.

Haydn and Mozart's ambitions for the symphony, the greater complexity they introduced as they wrote more, extending and uncovering possibilities, stretching the form, learning more about themselves and the form, transformed it into a bigger, more serious project, and it isn't until Mozart's last ten or so symphonies that they connect with what the symphony would become.

He had written thirty of what are now called symphonies before he was twenty, the first, of course, when he was eight. They were more functional orchestral diversions, exercises that pushed him deeper into developing the more epic nature of the symphony. The next eleven took thirteen years. The first ones were like decoration, perhaps – astonishingly adept for a young teenager, but still within human reason – of small rooms, pathways, and over time they became houses, and then bigger houses, even castles, with the idea they could even stretch to the heavens.

Haydn and Mozart's efforts led to Beethoven's view of the symphony as the essence of his work, the music that would create his legacy. He had to follow Haydn and Mozart — with Schubert close by — and by resisting their formulas and techniques and developing his own solutions and ideas, the symphony became a grander, loftier performance, with a more ideological sensibility, and took far more emotionally and creatively to imagine and build, and then to do again. Symphonies became huge, exuberantly designed bridges with fantastic views stretching across vast areas of land and sea. They became cathedrals, imagined versions of great buildings designed to celebrate and articulate the spirit and the spiritual, the sort of buildings, if they could be built, that would be the ideal place for the music to be played inside.

Symphonies in 1781 not yet being the landmarks they would become, for Mozart it is a year of violin sonatas: he writes his Twenty-Fourth — K. 376, Twenty-Fifth — K. 377, Twenty-Seventh — K. 379 and Twenty-Eighth — K. 380, so begin your tour of the sonatas with K. 377 played by Mitsuko Uchida (piano) and Mark Steinberg (violin).

The next year, Haydn completes four more symphonies: the Seventy-Third, Seventy-Sixth, Seventy-Seventh and Seventy-Eighth; and Mozart is flying through three piano concertos: the Eleventh — K. 413, Twelfth — K. 414 and Thirteenth — K. 415; his Thirty-Fifth Symphony — K. 385; a Horn Quintet — K. 417; and his Fourteenth String Quartet — K. 387. The year after that, as though it's a natural part of the growing process, as if it is him changing shape, or merely breathing in time, or outside time, and all this music can only be what it is, a sanctified articulation of material energies released at the beginning of time, he's on to his Fifteenth — K. 421 and Sixteenth Quartet — K. 427, his Thirty-Sixth Symphony — K. 425, his Seventeenth Mass — *The Great* Mass — K. 427, a Second Horn Concerto — K. 417 and a Fugue in C minor for two keyboards — K. 426.

In 1784, with twelve-year-old Beethoven as a promising young court musician already beginning to compose for the piano in Cologne and perform in concert in cities such as Rotterdam for considerable amounts of money, with Haydn moving into the eighties with his symphonies, like a cautious cricketer carefully inching towards a century, Mozart moves through six piano concertos, 14 to 19 — K. 449, K. 450, K. 451, K. 453, K. 456 and K. 459 — as though he just had to open the piano lid to find them, and there is still time somehow for other works including a Quintet for Piano and Winds – K. 452, his Thirty-Second Violin Sonata – K. 454, a Fourteenth Piano Sonata – K. 457, and a Seventeenth String Quartet – K. 458.

In 1787, in the twilight of the Enlightenment, eleven years after the American Revolution and two years before the French Revolution, as the fifty-five-year-old Haydn reaches his Eighty-Eighth and Eighty-Ninth Symphonies, the sixteen-year-old Beethoven is visiting Vienna to receive some lessons from the thirty-one-year-old Mozart, a trip he has to abandon in order to attend to his frail mother in Bonn, who dies in July at forty from tuberculosis. (His one-year-old sister also dies this year; his father's response is to sink further into alcoholism, and Beethoven, as the eldest surviving child, takes on the responsibility of head of the family.)

Mozart's major works that year include the Third and Fourth String Quintets – K. 515 and K. 516; the Thirty-Fifth Violin Sonata – K. 526; the completed the Third Horn Concerto – K. 447; the opera *Don Giovanni* – K. 527; and *Eine Kleine Nachtmusik*, Divertimento for String Quartet – K. 525. In 1788, while Haydn with his symphonies makes the nineties, Mozart is writing, among other works, his Thirty-Sixth and final violin sonata – K. 547, the Fifteenth, Sixteenth and Seventeenth Piano Sonatas – K. 533, K. 545 and K. 570, a String Quintet transcription of his Wind Octet, K. 388, the Third Piano Trio – K. 543, Fourth Piano Trio – K. 548 and final Fifth Piano Trio – K. 564, and the Thirty-Ninth, Fortieth and Forty-First – the final – symphonies. The last works in certain styles and series are now starting to arrive regularly as the life and travels of Mozart come to an end, and he is struggling to earn a freelance living, writing as much as possible, as much to alleviate his cash-flow problems as to create great art, even as the great art keeps coming.

In 1789 he composes the last three string quartets: the Twenty-First – K. 575, Twenty-Second – K. 589 and Twenty-Third – K. 590, and his last two keyboard sonatas, the Eighteenth – K. 576 and Nineteenth – K. 547. *Cosi Fan Tutte* – K. 588 premieres at the beginning of 1790, and later in the year he completes Adagio and Allegro in F minor for a mechanical organ clock – K. 594, one of three pieces Mozart wrote for a popular eighteenth-century object that combined a clock with a small mechanised organ. A financially desperate Mozart, complaining to his wife Constanze that he was only doing it for the money, wrote that the sound was too shrill and high-pitched.

In 1791 he writes numerous lively, zestful works, including pieces for a glass harmonica conceived by Benjamin Franklin, and completes K. 595, the B-flat Piano Concerto No. 27, which he had begun working on three years before. Performing it in March, he makes his final appearance as concerto soloist with no sign, whatever that might mean, that this year would be his last. He wasn't making plans about what he would write, or play, at the end of his life.

It is easy to hear significant things in this final piano concerto, and his final orchestral piece, the intimate Clarinet Concerto in A major, K. 622: a faintness, a joyousness, a resignation, a dread, a melancholy, but any of those moods are introduced after the fact by interpreting musicians who know only too well the end of the story and are playing it with significant end-ness in mind.

Despite not being written with a sense of impending death, K. 595 can be played – and listened to – as a farewell, but it can also be played as a Mozart piece from a life that wasn't about to end, that was still moving forward, as can K. 608, another composition for beautifully made if twee-sounding mechanical clock. The serious, serene Fantasia in F minor evocatively filters baroque techniques and classical themes through a modern Mozart mind, seriously matching the technical precision of the fugue with the complex interlocking gears of the mechanism he wrote it for. What could have been kitsch is an unlikely late masterpiece, but not because it was the end, simply because of his constant application to the task in front of him, where he could disappear, whatever was happening around him, into pure process, and whatever it was that his mind was doing.

Earlier pieces could be played with the same sense of melancholy, or dreaming into the distance, of sensing the end of all ends, and the final pieces would make as much sense as midlife works, filled with art, fire and fancy, with a still often thrilling, infectious sense of apprehending what happens next, a constant ability to take the listener by surprise, not at all overshadowed by death.

Mozart composes his final opera – *La Clemenza di Tito*, K. 621 – and the more famous, overstuffed and less serene *Die Zauberflöte* (*The Magic Flute*) – K. 620, which premieres on 30 September at the Theater an der Wien outside Vienna, and is soon a hit, the cult veneration starting before his death. The secular *Magic Flute* becomes endlessly worshipped, to the point of it being hailed in 1961 by music critic – and great sportswriter – Sir Neville Cardus as the 'only opera in existence that might have been composed by God', an over-the-top response to an over-the-top opera.

Mozart is unable to complete the last composition he is working on, some reports said feverishly, which happens to be his sacred Requiem Mass for the dead, where the childlike quality that had lingered in Mozart into his twenties and thirties was eradicated once and for all, if more for the sake of the commission than any sense of his own fate. There is little evidence during November 1791 to say the work was causing him any particular anguish; domestic life remained largely normal. After a few weeks of undramatic-seeming illness, he had been rehearsing parts of the Requiem on 4 December and felt worse than usual. His doctor applied cold compresses, which sent him into shock. He never recovered consciousness.

Gossip melodramatically exaggerated over time suggested he was poisoned using a seventeenth-century potion mostly containing arsenic by a rival composer, Antonio Salieri, who was a little unstable – actually on his deathbed – when he made his confession, or perhaps by the Masons in revenge for his disclosure of Masonic practices and secrets in *The Magic Flute*. He might have died from rheumatic fever, deadly to someone who had been notoriously frail since childhood, with all that arduous travelling, or 'dropsy of the heart', a swelling of the body due to water retention as a result of kidney failure. According to his death certificate, Mozart died of 'heated millary fever', which was eighteenth century for 'haven't a clue'. Newspaper obituaries immediately noted that the musical world mourned the early loss of this 'immortal man'.

It was a sudden ending, in a flash of history, one that turned the shape of Mozart into something very different from someone who lived perhaps another thirty years into the nineteenth century, as Beethoven and Schubert pulled music even more into the future, and he was alive to react, to keep adapting. He was outlived by Haydn – making it into the nineteenth century, dying in 1809 – who had taught the wildling Mozart economy and discipline, and influenced him if only as an example of a great composer he needed to equal, and in the end outshine. In 1798, Haydn wrote: 'If I could only impress on the soul of every friend of music ... how inimitable are Mozart's works, how profound, how musically intelligent, how extraordinarily sensitive!'

Mozart can easily be turned into the perfect emblem of the perfect composer, who worked miracles and even had a miraculous influence on the world, with so much prolific, versatile skill to admire – his ability, so it has come to pass, to write in every musical genre of his time, including a few not yet completely defined, needing his own transformative contribution to complete their identities, writing subtle, complex, moderate, facile, resonant pieces that were both secular and sacred, instrumental and vocal, intimate and epic, intended for home, court, concert hall, church, theatre, opera house – and wax cylinder, record, cassette, eight-track, elevator, radio, studio, cinema, café, television, phone, DVD, MP3, iTunes, Spotify, the cloud, somewhere else, encompassing the beginning and end of music, of life itself.

One thing Mozart really understood was how to end any kind of invention or performance, any composition, any series of compositions: there must always be an ending, a final breath, a final note, a final pause, a last lingering moment... and the silence that follows, invisible as music, is still Mozart.

5. THE PREPARATION

With the story of 'the piano', there are numerous other points of entry. I've flirted with collecting music produced using toy pianos, not least because John Cage made tantalising use of the idea of the toy version in his 1948 composition *Suite for Toy Piano*, drawn to how the stiffened, conventional classical piano sound was distorted, diminished and remade through the reduction of the real thing to a kooky, twinkling child's version. For Cage in the late 1930s, the idea of the classical piano had become overfamiliar and in any experimental context fairly ossified, with mostly jazz players like Earl Hines, Art Tatum and Duke Ellington finding ways to take it forward, with Monk, Jamal, Evans and Cecil Taylor on the horizon, Glenn Gould not yet dreamt up, and Cage used his natural critical blend of playful whimsy and self-conscious trial and error to subvert the classically based instrument.

Potentially troubling notions of how modernist music feels unfamiliar and disconcerting to a casual listener are contradicted, even soothed, by using sounds that have a nostalgic, unthreatening, nursery quality. On the other hand, the toy piano's awkward, otherworldly music-box charm enhances a sense of the alluring ghostliness of the unexpected, and perhaps generates a haunting sense of the tentative, vigilant moves of the earliest pianists playing instruments being built around them and their fingers as they got used to this new object, working out what exactly could be done with it.

The toy piano can be a good, hopeful place to begin taking on experimental music, where the tendency is to find other places, positions and sound sources to remake and positively deform musical potential. It can take you to dramatic pieces by George Crumb and Mauricio Kagel, itself a route into a wider, greater universe, and the slightly jauntier but still moving *Art of the Toy Piano* where Margaret Leng Tan toys up Cage, Satie, Beethoven and, just in case you might waver, 'Eleanor Rigby'.

It can take you to Christopher Hobbs, a member of Cornelius Cardew's Scratch Orchestra and AMM, who was a part of the Promenade Theatre Orchestra, inheriting Satie's desire to deflate pomposity, his mischievous argument that serious music did not need to be interesting and dominating at all costs, and who used toy pianos to perform rigorously processed systems music.

The Malaysian pianist Mei Yi Foo won the 2013 *BBC Music Magazine* Newcomer of the Year for her second album, called *Musical Toys*, titled after fourteen short miniatures inspired by childhood toys and nursery imagery written by the formidable spiritual modernist Sofia Gubaidulina.

Foo imagined the kind of pieces she would have liked to play as a child – the kind of awed, awe-inspiring child who would also have been able to play as though they were toys Ligeti's profoundly playful *Musica Ricerata* and South Korean Ligeti student Unsuk Chin's wonderfully restless, charmingly strange Six Piano Études, which are also featured on the album.

Both Ligeti and Chin were fascinated by the fantastical, captivating game-playing of *Alice in Wonderland* – Ligeti planned over thirty years to write an *Alice* opera, and Chin brought the idea to fruition. Both carried into their music Carroll's literary methods of changing perspectives, merging the simple, attractive and innocent with the complex, distorted and unsettling, sometimes the severely absurdist, which Foo connected with the transformative fantasies of *Musical Toys*.

Gubaidulina treats the imagination of a child in much the same way as Lewis Carroll treated it, as something that can be deep and mysterious, poetic and puzzling, wild and intoxicating. The childish isn't cuddly here: it's vivid, disconcerting and even nightmarish. Childish thoughts and childish activities can be as weird as anything, and often a direct influence on general avant-garde pursuits.

Foo used a standard, unprepared piano to play these dynamic miniatures, but the idea of imagining demanding pieces filtered through childlike imagery abstractly parallels the principles of the prepared piano by framing the intricate compositions inside an imagined world of innocent, unhindered, random play. The piano is played with immense skill, but somehow as though it is being experienced for the first time, the equivalent of a child encountering something initially strange and puzzling. Piano playing becomes a series of bizarre events, and even when it all becomes familiar, the tantalising bizarreness lingers. Technically demanding works are presented without sacrificing a near-prankish, Cageian sense of mischief, so that possibly intimidating, structurally complex, reflective seriousness is played with a light, fluent sense of joy and adventure.

There is a lovely version of Cage's *Suite for Toy Piano* on Stephen Drury's 1995 collection of John Cage piano music, named after Cage's beautifully charged *In a Landscape*, a tentative yet certain 1948 piece that astonishingly anticipates the pace, peace and time-consuming pleasures of post-minimalist electronic ambient music. There is no better place to start working through classical music than from this record, in a way that will, if you've got the inclination, eventually take you to, say, Mozart's piano concertos, Charles Ives's *Concord* Sonata, Debussy's preludes, Nancarrow's Studies for Piano Player, La Monte Young's *The Well Tuned Piano* and Shostakovich's Preludes and Fugues. (That Cage will also, if you've got an open mind, take you to, say, Alice Coltrane, Matching Mole, Miles Davis, Scott Walker, Laurel Halo, Chris Watson and Sarah Davachi shows something about how amazing he was at not only forecasting the weather but also pretty much creating it.)

Drury's *In a Landscape* also contains examples of Cage compositions for prepared piano. Cage is often considered eccentric, weird, difficult, non-musical, perverse, silly, charlatan, chaotic, but he suffers to this day from being turned into something that reflects wider prejudices about the experimental and theoretical, even as all popular entertainment is essentially based on ideas and thinking that was originally avant-garde, open-ended and utterly, scarily fresh.

Cage is more an unorthodox, highly independent mixture of philosopher and entertainer, and he also spliced together spiritual imagining with a show-business dimension that will probably remain ahead of its time for a few decades yet. Prepared piano music is definitely one of the things I like to 'collect', and although Cage's way of preparing the piano has remained a marginal process, the few places where it can be found are usually worth the search. The prepared piano can take you to Radiohead, Richard Carpenter, Yann Tiersen – who would hate to be just known as the composer of the *Amélie* soundtrack – and the B-52s, and also, where it comes closest to being the scratchy, sketchy, kiddy-giddy soundtrack to an eerie and/or quirky puppet show, the French duo Klimperei.

Cage decided to change the sound of the piano because, obliged in 1940 to write a piano piece for an African-themed dance and unable to use percussion, his preferred choice for such a commission, he realised that for his immediate purposes the piano was 'wrong'. The normal and normally played piano would not give him the appropriately styled noise and rhythms he wanted. Limited to using the piano in a performing space with no pit or wings, he was compelled to mix up the technique he would use for writing orchestral pieces with the technique he would use writing for small percussion ensembles while using the piano alone to generate the sound.

He had studied with American theorist and composer Henry Cowell – at another extreme from his other teacher, the deviant traditionalist Schoenberg – who wrote his first piece for piano in the year Cage was born, 1912. Cage recalled how Cowell, keen on inventing unprecedented ways to play the piano, to break away from the European traditions, would change traditional piano sound by effectively attacking it – climbing inside and plucking, scraping and muting the strings using his fingers, fingernails and hands. Sometimes he would stroke the strings inside with a darning needle while playing the keyboard. He would play it like a harp, as though it was everyone else that was mad for using the keys. This combination of the impish and the inquisitive appealed to Cage and turned a practical restriction into a creative opportunity.

Cage explored ways to alter the sound of the piano, and after false starts with plates, which moved around too much, he quickly arrived at using nuts, bolts and pieces of 'weather stripping' (short strips of felt-covered plastic used for draught-proofing windows) between and bound around the strings. Sometimes the interference produced a more percussive, banging-type sound, conjured up from some imagined ancient past when early humans learned how noise could be made into consoling pleasure and inspiring ritual, sometimes a more resonant, ringing and enigmatic gong-like sound, from the hidden, captivating Eastern worlds that were one of Cage's prime fascinations.

There was the added element of the objects placed onto and into the strings vibrating with their own supplementary rhythmical and musical quality. The limitations of the piano, when played as it seemed it must be played, as if there could be no other way, were released by this simple act of enforced disobedience. From the muting and the production of more complex, dissonant timbres, a new instrument materialised, one that contained all manner of delightful unplanned surprises, something else Cage found attractive.

Cage was consistently chasing uncommon sounds beyond the range of traditional instruments that the invention and refinement of electronic instruments later in the century would more comprehensively satisfy. He wanted noise and effects he could hear in his head but which no available instrument achieved. By 'preparing' the piano, interfering with its logic, Cage was effectively creating a primitive, acoustic home-made version of a synthesiser, producing noises that were as otherworldly as any eventually generated by machine.

For a few years, during the 1940s, especially when he had no access to the percussive instruments that led to the more unruly, or more controlled, sound he wanted, the prepared piano was effectively Cage's favourite way of pursuing the incongruous and unrecognisably vivid. And, radically rekindling Mozart's indecipherable feeling for sonic exploration, mirroring how, as the piano was initially evolving and provisional, it had qualities of being 'prepared', made up, reset, open-ended, Cage was excited by how much the prepared piano's indefinite, unconventional sounds inspired his appetite for composing new pieces, to make use of how the adapting of the customary opened up a new world of sound. That new world of sound led to new types of structure, and a blurring and realigning of the familiar that again suited Cage's nomadic temperament. Music was produced by concentrating on the duration of a sound, and on the elastic silence and fluctuating not-quite-silence in between one sound and another, and there was an extreme modification of what a piece of music could be, how random and abstract, how quiet and un-climactic, how non-musical, and therefore how astonishingly re-musical.

Compared to what was happening elsewhere in serious music during this 1930s and 1940s period, the overwhelming, strident complexity, smashing up against the horror and fierceness of the times, aggressively confronting ultimately useless sentimentality, dislocating sense at a time when reason was being brutally smashed apart, this music was oddly, dreamily reduced, seeking exquisiteness and spiritual relief from the surrounding mayhem, and achieving a brave, almost amoral, level of timelessness that means the music makes more sense as time passes.

Cage wasn't thinking particularly about what was going on in the world at the time he was preparing the piano, nor really what had happened in the past, except to avoid repeating it – and consequently he evokes a transcendent, meditative timelessness, which induces a necessary sense of optimism if only because, in the darkest, most unnerving of times, there was still this perhaps naive, misfit level of faith in the future and in the importance of individual freedom, however delicately, even indulgently expressed.

Pieces written for dances, such as *Primitive*, *A Room*, *In the Name of the Holocaust*, *Our Spring Will Come* and *Root of an Unfocus*, and the wonderful culmination of his prepared piano period, the sonatas and interludes, which he worked on between 1946 and 1948, demonstrate the richness of what the conceptualist Cage did with his reinvented piano. He used techniques that paradoxically scaled down the piano's expressive power and basically turned it into a polyrhythmic percussion instrument (the equivalent of a percussion ensemble), a utilitarian purpose later transposed to his String Quartet (1950).

The piano as an orchestra in miniature is transformed into an alternative, hallucinatory version, where the sound of the piano is not messed up or damaged but converted and somehow sympathetically impaired. Whispering allusions to how Satie developed a new secretive melodic language for the piano by draping notes around the edge of silence merged with a vision of where music could go once it could be made using equipment and sonic sources beyond the range of established instruments.

Cage moved on as the 1940s became the 1950s, as he was destined to do, transferring the structural ideas the prepared piano inspired into other instrumental arrangements, which in turn inspired his investigations into the uses of chance and randomness in composition, to explore and expand the organising of structural dimensions, durational proportions and sound materials he now considered to be the fundamental properties of musical composition. By the early 1950s he had fully discarded the prepared piano, eventually, of course, in 1952, after slowly throwing less and less sound into a version of pure silence, he opened up *4'33''* of potential silence as a complete compositional conclusion to his investigations into where music begins and ends and begins again. In a world about to leap into what on the one hand was rock 'n' roll, and beyond, and on the other was electronic music, and beyond, both leading to an extraordinary development of sounds generated in recording studios unique to their late twentieth-century time, there seemed little point any more for him to use the prepared piano.

The principle of the prepared piano quickly gathered dust, and an alternative history of soundscaping was abruptly turned into something of a secret, stuck in a corridor, filed away out of sight and mind, with only the rare, occasional explorer like George Crumb breaking into the piano to make a noise rather than sitting where you were told and, mostly, certainly outside improvised music, following orders. There were the occasional affectionate homages paid by those who had their mind turned by Cage, such as John Adams, who from a position of being the most famous living mainstream classical composer in the world following *Nixon in China*, took the prepared piano of Cage and in 1994 placed it inside his *John's Book of Alleged Dances* string quartet, communicating the concept way beyond the reach of Cage, proving yet again how the influence of Cage never stops humming.

A little later, decades after Cage had finished preparing pianos, post-electronic conceptualist Richard James, a.k.a. Aphex Twin on the electro-specialist Warp Label of Sheffield, heard some gorgeously decaying Cage pieces from the 1940s while working on his 2001 album *Drukqs*, and, clearing away the dust, recognised in their enchanting strangeness, which by the end of the twentieth century was both antique but also still from a wiped-out future, something of the mysterious otherness he also desired. It gave him access to the production of ravishing, spectral melodies usually beyond the reach of the calculating, bedroom-computer musician mostly concerned with shaping and shattering sonic surfaces, slicing up internal tension and shredding basic rhythms.

The sound of electronic music had become by the end of the century as fixed and regulated as the classical piano had become by the middle of the century, and James was more liberated by his discovery of Cage and his repossession of the piano than he was at the time by the computer. His response was to use a grand piano that could be played by computer and programme his own equivalents of prepared intrusions to reproduce, to re-find, the unearthly noises Cage was moving towards back in the 1940s. *Drukqs* randomly, near satirically skipped and skittered between the expected, demented Aphex transmissions, cracking up time and space, and stark, gauzy impressions of piano impressions that linked him with the special, manipulating mind of Cage. Some listeners, including fans, were baffled by the contrast between the splintered frenzy and the shrouded tranquillity, but there was deep logic in the connection between the different ways of investigating and making up motion, energy and stillness.

Drukqs makes for an illuminating, anomalous addition to any prepared-piano collection, but for a while appeared to lead to another cul-de-sac, a small addition to the world of prepared piano that itself went nowhere, followed up by very few.

One member of the 'very few' was Paul Corley, whose gorgeously, nervously lucid debut album *Disquiet* was released on the shyly present Bedroom Community label, formed in Iceland in 2006, where he worked as a recording engineer not only with furtively forceful Bedroom Community artists such as Ben Frost, Daníel Bjarnason, Valgeir Sigurðsson and Nico Muhly, but also other electronic, experimental and wilful outsider acts like Tim Hecker. Studio work enabled him to make things, sometimes just for the sake of it, hiding behind the work and expression of others, so that he could work out what kind of shapes he wanted to make for himself, how to sonically combine thought with flows of feeling.

Disquiet features plotless, actionless, deeply absorbing instrumental songs that sound as though they leak from the emotions of someone who has moved around the planet in search of, if not a place to call home, then a place pointing in the right direction, which is always just out of reach. The album title comes from a book written in Lisbon between 1912 and 1935, Fernando Pessoa's fragmentary, incomplete melancholy masterpiece *The Book of Disquiet*, where someone says, 'I feel as though I am always on the verge of waking up,' and this helps with any description of the music, as does another quote from Pessoa, 'The moment I find myself, I am lost.'

The proactive, interconnected Bedroom Community drew Corley in, and suited his own sensibility and artistic desires. A kind of insulated North Atlantic relative of ECM Records, specialising in vulnerable and visceral metaphysical electro-acoustic music, and yet also close to the conceptual wavelengths of Warp and Mille Plateaux, specialising in radically self-conscious electronic music, the label appealed to Corley. It produced music that seemed as influenced by, say, the thought of emotion and the emotion of thought, birds, marine animals, weather changes, brainwaves, earthquakes, plants, planets and the stars themselves, as much as it is inspired by Webern, Eno and the glitch specialists Oval, creating sounds from the skips and errors of purposefully damaged compact discs.

Corley started work behind the scenes in the BC studio – closer to the top of the world than most, actually nestling in the settled, anonymous suburbs of Reykjavík, set well apart from general clichés of icy, isolated Icelandic existence. A year or two later, slipping into the label's mindset, he started thinking about his own music and what would become his debut album. He began improvising, often in the early hours of the morning, the early, provisional sounds that would over time become the fully formed compositions on *Disquiet* that exist between the intentional and the unintentional. He'd often experimented with making his own music but produced nothing he felt proper enough to ever be played to anyone else, nothing that didn't sound simply like he was just haphazardly working out if he had his own voice, something that might be distinct and separate from his influences.

The new pieces that became *Disquiet* felt different, and didn't need abandoning. He didn't plan for it to be a Bedroom Community album, didn't dare hope that what he was doing would be up to their discriminating standards, but when he played the music to Sigurðsson at the label, for a little guidance, he could immediately hear it was one of theirs, that it belonged in the Community. In his own way Corley had already taken the label's advice, which isn't written down, but can be read through the music they release, which is a constantly unfolding manifesto. The music they specialise in is spectacular northern music, from up and out there, where all forms of psychic and physical protection become completely necessary faced with the weather, and the isolation, and the secret, disorientating movements of the invisible. The label's Icelandic-born and/or-based musicians are a little nonplussed, even offended, when writers like me make such a fuss of the relationship between location and music, as to them Iceland is just were they happened to be, nothing special, even as it brings them closer to elemental forces and the beginning – or a quiet, spaced-out end – of time than most. It's an inevitable influence, a contributory factor, but they don't want to think it controls the music, or is all it is, as if they have no say and do nothing but neurotically recreate the sound of dramatic waterfalls, bubbling springs and cracking ice.

I hear *Disquiet* as a solo piano album, with Corley playing prepared piano in the tradition of Henry Cowell and John Cage, approaching the instrument as being percussive and musical, functional and exotic, so that it creates pulse, and pitch, and tone, which can lead to any number of directions. The piano becomes other than a piano, and Corley plays it with what he calls an inexpert, non-musician sensibility – admitting that he is 'a horrible piano player' – with a liberating, capricious disregard for technique. He gets inside the instrument, under the lid, and plucks, strokes, cajoles, digs, meddles, needles, searching for he doesn't know what until he finds it, searching for the impossible via the everyday.

It's not the only instrument he plays, and the studio itself, his computer, various plug-ins, the space he throws into and around the sounds he produces, are also part of the overall instrumental line-up, but the piano is the lead instrument. The piano is where the melody reveals itself, as the essence of the experience, notes and feelings tentatively coming to a conclusion, with all other noises becoming the rhythm, a shimmering, abstract halo around the piano performance.

In that sense, the music, which, if it belongs in any fixed genre, exists where you rub together glitch, drone, sound art, post-rock, sound art and alt-classical, and one or two downstream Cageian genres not yet invented, is also a vagrant kind of post-jazz. It follows a trail, or perhaps creates the trail, towards an imaginary shore that Morton Feldman might have found if he'd been influenced by Thelonius Monk, post-rock chamber group Labradford, and Autechre.

Corley himself admits to the improvisational influence of abstract avant-blues master Loren Connors – from a fluky universe where Bach jams with Muddy Waters – and the capricious, elaborate minimalists Dirty Three – like an aggressively stagnant Spontaneous Music Ensemble with special guest John Cale – in the way his playing embraces a sort of spare, rattled energy. I hear tender, defiant late-period Keith Jarrett, breaking down familiar show tunes into fractured, lonely focus, confessing himself through carefully aligned fragments, where piano notes, some verging on the bell-like, some falling towards the drum-like, maintain resonant tension between structure and collapse, energy and its eventual erasure.

Corley also admires the obsessively patient, set-apart work of wildlife sound recordist Chris Watson, once of electronic aggressors Cabaret Voltaire, and makes sound out of the noise of the time, whether natural or supernatural, organic or fabricated, synthesised or dreamlike. Then again, Corley's other main instrument is a microphone, with which he can pick up, one way or another, all of the sounds that he can then turn into information. A third main instrument is a pair of headphones, through which he hears the sound he is making, and then hears the slow, reflective songs he turns these sounds into; and then there is the room he sits in as he makes noise, and manipulates and scrutinises it, which is also an instrument, which you can play and make changes to.

He is the first person to listen to what he is doing, and by the time others listen, they are listening to Corley listening to himself, and to what he has recorded and treated and processed, as if we are eavesdropping on his imagination. We are collaborating with his Pessoanistic concern, felt especially at 3 a.m. in a distant, still recording studio set in far-off Iceland while the whole world sleeps, that he might be imaginary, and the sounds he makes from inside the piano are the only things that are real.

In 2004 the amiable, ambitious thirty-eight-year-old Düsseldorf musician and film composer Volker Bertelmann, writing and performing as Hauschka, stumbled across the non-existent esoteric map that linked the echoing footsteps and fading fingerprints of John Cage with electronic curiosity-seeker Aphex Twin.

Bertelmann was a classically trained musician who had tired of studying and playing classical music, turning to electronic music, and an increasing number of collaborative, electronically based projects. He then ran out of enthusiasm for how the once endless possibilities of electronics were becoming limited, not so much repetitive, which he was drawn to, as more and more of the same. As James of Aphex had noticed a decade earlier, the prepared piano as refined by John Cage suggested a new opportunity to tamper with music and forge unique sounds in ways that were all at once absurd, profound, even profane, and on the edge of the uncanny. Bertelmann noticed, as Cage had prematurely and accidentally, and James more knowingly, that there was a way of playing electronic music without using electronic instruments, by taping up, tinkering with and invading the traditional, solemn grand piano as sedately set in place inside twentieth-century concert halls.

Hauschka's records, following his rediscovery of those earlier discoveries, have remained loyal to the notion of distressing the piano while retaining a measure of dignity, so that what could end up being inconsequentially nutty and even horribly cute reflects more the minimalist grace and poise of Harold Budd. The prepared piano has become his instrument, and although there is a playful, wacky-scientist element to how he treats his piano, and fiddles about with the strings and tonal quality in order to remake the instrument, there is also a deep seriousness, and a self-aware, emotional channelling of the prime 1960s minimalists through a personal musical history filter that stretches from Erik Satie through to Michael Nyman, John Fahey, Oval, Matmos and Fennesz.

One of his albums is actually titled *The Prepared Piano*, taking an unashamed pride in the fact that he was setting out to become an expert, if not *the* expert in the far-off field, and this with *Room to Expand*, where he unashamedly announces he will not be penned in by what could be seen as a novelty act, are worth trying first.

Ferndorf is where he leaps beyond the idea of piano preparing being merely a nice, temporary trick, a whimsical variation on something almost vaudevillian, and delightfully demonstrates how he has found a decisive, random way of making personal music that can express yearning, melancholy, rapture and boldness. With *Salon des Amateurs* Hauschka draws from his experiences of where experimental electronic music breaks, however capriciously or unpredictably, into underground dance clubs, while sticking to his favourite instrument, the prepared piano. He positions his idiosyncratic, idealistic acoustic take on the idea of the synthesiser with programmed beats and more orthodox instrumentation.

Repetition is delicately layered over repetition and given a repetitive twist and a charming restorative melodic longing that ends up moving the Aphex venture a little further on, and over, another boundary.

He collaborated with others on *Salon*, including members of Múm and Calexico, suggesting the prepared piano could be part of an ensemble where whole new worlds revealed themselves, not just a quizzical solo project balancing the books between indie pursuits, classical strategies and light-hearted stunts. Former *Time* Best Young Classical Musician in the World, the violinist Hilary Hahn travelled from her more formal world into Hauschka's wilfully quixotic zone. Her wistful solo on 'Girls' led to a whole album by the pair, where a new world did unfold, the spare, improvised *Silfra*.

Hahn fused her own sophisticated love for Bach — and her attraction to less-known works like Schoenberg's Piano Concerto and Ives's sonatas — with Hauschka's knack for inserting ping-pong balls, marbles and mini vibrators into the belly of a piano without sacrificing integrity and sensitivity. Her unerring, graceful articulation of loneliness and concentration was framed inside his scoreless, Cageian, even creepy flair for binding playfulness with solemnity, just to see where things might go. *Silfra* wasn't necessarily earth-shattering, as much as it suggested a few routes you could take towards the earth-shattering, not least the modest, un-crossovery combining of disciplined classical brilliance with an experimental indie sensibility. But it took the prepared piano over yet another border, into another country, one imagined by Hahn and Bertelmann, based on their developing relationship with each other, which was both strange and comfortable, scratchy and sensual, set inside a troubling dream they were having about the country they recorded it in, Iceland, which already has, whatever Bedroom Community might say, dreamlike qualities.

Hauschka is right on the contemporary dream sweet spot where classical, electronic, pop, sound art, novelty, camouflage and the avant-garde meet, nostalgic for a compromised notion of authenticity and often weirdly sentimental, but with a militant edge, as much a part of the modern festival circuit as an ingredient in any curating of Riley, Reich, Glass, Eno and co. that sets them into the history of music right between John Cage and Björk, trip hop and glitch.

If you can thin down the torrential, distracting glut of music automatically pouring in and out of machines, screens and ravenous social media right now, much of which resembles and reassembles the major trends and indie versions of popular music mixed and remixed since the 1950s, this is where there is a possible emergence of a distinctive, transformative and mutating scene, reflecting and monitoring the post-traumatic and post-pandemic twenty-first century.

It is not of and from rock 'n' roll, with those particular antecedents and expectations, or shiny, seductive pop, with that spiralling accumulation of commercial pressures, which will lead to a different kind of post-pandemic response, although it refers to it in however fragmented a way, but it does seem to be where a progressive music for the twenty-first century seems to be heading. A music percolating from the speculative edges of classical history that comes from and refracts the distorted, distorting technological and transformed cultural environment, that becomes a soundtrack to how our minds, brains and time itself are changing because of the constant way new systems and routes – and battles – are emerging via the computer, the internet and social media.

In this scene, or variable fractions of an abstract scene overlapping each other, something that is from all over the world and simultaneously deep inside the new same-place intimacy of the computer, containing new territories changing shape all of the time, you can place: Hauschka, and other acts on his label Fat City, such as Max Richter, Johann Johannsson and Dustin O'Halloran, and those on labels such as Bedroom Community – including Valgeir Sigurðsson, who produced *Silfra* with shape-shifting, dimension-manipulating Hendrix and 1970s Miles Davis on his mind, and Ben Frost, with his slipping and slamming together of a classical commitment to structure and atmosphere with a near death-metal take on volume and attack – and Erased Tapes, with Nils Frahm, Peter Broderick and Ólafur Arnalds.

This connects to a whole array of approaches to the arranging and representing of a music for and of the times we find ourselves in, where sportive rock clichés and big-time, glamorous pop gestures actually seem a little old-fashioned and done with. In this scene, which arrives when the idea of scenes is all but over, or too self-consciously faked, there is the blurring of lines between music and art, between parts of the world, between old and new, between instruments and electronics, between silence and disturbance, between composition and improvisation, between mood and desperation, between architecture and daydreaming, between history and tomorrow, between community and privacy, between weight and lightness, between Feldman and his shadow, between Miles and what is missing in general, and a list that would take in Tyshawn Sorey of Pi, one step forward from AMM and Braxton — two steps across and off the floor from Spontaneous Music Ensemble, Earle Brown and Popol Vuh — Food and Eivind Aarset of ECM, the Portico Quartet of Real World, Travis and Fripp of Panegyric, Ulrich Schnauss of Scripted Realities, Daniele Mana of Hyperdub, Lapalux of Brainfeeder, Jon Hopkins and Marconi Union of Just Music, Forest Swords of Ninja Tune, the self-releasing (once Startled) Insects of Bristol, Esmerine of Constellation, Lisa Moore of Cantaloupe, Unsuk Chin of Deutsche Grammophon, John Talabot of Permanent Vacation, Cosmo Sheldrake of Transgressive, wzrdryA,V of Digitalis, Agnes Obel of Play It Again Sam, Christian Scott aTunde Adjuah of Ropeadope, George Benjamin of Nimbus, Colin Stetson of 50HZ, Toshio Hosokawa of ECM, Poppy Ackroyd of One Little Indian, Ryuichi Sakamoto of Milan, Sarah Davachi of Students of Decay, Missy Mazzoli of New Focus, Holy Other of Tri-Angle, High plains of Kranky, Lustmord of Touch, Biosphere of Biophon, Touch of Smalltown Supersound, Deathprod of Smalltown Supersound, Main of Editions Mego and These New Puritans of Infectious, whose album *Field of Reeds* is a near-rock album made using classical instruments without losing directness, mixed with glamorous post-hip-hop ceremony, as if Britten haunts Ghostpoet and, on the quiet, there is a piano element eccentrically related to how the prepared piano produces exotic, clandestine sounds that seem as though they could only be created electronically...

This music's hint of a hint of a sign of a sign of a future that may yet materialise at the edge of vision has roots that are, if you like, as detected in the studies, preparations, energy and performance of Hauschka, in a composing and decomposing world that began in darkness and mud, wood and travel, fear and transgression, melody and transcendence, mind and body with Mozart, from where everything was possible, and accelerated, meandered, dissolved, reversed, distressed all the way to John Cage, from where everything again became possible, if inside out, and Aphex Twin is a transitional, operational descendant of Mozart and Cage, extremes of the same but different thing, as much as he swooned out of machines and the world as one big noisy, nosy and moving collage.

Spotted in Hauschka, and the suggestion of some sort of musical movement that can be filed under post-classical, not pop or more preferably something else altogether, to be filed under 'beyond', for those who believe there is still some progress left, even if it comes via the past, is something that is one way of measuring the nervy, nerdy, shattered, pleasure-seeking tone of the times. It could not exist without a certain layering of what has happened before, more than once, even if in different ways, nor without a belief in searching for new ways of advancing and experimenting, even if everything does seem to have all been done and redone before – it is a coming together of tradition and innovation, of the fixed in place, and the need to rearrange, a refurbishment and refreshment of the old using the technology and social contexts of today, with a sense that what hasn't been done before is to exist where we are now, surrounded by so much difficult history, and so much demanding precedent, and to work out whether art and music can still show us where we might be going, rather than simply where we have been.

Perhaps Hauschka and his prepared piano, as daft as it can be, as fiddly, as romantic, as old-fashioned, as marginal, as delightful, is much more of a clue than it seems about where music goes next, one sure timeline emerging unexpectedly out of a spiralling, time-crossing tangle of timelines, a metaphor for how the whole history of music can itself be prepared, interfered with, messed up, and, while being itself, turned into something else, which few saw coming next.

And whatever that 'next' is it will still involve the piano, a machine for making sound that has lasted for centuries.

As I listened to more classical music, discovered and made up more histories and connections, it seemed more likely that the last piece of music that I would ever hear, if I had the choice, was going to come from the eighteenth century, or the 1920s, or from the minimalist edge of the avant-garde – something an hour or so long that might delay the moment of my death, because after all I had to hear it to the end.

Maybe, for that reason, something that might take me through to the next day. It seemed increasingly likely that it might be something from a curated ECM New Series consideration of a postmodern investigation of the connection between modernism and the baroque. Something that let me finish things off in the proximity of the astonishing, or, if I preferred, because after all that it seemed more appropriate, the immensely inconsequential.

I was still listening to the albums of the year that the many pop critics were mentioning, and, I had to be honest, as much as they often sounded like the kind of treated, elasticated electronic music, with voice and verve, that I have always liked, nothing, outside the effects and slang used, and the comments made about local circumstances, the rhymes cut out of the temper of the times, the knowingness engraved into the texture and tones, none of it sounded like anything I hadn't come across before.

It was static progressive music in some sort of limbo between the album era and whatever comes next, which still isn't clear. It lacked a stage, a position, a context — it was just a part of everything else, and it might have been a failure of mine, but I still couldn't get used to all music being packed together and turned into an amorphous mass of urges and revivalism that was designed to be selected for certain times of the day, and for certain moods, journeys, tasks and functions. It enabled me to find all the classical music I needed, and use it for my own purposes, including making up history that made sense to me, but elsewhere the new system seemed to be squeezing the life out of the future of music, which now arrived immediately surrounded by an immense amount of existing music. It was making it so available that it got in the way of music, unless you knew what you were looking for, and had a plan, and could ignore the maps, organisation and calculations that the sites had designed.

Brought up on music scenes, on the stimulating fresh new energy they introduced, I was using the new technology to make my own new scene — one that covered centuries and countries — at a time when music scenes as we once knew them were over or consisted of numerous fragmented music micro-scenes all happening at the same time. They'd washed up as polite, stagnant tributes in music festivals, in playlists, as endless choirs.

Music scenes with unprecedented performers and exciting records at their centre had been replaced by other sorts of mobile scenes paraded through social media, scenes based around the self, selling, reviewing, influencing, gaming and curating. Absorbing, distracting, often somehow isolating cultural scenes were now packed inside the new convenient stores of YouTube and Netflix and the new scenes generated by apps. Scenes were over in a flash on Twitter, transformed into transitory TikTok time and an Insta instant. The old-fashioned idea of a music scene with a militant new sensibility emerging over time off-line within a particular city, club or mutant new genre, didn't stand a chance, and a new age of social distancing either means total extinction or exceptional, deeply unrecognisable post-pandemic revisions.

Missing these sort of cathartic scenes and communities I used all the information that is now out there, assiduously collected by the streaming sites, to invent my own personal music scene with its own uncompromising timing and complicated meaning. A scene in the region of my mind only. And what I was used to doing when I had been engaged with a contagious, revelatory music scene as a pop critic, responsibly passing on my enthusiasm and new know-how, was interviews. And for the music scene I had created, if only for my own benefit, that meant I needed to interview classical musicians.

As a writer, now I was moving deeper and deeper into classical music and learning its ways, in my own way, it seemed that a big breakthrough for me was if and when I started to interview classical musicians and was able to talk with them in a way I had with pop and rock musicians for forty years. I have interviewed some of the most notoriously difficult rock stars, including, for heaven's sake, the journalist-loathing Lou Reed, twice, and I still have nightmares where he pulls out my tongue and feeds it to his ravens whilst humming 'Perfect Day'. I have interviewed Mick Jagger, Iggy Pop, Debbie Harry, Patti Smith, John Lydon and Morrissey, more than twice, but there was definitely something intimidating about the thought of interviewing a classical musician. What would we even talk about? They seemed to come from another planet. I couldn't imagine knowing enough about their habits, language, drives, sensitivities to ever have a proper conversation with one.

I had interviewed Brian Eno a few times, but that was cheating, because even though he had created a lot of music that was on the border between art and rock, classical and pop, and was increasingly acting as a visual artist, he was essentially a pop personality, an iconoclastic rock artist, increasingly known as an adventurous producer of commercially spectacular alternative rock acts. And a conversation with Eno was usually about ideas, and it was another sign of a lost future where Cornelius Cardew didn't die young, and lived for another thirty years, and passed through many other channels and possibilities in terms of making music as art and for a reason. A conversation with Cornelius Cardew wouldn't have been a conversation with a classical composer.

A conversation with Brian Eno is a conversation with someone who happened to make music in various settings for various reasons, ranging from 'to see what happened' to 'seeing what happened next' and at some points you might glance against something to do with classical music, but only in the most abstract sense. It did seem though as if this was the closest I would ever get to interviewing a classical musician, even if he was not classical, and not, as such, a musician.

6. WITH BRIAN ENO

Extracts from a conversation with Brian Eno, which continues a 'long' conversation he has been having with culture in general since about 1967 and which is like dipping into where his thinking is on a given day, depending on his mood and what he is planning at the time, and where he is about to travel, or has just been, who he has just met, and has nothing to do with the kind of interview that plugs a product, confesses feelings, reveals personal details, explains a biography, fills in gaps, admits motives, confirms facts and which leads an observer to consider that one word to describe Brian Eno is 'precise' and another would be 'clandestine' and a third, why not, would be 'attentive'. He never stops talking about what he does, and why, working out his place, the place of art, the history of progress, the enigma of meaning, the mechanics of creativity, the mystery of aesthetics, the fiction of music, reluctant to think too much about his past in case, as he says, he starts to feel 'useless awe towards his former self' but is politely prepared to look back at his work if he thinks someone might find it useful. When you meet him to discuss something or other to do with his always perfectly organised research and development thoughts about something or other, you arrive as he is finishing one conversation with someone about, say, how technology changes the way our brains work, and as you leave someone else is arriving for a conversation about, say, the shrinking divisions between art and science. Or how Jeremy Clarkson almost moved in to the house next to his office, which was previously owned by Jason Donovan.

On talking (1)

I heard a recording that had been made of me thirty-five years ago chatting with some friends and when I heard myself, I thought that the tape must have sped up because I sounded so fast. When others spoke, they were at a normal speed. It was me — I was the one speaking this fast. What I find both disappointing and reassuring is that I was saying exactly those things I will be saying today. I don't know what to make of that. A few different references, but the basic ideas haven't changed at all. No difference whatsoever! I suppose it's good to see I've been consistent as sometimes over the years it seems as though it's all been a bit incoherent, a bit of this, a bit of that, a while doing this, then one of those, followed by three of those and a bit of the before. It seems all over the place when I'm doing it. Listening to me now talking then suggests there has been a pattern.

On the intensity of ideas
If you grow up in a very strong religion like Catholicism you certainly cultivate in yourself a certain taste for the intensity of ideas. Being in church means you are surrounded by art from an early age. You expect to be engaged with ideas strongly whether you are for or against them. If you are part of a religion that very strongly insists that you believe, then to decide not to do that is quite a big hurdle to jump over. You never forget the thought processes you went through. It becomes part of your whole intellectual picture.

On listening
If you think of the mid- to late 1950s when all of this started to happen for me, the experience of listening to sound was so different from now. Stereo didn't exist. If you listened to music outside of church apart from live music, which was very rare, it was through very tiny speakers. It was a very nice experience, but it was a very small experience. So to go into a church, which is a specially designed and echoey space, and it has an organ, and my grandfather built the organ in the church where we went, to suddenly hear music and singing was amazing. It was like hearing someone's album on a tiny transistor radio and then you go and see them in a 60,000-seater. It's huge by comparison. That had a lot to do with my feeling about sound and space, which became a big theme for me. How does space make a difference to sound, what's the difference between hearing something in this room and then another room? Can you imagine other rooms where you can hear music? It also made a difference to how I feel about the communality of music in that the music I liked the most, singing in church, was done by a group of people who were not skilled – they were just a group of people. I knew them in the rest of the week as the coalman and the baker.

On destiny
It was a real dilemma for me at the end of my time at school. Am I going into music or am I going into painting? Funnily enough, the

Who were important to me when I was working out whether I would go into fine art or popular art. I felt they had found an important position between the two and then the Velvet Underground came along and also made it clear how you could straddle the two somehow. It helped make my mind up to go into music, which could still be a form of painting.

On recording
I came out of this funny place where I was interested in the experimental ideas of Cornelius Cardew, John Cage and Gavin Bryars, but also in pop music. Pop was all about the results and the feedback. The experimental side was interested in process more than the actual result — the results just happened and there was often very little control over them, and very little feedback. Take Steve Reich. He was a very important composer for me with his early tape pieces and his way of having musicians play a piece each at different speeds so that they slipped out of synch with each other. But then when he comes to record a piece of his like, say, *Drumming*, he uses orchestral drums stiffly played and badly recorded. He's learned absolutely nothing from the history of recorded music. Why not look at what the pop world is doing with recording, which is making incredible sounds with great musicians who really feel what they play? It's because in Reich's world there was no real feedback. What was interesting to them in that world was merely the diagram of the piece, the music merely existed as an indicator of a type of process. I can see the point of it in one way, that you just want to show the skeleton, you don't want a lot of flesh around it, you just want to show how you did what you did. As a listener who grew up listening to pop music, I am interested in results. Pop is totally results-oriented and there is a very strong feedback loop. Did it work? No. We'll do it differently then. Did it sell? No. We'll do it differently then. So I wanted to bring the two sides together. I liked the processes and systems in the experimental world and the attitude to effect that there was in the pop; I wanted the ideas to be seductive but also the results.

On being like nothing else
In my house in Oxfordshire we have this big beautiful Andrew Logan sculpture of this lovely Pegasus horse with blue-glass wings. And when I get a taxi from the station a driver will always comment on it because

it is so striking. What they often say is – what does that stand for then? Or what does that mean? They ask a question based on the idea that something exists because it has to tell you something, or it refers to something else, and I realise that this notion is completely foreign to me. The earliest paintings I loved were always the most non-referential paintings you can imagine, by painters like Mondrian. I think I was thrilled by them because they didn't refer to anything else. They just stood alone, and they were just completely charged magic objects that did not get their strength from being connected to anything else.

On singing

I belong to a gospel choir and they know that I am an atheist, and they are very nice to me, and they say that one day you might change your mind but if you don't it doesn't matter. They are very tolerant. Ultimately the message of gospel music, if you think about it, is that everything's going to be all right. If you listen to millions of gospel records – and I have – and try to distil what they all have in common, it's a sense that somehow, we can triumph. We can win through. We can make it. It doesn't matter through to what. There could be many thousands of things. But the message... well, there are two messages... one is a kind of optimism for the future rather than a pessimism. Gospel music is never pessimistic, it's never oh my God it's all going down the tubes, like the blues often is. Gospel music is always about the possibility of transcendence, of things getting better. It's also about the loss of ego, that you will win through or get over things by losing yourself, becoming part of something better. Both those messages are completely universal and are nothing to do with religion or a particular religion. They're to do with basic human attitudes and you can have that attitude and therefore sing gospel even if you are not religious.

On talking (2)

I like to talk about all sorts of things. I've never seen the downside of it. I've never minded the egghead tag. It makes sense with my physiognomy anyway. I've fought for years the idea that rock and popular art is only about passion and fashion and nothing to do with thinking and examining and if you do think, there is something suspicious about you.

On the synthesiser (1)

One of the important things about the synthesiser was that it came without any baggage. A piano comes with a whole history of music. There are all sorts of cultural conventions built into traditional instruments that tell you where and when that instrument comes from. When you play an instrument that does not have any such historical background, you are designing sound, basically. You're designing a new instrument. That's what a synthesiser is, essentially. It's a constantly unfinished instrument. You finish it when you tweak it, and play around with it, and decide how to use it. You can combine a number of cultural references into one new thing.

On the synthesiser (2)

Instruments sound interesting not because of their sound but because of the relationship a player has with them. Instrumentalists build a rapport with their instruments, which is what you like and respond to. If you were sitting down now to design an instrument you would not dream of coming up with something as ridiculous as an acoustic guitar. It's a strange instrument, it's very limited and it doesn't sound good. You would come up with something much better. But what we like about acoustic guitars is players who have had long relationships with them and know how to do something beautiful with them. You don't have that with synthesisers yet. They are a very new instrument. They are constantly renewing so people do not have time to build long relationships with them. So you tend to hear more of the technology and less of the rapport. It can sound less human. However! That is changing. And there is a prediction that I made a few years ago that I'm very pleased to see is coming true – synthesisers that have inconsistency built into them. I have always wanted them to be less consistent. I like it that one note can be louder than the note next to it.

On the naming of things

A way to make new music is to imagine looking back at the past from a future and imagine music that could have existed but didn't. Like East African free jazz, which as far as I know does not exist. To some extent, this was how ambient music emerged. My interest in making music has been to create something that does not exist that I would like to listen to, not because I wanted a job as a musician. I wanted to hear music that had not yet happened by putting together things that suggested a new thing that did not yet exist. It's like having a ready-made formula if you are able to read it. One of the innovations of ambient music was leaving out the idea that there should be melody or words or a beat... so in a way that was music designed by leaving things out – that can be a form of innovation, knowing what to leave out. All the signs were in the air all around with ambient music in the mid-1970s and other people were doing a similar thing. I just gave it a name. Which is exactly what it needed. A name. Giving something a name can be just the same as inventing it. By naming something you create a difference. You say that this is now real. Names are very important.

On hindsight
Instead of shooting arrows at someone else's target, which I've never been very good at, I make my own target around wherever my arrow happens to have landed. You shoot your arrow and then you paint your bullseye around it, and therefore you have hit the target dead centre.

On reporting in the 1990s that there was too much music being released and he was not going to add to it any more
I didn't think it through, to be honest.

On the end of an era
I think that records were just a little bubble in time and those who made a living from them for a while were really lucky. There is no reason why anyone should have made so much money from selling records except that everything was right for this period of time. I always knew it would run out sooner or later. It couldn't last, and now it's running out. I don't particularly care that it is and I like the way things are going. The record age was just a blip. It was a bit like if you had a source of whale blubber in the 1840s and it could be used as fuel. Before gas came along, if you traded in whale blubber you were the richest man on earth. Then gas came along, and you'd be stuck with your whale blubber. Sorry mate – history's moving along. It's a little like that with recorded music. Recorded music equals whale blubber. Eventually something else will come along to replace it.

On the idea of what Eno calls scenius

Scenes are always important in terms of creating the sort of collective energy that makes something happen, with people watching each other and encouraging each other, and scenius is a way of creating scenes that are not necessarily geographic, but where like-minded people find a way of generating a scene connected to their thinking, and helping that become known. Scenes used to be all about location, but that is changing now because of the internet, which is itself a whole new location, so I am interested in what that means in terms of new scenes and new fashions. How does music now become part of a scene other than the fact its part of this global but very thin web — and how can you now make a piece of music that you can release as though it has greater meaning than just being something which at best just floats above every other piece of music that's out there in this inconsequential sea of sound. This is what I am concerned with at the moment — how you might recreate certain experiments that there are in terms of solving maths problems on line, and mixing the input of the Nobel Prize winner and the everyday person with sometimes the everyday person contributing something as important to the problem-solving as the prize winner. Can you imagine applying that idea to culture, the creation of a sort of collective problem solving creative community that generates innovative ideas that exist as single works of art? I like collaborating a lot and I think I am very good at it but I think the whole idea has to change now that things are so different in terms of how you collaborate and who with. But I still want there to be some sort of expert in control, someone who is good at what they do.

On the idea of a whole new way of composing, packaging and distributing popular music in a way that continues the recent twentieth-century narratives, but that belongs to the flexible new spaces and fluid, pulsating, adaptive dimensions of the post-internet twenty-first century.

I want to think that it is possible. That somehow a piece of music can be made that enters the world and somehow inside the world it is constantly refreshed by how people interact with it and they actively change it because of how and where they listen to it. So that a piece of music is continually changed by its contact with the world and yet is recognisably still that piece of music, like a remix but beyond.

PART TEN

The Answer – The Place Where the Story Stops

Harrison Birtwistle 1994: *'I wanted to write music that didn't exist.'*

1. I TRY NOT TO REPEAT MYSELF

Interviewing Brian Eno and Gavin Bryars seemed to be safely close enough to the Obscure label to be closer to pop than classical. I could cope, without panicking that I lacked the technical language to be able to engage completely with a more conventionally classical composer. My first move into interviewing that kind of classical composer, one regularly described as 'one of the world's leading composers', still had Obscure links, so it wasn't a complete break for me.

This was, though, the first composer I interviewed in what was essentially a completely classical context. John Adams moved on from his Obscure debut, after some early clearly post-minimalist pieces, not least because of the ground-breaking docu-opera *Nixon in China* from 1987, glassy minimalism multiplied by *Aida* blown up into high political drama, which became a celebrity in its own right, and *The Death of Klinghoffer* in 1991, which established his speciality, eloquently if expediently setting recent historical events to music. These operas in particular made him about as internationally renowned as a modern classical composer can become while not losing the sense that he remains a classical composer – largely unknown in a wider sense, but a giant in his field.

Minimalist emancipation and a post-serial problem-solving mind had been important in his development, including the shaking away of the brainy, domineering aloofness of Boulez, but he never lost his passion for tonal music, for the usual masters, for the succulent power of melody, as can be heard on his 1978 string septet *Shaker Loops*, where he shackled the energy and emancipation of self-determining American minimalism, which had peaked in the 1970s with unashamed, extremely pleasing melodic purpose.

A technically ingenious twenty-five-minute solo piano piece from 1977, *Phrygian Gates*, – self-certified as his Op. 1, showing before the operas that the blockbuster held no fears for him but which in its maths shows lingering traces of serialist calculations, confirming minimalism was a scenic tributary of serialism – begins with classic, sonorous minimalist rhythm but by the end is coiling around pumped-up memories of Beethoven. As he once said, the minimalist was already bored by minimalism.

Working as composer-in-residence for the San Francisco Symphony in the early 1980s gave him prized access to a full orchestra – taking him far beyond the modest, make-do ensembles, percussion line-ups and unorthodox, mobile instrumental units of the inquisitively limited minimalists – which supercharged his development and enabled him to use an orchestra to analyse and animate his favourite composers in history. The previously assumed unobtrusive post-minimalist weaned on John Cage and sundry postmodern progressives and educators demonstrated an unabashed desire to romanticise the romantics.

A truly romantic, expressive composer emerged from what turned out to be a fragile new music shell, one that without the early minimalist leanings and technical fascination with the techniques and treatments of the experimental mavericks and electronic music might well have been underwhelmingly conventional, even miserably nostalgic. The journey to San Francisco to escape the intricate, vice-like rigours of serialism, and his running of a new music ensemble alert to the radical, visceral currents of the 1960s and 1970s generated a composer who established a unique, if controlled blend of tart, cheering romance and stirring, considerate repetition, with subject matters that smartly and emotionally reflected the politicised conceptual ideals of the 1960s and 1970s underground.

His receptive musical references, taking in the baroque, Bach, Beethoven, Schubert, the pomp and circumstance of opera, including Wagner and Verdi, the monumentalised symphonic sweep of Mahler, Sibelius, Bruckner and Strauss, the provocations and proposals of Cage and his haunting antecedent Satie, and twentieth-century popular song from jazz standards to rock dynamics all became modified by his appreciative and expert handling of the raptures of minimalism and computer solutions. Passing a traditionalist approach through the filter of minimalism and being open-minded towards amplification and electronics gave a contemporary sheen to whatever he did, wherever he borrowed his music, instantly placing it in a new context, so that what might have otherwise seemed old-fashioned teemed with slickly appropriated and constantly renewed inventive energy.

He applied a sensibility taken from the experimental exploration and appropriation of the 1960s and 1970s to the taking and repositioning of traditional classical genres. Patterns from the past took off in new directions, because he began composing during the lifespan of minimalism. Steve Reich, he once said, hadn't invented the wheel, but 'he had shown us a new way to ride'. Adams went for a ride throughout history, always using the spinning wheels of minimalism to get him to wherever he ended up.

It was an act of almost administrative genius, using rapt, fastidious minimalist styles and kinetic effects as a creative process through which he could pass his thoughtful, evocative ideas and compositions. This process ensured whether opera, concerto, symphony or string quartet, his music came out dressed not as official minimalism or resonating with experimental originality but as an accessible, seductively decorative elaboration of the music that had, through Terry Riley, Steve Reich and Philip Glass rejected or redirected the dogmas of serialism. Adams produced crossover music, but what elevated it was its roots in the premises and aphorisms of Cage, minimalist pulsation and militant English playfulness.

Along with the death of Zappa, he's another marker of an end, or a beginning of an end, to classical momentum, with his major works in the 1980s and 1990s, after which there comes Max Richter's more fluid, eclectic, informal 'post-classical era'. Classical history leads to John Adams's studious gathering and weaving of classical periods from the baroque to the minimalist and postmodernist, and an ability, an ambition, to create some pieces that will lodge in the memory of those around at the time paying attention. For technological and cultural reasons, the widening of choice, narrowing of reach and shredding of collective judgement, he might be one of the last such composers to manage this, to have a *Nixon in China* moment, where a classical music project emerging from almost wholly inside classical history becomes part of a wider, more publicised narrative.

The generation or two after his, exemplified by Nico Muhly and Anna Thorvaldsdottir, is introducing into orchestral music for the first time a permanent sensibility from beyond the classical borders, a sensibility that Americans call 'indie'. It's an approach to classically based performance, collaboration and an organisation of influences that is as much driven by the idealistic spirit of alternative rock music, post-rock, ambient and electronic pop as it is by experimental spirits from Purcell to Webern and beyond.

Adams was extremely collected as we began our interview, very comfortable with such social obligations, and I was nervously wondering if I would remember all of my notes and manage to get across, without faltering, some of the thoughts I had about his music. With his background in academia, and his solid reputation as a world-renowned composer, he wanted to take control of the interview, which was fair enough, and I was a mere vessel through which questions were channelled, which he could then do with what he wished.

I count it as my first interview with a bona fide classical musician. (There had been a brief, filmed conversation with Peter Maxwell Davies during my television year at the Royal Academy, but I was helped along by my composition teacher Chris Austin, a close friend and colleague of Davies, and didn't yet feel that I was flying solo.) I had an hour. In my rock-critic days this would have seemed extremely mean and limited, but, count the ways, it is now a very different world.

Adams comes across as a little defensive, but then he is as reviled as he is revered, and probably detected, quite accurately, that I couldn't quite make my mind up on which side I fall – is he the John Cage of the middle-of-the-road, or the Andrew Lloyd Webber of the avant-garde? Both may well have their benefits, or not.

Having done plenty of reading about your life and times, I was initially interested in what the difference was between the 'John Adams' that has been assembled online – the internet biography orbiting Wikipedia – and your own perception of yourself.

Well, I'm much better at telling you about me than Wikipedia.

How accurate is your Wikipedia page?

It's no secret everyone looks at their Wikipedia page. I hadn't for a while and then I did, and I was horrified. I was credited with several things I've never even done! The technology philosopher Jaron Lanier, who wrote *Who Owns the Future?*, talked about Wikipedia and information and he said that Wikipedia is best for popular culture and science but other factual things, especially about people, are highly suspect.

Doing my research, I became interested in this endless information and opinion in the context of you writing a new piece – are you aware of the versions of who you are, the interpretations and expectations there are of who you are, that complex, ever-present history, the John Adams content assembled by many, creating your identity whether you like it or not? Does it make a difference to how and what you write?

Well, I do also have the issue of having a very well-used name, and there are two American presidents called John Adams, and the first was a Founding Father. If you Google my name, that's who you come across first. I'm quite a way behind them.

I'm not named after them. I'm named after my Swedish grandfather whose name was Jan Adamsson. He dropped the 'son' when he immigrated to the United States, and then of course there's John Luther Adams, the wonderful composer who lives in Harlem now, although he had a period in Alaska, which deeply inspired him. What you're getting at is my age when I sit down to compose, am I aware that I have the burden of writing a John Adams piece?

I don't look at it that way. I tell young composing students that it's never easy. Starting a new piece is always just hell, and I may think that I have a great idea, but then what? I've decided I want to write an opera or, I don't know, a violin concerto or a piece that will be choreographed. In the abstract, it sounds like a wonderful idea and I may even have images for how it will sound, but the day that I sit down to do the first sketch, it's always a terrible confrontation, and I'm sure anyone in this room who's a creative person, whether you're a composer, or a painter, or a writer, that you understand that.

What I have to remind myself is that I must become a beginner again. Zen Buddhism has this great phrase, 'beginner's mind', and I always have to remind myself that I have to adopt a beginner's mind, because the first scratches, the first jabs are always just incredibly humiliating. If

I thought, after all that's written about me, 'Oh, no. I'm an important composer', that would only make things worse. I have to be intensely grateful that I'm able to do this and I don't have to go to work nine to five in a job that I hate, and a lot of people have to do that. I feel very privileged about that.

Tell me about those first 'jabs'.

You'd be amazed at how awful my first sketches are. We all love to look at composers' sketches and some composers left more unfinished sketches than others, Beethoven, for example. But it's just amazing how primitive and humiliating the very first gestures towards a new piece are. You just can't believe that this awful, childish thing that you've put out there on your desk is potentially going to end up being played by the London Symphony Orchestra or being heard by tens of thousands of people.

Often the question to a composer like yourself is, when do you know a piece is finished, but as much as that is interesting, I'm also intrigued by when do you know a piece has actually started?

Well, I think, sometimes I just have to run with what I have. I think, there's nothing in the world like a deadline, that's something to keep you sober and focused. Sometimes I haven't found what I think is the gold nugget, I haven't found the key into the piece, or I think I haven't. What I'm looking for is the DNA, the code that will crack what this piece is going to be. For me, that's usually harmony, it's usually a harmonic field that the piece is going to live in, and then, of course, the gesture. Schoenberg has a wonderful description in his *Fundamentals of Musical Composition* book that he wrote for students when he got to California and realised that they had so little sophistication. It's a really wonderful book and he talks about composing being this combination of melodic intervals that are united by a characteristic rhythm. I always think of the opening to Beethoven's Fifth, but it could be anything. There are pieces of music that just begin with a harmonic field, your standard Bruckner symphony. But generally, for me, they begin with some kind of harmonic and rhythmic idea.

My father gave me, as a present when I was in high school, a book by Hindemith called *A Composer's World* and there was a sentence in that book that just terrified me. It said, 'A composer should never put a note down until he knows everything about the piece.' It was one of those kind of Germanic edicts, 'This is the way it is!' Like it is the only way. I still don't know what I'm doing when I start a piece. I have to say, I still feel like I'm lost at sea. I figure there is land somewhere, but I'm not sure how to reach it, and I just take off in some direction or another and sometimes I run into sea monsters.

I do have a flow chart when I write an opera. I have a flow chart of the whole act that I'm writing right now, so I know what the events are, and I know that I'm going to have to find some sort of transitional material here and something needs to happen here. Basically, I want to make sure that I don't leave something around so that this particular singer doesn't sing until the last ten minutes of the opera – which happens, you just forget. Or somebody else ends up singing for seventy minutes without stopping, so those are important things. You have to plan for that. But I would not say that generally I start with preconceived plans, so Hindemith would dismiss me out of hand.

Does your past music in a way get in the way of your new music, or does it liberate you to new possibilities? Have you left behind trails sometimes, that you want to pick up again; sometimes you feel you've reached the conclusion so that you've done that? How does that feed into what you do next?

The one nice thing about getting older is, if you're having a really, really bad time, a bad day, a bad week, a bad month, if you have a history and you're my age, you can remember that you've had this before and you've got out of it somehow. You don't know how you did, but you know you got out of it. That is the difference between me and a graduate student. I have to tell the graduate students, 'Don't despair, you'll figure this out.' Because when you don't have a history to comfort yourself, you really can despair. You really can think, 'Well, it's not going to happen for me. I'm not going to be a composer.' As we say in the US, 'You have to tough it out.'

As for my own works, I try not to repeat myself, and one of the things I object to in a lot of contemporary art, contemporary music, is what I would call 'branding' oneself. You see that particularly in the art world, where a painter or a sculptor has hit the bullseye, and it's a sudden success. Of course in the art world, millions of dollars accompany that sudden success, which we contemporary musicians never have to worry about. But I would think in a way that's the worst kind of compromise and bargain, because not only are you seduced into wanting to repeat yourself, to repeat the success, but you've got all kinds of pressure: your gallery, your management, your audience and whatever. People don't really care a great deal about what we do in the world of contemporary music, so there is not quite that pressure on us.

The idea of branding is interesting because to some extent, one of the important components in what you do, and I think it's reflected in your official blog, is that you are not just a composer or musician but also a thinker, a cultural commentator, if you like. It seems to be an important element of what you do, going back to when your graduation present from your parents was John Cage's book Silence. *So there's that element that you also think very deeply about the meaning of music, what music is. You write about it a lot. That suggests, to an extent, a kind of awareness of the idea of branding yourself to achieve permanence, because that also must become part of being a composer, because you understand the historical chronology of music and where you might or might not fit in. There is an element that a certain momentum must have been created as you worked where you suddenly realised you had a chance of attaining that, being self-conscious about the way you would fit into history and that must make a difference as well when you suddenly think,* I've got this momentum, I can now start to design my musical progress, *and therefore it influences certain choices you make about what you do and why you do it.*

This is terrifying me… It's funny, I went to a bookstore the day I got to London, mindlessly looking through the shelves, and I fell on a book by a writer I never heard who was obviously well known in England and the book's called *The History Man* by Malcolm Bradbury. The book takes place in an era when I was the age of the students here back in the seventies, and I haven't finished it, so I can't speak terribly authoritatively about it. But I'm reminded of it in your question because it's largely about a very left-wing college professor in the most full blossoming of the liberal New Age, a consciousness explosion of Freud, Marx, Jimi Hendrix, the Beatles, Mick Jagger, that period, and his problems relating in a normal human way, not only to his friends but even to his wife and family, because he had such a historical view of life. It's tainted by intellectual Marxism and I read a great deal of history and I sort of compulsively follow current affairs, but I don't let it dictate my work or my thoughts about what I write. I read about politics, particularly American politics, which has now become a blood sport. I've reached a point where I think that historical thinking can be very damaging and I'll give you an example, because when I was a student in my early twenties, that was the period of what we now call high modernism and particularly in music, where composers and theorists had discovered atonality and they had taken very seriously what Schoenberg had said about owning the future and the inevitability of the twelve-tone method and the triumph of a certain kind of progress. It's a kind of Darwinian interpretation of art. So that art, as it moved through history, became more and more complex, as if there was some kind of inevitable one-way movement or inevitable evolutionary direction forward, like time's arrow. It was as though it would always move that way. And if you weren't on the train going in the right direction at the right time you were useless, and your music had no historical weight. I wrote about this in my book *Hallelujah Junction*, because it was a major freak-out moment for me as an impressionable young man. It took me a good ten or fifteen years to realise that was actually very blinkered and, I think, actually a very warped view.

That's why I'm very entertained by this book by Malcolm Bradbury because I do recall thirty-five, forty years ago that people felt – on the one hand they felt very bullish, very optimistic, when John Lennon was alive, and the Soul Psychedelic generation were discovering Zen Buddhism and good food. There was a revolution in sexuality. A lot of things have carried on and continue to fulfil themselves, but many things have unfortunately gone in the wrong direction. But I think to take art and to lump it in with that kind of historical inevitability is a really problematic thing. Because art is as unpredictable and as varied and experienced as every individual is. Every piece of art is different and there shouldn't be an elite or a certain kind of art that is the right way to do it. For every very complicated composer, whose work is extremely intellectual and takes hundreds of hours to learn, there's a musical experience that is as simple as a Bartók *Mikrokosmos* or a Schubert impromptu, about which you can't say much, you simply experience it. You can't write a 200-page analytical tome about it and yet its value is every bit as important as the complex piece.

I can't work out whether you're avoiding the question about whether you've designed your own career or answering it.

No, I'm sorry, I wasn't trying to be coy there. The idea of designing a career is just an anathema to me. It's like designing a marriage or designing a baby, or something. There are people who are intensely conscious of how to massage their historical image. I'm sure there are many composers who, if they had my Wikipedia page, would be immediately on the phone trying to get things corrected. Maybe I am too relaxed about it. I just feel that in the end, the value of what you do will come through and that trying to paint my picture carefully, control my image, it's just not the sort of thing I do. But I acknowledge there are people like Stravinsky and Wagner and a couple of contemporary composers I know who are intensely conscious of their place in history and maybe the critics buy into that or maybe audiences buy into that. They open a programme and they say, 'It says this is the greatest composer of the latter part of the twentieth century, I'd better pay attention.' If it doesn't say that, they start with a different, less persuaded attitude. But I keep thinking of people like Herman Melville or Emily Dickinson, or Walt Whitman, who were virtually unknown in their time, and those are the three great American writers.

There's an element, the American side of making contemporary music, even as extreme or as radical as it can be, because it's American there still has to be a kind of, a component of the showman, the entertainer. Cage was a showman, Elliott Carter, they are showmen, they want to appeal. however obscure they are in a mainstream sense.
     Elliott Carter?

Yes. There's a glamour about it, isn't there? Intellectually, perhaps, but it's definitely something that is part of the American drive to make a difference. You have to be aware of that too, it is to be American, in a way, to have success even in the margins, to become a recognised name. There is some way you decided that as a contemporary composer with an in-built limited audience that it's important to be an entertainer, to see if the audience can be extended?
     Well, to go back to my formative years, I was in college during a time of extraordinary schizophrenia, a cultural schizophrenia. Because in my music classes we were studying absolutely the most dour, serious, cerebral music. The models there were late Webern and Boulez and the art of the few, and I guess that music classes were really very serious occasions, and nobody laughed. I would go back to my dorm and my roommates would be in some altered state and they'd be listening to Jim

Morrison or Janis Joplin or Bob Dylan. And there was such fantastic richness and such provocative misbehaving in this music and, again, I wrote about this in my book that I finally just had to come head to head with that, that there was something wrong with this picture. That you sort of either had a choice of this rigorous sort of humourless post-war avant-garde or of the music of the counterculture. Even John Cage, who was always smiling and such a public figure. His music was just amazingly didactic. If you got down, nitty-gritty with John Cage, it was every bit as intellectual and every bit as sort of cerebral and cold as anything created by a serialist. For me, actually finding myself, finding my voice had to do with understanding the components of my personality. And, yes, I do have a sense of being, as you say, I'm not sure how you're using the term, 'the entertainer'. But I think that many of the great artists had that capacity. Certainly Dickens was a fantastic entertainer, and so is Cervantes, and for sure, Shakespeare was. At the end of quite a few Shakespeare plays, somebody comes out on stage and says to the audience, 'I hope you liked it, and if you didn't, please let us know and we'll fix it,' until he finally gets to the end of *Troilus and Cressida* where Pandarus comes out and says, 'If you didn't like it, I hope you'll catch my disease.' Even the loftiest of musical statements should have a capacity to entertain as well as elevate.

Do you feel differently now about the post-war modernist music you found so difficult when you were a young man?

That's a real tough one. I've been thinking a lot about Boulez lately, and once it seemed like he was going to be around for ever as one of the great, great conductors and when I do a piece and I am considering, for example, Ravel or Debussy, I always study his recordings, and they're so wonderful. They're so warm, and so human, and delicate, and subtle, and I've never been able to in my mind understand how he can go from that to the kind of music that he wrote. His compositions were so removed from his conducting.

But then I realise in a way, we all are still children of the times when we grow up, and he grew up in that very difficult time, in the 1940s when Europe was just so deeply traumatised by the war. I realise as an American, where aside from our Civil War we've just never had that kind of trauma like you had here in England and that happened all over Europe, and right now is happening in Syria and elsewhere. Because of those circumstances I have to give him the benefit of the doubt. I think that that kind of very severe, intellectually controlled modernism in the forties, in the fifties, and into the sixties was probably what composers felt they needed to just hold the world together. People at the time probably associated grand romantic German music with something bad. I don't know, but fortunately, in the end, there are no rules, and I once thought that European modernism was the only answer, and now I realise in a way that it was just a little moment in history.

Once you'd come out of Harvard after studying a highly serious, ultimately alienating world, and there was Hendrix, and there was this hippy thing going on, why weren't you tempted like many your age, born after the war, even in the experimental world, to be in a group or even to pursue jazz, which you had an interest in? You stayed loyal to classical music, and that led to all kinds of breakthroughs, but at the time the rock 'n' roll must have been extraordinarily tempting in a way. You stuck to your beliefs. That other world didn't completely seduce you, even as you drove out to California seeking the less oppressively serious.

I know, it's a terrible black hole in my biography that I didn't have a band. I did play jazz, but to be very honest, I wasn't very good at it. I was a wind player and I played the clarinet and the clarinet was definitely out of style in the sixties. The only example I can think of it was Paul McCartney used it in his song called 'When I'm Sixty-Four' to give the feeling of something that was sadly old and out of date. That was not a popular song for us clarinet players. I was already very active as a performer. I played clarinet professionally when I was still an undergraduate, and even in some instances played with the Boston Symphony Orchestra as a substitute. I played clarinet in the American premiere of Schoenberg's *Moses and Aaron*, which had waited many years before it was done in the US, and I was actually in the clarinet section with the Boston Symphony for that performance, and I was also starting to conduct.

The one wonderful thing about Harvard University is that it has two orchestras. It has a large symphonic orchestra that was always conducted by a faculty member, but a smaller, sort of Haydn-sized orchestra that traditionally is conducted by a student who wins a competition, and some of my other colleagues later on who conducted include Alan Gilbert, the conductor of the New York Philharmonic. It was a great opportunity to make a lot of mistakes in public, and there's no better way to learn than to not have anybody there telling you what to do, and I think I probably grew in those two years that I was conducting. I also did a couple of opera productions in the dining hall of our house at Harvard, including a complete *Marriage of Figaro*. Again, as I say, you don't know what you're doing. People are screaming at you and telling you this is wrong or that's wrong. There's just no quicker way to learn than being involved in something. And once I'd found the orchestra I wasn't going to leave it behind.

It was an incredible time for a young composer to start work because of the combination of things that were in the air. The experimental side of American music that became known as minimalism was beginning; you had the liberating social and cultural experiments that were involved in the counterculture. This gave you an extraordinary context in a way to begin work, didn't it? To find yourself?

I left the East Coast. I'd never been to Europe, actually. I had hoped to go but the Vietnam War got in the way. By the time that I had finally gotten free of that problem, whether I was actually going to have to deal with being drafted, it was 1971, I think, and I just decided to go to California. I didn't know anybody out there, but it seemed far enough away from where I'd grown up and from the intellectual Eurocentric scene in the East Coast universities. I went out not really expecting to stay very long, but I ended up working at so much that I stayed, and I remained there ever since.

I did become a big fan of John Cage when I was still in my last couple of years as a student. Part of it was just a way of taunting my professors, because you have no idea how provocative John Cage was to the university professors in the early seventies. They just thought he was a fool and a charlatan, and I read his books, his first two books. I could recite them word for word. I learned a great deal about a different way to think about music. I started doing concerts that were very much in the John Cage tradition. Sort of. Well, they weren't in the John Cage tradition because John Cage was actually extremely rigorous, and we were all kind of sloppy. It was a kind of feel-good sort of musical finger-painting. Yes, I think it was important for me because I had to go through that rebellious period. Then at some point, when I was in my late twenties, I realised the need for some kind of cohesive structure.

I needed a kind of discipline. Fortunately, that was exactly the time I started hearing some really great pieces of early minimalism by Steve Reich and Philip Glass. That really kind of hinted that there might be a direction for me.

What was it that was so attractive to you about what they were doing?
Minimalism was a term that had been bandied around in the arts. I don't know where it started. I suspect probably in sculpture or painting. I always have felt the marriage of musical minimalism to visual minimalism to be a very forced fit. It makes me very uncomfortable. A graduate at Princeton recently sent me an introduction of a thesis that they are writing about my operas. In the introduction, there's sort of a general overview of my work. I saw these names of very, very sparse minimalist painters. I couldn't even begin to identify with that kind of stripped-down, severe, aesthetically reduced language.

Minimalist music isn't about stripping back – almost the opposite.
A long time ago, for myself, I defined it as having essentially three qualities. The music has a regular pulse, it's tonal, and it uses repetitive methods to take very small motivic fragments and build them into large-scale structures. Now, why doesn't that describe Beethoven's Fifth Symphony? The reason is because of the use of harmonic language.

Has it been an impediment or an aid, in a way, that you've been branded and labelled a minimalist, because in one sense it is part of what you do, but on the other hand it's not what you align yourself with at all?
Well, writers love labels. It makes them feel they're in a comfort zone. I'll pick up a German newspaper and read about the leading minimalist John Adams. I know how comforting that is to feel that we can put artists in a box and this person is expressionist or neo-romantic or something like that. It actually makes you feel comfortable because you don't have to think so much. But certain composers can't and shouldn't be categorised. It might be handy, but it doesn't really help. I think genres in the arts can be helpful because they will at least put us in the same country or the same zip code, for the sake perhaps of programming music or booking tickets, but beyond that, it can be very off-putting. I certainly would easily say Steve Reich and Philip Glass and Terry Riley are minimalists. In that sense the label is very specific,

and we all know what it stands for. They'd be happy to agree with being called minimalists, especially Steve, because he feels he invented it, and in many ways he did. For me it was a kind of breakthrough to employ this language that was tonal and had a regular sense of pulsation and had repetition, because for me that was what music was about. I was just looking for a new way of saying something, which didn't mean I became one so clearly. They came out of this period of real aesthetic chaos you can experience if you listen to pieces like Boulez's two *Structures* or some Xenakis pieces or certainly a lot of John Cage. It was music, but it was right on the edge of aesthetic chaos, where the listener simply could not comprehend what the creator was doing, and to some extent the creator didn't mind that. Frequently the creator didn't know what they were doing either, because a lot of the musical choices had been given over to a magic square, or a tone row, or flipping of coins, or consulting the I Ching or whatever. I'm not saying this in a pejorative way at all, but it wasn't leading anywhere outside of itself.

Minimalism really just completely walked away from all of that and did a basic very healthy house-cleaning of ideology and sort of started up the beginner's mind all over again. It was very *very* important for me in some of my early pieces. I was restless and the ideas and intentions suited me, especially where I was as a young composer. But minimalism also entered a cul-de-sac. I like, among the masterpieces, Glass's *Einstein on the Beach*, Reich's *Drumming* and *Music for Eighteen Musicians*; those are absolutely masterpieces and they will always be significant events in the history of Western music, but where to go from that? For me, what was missing was a sense of unpredictability and drama. I wanted to have a music that was capable of suddenly exploding into a much wider, expressive bandwidth. I felt that minimalism was just itself stuck in its own rigour. It's interesting to see what's happened to those composers over the last forty years. How they have or have not dealt with that challenge.

You never got stuck in a purely minimalist groove — one way you broke free was with the operas, and indeed their subjects alone was a kind of weapon you used in not being locked into a genre that to some extent had run its course. What is it about you that always tackles such big subjects with your operas? What is it about that? Why has it become a John Adams thing?

It's so funny, because I am often asked that question and I find it just puzzling, because if I were a novelist or a film-maker, no one would think twice. They would figure dealing with such things is just normal. But somehow, if you are a composer and you are drawn to subjects like terrorism or the atomic bomb or politics or history or whatever, it's somehow considered to be somewhat unusual. But I think that's really what's going on in our psyches and music is there to represent and examine that. We all read the news, we all have deep, complicated, probably unresolved feelings about terrorism or totalitarianism or nuclear war. I think it's an absolutely natural thing to do and maybe if people are drawn to my music, it's in part because it makes them think about these things or, better still, it makes them work out their own feelings because I don't really have a political message. I'm not like Bertolt Brecht. I'm not trying to sell you an ideology. But I want to share feelings and I think music above and beyond everything else, it's about feeling. It's not about being told what to think but perhaps about helping you decide what you actually do think.

You end up being called both a radical and a conservative. There's a confusion of why you aren't more experimental in your appropriation of popular music, if you like, than you appear to be when you write songs that exist in that tradition.

I have a very strong intuition about singing that gets stronger as I get older, which is that singing atonal music is – it actually causes such physical effort for the vocal cords that the experience of listening to it is painful. I'm sure the experience of singing it is painful. I think that the voice – I know this sounds like bad science and it probably is bad science – but I think the voice naturally wants to sing tonal music because tonal music is based on the partial series. The voice, as any singer will tell you, it breaks in notes just like a brass instrument breaks in the notes. I think it's like a natural thing. I'm sorry, I sound like some life-to-life right-wing, Tea Party person here talking about politics or something. But I actually do think that we sort of want to hear the voice organised tonally. I'm just trying to find a way to write tonal music for the voice that feels new and feels fresh.

My greatest regret was that I never played the piano or sang, and I don't know which I regret most. In a way, I probably regret that I didn't sing, because I think if you sing, you just have a kind of physical knowledge of intervals and sound, and I just never sang, and it's interesting because my mother was a natural singer. We didn't have a piano in the house, so I learned the clarinet, and I don't know, if there'd been a piano and I'd grown up playing the piano, I may not have become a composer. I may have just been so saturated with scores and have been able to play Wagner operas, and Mozart concertos, and Beethoven, and Bartók, and whatever, and never felt the desire to compose myself. It's been a great problem not to have keyboard ability, but I became a very qualified clarinet player, and then that led to conducting, and I ended up being a performer, only not a conventional one.

It was a surprise to see you once discuss about how hard it is for you to write melody.

I had to teach myself how to write a melody when I was forty years old. It's hard to write a melody because, well, I must use the analogy of going up into the Sierra Mountains and panning for gold in 2015. There just isn't any left. Or not much. Because all the good nuggets were found a hundred years ago. In the circumstances it was really hard to be the kind of composer I wanted to be. How do you write a melody without being a retro or without sounding silly? It's a very tricky thing. I know that *Nixon in China* has some melodies and it would perhaps be a little coy in saying it didn't have melody. It's just a very imponderable thing, because as I said before, it's very hard to write a melody that hasn't already been thought of. The thing about *Nixon in China* is that it's an opera with great serious issues and a very, very great libretto by Alice Goodman. At the same time, it's sort of wry and tongue-in-cheek while also being very serious. That allowed me a freedom so I could do something like *I am the wife of Mao Tse-Tung*, which is basically kind of like a barn-burning verismo da capo aria, if there is such a thing, and there are melodies for the weightier parts of the story, which are very dignified and represented kind of a big historical view of the country. Yes, it has melodies. But they took some finding. And it didn't mean I had solved the problem of finding them again.

Is there also a feeling that a good melody can need a kind of soothing, sentimental, sweetening openness that you might be trying to avoid in certain pieces — a great melody is essentially a form of happy ending — glib even — which perhaps sits awkwardly in contemporary music?

I have no problem with happy endings!

A PLAYLIST THROUGH WHICH, POSITIVELY, JOHN ADAMS FLOWS

1. *Short Ride in a Fast Machine* (1986)
2. *Hoodoo Zephyr* (1993)
3. *Grand Pianola Music*, III. *On the Dominant Divide* (1982)
4. Violin Concerto, II. Chaconne – *Body Through Which the Dream Flows* (1993)
5. *I Was Looking at the Ceiling and then I Saw the Sky* (1995)
6. *Christian Zeal and Activity* (1973)
7. *Dewain's Song of Liberation and Surprise* (1995)
8. *City Noir*, II. *The Song is For You* (2009)
9. Saxophone Concerto, II. Molto vivo: a hard driving pulse (2013)
10. *Son of Chamber Symphony*, II (1997)
11. *John's Book of Alleged Dances: Hammer & Chisel* (1994)
12. *The Wound-Dresser* (1989)
13. *Lollapalooza* (1995)
14. *Shaker Loops* for String Septet, *Hymning Slews* (1978)
15. *Dr Atomic* Symphony, I. *The Laboratory* (2007)
16. *My Father Knew Charles Ives*, II. *The Lake* (2003)
17. *Gnarly Buttons*, III. *Put Your Loving Arms Around Me* (1996)
18. *Berceuse elegiaque* or *Cradle Song (of the Man at the Coffin of his Mother)*, Adams's arrangement for chamber orchestra of Busoni's 1907 Berceuse No. 7 of *Elegies* (1989)
19. *American Berserk* (2002)
20. *Naive and Sentimental Music*, III. *Chain to the Rhythm* (1999)
21. *Nixon in China*, Act 1, Scene 1. *News Has a Kind of Mystery* (1987)
22. *Light Over Water*, Part II (1983)
23. Chamber Symphony, II. *Aria With Walking Bass* (1992)
24. *Nixon in China*, Act 2, Scene 2. *It Seems So Strange* (1987)
25. *Harmonium*, 'Because I Could Not Stop For Death' (1980–81)

2. I RAN AWAY AND FOUND THE FUTURE

A few weeks after interviewing John Adams, I interviewed the extravagantly great composer, conductor and new music trainspotting geek Ollie Knussen, who in 2014 became the inaugural Richard Rodney Bennett Professor of Music at the Royal Academy – no off-world, Obscure associations at all, so this was in fact my first official interview with a purely classical musician deeply immersed in its language and heritage.

It was an interview I had wanted to do since I sat opposite him around a table at the Royal Philharmonic Society Awards at the Dorchester Hotel, where he seemed to exist both in splendid isolation and also embedded in the very reason everyone was there. There was nothing intimidating or aloof about him — he seemed completely approachable — but at the same time he was clearly charismatic and cheerfully occupying a world of his own that he was happy for others to visit if they had the time and inclination. He was some sort of star sailor who never left the ground. He found other ways to take off. I decided I could interview him without having to worry that I knew nothing about arpeggiated chords, harmonic shifts or the slippery world of key centres.

Here was one of the most significant British classical figures of the past fifty years, for his conducting as much as his composing, with a personally balanced combination of the traditional and the radical that echoes Adams's mix of conservative and experimental. As a conductor, he was a genial, enigmatic English equivalent of Euro-manic Pierre Boulez, with an unfailing instinct for the best new contemporary music — Thomas Adès, who like many of Knussen's younger colleagues viewed him as a father figure, said 'his ears were even better than Boulez'. Anyone who seriously wants to know what it is a conductor actually does should pay attention to what Knussen conducted, and why it made a difference that it was him in control rather than anyone else. The 'how' he did it is invisible, as it should be, but without his presence the music would be some sort of pale shadow of what it should or could be.

He conducted as an expert emissary of the dead or alive composer, with an unshowy, deeply soulful, acutely perceptive ability to be the fundamental yet spooky link between the impassive but all-important score and the shape-shifting human collective playing the orchestra. His job was to turn the score, mere marks on flat paper, into glorious action — turn the literal deadness of those marks, those madly or sanely organised signals, into extraordinary, pulsating, totally present and often incantatory life. Whatever wisdom he possessed, and he definitely knew things as a connoisseur of the marvellously modern, could be found through his conducting as much as his composing, and he gave nothing away about what that wisdom was, only that it existed, and it could be found if you want.

And whatever that wisdom was would certainly not come out in an interview, where it could often seem that he had forgotten what he was thinking, or thought in general, or indeed had forgotten how to speak. Many composers can be credited with the sentiment: 'Words fail me. Which is why I compose.' And it could certainly have originated with Ollie, with the addition of, 'And why I conduct. And listen. And advocate.' Followed by a significant hesitation, merging with a definitive pause, leading to a satisfied changing of the subject.

If he ever did interviews, he preferred to do them by email – so that he could be more in control of what he said, keep his guard up, and didn't, as he admitted he could do, run away with himself and reveal things he wished he hadn't. 'My mum, hah, when she was nervous just simply talked like you wouldn't believe. I mean you couldn't get a word in. My dad was the opposite. He was a man of few words, most of them ironic. I tend towards my mum.'

My Academy credentials – and a little gentle persuasion from his close friend, the multi-talented cellist Zoë Martlew – permitted a rare face-to-face hour in front of a few Academy composition students in the Henry Wood room, the size of a large, posh parlour just off the reception area at the front of the building, which boasts a forbidding bust of Sir Harrison Birtwistle sternly guarding proceedings. In the end, always generously keen on pleasing, he found some words, even if it sometimes seemed to cause him pain.

Knussen's music story, which began when he was a young child – a child that remained happily ensconced within, enjoying the ride – and bumpily travelled through teenage precocity, brings with it a way of moving through the musical history of the past fifty years in a more personal way, one that resists the standard, fixed, more academic and critical versions of how that history has formed and how it will be passed forward.

He lived it, and experienced it as a complex mix of absolute insider and permanent outsider – intimately aware of the accidents, coincidences, protagonists, enquiries, insularity, 'family' secrets, unlikely meetings, private visions, establishment impositions, erasures, quests, misunderstandings, shifting perspectives, fashions, traditions, counter-traditions, institutional, ideological and personality clashes and, as much as anything else, the gossip that was at the foundation of how classical music developed hither and thither since the 1950s, and even as he knew the major makers and shakers, and worked with some of the greatest post-war figures, he remained by temperament absolutely anti-establishment, however that manifested itself. Biographies will list how he was the artistic director of the Aldeburgh Festival, head of contemporary music at the Tanglewood Music Centre, home of the Boston Symphony Orchestra in western Massachusetts, music director of the London Sinfonietta and artist-in-association of the BBC Symphony Orchestra, but he wore all that very lightly behind a perhaps carefully organised, deflecting befuddlement.

He looked exactly like the sort of musician — as comfortably large, scruffily bearded, amiable and easy-going as he wanted to be, a little mischievous on the side — who would collaborate with a world-famous children's author in turning their beloved picture book about beloved monsters into an opera, where he would happily quote Ravel, Stravinsky, Debussy, Mussorgsky and Mozart, and pay empathic homage to Harrison Birtwistle and Benjamin Britten.

In fact, in the early 1980s, he did collaborate with Maurice Sendak on a children's opera based on Sendak's 1963 classic — and Barack Obama favourite — *Where the Wild Things Are*, which in its own way also paid homage to artists of the past, in this case illustrators, storytellers and artists, and which was created while listening to music.[1]

Knussen was sitting in on lessons given by Oliver Messiaen at Tanglewood when the unlikely circumstances developed that led to the unlikely collaboration. Ollie had little idea why he seemed such a good choice to be the composer, not least because of Sendak's passion for Mozart, which Ollie's flamboyantly austere music in no sense resembled or even seemed particularly aware of. When they first talked about the

---

[1]Sendak looked to the Germanic sublime of Mozart and Grimm to work through his post-Holocaust trauma after many of his family disappeared inside concentration camps. It was a children's book but didn't treat children as... children, or indeed adults as adults. If you were alive, whatever your age, you should be ready for what happens, which you will understand from dreaming dreams and having nightmares.

project, Ollie passed the 'audition', quickly answering Sendak's question about what the best children's opera ever written was by saying, 'The second act of Mussorgsky's *Boris Godunov*.' 'Right answer,' said Sendak.

Knussen had never written a piece longer than seventeen minutes, and now he was committed to writing an opera, two in fact – *Where the Wild Things Are* was quickly followed up with a second collaboration, *Higglety Pigglety Pop!*. 'It nearly killed me. I let him down appallingly. I was basically a year late with both operas and we had cross words and all that, but he never ever lost his faith.'

It seems strange and yet entirely natural, if not fateful, that the then young British composer of enlightened, graciously modernist contemporary music should end up working on a book reverberating on a number of different levels – adorable with dark undertones, beauty pushing and pulling with terror – that reflected how Sendak remained in contact with the child in himself, and dealt with how so much in life, whether dark or beautiful, remains untamed. There was much about Knussen, as gentle as he was, as lovely, that remained, wonderfully, untamed.

He was weaned on a generation of composers who were, for all their sins and faults – as well as their sorcery and self-possession – larger than life, and that's what he was, one of the last in line from when the idea of being a forward-looking contemporary composer meant you could cause enough noise to effect part of the change in a rapidly changing world. The kind of composer demanding to be heard, however much the general public thought what you were doing was in an uncrackable code. You wouldn't say Knussen was one of the last of a soon-to-be-extinct species, but it will take a considerable change in circumstances for such a significant personality with such knowledge and insight to emerge again. It might not even become an extinct species; just invisible, or in disguise, or discreetly planning a rebellion, a lost tribe receiving nourishment from the making of noise, the divining of feelings and the making-up of fantasies using sound.

Sendak at a particular point in the twentieth century examined how, through art and stories, through the imagination, we can dream up a place we'd like to be – one way of defining Knussen's commitment to the making of, conducting, finding, playing, sharing and listening to music, to rearranging, even making disappear a disappointing, dangerous world. There was no one better alive or dead to turn the

Where the Wild Things Are fantasy into music, which suggests, almost moment by moment, hundreds of other fantastic spaces and other musical places we'd like to be.

Knussen's classical associations were with a conventional, orchestral Britishness that contained both the exquisite and explicit Englishness of Britten, Bridge and Vaughan Williams and the less obvious, less tamed, more speculative Englishness of Birtwistle, Maxwell Davies and Tippett, but also a taste, somewhere between the hedonistic and the spiritual, for otherworldly post-war exotica, whether that came through some of his later-life favourites, Ligeti, Takemitsu, Carter, Berio, Henze and, again, Birtwistle, or from his obsessions from further back: Scriabin, Brahms, Ravel, Debussy, Berg, Schoenberg, Crawford. (One of his composing contemporaries, Simon Bainbridge, once said that he learned everything he needed to know about modern music from Knussen's discerning collection of modern music albums — music collecting as an art form, as the shaping of history, and/or as self-administered therapy — which became the central resource for Bainbridge's research into what exactly his research should consist of.)

Because of his commitment to conducting, and in general his endorsing and encouragement of young composers, there were fewer compositions than there might have been, and he developed a reputation for lateness and irregularity. Many commissions went unfinished. The work that did get finished is consistently brilliant; quixotic in mood, sublimely detailed and meticulously crafted with a Ravel-like orchestral mastery, combining accessible sounds with ingenious structural unorthodoxy, magically packing timeless, mind-bending intensity into brief passages of time. He worshipped the small, the tiny, and arranged little bursts of energy in order to build an edifice to the magnificent.

His pieces are not necessarily Webern-brief, but there is a resplendent conciseness about them that comes from an avoidance of padding and any formulaic tricks; the symphonies, all written before he was thirty, are all under twenty minutes — the effervescent Third seems to compress a lifetime's learning and his purposeful commitment to refusing certainty and rejecting the straightforward into fifteen dazzling, rigorously luxurious minutes — his masterful horn and memorable violin concertos are about twenty minutes, and even his operas last under an hour. It's not soulful music as a fan of Marvin Gaye might think of it, but it is music that, in its own way, asks you to look after your soul.

There is no difference in the levels and values between his composing and conducting as there is with Boulez. The energy, architecture and style he received from the composers he conducted embedded itself in his consciousness, determining, as he once said, 'the very notes that I write'. This didn't seem to happen with Boulez. With Knussen the energies and passions of the composer and the conductor were much more connected – they were obviously the same person, whereas the music Boulez wrote and the music he conducted, for better or worse, seemed worlds apart, rarely feeding into each other, as if the contrast, the competition almost between one and the other, the breaking up of the two sides almost into the social and the anti-social, was part of the overall Boulez mission. And as a composer, taking him away from actual composition, part of Knussen's creativity and his quiet, humble and stoical genius was in ensuring much difficult, uncommercial contemporary music was being recorded when its existence on record was being seriously threatened. Again, this promotion of other music – other in any number of ways – paralleled the altruistic allegiances of Boulez, who along with Leopold Stokowski was one of Knussen's conducting heroes. 'They both didn't use sticks. So I didn't use sticks. They hardly moved at all and got these incredible sounds. They didn't emote. They let the music do the emoting.'

Knussen was born in 1952, which seems to contradict my theory about the 'last' generation of purely classical composers, only lightly touched if at all by pop culture, being born before the Second World War. But Knussen, a teenager in the mid-1960s, when pop and rock reached its first great peak of seduction, but almost completely untouched by pop and rock, was an anomaly, the exception that proves the rule – almost the freakish child of a relatively benign cult that kept the insidious, or just plain corrupting, outside world at bay, seeing no need to engage with what was happening elsewhere. He was born into the swirling depths of classical music and was almost immediately expected to swim in it and know how to breathe underwater, even communicate with fish.

His father Stuart was the principal double bassist in the London Symphony Orchestra and would play in many of the premieres of Benjamin Britten's music. As a young child Ollie would sit in on rehearsals for the Proms at the Royal Albert Hall, which he would treat as a playground. Family friends tended to be all from the classical world, including many living legends. To Ollie, Leonard Bernstein was

'Lennie'. At twelve, he's meeting Benjamin Britten, 'Ben' to his dad, who congratulates him for winning a music competition in Watford for a string quartet called *The Skipping Rope* – 'ghastly name'. He sits with Britten in his famous Red House in Aldeburgh drinking ginger ale – Britten something stronger – discussing his favourite composers, Stravinsky, Mahler, Berg.

'Dad had to kick me under the table to make sure I mentioned Britten himself among my favourites. I did know a lot of his music, so it was true. He gently told me how important it was that I planned what I wrote before I started, which I didn't then do. He said I might find it useful. That was advice that stayed with me. I now appreciate what incredible privileges I had from when I was very young, and not really understanding then how incredible those privileges were. That was the world I grew up in. It's a bit like you read an interview with Carrie Fisher of *Star Wars*, and they ask her what it was like to grow up with two Hollywood film stars as your parents, and the answer is, "I don't know, they were just my mum and dad."'

His father gave a bass player lessons in return for him giving the five-year-old Ollie piano lessons and teaching him how to read music. As soon as he could read music, at about six, he started writing music. 'Or, rather, putting marks on papers that looked like they were pieces, because I knew what music looked like.'

The first conscious composition was when he was about ten, called *Sweet Nemo*. 'I must have been reading *20,000 Leagues Under the Sea*.' At thirteen he is discovering Purcell, and he couldn't believe his ears. 'He had a transformative effect on me as a composer, his music materialising like sudden miracles in my life.'

He would write a piece a week, and, he said, you could tell what records he had just bought. 'At that age you don't think about quality or anything. I was just venting, really. If you take it to your teacher, which I started doing when I was twelve, and a teacher makes a criticism of it, you don't fix it, you write another one. I wish that one a week was like that now for me ... the one a week has become one a few years. Going through these compositions years later, which I had carefully numbered, I could tell which records in my collection I had bought the week before, because I imitated like a magpie up until probably I was about seventeen or eighteen. I mean, I could literally compose what I had just heard.'

After that the rest was his musical life, which was, more than anything, an individual standing up for the history and future of classical music in increasingly instant, pleasure-seeking, fashion-conscious times, not as cosy tradition, opaque elitist property or a series of arcane super-white rituals, but as a constant imaginative revelation.

He breathed classical music and became a uniquely original interpreter and fantastic composer, able to transmit through sound and structure the fantastic bordering on – and he would have hated me to say this, and pretend I hadn't said it, and be quite accepting that I did say it as long as he didn't have to – the mystical. When I interviewed him at the Royal Academy in the autumn of 2016, he was keen to report that he had heard on the radio that some sort of estimate suggested he would live to be eighty-four. Nineteen more years! Still plenty to do, and see, and hear, and even, you never know, compose.

There were two more years. He died in July 2018 and to some extent the response to the death of this extraordinary musical artist reminded me of why I wanted to write this book. The brilliance of his work and commitment to intellectual and emotional brightness did not really penetrate the pop culture or mainstream cultural firmament – there was far more attention given on radio and television to the death of one of the Chuckle Brothers.

I'm not saying – although maybe I am – that the death of a Chuckle Brother, and a few months later of a sit-com comedian whose one musical contribution was a novelty hit 'Whispering Grass', should not be mentioned at length on the mainstream news. But the equivalent lack of some considerable acknowledgement of the life and work of Oliver Knussen, the non-existence of a celebration and interpretation of his immense contribution to musical thinking, is as much an indictment of the reduction and breakdown of modern moral imagination and the triumph of a general cultural infantalisation as any referendum result or tawdry *Sun* headline.

The best way to remember him is to make sure the music he loved so much, paid such attention to and understood more than most doesn't follow him out of this world. It would remove one form of possibility that tends to take other, perhaps more vital, challenging, urgent mind- and world-opening contemporary ideas of possibility with it. All forms of possibility, whatever their basis, whatever the cause, support each other. All weirdness dedicated in whatever transgressive, complex or abstract form to the idea of progress and difference has to be allowed its other space, where the wild things are.

We sat down in comfortable armchairs to begin our conversation. I discreetly turned on my tape recorder, and at first Ollie didn't notice. When he did realise the conversation was being taped, I detected a little wince. He had, though, decided there are a few things he might as well say. After all, there were only a dozen or so others in the room.

When did the moment come when you absorbed influences without imitation? I mean, what stage did you reach when you certainly realised that was happening?

I didn't realise when that was happening. I was just aware that people started to say to me that my stuff sounded like itself. I'm still very much aware or hyper-aware, always self-critical, of realising, oh I got that from this source, or I got that from that source. As a kid I never thought about it. I mean, the big thing early on for me was the first part in Schoenberg's *Five Pieces for Orchestra*, which is an amazing thing if you have never heard it before. I immediately wrote three pieces for orchestra that absolutely ripped it off, except for the slow movement, which is ripped off from whatever the latest Shostakovich symphony was at that time. I once decided that I would remove the pieces from my catalogue that were derivative. I discovered it would be practically my entire catalogue. I got over that one pretty quickly or there would be nothing left.

It is interesting that you were surrounded by music because of your father and it obviously makes a huge difference to who you are and what you are. Did you ever get a chance to pull back? It creates a very unusual world for you.

I didn't know there was another one. In fact, there was a teacher at school who said, 'All you care about is bloody music.' Well, she didn't say 'bloody', not in those days, she would have been fired. I thought she was bonkers. I knew that people were interested in other things, especially football and things like that, which I have no interest in at all. I think it was kind of a shock when I was in my late teens, and I gradually realised that actually this was only a little microcosm. I was able to stand back a little more when I got married, which was quite early on, and I spent a lot of time living with my in-laws, who had nothing to do with music at all.

There was no hint of a rebellion against your father, and this almost institutionalisation?

There was a hint of a rebellion. My father was an orchestral player, and as anyone who— I have to qualify that now. As I would have said fifteen years ago, as anyone who worked with orchestra players will know, they hate modern music. It's not so true any more. A lot of the orchestra players I meet actually enjoy playing modern music now. In those days it was very much something that you did because you were forced to because, apparently, it was good for you – like you took castor oil, and there were some people who were above criticism, which was Britten and Stravinsky, even though he was writing this really difficult, modern, plinky-plonk stuff.

Boulez became above suspicion because he was such a good conductor, and the players respected that. But woe betide you if you were a young composer, unless you wrote very conservatively, and even Webern was frowned upon. I remember my dad loved Schoenberg, which was unusual, and Dad used to say Berg was like a great big pot full of mud which, when you stirred it yourself, some beautiful colours that sounded like Mahler came to the top.

Webern was completely out of his purview, and my rebellion was getting interested in that sort of music at the expense of Stravinsky, at the expense of those other things that were more acceptable. But at the same time, I loved both Britten and Tippett, who was also a composer not above suspicion in those days, the early sixties. I've always had those two sides to my nature, being interested in, hopefully, avant-garde or at least some kind of avant-garde and also in the apparently more conservative side. The great composers of that time who were alive were Shostakovich, Copland, Britten, Messiaen, Stravinsky and there were more of course, but that's quite a lot and as modern as they were, they were actually writing for the repertory, so the whole notion of modern music things being either atonal or traditional is not really true. There were two kinds of modern music, that's what I'm trying to say. The establishment modern music composers, which was provocative and influential for a whole generation of composers, and the more controversial atonal stuff, the Stockhausen side, that tends to dominate the story as if it destroyed everything. Of course it didn't, it was also important and life-changing for many good musicians.

What I won't hear of, although I'm bringing it up, is this myth in the sixties and seventies we were all taught to write twelve-tone music, strung up by the wrists and flogged until we did so, and there was the tyranny of it that led to some sort of life-saving antidote. People like John Adams say stuff like that, and it's complete balls. If one was influenced by such things, and you couldn't not be, because it was around everywhere, it was because it was fascinating and then at a certain point you realise there was more to life than that particular thing. Some people wrote this so-called horrible atonal music, which was somehow morally wrong, some didn't, some did both, some thought of something else altogether, and a very messy story, where lots of different music was being written for lots of different reasons, where there were no simple good-and-evil conflicts, no clear morals, no bright lines of destiny, it all gets boiled down to a very simple and not entirely accurate story. A distorted history gradually settles, or is forced into place, which the future will believe.

It's like over time journalistically a huge scythe keeps whittling down the details, the messy, interactive to- and fro-ing, to a very digestible narrative. Contemporary music in this very fertile, active period was the same story told in many different ways. I'm on the warpath against it being turned into a simplistic narrative, because if you've witnessed all the different nuances and the ups and downs of the history of an era, which I was lucky enough to be active in when I was very young, you know it didn't happen like that. I saw the sixties at least from an artistic point of view. I was there. I didn't, unfortunately, manage to do all the drugs and everything else. Which probably made me see clearly that one thing didn't lead logically to another.

Those established and not-so-established, atonal and tonal composers seemed to be your glamour at a time when the pull for many people your age was pop music and rock 'n' roll — where the drugs were.

I don't know about glamorous, but they were sorts of super father figures for me. They were composer father figures, because I knew that was what I wanted to do, and they helped me. Dad never intended that I be a composer. I was supposed to be a conductor and I was supposed to become a string player, and then learn the piano enough to work in opera houses and then become a conductor. I wasn't having any of that. I hated string playing, because it made such a foul noise. I would

be the ten-millionth-generation string player in our family, and I'm
not good with my fingers and I was more interested in reading music
than practising it. I would sight read till the cows come home. I hated
repetition and I liked writing, so I did what I wasn't supposed to do.
I was brought up definitely to think that pop music was a bad thing,
and this was also borne out by the fact that I can't – this still holds
today – I cannot bear – this sounds philistine – I can't bear the sound
of electric guitars; I hate it. But on the other hand, I'm not particularly
fond of string quartets either. So I was being balanced.

*How did your taste, for lack of a better word, your sensibility, develop in the
fifties and sixties, because even when very young you were clearly knowing
the things you liked and things you didn't like? What made the difference in
terms of what you liked and what you didn't like? And why in general did
your choices seem the right ones?*

I don't know. I had and I like to think, if I do think about this at
all, I've got a nose, I've got a sort of an instinct for the things that are
going to be interesting. So, for example, you're going to say I'm bonkers
because I was about fourteen at the time, I was one of the first people
around who noticed that Ligeti was a rather interesting composer.
This was way before Kubrick's *2001*. I remember buying a recording
of Ligeti's *Atmosphères* in America, a very poor recording actually, by
Bernstein – it's too fast – but I was really taken by what Ligeti was
writing. Nobody had heard it at all when I brought it back, not even
my teachers. It was completely in the underground, which did have a
kind of glamour, I suppose. I saw a performance from manuscript by
the Stockholm Wind Ensemble of his Ten Pieces for Wind Quintet at
the Austrian Institute in about 1968 in front of less than twenty people.
When Ligeti became ultra-famous, it wasn't a surprise to me, because
the music was fantastic. I knew it as soon as I heard it. I'm using that
as an example, but there were always certain things that I was attracted
to that weren't necessarily what one was told was officially the best stuff
to listen to at the time. I think, that's also helped me – and perhaps I'm
patting myself on the back too much, that's also helped me, in a sense,
spot interesting young composers, when I've come across them, I've
got a kind of a nose sometimes, but – I don't know quite what it is, but
I think it's because I've been so immersed in that world. It can seem
obvious to me in a way I can't explain.

Why didn't you take to Haydn and especially Mozart during this formative period?

Because I took it for granted. An awful lot in my life I took for granted, because of my background. I don't want to trash it at all, because it was remarkable, and what my dad did for me was wonderful. But I still discover things that I took for granted and missed then because there was Schoenberg around the house, or because there was loads of Mahler around the house. People used to give me presents at thirteen, 78s of music by Shostakovich. Because of that, of course Mozart or Beethoven, stuff from the eighteenth century, seemed boring because it was less spicy. In the middle of all I was exposed to it seemed to me like ordinary music. It didn't have the allure, the immediacy, of all my favourites. I started to like the Mozart I heard where there was something odd about it, which I started to realise could be the case. There were weird things going on, after all, and then *Don Giovanni* hit me very hard at some point. I realised there was something much more powerful than I'd given him credit for. God, I sound so grand!

Maurice Sendak, who I worked with for years, was a complete Mozart freak. He once said, very sweetly, 'I know this is difficult for you, but this is a great, great artist, and you'll realise it one day.' He didn't add, 'young man', but he sort of did. About five, six years ago, I had the radio on one morning, and this music came up, and it caught me unawares – and I thought, *This is just incredible, and what the hell is it doing?* It was something I'd heard before and not really got excited about, and I realised it was Mozart's *Prague* Symphony. I suddenly heard it as if it was new, as if it was something that wasn't tied to the eighteenth century. It wasn't tied to any particular time or school, it didn't come loaded with off-putting associations and it was just an out-of-the-blue object to examine. I could suddenly see clearly what that extraordinary object was, and I was completely won over.

Very shortly after that I went to Paris and I saw in the window of a music shop near where I was working the complete works of Mozart. I bought the scores. I was doing a concert that week so for once I was flush. I bought this heavy collection of complete works, put them in a suitcase and as I was doing it pulled my stomach muscles so badly I have a hernia scar that you can still see to this day. So if somebody says why do you have a hernia scar on your stomach, I can say, 'There is a very good reason for that. I carried the complete works of Mozart all the way from Paris!' You can't say that Mozart hasn't had an effect on me.

Your teenage precociousness led to a particularly bruising experience in 1967, almost a kind of star-child, show-business-family, X-Factor experience where, as a fifteen-year-old, your First Symphony was performed by the London Symphony Orchestra at the Royal Festival Hall and what could have been amazing turned out very bruising. The kid composer was treated as some sort of freak.

It was terrible. It was fantastic to hear my piece and it didn't put me off composing, not one jot. You couldn't stop me from composing. What it did do, very emphatically, was put me off the world of Royal Festival Hall, or the world of the glamorous agents and promoters, that business side of things. I was well over forty before I got an agent of my own and that was for entirely practical purposes. It gave me an instinctive distrust of – excuse me – journalism. Because you would say something to somebody doing an interview and they would write any old stuff. We are talking *Daily Mail*, that sort of journalism.

You got that kind of tabloid attention?

When I came home, the morning after my symphony was performed, first of all, there were journalists outside my house. I lived in this ordinary suburban street in Watford. It was nothing special. There were journalists climbing up the side of the house trying to get a picture of me asleep in my bedroom. And when I went out, they followed me. I said to my mum, 'I have got to get out of here.' It was ridiculous. I detested it; I really detested the whole thing, although it was great to hear my piece. I was used, as I now see it, quite rightly, by some very influential critics whose work I admired, who were appalled at the whole idea of allowing a symphony by a fifteen-year-old to be played when these orchestras weren't doing their bit for new music. It was a perfectly right thing to say, but it hurt me like mad, because I thought what I was doing was all right. They said it was completely derivative and naive and all that, which it was, but I didn't know that. The fact I conducted it didn't help, because the scheduled conductor, István Kertész, was ill, and it was performed by my dad's orchestra.

That is what mainly all of the fuss is about. If I hadn't conducted it probably would have been much less fuss. Daniel Barenboim took over an American tour it was included in the following week because the original conductor was still very ill. And it was Barenboim's first ever concert tour, as I subsequently discovered. Can you believe it? He'd only made his debut as a recording conductor the year before. He asked me to conduct some of my piece on the tour. Just one concert in Carnegie Hall. I said, yes, great, but what really interested me about the idea was the record shops in New York, which were sensational, and I could never get enough of record shops.

At that time it was 1968, and literally all the record companies were cashing in on the fact there was this crossover thing happening in pop music, where the Beatles had been influenced by Stockhausen and he was on the cover of *Sgt. Pepper*. The result was that the recording companies were recording modern contemporary music by the ton. I had some money, because I had just done these concerts, and I bought everything modern I could find. It cost me more in overweight baggage to get them home than to actually buy the records. I mean, there was Carter, which I didn't know and there was Stockhausen. There was Schuller, who became my teacher later. There was Takemitsu. I would pore over them for hours. Listen to them until I became the music. You could virtually lay out my entire future from the records I bought then in New York. That was the benefit, indirectly, of the paparazzi chasing me — I ran away and found my future.

Going to America also sounded a good idea because my grandmother lived in Chicago, which meant I could get on a plane and go stay with her. Which was the smartest thing I ever did, visit my grandmother in Chicago to get away from the negative fuss caused by my First Symphony in London. I stayed there for a month. I knew nothing about what was going on in London. I just immersed myself in the modern music scene there. And I wrote a lot and just got back to normal. I don't know why the hell I had that instinct. It saved my life. I think that I would have gone bonkers. Slowly, I returned to normal — well, my kind of normal.

Tell me about the teachers in your life. What was the most important information that you were getting from the teachers?
Well, the first teacher was Johnny Lambert, who had been a pupil of the important French teacher and composer Nadia Boulanger, which connects one to the time of Stravinsky and Debussy, who were her

friends. He was supposed to teach me harmony and counterpoint, and he taught me harmony a bit. I was not so good at harmony, believe it or not, because the harmonics in my music is, if I say so myself, not the most uninteresting element. Counterpoint he was a little bit better, although I didn't get that far with it. Just enough to sort of keep me going. I remember Britten telling me I must make Lambert teach me counterpoint, because he said that counterpoint *is* harmony.

Lambert introduced me to Boulez's music, and I would introduce him to Ives's music, another of my big passions. Then, later on, I went to Tanglewood. Even going to Tanglewood relates back to me having written that First Symphony, because the person who told the orchestra that when the firm that had commissioned the piece through the LSO had folded, the person that told the orchestra management that they should play it anyway was Leonard Bernstein. Later on, when he was in London, I went to see him to say hello. He was recording Verdi's Requiem at the Albert Hall. Lennie was another great encourager like Britten – it's a magical quality and they both had it more than anyone else I knew – he asked me where I wanted to study, looking out for me. I said, 'I want to study abroad.' He said, 'Have you ever thought of going to Tanglewood?' I knew that Gunther Schuller taught at Tanglewood. He was one of the composers whose music I got into in this very formative record-buying period. And I knew he came from an orchestral background. His dad was a second violin in the New York Philharmonic for years. He was also an orchestral horn player and a jazz person. Not that that was particularly my thing, but it meant he was open-minded and also he was an incredible orchestrator. He was a major, major promoter of avant-garde music, and I thought, *That's my man*. I was dead right, because he understood my background and I understood his background.

I went into our first lesson and I can't remember how it came up, but within five minutes I mentioned Scriabin and his eyes, I mean, his eye, sorry, he only had one eye. His eye lit up. I couldn't tell which one was the functioning one, actually. He said, almost suspiciously, 'You like Scriabin!?' I said, 'Yes.' He said, 'Actually, when I was a kid I orchestrated all of the ten Scriabin sonatas.' He was completely obsessed with him and we hit it off from that moment on. He was a very tough teacher. I have to say, but he was tough in the sense that you know, if he thought you had magpied something that he thought wasn't up to snuff he'd say, you know, you are too good to be doing that kind of stuff, anybody can do that kind of thing, copying obvious things. He gently took me away from relying too much on taking stuff from elsewhere. The main thing is he encouraged me and made me think about my true worth. The First Symphony experience had made me doubt myself and removed any sense in myself of whether what I was doing was good or not, because if you are told by one or two people that you're a great genius, which I'm not, and then you are told by another set of people that your music is totally worthless and that you are being used as a political thing, which it was, then you feel more the idea you are worthless rather than being any good.

I used to go back over and over and over again to Tanglewood. I mean, I was lucky enough to get fellowships there. Well, initially twice, and then I found that Ligeti was going two years after that. So I twisted their arm so hard that I got an alternate fellowship for a third year, just so I could be there when Ligeti was. Then I used to get myself odd jobs. Just so I could go back and hear various people talking. It was quite a time. There was so much going on you couldn't fail to absorb it through the air. I mean, the composers I heard talking there, doing lecturing work, were amazing. George Crumb, Copland, Carter, Lennie Bernstein, Ligeti, you name it. People used to say when you went to the late, lamented Tower Records, as it was then, after going to Tanglewood, it was like everybody had crawled back into their record covers after coming out for the summer. It was a wonderful thing and these incredible student orchestras and student ensembles and students conducting and also the Boston Symphony Orchestra. I was in my element.

In the end, having become a composer, you then did what your father had hoped for and became a conductor.

Tanglewood had actually put me off the idea of conducting for ten years. I went into the conducting class and I realised that was a world I wanted nothing to do with. Because it was all about very laborious technical work, the gestures you made with your wrist, how you signalled the beat; it just didn't appeal to me at all. I was too shy to admit it. And I also thought that conductors tend to be very narcissistic – it's such a terrible thing to say, but it's true. When they're in that sort of environment, competitive, superficial, and in those days and in that period there were a lot of very un-nice characters doing that kind of thing and they weren't interested in new things. Nowadays things are quite a lot different; there's some very interesting young conductors, and they're good people.

You didn't do much conducting for ten years between 1975 and 1985 and when you look at the amount of compositions you produced, and the variety, obviously there's a connection with how once doing full-time conducting, the composition trails away.

Of course there is. The only conducting I did do was actually either if there wasn't anybody to take a rehearsal of something of mine or something, then I'd do that, or occasionally, I'd do somebody else's piece to help out. It's true, I did full-time composing and the result of course was that I was totally and utterly broke. I did some recording with the London Sinfonietta, and I ended up conducting my *Ophelia Dances* piece. The orchestra's conductor, Michael Tilson Thomas, was due to conduct it again after an earlier recording, but said why didn't I do it this time, which was actually a very nice gift, although I didn't realise at the time. The following week, when a conductor got sick, as people sometimes do, the Sinfonietta players had just worked with me and I'd never conducted them before, maybe once. They said to Michael, 'Why don't you get Ollie to take these things over?' and then I took more and more things over and eventually took over the performance of *Where the Wild Things Are*, the first big concert performance in his country, and then that was all set in motion. I was a conductor and that's how I've earned my keep all these years.

How did your relationship with conducting affect you as a composer?

I was in denial about it for a long time, because I said the fact that I don't get pieces done on time has nothing to do with this at all, because I didn't get pieces done on time before too and that was for neurotic reasons. At the same time I'm learning a tremendous amount about the relationship between what you write and how the sounds are produced, and I spent a hell of a long time writing the two operas. I still composed steadily pretty much up until the middle nineties, then it slowed right down, but at that time I was doing a lot of recording and I did all my own editing and a lot of my own production. I was definitely distracted, but by what seemed important work.

In terms of conducting, in general in classical music, there doesn't seem to be the equivalent collaborations that there are in other forms of music, and I was thinking is the great collaboration actually between the conductor and the composer?

I'll tell you the most wonderful collaboration I've ever had was with a librettist, and that was with Maurice Sendak, and it was incredible. He music-ed the libretto and I libretto-ed the music. He couldn't write the music, but it was very much by the both of us, in the sense that I did things in the music of those operas that I would never have done in a million years without him, some good and some I like a little less, and likewise in the librettos he probably had exactly the same feeling. He didn't like modern music and I didn't like Mozart and it shouldn't have worked and on the other hand he was incredibly musical and Maurice was one of these people who would decide within probably maximum one minute whether he likes you or not, and there was nothing you could do to alter that impression from that moment onwards and thank God – I didn't know this about him – he liked me, and we got on and from that moment I could do no wrong, but he'd allow you to do what you thought was right. He never impinged ideas on me, and only ever made me think better about what we were working on and music in general.

Where do you think the two operas fit in to your repertoire?

They weren't planned to be this, but they are central. They released various things in me that were there, probably stuff to do with the music I heard in my head when I was a kid that I would never have let out without doing them. What I'm most interested in those pieces, apart from the fact they do sound very good, is that stylistically they make no sense at all. I started to do things that would never have occurred to me without having the kind of freedom I had writing the operas. I was doing things that I wouldn't have listened to before.

But to go back to what you're saying about the collaborations between conductor and composer, when you're collaborating with somebody like Carter, that was interesting because there was a lot of feedback, and he was very precise about what he wanted – this should come out and that could come out, and he'd explain why, and Takemitsu was another one who was amazing, because he had a very particular aesthetic sense. It took me a year or two to understand it; he must have hated the performances I did before I had the feeling of how that music is paced, and that you've got to have a feeling for silence of a certain kind, because I tend to be quite literal in many respects at first. But then you get a composer like Henze, whose music I used to adore doing because he basically presents you with too much material, and you've got to sift it and make it sound coherent, and if you asked him a question about it, 'Which part do you want brought out here?' – 'All of them, darling,' he would reply, 'oh, they're so wonderful.'

The collaboration is perhaps more accurately with the score. The idea that you're actually communing with the score is something that is very inspiring – I've spent many hours alone looking at scores. Henze once said something marvellous to me. We were talking about – I don't know whether this is relevant to what you said about collaboration or not, but it feels like it is. We were talking about where the orchestra is placed in an opera house, and sometimes you have these productions where the players are put behind the set, you know what I mean? You have the stage set in front and the orchestra are hidden behind or they're on the side of the stage, and Henze said, you know, he sometimes understood the idea, practically or visually, why it was done, but it was quite wrong. I said, why was that? He said, 'The whole point is that there is the stage, and down there in front in the pit is the orchestra and right in the middle of it between singers and players is the score, and it radiates the whole work outwards.' The score can't be behind or to the side of the performance. It is the centre, the soul of it all, bringing together the singers and the music. I do have a sense of scores as being living, breathing things, and in that sense he just hit the nail very sharply on the head. Very touching, actually.

How do you feel in terms of all you've done and that you've done all that work and all those pieces you've conducted, that there is the inevitable limited audience?

I can't tell whether the actual audience has gotten smaller for the music I like and conduct and listen to, or whether the wider world has gotten bigger. Do you know what I mean? I am not talking about my music, because I have no right to talk about my music that way. But if you talk about all the kind of music that I have been involved with, I think it's a terrible shame that it doesn't reach lots of people. Because lots of people would find something in it and they might be put off by the brand name or the concert rituals or whatever the hell it is that tries to make classical accessible. Or they might be put off by the lack of the brand name or the ritual. I mean, I find the concert ritual – I have always done – ridiculous. I mean, it's all right for the kind of meat-and-two-veg programming that goes on at the Southbank and what have you. But I find wearing black ridiculous. I think when you are conducting at least, this is entirely personal, in order to do your best, you should be as comfortable as possible and able to move as quickly as possible or what have you. Why are we wearing Victorian costumes? Why, when the BBC upped the ante on the Proms broadcast, did they hire more ladies in more fancy full-length frocks? Why? It's totally stupid. I think that puts people off more than the sound of it, in many respects.

If you put on a piece of music that people think is very difficult and challenging or unpleasant to some people, it doesn't matter if you are told how wonderful it is by the lady in the red ballgown. The fact is, often you find that an audience that is not meant to be able to get, or appreciate, a so-called difficult, dark piece are quite prepared to listen if you just present it to them with no sense of danger. They are very unlikely to run away in fright, and I find reports of the riots that are claimed to happen at the premieres of avant-garde music to be often greatly exaggerated.

I anticipated you might ask me some stuff about that sort of a question. To some extent, I regret that what I do or what a number of us do doesn't go or doesn't get further or doesn't produce accolades of whatever – basically, get more attention. But I've accepted it now and what concerns me is just to keep doing it. And to hold on to the ground we have and if you have an opportunity to bring it to the wider audience, then grab it, for God's sake.

Where does your loyalty come from in terms of how you are so generous in the way you want to encourage and teach new generations? You have a commitment to something, to some idea of what the music is and how important it is. What is that? Why is your faith so strong?

I have no idea. I had a chat with John Tavener once over dinner. He's a very funny man, which is what I liked about him. We were chatting about early music, if it went wrong when harmony was introduced. At some point he suddenly said something like, 'Are you religious?' I said, 'No.' He said, ' What do you believe in?' I said, 'Nothing really.

Not that I'm aware of.' He said, 'Come on, there must be something.' 'Well, no, not really.' Then he said, 'Well, you believe in music, don't you?' and I said, 'Yes.' He said, 'Well, that's God in some sort of a way.' In other words it's the thing itself. When you put it in words now, it sounds dinky, but he was right.

So I believe in music, the thing itself. We're posing puzzles. We're asking questions. We're considering answers. It does correspond to a kind of faith. That overrides any rational stuff and no matter what you say your music is about, you can't really say what it's doing. I can listen to Boulez conducting Bruckner, and if you ever lost sight of what this kind of music is about, you will be reminded, in that combination of Boulez and Bruckner. It's trying to show what the idea of the infinite is. Which is a mystery worth pursuing. That's what we can do in ways that other artists and art forms can't do. And that's why it's important. That's why people who aren't interested in music in— I want to say in a spiritual, in a non-materialistic way, they'll never understand what we do.

If you could put into words what you are trying to achieve with a piece, apart from the technical elements, which is a kind of evasion from the true meaning, then you didn't need to write the music. You could have just written the text. But there are more than words. That's the music. I'm writing a piece at the moment. It's taking time but I am very excited about it. It's a thing; it's probably quite capricious. There is no particular reason in the great scheme of things for it to exist or not exist. The world won't be changed by it. The world might not, on the whole, even notice. At the same time, it's tremendously important for me to communicate the particular vision of what this piece is about. I really don't want to say any more about it. I have said far too much.

Composing for you seems to be a combination of the most natural thing in the world and at the same time a kind of torture.
My favourite analogy these days to what gets me composing is the oyster. You put a grain of sand inside the shell and if the grain of sand doesn't irritate then you don't get the pearl. I'm not saying that every note is a pearl, but it's very interesting. I find that fascinating, all that stuff. I admire people very much like Hindemith, who could sit down and write a sonata for say – off the top of his head – tenor euphonium and piano and do it very quickly and very well. I can't do it. I can't do it. I could do it, I suppose, but I can't.

The more I work over something, the better it gets. I'm not one of those people for whom the first idea is fantastic, and you just stick with that. Occasionally you get very lucky and something just happens. It's what the French call the '*donne*', the given, a gift that you are given. You get given the idea from somewhere. It's given to you, somehow. It doesn't happen very often. More often than not you work to come up with some sort of concept. That concept that you have in mind somehow has to be inhabited so that it can occupy space and time. So it's got to have occupants and the occupants are eventually the notes and whatever else I write.

Now, for me in order to get to that point it's like having a little array of things that you have by you all the time when you work, let's say. So, there are — perhaps a text, perhaps a painting, perhaps a particular kind of music; more often than not two particular kinds of music that shouldn't really live together. But you think that they actually should. Somehow this all gets together in a big knot and they produce some sort of fission in my head. That fission is what gets me going and until I've got that, I can't start. Once I've got it, of course you've already got yourself problems to solve. Once you've got problems to solve you've begun. And you're away. To a point.

When I'm teaching, I just encourage the students, and tell them to be precise. Is what they were putting in that place precisely what they wanted and is it in the precise place they imagined? Teaching is just having a conversation, really. Sometimes I feel like a benign shrink. You need to establish what they're trying to do, what their points of reference are, how they're going about doing it, whether they're confused, whether they've got incredible judgement, whether they're really going perfectly fine. The last thing you want to do is to get in the way. In the end they've either got it or they haven't. I can tell whether they have, I've had enough training, but there's nothing I can do about it one way or another apart from just being there if they need a hint, or a clue, or simply an answer to one of their questions, which might be as simple as, 'If it's not working, try again, and if it is…'

He finished our session by answering some questions that the students in the room had, and nothing was too trivial, or transcendent, for him to dismiss out of hand. He gave them his time. Time was on his mind, in fact. To some extent, he thought the main function of being alive is to pass the time.

He told me he was sort of enjoying one part of getting old, the part that does things to time that as one of the great conductors of the past hundred years – which is another way of saying he was a time lord – he seemed to be really intrigued by.

'The one thing I notice as you get older is that time moves faster. It is an obvious thing. I think you perceive time based on how much time you have experienced. When you were a baby and you were hungry, then probably a minute feels like an eternity. When you were five years old, a week felt like an eternity. When you are fifteen years, a year feels like an eternity. Well, now a year feels like a week used to do. I mean, really, it goes past so fast. I remember my father, who died when he was like my age, when he was in his sixties, once said, 'You cannot believe how fast time goes.' There are two things that are very good about this. It is much more difficult to get bored, because things move faster. So, if you have to wait for a train, it is not such a big deal if you wait half an hour. It used to make me want to jump onto the tracks, I was so bored waiting.

'Also, if you have to sit through a Bruckner slow movement, it is fine the older you get. The slower the better, really. There is a performance of the Eighth Symphony, which included a movement I used to hate. I would hear it, and it was so slow, I was literally counting the bars. There are four bars, okay, and that is another four bars, and by the time I got to bar 300 or something, I was ready to shoot myself. I've now found a performance that almost breaks the half-hour mark and the slowness is a very different thing. It is really very, very nice. You actually hear time being created.

'The other thing of course, when you sit down to work, there doesn't seem to be enough time to do anything, but it's all very pleasant – the other day I was composing and I'm not an early riser, putting it very mildly, and I sat down to work at around two. The phone rang and I chatted to somebody for about an hour or something, which went splendidly. Then I started working again and at a certain point I thought, 'Well, I should probably take a little break now and have a nibble.' I looked up and it was eight o'clock at night. I had noticed that it had gotten a little dark, but I thought it was six or five, something like that. Well, I will just do a few more minutes and then suddenly it was ten thirty. It had seemed like a few minutes. That was kind of nice, except that I couldn't sleep all night, but apart from that it was all very delightful. I hadn't wasted time. I'd used it very sensibly. And then there was the next day to consider, where I might do exactly the same again. Time changes things, sometimes when you want it to, sometimes when you don't.'

With that, he left the room, and its forbidding bust of Birtwistle, taking his time.

3. I CAN'T GO BACKWARDS

I've always wanted to interview Bob Dylan, but I never did, and I never will, not at least until after he's died and I can make it up, based on certain evidence. He's become a kind of fictional character, so it makes sense to make something up. In terms of the difficulty of such an idea, interviewing an artist who hates the idea of interviews, who is not interested in transmitting in simple forms the kind of simply described information necessary, interviewing the elusive, evasive, cranky, to some extent the potentially violent Lou Reed was as close as I got. An interview was something that made him feel cornered, and everything he had done as a musician was in order to resist being cornered. Volunteering to be cornered by what he considered the creepiest, slimiest, lowest of the lows — a journalist — seemed to him a ridiculous submission.

The musician I most wanted to interview as I built classical music around and inside me was Harrison Birtwistle, who I found to be the most astounding of all the living composers, and high up among all composers, not so much for solving any mysteries but for making the mysteries more spectacular. His music is an example of how the greatest classical music by the dead or alive composers is not only about life, it is life, organised into a mystical shape. It is the sound of life, and that is never going to be particularly straightforward.

Here was another endpoint to classical music before it becomes post-classical, or in fact doesn't end at all but takes on a new life of its own, even if it's just banged on a can or blown through a reed, sensationalising civilised thinking, summoning the gods or sounding the alarm, one more likely to cross the centuries and see the end of time — which of course it is often describing — than pop music, which is mostly of its time.

Birtwistle seemed to me to be an equivalent theatrical character to Dylan, a phantom genius using music simultaneously to conceal and reveal himself, inventing himself almost with every few seconds of his music, as it constantly shifts through dimensions and finds ways to break with tradition, keeping a distance from explanation, becoming, in the world he moves through, the reality he traces, a kind of myth. Occasionally spotted, even heard, surrounded by biographical material and detail, but only reluctantly confirming or denying elements of it, and keeping the meaning or not of his music a closely guarded secret. He doesn't really want anyone rummaging around in his affairs.

There is a *Sir* Harrison Birtwistle, because it suits the establishment to welcome him inside, even with a little apprehension, because he has the aura of being a trusted voice, and it was given because of his music, but it's a little like Dylan receiving the Nobel Prize – it adds even more engrossing weirdness to the presence rather than a compromising softening of it. Dylan will be called a singer/songwriter and Birtwistle will be called a modern composer, but even though both pilfer from genres and musical styles, even parody and reanimate certain conventions, and have the best sense of musical history, they constantly resist being pinned down, and live and love to slip into gaps between genres and musical eras, making up their own history, their own lines of enquiry. The music they make is of its time, but you get the feeling that whenever they were born, they would be thinking the same things and be outside the hurly-burly of the everyday.

They're pre-modern, from some ancient land, even as their imaginations and their understanding of the imagination make the most ingenious modernist and postmodern artists seem tame and predictable. And Birtwistle, like Dylan – and Lou Reed – has an ingrained reluctance to comment on his own work, and even though Birtwistle has politely done more conversation recently than he did in the period between the mid-1960s and the mid-1980s, when his musical reputation was consolidated and he was at his most publicly curt, he is unlikely to open up at length. There is no satisfying technical information or academic-pleasing spirited articulation of a specific radical manifesto, no publicising of his own artistic conviction; the music is somewhere and he is somewhere else, and prefers not to be dragged too closely to where the music is in case he's encouraged to explain it.

In a talk he gave in 1964 he was already confirming a position when he was clear – in a vague sort of way – that his music 'should really speak for itself. I cannot help wondering a little whether I have sufficient grounds for saying anything and whether I shall be able to do it right. For while as a composer I feel quite in command of the means to move others in the direction in which I myself am driven, I feel that it is not within my powers to map such paths so surely through words.' To theorise is the task of the critic and not the artist. And the artist is better off not bothering with those theories. Then again, Harry's not short of opinions, and has got plenty on his mind — which to some extent is where all those notes he has written come from — but not much that he is particularly inclined to share.

As composers set themselves problems that they must then solve, so as an interviewer I fancied setting myself the problem of interviewing a formidable musical artist whose work is in general as powerful and often stunning as it is precisely because he is not likely to treat interviews as anything other than an irksome, random, slightly amusing duty.

The biography of Birtwistle begins in 1934 in Accrington, east Lancashire, five miles from Blackburn, still lingering at the cheerless, blackened shores of a gnarled, crowded, world-changing Victorian Britain. 'I was born into another age. There were still horses and carts round my way.' The rhythm of clogs on cobbles constantly clattered around him as workers started and ended their shifts in nearby cotton mills; the chaotic clamour left permanent marks on his imagination, becoming almost a first musical influence.

The famous first industrial city of Manchester, twenty increasingly smoky miles to the south, is as far as the imagination stretched from such a small, lost-in-time town. By the 1950s, with an adventurous sense of wonder learned growing up in Accrington, he is part of an unofficial collective at the Royal Manchester College of Music filing a youthful rebellion against the idyllic, southern Englishness of Vaughan Williams and his acolytes, the charming colours of which made no sense in a damp industrial North, brimming with grey slate, ominous smoke and a super-strong rustic red brick that originated in Accrington and was used for the foundations of the Blackpool Tower, Battersea Power Station and the Empire State Building.

Birtwistle, along with other members of the Manchester Group, the most famous of which were Peter Maxwell Davies, John Ogdon, Alexander Goehr and Elgar Howarth, rejected the dominant acceptable face of English music that was safely held in the hands of Vaughan Williams and Elgar. They looked to the European avant-garde, which had an outsider sense of discontent – and an irascible dissonance – that seemed more northern. To work out their other, wilder, truer Englishness, and just work out their trans-national musical position, they turned to the twelve-tone revolution of Schoenberg and Webern that had regrouped after the interruption of the war, inspired by the furious energies of standard-bearer Pierre Boulez and the American Europeanness of Milton Babbitt.

Birtwistle's 'Opus 1' is a 1957 piece for wind quintet with a deadpan, clean-cut, modernist title, *Refrains and Choruses*, that announces the idea of Birtwistle as much as the music, and which, as some sort of seed, contains the DNA of everything he would subsequently write. Future no-frills titles like *Slow Frieze, Endless Parade, In Broken Images, Ritual Fragment, Panic* and *Secret Theatre* are also hints of the genre he is inventing as he goes along that doesn't really have a name, or if it does, it is never spoken aloud. Some call his music instrumental theatre, others call it deranged, and the truth seethes, writhes and settles into itself in the spaces – sometimes in a vacuum – between topsy-turvy theatre and harnessed disorder.

Even though *Refrains and Choruses* suggests moments that could label it post-Stravinskyan, post-Varèsian, serial, neo-tonal, emotionally, subversively English, avant-garde and even somehow medieval and postmodern, it is not directly any of those things. And even though it materialises from such worlds, and is not exactly accessible to the popular audience, there is nothing pretentious about it; it might lack an obvious punchline, but it's as down to earth as any raw, homespun and mischief-making northern comedian, using comedy to preserve his sanity faced with a constantly crazy, meaningless world.

Refrains and Choruses arrived midway between Boulez's mathematically liberated, or enslaved, *Structures I* (1951–2) and *Structures II* (1956–61), which for some exhausted the possibilities of serialism, a fitting punch line or an extreme anti-climax, or both. Birtwistle picked up from there, incorporating, sustaining and penetrating serialism rather than rejecting it, stimulated, not stymied by its sophisticated concept of form, and simultaneously summoning an avant-garde music he discovered had existed in the apparent lost Dark Ages before Bach, as though the baroque and the classical/romantic eras were both preceded and followed by a modern period. He worked out his own post-serial system – never named, never becoming a thing to own or disown, only meant for his purposes – where he could administer different processes, properties and situations and, within that, be totally free, embrace inevitable accidents, set in motion constant battles between different modes of action and generate his own randomness and, through that, his own logic.

He is already resisting standard genres, obliviously or with determined intent, and speaking pretty much his own language, somewhere between an 'Ur' language, absolutely pure and untouched by influence and, at the other extreme, one filled with recognisable syllables but unrecognisable words. And whatever that language is, it does have a broad northern tang – not just from the North of England, but from an elysian, transcendent north.

As he moved through the 1960s, he's completely separate from rapidly accelerating musical movements in pop culture and rock music, but also somehow completely separate from the established theories, consolidations, rebellions, progressions, diversions, solutions, fashions and deviations in classical music; across many borders from Cardew, totally apart from the concerted reaction of the Manhattan minimalists to serial severity and Stockhausen spirit-building. He finds himself where he is, sticking to certain resolutions, wonders what to do next, struggles for an idea, makes a discovery, totally inside his own head, his own version of music. He carried on speaking his language, and as someone obsessed with rituals and the ritualistic, he's describing and exploring them with his own musical rituals.

It's the same thing with his approach to perspective; all of his pieces, whether they are written for thirty-six trumpets, six percussionists, unaccompanied choir, orchestra, variously sized mixed ensembles or solo piano, play with perspective, as though he's using music to work out the true scale of reality, and also to capture how reality is a continual, fluctuating series of mysterious, juxtaposing energies, which often involves rampant, fruity repetition, enough to make him as much a champion of repetition as any early American minimalist. At the same time, often as he is playing with perspective and ritualistically examining ritual, he's playing with time: accelerating it, freezing it, distorting it, stretching it, superimposing it, wearing it down, working out its topology, convinced it's more than a straight line, and musically imagining the possibility of time consisting of multiple time streams. And then there is all that space out there that contains no lack of void.

At which point he might say, with a wink, and a sweet, deceptive little whine, 'I don't try and make my music difficult. I try to make it as simple as possible.' Of course, one person's simple is another person's attempt to capture the moment of creation – or the moment of creativity – in a series of sounds that unfold around themselves and tell a story you couldn't see coming. Even the composer couldn't see the story coming and is very surprised by how it ends. Somehow, a few notes, or a lot more, the correct balance between precision and spontaneity, the peering into dark places illuminated by his subjectivity, finding form to accommodate the mess of existence, and, abracadabra, *voilà*, ee bah gum – a bit of magic.

His music as a pure manifestation of spirit is never particularly meant to be musical, but it sometimes can't help it, the way he harmonises space with time, and in the end, once the clarinet was left behind, it becomes his chosen medium. Birtwistle can sometimes seem a bit reluctant about this, as though music might not have been where he belongs, even as a musician. It might have been the ever-increasing availability of music that puts off highly sensitive musical minds like Birtwistle.

Pianist Joanna MacGregor told me: 'Composers of the Maxwell Davies and Birtwistle generation very quickly stopped listening to music because they were driven mad by the availability of it, and this was nearly half a century before Spotify. There are many, many composers who crave silence and they put themselves in environments where they can't get hold of music. Both Maxwell Davies and Birtwistle spent time in the Orkneys, almost purposefully off the grid. They're fed up with music. There are two things going on. I think one is that they stopped listening to a certain type of music because they know that it's not theirs and they just don't like it. They're just going to make sure they're never around it and they just deliberately cut it out of their lives. They're also doing that because they feel that in some way too much awareness of certain other music is corroding what they want to do. I mean, someone like Ligeti, he hadn't heard Stravinsky's *Rite of Spring* until he was twenty-three – it wasn't easy to hear new music on record, and so when you did, you really felt it, the great new music would cut into you like a scalpel, it would be such a shock. And it's these shocks that make you as an artist. You need music to be a shock, to really come up with the goods, not simply be there all the time.

'But I think quite literally, composers like Birtwistle, they're aware that their ears are getting tired and there's just too much noise around. There's too much muzak, which all music is becoming, there's too much everything. Of course, you've got to be quite a purist to do that.' Something more, or other, than a mere musician.

Birtwistle's music evolves within each piece and from piece to piece, so that as you go through the tremendous amount of music he has written throughout his life, in bits and pieces, in coherent slabs, in bursts of activity, between pauses for thought, from the profoundly slight to the exquisitely mighty, you notice the changes, but the changes seem to be both invisible and happening all the time, in the way he can in one piece merge the static and the propulsive, the massive and the miniature, the gritty and the graceful, the sacred and the profane, a closed loop and a continuous line. There is never a moment where he dramatically alters what he's doing; he just keeps speaking the language he invented, but over time, everything has changed, and a new language has emerged. All the way through, whatever happens in his music, it can only be what it is, but he still has to make sure that it is, grabbing hold of the essential, which never changes. There are greater cosmic laws in motion, but there have to be the right minds to interpret and refine them, knowing in their own way, on their own terms, how to break them and create new precedents.

The antecedents for such a spirit are also artistic loners and prophets who don't fit in, and don't want to fit in, the accepted academic and cultural grooves and genres, thinkers and makers who tended towards the solitary – the continuous change and variety of Edgard Varèse dropping his and Debussy's Frenchness and Stravinsky's neoclassicism into a 1930s New York mixer, treating chaos as an event, extinguishing worldly time; Antonin Artaud's commitment to presenting art as an ordeal, his image of the world's madness incarnated in the tortured human; the deconstructed musical hall of master of the comic grotesque Max Wall; modernist pioneer Paul Klee's Bauhaus structural organisation of colour and exploration of form, the way the creative force eludes every denomination; early twentieth-century American composer Charles Ives's lusty appreciation of the thrill of losing control, his capacity to shuffle the continuity of his thoughts, all the better to disorientate his audience, his fascination with the thin line between order and disorder, between sense and nonsense, taking a great delight in allowing his music to approach, even descend, into chaos, using dissonance as a sign of moral integrity; nineteenth-century essayist Thomas De Quincey's dreamworld 'combinations of concrete objects recurring in time' and his chipping away at the sublime; the secular, church-troubling fourteenth-century composer Philippe de Vitry's new method of measuring rhythm, his revolutionary form of notation, his using music to express non-sacred business; strange carnival master David Lynch's artistic managing of our fear of the void, reconciling a world of opposites, hope and cosmic terror, an impersonal universe and our personal selves; the feverish, contrary, northern English imagination of Anthony Burgess, spiked with northern airs and disgraces, chasing adventure as if to repair the devastation around where he was born.

Of other musicians of Birtwistle's time, the closest to his way of working, and stubbornly evading the obvious, was his Salford-born student friend Peter Maxwell Davies. Who knows what they talked about in their early twenties, based in broke, post-war, post-industrial Manchester, filled with ghosts, its history stalled, its buildings bombed, and at the same time in their minds existing in an unnamed territory where music was both a way out and a way in, a method of creating purpose or evading fixed responsibilities?

With each of Birtwistle's pieces, whatever it is, whether chamber or opera, small unorthodox ensemble or larger and more traditional, he constructs a carefully careless framework within which he represents a mind working out its experience of reality. At which point, if he heard such a statement, he would do a perfectly timed double take and smartly slip in one of his catchphrases – a mock-bewildered 'What?' with a little curl of the lip, a helpless shrug and tacked-on roll of the eyes, uttered by someone who would have heard comedian Sandy Powell on the radio in the 1930s and 1940s asking his hard-of-hearing mum, 'Can you hear me, mother?' It's now Birtwistle who is hard of hearing – 'What??' – which adds a further absurd edge, and intermittent light relief, to any conversation with him.

As things stood, in the early 1960s there was nowhere to put this music, which existed as a new kind of performance as much as anything else, and which seemed to the casual listener to provoke the same sort of heebie-jeebies as free jazz, both founded on the dynamism of transformation, but it inevitably ended up in the studies, halls and pages of classical music, even as it ruthlessly steered clear of the sonata and the symphony forms and tossed all sorts of matter and material over and into tonality, not completely destroying it, but not spending Sundays kneeling in front of it. As conservative as that world could be, it remained where the avant-garde at least got a hearing. Even if just the one.

It was a few hard years before Birtwistle made it to a first level of being noticed by more than the cognoscenti and his colleagues, breaking through with 1965's obscure but lucid *Tragoedia*, which abstracted Greek theatre, placing a string quartet on the left, a wind quartet on the right, and a harp in the middle. He completed his savagely satisfying *Punch and Judy*, his sadly mad, madly sad, cheerfully violent, violently cheerful first opera, or anti-opera, skinning alive the usual properties, which debuted at Benjamin Britten's Aldeburgh Festival in 1968 – reputedly to the un-bloodthirsty Britten's horror, but it probably tickled his funny bone as well, or perhaps he noticed and was flattered that buried in all that carnal blood and mayhem there was a bittersweet trickle of Britten. Wipe away all the apparent mess, and there he was, as clear as day.

After that, catching the ears of Boulez, who would become a committed supporter, there was *Verses for Ensembles*, an exhilarating snapshot of a teeming universe filled with mystery and creatures, and 1975's awesome, deathless atonal masterpiece almost praying to Brueghel's uncompromising depiction of the remorselessness of time and death, *The Triumph of Time*, which is both scattered and coherent, contingent and eternal, dead to the world and alive to the cosmos, finding its bearings between damnation and salvation, between the boundless universe and unfathomable transcendence, with mind-widening hints of glory. Just Boulez's goblet of interconnectedness, right up his boulevard of being-ness and becoming-ness.

It was far-sighted conductors like Boulez and Knussen that helped locate Birtwistle in a classical world needing the wildly new in order to freshen the repertoire, plot the development of the once new and maintain a search for beauty and, on the other hand, the cruel and ugly. If the once new grinds to a halt and leads nowhere, then its purpose is debatable; after Debussy, Stravinsky, Bartók and Messiaen, as formidable and fiercely engaged as they were, someone like Birtwistle extends the line, plots a trip from dead Accrington to diverting anarchy, creates a new context, shines new light on the once new, and still works out what it is that happened, and what could still be happening.

Birtwistle was even more exuberantly monumental in 1986 on the space-shattering, symphonically unsymphonic *Earth Dances*, a contemporary classic that could only be dedicated to Pierre Boulez. In his own way, keeping himself occupied, he had the dislodged time of his life with a series of concertos between 1987 and 1995, which of course upended the notion, offering a parallel universe, mythical-seeming concertos, inventing structures that are impossible to describe except with music, essentially having visions, for trumpet (*Endless Parade*), piano (*Antiphonies*), tuba (*The Cry of Anubis*) and saxophone (*Panic*).

He writes a brutally unpretty, irresistible violin concerto in 2007 because he decided to write the last thing he imagined he would ever write, and the most difficult thing he could think of. He likes a challenge. He likes contradicting himself, even winding himself up; if he decides he won't do a certain thing, he then goes ahead and does it. He likes to see how he can make it through such a commission without including any clichés. Forcing himself to deal with his own neuroses, or confusions, is one way of dealing with the self-doubt that has continually plagued him since the 1950s.

One of his five operas – he considers himself an occasional opera composer, but he's an idiosyncratic specialist, an otherworldly master, splitting the idea apart and extravagantly fastening it back together, doing the same to time, replacing traditional opera rituals with cosmic rituals based on his private language – was the insanely complicated and divinely sure-of-itself *The Mask of Orpheus*, which is as much about the immense imagination of the composer as another artistic take on the Greek myth. This version of the Greek myth is chucked at us from the edge of the solar system. Surely not the work of someone who sometimes considers he is a failure as a musician? Actually, totally the work of someone making sure that what he does has not been a waste of time, even if few people, in this lifetime, will ever get to see or hear it.

Any rare performance lasts about four hours, just about long enough to deal with all the myth and death, the birth of music, the use of musical expression to win over creation, and to fully understand its multidimensional combination of spectacle and transcendence would take four years. There are a couple of Wikipedia lines that for once are really helpful in describing its subject. 'The structure of the opera's plot is complex. It is difficult to provide a detailed synopsis.' Offered it as a whole, the mind might surrender, but the music, moment-to-moment, is a dream of a dream, a reforming of music with a logic best surrendered to. It's Wagner coming after Stockhausen, Mozart after Webern, in the way his other music can be Telemann after Bartók, Purcell after Gubaidulina, Beethoven after Babbitt, Schubert after Zappa and, bizarrely, Birtwistle after Birtwistle.

You might get the feeling that Birtwistle does not expect to be understood in his lifetime, if ever, and he doesn't particularly care. He's not bothered whether or not time will catch up with him. What he does care about is getting something done once he's had an idea, even if it does involve presenting Orpheus as a singer, a mime, a dumb-show act and a puppet.

My Royal Academy credentials get me my interview with Harry Birtwistle, one of classical music's most iconic figures, with an intellect powerful enough to make you think he sees more of reality than most other people. He has a brutal dislike of small talk that combines no-nonsense northern brevity with the intolerance of an artist who really doesn't want to waste any of his time, especially when that time is rapidly shrinking by the day, with stupid questions, which of course tend to lead, if you're not careful, to stupid answers. Interviews irritate him because it's all very well promoting yourself, but you end up squabbling over petty details, the pair of you feigning interest, talking past each other, while the larger issues remain undefined and unresolved.

When I 'studied' at the Royal Academy as a classical music Bambi for the BBC, I never imagined I would ever know enough about classical music to be able to handle an interview with Sir Harrison Birtwistle, who seemed as distant as high modernist priests like James Joyce or Jean-Luc Godard. Actually, I don't know enough. But I know more than I did. Perhaps enough for it to be like a GCSE physics student interviewing Stephen Hawking. Perhaps enough of the history – even if it's a history I made up – if not of the technical components. Perhaps enough of the North to be able to at least reminisce. And after all, from my own dark northern quarters, twenty years after the Manchester School, when it was the Sex Pistols and Patti Smith coming to Manchester, not Schoenberg and Messiaen, climbing out of my provincial background through the loving of and listening to music, I now find myself a staff member at the Royal Academy of Music, where Birtwistle also teaches. So he is a kind of colleague. We can swap notes. Well, I would have some notes. Birtwistle would have a blank piece of paper. Actually, he would have forgotten to bring it. He would never have had it in the first place. It's all in the mind. It's on the tip of his tongue. It never occurred to him.

I meet him for the first time in the unceremonious teacher's room in the Academy's basement, and he approaches me with the soft-shoe shuffle of an old music-hall act, Mr Disgruntled of Accrington, the top of his baggy trousers loosened, just in case a pratfall is called for, and the look in his eye of someone who finds just about everything in life highly amusing, and also a little disappointing, the look of someone who had quite a cockiness when he was young, knowing where he was going on the hunt for a ray of sunshine and a free bench, and then got to know despair.

He looks for a moment as though he recognises me from my appearances as a pundit on arts television, or maybe from my occasional appearances on daytime television, always there for those in enforced or creative isolation. Then it seems as though he's sure he doesn't know me from Adam. Maybe he's just amused and disappointed with me, knows all about my 'how to be a composer' dabbling, seeing in me the absolute shape of a dumbed-down world. Maybe he's seen my type before, vainly, sentimentally looking for answers and even for help, and he is only too aware that I might ask him for help about what exactly music is – is it a way of expressing something so deep about life that neither religion nor science get close to revealing it? Is it a way of communing with ghosts from another dimension, which is why those of us who take it seriously do take it so seriously, and often need it to be special, and surprising, and original? I might ask him if he makes music to make sense of a life that otherwise would make no sense at all. By the end of such a question, his mind would have drifted off.

He looks like he might chuck a custard pie in my face, and then take pity on me, and shoot me through the heart to put me out of my misery. Perhaps he'd rather chat with a puppet.

I imagine him enjoying being in the company of Bob Dylan, and not so much not knowing who the other character in the room is, but always forgetting and having to find out again, and enjoying the moment of reunion. Until the next time. There is a faint hint of him instantly forgetting who I am if we don't interact for a few seconds. His memory is breaking down and breaking up, not necessarily because of age, but perhaps because of such close, constant exposure for fifty years to his breaking down and breaking up of time and experience in his music. There are psychic dangers getting this close to the inside of everything and being so acutely aware of everything we know moving relentlessly towards some tenuously receding end.

For some reason, the subject of Captain Beefheart comes up — maybe I misheard him, or he couldn't hear me, or something. Maybe the Academy's head of composition, Phil Cashian, doing the introductions, mentioned him, as if to point out to Birtwistle that I might be from the pop world, but that stretches as far out as Beefheart, so it's not all sweetness and light.

I get excited at the whole idea of a world where at the same time Captain Beefheart and Harry Birtwistle were changing the very internal shape of music, even if the two spheres of musical collisions never seemed to collide with each other — and at the very idea that Birtwistle had heard of Beefheart. I ask him if he's heard any music by Beefheart.

'No,' he smirks, with a jolly sort of 'as if' look about him, which I decide to interpret, as the critic in this relationship, as him saying that the very act of listening to something outside his carefully cultivated space and time might indeed ruin music for him, if not life itself.

The two of us take our place on a small stage, which is bare apart from two chairs, a table in between and a lone, leafless tree. There is a small tape recorder to take in the past, in whatever fragments it reveals itself. We are two characters in a play where there is no past or future, only the maddeningly temporary here and now. There is a small audience, there to play the role of a small audience.

I am on a quest to discover what the final piece of music I will ever listen to will be, which has involved a late-fifties crisis-of-faith crash course in classical music, which has taken me to places, to here, and there, and somewhere, where there is quiet, to escape a noisy world, but also noise, full of meaning and direction, which crushes the empty, distracting, conditioning noise of a world repeating itself, going round and round in circles, losing its way, what with one thing and another. He is on a quest to avoid the question, any question, and keep himself to himself, a closed book, to be simply here and nothing more, sharpening his wits, collecting data, finishing tasks, until his time comes.

There is the time that moves forward, and the time that, as it reaches inward and turns into memory, becomes erratic and eroded. Naturally,

I begin in the North. A small smile plays around his lips and, without actually saying the words, he adopts a position in his chair that clearly means: 'Mind your own business.'

The beginning. Or the end.
Time is a funny thing. I can remember things. Not necessarily what order things happened.

The first memory. It might be true; it might be what he's read that he's said before.
I am sitting in a highchair and because my father was a baker I was given lumps of dough to keep me quiet while they got on with their things. I don't know whether you've ever played with bread as opposed to just baking it. The dough turns grey.

How did music appear? When did you first become aware of music?
Well, my mother said it was to keep me off the streets. To keep me out of trouble. She heard that there was somebody who played the flute in the next street, Mosley Street. I don't know why I remember that, but it was Mosley Street and this guy played the flute and it didn't matter what the instrument was, he could teach me. It turned out that he played the clarinet. So I started to learn the clarinet. Small and easy to play. A nice sweet sound. I worked hard at it. In that society it was seen as a way of getting further education. Something to aspire to. It didn't come natural to me. I didn't become any good at it. Good enough, but I wasn't cut out to be an instrumentalist.

I failed the eleven-plus – most people who were poor didn't pass the eleven-plus. I remember a girl at eleven called Mary Carr, the first girl I fancied, secretly, the first girl I fell in love with, and she had to go to the grammar school; she passed the eleven-plus.

What was music like in Accrington?
Usually the North is famous for its brass bands, but Accrington had a military band. I don't know of any other place nearby where they had reed instruments as well as brass. That's why there was a clarinet player in the next street. It was called the North East Lancashire Military Band. I ended up playing with them. It used to rehearse on Sunday morning above a local pub. They used to open the pub where we played quite early on, a bit

too early, and there were a few pints went down before rehearsal, which had an effect on how we sounded one way or another. The bandmaster was called Wilmot Dewhurst — you ever heard of anyone called Dewhurst? I can see Wilmot now. They all wore uniforms, but he had a special officer's uniform from, I would say, the nineteenth century. Very smart.

How do you break into composition from that kind of background?
    Well, now we're talking about creativity. There's a difference between learning to play an instrument and becoming a composer. Lots of kids were taught to play instruments. Not many became composers. That involves something else altogether. How do you become a composer? Is that the question? Well, I'll tell you that it never occurred to me not to. I've still got some things from when I was about ten, eleven years old, where I couldn't actually make the notes, but I made it sort of look like notes. I knew what they looked like. I was getting music lessons. It took a few seconds to make some notes and then you still don't know what they are or why they go on the music manuscript, because the crotchets and quavers I made were too big and they sat there over the lines, and you can't really tell where they're meant to be. It seemed silly to those on the outside. I was deadly serious. It's what I did.

How come that has happened, this eleven-year-old has the pen and the paper and he's writing music?
    I have no idea. I always felt that I was musically educated via the Third Programme.

Which starts in 1946 straight after the war, in the progressive spirit of changing and remaking a ruined world that led to the ambitious creation of the NHS a couple of years later. The Third Programme was for the creative — and mental — health of the nation. The BBC were aiming high — highbrow — purposefully, as a patron of the arts dedicated to the refinement of society, and for a good twenty or so years it is much more intellectually minded and self-consciously 'culture conscious' than its updated version, Radio 3, becomes: the Third Programme was for the new, for the experimental, for advancement in the arts, and in an introduction to the service the then director of the BBC, Sir William Haley, announced it would have 'no fixed points and will devote to the great works the time they require. It will seek every evening to do something that is culturally satisfying and significant.

Its whole content will be directed to an audience that is not of one class but that is perceptive and intelligent.'

I heard music that wouldn't have reached me any other way. I didn't know who it was by, but later I identified composers such as Schoenberg or Hindemith, Mendelssohn's *Songs Without Words*... It didn't matter who it was by. Things stuck in my head – I didn't know one from the other, it was all the same to me, but I would think, *Oh, I'll have a bit of that* – it seemed more interesting than playing scales on the clarinet.

My father, Fred, had a radiogram – a gramophone with a built-in radio. There were gramophone records in our house. He liked 'The Donkey Serenade', Paul Whiteman and his orchestra – does anyone know that? It wondered what the point was of singing to a mule . . . something like that. It's a good question, of course.

My father was a dreamer, frustrated by being uneducated. I was his only son. He was from another world, so we could never be the same even if we were. There was something about him that meant he became interested in photography... and in music. He was such a dreamer, wanting things to be better, that when the war finished he bought a farm! What you call a smallholding... with about twenty acres of land. I lived there until I left home. My father and mother died there. I used to milk the cow once a day before I went to school.

When I was about fourteen I was allowed to leave school on a Monday afternoon because I had a musical talent. I didn't know I had. I would make my way to Manchester to the Northern School of Music where people paid to have lessons. I was given lessons in counterpoint and all that nonsense. And they had a class where you could get a scholarship. I applied and I got the scholarship – a county major scholarship.

Manchester was where it was all happening if you lived in east Lancashire. There was the Hallé Orchestra, and I suppose then I was being trained to become the clarinettist in the Hallé Orchestra. That would have been the ambition of my family – there was no sense of creativity; that was my secret. You didn't let on. It was too weird. Play an instrument, yes, that was a craft, a job, but do not think you can write something. Who do you think you are? I kept all that to myself. Eventually, the clarinet playing stopped and the composing took over.

Perhaps keeping it inside contributed to the music you would write — it was allowed to sort of ferment, fester, evolve in your imagination while you kept it a secret. Even when it appeared in public it kept its secrets.

Perhaps.

You're not convinced.

I had somehow become fascinated by the whole notion of writing music. It was just there. I cannot tell you where that came from and I do not acknowledge that this was a very unique thing for a young boy from Accrington with my background — go on then, it probably was. I'll agree there were not many of us around! But it was nothing special. It didn't seem to be special. It's just what I did. Like milking cows.

I suppose I am wondering if this sort of forbidden nature of composing contributed to your compositional separation from everything else — the way you resisted the cultural and musical currents and grooves and genres that are around you. You're in your own world, in the way, it seems, as you grew up you were in your own head, and not letting on what you were really up to.

But is there really anything special there, though? We're all products of our environment — it's all grist to the mill. Things are put into a pot and those are the ingredients you have to make something from. What I can say is that I was totally unpretentious about it. It wasn't until I was eighteen that I became arrogant, but then that arrogance was a necessary part of the rebel and I did become the rebel, the outsider.

How did that articulate itself?

Dress. Dylan Thomas was a big influence on how I dressed — bright red tweed suits. Green shirts. Hawaiian shirts.

Were you consciously a musical rebel?

The musical revolution that was happening in Europe was curtailed by the war. Twelve-tone music, serial music, the revolution of Schoenberg, this was all interrupted, and I became born into an English continuation of what was happening here before the war, that Vaughan Williams thing, who as a composer didn't interest me. There was a strong division at the time between a very English music and a very European music and in a sense I went to Europe. It was necessary for me to reject the Englishness, which didn't mean much round our way. Serialism pointed in a different direction, which made more sense to me. The idea of an alternative attitude connected with my own thoughts. That was where I was self-consciously a rebel, and arrogant with it. I was against this idea of the symphony and the sonata form. I think Vaughan Williams was actually in the same predicament and there was music he did that didn't teach me anything new but which I admired, and that's when he wrote pieces that were not associated with the symphonic form, like *A Lark Ascending*, which is unique to itself, and there was *Norfolk Rhapsodies* and *Fantasia on a Theme by Thomas Tallis*. They're like nothing else, and I think Britten and Tippett came from that. In the end excellence isn't what you do, it's how you do it. Vaughan Williams could be extraordinary, but it didn't interest me, not as a composer.

What kind of composer did you want to become?

The answer to how or why I became what I am is always— I don't really know. You can keep asking but you're asking the wrong person. I was there, so I didn't see it happening. It just happened. There it was. There I was. I took the language that was handed down to me, which was largely serialism, and once I had begun with that, there was no going backwards. I can't go backwards. Once you move on from twelve-tone, it's never going to be easy, believe me.

Was it important that you were born too early to be bothered with the temptations of popular culture?

That all happened a few years after I had been taken where I had been taken, so it wasn't going to be interesting to me. I might not have been interested anyway.

I did my national service in the early 1950s, two years in the army, and after the army I'm playing in an orchestra. I played in the orchestra, but I was somewhere else in my mind. I was a composer in my head. It took my time in the army to really come to the decision that I want to compose, not just play the music of others.

Don't ask me why.

Your first official piece, Refrains and Choruses, *seems so out of time from anything that was happening around you, and that has never changed — you're part of no school, no genre, no movement.*

It wasn't designed to be different, or at least not for the sake of it. That this is how I wanted to be. I wasn't showing off or anything. I didn't know what I was doing – well, it's wrong to say I didn't know what I was doing. I knew exactly what I was doing. I knew that I was composing music and I looked for things that would help me do that. At the college you were trained to be an instrumentalist, and you were creative on the side, after hours, and that's where you met others like you. Having won this scholarship, I went to the Manchester School of Music, where I met Alexander Goehr, Peter Maxwell Davies, John Ogdon and a lot of other people, and the natural thing was to set ourselves aside from all the weak academia, to be actively new.

Was there anything useful that you were learning?
It never seemed to have much to do with what I had been writing since I was eleven. There was something in Messiaen I recognised, but I was finding that for myself. Also, there was a history of music course, and each week there was a lecture on a particular period of music and there were two things that stuck out for me. The first was the modern music one, talking about twelve-tone music, and it consisted of the teacher saying give me a pitch, give me a tone, give me twelve, anything you like, and then we can use them to write something. This was his explanation of it all, and we were meant to just follow what we were told – and then a voice came out of nowhere, which turned out to be Sandy Goehr, and he took this guy on. He knew more than the teacher and he gave him a hard time. That was interesting to me. It didn't have to be what you were told. There were other ways. Nothing was fixed. And in this history we were being taught it was accepted that music began with Bach and whatever was before Bach was only known as the Dark Ages and they knew nothing about it at all. I decided there must have been something going on before. Where's it gone? I went out to find out more, read some books, and found out there were at least 300 years before Bach. They didn't teach it, because they decided it didn't help you as a player, so you found it on your own. It fascinated me about what happened before Bach, especially because it wasn't a part of formal education, like it was banned or something. Questioning what you were told and filling in blanks for yourself made sense to me as a composer.

What did you discuss among yourselves as the Manchester School? The myth is one of a group of insurgents angrily tearing up the rulebook.

We spent all our time together. We got up to no good.

What did you talk about?

We talked about modernism. It was the time to be new. Move away from an awful past. Rebuild.

I've forgotten the question.

So have I.

Ask me something else, then. Go on.

Thinking about how your music exists in its own space and time, you once said that if music didn't exist, you could have invented it. Is that you explaining the difference of your music in hindsight, to not be like anything else, at risk of sounding too strange for words, or does this otherness come naturally to you?

Yeah. That was very pretentious. I like it, though, but I think I could rephrase it. (Pause.) Maybe not. I wanted to write music that didn't exist, not so much invent music itself. Perhaps it's the same thing. I got interested in the artist Paul Klee; a lot of composers have written music about Klee, but they call them picturesque things like *The Twittering Machine*. I wasn't interested in the colours or the patterns. I was interested in when he was teaching the Bauhaus people, and I felt that he was inventing painting as though it had never existed. The way he talked about line, the balance between shapes and – the nature of nature... the complex examination of very simple things, the simple rendition of very complicated things. Once I got rid of the arrogance, the sense I was fighting something or for something, all that side of me fell into place. Based on that kind of thing Klee was talking about, there was so much to do that hadn't been done. Not to argue something, merely to present it.

Not everything I've done works. I hate the expression 'experimentation'. I don't like the idea of saying something was an experiment, because that gives you the excuse to fail – oh, it was an experiment. If I made a mistake I would try and correct it in later pieces... music has to work... there are certain things you do in music that if you are not hearing it, if you don't know where you are in time – the time of the piece – then it's not working… I can write what I would call a very interesting failure…. *Slow Frieze* is a very interesting failure.

Do you feel that when you listen again to your old pieces that there is something you wish you'd not done or changed?

I am always suspicious of the pieces that do work. They are the real failures. I know that it means that to some extent I've relied on a clichéd solution to a problem. Does that make sense? I've not come up with an original solution, I've repeated a well-used solution. And I know I do that. I'm just writing a piece for two pianos and in a sense it is, it is a big um, uh, experiment, because it's an experiment in the sense if there's one thing in it that doesn't work, none of it will; it's all a failure beginning to end. I realised that when I thought of it, but I knew that if I didn't do it at the time I was given the opportunity, I never would, and it's always been to some extent about setting up problems, you know, and finding the solution to those problems.

That basic. No inspiration?

No. I don't need inspiration.

You say this a lot. No inspiration, no expression.

Yeah. And?

So what are we left with?

My intuition and my art, which you have no control over. You can't just decide to be original; you can't sit down in the morning and think what I'm doing today is going to be original. Now I'm going to show them all, Beethoven hasn't got a chance. You can't do it.

But you want to be original?

It's not something you can think about. I want the *idea*, whatever it is, to work. I remember at school they always used to say to me – could do better, could do better. I'm doing my best, miss! Promise! Bloody doing it. That's still how it is. I'm bloody doing it. What more do you want? There's this new piece called *Keyboard Engine* I'm writing for two pianos, and that in itself is a problem – there are a lot of problems leading on from the two pianos. You've got one piano for an imaginary big left hand and a big piano for a big right hand, so there's a sense of this monster pounding away... and I wanted to write a piece that was permanently three against two... sort of independent from each other, but connected. The idea of the engine is as though they are mechanisms that are going through a process, and I composed a couple of minutes of that, of this, and then I took scissors and cut into the music, and then I wrote some other music – and it all comes back to Paul Klee. He talked about something dividual and something individual. He talked about something like a piece of wallpaper, where if you cut a bit out it is still dividual, it can still exist, but something individual, like a bottle, if you take a piece out you fundamentally destroy the form, so the two parts are reflected in the two pianos, the dividual and the individual combined... individual is in the dictionary, the other one isn't... You can tell I need to write this piece because finishing it is the only way to explain it. That's always the way. Music explains music, not words.

Words don't explain music and music doesn't explain words.
   (Silence.)

Each of your pieces has a distinct, individual form but could be part of an overall form, as if all of your separate compositions are really one work, a continual work in progress, part of a lifelong dialogue between you and your material.
   It's not set up. It's not what I think about. It's just the way it is. I love the idea of Messiaen, who writes this music where he invents a mode when he's twenty-one and that's it, he stays within that, but he manages to always change the music as he goes along. *Chronochromie* is one of my favourite pieces, but don't ask me what my other favourite pieces are.

If Refrains and Choruses *was your first work, the first work that got you really noticed was* Punch and Judy *in 1965.*
   The narrative was exactly the kind of opera I wanted to write; it fitted me like *Don Giovanni* fitted Mozart, and it's a real theatre of cruelty – Punch just kills people and then he kills the devil and says, 'Where is the woman I love?' and then takes her away. It's got all the ingredients – they are not real people, but they are emblematic of real people. I could write the music to that.

Cultural attention is generally elsewhere as you write this extraordinary piece — does this sort of indifference and celebration of popular culture contribute to your testiness that everyone is looking over here while you are doing niche stuff?

I don't make the niche. The niche is made by others. Oh dear — this is an old bloody thing; I get into trouble, too much champagne at an award ceremony and I say too much, just being grumpy… oh dear… is this your world? I have to be careful, I mustn't say anything naughty… like, it's amazing what they've done with four or three chords. Must not say that.

The Triumph of Time seems to me the kind of thing the great prog bands — King Crimson, Magma, Van der Graaf Generator — were desperate to do, and here you are in the mid-seventies doing it, and it's completely separate from that world and it's only noticed inside its own world.

We come back to… it was all from a situation that wasn't calculated — I know what I've got and I can't do anything else and it's good enough for me, and that's good enough… pop and rock was on a different timeline to me, which is okay. There is this question in that world of who is at the top. Someone has 5 million number ones, it's all so exciting, of the moment, and then it's gone. Meanwhile, I keep on doing what I'm doing, and it's not about that… pop culture is like a huge monster that needs feeding every week and one or two things are marvellous, but the fundamental difference is the music I am involved in is about a wider sense of time, a timelessness, and the pop song is at best about five minutes, at the time, it's here and now, it won't last, it's not made to last… Mahler wrote symphonies that are on a completely different and higher level and I know there are moments in pop music that are phenomenal… but I am elsewhere. I exist where I exist.

From another time. For another time.

What? My world won't disappear — I will always be here. The work can't be unsaid, but it's not my problem what happens to it. It's pop's problem when it becomes fish and chips, when its time has gone. My time is another time. All right.

What's changed about the way you perceive music?

One thing I have learned in my late years is that Beethoven is completely original in that they are symphonies and he deals with tonality, which often means it is all going to be entirely predictable, because the rules make it so, but you never know what he's going to do. He's constantly doing things you don't expect, and he does something that seems to trap him, and you wonder how he is going to get out of that, and he does – and it's always a surprise.

I always feel with your music that I have no idea what on earth can happen next, but I am always dying to find out.
    That's not bad.

Is that the kind of thing you're aiming for?
    I don't think about an audience or any kind of reception or reaching people, that doesn't mean anything when you're composing... it's an abstract narrative and it's got nothing to do with anything but music. My music is about the nature of music.

Is that what The Mask of Orpheus *was about – one of the things?*
    My interest in Orpheus is not as such in the myth of Orpheus – the story is about someone who is given music, it becomes his power, so it is still about my interest in music, but to some extent the subject doesn't matter. It's irrelevant in a way. You choose something that has an interest, that suits you, but that's just to get a canvas, so you can make marks, get shapes, find balance. It's not the story, it's how you tell a story. Before I wrote *Orpheus* I had an idea of writing an opera about Faust. There was a famous moment at the Royal Opera House where there was a big meeting – producer, the director, the designer – and they all wanted to know how I was getting on, and they all went on about Faust, as if this was the point of the project. I said, 'Can I stop you there? I've changed the subject. It's not Faust any more.' Their faces dropped. Uh? I said, 'Don't worry, it's the same opera, just a different subject.' The subject didn't matter. That's just a way for me to get to what the thing is really about. And it will be about music. The subject just presents some problems to solve musically. I still need to like the subject, but it's not the real story of the piece.

How does this subject, music, and your interest in where it comes from change over time?

It evolves. Influences come and go as well, which means I see music differently. People always ask — what are your influences? Well, it's none of their business, but apart from that, it's more complicated than they think. Influence can be something you like by the usual names that you consciously steal — you take somebody's idea and you hope you can give it a new slant. But there is also the influence that, if you like, comes under the door, like a draught, which you have no control over. And as a thinking man I like to think that is always changing, because I am always interested in different things, in different priorities. Some new things come into focus, some things become relevant, some become irrelevant. The influence that comes under the door without you knowing is what's interesting. So the answer to the question, what are your influences is, genuinely, I don't know. I'm not being difficult. They sneaked up on me. I'm not copying them because I don't know what they are.

Why does a wider audience have so much trouble with abstract music?

I was talking to somebody about abstract expressionism in America, and the idea when people see a Jackson Pollock and they go, oh well, I could do that. The truth about expressionism is that it was the context and the journey that got painting to that point. What makes it honest is that it belongs to that context. It comes from somewhere and something, but you couldn't see it coming. You might think, *Well, I can throw some paint at a canvas*, but you're doing it from the wrong impulse, and because you now know what it is. And that's the same with my pieces — it's not just doing it because I can or because I want to, it comes out of something and somewhere, and it makes sense at the time I am doing it of certain musical journeys, including my own. There is a context for it, it is not just making shapes. This piece for two pianos to do with pieces cut out, where I am writing a piece about continuity that is discontinuous — there's my perversity, but it's where I am at the moment, and that's the truth, its realness. Once it's done it's not honest to repeat the ideas or the solution. I then need to find another problem and another solution, and if I can't, the doubts begin. Sometimes I have no confidence in what I do. Then I have an idea, and it is a euphoric feeling.

Abstract art becomes more cherished than abstract music – and abstract art, often as weirdly put and as contemporary as the most abstract music, has a value in the millions.

You can't own abstract music. If I was looking for money I chose totally the wrong field of abstraction. David Sylvester, a great friend of mine, he said, 'Do you realise if you were a painter and you were as famous as you are, you'd be worth millions?' The painting equivalent of the music would have real value, because it can be owned by one person with the sort of money that wants to show itself as knowing the value of even the most unorthodox thing. You can be rich and pretend you're interesting enough to understand interesting things. You can't take the music home and have it for yourself, and it requires time. You can look at an abstract painting for a few seconds and then move on. Abstract music needs attention, and then if it's any good it will get under your skin. It's out of control. The picture on the wall is under control. The abstract there becomes a luxury, a commodity. It becomes an object of desire, because it is so unlike anything else. Abstract music that is unlike anything else is mostly ignored.

What's your view of modern classical music since the 1950s?

There have been some wonderful things in music since the war. Some of Stockhausen's ideas are mad but brilliant. So-called minimal music – that was the end for me. The thing about minimalism is it's the end of the wedge and after that all you can do is back out of it and add a bit more to it. Of course within there are some good things, but in general it was the end of something, especially in terms of how fashionable it became. That makes it something to become suspicious of… a few years ago all the kids were writing it and you could teach your granny to do it. It was a reaction of its time to the maximalism of serialism. A bit too simple, a bit too easy to teach, the obvious next stage from the serialist set theories.

I like minimalism.

That's your problem.

What does the name Sir Harrison Birtwistle mean to you?

Who he?

I have a terrible insecurity linked with a terrible arrogance… I can bring one in front of the other and they tend not to belong at the same time. I move from one to the other quite freely, but in the end I'm not impressed by me.

One truth is that he writes uniquely original music.
I never think this. I am very pleased it is original, if it is. Who's to say? I've had ideas and they might be fresh, but I don't know about original. I have no sense of it being original or not. We're going round in circles. (*His voice faltering in exasperation.*) It's a more mysterious thing than it being original or not.

When I hear pieces I've done there are what I call wounds. I can hear them and I think — why didn't I get rid of those? And then I tried to do that with some pieces, and I couldn't do anything about them. I couldn't make changes. The wounds were part of the piece. Sometimes I might hear a piece of mine I haven't heard for a while and I'm expecting the wound I remember, and I don't hear the wound. It's healed somehow. But another wound has taken its place somewhere else. Why did I do that? It is a sore you can't get rid of. One gets better but another one appears. It's where something doesn't work. No one else notices. You wouldn't hear a piece and go, oh, there's a Birtwistle wound. But Birtwistle knows.

Talking about time and where we came in, what difference does your age make in terms of how and what you write? Because you like to look forward. You're not sentimental. What difference does it make that you have less time ahead of you and therefore the looking forward becomes something different?
(*Sigh.*) I'm not looking to do anything different. It was never about looking forward. It was about doing something that was on my mind at the time. I trusted my creativity and that's as far as it goes. Being older makes no difference. The music isn't older. It's in a time all of its own.

But what about the sense that you know, you're coming close to the last piece, and perhaps everything you've done has been a commentary on your mortality, and soon it will be over.
So yeah, it will totally be for you as well.

I'll probably go before you.
Maybe. It doesn't matter. And yet you go on.

Does the stage you're at in your life make a difference in terms of any new composition, though?

No, not at all. Same as ever. I'm always at the end of my time until the next piece. Always have been. Every piece could have been the last piece. Or the first.

The end of life doesn't make a difference to your music?

It is what it is. I haven't got anything else. I can only do what I can do. What else is there?

There is a question from the audience, which takes us back to what Birtwistle was saying about discovering the music that was there before Bach. He would find it in the libraries, music written down in copies of manuscripts of the complete artistic output of Guillaume de Machaut, produced for members of the French royal family. Those on the hunt for this apparent musical pre-time could locate written music preserved from the 1300s, and discover the kind of subtle personal touches, detailed rhythmic notation and dramatic presentation that seemed centuries ahead of its time.

It is, though, of its time, and as much about the mystery, the mechanics, of music as any modern avant-garde piece. Why wouldn't it be? It was being produced when the world was as modern as it had ever been. And if this was the beginning of modern music, of the shape, structure and development of the song, you get the feeling there were other beginnings before and after this beginning and it meant that Birtwistle never felt he was a part of anything new, whether recently new, or new from ancient times, but simply a continuation of something that both never changed and always changed. The music comes from the same places as Birtwistle's. The imagination. A life spent living. A life spent noticing things. It's the air of another planet. The sound of things coming to life.

'There was a piece by Machaut, *Mass of Our Lady* from the fourteenth century, medieval counterpoint, which is the most enigmatic piece in the history of music because nobody knows what the rationale was for how and why one note came after the other. I mean, it's a very formal piece. So it should have a pretty clear structure, but it's completely of itself, there is no reference to anything else before or after. The interesting thing about the music that is before Bach, when you get really back in time, I've no idea why it has the characteristic flavour that it has. It's easier to understand Bach because you can analyse the harmony. You can see why one thing is after another. You can understand his mind working. Whereas a lot of the pre-Bach, I have no way of knowing.'

It's the end of our allotted hour. He looks at me with tragi-comic weariness and at the same time iron-hard strength. Because we're done, all talked out, I now need not be worried about a curt reply and a sigh of irritation; I ask him an interviewer's classic cliché question. I am, after all, looking to him for help — how to finish a book about classical music, perhaps, or some clue about what music is becoming. I ask him how he would like to be remembered. The answer does not snap back with a bitter relish. There is a pause. A long pause. A pause that becomes a hole in space and time. A pause that you imagined could be filled with sound and fury, or silence and self-scrutiny.

Eventually, he answers.

'Well, I'd like to think that what I have done has had a degree of relevance... And that I found a tiny corner of fairyland.'

It doesn't seem much; he can be a self-deprecating, deceptive bugger, but he's not totally avoiding the question. The more you think of it, the more amazing it is — to have been such a discoverer, to find, even populate other magical worlds, to see beauty where others don't, to constantly re-enchant the world, to have such energy, to know so well your own mind, where anything can happen and often does, to find your gift and then give it away.

I am about to try one more question — the very final piece of music he would like to hear before he dies — but before I can ask it he turns to me and softly brings things to a close.

'I've said enough.'

The Coda...

Sound Out of Sound – Music to Listen to While Reading a Book

A PERMANENT CLASSICAL MUSIC CHART IN NO PARTICULAR ORDER

Use any or all pieces as a path or paths into classical music which will take you all the way, which includes knowing what 'all the way' actually means in this context.

- Maurice Ravel: String Quartet in F major (1903)
- Jean Sibelius: *Finlandia* (1899)
- Camille Saint-Saëns: Symphony No. 3 (with organ) in C minor (1886)
- Pauline Oliveros: *In Memoriam: Nikola Tesla, Cosmic Engineer* (1969)
- Igor Stravinsky: *Symphonies of Wind Instruments* (in memoriam Claude Debussy) (1920)
- Johannes Brahms: Horn Trio, Op. 40 (1865)
- Dmitri Shostakovich: *The Gadfly* (1955)
- Malcolm Arnold: Serenade for Guitar and Strings (1955)
- Edgard Varèse: *Hyperprism* (1923)
- Robert Schumann: *Konzertstück* (1849)
- Richard Strauss: *Death and Transfiguration* (1889)
- Edward Elgar: Cello Concerto in E minor (1919)
- Harry Partch: *Castor & Pollux* (1952)
- Ralph Vaughan Williams: *The Lark Ascending* (1921)
- Orlando Gibbons: Fantasia in C major
- Sergei Rachmaninov: Sonata in G minor for Cello and Piano, Op. 19 (1901)

- George Crumb: *Makrokosmos, Vol. I, Crucifixus* (Capricorn) (1972)
- Richard Wagner: *Siegfried Idyll* (arr. Glenn Gould, piano) (1870)
- Morton Feldman: *Coptic Light* (1983)
- Bela Bartók: *Two Portraits* (1908)
- Iannis Xenakis: *Akrata* (1964–5)
- Tōru Takemitsu: *Twill by Twilight* (1988)
- Hans Abrahamsen: *Let Me Tell You* (2013)
- Franz Liszt: *Mazeppa* (1852)
- Ludwig van Beethoven: Symphony No. 3 (1803)
- Alexander Scriabin: Piano Sonata No. 7, Op. 64 (*White Mass*) (1911)
- Luc Ferrari: *Archives Génétiquement Modifiées* (2000)
- Conlon Nancarrow: Study for Player Piano No. 3a (1948–9)
- Igor Stravinsky: *Pulcinella*, II. Serenata (1922)
- Wolfgang Amadeus Mozart: Divertimento for String Trio in E-flat major, K. 563
- Henryk Górecki: Symphony No. 3 (*Symphony of Sorrowful Songs*) (1991)
- Igor Stravinsky: *Symphony of Psalms* (1930)
- Dmitri Shostakovich: String Quartet No. 13 in B-flat minor, Op. 138 (1970)
- Samuel Barber: *First Essay for Orchestra* (1938)
- Alban Berg: Violin Concerto (1935)
- Aaron Copland: *Quiet City* (1939)
- Milton Babbitt: *Vision and Prayer* (1961)
- Peter Maxwell Davies: *Eight Songs For a Mad King* (1969)
- Paul Hindemith: Concert Music for Brass and Strings (1930)
- Claude Debussy: *La Cathédrale engloutie* (*The Sunken Cathedral*) (1910)
- Wolfgang Amadeus Mozart: Sinfonia Concertante for Violin, Viola and Orchestra (1779)
- Pierre Boulez: *Messagesquisse* (1976–7)
- Harrison Birtwistle: *Fantasia Upon All the Notes* for Flute, Clarinet, Harp and String Quartet (2011)
- Steve Reich: *New York Counterpoint*, II: Slow (1985)
- Edvard Grieg: *Two Elegiac Melodies* (1880)
- Iannis Xenakis: *Tetora* (1990)

- Elizabeth Maconchy: *Ophelia's Song* (1926)
- Alexander Scriabin: *Prometheus: The Poem of Fire* (1910)
- George Crumb: *Ancient Voices of Children* (1970)
- Unsuk Chin: *Xi*, for ensemble and electronics (1998)
- César Franck: Symphony in D minor (1889)
- Ludwig van Beethoven: String Quartet No. 14 in C-sharp minor, Op. 131 (1826)
- Francis Poulenc: *Stabat Mater* (1950)
- Arnold Schoenberg: Chamber Symphony No. 1 (1907)
- John Cage: *In A Landscape* (1948)
- Franz Liszt: *Hungarian Rhapsody* No. 5 (1853)
- W. A. Mozart: Divertimento for String Trio in E-flat major, K. 563: Allegro (1788)
- Galina Ustvolskaya: Twelve Preludes for Piano, III (1953)
- Earle Brown: *Novara* (1962)
- György Kurtág: *Zwiegespräch*, V: *Solace* (2007)
- Peter Maxwell Davies: *Judas Mercator* (2004)
- Krzysztof Penderecki: *Threnody to the Victims of Hiroshima* (1960)
- Erkki-Sven Tüür: *Crystallisatio* (1995)
- Elisabeth Lutyens: Motet, *Excerpta Tractatus Logico-Philosphicus* (1964)
- Harrison Birtwistle: *Tragoedia* (1965)
- Erik Satie: *Relâche* (1924)
- William Byrd: *Ye Sacred Muses*
- Ruth Crawford Seeger: *Rissolty Rossolty* (1939)
- Johannes Brahms: Symphony No. 2 (1877)
- Franz Liszt: Two Concert Études, I: *Forest Murmurs* (1862–3)
- Morton Feldman: *The Viola in My Life* (1970)
- Louis Andriessen: *De Staat* (1972–6)
- Duke Ellington: 'Way Early Subtone' (1959)
- Nadia Boulanger: Three Pieces for Cello and Piano, No. 1: Modéré (1914)
- Edgard Varèse: *Octandre* (1923)
- Ferruccio Busoni: Chaconne in D minor, after Chaconne, BWV 1004 by Bach (1893)
- Krzysztof Penderecki: *Largo* for Cello and Orchestra, III: Adagio (2005)
- Anton Webern: *Passacaglia* for Orchestra (1908)

- Rebecca Clarke: Viola Sonata, I: Impetuoso (1919)
- La Monte Young: *Dream House* (1997)
- Franz Schubert: Overture in the Italian Style (1817)
- Erik Satie: *Trois Gnossiennes* (1893)
- Leoš Janáček: Glagolitic Mass (1926)
- James Dillon: *Tanz/haus: triptych* (2017)
- Dmitri Shostakovich: Symphony No. 5 (1937)
- Sofia Gubaidulina: *Silenzio* (1991)
- Olivier Messiaen: *Turangalîla-Symphonie* (1946–8)
- Wolfgang Amadeus Mozart: Symphony No. 41 (1788)
- Franz Schubert: Piano Sonata No. 21 in B-flat major (1828)
- Mauricio Kagel: *Match* (1964)
- Nicholas Maw: *Life Studies* (version for string orchestra), Study I (1973)
- Elliott Carter: *Figment No. 2, Remembering Mr Ives* (1994)
- Gyorgy Ligeti: *Poème symphonique for 100 Metronomes* (1962)
- Arvo Pärt: *Cantus in Memoriam Benjamin Britten* (1977)
- Claude Debussy: *Hommage à Haydn* (1909)
- Lili Boulanger: *Nocturne* (1911)
- Tyshawn Sorey: *In Memoriam Muhal Richard Abrams* (2018)
- Harrison Birtwistle: Three Fugues from *The Art of Fugue* (after J. S. Bach, 2008)
- Johann Sebastian Bach: Great Fantasia and Fugue in G minor (c. 1720)
- Leos Janáček: *On an Overgrown Path*, VI: *Words Fail!* (1905)

Acknowledgements

This book is inevitably a solo performance, but it only exists because of a series of collaborations.

Thanks, as always, to everyone at my agents DGA, especially the maestro David Godwin and the ever-calm Philippa Sitters. Thanks to everyone who has helped me as part-time student, tentative composer and contributing lecturer at the Royal Academy of Music, especially my teachers: the irrepressible, Tony award-winning Christopher Austin and the brave Hannah Riddell. Thanks to Philip Cashian, the unflappable Head of Composition, at the Academy for giving me the confidence to conduct interviews with scrupulous, intimidating Scandinavians, and helping me on my quest to know new things about music. Thanks also to Emily Mould for organising the RAM interviews and the students and staff who helped make them an event. Thanks to the various editors who commissioned pieces from me that were never quite what they thought they had asked for, including at *Sinfini* Emma Bharj, Emma Baker, Tricia Boczowski, Amanda Holloway, Tina Poyser and Fiona Maddocks. Thanks to *Sinfini's* original editor John Evans for believing I could help with their mission to appeal to the culturally curious before I drove him into the arms of Jeremy Clarkson at the *Sunday Times*. Thanks to Justine Willett at the BBC for asking me to write about The Planets, and Brian Donaldson at *The List* for asking what I thought about Frank Zappa. Thanks to Sarah Donaldson and Julian Coman at the *Observer*, and to Caspar Lewellyn Smith at the *Observer Music Magazine* for still publishing me even after he had heard some of the music I wrote at the Academy. And thanks to the farsighted producer Roy Ackerman, who thought it would be a good idea for me to find out on television how to be a composer, and to director Paul Yule and assistant producer Poppy Edwards.

Thanks to those musicians whose interviews appear in the book, and also to those I interviewed that do not appear, including James Dillon, Andrew Norman, Anssi Karttunen, Hans Abrahamsen, Georg Haas, Magnus Lindberg, Edmund Finnis and Andrew Poppy. Another time, another book, perhaps.

Thanks to the fantastic team at Bloomsbury, especially after the world took a strange turn, starting with my wise editor Michael Fishwick for taking on the project and going with the flow while at the same time patiently suggesting new routes. Thanks to Lilidh Kendrick for making sure the important things got done. Thanks to managing editor Lauren Whybrow for the unwavering care and attention that turned the manuscript into a book with the tenacious, invaluable help of copyeditor Kate Quarry and proofreader Catherine Best. Any mistakes left over are all mine or, you never know, entirely meant to be. Thanks to David Atkinson for the index. Thanks to Jo Forshaw on audio, Jonny Coward on publicity and Grace McNamee at Bloomsbury New York.

Thanks to the Art of Noise of the recording studio, James Banbury of Infantjoy, the Bedroom Community of Iceland and Ian Hazeldine of Antonymes. Thanks to Kevin Cummins for the jacket photograph, taken at the Motel One, Manchester, 26 November 2019, two hours before Manchester City versus Shakhtar Donetsk in the Champions League.

Love and thanks to Madeleine and Carol Morley for their constant encouragement and the inspiration of their own writing and thinking. Also to the Morleys of France and the Mitchells of North Wales.

Love and thanks and beyond to Elizabeth Levy, my closest collaborator, with her fantastic mind, who was there with me all the way from the first word to the final full stop. Love kept things going.

Index

A Note on the Author

Writer, critic and broadcaster Paul Morley grew up in Stockport and wrote for the *New Musical Express* between 1976 and 1983. A founding member of the electronic ensemble Art of Noise, he collaborated with Grace Jones on her best-selling memoirs and was an artistic advisor to the *David Bowie Is* exhibition at the V&A. He is the author of a number of books on music including biographies of Joy Division and David Bowie, as well as the psychedelic history book *The North* and the acclaimed memoir *Nothing*.

A Note on the Type

The text of this book is set Adobe Garamond. It is one of several versions of Garamond based on the designs of Claude Garamond. It is thought that Garamond based his font on Bembo, cut in 1495 by Francesco Griffo in collaboration with the Italian printer Aldus Manutius. Garamond types were first used in books printed in Paris around 1532. Many of the present-day versions of this type are based on the Typi Academiae of Jean Jannon cut in Sedan in 1615.

Claude Garamond was born in Paris in 1480. He learned how to cut type from his father and by the age of fifteen he was able to fashion steel punches the size of a pica with great precision. At the age of sixty he was commissioned by King Francis I to design a Greek alphabet, and for this he was given the honourable title of royal type founder. He died in 1561.